DEFENSE AND SECURITY

DEFENSE AND SECURITY

A Compendium of National Armed Forces and Security Policies

Volume 2: New Zealand–Yugoslavia

Edited by

Karl DeRouen, Jr.
Uk Heo

A B C ⬤ C L I O

Santa Barbara, CA   Denver, CO   Oxford, UK

Cataloging-in-Publication Data is available from the Library of Congress.

08   07   06   05   10 9 8 7 6 5 4 3 2 1

This book is also available on the World Wide Web as an eBook. Visit abc-clio.com
for details.

ABC-CLIO, Inc.
130 Cremona Drive, P.O. Box 1911
Santa Barbara, California 93116-1911

Production Team

Acquisitions Editor	Alicia Merritt
Project Assistant	Wendy Roseth
Production Editor	Anna R. Kaltenbach
Editorial Assistant	Alisha Martinez
Production Manager	Don Schmidt
Manufacturing Coordinator	George Smyser

It was set in typeface Trump Medieval.

This book is printed on acid-free paper ∞ .
Manufactured in the United States of America

Dedicated to the memory of Karl DeRouen's grandparents
and to Uk Heo's parents:
Fernand, Agnes, Rosemary, and Sam
and
Mansik and Sunok

CONTENTS

New Zealand

Paul Bellamy

Geography and History

New Zealand is located in the southwest Pacific Ocean, 1,600 km east of Australia. The total land area is 268,021 sq. km with the landscape dominated by mountain ranges and hill country. New Zealand's maritime Exclusive Economic Zone (EEZ) is 1.3 million sq. nautical miles (fifteen times New Zealand's landmass), making it one of the largest such zones in the world. In addition to the main islands—the North Island, South Island, and Stewart Island— New Zealand territory also includes a number of small islands (the Chatham Islands, Raoul Island, and Campbell Island), and jurisdiction is held over the Ross Dependency in Antarctica. Tokelau, a small island grouping in the central Pacific, is a New Zealand dependency, but in practice enjoys a large measure of administrative and political autonomy as the New Zealand administrator has delegated most powers to local authorities (Henderson and Bellamy 2002, 17).

New Zealand also has a constitutional relationship with two other Pacific islands: the Cook Islands and Niue. These are self-governing states in free association with New Zealand. This relationship provides for the exercise by New Zealand of certain responsibilities for defense and external affairs, but in practice these powers are exercised only on the request of the island governments (see the section on alliances).

New Zealand is an independent state with a parliamentary democracy and is a member of the Commonwealth, the inter-governmental organization of fifty-three countries that accept the British sovereign as the "Head of the Commonwealth." The current head of state, Queen Elizabeth II, is represented by the governor-general (currently Dame Silvia Cartwright), who summons and dissolves Parliament and assents to legislation. Following the British tradition, New Zealand does not have a single overriding formal written constitutional document. Its constitution is made up of the statutes of the New Zealand Parliament, common law, constitutional convention, the law and custom of Parliament, and the heritage of British constitutional history. New Zealand has a mixed member proportional (MMP) electoral system with a 120-seat unicameral Parliament. Parliamentary terms are triennial. The most recent election was held in July 2002, after which a coalition government consisting of the New Zealand Labour Party and Progressive Party, supported by the United Future New Zealand Party on confidence and supply, was established. The Green Party of Aotearoa/ New Zealand and the Labour Party signed an agreement to cooperate. The prime minister currently is the Right Honourable Helen Clark (see Sidebar 1), and the deputy prime minister is the Honourable Dr. Michael Cullen. The opposition leader is Dr. Don Brash, the National Party leader.

Archaeological evidence indicates that Polynesian settlement was established by 1300. European contact dates from the eighteenth century and European settlement from later that same century. New Zealand became a British colony in 1840 (for information on the New Zealand relationship with Britain, see the section on alliances) after the Treaty of Waitangi was signed by over 500 Maori chiefs and the British Crown. The treaty, which was written in Maori and English, has three articles that:

- cede the Maori right to govern to the Crown.
- guarantee to the Maori "full, exclusive and undisturbed possession" (English version) or "*Te Tino Rangatiratanga*" (Maori version), which can be translated as full chieftainship or "kingdom, principality, sovereignty, realm" of their lands, estates, forests, fisheries, and other properties, as well as their "*Taonga*" (treasured possessions).
- recognize Maori as British citizens (Orange 1990, 25).

Conflict between the Maori and settlers resulted in the New Zealand Wars, fought in New Zealand between 1843 and 1872 (there is some debate regarding the exact

---

Sidebar 1   The Right Honourable Helen Clark, Prime Minister of New Zealand (1999 to Present)

The Right Honourable Helen Clark is the first woman to be elected prime minister of New Zealand. Helen Clark was born in Hamilton in 1950. Clark studied at the University of Auckland, and lectured in political studies at the university from 1977 until her election to Parliament, in 1981, as a member of the Labour Party.

During the second term of the Fourth Labour Government (1987–1990), Clark was minister of conservation (1987–1989), minister of housing (1987–1989), and, in 1989, she became minister of health, minister of labour, and deputy prime minister. After the defeat of the Labour Party in the 1990 election, Clark became deputy leader of the opposition, a position she held until 1993 when she became the leader of the opposition. In 1999, Clark was elected prime minister of New Zealand. Clark is also the minister for arts, culture and heritage, and is responsible for the New Zealand Security Intelligence Service and Ministerial Services.

Sources
Edwards, Brian. 2001. *Helen–Portrait of a Prime Minister.* Auckland, NZ: Exisle Publishing.
New Zealand Labour Party. *Right Honourable Helen Clark—Biography (school).* http://www.labour.org.nz/labour_team/mps/mps/helen_clark/biography_school/ index.html (accessed May 14, 2005).
New Zealand Labour Party. *Right Honourable Helen Clark—Biography (work).* http://www.labour.org.nz/labour_team/mps/mps/helen_clark/biography.html (accessed May 14, 2005).
Official Website of the New Zealand Government. 2005. *Right Honourable Helen Clark—Biography.* http://www.beehive.govt.nz/Minister.cfm?MinisterID=1 (accessed May 14, 2005).

time frame). The New Zealand Parliament had first met in May 1854, and responsible government was established in 1856, under which the governor accepted that he would be guided by the views of ministers responsible to Parliament. The first premier was Henry Sewell. Four Maori seats in Parliament were established in 1867, and women were given the same voting rights as men in 1893. A basic feature of New Zealand's economy during the nineteenth century was its dependence on the United Kingdom (Rice 1992, 57). Wool, grain, and, later, frozen meat were major exports (King 2003, 236).

By 1901 the total New Zealand population numbered 815,862 (an increase from 115,461 in 1858). However, the Maori population had fallen from no more than 100,000 in 1840 to a low of 42,000 in 1896 (Statistics New Zealand 2002, 96 and 112). New Zealand fought in World War I, experienced economic and social hardships due to the Great Depression in 1929, and fought again in World War II (for information on New Zealand's involvement in both wars, see the section on conflict). The New Zealand population passed 2 million in 1952 and reached 3 million in 1973. Until 1975, the terms of trade for the country's primary exports (wool, meat, dairy products, and timber) were high. After the energy crisis of the 1970s, the terms of trade turned against most primary products and unemployment increased (Statistics New Zealand 2002, 18 and 2122).

Major changes occurred during the 1980s and 1990s. The government undertook wide-ranging social and economic reforms, and under 1987 legislation, New Zealand became nuclear-free (see the section on the military). In 1993 a binding referendum on the electoral system was held. This resulted in a move away from the first-past-the-post electoral system to MMP, the first election under this system taking place in 1996. A Labour-led coalition government took power in 1999, and the Labour Party continued to lead a coalition government after the 2002 election.

New Zealand's small economy is heavily dependent on overseas trade. Australia, the United States (see the section on New Zealand's relationship with the United States), and Japan are currently New Zealand's largest trading partners. Although dairy and meat exports continue to make a large contribution to the economy, forestry and manufacturing exports have become increasingly important, while wool has declined. New Zealand has developed its agriculture and manufacturing industries to meet the needs of niche markets (Statistics New Zealand 2004a). Annual growth in gross domestic product (GDP) for September 2003 was 3.9 percent (Statistics New Zealand 2003). For the December 2003 quarter the seasonally adjusted unemployment rate was 4.6 percent (Statistics New Zealand 2004a).

Regional Geopolitics

The Asia-Pacific region is very important to New Zealand. New Zealand's association with Asia dates back to the country's involvement in World War II, and New Zealand provided significant development assistance to many Asian countries in the 1960s and 1970s. Assistance to the region continues, and trade with Asia is extensive. In the year ending June 2001, Asia took 37 percent of all New Zealand's exports and provided 31 percent of imports (Statistics New Zealand 2002, 66). In addition to economic ties, New Zealand has cultural and security ties with Asia (with regard to security

Table 1   New Zealand: Key Statistics

Type of government	Parliamentary democracy
Population	4,009,100 (2003). In 2001 Maori represented 14.1% of the population.
Religion	Christianity, including Maori Christian (61%) (2001)
Main industries	Agriculture is the largest industry. Forestry, fishing, and tourism are also important
Gross domestic product (GDP)	NZ$122 billion (2002)
Growth	3.8% (2002)
Inflation	2.6% (2002)
Main security threats	Threats include terrorism, transnational crime, the illegal movement of people and goods, and regional civil instability
Defense spending (% GDP)	1.1% (2002)
Size of military	12,904 personnel (2003)
Number of civil wars since 1945	0
Number of interstate wars since 1945	4

Wars are based on the number of wars where New Zealand forces have served in combat abroad. The four are: the Korean War, the Vietnam War, the Malayan Emergency, and the confrontation between the Federation of Malaysia and Indonesia. Peacekeeping operations are not included.

Sources
International Institute for Strategic Studies (IISS). 2003. *The Military Balance 2003–2004*. London: IISS and Oxford University Press, p. 300.
New Zealand Ministry of Defence. 2003a. *Annual Report for the Year Ended 30 June 2003*. Wellington New Zealand Ministry of Defence, p. 3.
New Zealand Defence Force. 2003. *Annual Report of the New Zealand Defence Force for the Year Ended 30 June 2003*. Wellington New Zealand Defence Force, p. 32.
Statistics New Zealand. 2002. *New Zealand Official Yearbook 2002*: 118. Auckland, NZ: David Bateman Ltd., p. 118.
Statistics New Zealand. 2004b. *Top 20 Statistics*. http://www.stats.govt.nz/domino/ external/web/prod_serv.nsf/htmldocs/Top+20+statistics (accessed February 17, 2004).

ties, see the section on alliances). Regional stability and peace is central to New Zealand's interests.

North Korea and its nuclear program pose the main security issue in eastern Asia. Tensions on the Korean peninsula have increased with the threat of a potentially nuclear capable North Korea. New Zealand has historically had little contact with North Korea. However, a semiofficial dialogue developed in the late 1990s, and diplomatic relations were formally established in March 2001. Relations between the People's Republic of China and the United States have sometimes been tense, especially after a U.S. maritime-patrol aircraft landed on Hainan Island following a collision with a Chinese fighter in April 2001, but more recently have improved. The relationship between China and Taiwan remains problematic (International Institute for Strategic Studies [IISS] 2003, 145–149). New Zealand established diplomatic relations with China in 1972, and this relationship is now one of New Zealand's most important.

In Southeast Asia, there are tensions between governments (notably Singapore and Malaysia, Malaysia and Brunei, and Thailand and Cambodia). The October

12, 2002, terrorist bombings in Bali, which killed 202 people (including three New Zealanders), graphically illustrated the threat of terrorism. The bombings prompted the Indonesian government (Indonesia is an important trading partner for New Zealand) to take action against Jemaah Islamiyah, a regional Islamic terrorist organization. In May 2003, the Indonesian government also imposed martial law and launched a major military operation in the province of Aceh aimed at eradicating the Free Aceh Movement (Gerakan Aceh Merdeka, or GAM), a separatist movement. Elsewhere, the Philippines military has conducted operations against various groups (IISS 2003, 147–149).

Pacific island states form the immediate neighborhood for New Zealand. New Zealand has very close links with the Pacific, especially Polynesia. New Zealand has eleven diplomatic missions and consulates in the Pacific and accreditation to a further eight (Statistics New Zealand 2002, 63). According to the New Zealand Minister of Foreign Affairs, Phil Goff, "New Zealand is a Pacific nation. We have growing interdependence with the region through significant trade and people-to-people links, and the growing part that Pacific Islands play in New Zealand's national identity" (New Zealand Ministry of Foreign Affairs and Trade [MFAT], *Pacific Division Introduction* 2003). Approximately 6.5 percent of New Zealand people are of Pacific Island origin, and Auckland is the biggest Polynesian city in the world. New Zealand is further connected with the region through trade (exports were $856 million and imports $155 million during 2002), development assistance, and foreign policy (MFAT, *Pacific Division Introduction* 2003). The New Zealand Ministry of Defense (MoD) also states that

"New Zealand shares many security interests with the Pacific Islands. They comprise a wide range of responsibilities and, more recently, the need to address an emergent range of risks such as illegal movement of people and goods, international terrorism and other transnational security threats" (MoD 2003a, 10).

Regional geopolitics influence various issues facing the Pacific. Political issues include questions over the legitimacy of political systems and demands for political change and transparency. For example, Tonga has a monarchy with the king holding considerable status and power, and there have been calls for greater democracy (including calls from some in New Zealand). Corruption and questionable accountability in the Pacific region are also issues. These problems are compounded by economic issues that include an overreliance on some industries and exports, vulnerability to international developments, questionable business practices, demands for reform, debate over resources, and aid dependency. Regional security issues that have been a source of concern include terrorism, money laundering, poaching, the arms trade, people smuggling, and military insubordination.

Violence and instability have been particularly evident in some Pacific islands. For instance, during 1999 in the Solomon Islands, tensions led to violence between the local Gwale people on Guadalcanal and migrants from the neighboring island of Malaita. The Townsville Peace Agreement was signed in October 2000, and unarmed peace monitors of the International Peace Monitoring Team (IPMT) were deployed, including New Zealanders. The IPMT deployment ended in June 2002 but problems remained, such as the availability of weapons and the threat former militants posed to law and order. In July 2003, under the Regional Assistance Mission to the Solomon Islands, 2,225 military and police personnel were deployed from Australia and other Pacific states (IISS 2003, 148). New Zealand personnel remain in the Solomon islands. A platoon of thirty-three soldiers from the Burnham Military Camp flew to the islands in February 2004 to take over from a North island platoon ("The Burnham Troops Depart" 2004, 5). New Zealand's assistance has also included grants to secondary schools, the provision of doctors and emergency medical supplies, and provincial development funds.

Coups occurred in Fiji during May and September 1987, and more recently in May 2000. During the May 2000 coup, armed gunmen led by George Speight entered Parliament and took the majority of the government hostage. The last hostages were not released for some eight weeks, following the signing of the Muanikau Accord. As a result of the political crisis, the 1997 constitution was purported to have been abrogated. An interim civilian government was eventually appointed to run the country, during which time there was a state of emergency. In March 2001, the Court of Appeal ruled that the 1997 constitution remained the supreme law of Fiji, and an election was held in August 2001. The sanctions New Zealand had in place due to the 2000 coup were lifted in December 2001, and the bilateral relationship with Fiji is among New Zealand's most important in the South Pacific. However, Fiji continues to experience various problems, and tension between Indians and ethnic Fijians remains.

In Papua New Guinea, the status of the island of Bougainville and its relationship with the mainland has been a key issue. From 1989 to 1997, conflict occurred between Bougainvillean militants and the Papua New Guinea Defense Force. This conflict was encouraged by landowner concerns and Bougainvillean views of their separateness from mainland Papua New Guinea. Negotiations between the Papua New Guinea government and Bougainvillean leaders on the future status of the island led to the conclusion of the Bougainville Peace Agreement in August 2001, which was given legal effect in March 2002. New Zealand was instrumental in facilitating talks between warring factions in the late 1990s, led the Truce Monitoring Group that deployed to Bougainville in 1997, and in May 2003 was the second-largest contributor after Australia to the seventy-five-member Peace Monitoring Group. Despite these developments, law and order is poor in areas of Papua New Guinea , and there is some possibility of terrorism (MFAT January 12, 2004).

Social and environmental issues are wide-ranging. A major health concern is the spread of HIV/AIDS. Known infection rates are already as high as 430 per 100,000 in Papua New Guinea and other countries, notably Kiribati, the Marshall Islands, and Tuvalu have sharply increasing infection rates (MFAT, *Key Pacific Issues—Social and Health*, July 2003). Additional concern has been voiced over domestic violence, rapid population growth, inequalities, the pressure of customs and traditions, crime, drug and alcohol abuse, and migration. New Zealand supports HIV/AIDS initiatives in the Pacific and has sought to address social issues through its multilateral, regional, and bilateral programs. Associated with these issues are the interethnic conflicts and tensions visible in countries such as Fiji. Finally, there are threats to the environment. Climate change is a major concern and an environmental priority for New Zealand, as many Pacific island populations are concentrated in low-lying coastal zones. Hence, islands such as Tuvalu are vulnerable to climate variability and rising sea levels.

Conflict Past and Present

Conflict History

New Zealand acquired dominion status in 1907 to mark its autonomous status in domestic affairs and has been involved in various conflicts since that time, the largest being the two world wars.

As part of the British Empire, New Zealand was formally involved in World War I (1914–1918) following King George V's declaration of war on Germany on August 4, 1914. New Zealand involvement ranged from the 1914 capture of German Samoa and participation in the 1915 attack on the Gallipoli Peninsula to fighting on the Western Front and naval action in the North Sea. Some 100,000 soldiers were sent abroad with about 18,000 being killed and 41,000 wounded (Rolfe 1999, 8) (for World War I and other wars, see the table on casualties).

New Zealand was one of the first countries to become involved in World War II (1939–1945), formally declaring war on Germany on September 3, 1939. New Zealand was actively involved in many campaigns against the Axis powers with about 140,000 men and women being dispatched overseas to serve in fighting formations. Of these, 104,000 were in the Second New Zealand Expeditionary Force and the rest in the British or New

Table 2   New Zealand War Casualties

Conflict	Total Casualties*	Total Dead
Boer War	398	230
World War I	59,483	18,166
World War II	36,038	11,625
Korean War	115	35
Malayan Emergency	38	15
Confrontation**	1	—
Vietnam War	224	37

Private Leonard Manning, who was killed in East Timor in July 2000, was the first New Zealand soldier to die in action in nearly thirty years. In February 2002 in Jakarta, the private's killer was found guilty of second-degree murder and was sentenced to six years in jail.

* The term "casualties" refers to those who by death, injury, illness, or capture become "ineffective."

** The confrontation between the Federation of Malaysia and Indonesia.

Sources

McGibbon, Ian ed. with the assistance of Paul Goldstone. 2000. *The Oxford Companion to New Zealand Military History*. Auckland, NZ: Oxford University Press, Table 3, p. 80.

Official Website of the New Zealand Government, *Right Honourable Helen Clark—Private Manning Verdict*, February 7, 2002, http://www.beehive.govt.nz/ViewDocument.cfm?DocumentID=13224 (accessed May 15, 2005).

Official Website of the New Zealand Government, *Honourable Jim Anderton—Death of Private Manning*, July 25, 2000, http://www.beehive.govt.nz/ViewDocument.cfm?DocumentID=8027 (accessed May 15, 2005).

Zealand naval or air forces. Postwar calculations indicated that New Zealand's ratio of killed per million of population (at 6,684) was the highest in the Commonwealth (McGibbon 2000, 484).

New Zealand was one of the first countries to answer the UN Security Council's call to aid South Korea with combat assistance after its invasion by North Korea. About 4,700 men served in Kayforce, New Zealand's ground force contribution, and another 1,300 served on frigates during the seven years of New Zealand's involvement. During this period, forty-seven men were killed (thirty-three of them during the war) (McGibbon 2000, 270).

New Zealand was actively involved in the Malayan Emergency (1948–1960), a conflict that arose in the Malayan peninsula with the Malayan Communist Party attempting to overthrow the British colonial administration. During the emergency fifteen servicemen lost their lives (McGibbon 2000, 294). New Zealand provided forces to operations in support of the new Federation of Malaysia during its confrontation with Indonesia (1964 to 1966) and deployed combat forces in Vietnam. This combat involvement began in 1965 and ended with the withdrawal of the First Australian Task Force in December 1971. A total of 3,890 personnel served with V-Force, the New Zealand army's contingent, of whom thirty-seven were killed (McGibbon 2000, 563). New Zealand was not directly involved in the 1982 Falklands War, but did deploy a frigate in the Indian Ocean so that the British could redeploy a similar vessel to the South Atlantic.

New Zealand committed personnel to the coalition against Iraq in the 1991 Gulf War, their number reaching 112 in February 1991. However, combat troops were not deployed, the first time that New Zealand had not committed such forces to a major conflict involving the United Kingdom or the United States during the twentieth century (McGibbon 2000, 211). New Zealand did not commit combat forces to the U.S.-led coalition against Iraq in the 2003 Iraq war. However, in June 2003, Prime Minister Helen Clark announced the contribution of a New Zealand Defense Force (NZDF) engineering group of sixty-one personnel, inclusive of support staff, to work alongside the United Kingdom and other countries on reconstruction and humanitarian tasks in southern Iraq. The engineering group was deployed in September 2003. The Light Engineer Group left New Zealand in March 2004 to replace personnel who had served in southern Iraq. This group was tasked with working alongside British forces in the Basra region to repair bridges, schools, hospitals, and water supplies ("Army Engineers Head for Iraq" 2004, 7).

Since July 1950, New Zealand military personnel have been involved in many UN peacekeeping operations. New Zealand had a particularly important role in international peacekeeping efforts in East Timor (now the Democratic Republic of Timor-Leste). East Timor was invaded by Indonesia in 1975 and formally annexed the following year. In January 1999, Indonesian President Bacharuddin Jusuf Habibie announced that he was willing to consider granting independence to East Timor if its people did not want to accept autonomy within Indonesia. In August 1999 an election was conducted by the UN mission to East Timor, and the majority voted for independence. Widespread violence followed this decision, and in September of that year a UN-sanctioned multinational peacekeeping force, International Force East Timor (INTERFET), was deployed. At its peak, New Zealand contributed 830 troops to INTERFET (MFAT March 2005). INTERFET's responsibility for maintaining security was transferred to the UN Transitional Administration in East Timor in February 2000, which New Zealand continued to support through successive battalion groups until November 2002. After that time, support continued with twenty-one personnel being deployed in Timor-Leste in June 2003.

Current and Potential Military Confrontation

Although New Zealand does not face a direct military threat (MoD 2003a, 3), security threats have been identified. Various circumstances have been identified by the MoD under which the New Zealand government could expect to deploy the NZDF. For the year ending June 30, 2003, five contexts were identified.

Security challenges to New Zealand and its environments provide the first context for employment of the NZDF. Events that could pose such security challenges are identified as civil disturbances and industrial actions affecting essential services; disasters posing a serious threat to life, property, or the environment; incursions into and through New Zealand's EEZ and threats within other areas under New Zealand's jurisdiction; terrorism and acts of sabotage; and asymmetric attacks on New Zealand territory (such as information warfare attacks and the mining of ports).

Security challenges to New Zealand's interests in the South Pacific constitute the second employment context for the NZDF. Relevant events would be disasters posing significant risks to life, property, or the environment; illegal incursions into South Pacific island EEZs and

territories; civil disturbances leading to a breakdown in law and order and/or posing risks to New Zealand nationals; terrorist acts; and challenges to legitimate governments, including civil war and secessionist conflict.

The third context comprises security challenges to the Australia–New Zealand strategic area. These challenges are identified as short-warning attacks against maritime approaches and terminuses and land incursions on Australian territory, serious attacks on the physical security of the New Zealand–Australia strategic area from a broader regional conflict, asymmetric attacks, and major conventional conflict (such as an invasion of Australia).

Security challenges to New Zealand's interests in the Asia-Pacific region represent another context. These challenges involve disasters posing significant risks to life or the environment, acts of piracy, impeded rights of passage through contested sea-lanes, significant internal unrest or insurgency that spills to other states and/or poses risks to New Zealand nationals, aggression affecting maritime boundaries or seizure or expropriation of resources, and interstate conflict.

Finally, security challenges to New Zealand's interests in global peace and security might also lead to the employment of the NZDF. Relevant events would be unresolved conflict where protagonists have sought third-party resolution assistance, act(s) by states or nonstate actors that contravene international norms of behavior or threaten international security or stability, impeding supplies of essential resources (such as oil, water, and electricity) to force political concessions or threaten the security of a nation or group of nations, significant internal conflict with risks to the stability of surrounding states or involving large-scale suffering, aggression affecting maritime or land boundaries or seizure or expropriation of resources, and a major breakdown in international security leading to wide-scale war (NZDF 2003, 15).

With regard to the threat of terrorism, also see the section on terrorism.

Alliance Structure

The first Europeans to reach New Zealand probably belonged to Abel Tasman's Dutch East India Company expedition in 1642. In 1769 the English explorer James Cook made his first visit to New Zealand and claimed it for King George III, and the first British residents arrived in the 1790s. In 1833 the Crown appointed the first British resident to look after British settlers, and New Zealand became a British colony in 1840 after the Treaty of Waitangi was signed. In 1852 New Zealand became a self-governing colony, Parliament first met in 1854, the provincial government was abolished in 1875, and in 1899 New Zealand sent troops to assist Britain in the Anglo-Boer War. This was the first overseas conflict to involve New Zealand troops. In 1900 New Zealand decided not to join with the Australian states in the new Australian Federation, and in 1901 Britain allowed New Zealand to annex the Cook Islands and Niue. New Zealand was constituted a Dominion of the British Empire in 1907.

New Zealand went to war alongside Britain in 1914 (see the section on conflict) and fought closely with allies such as Australia. In 1914 the Australian and New Zealand Army Corps (ANZAC) were established by grouping the Australian Imperial Force and New Zealand Expeditionary Force stationed in Egypt under the command of Lieutenant General William Birdwood. The corps made its operational debut the following year in Gallipoli. The cooperation of the ANZAC forces continues to denote a sense of Australian and New Zealand community of interest (McGibbon 2000, 26).

After World War I, New Zealand signed the 1919 Treaty of Versailles and joined the League of Nations. Since the Treaty of Versailles, it has been recognized that United Kingdom treaties applied to New Zealand only with New Zealand's concurrence. The signing of an Exchange of Notes with Japan in 1928 was the first independently concluded bilateral treaty formed by New Zealand with a foreign country not involving the agency of the United Kingdom (MFAT 1997, 8–9). New Zealand again fought alongside Britain in World War II (see the section on conflict). However, the fall of Singapore in 1942 symbolized the end of British protection and a turn to the United States for Pacific security. In 1944 the Australian–New Zealand Agreement, or Canberra Pact, was signed. This signaled to the United States and Britain the intention of the signatories to play an active collaborative role in maintaining South Pacific security after the defeat of Japan (Hoadley 1992, 18).

New Zealand has placed considerable reliance on alliance relationships for security since World War II. In 1947 the Statute of Westminster dissolved the British Empire and replaced it with the Commonwealth. The statute also meant that Parliament achieved the power to make its own constitutional changes.

As a member of the Commonwealth, New Zealand's security concerns immediately after World War II were focused on the Middle East. However, this focus turned to the Far East (now Southeast Asia) in the early 1950s with New Zealand joining Britain and Australia in the Commonwealth grouping ANZAM (Australia and New Zealand in the Malayan Area). In 1954 New Zealand signed the South East Asia Collective Defense Treaty and became a member of the South East Asia Treaty Organization (SEATO) directed against China and North Vietnam (SEATO ceased to exist in 1977). During this period New Zealand security was further aligned with the United States with the Australia-New Zealand-United States Treaty (ANZUS) signed in 1951 (see the section on the relationship with the United States).

New Zealand formally became associated with the security of Malaysia and Singapore via the Anglo-Malayan (later Malaysian) Defense Arrangements (1957–1971) and the Five Power Defense Arrangements (1971–present). The member nations of these arrangements—Australia, Malaysia, Singapore, the United Kingdom, and New Zealand—agreed to consult on what steps to take in the event of any external threat to Malaysia or Singapore. In peacetime, the parties exercise their forces together and undertake other training activities, and the defense ministers have met every three years since 1991. New Zealand involvement in the Asia-Pacific is reinforced by its membership of the Asia Pacific Economic Cooperation Forum and the Association of South East Asian Nations Regional Forum. The 1991 Closer Defense Relations arrangements were signed between Australia and New Zealand in an attempt to formalize the process of defense cooperation. However, disagreements between Australia and New Zealand over defense and security have occurred.

New Zealand currently has fifty-six diplomatic and consular posts in forty-two countries and territories and more than fifty honorary consuls. Multiple accreditation allows New Zealand representatives to cover seventy-six other countries and states from their bases (Statistics New Zealand 2002, 63).

New Zealand was a founding member of the United Nations and has actively supported the organization. New Zealand has served three terms on the UN Security Council (in 1954–1955, in 1966, and in 1993–1994), and New Zealanders are currently members of high-profile bodies within the UN system. William Mansfield is a member of the International Law Commission, Sir Kenneth Keith is a member of the International Humanitarian Fact Finding Commission, and New Zealand is a deputy member of the International Labor Organization's Governing Body.

Size and Structure of the Military

Civilian control of the NZDF and its accountability to the government is established by the Defense Act of 1990 (see the section on civil-military relations). The three services of the NZDF are: the New Zealand army, the Royal New Zealand Navy, and the Royal New Zealand Air Force. Individual service chiefs, along with the Commander Joint Forces New Zealand, report to the chief of the defense force, who is at the top of the NZDF organization. The Defense Force New Zealand Headquarters (HQ) was opened in July 2001, bringing together the operational command of all three services.

As of June 30, 2003, the NZDF command structure was comprised of Chief of Defense Force Air Marshal Bruce Ferguson, Chief of Navy Rear Admiral Peter McHaffie, Chief of Army Major General Jerry Mateparae, Chief of Air Force Air Vice Marshal John Hamilton, and Commander Joint Forces New Zealand Major General Martyn Dunne.

NZDF personnel as of June 30, 2003, totaled 12,904. The army is the largest service with 7,053 personnel (7,227 in 2002), followed by the navy with 2,773 (2,735 in 2002) and the air force with 2,674 (2,644 in 2002). The NZDF HQ staff number 578 personnel (560 in 2002), and Joint Forces New Zealand include 213 personnel (204 in 2002). The total number of personnel declined throughout the 1990s, falling from 20,911 in 1990, to 16,156 in 1996, and to 13,015 in 2002 (NZDF 2002, 36; NZDF 2003, 32–33). Concern has been expressed by some regarding the loss of personnel, and the government has sought to address the issue (MacLeod 2003, A16–17; Burton 2003, A17).

The NZDF HQ is located in Wellington, the nation's capital, and the Joint Forces New Zealand in Trentham. The army is located in Papakura, Waiouru, Linton, Trentham, Burnham, and Tekapo. The navy is located in Auckland, and the air force is located in Auckland, Ohakea, and Woodbourne.

New Zealand forces are actively involved in a wide range of international operations. For the year ending June 30, 2003, NZDF personnel were deployed in the following operations:

- Afghanistan: Four staff officers and an Air Loading Management Group supported the International Security Assistance Force in Kabul. Special Air Service forces and staff officers participated in Operation Enduring Freedom (OEF).
- Antarctica: Ninety-two NZDF personnel provided terminal and logistic support at Christchurch, Mc-Murdo Station, and Scott Base from October 2002 to February 2003 in support of Antarctic New Zealand.
- Arabian Sea: Approximately 170 personnel were deployed in the Arabian Sea for maritime interdiction operations in support of OEF. A P-3-K Orion aircraft and forty personnel were deployed to the region in May 2003.
- Bosnia: Seven staff officers are assigned to the HQ Multinational Brigade of the Stabilization Force in Bosnia (SFOR). A twenty-person NZDF contingent was attached to British units of SFOR during the northern summer months. The previous contingent returned to New Zealand in September 2002, and the current contingent was deployed in Bosnia in March 2003.
- Bougainville: Nineteen NZDF personnel served in the Peace Monitoring Group (PMG) in Bougainville. NZDF contributions ceased following the withdrawal of the PMG on June 30, 2003.
- Cambodia: Two officers serve in the Cambodian Mine Action Center HQ in Phnom Penh.
- Croatia: One officer worked as an observer in Croatia with the UN mission of observers in Prevlaka until December 2002.
- East Timor/Timor-Leste: Approximately 700 NZDF military and civilian personnel, including an infantry battalion group and an air force helicopter detachment, supported the UN mission in support of East Timor. These NZDF units were withdrawn in November 2002. Twenty-one NZDF personnel remain in support of the mission.
- Iraq: Thirteen NZDF personnel provided medical and communications

support to the UN monitoring, verification, and inspection commission in Iraq from November 2002 to March 2003.

- Israel/Lebanon/Syria: The NZDF provides seven UN military observers to the UN truce and supervisory organization. They are based in Jerusalem and serve at a variety of locations in Israel, Lebanon, and Syria.
- Korea: An eleven-person contingent provides support for the UN Command Honor Guard Company in Seoul.
- Kosovo: One staff officer serves as a military liaison officer with the UN interim administration mission in the Kosovo headquarters in Pristina.
- Laos: Two officers served in the UN unexploded ordnance program in the Laos headquarters in Vientiane until May 2003.
- Mozambique: Two NZDF personnel support the accelerated demining program in Mozambique.
- Sierra Leone: The NZDF provides two UN military observers to the UN assistance mission in Sierra Leone.
- Sinai Peninsula: A twenty-seven-person contingent provides expertise in force operations and training to the Multinational Force and Observers in the Sinai Peninsula (NZDF 2003, 22–23).

Budget

Defense expenditure for the year ended June 30, 2003, was NZ$1.427 billion ($1.423 billion in 2002). The navy received $445 million ($452 million in 2002), the army $435 million ($411 million in 2002),

the air force $413 million ($414 million in 2002), and headquarters (this includes HQ NZDF and HQ Joint Forces New Zealand) $134 million ($146 million in 2002) (NZDF 2003, 33; NZDF 2002, 37). The navy received $402 million in 1999, $402 million in 2000, and $439 million in 2001. The army received $442 million in 1999, $456 million in 2000, and $400 million in 2001. The air force received $490 million in 1999, $493 million in 2000, and $518 million in 2001. Finally, HQ received $68 million in 1999, $68 million in 2000, and $71 million in 2001 (NZDF 1999, 19; NZDF 2000, 31; NZDF 2001, 28). There has been debate regarding whether the NZDF is adequately resourced, especially given its various peacekeeping operations (MacLeod 2003, A16–17; Burton 2003, A17).

The defense industry is limited. A defense industrial sector has existed to any extent only since the mid- to late 1980s. Prior to this, some individual industries had provided equipment and maintenance support to defense. The Defense Industry Committee of New Zealand was established in 1994 to improve communication between the MoD and local industry. The main conduit for MoD assistance to support local companies seeking defense work has been through the group of local companies, the Defense Technologies New Zealand Joint Action Group, which is now the New Zealand Defense Industries Association (MoD 2003a, 21).

The construction of ANZAC frigates with Australia has been a major defense project that has involved New Zealand companies. In early 1997 the Minister of Defense, Paul East, estimated that New Zealand participation in the ANZAC frigate project had resulted in $470 million directly being injected into 417 New

Zealand companies. A further $126 million had been gained by New Zealand companies from other Australian defense work as a result of the project (Rolfe 1999, 172). In 1999 New Zealand companies exported $100 million worth of defense-related products (McGibbon 2000, 241).

Access to advanced weapons systems is limited, but there have been moves to modernize the NZDF (see the section on the future). Key pieces of army equipment include 105 lightly armed vehicles III (the first vehicles were delivered in August 2003), 41 M-113 armored personnel carriers (plus variants), and 24 Hamel towed 105-mm artillery. With regard to the navy there are three principal surface combatants (three frigates—two ANZAC class and one Canterbury [Leander]), one tanker for logistic support, four inshore patrol craft, one diving support vessel, and one survey ship. Naval aviation consists of five Sea Sprite helicopters that are maintained by the air force. Finally, the air force is comprised of six P-3-K Orion aircraft that provide maritime surveillance and reconnaissance, two Boeing 757s and five C-130 Hercules aircraft for long-range and tactical air transport, and fourteen UH-1-H Iroquois helicopters for helicopter support (IISS 2003, 166–167; NZDF 2003, 20; Royal New Zealand Navy 2004). In May 2001 Prime Minister Helen Clark confirmed speculation that the government would scrap the air force's air combat capability, an announcement that caused debate (Watkins 2001, 1). This capability consisted of seventeen A-4-K Skyhawk fighters and seventeen Aermacchi MB-339CB jet trainers, which flew for the last time in December of that year. This was in line with the policy of giving priority to the army's ability to participate in peace support operations and other multinational operations.

New Zealand does not have nuclear weapons. Under the New Zealand Nuclear Free Zone, Disarmament, and Arms Control Act of 1987, the manufacturing, acquiring, possession, or control of any nuclear explosive device in New Zealand is forbidden. Visits by nuclear-propelled or armed vessels are also forbidden (see the section on the relationship with the United States).

Civil-Military Relations/The Role of the Military in Domestic Politics

Civilian control of the NZDF and its accountability to the government is established by the Defense Act of 1990. This act stipulates that the governor-general is the commander-in-chief of the NZDF. The minister of defense is responsible for the armed forces and operates under the prime minister. The secretary of defense is the principal civilian adviser to the minister of defense. The chief of the defense force is the principal military adviser to the minister of defense. Currently the minister of defense is Mark Burton, and the secretary of defense is Graham Fortune.

Civilian control is widely recognized and accepted. There have been no occasions when the armed forces have directly challenged the authority of civilian rule, and they have remained ultimately accountable to the civilian government. The armed forces are charged with carrying out the lawful orders of the civil authority, and there is a convention that the armed forces stay out of the political arena. Members of the regular armed forces are classified as public servants by the Electoral Act of 1993. Thus, election candidates must take leave and vacate their public service office if they are elected. Former members of the armed forces may enter Parliament. In recent years, few have been candidates and fewer still have won election.

Although defense has not generally been a major issue in recent elections, some personnel have publicly commented on government policy. In 1938, four senior Territorial Force officers issued a statement criticizing government policy, and in October 1985 sixteen retired service chiefs criticized the government's approach to defense, especially with regard to ANZUS (see the section on the relationship with the United States). More recently, in April 2001 seven former defense chiefs called for public debate on defense policy.

Some differences have arisen over policy matters between the government of the day and personnel. For instance, there were differences of opinion between Chief of Defense Staff Air Marshall David Cooks and Prime Minister David Lange over New Zealand's response to the May 1987 coup in Fiji. A Territorial Force officer who openly questioned government policy was rebuked by the chief of general staff in 1997.

Terrorism

Terrorism is recognized as a security threat to New Zealand. In July 1985, agents of the French secret service bombed and sunk the *Rainbow Warrior*, the flagship of the environmental group, Greenpeace. The ship had been about to sail from Auckland to Moruroa Atoll in French Polynesia to protest against French nuclear testing (French testing ended in 1996). One person was killed in the incident, and it has been described as "the first act of state-sponsored terrorism in New Zealand" (King 2003, 443) (see Sidebar 2). More recently, according to the NZDF in 2003:

The destruction of al-Qaeda's sanctuary in Afghanistan has not diminished the threat of terrorism. Instead, al-Qaeda has adapted and evolved into widely dispersed smaller cells. The Bali bombings demonstrated that al-Qaeda's

---

Sidebar 2   The Sinking of the *Rainbow Warrior*

On July 10, 1985, the *Rainbow Warrior*, a Greenpeace vessel, was sunk in Auckland Harbour by two bombs laid by the French secret service. One crew member, a Dutch citizen, was killed. The operation had been authorized by French Minister of Defence Charles Hernu to prevent the vessel from sailing to Moruroa Atoll where it was to protest against French nuclear testing. Two of the French agents involved in the operation were apprehended. The agents pleaded guilty to manslaughter charges and were sentenced to ten years' imprisonment. However, a diplomatic settlement was negotiated by the United Nations secretary-general. This led to the agents being handed over to French custody, and the agreement that the agents would be held on Hao Atoll for three years (the French government later broke this agreement). New Zealand received an apology for the violation of its sovereignty and monetary compensation, but the incident had a negative impact on New Zealand–French relations.

Sources
King, Michael. 1986. *Death of the Rainbow Warrior*. Auckland, NZ: Penguin.
McGibbon, Ian (ed.) with the assistance of Paul Goldstone. 2000. *The Oxford Companion to New Zealand Military History*. Auckland: Oxford University Press.
Robie, David. 1986. *Eyes of Fire—The Last Voyage of the Rainbow Warrior*. Auckland, NZ: Lindon Publishing.

affiliates are active in our own region. Terrorism thus remains a significant and serious threat. (NZDF 2003, 7)

The New Zealand Security Intelligence Service (SIS) provides the government with intelligence and advice on national security issues. In the year up to June 30, 2003, the SIS investigated issues that included the provision of financial support from New Zealand for organizations that undertake terrorist acts overseas and links between individuals in New Zealand and terrorist organizations abroad (New Zealand SIS 2003, 9).

The New Zealand government has been involved in the international campaign against terrorism. New Zealand has supported OEF against al-Qaeda and the Taliban in Afghanistan. This has involved the use of special forces in Afghanistan, and New Zealand has been one of the largest per capita contributors to the operation (NZDF 2003, 7). From October 2001 to October 2003, New Zealand contributed $4.6 million in humanitarian aid to Afghanistan. This aid was in support of UN and nongovernmental organizations' reconstruction efforts in education and drug management, demining, and water supply purification (MFAT October 2003).

In addition to New Zealand's international efforts, domestic counterterrorism measures have been taken. For instance, the Terrorism (Bombings and Financing) Bill, already under consideration before the September 11, 2001, attacks, was amended to ensure that New Zealand could meet its international obligations to suppress the financing of terrorism. After September 11, 2001, the government also announced measures to boost its counterterrorism efforts, and increased funding of $30 million over three

years was approved. This funding was targeted at border protection efforts, an increased capacity for the collection and evaluation of intelligence, the establishment within the police of an intelligence and investigation unit dedicated to counterterrorism, and the provision of police liaison officers in London and Washington, D.C. Funding was also targeted at the establishment of capability to respond to a chemical or biological terrorist emergency and stronger security for the parliamentary complex (MFAT).

Relationship with the United States

The first recorded American–New Zealand contact occurred in 1797, and in 1839 the U.S. flag was first officially raised. New Zealand's earliest treaty with the United States was signed in 1842, but this was signed by Britain on behalf of its colony. New Zealand and the United States were allies during World War I, and by the 1920s the United States was New Zealand's second-largest customer and supplier (Hoadley 2000, 22). In 1937 New Zealand negotiated and signed its first direct bilateral agreement with the United States, an exchange of notes for the mutual reduction of visa fees. Relations grew stronger during World War II. U.S. servicemen were stationed in New Zealand, and New Zealand contributed to the Pacific campaign. After the war, New Zealand participated in the occupation of Japan, assisted the United States during the Korean War, and in September 1951 signed the ANZUS Treaty.

> At the center of the Treaty was Article Four: Each party recognises that an armed attack in the Pacific Area on any of the Parties would be dangerous to its own peace and safety

and declares that it would act to meet the common danger in accordance with its constitutional processes.

The Treaty enjoined its parties to consult when territorial integrity, political independence, or security was threatened and to maintain and develop their individual and collective capacity to resist armed attack. The treaty also established a council of foreign and defense ministers.

In the ensuing years, the ANZUS Treaty came to be regarded by some as the cornerstone of New Zealand's security (Hoadley 2000, 22). From the 1950s the council met annually, and council deliberations, along with consultations and exercises conducted in the context of the treaty, indirectly facilitated cooperation in Vietnam. From 1960 U.S. warships also began to regularly visit New Zealand. However, opposition to nuclear ship visits increased in the 1970s, and the Fourth Labour Government was elected in 1984 with an antinuclear policy. This led to tension as the U.S. policy was to "neither confirm nor deny" the presence of nuclear weapons on any vessel. The United States did not make an operational distinction between nuclear and nonnuclear vessels and believed that access to ports was an obligation implied by the treaty (Hoadley 2000, 43–44). The New Zealand government would not back down from its policy and declined the USS *Buchanan*, a guided missile destroyer, a request to visit in February 1985. The United States reacted by discontinuing joint exercises and the flow of an undisclosed quantity of intelligence. In June 1986 the United States suspended its security obligations. Relations gradually improved in the 1990s with a restoration of senior-level contact in 1994 and some improvements in de-

fense ties, such as the resumption of some exchanges of military personnel. President Bill Clinton visited New Zealand in 1999.

The United States and New Zealand currently cooperate on a wide range of issues including international trade, regional multilateral matters, the Antarctic, natural resources, and security. Prime Minister Helen Clark met President George W. Bush at the White House in March 2002. However, some differences of opinion arose between the two countries over the 2003 invasion of Iraq (Watkins 2003, 1).

Although there are restrictions because of its antinuclear stance, U.S.–New Zealand security ties have increased since the ANZUS dispute. New Zealand has assisted U.S. efforts against terrorism (see the section on terrorism), and this assistance, along with other actions by New Zealand, such as its contributions in the Pacific region, has been acknowledged by the United States.

New Zealand is a member of a collaborative international partnership for the exchange of foreign intelligence and the sharing of communications security technology that includes the United States.

The United States is an important trading partner. In the year ending June 2002, New Zealand's total trade with the United States was $10.8 billion (16.8 percent of total trade). The United States is New Zealand's second-largest export destination with exports increasing by 5.5 percent to $4.9 billion in the year ending June 2002 (frozen beef was the main export). The United States is also the third-largest source of imports. New Zealand imported $4.8 billion in merchandise goods from the United States in the year ending June 2002, down 9.6 percent from the previous year (aircraft topped the list of imports) (MFAT June 2003). Provisional figures for the year ending June, 2003, indicate that exports to the United States were valued at $4.3 billion and imports at $4 billion (Statistics New Zealand 2004a). Since 1998 the United States has been the third largest international investor in New Zealand (MFAT June 2003).

The Future

New Zealand does not face a direct military threat from another country in the foreseeable future. However, issues such as interstate tension and domestic discontent in the Asia-Pacific region, a region that will remain important to New Zealand, are likely to continue to be a concern. Of particular concern is the potential of such issues to destabilize the region and ultimately threaten New Zealand's interests. The 2002 Bali terrorist bombings graphically illustrated the threat posed by terrorism, a threat that will remain a concern. Potential threats to New Zealand's interests and its limited resources make it likely that strong relations with allies, and the membership of alliances and international organizations, will remain important. The relationship with both the United States and Australia will be particularly important. The security relationship with the United States will remain restricted due to the low likelihood of a change in New Zealand's antinuclear policy. Active involvement in peacekeeping operations is likely to continue.

In the Defense Long-Term Development Plan released in 2002, and updated in June 2003, the government directed that the NZDF receive up to $1 billion, in nominal terms, in capital injections over the next ten years (MoD 2003b, 3). The need to ac-

quire equipment has also been recognized. Projects that the government has approved in principle include the acquisition of light operational vehicles. This is in line with the need for the army to replace obsolete vehicles. The need for a tactical sealift capability, disaster relief and peace support operations, resource protection patrols, and increased surveillance capabilities has been recognized, and the government has approved in principle the acquisition of a multirole vessel and patrol vessels. Upgrades to air force aircraft have also been approved in principle (MoD 2003b, 12–25). More generally, the importance of the ministry of defense and NZDF working together effectively, as well as the individual services of the NZDF, has been recognized (Hunn 2002, iii). A challenge to civilian supremacy is not foreseen.

Paul Bellamy is a research analyst at the New Zealand Parliamentary Library. Please note that the views expressed in this chapter are those of the author and not necessarily those of his employer.

References, Recommended Readings, and Websites

Books
Baker, Richard, ed. 1994. *The ANZUS States and Their Region: Regional Policies of Australia, New Zealand, and the United States.* Westport, CT: Praeger.
Bercovitch, Jacob, ed. 1988. *ANZUS in Crisis : Alliance Management in International Affairs.* Basingstoke, UK: Macmillan Press.
Crawford, John. 1996. *In the Field for Peace: New Zealand's Contribution to International Peace-Support Operations, 1950–1995.* Wellington: New Zealand Defense Force.
Crawford, John, and Glyn Harper. 2001. *Operation East Timor: The New Zealand Defence Force in East Timor 1999–2001.* Auckland, NZ: Reed.
Edwards, Brian. 2001. *Helen—Portrait of a Prime Minister.* Auckland, NZ: Exisle Publishing.

Fraser, Bryce, ed. 1986. *The New Zealand Book of Events.* Auckland, NZ: Reed Methuen Publishers.

Henderson, John, and Paul Bellamy. 2002. *Democracy in New Zealand.* Christchurch, NZ: Macmillan Brown Centre for Pacific Studies; Stockholm: International Institute for Democracy and Electoral Assistance.

Hoadley, Stephen. 1992. *The New Zealand Foreign Affairs Handbook.* 2d ed. Auckland, NZ: Oxford University Press; Wellington: New Zealand Institute of International Affairs.

———. 2000. *New Zealand United States Relations—Friends No Longer Allies.* Wellington: New Zealand Institute of International Affairs.

Hunn, Don. 2002. *Review of Accountabilities and Structural Arrangements between the Ministry of Defence and the New Zealand Defence Force.* Wellington, NZ: Ministry of Defence.

International Institute for Strategic Studies (IISS). 2003. *The Military Balance 2003–2004.* London: IISS and Oxford University Press.

King, Michael. 1986. *Death of the Rainbow Warrior.* Auckland, NZ: Penguin.

———. 2003. *The Penguin History of New Zealand.* Auckland, NZ: Penguin.

McGibbon, Ian, ed. 2000. *The Oxford Companion to New Zealand Military History.* Auckland, NZ: Oxford University Press.

New Zealand Defence Force (NZDF). 1999. *Report of the New Zealand Defence Force for the Year Ended 30 June 1999.* Wellington: New Zealand Defence Force.

———. 2000. *Report of the New Zealand Defence Force for the Year Ended 30 June 2000.* Wellington: New Zealand Defence Force.

———. 2001. *Annual Report of the New Zealand Defence Force for the Year Ended 30 June 2001.* Wellington: New Zealand Defence Force.

———. 2002. *Annual Report of the New Zealand Defence Force for the Year Ended 30 June 2002.* Wellington: New Zealand Defence Force.

———. 2003. *Annual Report of the New Zealand Defence Force for the Year Ended 30 June 2003.* Wellington: New Zealand Defence Force.

New Zealand Ministry of Defence (MoD). 2003a. *Annual Report for the Year Ended 30 June 2003.* Wellington: New Zealand Ministry of Defence.

———. 2003b. *Defence Long-Term Development Plan.* Wellington: New Zealand Ministry of Defence.

New Zealand Ministry of Foreign Affairs and Trade (MFAT). 1997. *New Zealand Consolidated Treaty List as at 31 December 1996—Part One.* Wellington: New Zealand Ministry of Foreign Affairs and Trade.

New Zealand Security Intelligence Service (SIS). 2003. *Report of the New Zealand Security Intelligence Service—Report to the House of Representatives for the Year Ended 30 June 2003.* Wellington: New Zealand Security Intelligence Service.

Orange, Claudia. 1990. *An Illustrated History of the Treaty of Waitangi.* Wellington, NZ: Allen and Unwin.

Pugsley, Chris, Laurie Barber, Buddy Mikaere, Nigel Prickett, and Rose Young. 1996. *Scars on the Heart: Two Centuries of New Zealand at War.* Auckland, NZ: Bateman.

Rice, Geoffrey, ed. 1992. *The Oxford History of New Zealand.* 2d ed. Auckland, NZ: Oxford University Press.

Robie, David. 1986. *Eyes of Fire—The Last Voyage of the Rainbow Warrior.* Auckland, NZ: Lindon Publishing.

Rolfe, James. 1999. *The Armed Forces of New Zealand.* New South Wales, AU: Allen and Unwin.

Statistics New Zealand. 2002. *New Zealand Official Yearbook 2002.* Auckland, NZ: David Bateman.

———. 2004. *New Zealand in Profile 2004.*

Stockholm International Peace Research Institute (SIPRI). 2003. *SIPRI Yearbook 2003.* New York: Humanities Press.

Taylor, Richard. 1996. *Tribe of the War God—Ngati Tumatauenga.* Napier: Heritage New Zealand.

Thomson, John. 2000. *Warrior Nation: New Zealanders at the Front, 1900–2000.* Christchurch, NZ: Hazard Press.

Articles/Newspapers

Ansley, Greg. 2003. "In the National Interest—Fighting Blind." *New Zealand Herald,* August 1:A14.

"Army Engineers Head for Iraq." 2004. *The Dominion Post,* March 6:7.

Bellamy, Paul. 2005. "Cambodia: Remembering the Killing Fields." *New*

Zealand International Review 30, no. 2:17–21.

"Burnham Troops Depart for Solomons Duty." 2004. *The Press*, February 24:5.

Burton, Mark. 2003. "Forces Plans Couldn't Be More Explicit." *New Zealand Herald*, August 15:A17.

Henderson, John. 2000. "Fiji: Coups and Conflict in Melanesia." *New Zealand International Review* 25, no. 4:17–20.

Henderson, John, and Paul Bellamy. 2002. "Prospects for Further Military Intervention in Melanesian Politics." *World Affairs* 164, no. 3:124–134.

MacLeod, Scott. 2003. "In the National Interest—The Big Battle: Maintaining the Peace on a Shoe String." *New Zealand Herald*, July 31:A16–17.

Mcloughlin, David. 2002. Tonga's Money Pit. *The Dominion Post*, February 9:2.

O'Sullivan, Fran, and Greg Ansley. 2003. "In the National Interest—Promises, Promises, and Reality." *New Zealand Herald*, July 30:A20–21.

Reilly, Ben. 2000. "The Africanisation of the South Pacific." *Australian Journal of International Affairs* 54, no. 3:261–268.

Watkins, Tracy. 2001. "Clark Downs Skyhawks and 600 Jobs." *The Dominion Post*, May 9:1.

———. 2003. "US Will Not 'Get Over' NZ Stance." *The Press*, October 9:1.

Websites

Australian Department of Foreign Affairs and Trade: http://www.dfat.gov.au/.

Australian High Commission, Wellington, New Zealand: http://www.australia.org.nz/index.php.

Central Intelligence Agency (CIA). 2003. *World Factbook—New Zealand.* http://www.cia.gov/cia/publications/factbook/geos/nz.html (accessed December 22, 2003).

New Zealand Army: http://www.army.mil.nz/.

New Zealand Central and Local Government Services: http://www.govt.nz/en/home/.

New Zealand Defence Force: http://www.nzdf.mil.nz/.

New Zealand Labour Party: http://www.labour.org.nz/.

New Zealand Ministry of Defence: http://www.defence.govt.nz/.

New Zealand Ministry of Foreign Affairs and Trade (MFAT): http://www.mfat.govt.nz/.

New Zealand Ministry of Foreign Affairs and Trade (MFAT). 2003. *Afghanistan Country Paper.* October. http://www.mfat.govt.nz/foreign/regions/mideast/countrypapers/afghanistan.html#Visits (accessed November 1, 2003).

———. *Democratic Republic of Timor-Leste Country Paper.* March 2005. http://www.mfat.govt.nz/foreign/regions/sea/countrypapers/timorlestepaper.html (accessed May 24, 2005).

———. *Key Pacific Issues—Economic.* July 2003. http://www.mfat.govt.nz/foreign/regions/pacific/keyissues/economic/economic.html (accessed August 1, 2003).

———. *Key Pacific Issues—Social and Health.* July 2003. http://www.mfat.govt.nz/foreign/regions/pacific/keyissues/health/health.html. (accessed May 28, 2005).

———. *New Zealand and the Campaign against Terrorism.* http://www.mfat.govt.nz/foreign/spd/terrorism/campaignterrorism.html (accessed May 28, 2005).

———. *New Zealand and the United Nations.* http://www.mfat.govt.nz/foreign/unc/general/unandnz.html#Today (accessed May 28, 2005).

———. *New Zealand's Policy on Iraq.* http://www.mfat.govt.nz/foreign/regions/mideast/faq/iraqfaqupdate.html (accessed May 28, 2005).

———. *Pacific Division Introduction.* July 2003. http://www.mfat.govt.nz/foreign/regions/pacific/generalinfo/pacintro.html (accessed December 1, 2003).

———. *Solomon Islands Country Paper.* June 2002. http://www.mfat.govt.nz/foreign/regions/pacific/country/solomonislands.html (accessed December 1, 2003).

———. *Travel Advice: Papua New Guinea.* http://www.mfat.govt.nz/travel/countries/png.html (accessed January 12, 2004).

———. *United States Country Paper.* June 2003. http://www.mfat.govt.nz/foreign/regions/northamer/usa/usacp.html (accessed December 17, 2003).

New Zealand Ministry of Social Development: http://www.msd.govt.nz/.

New Zealand Parliament: http://www.parliament.govt.nz/.

New Zealand Security Intelligence Service: http://www.nzsis.govt.nz/.

Official Website of the New Zealand Government: http://www.beehive.govt.nz/home.cfm.

Royal New Zealand Air Force: http://www. airforce.mil.nz/home/main.htm.

Royal New Zealand Navy: http://www. navy.mil.nz/.

Royal New Zealand Navy. 2004. *A Quick Voyage Around.* http://www.navy.mil. nz/rnzn/voyage.cfm (accessed February 12, 2004).

Statistics New Zealand: http://www.stats. govt.nz/.

Statistics New Zealand. 2003. *Gross Domestic Product September 2003 Quarter.* http://www.stats.govt.nz/ domino/external/pasfull/pasfull.nsf/ 7cf46ae26dcb6800cc256a62000a2248/ 4c2567ef00247c6acc256e000018bc40? OpenDocument (accessed December 19, 2003).

———. 2004a. *Quick Facts—The Economy.* http://www.stats.govt.nz/ domino/external/web/nzstories.nsf/ htmldocs/Quick+Facts+-+Economy (accessed January 24, 2004).

———. 2004b. *Top 20 Statistics.* http:// www.stats.govt.nz/domino/external/ web/prod_serv.nsf/htmldocs/Top+20+ statistics (accessed February 17, 2004).

Nigeria

Trevor Rubenzer

Geography and History

Nigeria is situated in western Africa and shares borders with Benin, Cameroon, Chad, and Niger. Its access to the sea is in the south at Port Harcourt and in the southwest at Lagos. The most extreme topography in Nigeria lies in the east, while a large plateau dominates the central portion of the country. The climate is tropical in the central portion of the country, arid in the north, and equatorial in the south. The Niger and Benue are the two longest rivers in Nigeria, which meet and flow into the Gulf of Guinea. Many portions of these two rivers, and their various tributaries, are navigable, culminating in a waterway system of significant length (approximately 8,500 km). The Nigerian highway system consists of nearly 200,000 km of road, of which 60,000 are paved (CIA *World Factbook* 2003). Nigeria also has over 3,500 km of rail.

The Niger and Benue rivers also roughly define Nigeria's political geography, which is complicated by a variety of ethnic divisions. The Ibo ethnic group dominates the eastern portion of Nigeria. It is this region of the country that attempted secession from Nigeria in 1967. The western segment of Nigeria comprises primarily members of the Yoruba ethnic group, while the Hausa and Fulani, often referred to as a single group, are the principal peoples inhabiting the northern portion of Nigeria.

When Nigeria became an independent state, its capital city was Lagos, which is located in the southwestern portion of the country. The seat of government was eventually moved to the city of Abuja, in central Nigeria. This reflects a desire to avoid regional ethnic bias in the location of the government. Ethnic divisions within Nigeria are a source of continued concern as the country attempts to consolidate democracy within a diverse federal system.

The British colonized most of what is now known as the Federal Republic of Nigeria in the late 1800s. Nigeria became an independent state, with a constitutional monarchy form of government, in October 1960. The governmental structure changed in 1963, transitioning to a federal republic. The current head of state is Olusegun Obasanjo, who was initially elected in 1999 and reelected to the office of president in April 2003. Despite some irregularities, the April 2003 elections marked the first civilian transfer of power in Nigeria's history (CIA *World Factbook* 2003). The federal system is divided into thirty-six states, which are further separated into 768 local administrative units (Synge 2003a, 844). The constitution provides for democratic elections in each of these local governments.

The Nigerian economy is dominated by dependence on oil and oil derivatives. Oil accounts for 95 percent of export earnings and 65 percent of government revenue. In spite of its vast resources, Nigeria is an impoverished country, with a per capita gross national product of less than U.S.$300. As is the case in many developing countries, there are wide disparities in income between the poorest and wealthiest segments of the nation. Sixty-six percent of Nigerians live below the poverty line (Van Buren 2002, 829). The economy has experienced moderate levels of growth, expanding by approximately 3 percent a year in recent years. Key industries include petroleum extraction and refining, as well as the exploitation of coal and tin resources. Given its dependence on oil, the Nigerian economy is highly vulnerable to fluctuations in oil prices. Continued economic growth will depend on the success of the government's diversification policies.

Nigeria's population is estimated at 134 million. The population growth rate is estimated at around 2 percent. Both the population and growth rate are adjusted for AIDS-related deaths. Approximately 3.5 million Nigerians were living with HIV/AIDS as of 2001 (CIA *World Factbook*

2003). Although this is a large number, it is not as high per capita as many states in south and southeastern Africa. A majority of Nigerians are Muslims, while a significant minority practice Christianity. Islam is the predominant religion in the northern portion of Nigeria. English is Nigeria's official language.

Regional Geopolitics

Regardless of whether the measure employed is military might, economic output, or population, Nigeria is the most powerful country in West Africa. There is no grouping of regional conventional forces that could threaten the country. However, Nigeria's internal political stability is closely tied to that of the nation's West African neighbors (Abegunrin 2003, 187). The region has experienced a great deal of instability, including conflicts in Liberia, Sierra Leone, Côte d'Ivoire, and Guinea Bissau. In 2003, Obasanjo granted Charles Taylor, the former leader of Liberia, exile in Nigeria. Taylor is an indicted war criminal and is on the Interpol most-wanted list for his role in support-

Table 1   Nigeria: Key Statistics

Type of government	Republic
Population (millions)	133.8 (2003)
Religion	Muslim 50% (2003); Christian 40% (2003)
Main industries	Crude oil, coal, tin (2003)
Main security threats	Internal instability
Defense spending (% GDP)	1.00 (2002)
Size of military (thousands)	78 (2002)
Number of civil wars since 1945	3
Number of interstate wars since 1945	0

Sources

Central Intelligence Agency Website. 2003. CIA *World Factbook*. http://www.cia.gov/cia/publications/factbook/ (accessed December 15, 2003).

Correlates of War Interstate War Dataset Website. http://cow2.la.psu.edu/ (accessed December, 2003).

Stockholm International Peace Research Institute (SIPRI). 2003. *SIPRI Yearbook 2003: Armaments, Disarmament and International Security.* London: Oxford University Press.

ing rebels who committed war crimes in Sierra Leone. Nigeria refuses to turn Taylor over to international authorities and questions the legality of the arrest warrant. Many Liberians are wary of the Nigerian role in Liberia. They point to the fact that Nigeria did not maintain neutrality when it entered Liberia as the dominant component of a peacekeeping force in August 1990. In spite of these concerns, Nigeria has provided support for the transitional government of Liberia and humanitarian assistance both to rebel and government groups. As of February 2004, the principal rebel group remaining in Liberia has begun the process of disarmament and reintegration. Democratic elections are scheduled in Liberia for some point in 2005. For the moment, Liberia enjoys a certain degree of political stability. The full reintegration of rebels into Liberian society, as well as political and economic reconstruction, will continue to be major issues for the next several years.

The prospects for a lasting peace in Sierra Leone will also depend on reintegration, reconstruction, and development. Although the peace process initiated in 2001 has resulted in successful elections and demobilization of the principal rebel group, food shortages and continued unrest leave open the possibility of a return to violent conflict. In addition, the rebels recruited thousands of child soldiers, and their reintegration poses special challenges to the country.

The situation in Côte d'Ivoire is equally unstable, with rebels holding power in the northern portion of the country in spite of a peace agreement that contained provisions for power sharing. Peacekeepers from France, Côte d'Ivoire's former colonial power, have formed a buffer zone between the rebels in the north and the government in the south. The Economic Community of West African States (ECOWAS), of which Nigeria is the dominant member, has also provided over 1,000 troops to the mission (Nigeria itself has not contributed troops). As of late February, the UN Security Council has agreed to deploy a peacekeeping force to the country. At this point the prospects for stability in Côte d'Ivoire are uncertain.

Regional security in West Africa would also benefit from a return to stability in Guinea Bissau. After a civil war in the late 1990s, the country experienced another military coup in September 2003, after the country's president, Kumba Yala, postponed a scheduled election. Nigeria, along with several other African states, condemned the coup and has pressured the coup leaders to reinstate the elected president. Nigeria is also opposed to attempts by the military to create its own transitional government. The military, for its part, accuses the former administration of plundering the country, a charge that is supported by many citizens. Even though a return to the bloodshed of recent years appears unlikely, the overall political instability in Guinea Bissau is a concern for Nigeria's young democracy.

Conflict Past and Present

Conflict History

Nigeria has experienced three civil wars since its independence. The most costly of these, both in terms of human life and political stability, was the Biafran secession. This conflict lasted from July 1967 to January 1970. In 1966, a group of junior Ibo officers overthrew the government of Tafawa Belewa. The rapid transfer from British to indigenous rule had created instability in the structure of the armed forces (Aborisade and Mundt 2002, 14–15). The first coup resulted in a countercoup that took place in July of the same year. At the same time, riots and murders in the north were directed against the Ibo, who were a minority in that region. The result was a mass migration of the remaining Ibo eastward, to the area of Nigeria where they constitute a majority. The new leader of Nigeria, Colonel Yakubu Gowon, proposed a plan to divide the country into twelve states, replacing the four-region system inherited from British rule. The Ibo recognized that the new division of territory would result in three eastern states, two of which would contain only a minority Ibo population. In this sense, the Ibo viewed the new system as an attempt to dilute their power.

Colonel Gowon met with the leader of the eastern forces, Colonel Chukwuemeka Odumegwu-Ojukwu, in January 1967 in an attempt to diffuse the rapidly escalating situation. Though Gowon agreed to many of his counterpart's demands for a decentralized power arrangement in Nigeria, both sides were under immense pressure to achieve total victory in the negotiations. The result was diverging interpretations of the document produced at the conference (De St. Jorre 1972, 92). In May 1967, Colonel Ojukwu declared independence for the Republic of Biafra.

The Biafran forces were outnumbered and geographically marginalized from many of the country's resources. The basic strategy was to pursue support from friendly governments and international organizations. Côte d'Ivoire, along with its French patron, provided support to the secessionists, while the Soviet Union provided equipment and experienced Egyptian pilots to fight alongside government forces to supplement the government forces. Several international aid organizations lent humanitarian aid to civilians in Biafra, who were suffering under a government blockade. By the end of the war, as many as 2 million civilians in the east had died either as a result of the fighting or (more commonly) as a result of the blockade. Approximately 100,000 soldiers on both sides died during the course of the conflict. By late 1969, the eastern secessionists had been cut off from most of their support and were suffering major defeats on the battlefield. The eastern forces surrendered in January 1970.

During late 1980 and early 1984, Nigeria experienced violence between government forces and Islamic groups in the north that resulted in a total of 6,000 battle deaths. Government corruption was a partial catalyst for both of these conflicts, as was the desire by Nigerian officials to maintain a balance between the Muslim north and the Christian south. However, the government reversed this policy to some extent in 1986, when it gained admission into the Organization of the Islamic Conference. The divide between Islam and Christianity is a constant source of potential conflict in Nigeria.

Nigeria has also intervened in several regional civil wars. Its most prolonged involvement was in the Liberian civil war and its aftermath, lasting from 1990 until the present. The civil war in Liberia began in 1989, when rebels from the National Patriotic Front of Liberia (NPFL) crossed into Liberia from neighboring Côte d'Ivoire. The initial goal was to overthrow the regime of Samuel Doe, who had forced many of his political opponents to flee the country. However, the war soon became a battle between rival ethnic groups. When the NPFL began its campaign in the area inhabited by the Gio and Mano ethnic groups, Taylor was welcomed as a liberator by the local population (Outram 2002, 603). Doe, who was from the Krahn ethnic group, soon instituted a policy of exterminating the Gios and Manos. The NPFL responded by attacking members of the Krahn and Mandingo ethnic groups. Both sides committed many human rights abuses, including torture and arbitrary execution. Upon successfully reaching the capital city of Monrovia, Prince Yormie Johnson, leader of one of the groups that had merged with Taylor, separated from the NPFL and formed the Independent National Patriotic Front of Liberia (INPFL).

The reality of two rebel groups advancing on the capital set the stage for Nigerian involvement via the ECOWAS military observer group, ECOMOG. Nigeria provided most of the personnel, equipment, and financing for the mission, which resulted in its domination of the operation. Although most peacekeeping operations maintain strict neutrality in conflict, ECOMOG quickly allied itself with the INPFL. With the support of ECOMOG, the INPFL gained an advantage over both government and NPFL forces. Monrovia officially fell to the INPFL in September 1990, when Samuel Doe was captured, tortured, and executed. The first year of the conflict resulted in millions of refugees and internally displaced persons.

After two years of relative calm facilitated by a cease-fire agreement, the NPFL launched a new offensive against the capital. One of the reasons commonly cited for the failure of the cease-fire was the decision of ECOMOG to install its own government of national unity. The Interim Government of National Unity drew little support from any of the various ethnic factions and was dependent on ECOMOG for its legitimacy and survival (ibid.). As a result, ECOMOG was forced to defend the capital after learning of Taylor's attack. The NPFL also came under attack from the United Liberation Movement for Democracy (ULIMO), an alliance between some members of the Krahn and Mandingo ethnic groups.

After several failed cease-fire attempts and the division of ULIMO into two competing factions, a new agreement was signed in 1996. ECOMOG reasserted its military dominance and elections were scheduled for 1997. During this period, ECOMOG also dropped its most serious forms of opposition against Taylor. Taylor formed the National Patriotic Party and obtained an overwhelming majority in the general election of July 1997. Taylor, who initially made conciliatory gestures toward the opposition, quickly hardened his stance and began to oppress all opposition. Elections scheduled for 2003 never took place, and rebel groups again descended on Monrovia. Although Taylor's military organization was able to defeat the rebels in the capital, he was losing even his marginal control in the remainder of the country. In addition, the UN arms embargo on the Taylor government, in place since 2001, began to take its toll on Taylor's forces. The sanctions were imposed in response to the discovery that Taylor had been trading weapons for diamonds with the principal rebel group in Sierra Leone. On August 11, 2003, Taylor stepped down as president of Liberia and went into exile in Nigeria.

Nigeria's involvement in the civil war in Sierra Leone was once again carried out under the auspices of ECOMOG. At one point in the conflict, Nigeria represented the sole contributor to the ECOMOG contingent in Sierra Leone. Nigeria's role in the civil war began when NPFL rebels from Liberia began incursions into Sierra Leone. These rebels allied themselves with an indigenous group known as the Revolutionary United Front (RUF). Nigerian troops were deployed around the border between Liberia and Sierra Leone in order to assist the government in its attempt to repel the NPFL/RUF force. However, internal dissension in Sierra Leone was not limited to the rebel groups. As a result, dissatisfied members of the armed forces staged a successful coup in 1992.

After successive coups in 1996 and 1997, the new leader of Sierra Leone, Johnny Paul Koroma, made peace with the RUF. Nigeria had maintained a significant military presence in the country and attempted to force the new leader to step down by bombing the capital city. The RUF/military alliance thwarted the Nigerian attack and set up its own governing council to administer the country. However, the United Nations and the Commonwealth both refused to recognize the new government and supported the arms embargo imposed by ECOWAS (Synge 2003b, 971). The United Nations applied its own sanctions in August 1997. In February 1998, ECOMOG successfully gained control of the capital city, and Nigerian troops concentrated on neutralizing the rebel forces in the countryside. Later that year, the United Nations established the United Nations Observer Mission in Sierra Leone.

By October 1998, the rebels had launched a new offensive, once again closing in on the capital. However, the costs of the war led Nigeria to announce the withdrawal of its forces from the country. The government, which had relied on Nigerian support to retake the country, was forced to enter into negotiations with the RUF. The UN Security Council authorized a peacekeeping mission to replace its earlier observer group and the Nigerian contingent. However, increasing hostilities forced the Nigerians to remain engaged in the conflict in order to avoid the collapse of the government as the UN mission deployed.

In 2000 and 2001, the government made further efforts to make peace with the RUF and integrate the rebels into the political process. In this context, the government agreed to take steps to ensure that the rebels would be able to compete in eventual elections. Elections were held in May 2002, with Ahmad Tejan Kabbah, the reinstated head of state, achieving a clear victory. The elections were certified by the United Nations, which began to decrease its military presence in late 2002. The Nigerian forces that had comprised the ECOMOG contingent were assimilated into the command and control structure of the UN peacekeeping mission.

Current and Potential Military Confrontation

Averting interethnic conflict remains the greatest challenge to long-term Nigerian security. Nigeria is home to over 250 distinct ethnic groups, a level of diversity that continues to foster instability. Table 2 lists the major ethnic groups that currently vie for power within the federal system. One common government response to interethnic tensions within Nigeria is the creation of new states (see Sidebar 1). In the year 2000, hundreds died in ethnic clashes in the north and south. The state of Sokoto adopted the Sharia as its legal code in May 2000, resulting in pitched battles between Muslims and Christians. A common source of fear is the prospect of Nigeria's disin-

Table 2   Nigeria: Largest Ethnic Groups (as Percentage of Total Population)

Hausa-Fulani	29%
Yoruba	21%
Ibo	18%
Ibibio	5.6%
Kanuri	4%
Edo	3%
Ijaw	2%
Bura	2%
Nupe	1%

Sources

Badru, Pade. 1998. *Imperialism and Ethnic Politics in Nigeria, 1960–1996.* Trenton, NJ: Africa World Press.

Central Intelligence Agency Website. 2003. CIA *World Factbook.* http://www.cia.gov/cia/ publications/factbook/ (accessed December 15, 2003).

tegration, an image that remains in the minds of many Nigerians after the first civil war. Conflict between various ethnic factions is almost a daily occurrence in Nigeria. There are reports of interethnic violence in the state of Delta as recently as February 2004.

A second source of fear is the renewed prospect of direct military intervention in government affairs. The current level of violence in Nigeria makes it difficult for the civilian police to provide adequate protection to the population. The military is one of the few institutions

---

Sidebar 1   Extreme Federalism: The Proliferation of States in Nigeria

When Nigeria gained independence in 1960, the country consisted of three administrative regions. In less than fifty years, the number of states in Nigeria has increased to thirty-six. One of the principal reasons for the remarkable level of state proliferation within Nigeria is the quest for internal stability.

The three original administrative districts corresponded roughly to the regional hegemony enjoyed by the dominant ethnic groups: Hausa-Fulani, Yoruba, and Ibo. Concerns about regional domination led some of Nigeria's smaller ethnic groups to call for the creation of new states. The central government has been willing to create more states; however, substantive federalism has been absent in Nigeria during periods of military rule. Several requests for new states remain outstanding from the previous period of military rule, and further devolution usually is resisted by at least one of the three dominant ethnic groups. It also is unclear how far Nigeria can devolve, even within the framework of a democratic government.

Source

Suberu, Rotimi T. 2001. *Federalism and Ethnic Conflict in Nigeria.* Washington, DC: United States Institute of Peace Press.

equipped for this type of task. There is always the possibility that the military will decide not to leave the streets after quelling an episode of violence. Continued democracy will require an increase in the capacity of civil authorities for dealing with interethnic and intersectoral strife in the country.

A third potential source of conflict in Nigeria is the state of the economy. The president's decision to end fuel subsidies resulted in a series of riots in the most populous city of Lagos. However, ending fuel subsidies is vital to the Nigerian economy, which suffers under high levels of debt and debt service requirements. In addition, the decision by the government to levy an additional tax on the sale of fuel has resulted in strikes by Nigerian trade unions (Borzello 2003).

Although Nigeria has never been engaged in a full-scale interstate war, it has experienced conflict with Cameroon over the status of the Bakassi peninsula in the Gulf of Guinea. In 1996, several military personnel died in clashes between Nigeria and Cameroon on the peninsula. In 1998 Nigeria and Cameroon began to build a more significant military presence in the region. Meanwhile, Cameroon had submitted the dispute to the International Court of Justice (ICJ), asserting that its claim on the peninsula was legitimate based on the division of colonial territory between Germany and the United Kingdom. Nigeria denied that the court had jurisdiction over the case and continued its troop buildup. When the ICJ ruled in favor of Cameroon in 2002, Nigeria ignored the decision and continued its military exercises. However, in late 2002 Nigeria and Cameroon agreed to cooperate on the delineation of a precise boundary between the two countries. As of February 2004, it appears that Nigeria is prepared to settle the dispute with Cameroon by withdrawing from most of the disputed territory.

Alliance Structure

When ECOWAS was founded in 1975, it was viewed as an instrument of economic cooperation and development. Later, representatives from Nigeria and Togo suggested the addition of a formal defense treaty. This treaty ultimately entered into force in 1986. However, in 1978 and 1981, the members of ECOWAS signed security protocols that required mutual assistance in the event of external or internal attack on any of the member states. The special character of the protocols stems from the provision requiring mutual assistance in response to civil war. Most defense pacts are only activated in cases of an interstate dispute. Including an intrastate provision was important to a group of states that is under the constant threat of internal instability. It is under the terms of these protocols that ECOWAS intervened in Liberia and Sierra Leone. The members of ECOWAS include Nigeria, Ghana, Sierra Leone, Liberia, Guinea, Benin, Gambia, Guinea Bissau, Cape Verde, Togo, Burkina Faso, Côte d'Ivoire, Niger, Mauritania, Senegal, and Mali. This alliance is also important to Nigeria in that it includes in its membership both francophone and anglophone states.

Size and Structure of the Military

The Nigerian armed forces consist of an army, a navy, and an air force. The Nigerian army claims an active force of approximately 60,000 personnel. However, this number is difficult to verify given the high number of "ghost personnel" in the armed forces. The use of ghost personnel is a form of corruption where fictitious names are added to the ranks of the armed forces in order to generate salary and benefits for someone who is not serving in the army (British Broadcasting Corporation 1999). Lieutenant General Alexander Odareduo Ogomudia heads the army. This force is divided into two mechanized infantry divisions, a composite formation, a garrison command, and a presidential guard (U.S. Department of State 2003). The 1st Mechanized Division possesses one mechanized infantry brigade and one motorized infantry brigade. Though its precise deployment location is unknown, it is thought to be located in the north (Jane's Information Group 2000, 527). The 2nd Mechanized Division is deployed to the southwest of the country. The 82nd Composite Division is located near the border with Cameroon and is the force that is in various stages of withdrawal from the disputed Bakassi peninsula. The Garrison Command is located in Lagos. At full strength, each division should consist of a brigade of engineers, an artillery brigade, a logistic and support brigade, and a signal battalion. Repeated budget crises, as well as the withdrawal of U.S. funding for military training, have had an adverse impact on military preparedness and overall strength. In spite of these setbacks, Nigeria has been able to purchase some older, refurbished Soviet equipment, including ten Mi–34S light helicopters and six Mi–24P Hind F combat helicopters (Stockholm International Peace Research Institute [SIPRI] 2003).

The Nigerian navy is made up of 7,000 active duty personnel. The chief of naval staff is Lieutenant General Agwai. At full strength, the Nigerian navy is able to call on several frigates, attack boats, convenes, and patrol boats (U.S. Department of State 2003). Even though aging equipment is also a problem for the navy, Nigeria did procure four new Balsom Class cargo ships from the United States in 2003 (SIPRI 2003). Nigeria uses its naval capabilities both for domestic defense and for deployment in multilateral peace missions. The Nigerian navy was heavily involved in the ECOWAS missions in Liberia and Sierra Leone.

The Nigerian air force consists of approximately 9,000 active duty personnel. At full strength, it operates helicopters and fighter aircraft. However, most of this equipment is not in working condition (U.S. Department of State 2003). The chief of air staff is Vice Marshal Jonas Wuyep. Of all of the branches of the Nigerian armed services, it appears that the air force is in the worst condition in terms of equipment operation and maintenance.

Each of the army divisions, as well as the presidential guard and the joint intelligence center, reports to the army headquarters in Lagos (Jane's Information Group 2000, 527). All branches of the Nigerian armed services report to the civilian minister of defense, Rabiu Kwankaso. In spite of the newly established level of civilian control over the military, the level of effectiveness of the new military bureaucracy is unclear. President Obasanjo enjoys a degree of respect from the military by virtue of his history of military service. However, Nigeria has yet to develop any real level of legislative control over the activities of the armed forces. Shortly after his initial election, Obasanjo announced plans to trim the armed forces by over one-third. Obasanjo, reacting to internal pressure and the reality of Nigeria's domestic situation, scrapped these plans late in the year 2000 (Peters 2002, 16).

In addition to its domestic deployments, the Nigerian military is heavily involved in international peacekeeping missions. Nigeria spent over U.S.$8 billion on the ECOWAS operation in Liberia and committed thousands of troops. With an increased UN presence in the region, the number of Nigerian troops deployed internationally has decreased. As of January 2004, Nigeria has 3,236 military personnel involved in UN peacekeeping. The bulk of these troops are deployed with the UN mission in Liberia and the UN mission in Sierra Leone. Additional Nigerian forces are deployed in Africa as part of UN missions in the Democratic Republic of the Congo and Ethiopia/Eritrea (United Nations Department of Peacekeeping Operations 2004). Contributing troops to these missions provides Nigeria with the additional benefit of training, economic assistance, and employment for its soldiers.

Budget

Military expenditure data in Nigeria from the military regime era are not always reliable, especially in terms of constant U.S. dollars and percentage of gross domestic product. This is due in part to the use of a different exchange rate by the military in calculating the costs of purchases (SIPRI 2003). As a result, data from the pre-1999 era are usually considered underestimates of actual government spending on the military. Although the return of democracy to Nigeria has brought increased transparency, there is still a paucity of data on specific spending breakdowns.

Military spending in 2002 accounted for approximately 65,000 million naira (Nigeria's local currency). This is approximately equal to U.S.$487 million. This represented a U.S.$66 million decrease over the year 2001. However, the figure is up from $369 million in 2000 (SIPRI 2003; CIA *World Factbook* 2003). There is no clear trend in Nigerian military spending, reflecting the government's need to react to various instances of civil unrest. Nigeria does not have a significant arms production capability and has imported arms and equipment at various times from the United States, China, Russia, Germany, and Great Britain.

Nigeria is presently not capable of producing a nuclear weapon, though it is rumored that the country considered the idea in the 1980s as a response to the South African nuclear weapons program (see Sidebar 2 for more recent develop-

---

Sidebar 2　Nigeria and Nuclear Weapons

Concerns about Nigeria's desire to pursue the acquisition of nuclear weapons resurfaced in early 2004, when Pakistan released a press statement claiming that the government "is working out the dynamics of how they can assist Nigeria's armed forces to strengthen its military capability and to acquire nuclear power." Nigeria later claimed that the press release contained a typographical error and that the country only seeks increased military cooperation with Pakistan. Nigeria continues to deny that it has nuclear ambitions. Nigeria has signed and ratified the Treaty of Pelindaba, which prohibits the development or possession of nuclear weapons in Africa.

Source
British Broadcasting Corporation. 2004. *Nigeria's Nuclear Power "Mix up."* http://news.bbc.co.uk/1/hi/world/africa/3533225.stm (accessed May 2004).

ments). Nigeria considers South Africa its only rival in sub-Saharan Africa, though the overall climate has changed with the end of apartheid. Nigeria has renounced the nuclear option through its ratification of the Nuclear Non-proliferation Treaty. Nigeria has also renounced the possession of chemical and biological weapons through ratification of the relevant international instruments. The overall level of available weapons technology is quite low. Most of the weapons and weapons systems that Nigeria purchases are antiquated. In spite of this fact, Nigeria remains the most powerful military force in the region by virtue of its advantage in personnel and access to some level of technology.

Civil-Military Relations/The Role of the Military in Domestic Politics

The political history of Nigeria since independence is replete with military coups. As mentioned earlier, the elections of 2003 witnessed the first civilian transfer of power in Nigerian history. There are three primary reasons that are often cited for the prevalence of coups. First, the British colonial policy in Nigeria cultivated the dominance of the Hausa-Fulani (Nwagwu 2002, 9). The Hausa-Fulani dominated the rank and file of the military, while the Ibo provided most of the officers. Most Nigerian military bases were also located in the north. Even before independence, there was a great deal of mistrust and mutual suspicion between these two rival ethnic groups. It is not surprising then that the Ibo were the first to stage a successful military coup in Nigeria.

In addition to the structure of the armed forces, British policy toward Nigeria placed most of the political power in the north. Britain divided Nigeria and used relocation programs to establish northern dominance. As the United Kingdom prepared to grant Nigeria independence, it cobbled together a series of political institutions designed to promote parliamentary democracy (Nwagwu 2002, 17). The problem is that this type of political arrangement primarily benefited the north. Faced with the prospect of being a perpetual minority, and without a set of democratic values to accompany democratic institutions, many members of the military elite decided that the best way to succeed politically was via a military coup.

Finally, while the British attempted to create a professional military in Nigeria, geopolitical circumstances at the time of independence made professionalism difficult to maintain. As it gained its independence, Nigeria was left with a number of relatively weak, impoverished neighbors. The development of significant oil resources only increased this disparity. As a result, the Nigerian military was not challenged with the traditional problem of external defense (Ojo 2000, 10). Since Nigerian military personnel had been readily used by the British to quell violence in the empire, they easily adapted to this role at home.

Although there is some division among sources as to the exact number, Nigeria has experienced at least ten military coups since independence. Seven of these coups resulted in leadership changes. As stated earlier, the first coup took place in January 1966, when the installed civilian government was overthrown by a group of Ibo junior officers. The counter-coup that took place in July 1966, led by Colonel Gowon, ultimately led to the Biafran secession. After the war, Gowon pursued several foreign policy initiatives, including leadership in the effort to end white rule in South Africa and Rhodesia, in a partial attempt to divert attention from events in Nigeria (Abegunrin 2003, 55). The diversion was ultimately unsuccessful, as Gowon called off scheduled elections as a result of political and economic instability. Murtala Ramat Muhammed led a successful coup against Gowon and replaced him as head of state.

A failed coup attempt in February 1976 resulted in the assassination of Muhammed. Muhammed's replacement was none other than Chief of Staff Olusegun Obasanjo. Obasanjo set the framework for a transition to civilian government. The transfer was completed in October 1979. The National Party of Nigeria, led by Alhaji Shehu Shagari, received a plurality of votes in the elections and assumed power. However, civilian rule ended again in December 1983, when Lieutenant General Muhammadu Buhari deposed Shagari. Nigerians welcomed the coup in many respects, given the corruption of the civilian regime.

General Ibrahim Babangida and his loyalists overthrew Buhari in August 1985. Babangida's regime in turn survived two coup attempts. Babangida ultimately announced the transfer of power to a civilian regime, to take place in 1992. Babangida annulled the results of the first round of elections in October 1992 and prohibited candidates in that election from contesting the new elections scheduled for 1993. Chief Moshood Abiola polled highest in the new elections, which were once again invalidated. Babangida's popularity plummeted and an interim civilian government replaced him. However, the civilian government was quickly replaced by military rule under the leadership of Sani Abacha.

General Abacha survived two alleged coup attempts and vowed to affect a transition to a democratically elected government. However, the fact that Abacha intended to retire from the military and contest the election as a civilian raised doubts as to the legitimacy of his transition program. When Abacha died suddenly in 1998, there was an opening for a more legitimate democratic transition. General Obasanjo won the election and has been the president of Nigeria since May 1999.

The transition to democratic rule has not resolved the issue of civil-military relations. The military retains a great deal of influence in the political process. Obasanjo's election is partial evidence in this regard, as is his inability to decrease the size of the military or to affect a sustained decrease in military spending. The government is often forced to call on the military for assistance in dealing with internal conflict between ethnic factions, which carries with it the specter of continued military dominance. In 1999, the United States announced that it would provide aid and technical assistance in professionalizing the Nigerian military. However, this aid was suspended in early 2003, due to a series of human rights abuses on the part of the military.

Terrorism

Nigeria does not have a terrorism problem in the sense that the government is not the only target of Islamic fundamentalism. Religious differences in Nigeria have resulted in conflicts with the government at various points in Nigerian history. However, these conflicts have not been commonly labeled as terrorist acts, but rather as ethnic and religious conflicts. In February 2003, the U.S. Treasury Department linked the Saudi Arabian charitable organization Al-Haramain to support for terrorist activities (Akande 2003). The group maintains a branch in Nigeria, resulting in a terrorist connection. There is no evidence that the government has encouraged such groups to operate within Nigeria. In addition, the U.S. government has in general been pleased by Nigerian diplomatic assistance in the war on terror, including its role in fostering support for the United States within Africa (U.S. Department of State 2003).

One area of disagreement with the United States is on the issue of a unified international convention on terrorism. Nigeria supports such a convention, in part because it would allow certain acts to be excluded from a negotiated definition of terrorism. This is consistent with the stance of the Non-aligned Movement (NAM). Specifically, the NAM would like to exclude what it calls "legitimate acts of self-determination" from the definition of terrorism. To the NAM, this would effectively exclude the actions of the Palestinians within the West Bank and Gaza Strip from the realm of terrorist acts. The United States disagrees with the NAM position, preferring the existing regime of individual agreements on various actions associated with terrorism.

Relationship with the United States

Nigeria is the fifth-largest supplier of oil to the United States. The fact that Nigeria, along with Venezuela, provides alternatives to Middle Eastern oil suppliers has helped to shape the relationship between the two countries. In addition, Nigeria is important to U.S. policy in sub-Saharan Africa. Despite the strategic importance of Nigeria to the United States, the relationship between the two countries has been strained on various occasions.

The fact that the Soviet Union was willing to provide overt support to Nigeria during the Biafran civil war resulted in Nigerian condemnation of both the United States and the United Kingdom. However, the United States considered Nigeria to be within Great Britain's sphere of influence and did little to counter Soviet influence. Given Nigeria's commitment to nonalignment, the various military governments always needed to maintain some distance in Nigeria's relationship with the Soviets. In general, the United States enjoyed a positive relationship with Nigeria, even considering the flare-up of anti-U.S. sentiment in the wake of the civil war (Abegunrin 2003, 70). Nigerian support of the Angolan government in its civil war also angered the United States. The Angolan government was allied with the Soviet Union and its Cuban proxy.

U.S.-Nigerian relations improved again under the Carter administration. Though Carter was concerned about human rights in Nigeria, he was more concerned with apartheid in South Africa. Carter found a valuable ally in Obasanjo in his efforts to push for majority rule in South Africa and Rhodesia (Abegunrin 2003, 72). Nigerian action in Zaire (now the Democratic Republic of the Congo) spared the United States from a potentially costly intervention in the country. Although Nigeria's nonalignment policies at times diverged from those of the United States, relations between the two countries were positive.

The relationship between Nigeria and the United States soured noticeably in

1993 in the wake of the military's annulment of the democratic elections. The United States, along with the United Kingdom and the Commonwealth, imposed military sanctions against Nigeria, including an arms embargo. The United States also recalled its diplomats from Nigeria after nine Nigerian political dissidents, including Ken Saro-Wiwa, were executed by the military. Relations between the United States and Nigeria improved after the death of Abacha and the transition to democracy. As mentioned previously, the United States committed financial and technical assistance toward military reform.

The current state of relations between Nigeria and the United States is mixed. Although the United States has received Nigerian support on the terrorism issue, Nigeria opposed the war in Iraq. In addition, the Nigerian military killed at least 200 civilians in the state of Benue (Synge 2003a, 827). The Bush administration announced a halt to military aid in 2003 based on the government's human rights practices. The Nigerian perspective is that the termination of aid is tied to its opposition of the war in Iraq.

The Future

Nigerian security in the medium term will continue to be tied to the government's ability to keep the country unified. There is no foreseeable external threat to Nigerian security on the horizon, a fact that further highlights the importance of internal security. The growth of Islamic fundamentalism in the north does not bode well for national unity. Given Nigerian history, the price of political unification may well be the end of democratic rule. As long as the military retains its influence within the political system, it will be difficult for the government to control military spending. In addition, military spending in the short and medium term may need to increase in order to accommodate the need for increased security. Nigerian democracy is caught in a bit of a conundrum in that it must try to decrease the role of the military while increasing security.

Not all of the signs are negative, however. The Nigerian military may well view the present as an inopportune time to assume control of the government given the country's economic and political problems. If Obasanjo can extend civilian control of the military beyond the office of the president, it may be possible to consolidate democracy in the country. It will be necessary for the government to tackle both its own corruption, as well as corruption in the military, in order to promote economic development. In addition, it will be necessary for the government to develop the capacity to deal with internal conflicts at the level of the civilian police. In the final analysis, internal ethnic political tensions will continue to be the primary threat to Nigerian security for the foreseeable future.

References, Recommended Readings, and Websites

Books
Abegunrin, Olayiwola. 2003. *Nigerian Foreign Policy Under Military Rule, 1966–1999*. Westport, CT: Praeger.
Aborisade, Oladimeji, and Robert J. Mundt. 2002. *Politics in Nigeria*. New York: Addison-Wesley Education Publishers.
Akinyemi, A. Bolaji. 1978. *Nigeria and the World: Readings in Nigerian Foreign Policy*. Ibadan, Nigeria: Oxford University Press.
Badru, Pade. 1998. *Imperialism and Ethnic Politics in Nigeria, 1960–1996*. Trenton, NJ: Africa World Press.
De St. Jorre, John. 1972. *The Nigerian*

Civil War. London: Hodder and Stoughton.

Edozie, Rita Kiki. 2000. *Jane's World Armies*. Alexandria, VA: Jane's Information Group.

———. 2002. *People Power and Democracy: The Popular Movement against Military Despotism in Nigeria, 1989–1999*. Trenton, NJ: Africa World Press.

Mabogunje, Akin L. 2002. "Nigeria: Physical and Social Geography." In *Africa South of the Sahara*. London: Europa Publications.

Matusevich, Maxim. 2003. *No Easy Row for a Russian Hoe: Ideology and Pragmatism in Nigerian-Soviet Relations, 1960–1991*. Trenton, NJ: Africa World Press.

Nwagwu, Emeka. 2002. *Taming the Tiger: Civil-Military Relations Reform and the Search for Political Stability in Nigeria*. Lanham, MD: University Press of America.

Ojo, Olusola. 2000. *The Nigerian Military: An Obstacle to Enduring Democracy?* Jerusalem: Hebrew University of Jerusalem.

Outram, Quentin. 2002. "Liberia: Recent History." In *Africa South of the Sahara*. London: Europa Publications, pp. 601–611.

Peters, Jimi. 1997. *The Nigerian Military and the State*. New York: Tauris Academic Studies.

Stockholm International Peace Research Institute (SIPRI). 2003. *SIPRI Yearbook 2003: Armaments, Disarmament and International Security*. London: Oxford University Press.

Suberu, Rotimi T. 2001. *Federalism and Ethnic Conflict in Nigeria*. Washington, DC: United States Institute of Peace Press.

Synge, Richard. 2003a. "Nigeria: Recent History." In *Africa South of the Sahara*. London: Europa Publications, pp. 840–851.

———. 2003b. "Sierra Leone: Recent History." In *Africa South of the Sahara*. London: Europa Publications, pp. 968–974.

Van Buren, Linda. 2002. "Nigeria: Economy." In *Africa South of the Sahara*. London: Europa Publications, pp. 829–937.

Articles

Gibler, Douglas M., and Meredity Starkees. Forthcoming. "Measuring Alliances: The Correlates of War Formal Interstate Alliance Data Set, 1816–2000." *Journal of Peace Research*.

Peters, Jimi. 2002. "Defense Sector Reform in Nigeria." Paper presented at a workshop on Security Sector Reform and Democratization in Africa: Comparative Perspectives. African Security Dialogue and Research, Accra Ghana.

Sarkees, Meredith Reid. 2000. "The Correlates of War Data on War: An Update to 1997." *Conflict Management and Peace Science* 18, no. 1:123–144.

Websites

African Union Website: http://www.africa-union.org.

Akande, Laolu. 2003. "U.S. links Saudi Group in Nigeria to Terrorism." http://www.ngrguardiannews.com (accessed December 2003).

Borzello, Anna. 2003. "Nigeria Strike Call over Fuel Prices." http://news.bbc.co.uk/1/hi/world/africa/3164688.stm (accessed December 15, 2003).

British Broadcasting Corporation. 1999. "Nigerian Ghost Army." http://news.bbc.co.uk/1/hi/world/africa/548371.stm (accessed December 15, 2003).

Central Intelligence Agency Website. 2003. CIA *World Factbook*. http://www.cia.gov/cia/publications/factbook/ (accessed December 15, 2003).

Nigerian Government Website: http://www.nigeria.gov.ng.

"Nigeria's Nuclear Power 'Mix-up.'" March 4, 2004. http://www.bbc.co.uk.

Oloruntola, Tokunbo. 2003. "Military Reform in Troubled Waters." *Daily Independent Online*, March 28. http://www.odili.net (accessed December 20, 2003).

SIPRI Database of Arms Transfers: http://www.sipri.se.

U.S. Department of State Website. 2003. "Background Note: Nigeria." http://www.state.gov/r/pa/ei/bgn/2836.htm (accessed December 20, 2003).

United Nations Department of Peacekeeping Operations. 2004. http://www.un.org.Depts/dpko (accessed May 17, 2005).

North Korea

Terence Roehrig

Geography and History

The division of the Korean peninsula that created North Korea is a relatively recent occurrence. Since 668 C.E. Korea existed as a united country under the rule of numerous monarchs. In 1910, Japan annexed Korea, where it remained under an oppressive occupation until the end of World War II. With the close of the war, the United States and the Soviet Union agreed to temporarily divide the peninsula at the 38th parallel to accept the Japanese surrender. According to the arrangement, the Soviets accepted the surrender north of that line while the United States did so in the south. Despite numerous efforts to bring the two regions back together, growing Cold War tension prevented reunification, and the north and south remained divided. In 1948, separate governments were created: first, in the south, a capitalist state allied with the United States under the leadership of newly elected President Syngman Rhee (Republic of Korea, ROK), and then in the north, a communist state with ties to the Soviet Union led by Kim Il Sung (Democratic People's Republic of Korea, DPRK).

North Korea has a population of approximately 22.9 million, ranking it forty-eighth in the world. With only minor exceptions, all residents of North Korea are ethnic Koreans. Most North Koreans are adherents of Buddhism and/or Confucian-ism. Though not a religious denomination in the traditional sense, the tenets of Confucianism that stress respect, obedience, and loyalty to family and the state have a strong influence over society. Religious practices, though not formally banned, are almost nonexistent. As a result, there are no divisions in North Korea along ethnic or religious lines. It is a homogenous society with a common culture and language.

North Korea is approximately 47,000 sq. miles (120,400 sq. km), roughly the size of the state of Mississippi. The terrain is mountainous with only 20 percent of the land suitable for farming. With the division of the peninsula in 1945, North Korea obtained most of the peninsula's mineral resources while the South received a greater share of the arable land. The DPRK is also prone to droughts and floods that have wreaked havoc on its agricultural production. Throughout Korea's history, the North has had difficulty being self-sufficient in agriculture and has relied on the southern regions to augment its own food production.

The 1990s were particularly serious for the economy as droughts and floods, beginning in 1995, decimated North Korean agricultural production. A massive international effort to bring food to the DPRK finally alleviated the crisis after several years of tragedy. Although a precise count is not available, estimates indicate that close to 2 million North Koreans may have died of starvation. These famines continue to have an impact as children, malnourished during this period, show stunted physical growth that is a symptom of the inadequate diet.

Though the crisis has subsided, it is likely that North Korea will remain dependent on international food aid for some time to come. Due to a failed economic policy and the decisions of the leadership, the North Korean economy is in horrendous condition. The economy struggles with outdated technology, a chronic energy shortage, a dilapidated infrastructure, and industrial production that operates at only 30 to 40 percent capacity. North Korea's gross domestic product (GDP) is $30.8 billion and $1,400 on a per capita basis, numbers that place the DPRK near the bottom compared to other countries in the world. Exports total only $1.2 billion since there is little North Korea produces that others want with the one exception of ballistic missiles and related technology that make up the bulk of its export earnings. North Korea also has over $12 billion in external debt, a significant sum given the state of its economy (CIA *World Factbook: 2005*).

From its foundation, North Korea has been a totalitarian, communist dictatorship with power centralized in the Korean Workers' Party and its leader, Kim Il Sung, who ruled from its inception in 1948 until his death in 1994. His son, Kim Jong Il, succeeded him and remains the leader of one of the few surviving communist states. The government is a rigid and repressive regime that maintains tight control over all aspects of society including the media, public security, and education.

The rule of the Kims has been supported by a cult of personality that glorifies, exaggerates, or fabricates the accomplishments of the "Great Leader" (Kim Il Sung) and the "Dear Leader" (Kim Jong Il). Loyalty to the government helps determine employment options, access to medical care, and education opportunities. Those who oppose the regime are sent to

Table 1   North Korea: Key Statistics

Type of government	Authoritarian, communist regime
Population (millions)	22.5 million (2003 est.)
Religion	Buddhism and Confucianism (traditional), independent religious activity almost nonexistent
Main industries	Ballistic missiles and other military equipment, machine building, electric power, chemicals, minerals, metallurgy, textiles, food processing, tourism
Main security threats	Deteriorating economy, United States and South Korea
Defense spending (% GDP)	33.9% (FY 2002)
Size of military (thousands)	1,082
Number of civil wars since 1945	1
Number of interstate wars since 1945	1

Source
Central Intelligence Agency. 2005. CIA *World Factbook*. http://www.cia.gov/cia/publications/factbook/ (accessed May 15, 2005).

one of a dozen labor camps for political dissenters. The regime adheres largely to the tenants of Marxism-Leninism with the state owning the means of production while controlling prices and production. Kim Il Sung crafted an important variant to this ideology called *juche* under which the DPRK pursues self-reliance in economic and political affairs. In recent years, the leadership has begun to undertake modest economic reforms including establishing special economic zones and allowing wages and prices to float according to market forces. However, to date, the reforms have been meager and produced few results.

Regional Geopolitics

Northeast Asia is a region where the interests of several important powers intersect, including China, Japan, Russia, and since the end of World War II, the United States. Regional relations are relatively stable with growing economic and political ties among the various countries in the area. There is a degree of rivalry between China and Japan, but it is relatively benign at the moment. There are two potential flashpoints that could bring conflict to the region. The first is North Korea, particularly its nuclear weapons program. A confirmed North Korean nuclear weapons program could prompt both South Korea and Japan to develop a nuclear option. Pyongyang's ballistic missiles, now capable of reaching Japan and perhaps in the future, the continental United States, has pushed Tokyo and Washington to pursue missile defense in a more vigorous manner.

However, China fears that any significant missile defense program would diminish the deterrent effect of its nuclear forces. A nuclear North Korea also raises concern that it would sell a weapon or the technology to keep its suffering economy afloat.

Finally, there is uncertainty regarding North Korea's intent to reunify the peninsula. The DPRK maintains a heavily armed conventional force that could be used in an effort to strike the South. However, North Korea would have a difficult time if it chose to challenge the modern, well-trained armed forces of South Korea along with the U.S. military stationed on the peninsula. A vigorous counterstrike is sure to follow any North Korean attack and could utilize other U.S. forces in the region. While Seoul has a firm alliance with the United States, North Korea is unlikely to receive similar support from its former patrons, China and Russia, should it initiate a conflict.

A second flashpoint in the region is Taiwan's relationship with China. Beijing has long maintained that Taiwan is a renegade province of the mainland, and any effort by Taiwan to assert its independence is viewed in a negative manner by leaders in Beijing. Should Taiwan push for independence, China has indicated it would use force to prevent such an action. Although the United States has recognized China's eventual sovereignty over Taiwan, Washington has insisted any move in this direction be done peacefully. Should China use force to impose its will on Taiwan, the United States has stated it would come to Taiwan's defense.

Conflict Past and Present

Conflict History

The division of the Korean peninsula was born out of conflict, first the end of World War II and later the Cold War. As

World War II drew to a close and the end of Japanese occupation neared, domestic factions on the left, right, and center began a struggle for power in what Koreans assumed would be a free and independent Korea. While the struggle played out, the dynamics of the Cold War through the United States and Soviet occupation were imposed on this domestic conflict, preventing the factions in Korea from finishing the battle for power. When efforts to reunite the North and South failed, separate regimes were established in 1948 but with both claiming eventual sovereignty over the entire peninsula. For the next two years, there were repeated efforts by both sides to destabilize its adversary including numerous armed incursions across the 38th parallel.

On June 25, 1950, North Korea, with Soviet and Chinese acquiescence, attacked the South in a bid to reunify the peninsula by force. The effort came close to succeeding as South Korean and U.S. forces were driven back to a small area in the southeast known as the Pusan perimeter. The United Nations, led largely by the United States, counterattacked, driving North Korean forces back across the 38th parallel, and presented an opportunity for "rolling back" communism by eliminating this regime. Despite warnings from China that this outcome was unacceptable, U.S.-UN forces continued their drive north. In November 1950, Chinese "volunteers" intervened and pushed U.S. and ROK forces back in a hasty retreat. A military stalemate ensued for the next two years along a line that approximated the old border of the 38th parallel.

The war ended on July 27, 1953, with the signing of an armistice between North Korea, China, and the United States. South Korea's president Syngman Rhee refused to sign, insisting the war should not end until the South was victorious. It is important to note that an armistice only brings an end to hostilities and is not a formal peace treaty. Thus, a state of war still formally exists on the Korean peninsula. Since the end of the conflict, both Koreas have maintained sizable military forces that face each other in a tense standoff along the demilitarized zone (DMZ) that separates the two sides.

Despite many years of relative peace and stability on the peninsula, numerous incidents occurred that could have sparked another conflict in the region (Nanto 2003). In the late 1960s, North Korea drastically escalated its efforts to infiltrate and destabilize the South, reaching a peak in 1967 and 1968 with bolder and more numerous acts of violence. In 1968, over 620 incidents occurred along the DMZ, and 224 DPRK infiltrators were killed while on missions in the South. (UN Command in Korea 1968, 788–790; Koh 1983, 277).

It was clear to North Korean leaders that efforts to reunify the peninsula during the Korean War had failed miserably. As a result, these actions by North Korea were likely signs that Pyongyang was fully aware of the costs of a direct confrontation with U.S.-ROK forces. Instead, the DPRK relied on less direct action that could be ratcheted up or down depending on the level of success and the response of Washington and Seoul.

Matters escalated further in 1968 when North Korea seized the U.S. intelligence ship USS *Pueblo* in an area that Washington maintained was international waters. Pyongyang held the ship and crew for more than a year. In 1969, North Korean jets shot down a U.S. EC-121 reconnaissance plane. After downing the plane,

Kim Il Sung quietly removed a number of the generals that had urged more militant actions toward the United States and South Korea. It was becoming clear to Kim that these actions were drawing North Korea too close to war with the United States and South Korea (Suh 1988, 238–242).

In the 1970s, the ROK military discovered three infiltration tunnels that crossed under the DMZ on the western side of the peninsula. U.S. and South Korean military officials feared these tunnels could be used to place special forces behind ROK lines either prior to or during an invasion. A fourth tunnel was discovered in 1990, and while all four have been neutralized, there are likely other tunnels that have yet to be discovered. Finally, in 1976, North Korean soldiers killed two American servicemen at Panmunjom in the DMZ over the pruning of a tree in an area that obstructed the view of a U.S. observation post. Despite the provocation and suggestions that a military response was appropriate, the United States opted for a more restrained reply as it conducted a "military operation" to trim the tree despite North Korean objections.

At several points, it appeared there might be significant improvements in relations between the North and South. In 1972, the two signed an agreement that recognized the unity of the Korean people and called for unification through peaceful means. Despite these efforts, little in the agreement was ever implemented. In the closing days of 1991, Seoul and Pyongyang signed two other accords that again brought hope for better relations. The first agreement called for reconciliation and nonaggression while the second banned nuclear weapons from the peninsula. But once

---

Sidebar 1 North Korean Tunnels under the DMZ

In the 1970s, the South Korean military discovered three North Korean infiltration tunnels that crossed under the demilitarized zone (DMZ) on the western side of the peninsula. Both U.S. and South Korean military officials feared that these tunnels could be used to place special forces behind Republic of Korea (ROK) lines either prior to or during an invasion. A fourth tunnel was discovered in 1990, and while all four have been neutralized, there are likely other tunnels that have yet to be discovered.

Sources
"North Korea Laying 80 New Tunnels." *Donga Ilbo.* July 8, 2004.
U.S. House of Representatives. *Impact of Intelligence Reassessment on Withdrawal of U.S. Troops from Korea.* Testimony of Nathaniel Thayer, CIA, and General John W. Vessey, Hearings before the Investigations Subcommittee of the Committee on Armed Services. 96th Congress, 1st Session, June 21 and July 17, 1979. Washington, DC: Government Printing Office, pp. 43–44 and 91.

---

again, little occurred toward implementing the accords.

In 1997, former dissident Kim Dae Jung was elected president of South Korea. Once in office, Kim led an effort to improve relations through greater diplomatic and economic engagement with the North in what became known as the Sunshine Policy. The high point of Kim's efforts came in June 2000 when he made an unprecedented visit to meet Kim Jong Il in Pyongyang for a high-level summit. For the first time, leaders of the North and South met face-to-face. When the two arrived at the state guesthouse in Pyongyang, Kim Jong Il remarked, "June 13 will be a day recorded in history," to which Kim Dae Jung replied, "Let's go on and make that history" (French 2000, A1).

Following several days of talks, the two Kims drafted an agreement that called for "promoting mutual understanding" and "achieving peaceful, national reunification." They also agreed to meet again, this time with Kim Jong Il visiting Seoul "at an appropriate time." The summit agreement also included a measure to resume family exchanges that brought relatives together who were separated during the Korean War. On August 15, 2000, 100 families each from North Korea and South Korea made the journey to visit family members separated after the war. Since then, Seoul and Pyongyang have conducted several more rounds of visits.

The June summit was followed by other important meetings in the fall of 2000, one between the defense ministers of North Korea and South Korea; another when first vice chairman of the National Defense Commission, General Jo Myong Rok, visited Washington, D.C.; and finally, Secretary of State Madeline Albright's trip to Pyongyang in November 2000. The latter two meetings held out the possibility of a deal with the North to end the development, testing, and export of its ballistic missiles. One more meeting was necessary to finish the deal, possibly a trip by President Clinton in the closing days of his administration. However, Clinton decided there was insufficient time to conclude an accord, and the incoming Bush administration was unenthusiastic about such an agreement. As a result, Clinton did not make the trip to North Korea and the deal fell through. Finally, Pyongyang made ambitious diplomatic moves establishing formal relations

with over 140 countries including Australia, Spain, Italy, Canada, the United Kingdom, and Germany.

Despite the optimism generated by the June summit, tough security and political issues remained. The optimism faded further when the new Bush administration took office in January 2001. Expressing doubts about the Clinton administration's approach, Bush suspended talks with North Korea prior to completing a review of U.S. policy. In May 2001, the United States finished its review and indicated a willingness to restart talks, though with a much broader security agenda that included limits on the North's ballistic missile program, early inspections of the North's nuclear facilities, and reductions in Pyongyang's conventional forces. The North Korean response was predictable: "We cannot construe this otherwise than an attempt of the US to disarm" North Korea "through negotiations" (French 2001, A3). Relations deteriorated further in January 2002 when President Bush in his State of the Union address identified the DPRK, along with Iraq and Iran, as part of the "axis of evil." When the Bush administration later indicated its willingness to wage preventive war to eliminate these threats and followed through by ousting Saddam Hussein from Iraq, North Korea believed they might be the next regime in the "axis of evil" to come under fire.

Much of the conflict with North Korea in the 1990s revolved around its efforts to acquire nuclear weapons. In 1982, U.S. intelligence pointed to early efforts by the DPRK to begin a nuclear weapons program. Fears diminished somewhat when North Korea signed the Nuclear Non-proliferation Treaty (NPT) in 1985, thereby committing to forgo a nuclear weapons option and open up its facilities to international inspectors. Despite signing the NPT, inspections were late in coming and were incomplete. By 1992, some inspections had occurred, but the results indicated Pyongyang had not been completely truthful in its declarations of the nuclear material it possessed. When further inspections were requested, the North balked, a sign to South Korea and the United States that the North might be hiding something. Tensions grew between the two sides as the DPRK threatened to pull out of the NPT altogether, and Washington pushed for sanctions if the North did not allow full inspections. By the spring of 1994, it appeared that the Korean peninsula might be headed for war.

A disastrous collision was averted in June 1994 when former president Jimmy Carter traveled to Pyongyang in an effort to break the impasse. In a dialogue that was not officially sanctioned by the Clinton administration, Carter obtained Kim Il Sung's tentative agreement to freeze his nuclear program in return for talks with the United States. Negotiations began again, and on October 21, 1994, North Korea and the United States signed the Agreed Framework (AF). The agreement was one between sides that had very little trust in each other. As a result, the AF had many intertwining and conditional steps that meant implementation proceeded slowly.

The accord contained several provisions. First, North Korea agreed to halt all operations at its nuclear facilities, including a five-megawatt reactor that was operational, two larger reactors under construction, and a plant to reprocess spent fuel. These facilities were sealed and monitored by international inspectors. In return, the United States agreed to organize a consortium, the Korean Peninsula Energy Development Organization (KEDO),

that would build two modern light-water reactors to replace the older models North Korea was abandoning. The old models were particularly problematic since they produced significant amounts of nuclear waste that could be turned into weapons. The light-water reactors produced far less spent fuel and a type of plutonium that was more difficult to reprocess into weapons-grade material.

Second, while these reactors were under construction, the United States agreed to provide 500,000 tons of heavy fuel oil annually. Third, North Korea assented to come into full compliance with the NPT, including inspections of all North Korean nuclear facilities. Finally, North Korea agreed to open talks with the South, Washington and Pyongyang agreed to move toward normalized relations including the end of U.S. economic sanctions, and the U.S. pledged to give a formal guarantee not to threaten or use nuclear weapons against the North. While the CIA continued to estimate that North Korea possessed one or two nuclear weapons, the agreement appeared to put a cap on the North's nuclear ambitions.

For several years, the parties struggled to implement the AF, a project that was plagued by numerous delays. The intended completion date of the reactors was 2003, but after a few years it was clear the project would not be finished until 2008. In addition, U.S.-funded fuel oil deliveries were late on several occasions, and efforts to normalize economic and diplomatic relations were not forthcoming. The North may have believed these were purposeful delays by the United States and KEDO in hopes that the North Korean regime would collapse before the agreement was fully implemented. As a result, Pyongyang began to explore other options to acquire nuclear weapons.

Sometime in the late 1990s, Pyongyang changed course and embarked on a different path to nuclear weapons. Receiving considerable help from Pakistan, North Korea began to acquire the necessary parts and material to develop weapons based on highly enriched uranium (HEU), a different route from its earlier plutonium-based program. Though intelligence sources did not notice North Korean efforts immediately, by the summer of 2002 the CIA believed it had convincing evidence of an alternative North Korean effort to acquire nuclear weapons.

At a high-level meeting in October 2002, U.S. officials confronted DPRK delegates with the evidence. North Korea's initial response was to deny the allegations. However, when the meetings continued the following day, Pyongyang admitted it had a nuclear weapons program and "more powerful things as well," possibly a reference to one or two nuclear weapons or its chemical and biological arsenal (Sanger 2002, A1). Although admitting the allegations, the North also declared its willingness to put all security issues—nuclear weapons, ballistic missiles, and conventional forces—on the table in return for a security guarantee, a peace treaty, and acceptance of North Korean sovereignty (Slevin and DeYoung 2002, A1). The United States rejected the North Korean offer, insisting Pyongyang fully comply with all the nuclear agreements it had signed before any negotiations could begin. Heavily involved with the problems in Iraq, the United States insisted these events were not a crisis and could be addressed through diplomacy. As one U.S. official remarked, "One rogue state crisis at a time!" (Roehrig 2003)

Soon after, the AF began to unravel. In November 2002, the United States halted shipments of heavy fuel oil, and the North responded by expelling international inspectors and restarting its nuclear reactor and reprocessing facilities. In January 2003, North Korea announced that it was leaving the NPT. Construction of the light-water reactors continued despite the 2002 allegations. However, in November 2003, further construction was suspended. Though North Korea has declared formally that it possesses nuclear weapons, Pyongyang has yet to conduct a nuclear test. In addition, the exact extent of its HEU program is also unknown, and the North has begun to deny its existence. Thus, the status of North Korea's nuclear capabilities is unclear.

Sidebar 2   North Korean Nuclear Weapons

North Korea is believed to be operating two nuclear weapons programs, one based on plutonium and the other using highly enriched uranium. Pyongyang has not conducted any definitive test of a nuclear weapon, but intelligence sources believe that North Korea may have approximately eight nuclear weapons. On February 10, 2005, North Korea made a formal declaration that it does indeed possess nuclear weapons, a measure it argued was necessary to defend against "the hostile U.S. policy." It is not clear whether North Korea would give up its nuclear capability for the right incentives, or if it instead is determined to develop a nuclear capability regardless of efforts taken by the United States and South Korea. However, the exact extent of North Korea's nuclear weapons capability remains unknown, and efforts continue to convince Pyongyang to give up this option.

*Current and Potential
Military Confrontation*

Resolving the nuclear crisis remains North Korea's chief security problem. Since Pyongyang could make the crisis vanish by declaring it has no intention to develop nuclear weapons and dismantling its program, an important question here is why the North might desire to have a nuclear weapons capability. Four reasons are likely. First, nuclear weapons help North Korea address some serious security threats. Pyongyang faces a formidable and modern ROK military supported by an alliance with the United States that has 33,500 troops stationed on the peninsula. The United States also has many other military resources it could bring to bear in a conflict with North Korea. These threats are magnified by the loss of its traditional Cold War allies, China and the Soviet Union, and a deteriorating economy that makes it increasingly difficult to match ROK defense spending.

Security concerns have become even greater since September 11, 2001, and the Bush administration's policy to prevent states that possess weapons of mass destruction from threatening the United States. In the minds of North Korean leaders, U.S. actions in Iraq indicate that they may be next in line for regime change. Nuclear weapons provide a hedge against these threats and a cheaper alternative to matching South Korea in conventional forces. Indications of Pyongyang's concerns may be most evident in its desire for a security guarantee from the United States in return for giving up its nuclear weapons program. As Donald Gregg, former U.S. ambassador to South Korea noted, "I think that they would like the United States to give them some assurances that we don't want to blow them out of the water" (Seo 2002).

Second, North Korea may be interested in selling a nuclear weapon or the technology to build one. Already a major exporter of ballistic missiles and technology to countries such as Pakistan, Libya, Syria, and Yemen, a nuclear weapon could provide additional export income for its struggling economy. Nuclear weapons and ballistic missiles are two of only a few salable commodities the North possesses, and the leadership may feel increasing pressure to sell these items in an effort to keep the regime in power.

Third, North Korea's nuclear ambitions may result from internal politics and help to bolster support for Kim Jong Il's rule. When Kim Jong Il came to power in 1994 after the death of his father, there were doubts that he would be accepted, especially by conservatives in the military. With the continued economic problems since 1994, there have been concerns regarding Kim's leadership and his control of the military. The acquisition of nuclear weapons may help to bolster his position, especially within the armed forces, and, in the minds of North Koreans, elevates the DPRK's status to that of an important player in the region.

Finally, North Korea may be using its nuclear program as a bargaining chip to obtain food, economic aid, and foreign investment. In an effort to play this bargaining game, the DPRK has been adept at crisis diplomacy that seeks to draw attention to Pyongyang and the issues that concern it. Critics often maintain the North Korean regime is crazy and irrational. Although its actions are sometimes puzzling and difficult to explain, the regime can also be characterized as making the most of what little leverage it has to focus world attention on its needs.

The crucial question that remains is whether North Korea is willing to give up its nuclear ambitions. Though signs seem to point to Pyongyang's willingness to do so, the final outcome of this issue remains in doubt and will require patient negotiations to achieve a final settlement. Most recently, the Six-Party Talks that include North Korea, South Korea, the United States, China, Japan, and Russia have tried to reach a diplomatic settlement, but so far progress has been slow. Despite efforts to bring North Korea back to the negotiating table, further talks have remained on hold since June 2004.

North Korea faces another serious security threat—an economy in desperate trouble. Slowly, the inefficiencies of a Marxist-Leninist command economy, the juche ideology that has frowned on involvement in the global marketplace, and the meddling of Kim Il Sung in economic policy began to take their toll. In one example of mismanagement, farmers were urged to clear hillsides in an effort to increase land under cultivation. However, removing this vegetation increased soil erosion and flooding.

The 1990s were particularly disastrous for the economy. First, with the end of the Cold War, Soviet and Chinese aid came to an end along with extensive trade links to the former communist bloc. Second, beginning in 1995, a series of floods and droughts rocked North Korea, producing large-scale famine in a region that historically has difficulty feeding itself. The country remains dependent on outside food assistance. In 2001, Catherine Bertini, executive director of the World Food Program, noted after a visit to North Korea, "There is no question that for the foreseeable future North Korea will be the recipient of international assistance. It is not possible for the country to be food self-sufficient in the next few years" (Rosenthal 2001, A7).

North Korean industry faces similar challenges as it needs to attract foreign investment and new technology and rebuild its decrepit infrastructure. However, without a resolution to the nuclear weapons issue and the anticipated outside assistance that will follow, it will be difficult to produce the economic improvements the DPRK desperately needs. Without economic reform, there is a danger that the deteriorating economy may destroy the country from within. Hence, the chief task facing Kim Jong Il is regime survival, threatened both by internal and external concerns.

Alliance Structure

In July 1961, North Korea signed two important security agreements, one with China and another with the Soviet Union. These treaties followed on the heels of an ROK coup by General Park Chung Hee in May 1961, a response to the new, strongly anticommunist regime in the South (Koh 1983, 270–271). According to these agreements, "in case one party of the pact is in a state of war, the other party will provide, without delay, military and other assistance, employing all measures in its power" (Yim 1983, 122). This is the exact wording in the agreement with the Soviet Union (signed July 6, 1961), and the language in the agreement with China is similar (signed July 11, 1961). Following the signing, Kim Il Sung condemned the United States, declaring "the American imperialists are the most rabid enemies of the Asian peoples as well as of the other nations that are fighting for peace and social progress" (Caruthers 1961, A1). Premier Khrushchev argued that the Soviet Union did not believe in military pacts, but "we had to sign this treaty of a defensive nature because the Governments of the United States, Japan and other powers have turned down all our proposals toward the relaxation of tension and insuring of security in the Far East" (ibid.).

The end of the Cold War brought a significant shift in relations between these former communist allies. Despite years of ideological ties, China and Russia sought to distance themselves from the North while cultivating a relationship with Pyongyang's nemesis in the South. Abandoning the old "one Korea" policy that recognized a single legitimate regime on the peninsula—the DPRK—China and Russia moved toward a "two Koreas" approach that sought improved relations with both North and South. In 1992, Moscow and Beijing established formal diplomatic relations with South Korea, a move that greatly disturbed Pyongyang. Ideological ties with the North were no longer as crucial as the trade and investment opportunities offered by a relationship with Seoul. Concerning DPRK-Russia relations, one scholar noted, "North Korea now has very little to offer Moscow. A democratic Russia . . . sees no ideological value in links with an unreformed Stalinist regime, which it regards as a lingering relic from its own tragic past" (Marantz 1993, 35).

Concerning the security treaty, China has continued to maintain the 1961 bilateral Treaty of Friendship, Cooperation, and Mutual Assistance with the DPRK. However, Beijing has made it clear that it will not support a North Korean attack on the South. The exact nature of Chinese support for North Korea in a future crisis is unclear. Yet China will go to great lengths to prevent a North Korean collapse and has been a defender of Pyongyang in international forums op-

posing efforts to pressure the North with economic sanctions.

For the Russians, the treaty has been a different matter. Although China was somewhat successful in maintaining balanced relations with the Koreas in the early 1990s, Moscow's ties with the North soured dramatically. After normalizing relations with Seoul, Russian president Boris Yeltsin announced the 1961 security treaty had little value for Moscow, and in 1995 Russia asked to renegotiate the alliance that was due to expire the following year. On February 9, 2000, North Korea and Russia signed a new Treaty of Friendship, Good Neighborliness, and Cooperation to replace the 1961 agreement. The security clause therein was more vague than in the 1961 document, "in the event of the emergence of the danger of an aggression against one of the countries or a situation jeopardizing peace and security, and in the event there is a necessity for consultations and cooperation, the sides enter into contact with each other immediately" (Joo 2001, 475). The agreement included no language that would commit Moscow to the DPRK's defense. Earlier, the Kremlin had also made it clear that assistance would only be possible if the North were attacked. In July 2000, Russian President Vladimir Putin traveled to North Korea where he and Kim Jong Il signed a joint declaration indicating "the willingness to get in touch with each other without delay if the danger of aggression to the DPRK or to Russia is created or when there is the need to have consultations and cooperate with each other under the circumstances where peace and security are threatened" (School of Hawaiian, Asian, and Pacific Studies 2000).

For China and Russia, the dangers and uncertainty of North Korea's future is a cause of great concern. Both fear a collapse of the aging communist regime since this could mean a torrent of refugees, conflict on their borders, and the likelihood that the new Korea would be governed from Seoul, placing a staunch U.S. ally on their borders.

Size and Structure of the Military

North Korea is often characterized as one of the most militarized countries in the world. As shown in Table 2, it has a standing armed force of almost 1.1 million active duty soldiers, making it fifth largest in the world behind China, the United States, Russia, and India. In addition, over 4.7 million people remain in the reserves.

Active duty personnel include 88,000 special operations forces trained for infiltration, reconnaissance, and subversion. Close to 70 percent of its forces are forward deployed to within 100 miles of the DMZ. Pyongyang maintains a sizable tank force of over 4,000, but this number is offset by age and inferior capability since most are either light tanks or old Soviet model T-34s, T-54/55s, or T-59s. Another significant dimension of the DPRK's conventional capability are 10,400 artillery pieces and 2,500 multiple rocket launchers. Many of these are also forward deployed in hardened or underground locations able to attack with limited warning. Given Seoul's proximity to the border,

Table 2   North Korean Military: Structure and Size, 2004–2005

Total active duty military personnel	1,106,000
Army	950,000 (includes 88,000 special forces)
Navy	46,000
Air force	110,000
Reserves	4,700,000
Tanks	4,060
T-34, T-54/55, T-59, T-62	3,500
Light tanks	560
Artillery tubes	10,400
Multiple rocket launchers	2,500
Combat aircraft	584
Bombers	
H-5 (Il-28)	80
Fighters	
J-5(MiG-17)/J-6(MiG-19)/J-7(MiG-21)	386
MiG 23	46
MiG 29	20
Su-7	18
Su-25	34
Submarines	26
Frigates	3
Patrol and coastal craft	310

Source
International Institute for Strategic Studies (IISS). 2004. *The Military Balance 2004–2005.* London: IISS and Oxford University Press.

North Korean artillery and rockets could destroy the South Korean capital without an invasion.

Finally, North Korea has 584 combat aircraft, but only 100 are the more advanced MiG-23, MiG-29, or Su-25. The remainder of the fleet consists of older Soviet-design planes that would be facing the more modern F-15s and F-16s used by the ROK and the United States. Also, due to a shortage of spare parts and fuel, DPRK pilots train considerably less than their counterparts, further reducing their combat effectiveness (*The Military Balance* 2003–2004).

According to most estimates, North Korea could launch a sustained offensive for thirty to ninety days. However, for any extended operation North Korea would be in serious trouble in the face of the ROK-U.S. counteroffensive that would be sure to follow. These problems are further complicated by the deteriorating North Korean economy. Despite a "military first" policy that diverts the country's scarce resources to national security, there has been significant degradation of North Korea's military capabilities. These limitations are likely well known to DPRK planners, and hence, the likelihood of an offensive military operation is remote.

The North Korean military structure begins with the National Defense Commission (NDC). In 1990, the NDC was established as an independent commission rising to the same level as the Central People's Commission (CPC), the top party organization. In the past, the NDC was one of six commissions reporting to the CPC. In 1998, the constitution was amended to make the NDC the highest-ranking organization in the government with the chair, currently Kim Jong Il, as the highest position of authority. The NDC controls all elements of North Korea including the military, the economy, and the political structure. Authority over the military extends down from the NDC through the Ministry of the People's Armed Forces and the State Security Department to the General Staff Department and on to the specific operational units and commands. Next to and intertwined with the military organization are parallel structures for the government and the Korean Workers' Party that ensure political control and oversight of the armed forces. Control of North Korean intelligence and security forces is included in this structure and follows a similar line of authority. Although the general outline of the military bureaucracy is available, the specifics and inner workings of these organizations remain unknown (Bermudez 2001, 20–21).

The military also plays an extensive role in the North Korean economy, providing manpower in agriculture, mining, construction projects, and industry while operating arms and munitions factories that produce supplies for its own use and for export. Although the DPRK is a recipient of significant UN assistance, the North Korean military does not contribute to any UN peacekeeping activities.

Budget
Though estimates vary, North Korea devotes close to $5.2 billion for defense, placing it twenty-first in the world. Defense spending represents 34 percent of GDP, the highest rate of any country in the world (CIA *World Factbook*: 2005). Most of the defense budget is devoted to maintaining a large conventional capability though the technology and quality of DPRK forces has deteriorated over the years. North Korea possesses chemical and biological weapons; however, the level of their stockpiles is uncertain. The

DPRK has signed the Biological Weapons Convention but has not signed the similar agreement for chemical weapons. As noted earlier, North Korea is believed to be nuclear capable; U.S. intelligence estimates maintain North Korea has built one or two nuclear weapons from material diverted in the early 1990s. Five to six additional weapons may be available from reprocessed material available after the collapse of the Agreed Framework. In February 2005, North Korea declared formally that it has nuclear weapons. However, North Korea has not conducted a nuclear test and intelligence sources have been unable to confirm the February declaration making the exact status of the North's nuclear program unknown.

An important contribution to defense spending comes from North Korean exports of ballistic missiles and technology and other conventional weapons. Pyongyang's arms industry, run by the National Defense Commission through the Second Economic Committee, operates approximately 130 factories. Most are located in hardened sites or built underground. These facilities produce a variety of items including ammunition, small arms, tanks that are based on old Soviet designs, armored fighting vehicles, artillery, multiple rocket launchers, and missile systems of varying size and range. Several types of naval craft are also produced including patrol boats, coastal and midget submarines, and amphibious craft. The DPRK does not produce its own aircraft, relying largely on Soviet and Chinese models. However, it does produce spare parts for its planes and is developing a line of helicopters based on a Soviet design (Bermudez 2001, 47–55).

The most important export is ballistic missiles. Pyongyang acquired missiles from the Soviet Union and Egypt and, in a process called reverse engineering, replicated the production process from a completed weapon. North Korea improved on these earlier designs and sold missiles and missile technology to Syria, Iran, Iraq, Yemen, and Libya, among others. The trade has been an important source of hard currency for the military and the North Korean economy, bringing in from $38 million to $500 million in a given year (Stockholm International Peace Research Institute [SIPRI] 2003, 470; Chun 2000, 28).

Civil-Military Relations/The Role of the Military in Domestic Politics

As in most authoritarian regimes, the military has played an important role in North Korean politics. In addition to protecting the country from external security threats, the military helps buttress the internal power of the state. During Kim Il Sung's rule (1945–1994), the military held a vital position but did not supercede that of the Korean Workers' Party and "the Great Leader," whose credentials as an anti-Japanese guerrilla fighter and revolutionary were legendary though amplified through state propaganda.

Despite designating his son, Kim Jong Il, as heir, Kim's passing in 1994 raised numerous succession questions, especially regarding the military's willingness to accept the younger Kim, who had little military experience, as the new leader. Under Kim Jong Il, the status of the military has risen considerably, most likely to cement its support for the new regime. In 1999 Kim declared a "military first" policy that ensured vital resources would be steered toward the armed forces. In honor of his father, Kim Jong Il did not take the titles once held by the elder Kim and instead assumed the position of chair of the

National Defense Commission, elevating the military to the top place in the government structure. Kim further politicized the military through numerous promotions to ensure the command structure remained loyal to him. Though the level of support from the military for Kim Jong Il is not entirely clear, it is unlikely that the armed forces would do anything to remove him from power. However, Kim must continue to court military leaders and pay attention to their concerns in order to maintain his position in the regime (Oh and Hassig 2000, 106–124).

Terrorism

North Korea's participation in terrorist activities has been a mixed story. Following the events of September 11, North Korea supported several UN and U.S.-sponsored actions to combat terrorism. These included signing the UN Convention for the Suppression of Financing Terrorism and the Convention Against the Taking of Hostages and indicating that the regime intended to sign five other accords on terrorism. However, the North Korean response has been poor in other areas. According to the 2002 U.S. State Department *Patterns of Global Terrorism* document, Pyongyang's report to the UN Counterterrorism Committee under UN Security Council Resolution 1373 was "largely uninformative and nonresponsive" (U.S. Department of State 2002). The following year, the U.S. State Department noted that despite being "a party to six international conventions and protocols relating to terrorism, Pyongyang has not taken substantial steps to cooperate in efforts to combat international terrorism" (U.S. Department of State 2003).

The U.S. State Department continues to include North Korea on its list of countries that support terrorism, largely from DPRK actions prior to 1987. The most serious acts of terrorism include numerous infiltration and assassination attempts in the South, most notably in 1968 when a thirty-one-man team infiltrated Seoul and attempted to kill ROK president Park, and in 1974 when an assassin, presumably a North Korean agent, again attempted to shoot Park. The bullet missed its intended target and killed the president's wife.

In the late 1970s and early 1980s, North Korean agents abducted thirteen Japanese citizens and brought them to Pyongyang to assist in training DPRK agents in the Japanese language. Several of these died in the intervening years, but in 2002 Kim Jong Il permitted the five survivors to return to Japan. However, he did not allow their children to accompany them. In May 2004, Japanese president Junichiro Koizumi secured the return of five children of those abducted after pledging $10 million and 250,000 tons of food aid. However, the fate of possibly twenty to thirty others also kidnapped to train North Korean agents remained uncertain (Brooke 2004, A1). In 1983, a North Korean agent planted a bomb in Rangoon, Myanmar, in an effort to kill ROK president Chun Doo Hwan. The bomb detonated prematurely, missing Chun but killing four cabinet ministers and thirteen others in the president's party. Finally, in 1987, a North Korean agent stashed a bomb on Korean Air Lines Flight 858 that exploded over the Gulf of Thailand killing 115 people on board. Other events have occurred since, including a 1996 incident when a North Korean submarine lost power off the eastern coast of the peninsula, presumably on a mission to land DPRK agents on the ROK coast. Thirteen North Korean commandos escaped from the disabled submarine and led ROK authorities on a chase that resulted in the deaths of eleven North Koreans and eleven ROK soldiers and civilians.

Though North Korea has refrained from any recent terrorist actions, it remains on the U.S. State Department's terrorist list for several reasons. First, Pyongyang continues to harbor four members of the Japanese Communist League–Red Army Faction who hijacked a Japanese airline flight in 1970. North Korea maintains it has the sovereign right to provide political asylum for these individuals (Nanto 2003, 20). Second, North Korea may have sold weapons to terrorist groups, despite its pledge to support UN antiterrorist measures. According to Philippine officials, the Moro Islamic Liberation Front purchased weapons from North Korea in 1999–2000. Third, North Korea has not resolved the issue of the Japanese abductees; the fate of several of these individuals remains unknown. Finally, North Korea continues to sell ballistic missile technology to other states on the U.S. State Department's terrorism list, namely Libya and Syria (U.S. Department of State 2003). Until these matters are resolved, North Korea is likely to remain on the list.

Relationship with the United States

For most of its history, North Korean relations with the United States have ranged from strained to tense. From 1950 to 1953, North Korea fought a war with the United States that nearly ended the communist regime. Incidents such as the seizure of the USS *Pueblo*, the shooting

down of the EC-121 reconnaissance plane, and the killing of two U.S. soldiers at Panmunjom in 1976 further inflamed relations. Since the Korean War, the DPRK has been the target of a U.S.-ROK deterrence policy that includes the presence of U.S. troops stationed on the peninsula, joint military exercises (Operations Team Spirit and Foal Eagle) that indicate counterstrikes deep into North Korean territory should the North initiate another war, and until 1991 the positioning of U.S. nuclear weapons in South Korea. For Pyongyang, this has been a serious security threat, one that has gotten worse after its traditional allies, China and Russia, established strong economic and political relationships with the South.

Relations with the United States remain problematic and a source of great anxiety for DPRK leaders, particularly as they relate to the nuclear weapons issue. In addition to improving security concerns, better relations with the United States would open important economic doors that could provide hope for improving the North Korean economy. U.S. trade and investment, along with an economic aid package, are the likely results of North Korea settling the nuclear issue. Another important result would be the lifting of economic sanctions in place since the Korean War, including the release of $9.1 million in DPRK assets frozen in the United States (Noland 2000, 107). One of the provisions of the AF called for the lifting of sanctions, but it was not until 1999 that the Clinton administration removed some of them. North Korean leaders were angry at the tardiness of these actions and that other sanctions remained. Since North Korea is a communist state, sanctions remain under the U.S. Trading with the Enemy

Act. Also, as a member of the state department's list of countries that support international terrorism, the United States is required by law to block any assistance that might be available through the International Monetary Fund and the World Bank.

The Future

North Korea faces a bleak future unless it can implement significant economic reform and establish a less adversarial relationship with the United States, two items that are closely related. Without further reform, the economy will continue to struggle, providing only a minimal standard of living and keeping the North Korean people on the edge of survival. North Korea remains dependent on outside food aid, a reality that is unlikely to change without serious economic reform.

Poor relations with the United States, particularly its continued presence on the U.S. State Department's terrorism list, impede Pyongyang's access to international development funds and drains off scarce resources earmarked for the military that could be better utilized for economic development. Many critics of the North Korean regime hope and anticipate its collapse sometime in the future. However, this raises the possibility of a host of problems including regional instability, refugees, and a danger the failing regime may lash out in desperation. More importantly, it is unlikely that a collapse will materialize in the near future. Analysts have been predicting the collapse of the regime since the mid-1990s, yet North Korea has displayed a tenacious ability to survive. Moreover, South Korea, China, and Russia fear the uncertainties a collapse would bring and are likely to exert great effort to avoid that result. Thus, the world may need to deal with North Korea as it is and, rather than promoting drastic change, be content to nudge the regime toward political and economic reform that may one day bring a more permanent peace to the Korean peninsula.

References, Recommended Readings, and Websites

Books

Bermudez, Joseph S., Jr. 2001. *The Armed Forces of North Korea.* New York: I. B. Tauris.

Cha, Victor D., and David C. Kang. 2003. *Nuclear North Korea: A Debate on Engagement Strategies.* New York: Columbia University Press.

Cumings, Bruce. 1981. *The Origins of the Korean War: Liberation and the Emergence of Separate Regimes, 1945–1947,* Vol. 1. Princeton, NJ: Princeton University Press.

———. 1990. *The Origins of the Korean War: The Roaring of the Cataract, 1947–1950,* Vol. 2. Princeton, NJ: Princeton University Press.

———. 2003. *North Korea: The Hermit Kingdom.* New York: New Press.

Eberstadt, Nicholas. 1999. *The End of North Korea.* Washington, DC: AEI Press.

Gleysteen, William H., Jr. 1999. *Massive Entanglement, Marginal Influence: Carter and Korea in Crisis.* Washington, DC: Brookings Institution.

Harrison, Selig S. 2002. *Korean Endgame: A Strategy for Reunification and U.S. Disengagement.* Princeton, NJ: Princeton University Press.

Henriksen, Thomas H., and Jongryn Mo, eds. 1997. *North Korea after Kim Il Sung: Continuity or Change?* Stanford, CA: Hoover Institution Press.

Heo, Uk, and Shale A. Horowitz. 2003. *Conflict in Asia: Korea, China-Taiwan, and India-Pakistan.* Westport, CT: Praeger.

Kim, Samuel S., and Tai Hwan Lee. 2002. *North Korea and Northeast Asia.* Lanham, MD: Rowman and Littlefield.

Koh, Byung Chul. 1983. "Unification Policy and North-South Relations." In *North Korea Today: Strategic and Domestic Issues*, Robert A. Scalapino and Jun-Yop Kim, eds. Berkeley: Institute of East Asian Studies, University of California.

Marantz, Paul. 1993. "Moscow and East Asia: New Realities and New Policies." In *East Asian Security in the Post–Cold War Era*, Sheldon W. Simon, ed. Armonk, NY: M. E. Sharpe.

Mazarr, Michael J. 1995. *North Korea and the Bomb*. New York: St. Martin's Press.

Nanto, Dick K. 2003. *North Korea: Chronology of Provocations, 1950–2003*. Washington, DC: Congressional Research Service.

Natsios, Andrew S. 2001. *The Great North Korean Famine*. Washington DC: U.S. Institute of Peace Press.

Noland, Marcus. 2000. *Avoiding the Apocalypse*. Washington DC: Institute for International Economics.

Oberdorfer, Don. 1997. *The Two Koreas*. Reading, MA: Addison-Wesley.

Oh, Kongdan, and Ralph C. Hassig. 2000. *North Korea: Through the Looking Glass*. Washington, DC: Brookings Institution.

O'Hanlon, Michael, and Mike Mochizuki. 2003. *Crisis on the Korean Peninsula: How to Deal with a Nuclear North Korea*. New York: McGraw-Hill.

Roehrig, Terence. 2005. *From Deterrence to Engagement: The U.S. Defense Commitment to South Korea*. Lanham, MD: Lexington.

Sigal, Leon. 1998. *Disarming Strangers: Nuclear Diplomacy with North Korea*. Princeton, NJ: Princeton University Press.

Snyder, Scott. 1999. *Negotiating on the Edge: North Korean Negotiating Behavior*. Washington, DC: U.S. Institute of Peace Press.

Stockholm International Peace Research Institute (SIPRI). 2003. *SIPRI Yearbook 2003*. New York: Humanities Press.

Suh, Dae-Sook. 1988. *Kim Il Sung, the North Korean Leader*. New York: Columbia University Press.

Suh, Dae-sook, and Chae-Jin Lee, eds. 1998. *North Korea after Kim Il Sung*. Boulder, CO: Lynne Rienner.

The Military Balance, 2004–2005. London: International Institute for Strategic Studies.

UN Command in Korea. 1968. "North Korean Violations of the Korean Military Armistice Agreement." In *American Foreign Policy Current Documents, 1967*. Washington, DC: Government Printing Office.

Wit, Joel S., Daniel B. Poneman, and Robert L. Gallucci. 2004. *Going Critical: The First North Korean Nuclear Crisis*. Washington, DC: Brookings Institution.

Yim, Yong Soon. 1983. "The Dynamics of North Korean Military Doctrine." In *The Two Koreas in World Politics*, Tae-hwan Kwak, ed. Seoul: Kyungnam University Press.

Articles/Newspapers

Brooke, James. 2004. "North Korea and Japan Sign a Deal on Abductions," *New York Times*, May 23:A1.

Caruthers, Osgood. 1961. "Khrushchev Signs Defense Treaty with Korea Reds." *New York Times*, July 7:A1, A2.

Chun, Chae-sung. 2000. "Missile Technology Control Regime and North Korea." *Korea Focus* 8:15–29.

French, Howard. 2000. "Two Korean Leaders Speak of Making 'A Day in History.' " *New York Times*, June 14:A1.

———. 2001. "North Korea Rebuffs US on Troop Talks," *New York Times*, June 19:A3.

Joo, Seung-ho. 2001. "The New Friendship Treaty between Moscow and Pyongyang." *Comparative Strategy* 20:467–481.

Kang, David C. 2003. "International Relations Theory and the Second Korean War." *International Studies Quarterly* 47:301–324.

Mazarr, Michael J. 1995. "Going Just a Little Nuclear." *International Security* 20:92–122.

O'Hanlon, Michael. 1998. "Stopping a North Korean Invasion." *International Security* 22:135–170.

Roehrig, Terence. 2003. "'One Rogue State Crisis at a Time!' The United States and North Korea's Nuclear Weapons Program." *World Affairs* 165:155–178.

Rosenthal, Elisabeth. 2001. "North Korea Still in Need of Food Aid," *New York Times*, August 22:A7.

Sanger, David. 2002. "North Korea Says It Has a Program on Nuclear Arms." *New York Times*, October 17:A1.

Seo, Hyun-jin. 2002. "Pyongyang Ready to Act in Concert with Washington over Nuke Issue," *Korea Herald,* November 8.

Slevin, Peter, and Karen DeYoung. 2002. "N. Korea Admits Having Secret Nuclear Arms." *Washington Post,* October 17:A1.

Websites

Central Intelligence Agency (CIA). *The World Factbook: 2005.* http://www.cia.gov/cia/publications/factbook/geos/kn.html.

Federation of American Scientists: http://www.fas.org.

Korea Web Weekly—North Korea: http://www.kimsoft.com/dprk.htm.

Korean Central News Agency: http://www.kcna.co.jp.

Korean Peninsula Energy Development Organization: http://www.kedo.org/.

Monterey Institute of International Studies: http://cns.miis.edu/research/korea/.

National Defense University—North Korea Military Policy Awareness Links: http://merln.ndu.edu/mipal/nkorea.html.

Nautilus Institute: http://www.nautilus.org/.

New Zealand Korean Peace Committee: http://www.vuw.ac.nz/~caplabtb/dprk/.

North Korea Virtual Library: http://www.duke.edu/~myhan/s-nk.html.

School of Hawaiian, Asian, and Pacific Studies. 2000. *DPRK-Russia Joint Declaration.* July 19: http://russia.shaps.hawaii.edu/fp/russia/russia_dprk_jd_e_20000721.html.

U.S. Department of State. 2002 and 2003. *Patterns of Global Terrorism.* http://www.state.gov/s/ct/rls/pgtrpt.

Oceania: Fiji, Papua New Guinea, Tonga, and Vanuatu

John Henderson and Sheryl Boxall

Introduction

This chapter covers the Pacific island countries that maintain military forces: Papua New Guinea (PNG), Fiji, Tonga, and Vanuatu (paramilitary force). In the other ten independent or self-governing Pacific island members (excluding Australia and New Zealand) of the main regional organization, the Pacific Islands Forum (previously the South Pacific Forum), security-related duties are the responsibility of the police forces. The Vanuatu paramilitary Vanuatu Mobile Force (VMF), which is part of the Vanuatu Police Force (VPF), is included in this survey as its command and operations have been controversial over the past decade. (The "M" is sometimes translated as meaning "Military" rather than the correct word, "Mobile".) There were plans to transform elements of the Royal Solomon Islands Police (RSIP), which had operated as a paramilitary field force, into a military force, but these were overtaken by the internal instability that engulfed the Solomon Islands, and in 2000 the RSIP's paramilitary wing was disbanded. In 2004, the Regional Assistance Mission to Solomon Islands (RAMSI)—a 2,400-strong police-led regional intervention backed by military forces—helped to restore law and order. It is unlikely that further armed forces will be formed in the region. The experience of the region is that the military contribute to rather than help resolve problems of internal security (Fry 1999, 29). Forces are also costly to maintain, and the majority of security challenges in the Pacific are of a nonmilitary nature.

Brief details of the four countries are summarized in the following table.

Papua New Guinea, a parliamentary democracy, gained its independence from Australia in 1975. With a population of over 5 million, it is by far the largest Pacific island country. PNG has a diverse and fragmented society, as is highlighted by its more than 600 languages. The country is well endowed with natural resources, particularly minerals and forestry. But corruption, poor governance, and political instability have prevented the exploitation of these resources for the country's economic benefit. PNG remains heavily dependent on aid, principally from Australia. Problems of governance have been identified as the main threat to the country's stability (Jane's Sentinel 2003, 278). Despite extensive Australian aid, the military forces are poorly equipped, lack discipline, and are largely ineffective (Laki 2003, 69). Currently Australia is assisting the reformation of the forces through the Defence Cooperation Programme aimed at downsizing and upskilling the PNG Defense Force (PNGDF) to improve its professionalism and efficiency.

Fiji was granted independence by the United Kingdom in 1970. It has a popula-

Table 1   Fiji, Papua New Guinea, Tonga, and Vanuatu Demography

	Fiji	Papua New Guinea	Tonga	Vanuatu
Type of government	Republic/ bicameral parliamentary democracy	Constitutional monarchy parliamentary democracy	Constitutional monarchy	Republic/unitary parliamentary democracy
Population	868,531 (July 2003 est.)	5.3 million (July 2003 est.)	108,141 (July 2003 est.)	199,414 (July 2003 est.)
Religion	Christian 52%, Hindu 38%, Muslim 8%, other 2%	Christian 66%, indigenous 34%	Christian	Christian, local religions
Main industries	Tourism, sugar, clothing, copra, mineral resources	Mineral resources, agriculture, timber, fish	Tourism, agriculture	Tourism, agriculture
Main security threats	No external threat; internal tension caused by ethnic and regional divisions	No external threat; internal tension caused by corrupt governance; neglected military forces–secession tendencies	No external threat; internal tension related to pressure for constitutional change	No external threat; internal tension caused by corrupt governance and secession tendencies
Defense spending % GDP	2.2 (2002)	1.4 (2002)	2 (2001)	2.5 (2002)
Size of military	3,500	4,400	430	300
Number of civil wars since 1945	Two military coups 1987; part-military coup 2000; military mutiny 2000	Bougainville Secessionist war 1988–1998	0	Santos secession attempt 1980
Number of interstate wars since 1945	0	0	0	0

Sources
Asian Development Bank. 2003. *Key Indicators of Developing Asian and Pacific Countries.* http:// www.adb.org/Document/Books/Key_Indicators/2003/pdf/VAN.pdf. (accessed February 26, 2004).
Central Intelligence Agency Website. 2005. CIA *World Factbook.* http://www.cia.gov/cia/ publications/factbook/ (accessed May 15, 2005).
Europa. 2003. *The Europa Year World Book.* "Oceania." London: Europa Publications.
Jane's Sentinel. 2003. "Jane's Sentinel Security Assessment: Oceania." *Jane's Sentinel.* Surrey, UK: Jane's Information Group Ltd.
Tongan Reserve Bank. 2003. *Government Recurrent Expenditure, by Function.* http:// reservebank.ton/docs/QtrlyBulletin/sep_Bulletin03/sep_Bulletin.2003.pdf (accessed March 5, 2004).

tion of around 800,000, making it the second-largest Pacific island state. The population is divided between indigenous people groups (54 percent) and the immigrant Indian population (40 percent) who are the descendants of indentured laborers brought from India by the British to work on the sugar plantations. Currently sugar production takes second place to tourism in economic importance. Fiji's military, in stark contrast to PNG, is well trained and has proved to be highly effective as international peacekeepers. It is also highly politicized and has staged three military coups. Past high levels of discipline have been shattered by deep divisions that gave rise to a mutiny in November 2000. The country has returned uneasily to democratic rule.

Tonga, which has a population of around 100,000, is the only Pacific island state to avoid colonial rule (although it was a British protectorate until 1970). Tonga continues to be governed under the 1875 constitution, which in effect legitimizes an undemocratic feudal monarchy. Elections cannot change the government. Power is concentrated in the hands of the monarch, who personally appoints a cabinet of twelve who also sit in Parliament. A further nine nobles (or chiefs) are elected by the thirty-three noble families. Just nine of the thirty-member Parliament are directly elected by universal suffrage to represent the commoners. A pro-democracy movement is pushing for constitutional change and the protection of human rights. In early 2005, the king agreed to appoint two elected peoples representatives to the cabinet. Further change may occur following the death of the aging monarch, King Taufa'ahau Tupou IV. The economy is heavily dependent on aid and remittances paid by the large number of Tongans living abroad. The armed forces, known as the Tonga Defense Service (TDS), are small and have been described as more ceremonial than military (Jane's Sentinel 2003, 376). However, in recent years the TDS has made small but important contributions to a number of regional peace support operations, including in Bougainville and the Solomon Islands.

Vanuatu, which has a current population of around 200,000, was jointly ruled by Britain and France until it gained independence in 1980. Politics in this volatile parliamentary democracy continue to divide the country along the anglophone-francophone division. Vanuatu has pursued a more radical foreign policy than most Pacific island states. It attended meetings of the Non-aligned Movement (NAM) during the Cold War period and established links with Libya and Cuba. More recently, alone among the members of the Pacific Islands Forum, it has openly supported independence for West Papua. The economy is based on tourism and aid. The responsibility for defense is uneasily divided between the VPF and the VMF with the police commander having formal command.

Regional Geopolitics

The Pacific island region, which is also referred to as Oceania, is made up of three subregions: Polynesia to the south, which has been the main concern of New Zealand; Melanesia to the west, which is principally under Australian influence; and Micronesia to the north, which remains strategically important to the United States. This analysis concentrates on Polynesia and particularly Melanesia, where three of the four states with armed forces are located (PNG, Fiji, and Vanuatu in Melanesia and Tonga in Polynesia).

Until the mid-1980s the South Pacific was one of the most peaceful regions of the world. Outside of Melanesia, it still is, to a large extent. The region faces no external threat. Armed forces are maintained for a variety of reasons, including internal security, prestige, and foreign policy considerations.

Economic and environmental issues, rather than military matters, have constituted the main security concerns for most of Polynesia and Micronesia. There is regionwide concern about protecting fishery resources. Regional efforts to ensure the island states benefit from the rich marine resources are coordinated by the Forum Fisheries Agency in Honiara, the capital of the Solomon Islands. Other nontraditional security concerns include preventing smuggling of people and drugs and other forms of international crime, such as piracy.

Terrorism has also begun to appear on the regional security agenda, especially in Melanesia. Australia, particularly since the Bali terrorist bombings of October 12, 2002, has been increasingly concerned about the deteriorating security situation to its north. It is alarmed by what is referred to as the "arc of instability" that starts with Indonesia and the Philippines, moves through East Timor and West Papua, and on through the Melanesian states of PNG, the Solomon Islands, Vanuatu, New Caledonia, and Fiji (May et al. 2003). In July 2003, Australia, at the invitation of the Solomon Islands government, led RAMSI into the Solomon Islands in a successful (at least in the short term) bid to restore law and order. However, it is expected that the Solomon Islands will require external police and administrative support for much of the next decade.

The roots of internal strife in Melanesia lie in the ethnic divisions generated in large part by the artificial boundaries established during the colonial era that took no account of local culture. Melanesian politics is fragmented and there is little or no sense of nationalism. Secession attempts have sparked conflict in PNG, the Solomon Islands, and Vanuatu, and to a lesser extent, Fiji.

The secession war fought by the island of Bougainville against PNG from 1988 to 1998 spilled over into the neighboring Solomon Islands. The PNG government accused the Solomon Islands of harboring members of the Bougainville Revolutionary Army (BRA). The PNGDF made several incursions into the Solomon Islands that resulted in casualties.

The May 2000 attempted coup in Fiji was followed two weeks later by an armed uprising in the Solomon Islands, giving rise to concern about the contagious effect of regional instability. ("Copy cat" coups have been a feature of African politics.)

The current struggle for independence in West Papua (formerly Irian Jaya and sometimes referred to as Papua) waged by the Organisasi Papua Merdeka (Free Papua Movement or OPM) has a destabilizing effect on PNG, with which it shares a long border. Refugees and OPM members have sought refuge in PNG, and border crossings by the Indonesian military have been frequent (Fry 1999, 10). Most go unchallenged by the poorly equipped border protection force as PNG has sought to avoid conflict with Indonesia.

Australia and New Zealand are the two outside powers most concerned about instability in Melanesia. Military assistance has been provided under Australia's Defense Cooperation Program and New Zealand's Mutual Assistance Program (MAP). In 2004, Australia and Papua New Guinea agreed on a development assistance package, the Enhanced Cooperation Package (ECP), to strengthen law and order and other reforms of the PNG public sector. Nearly one year into the program it was suspended after the PNG supreme court declared sections of the agreement, relating to the granting of immunity from prosecution to Australian police, as unconstitutional and invalid.

Notwithstanding the help from Australia and New Zealand, Pacific island states are increasingly looking north to Asia for assistance. Japan, China, Taiwan, Indonesia, Malaysia, and the Philippines are all showing a growing interest in the

South Pacific, which is bringing about a change in regional geopolitics. For instance, both PNG and Tonga have established low-level military ties with China.

The United States has reduced its presence in Polynesia and Melanesia but remains the unchallenged power in Micronesia. France maintains a significant (in regional terms) military presence of 7,000 troops in its Pacific territories of New Caledonia, Wallis and Futuna, and French Polynesia (Crocombe 2001, 577). It is noteworthy that France, the United States, and Britain continue to recruit armed forces from their existing or former Pacific dependencies. There are currently 1,600 Fijians serving in the British army (Jane's Sentinel 2003, 99).

Conflict Past and Present

Conflict History

During World War II, Pacific islands in Melanesia and Micronesia, including PNG, the Solomon Islands, Kiribati, and Palau, were the site of a number of major battles between U.S. and Japanese forces. Since 1945 there have been no external threats to the region with the possible exception of terrorism. Internal conflict has resulted mainly from struggles for independence and ethnic strife.

From the 1960s the movement to independence by the island states was generally a peaceful process. However, this was not always the case. Vanuatu, with the help of PNG forces, suppressed a secession attempt from Santos Island at the time of independence in 1980. East Timor's UN-assisted path to independence in May 2002 was particularly violent.

The independence process remains incomplete. In the 1980s, the struggle for independence in the French territory of New Caledonia turned violent. Fighting ended with the Noumea accords of May 1998, which paved the way for a future referendum on independence. In the mid-1990s rioting broke out in French Polynesia, sparked by the resumption of French nuclear testing. West Papua's current struggle to break away from Indonesia, which is complicated by deep internal divisions between the pro-independence forces, has been accompanied by considerable violence.

Ethnic tension has been the main cause of internal conflict in the South Pacific. It has been accentuated by artificial boundaries that reflected the interests of colonial powers but took little account of local culture. Bougainville rebels fought a decade-long civil war from 1988 to 1998 in an attempt to establish a separate island state from PNG. A 2005 constitution granted Bougainville considerable local autonmy and a future vote on independence. Further breakaway attempts are likely as PNG is a country deeply divided between more than 600 language groups. Intertribal warfare remains common, particularly in the Southern Highlands, and has become bloodier with the availability of modern weaponry.

The lawlessness and fighting between opposing militia in the Solomon Islands has its roots in the ethnic rivalry between people from the islands of Malaita and Guadalcanal. The Fiji coups were motivated in part by the indigenous Fijians' determination to keep political power from the Indo-Fijians. Regional and tribal divisions within Fiji were also important. There are deep divisions between the Kanak pro-independence movement in New Caledonia, which is further complicated by strife between the Melanesian Kanaks and immigrants from the French Polynesian territories. In Vanuatu disputes over land have become violent (Jowitt 2001).

Concern about land has often been at the core of these conflicts. In the Solomon Islands the people of Guadalcanal resented the influx of Malaitans who squatted or bought land around the capital of Honiara. The Fiji coups were sparked in part by indigenous Fijian fears that the Indo-Fijian-dominated government might interfere with their land rights.

Poor governance is another factor fanning internal conflict. Corruption is endemic throughout much of Melanesia and remains a problem in Polynesia and Micronesia. The political systems inherited at independence have proved to be divisive and have not generally blended well with traditional systems. Political parties tend to divide along racial or tribal lines.

Parts of the Pacific island region remain strategically important to the larger Pacific Rim states. Kwajalein Atoll in the republic of the Marshall Islands is the site of a major U.S. missile testing facility. It is playing a vital role in the development of the Bush administration's missile defense program. China and Taiwan compete (with checkbooks rather than military threats) for the diplomatic backing of the island states. Currently Taiwan is recognized by the Solomon Islands, the Marshall Islands, Tuvalu, Palau, and Kiribati. In May 2005, after a change in government, Nauru switched allegiance from China back to Taiwan. Outside powers also have important economic interests. Japan wishes to protect its interests in the region's rich fishing stocks and, in the future, seabed minerals. France seeks to ensure its access to the rich mineral deposits, particularly nickel, in New Caledonia. Australian companies have major interests in PNG's extensive mineral resources, including petroleum, oil, copper, and gold. A U.S. company has a major financial interest in the Freeport copper and gold mine in West Papua. Malaysian logging companies are exploiting Melanesia's vast forests (Fry 1999, 12).

Current and Potential Military Confrontation

With the exception of West Papua's violent struggle for independence from Indonesia, there are currently no military conflicts in the South Pacific. The 2003 Australian-led RAMSI intervention into the Solomon Islands ended (at least for the time being) the most recent conflict between rival militia groups and the resulting breakdown in law and order. The Bougainville Peace Agreement that ended the conflict in 1998 is maintaining a tenuous and uneasy peace. However, elections held in June 2005 peacefully elected former BRA leader Joseph Kabui, the first president of Bougainville.

The potential for further internal conflict remains high in the regional trouble spots. Given the deep roots of past conflict, Melanesia seems headed for a future of chronic instability. The Solomon Islands face an uncertain and possibly violent future following the withdrawal of the RAMSI intervention force. The struggle for independence in New Caledonia by the Kanak Socialist Front for National Liberation (FLNKS) is likely to reignite if the promised referenda, which are still a decade away, do not deliver autonomy. As is the case elsewhere in Melanesia, deep internal divisions remain. Tribal fighting in PNG is increasing and likely to continue. Fiji has yet to find a way to reconcile the indigenous rights of Fijians and the democratic rights of the Indo-Fijian population.

Alliance Structure

Although the Pacific Islands Forum does not extend to a formal military alliance, it is playing a growing role in regional security matters. All fourteen Pacific island states, along with Australia and New Zealand, are members of the forum, which has a secretariat based in Suva, Fiji. It meets annually at the head-of-government level. The 2000 Biketawa Declaration authorizes the forum secretary general to initiate an appropriate response in the event of a regional crisis; this was restated following a major review completed in 2004. The Melanesian members of the forum (PNG, the Solomon Islands, Vanuatu, Fiji, and the New Caledonia Kanak party, the FLNKS) have formed their own subgroup, the Melanesian Spearhead Group. There is an agreement to form a Melanesian peacekeeping force, but it has yet to be acted on. The long-standing proposal of the former PNG prime minister, Sir Julius Chan, for a wider South Pacific peacekeeping force has yet to receive forum endorsement. However, at the thirty-fourth Pacific Islands Forum held in Auckland in 2004, Solomon Islands Prime Minister Allan Kemakeza restated the Melanesian objective of establishing a standing regional force. Ad hoc regional forces have been successfully deployed to trouble spots in Bougainville and the Solomon Islands.

The Pacific island states have generally remained firmly in the Western camp, although they are not members of any formal Western alliance. Only Vanuatu and PNG are members of the Non-aligned Movement (NAM).

Under the Compact of Free Association, the United States has responsibility for the defense of the Micronesian states of the Marshall Islands, the Federated States of Micronesia, and Palau. The United States exercises the right of strategic denial, under which it can prevent the armed forces of any other nation from operating in the Micronesian region covered by the compact states. It also has the right to establish military bases.

During the period until the mid-1980s when the Australian-New Zealand-United States (ANZUS) Treaty was operative for New Zealand, island states with close New Zealand links—Samoa, the Cook Islands, and Niue—were generally assumed to be covered by the alliance. However, it was an informal arrangement that was not put to the test.

Western Samoa, alone among the Pacific island states, has a Treaty of Friendship with New Zealand. This obliges New Zealand to provide assistance in the areas of defense and foreign affairs. The Cook Islands and Niue constitutions make defense the responsibility of New Zealand, although in practice New Zealand acts in accordance with the wishes of the self-governing states.

Pacific island ties with Asia are expanding, but do not extend to formal alliances. PNG has observer status with the Association of Southeast Asian Nations and is a member of Asia-Pacific Economic Cooperation (Jane's Sentinel 2003). Although these organizations are not formal military alliances, they provide PNG with a valuable forum for discussing defense and security issues with neighboring Asian states.

Size and Structure of the Military

The size of the military in Oceania is small and insignificant by international comparisons. PNG has the largest armed force, the PNGDF, totaling 4,400 members (Jane's Sentinel 2003, 278). Fiji is next, with the Republic of Fiji Military Forces (RFMF) consisting of a military force of 3,500 including reservists (Jane's Sentinel 2003, 83). The other two states have minimal forces. The TDS totals 430 (Jane's Sentinel 2003, 375). The VMF consists of around 300 personnel (Europa 2003, 4535).

PNG

The origins of the PNGDF can be traced back to the Pacific Island Regiment, which served with considerable distinction in the World War II battles against Japan. Indeed its effectiveness in the Pacific war contrasts starkly with the largely ineffective force today.

The PNGDF currently consists of the army, which has a strength of 3,800. The navy has 400 personnel and the air force has 200. There is also a special forces unit (Jane's Sentinel 2003, 278). The PNGDF is responsible to the minister of home affairs. The force has been mainly deployed on internal security duties (May et al. 2003, 5).

The PNG army is made up of two infantry battalions, equipped with light weapons. There is also an engineering battalion. The navy has four Australian-supplied patrol boats and two heavy amphibious landing craft. Maintenance problems mean that usually only one patrol boat can be deployed at any time. The air wing has six transport aircraft and four helicopters, none of which were airworthy in 2003 (Jane's Sentinel 2003, 299–303).

Despite extensive assistance from Australia, including the Defence Cooperation Programme, the PNGDF remains poorly trained, ill equipped, and lacks discipline. The force suffers from low morale. As its performance in the Bougainville conflict demonstrated, it is ineffective as a military force. It is alleged that the PNGDF committed human rights violations during the Bougainville operation.

The force has a serious imbalance between the ranks. Senior servicemen are retained to the detriment of lower-ranked servicemen. In 2000 the average age of the PNGDF was around forty, and twenty years was the average length of service (Jane's Sentinel 2003, 279). After a Commonwealth-assisted Eminent Person's Group Review, the PNG government's 2001 decision to radically cut the force by 1,500 has proceeded cautiously in the wake of a 2001 mutiny, which was sparked by opposition to the cuts (Jane's Sentinel 2003, 298).

PNG armed forces have not been deployed on UN or regional peacekeeping duties in recent years on the basis that it does not have the resources. The force also lacks the necessary training and discipline. However, in 1980 it carried out the region's first peacekeeping mission when PNG forces were deployed to Vanuatu to put down a secession attempt on the Vanuatu island of Santos. In 2003 PNG offered armed forces for service in the Solomon Islands, and in early 2004 the country entered talks about contributing forces to Iraq.

The PNGDF, and particularly the engineer battalion, has been widely used on public works activities, including the building of bridges and roads. This includes the maintenance of government assets such as schools and health centers. Much of this work could be undertaken by the private sector. For instance, the navy's landing craft are often used in civilian roles.

Fiji

Fijian military forces trace their origins back to the formation in 1871 of a royal army of 1,000 ethnic Fijians loyal to Chief Ratu Seru Cakobau, the head of the precolonial government. During World War II the Fijian forces were expanded and mobilized by Britain to fight in the Pacific war against Japan. Fijian troops played an important role on Guadalcanal and Bougainville. It remains a sore point that Indo-Fijians did not volunteer for service.

The RFMF is under the administrative authority of the minister of home affairs, who is also minister of defense. The RFMF is under the command of Commodore Voreqe (Frank) Bainimarama, who in early 2004 was controversially reappointed for another five years. The force is made up of a regiment-size army of around 3,200 (including reserves) consisting of six infantry battalions, one engineering battalion, and a logistics battalion (Jane's Sentinel 2003, 99). There is also a small naval contingent of about 300 that crews nine patrol craft. Financial restraints have forced the small navy to effectively curtail its main role of surveillance and policing of Fiji's territorial waters including its large exclusive economic zone (Jane's Sentinel 2003, 102). There is no air force. A small army aviation wing has two utility helicopters, which are largely used for civil duties (Jane's Sentinel 2003, 101). The armed forces are mainly made up of indigenous Fijians and include only a small number of Indo-Fijians.

Fiji has undertaken extensive peacekeeping operations for the United Nations, maintaining around 1,000 members of the armed forces abroad on UN duties. Two battalions were stationed with the UN interim force in Lebanon from 1972 to 2003. Troops also served with the U.S.-led multinational force. Military observers have served on the

---

Sidebar 1   Fijian Commander of the Army, Commodore Voreqe (Frank) Bainimarama

On May 19, 2000, Fijian nationalist George Speight and the counterrevolutionary warfare unit of the army took the Indo-Fijian prime minister, Mahendra Chaudry, and other members of Parliament (MPs) hostage in the Parliament buildings. Ten days later, Fiji armed forces commander, Frank Bainimarama, declared martial law. President Ratu Sir Kamisese Mara was forced to resign. On July 3, Commodore Bainimarama appointed Laisenia Qarase as interim prime minister, and negotiated the release of the hostages.

In November 2000, pro-Speight sections of the army staged an abortive mutiny. Bainimarama, who survived an assassination attempt, has insisted that those responsible for the coup and mutiny be bought to trial. In February 2004, he forced the government to reappoint him commander for another five years. Bainimarama also forced the government to drop an inquiry into a coup that he'd allegedly planned in late 2003 to secure his reappointment. Although these actions cross the boundary between military and civilian responsibilities, Bainimarama enjoys wide support from both civilian society and business for maintaining political stability, and upholding the rule of law.

Source
Henderson, John, and Greg Watson (eds.). 2005. *Securing a Peaceful Pacific*. Christchurch: Canterbury University Press.
Te Karere Ipurangi. 2000. *Fiji Coup Supplement—May/September 2000.* http://maorinews.com/karere/fiji/.

Iraq/Kuwait border and in the Sinai. Further UN tasks have been undertaken in Afghanistan, Bosnia, Cambodia, Somalia, and Liberia.

These deployments have provided much-needed employment and government revenue. It has provided the rationale for a small state to maintain a disproportionately large army. The Fijian forces are sought after as particularly effective peacekeepers. Retired military have also been hired by private security firms for protection duties in Iraq.

Fiji has also played an important role in regional peacekeeping, including service in Bougainville and the Solomon Islands. A force of around 250 was dispatched to join the UN's transitional authority in East Timor.

The Fiji military have also been deployed on domestic security matters within the Fiji islands. This was particularly the case following the coup in 2000. Forces were also deployed internally during the strikes of sugarcane laborers.

The Fiji forces have undertaken extensive development activities within Fiji. Schools, health centers, roads, and bridges are among the many projects the engineering regiment has completed in rural areas. Trade schools and youth training courses are also part of the forces' nation-building activities (Fiji Government Online).

Tonga

The TDS has its origins in World War II. The force was trained by New Zealand officers and fought in the Solomon Islands.

The TDS has a total military strength of 430 personnel (Jane's Sentinel 2003, 388). The forces are divided into the Royal Tongan Marines, the Tongan Royal Guards, and the Maritime Force. The TDS, which includes a territorial force and active reserve, is divided into three geographic areas: two for the main island of Tongatapu and one for the smaller islands. The maritime force maintains three patrol craft supplied by Australia, a tanker, and two aircraft (Jane's Sentinel 2003, 389–391) and is mainly used for maritime surveillance. It also carries out important search and rescue and civil defense duties. Other roles are ceremonial. However, the TDS could play a crucial domestic role should the pressure for democracy result in widespread instability.

Tonga has not taken part in UN peacekeeping duties but has supported a number of regional peace support operations. In 1994 it played a leading role in the abortive Pacific island peacekeeping mission to Bougainville. A TDS platoon was deployed to the Solomon Islands in 2003 to support the Regional Assistance Mission to the Solomon Islands. In June 2004, the Tongan government sent forty-four troops to Iraq as part of the U.S. "coalition of the willing."

An important role of the TDS is to contribute to nation-building roles related to the socioeconomic development of Tonga. For instance, in 1998 the TDS established the Royal School of Science for Distance Learning. It also has a leading role in providing civil defense. The TDS barge is widely used to provide transport services for the public and private sectors.

Vanuatu

The VPF is the country's principal security force. It comprises regular police, a maritime wing, and a paramilitary force known as the VMF. However, there has been a prolonged period of tension between the VPF and the VMF. In August 2002 this tension resulted in an armed standoff between the two groups. A joint planning and operations center was established to coordinate the work of the security agencies.

Australia is the main contributor in the security areas through the Defense Cooperation Program. It continues to support the Pacific patrol boat program it initiated in 1987. New Zealand also provides capacity-building support to the VPF through the New Zealand Defense Force's (NZDF's) MAP.

Vanuatu forces have served on peacekeeping duties for the United Nations in East Timor and Bosnia. They also served with the regional Peace Monitoring Group in Bougainville and RAMSI.

In Vanuatu, the VMF have been involved in development work. The impression gained from visiting their base was that it seemed more suitable for a public works ministry than a military force.

Budget

The Stockholm International Peace Research Institute (SIPRI) calculated total annual military expenditure in Oceania (defined as Australia, New Zealand, Fiji, and PNG) as between U.S.$7–$8 billion during the period 1993–2002 (SIPRI 2003, 302). In 2002 the expenditure was U.S.$7.4 billion, a decrease of 4 percent from 1993, with Australia spending 91.3 percent; New Zealand, 8.2 percent; and Fiji, 0.4 percent. PNG spent over U.S.$30 million or 0.52 percent of the total regional expenditure for 2000 (SIPRI 2003, 302, 348; SIPRI 2004b). The global average of gross domestic product (GDP) spent on military expenditures for 2002 is 2.3 percent, Australia's figure is above this at 2.9 percent, and New Zealand's significantly less at 1 percent. The average for Fiji, PNG, Tonga, and Vanuatu is 2.02 percent (SIPRI 2004a; CIA *World Factbook* 2003). (The GDP percentages for Australia, New Zealand, Fiji, PNG, and Vanuatu are 2002 figures; the figure for Tonga is from 2001.)

Regional military aid from Australia for the period 1999–2002 totaled AUS$55.91 million (Australian Department of Defense 2002). This included assistance to Fiji, Vanuatu, Tonga, the Solomon Islands, Samoa, Kiribati, Tuvalu, the Marshall Islands, the Cook Islands, the Federated States of Micronesia, and Palau. Under the MAP, New Zealand gave nearly NZ$11 million to the Asia-Pacific region in 2001, just over NZ$8 million in 2002, and an estimated NZ$8.5 million for 2003 (NZDF 2003). (MAP participants

---

Sidebar 2 Vanuatu Mobile Force versus Vanuatu Police Force

In August 2002, the Vanuatu Police Force arrested the controversially newly appointed police commissioner. Later that same month, the Vanuatu Mobile Force surrounded the Port Vila Police Headquarters to serve arrest warrants on the officers involved in the earlier raid. This led to an armed standoff between the two groups. It is reported that unarmed ni-Vanuatu defused the standoff by interposing themselves between the two armed factions and threatening to riot should the Vanuatu Mobile Force take any further violent action.

Sources

Jowitt, Anna. 2003. "Melanesia in Review: Issues and Events." *The Contemporary Pacific* 15, no. 2 (Fall 2003):463–471.

Pacific Islands Reports. 2002. *Vanuatu's Police Crisis Continues.* http://archives.pireport.org/archive/2002/august/08%2D29%2D03.htm (accessed June 8, 2005).

extend to Southeast Asia and include Tonga, PNG, Western Samoa, Vanuatu, the Solomon Islands, the Cook Islands, Niue, Malaysia, Singapore, Thailand, the Philippines, and Brunei.)

PNG
Defense expenditures for PNG were U.S.$40.21 million in 2002, equivalent to 1.4 percent of GDP (CIA *World Factbook* 2003). Military aid from Australia under the Defense Cooperation Program between 1999 and 2002 totaled AUS$51.15 million (Australian Department of Defense 2002). In 2004, the United States provided International Military Education and Training (IMET) worth U.S.$300,000 to PNG (Federation of American Scientists [FAS] 2004). In 2002, the German government funded improvements to the satellite communications system and infrastructure development of government assets by the PNGDF. The following year, in 2003, the German government donated U.S.$7.6 million worth of construction equipment to the PNGDF.

Fiji
Defense expenditures in 2002 totaled U.S.$39.21 million, which made up 2.2 percent of GDP (CIA *World Factbook* 2003). This was an increase of more than U.S.$12 million from 2001, when defense expenditures made up 1.6 percent of GDP (Jane's Sentinel 2003, 97).

Australian sanctions against Fiji were lifted in October 2001, fifteen months after the May 2000 coup. For the period 2000–2001, Fiji received military aid of AUS$1.1 million under the Defense Cooperation Program (Australian Department of Defense 2003). Under this program, Fiji has received a total AUS$11.4 million dollars since 2000. After lifting

sanctions in August of 2002, two years after the coup, New Zealand's aid to Fiji has continued to concentrate on development assistance (New Zealand Ministry of Foreign Affairs and Trade 2003). New Zealand and Fiji will be looking to resume defense cooperation in 2005. Prior to the suspension of defense ties in 2000, the NZDF's MAP support to the RFMF was the largest in the Pacific region.

U.S. IMET aid to Fiji in 2004 totaled U.S.$200,000 (FAS 2004). In 2000, China supplied a military aid package worth U.S.$1.8 million but confirmed that figure did not include weapons. China contributed a further U.S.$50,000 of military equipment in 2002, which included nonlethal items such as tents and footwear.

The 2003 Fijian budget cut military funding by U.S.$1.3 million dollars. This included a reduction in capital expenditure. Military funding remained static in the 2004 budget.

Tonga
Expenditure on law and order and security for 2001 was U.S.$4.81 million, which is equivalent to 2 percent of GDP (Tongan Reserve Bank 2003; CIA *World Factbook* 2003). From 1990 to 2003 there has been as steady increase in police and defense expenditures.

U.S. IMET aid for 2004 totaled U.S.$125,000 (FAS 2004). Under the Australian defense cooperation program for the years 2000–2004, it is estimated Tonga will have received AUS$10.9 million (Australian Department of Defense 2003). Tonga is also a recipient of the NZDF's MAP.

Vanuatu
Police and security expenditures increased from V$645 million or 2 percent of GDP to V$766 million in the period

1989–2002. This is equivalent to 2.5 percent of GDP (Asian Development Bank 2003).

The Australian Defense Cooperation Program continues to fund five Australian defense force advisers in Vanuatu and contributed an estimated AUS$10.3 million from 2000 to 2004 (Australian Department of Defense 2002, 12; 2003). These funds assisted the VPF and VMF. Vanuatu has participated in NZDF's MAP since 1986. These funds have been focused on training assistance and engineering support. U.S. IMET aid for 2004 was $100,000 (FAS 2004).

Armaments and Trade

SIPRI calculated the volume of transfers of major conventional weapons for Oceania (defined as Australia, Fiji, Kiribati, the Marshall Islands, Micronesia, New Zealand, Palau, PNG, the Solomon Islands, Tonga, Tuvalu, and Vanuatu) as totaling U.S.$631 billion for 2002, which was down slightly from U.S.$733 billion in 2001, but nearly double the 2000 figure (U.S.$ 327 billion). Exports of major weaponry totaled U.S.$30 billion in 2002 and were too small to record in the previous two years (SIPRI 2003, 472–473). Nearly all the expenditures relate to Australia.

The United States, Australia, and New Zealand have not provided military arms to Pacific island states in recent years (Capie 2003, 11). After consultation with Australia and New Zealand, the United States allegedly refused the sale of 300 M-16 rifles to Tonga in 2001 (Capie 2003, 68). This does not, of course, prevent Pacific states turning elsewhere for commercial arms purchases. Modern weaponry has been used in insurrections and coups in Fiji and the Solomon Islands.

No Pacific island state has the capability to manufacture weapons. The exception has been rebel militia groups, notably the BRA in PNG, the Isatabu Freedom Fighters (IFF), and Malaitan Eagle Force (MEF) in the Solomon Islands, which have manufactured homemade weapons and reconditioned World War II weaponry.

A recent study showed over twenty-six countries in 2000 legally exported small arms valued at U.S.$44 million to the Pacific with approximately half coming from U.S. sources (Alpers and Twyford 2003, xvi). Most (over 94 percent) were imported by Australia and New Zealand. French Polynesia and New Caledonia received 4.6 percent, leaving less than 1 percent for Fiji, PNG, Tonga, and Vanuatu. In 2000, the declared small arms and ammunition imports to Pacific islands were valued just over U.S.$300,000. All these arms came from Australian sources (Alpers and Twyford 2003, 5–7).

Trafficking of small arms remains a serious regional problem. Illicit trading of guns for drugs from PNG to Australia takes place across the Torres Straight around the Daru region, where high-grade marijuana is traded for automatic and semiautomatic weapons (Capie 2003, 78). However, another study has reported that the volume is low (Alpers and Twyford 2003, 21). Australian Customs have increased monitoring of the area. Accusations of illegal trading of guns across the West Papua–PNG border from Sanduan provincial authorities and police have been met with "a word of caution" from the Indonesian Embassy in Port Moresby, who claim Indonesia has a strict gun control policy (*Pacific Magazine* 2005; Pacific Islands Reports 2005). Since the Bougainville peace process, weapons are reportedly being sold by the

BRA and the PNGDF to Solomon Islands militants such as the IFF (Capie 2003, 81–83).

The security of police and military armories in the Pacific has been inadequate, especially in Melanesia. During the 2000 Solomon Islands uprising, the rebel MEF, with the help of the Solomon Islands police, armed themselves with approximately 500 assault rifles and machine guns taken from the police armory (Alpers and Twyford 2003, 24). In 2004 a small arms seminar in Fiji organized by the UN's Department for Disarmament Affairs presented a program titled, "To Prevent Combat and Eradicate the Illicit Trade in Small Arms and Light Weapons in All Its Aspects." The Pacific Islands Forum Model Weapons Control Bill was also considered.

PNG
The PNGDF are poorly equipped. Most of their budget has gone toward wage payments. The PNGDF inventory is aged. The M-16A2, the infantry's standard weapons, are nearing the end of their operational life. There have been trials of several replacement infantry weapons, but Australia has refused to supply them (Capie 2003, 64–65).

Between the years 1996 and 2001, under the U.S. Arms Licenses and Agreements with PNG, the combined value of direct commercial sales (DCS) and foreign military sales (FMS) of defense equipment, services, and training totaled U.S.$6.2 million (FAS 2001).

Fiji
Due to embargoes on arms sales since the 2000 coup, RFMF stocks of arms and ammunition is reportedly low.

Fiji procures small amounts of military equipment from Australia, Korea, New Zealand, Singapore, the United Kingdom, and the United States (Jane's Sentinel 2003, 104). Between the years 1995 and 1998, under the U.S. Arms Licenses and Agreements with Fiji, both direct commercial sales and foreign military sales defense equipment, services, and training totaled U.S.$627,000 (FAS 2001).

Tonga
The TDS reportedly holds stocks of armaments in pristine condition despite their age. A sale of upgraded infantry weapons was refused by the United States on the recommendations of Australia and New Zealand. It is reported that Israeli Galil rifles are being considered instead (Capie 2003, 68).

Between the years 1991 and 2001, under the U.S. Arms Licenses and Agreements with Tonga, both direct commercial sales and foreign military sales totaled U.S.$968,000 (FAS 2001).

Vanuatu
The VMF are poorly equipped, as most of their weaponry is unserviceable. Due to lack of funds, it is unlikely the Vanuatu government will be able to upgrade its armory. The Australian government has supplied ammunition for patrol boat exercises (Capie 2003, 67–68).

Civil–Military Relations
Fiji
Fiji has experienced three military coups: in May and September 1987 and May 2000. The 1987 coups were led by Sitiveni Rabuka, who justified his actions as necessary to ensure political power was not lost to an Indian-dominated government. A race-based constitution was introduced in 1990 to entrench Fijian political domination, but was changed in 1997 following

international pressure. The 2000 coup followed a year after the election of Fiji's first Indo-Fijian prime minister, Mahendra Chaudhry. The coup was fronted by businessman George Speight and was backed by the army's elite counterrevolutionary warfare unit, which was linked to the nationalist Taukei movement. The military commander, Frank Bainimarama, opposed Speight and appointed a civilian prime minister pending new elections. The army was (and remains) deeply divided by the coup. A November 2000 mutiny was viciously suppressed. Prosecution of those involved in the 2000 coups and mutiny continue to be vigorously pursued.

PNG

PNG has not experienced a coup although there have been several military rebellions and mutinies. The most serious case occurred in 1997 in response to the government hiring of mercenaries to resolve the Bougainville conflict. The PNGDF, annoyed that the government could find funds for a foreign army but not its own ill-equipped force, mutinied and expelled the mercenaries. The prime minister was forced to step aside pending an inquiry and new elections.

There are several earlier examples of ruptures between the government and the military. In 1989, 400 soldiers marched on Parliament to demand an increase in pay. In 1988, the military defied the government's stated intention of closing the Lae air base and occupied the airfield. In 1994, the maritime unit went on strike in protest against the lack of maintenance of naval vessels. There were frequent differences between the government and the military during the Bougainville conflict, with the military believing they had been denied essential resources. In 1996, members of the military were implicated in the

assassination of the pro-government premier of Bougainville, Theodore Muriung. In March 2001, the army revolted on learning of extensive cutbacks in personnel (May et al. 2003, 6). The reductions were reduced and the mutineers pardoned.

Although further military revolts are likely, a full-scale coup is not anticipated. This is because of rifts within the military and poor discipline. There is also considerable tension between the police and the military. Should a coup occur, it would likely be followed by a succession of countercoups.

Tonga

The Tongan military forces have remained strongly loyal to the nation's king. In the early 1990s there was speculation about the possibility of a coup. This seems unlikely, given the conservative nature of Tongan society. The one possible trigger for intervention would be if the monarchy was under threat with the military intervening to protect, not challenge, the king. Tonga's king has warned that radical change could provoke a coup. A leaked assessment by the New Zealand High Commission in Tonga noted that some of the military regarded the pro-democracy movement as the enemy, but added that the TDS would not obey an order to fire on a crowd (*New Zealand Herald* 2003).

Vanuatu

Vanuatu has had military rebellions but no coups. In September 1996, amid rumors of a planned coup, elements from the VMF abducted the president and acting prime minister in order to force settlement of a long-standing dispute over pay and allowances. The dissidents took control of the radio station to announce they were not mounting a coup. One month later, impatient for results over the pay dispute, an official from the department of finance was kidnapped. In November of the same year, mass arrests of VMF personnel were made in a move to head off a rumored military coup. In August 2002, police who objected to the choice of a VMF officer as police commissioner arrested the attorney general and fourteen senior civil servants. The VMF later staged a raid on police headquarters and arrested police involved in the earlier incident. There were reports that the VMF were training a separate militia to help maintain order.

The Role of the Military in Domestic Politics

The high public standing of the Fiji military gives it considerable political clout. The powerful influence of the military was highlighted in early 2004 when the commander, Frank Bainimarama, refused to step down at the end of his five-year term of office. The government backed down rather than force a confrontation that could have sparked a further coup. The government also agreed not to proceed with an announced inquiry into allegations that Bainimarama had planned a coup in late 2003. Bainimarama, as well as being concerned about his reappointment, objected to cuts in the military budget and to rumors that his opponents from the 2000 coup and mutiny were to be pardoned.

The PNG military demonstrated their political clout over the 1996 Sandline mercenary affair. During much of the Bougainville conflict, the PNGDF operating in Bougainville were often their own masters and were not under effective civilian control.

In Vanuatu, as has been noted, the ten-

> ### Sidebar 3   Sandline Affair in Papua New Guinea
>
> In early 1997, deterioration of the Bougainville crisis led Papua New Guinea (PNG) Prime Minister Julius Chan to engage the services of mercenary providers Sandline International, a subsidiary of Executive Outcomes, an African private security company. The company was hired to train the Papua New Guinea Defense Forces (PNGDF), accompany the forces on missions, and supply large-scale weaponry. The commander of the Defense Force, Brigadier General Jerry Singirok, opposed the mercenary program and demanded the resignation of Prime Minister Chan. International and regional condemnation and violent demonstrations in PNG caused the deal to be suspended. Accusations of bribery and of Sandline having financial interest in the Panguna Mine were made during two inquiries. In 1998, the PNG government was ordered by an international tribunal to pay AUS$28 million to Sandline in outstanding debts.
>
> #### Sources
> Sinclair, Dinnen. 1999. "Internal Security, Private Contractors and Political Leadership in Papua New Guinea." *The Contemporary Pacific* 11, no. 2:279.
> Sinclair, Dinnen, Ron May, and Anthony Regan (eds.). 1997. *Challenging the State: The Sandline Affair in Papua New Guinea.* Canberra, ACT: National Centre for Development Studies, Research School of Pacific and Asian Studies, and Department of Political and Social Change, Research School of Pacific and Asian Studies, Australian National University.

sion between the paramilitary VMF and the police has frequently bubbled into the political arena. The VMF is mainly recruited from the anglophone community.

In Tonga to date, the military have not played a significant role in the political process and remain loyal to the king.

Terrorism

The threat of terrorism is generally low in the Pacific island region. There has been concern that relatively lax border controls might lead terrorist groups to consider the island states to be a soft touch. On the other hand, outsiders stand out in small and intimate communities, and potential terrorists would likely be detected. Only Fiji has a small Muslim community, which makes up about 8 percent of the population. Although there has been a report of an al-Qaeda connection, there is no evidence that it is active. PNG shares a border with Indonesia, the world's largest Muslim state.

In the 2002 Nasonini Declaration, Pacific Islands Forum leaders committed themselves to develop and enact antiterrorism and transnational crime legislation. An expert working group was convened to "coordinate the development of a regional framework including model legislative provisions to address terrorism and transnational organized crime."

Some of the dubious activities of the Pacific island governments have been exploited by terrorist groups. These include money laundering and passport sales. Tongan-registered ships have been connected to the al-Qaeda network, resulting in an embarrassed Tongan government declaration that it would close its shipping registry.

Relationship with the United States

Although U.S. President George Bush met with Pacific island leaders in Hawaii in late 2003, the U.S. interest in the South Pacific has declined since the end of the Cold War. The U.S. Embassy in the Solomon Islands was closed in 1993, along with an aid station in Fiji in 1994. Although concerned at the growing instability in Melanesia and the possibility of terrorist attacks, the United States was content to leave regional security matters in the hands of its "deputy sheriff," Australia. However, at the 2004 Pacific Islands Forum in Apia, the United States warned the Pacific island leaders that the threat of terrorism in their region was a daily reality. The U.S. Congress approved U.S.$1 billion for the Millennium Challenge Account, under which five Pacific island countries are eligible for development assistance. The United States also announced that a new Pacific island fund had been established and that an anti-money laundering and counterterrorist financing training program had been proposed. This program is to be administered by the Pacific Islands Forum Secretariat in Suva, Fiji.

The United States maintains important strategic interests in Micronesia, particularly the military bases in Guam and Kwajalein in the Marshall Islands.

PNG

The United States has an embassy in Port Moresby. It maintains an interest in PNG as the largest and most populous island state of the South Pacific. PNG is also richly endowed with mineral and forestry resources. Strategically it is important because of its land border with the turbulent Indonesian province of West Papua where the United States has significant interests in the mining industry. U.S. aid has funded the training of a more professional and disciplined PNGDF.

Fiji

Fiji's generally good relations with the United States have been disrupted by three military coups. The two countries exchange resident ambassadors. Fiji's policy of not allowing visits by U.S. nuclear ships (as is still the case for New Zealand and Vanuatu) was reversed following the coup in May 1987. The U.S. Peace Corps were withdrawn in 1998, but the program was restored in January 2004. Military assistance was halted after the 2000 coup. The 2002 U.S. Foreign Military Training Report noted that Fiji was excluded from training because of its antidemocratic behavior. In 2003, the guided missile destroyer USS *O'Kane* visited Suva and signaled a renewal of military ties.

Tonga

The United States has only limited ties with Tonga and does not maintain a resident diplomatic representation. The Tongan ambassador to the United Nations is accredited to the United States. A consulate is maintained in California largely for the recreation of the Tongan royal family. Some U.S. training has been provided to the TDS regarding respect for human rights and the need to maintain civilian control over the military.

Vanuatu

The United States does not maintain an embassy in Port Vila, but is represented by its ambassador to PNG. The United States lists its principal interest in Vanuatu as strengthening democratic institutions.

The Future

The squeeze on defense budgets in PNG and Fiji are likely to continue. The forces of both countries face severe cuts. Mu-

tinies in the armed forces of PNG, Fiji, and Vanuatu have lowered the standing of the military in the eyes of the public. The growing instability has not resulted in increased forces as the military have proved to be part of the security problem rather than the solution. No other Pacific island countries are likely to establish armed forces.

With the possible exception of terrorism, as noted previously, there is no discernable present external threat to the Pacific island region, and none is likely to emerge in the next five to ten years. Internal conflict will continue as Melanesia is likely to be politically unstable for the foreseeable future. The causes of the conflicts are deep rooted (see the Current and Potential Military Confrontation section). In Polynesia, pressures for constitutional reform in Tonga are likely to increase when the current eighty-five-year-old monarch passes away.

Under the 2000 Biketawa Declaration, the Pacific Islands Forum has mandated the forum secretary general to become more proactive during times of regional crisis. The 2004 review of the Pacific Islands Forum proposed that the Pacific Plan include a "more comprehensive regional approach to shared security interests."

The involvement of outside powers in Pacific island affairs is likely to increase. The civilian and police components of the Australian-led intervention force into the Solomon Islands are expected to continue for much of the next decade. Australian police are becoming increasingly involved in attempts to maintain law and order in the other Melanesian states of PNG, Vanuatu, and Fiji. Australian nationals hold the positions of police commissioner in Fiji and deputy commissioner with the Royal Solomon Islands Police.

Asian states, including Japan, China, and Indonesia, and Southeast Asia are likely to become more actively involved in the South Pacific. Island states are increasingly looking north for economic and political security (Henderson and Reilly 2003). China is likely to emerge as a major regional power in the next few decades. Its interests extend beyond rivalry with Taiwan to securing wider strategic advantages. This, in turn, is likely to attract a return of U.S. interests in the region.

References

General

Alpers, Philip, and Conor Twyford. 2003. *Small Arms in the Pacific.* The Small Arms Survey. http://www.smallarmssurvey.org/OPsOP08Pacifics.pdf (accessed March 16, 2004).

Australian Department of Defense. 2002. *Inquiry into Papua New Guinea and the Island States of the South-West Pacific.* http://www.aph.gov.au/Senate?committee/fadt_ctte/PNG/submissions/sub49.pdf (accessed March 13, 2004).

———. 2003. *Defense Cooperation.* http://www.defense.gov.au/budget/02–03/dar/02_06_05defcoop.htm (accessed March 14, 2004).

Capie, David. 2003. *Under the Gun: The Small Arms Challenge in the Pacific.* Wellington, NZ: Victoria University Press.

Central Intelligence Agency (CIA). 2003. *World Factbook: Australia, New Zealand, Fiji, PNG, Tonga, Vanuatu.* http://www.cia.gov/cia/publications/factbook/print/as.html (accessed March 17, 2004).

Crocombe, Ron. 2001. *The South Pacific.* Suva, Fiji: University of South Pacific.

Defense Reporter. 2001. *The Defense Reporter: Australia and Asia Pacific.* Engadine, NSW: Asia Pacific Defense Publications Party.

Europa. 2003. *The Europa World Year Book.* "Oceania." London: Europa Publications.

Federation of American Scientists (FAS). 2001. *US Arms Licenses and Agreements for 1990–2001. Fiji, Papua New Guinea, Tonga.* http://www.fas.org/asmp/profiles/sales_db.php?region=eapc&ctryin=png&fy1in=1990&fy2in=2001 (accessed March 5, 2004).

———. 2005. *Country/Account Summaries.* http:www.fas.org/asmp/profiles/aid/fy2004/cbj01-intro.pdf (accessed June 7, 2005).

Fry, Greg. 1999. *South Pacific Security and Global Change: The New Agenda.* Working Paper No 1999/1. Canberra, ACT: Australian National University.

Henderson, John, and Benjamin Reilly. 2003. "Dragon in Paradise: China's Rising Star in Oceania." *National Interest* 72: 92–104.

Jane's Sentinel. 2003. "Jane's Sentinel Security Assessment: Oceania." Surrey, UK: Jane's Information Group.

May, Ron, Anthony Regan, Sinclair Dinnen, Michael Morgan, Brij Lal, and Benjamin Reilly. 2003. *Arc of Instability: Melanesia in the Early 2000s.* Canberra, ACT: State, Society and Governance in Melanesia Project, Research School of Pacific and Asian Studies, Australian National University; Christchurch, NZ: Macmillan Brown Centre for Pacific Studies.

New Zealand Defense Force (NZDF). 2003. *Vote Defense Force.* Part B, Statement of Appropriations. http://www.nzdf.mil.nz/public-documents/downloads/DefenseForceEstimates.pdf (accessed March 13, 2004).

Pacific Islands Reports. 2005. "Drugs, Guns Rule Neglected PNG, Papua Border." http://pidp.eastwestcenter.org/pireports/205/May/05-12-ed1.htm (accessed June 7, 2005).

Pacific Magazine. 2005. "Region: Indons Wants Care on Drugs-for-Guns Claim." http://www.pacificmagazine.net/pina/pinadefault2.php?urlpinaid=15294 (accessed June 7, 2005).

Stockholm International Peace Research Institute (SIPRI). 2003. *Armaments, Disarmament and International Security.* Solna, Sweden: SIPRI.

———. 2004a. *Recent Trends in Military Expenditure.* http://projects.sipri.org/milex/mex_trends.html (accessed March 17, 2004).

———. 2004b. *World and Regional Military Expenditure Estimates 1993–2002.* http://projects.sipri.org/

milex/mex_wnr_table.html (accessed March 17, 2004).

Fiji
Fiji Parliament. 1997. "Defending Fiji, Defense White Paper 1997." Parliamentary Paper No. 3.
New Zealand Ministry of Foreign Affairs and Trade. 2003. *Republic of the Fiji Islands Country Paper—July 2003.* http://www.mft.govt.nz/foreign/regions/pacific/country/fijipaper.html (accessed March 14, 2004).

PNG
Laki, James S. 2003. "PNG Defense Force: An Analysis of Its Past, Present and Future Roles." In *Building a Nation in Papua New Guinea*, David Kavanamut, Charles Yala, and Quinton Clements, eds. Canberra, ACT: Pandanus Books, pp. 69–89.
May, R. J. 2003. "Disorderly Democracy: Political Turbulence and Institutional Reform in Papua New Guinea." In *State Society and Governance in Melanesia.* Canberra, ACT: Australian National University.

Tonga
New Zealand Herald. 2003. "Brian Smythe's Report on Tonga, September 2001." http://www.nzherald.co.nz/storyprint.cfm?storyID=3506638 (accessed February 11, 2004).
Tongan Reserve Bank. 2003. *Government Recurrent Expenditure, by Function.* http://reservebank.ton/docs/QtrlyBulletin/sep_Bulletin03/sep_Bulletin.2003.pdf (accessed March 5, 2004).

Vanuatu
Asian Development Bank. 2003. *Key Indicators of Developing Asian and Pacific Countries.* http://www.adb.org/Document/Books/Key_Indicators/2003/pdf/VAN.pdf (accessed February 26, 2004).
Jowitt, Anita. 2001. "Vanuatu: Politics." *The Contemporary Pacific* 13, no. 2:557.

Recommended Readings
Ambrose, David. 1996. *A Coup That Failed? Recent Events in Vanuatu.* Canberra, ACT: National Centre for Development Studies, Australian National University. Also available at: http://ww.vanuatu.usp.ac.fj/library/online/Vanuatu/coup.htm.
Crocombe, Ron. 2001. *The South Pacific.* Suva, Fiji: University of South Pacific.
Dibb, Paul, and Rhonda Nicholas. 1996. *Restructuring the Papua New Guinea Defense Force.* Canberra, ACT: Australian National University.
Dorney, Sean. 2000. *Papua New Guinea: People, Politics and History since 1975.* Sydney: Australian Broadcasting Corporation.
Hegarty, David, and Peter Polomka, eds. 1989. *The Security of Oceania in the 1990s. Vol 1: Views from the Region.* Canberra, ACT: Australian National University.
Henderson John, and Greg Watson, eds. 2005. *Securing a Peaceful Pacific.* Christchurch, NZ: Canterbury University Press.
Henningham, Stephen. 1995. *The Pacific Island States: Security and Sovereignty in the Post–Cold War World.* London: Macmillan Press.
Henningham, Stephen, and Desmond Ball. 1995. *South Pacific Security: Issues and Perspectives.* Canberra, ACT: Australian National University.
Laki, James S. 2003. "PNG Defense Force: An Analysis of Its Past, Present and Future Roles." In *Building a Nation in Papua New Guinea*, David Kavanamut, Charles Yala, and Quinton Clements, eds. Canberra, ACT: Pandanus Books, pp. 69–89.
May, Ron, Anthony Regan, Sinclair Dinnen, Michael Morgan, Brij Lal, and Benjamin Reilly. 2003. *Arc of Instability: Melanesia in the Early 2000s.* Canberra, ACT: State, Society and Governance in Melanesia Project, Research School of Pacific and Asian Studies, Australian National University; Christchurch, NZ: Macmillan Brown Centre for Pacific Studies.
Molloy, Ivan, ed. 2004. *The Eye of the Cyclone: Issues in Pacific Security.* Queensland: Pacific Islands Political Studies Association.
Ross, Ken. 1993. *Regional Security in the South Pacific: The Quarter-Century 1970–1995.* Canberra, ACT: Australian National University.

Sanday, Jim. 1989. *The Military in Fiji: Historical Development and Future Role.* Canberra, ACT: Strategic and Defense Studies Centre, Australian National University.

Shibuya, Eric, and Jim Rolfe, eds. 2003. *Security in Oceania in the 21st Century.* Honolulu: Asia-Pacific Center for Security Studies.

Websites

Asia Pacific Network: http://www.asiapac. org.fj/cafepacific/resources/david_aspac. html.

Fiji Government Online: http://www.fiji. gov.fj.

Pacific Islands Reports: http://pidp.ewc. hawaii.edu/pireport/text.htm.

PNG Government: http://www:// pngonline.gov.pg.

State, Society & Governance in Melanesia: http://rspas.anu.edu.au/ melanesia.

Tongan Government: http://www.pmo. gov.to.

Vanuatu Government: http:// vanuatugovernment.gov.vu.

Pakistan

Kanishkan Sathasivam

Geography and History

Geographically, Pakistan delineates the northwestern boundary of the Indian subcontinent, separating the south Asia region from the Middle East to the west and from central Asia to the northwest. Pakistan comprises 803,940 sq. km of total area, of which land area comprises 778,720 sq. km. This makes Pakistan about twice the size of California. Pakistan shares land borders with four other countries: a 2,912-km-long border with India to the east and southeast, a 523-km-long border with China to the northeast, a 2,430-km-long border with Afghanistan to the north and northwest, and a 909-km-long border with Iran to the west. Pakistan also possesses a 1,046-km-long coastline on the Indian Ocean to the south.

Pakistan experiences a wide range of climatic conditions, ranging from mostly hot and dry conditions in the south to temperate conditions in the northwest to extremely cold and snowy conditions in the north. However, in general terms Pakistan's climate is classified as arid subtropical, with three-fourths of the country receiving an average annual rainfall of less than 250 mm (IUCN-Pakistan). The Chagai and Sibi desert areas receive less than 30 mm of rainfall annually, while the northern areas are inundated with over 2,000 mm of annual rainfall. Much of the rainfall across the country occurs as the result of the southwest monsoon, experienced between June and September each year. Average pre-monsoon temperatures in the low areas range from 35 to 40°C, with high points close to 45°C in the deserts. Winter temperatures in the mountains remain below 0°C for many months.

As with its climate, Pakistan's terrain also varies considerably, from the flat Indus plains in the east to the Balochistan plateau in the west to vast, soaring mountain ranges in the north and northwest (IUCN-Pakistan). The mountains of Pakistan are a combination of parts of the Himalayan, Karakoram, and Hindu Kush mountain ranges and include Mount Godwin-Austen (commonly referred to as K2), the second tallest mountain in the world. The mountains separating Pakistan from Afghanistan to the northwest are traversed by the Khyber Pass and the Bolan Pass, two historical invasion routes from Central Asia into the Indian subcontinent. The Balochistan plateau in the western part of the country—often referred to as the "Western Highlands" of Pakistan—comprises a series of smaller hills in a dry climate. The eastern plains of Pakistan are defined by the floodplain of the Indus River, a large river system with several major tributaries and a vast network of irrigation canals. According to IUCN-Pakistan, the following ecological zones are found in Pakistan to some degree: permanent snowfields and cold desert, alpine meadows, Himalayan temperate forests, subtropical pine forests, tropical deciduous forests, alpine dry steppe, arid subtropical habitat, tropical thorn forests, and riverine plain.

The 1947 partition of British India into two states on the basis of religion resulted in the creation of the mostly Muslim state of Pakistan. Pakistan became an independent state on August 14, 1947, preceding mostly Hindu India's independence the following day, August 15, 1947. Officially named the Islamic Republic of Pakistan, the country is politically organized as a federal republic with the city of Islamabad as its capital. Administratively, the country is divided into four provinces (Balochistan, North-West Frontier Province, Punjab, and Sindh), one territory (Federally Administered Tribal Areas), and one capital territory (Islamabad Capital Territory). These administrative areas do not include the Pakistan-administered parts of the disputed territory of Kashmir (Azad Kashmir and the Northern Areas).

Pakistan was formally declared a republic on March 23, 1956. Its first constitution did not last very long and was abrogated in October 1958. Pakistan's current constitution was adopted on April 10, 1973, following an extended period of military rule. This constitution has since been modified and amended on several occasions and has also been suspended during subsequent periods of military government. The government structure is organized along the traditional three branches (executive, legislative, and judicial), with the head of state and head of government functions within the executive branch being performed by separate officials (the president and the prime min-

ister, respectively). However, with respect to national security and defense affairs, the president dominates the decision-making process, with the prime minister and other security-related cabinet ministers playing clearly subordinate roles.

In July 2003, the Central Intelligence Agency (CIA) estimated Pakistan's population at 150,694,740 people. Annual population growth is estimated to be about 2 percent. Ethnically, Pakistan's population consists of four historically recognized groups—Baloch, Pashtun (Pathan), Punjabi, and Sindhi—corresponding to its four administrative provinces. Linguistically, these communities comprise roughly 3, 8, 58, and 12 percent of the population, respectively. A fifth language, Urdu, the primary language of about 8 percent of the population, is the official language of Pakistan, along with English. The literacy rate for the Pakistani population is estimated to be about 46 percent.

In terms of religion, 97 percent of Pakistanis are Muslim, subdivided into Sunni Muslims (77 percent of the total population) and Shi'a Muslims (20 percent of the total population). Very small numbers of Christians, Hindus, and other religious groups make up the remainder of the Pakistani population. Although Pakistan often identifies itself as an Islamic state, it also considers itself to be and is constitutionally organized as a secular republic. Its legal system is based generally on English common law, with elements of Islamic law intermixed to accommodate the country's Islamic character and identity.

Pakistan is a poor developing country with serious economic problems and structural weaknesses that continue to hamper its development and modernization. Significant increases in foreign aid inflows in the 2001–2002 period, along

Table 1   Key Statistics

Type of government	Federal republic
Population (millions)	150.7 (2003)
Religion	Islam (97%, 2003)
Main industries	Textiles and apparel (2003)
Main security threats	Historic and ongoing conflict with India, border instability from recent war in Afghanistan, domestic sectarian violence and Islamic terrorism
Defense spending (% GDP)	3.97 (2002)
Size of military (thousands)	1,133 (2003)
Number of civil wars since 1945	3
Number of interstate wars since 1945	3

Sources

Central Intelligence Agency Website. 2003. CIA *World Factbook*. http://www.cia.gov/cia/publications/factbook/ (accessed May 15, 2005).

Correlates of War (COW) 2. *COW Formal Interstate Alliance Data Set, 1816–2000 (v3.03).* http://cow2.la.psu.edu.

International Institute for Strategic Studies (IISS). 2003. *The Military Balance 2003/2004* (annual yearbook). Oxford, UK: Oxford University Press (for the IISS).

with other fortuitous circumstances and some governmental reforms, have improved Pakistan's prospects considerably in the short term. However, long-term prospects for continued reform and growth remain uncertain at best. Using purchasing power parity conversions, the CIA (CIA *World Factbook* 2003) estimated Pakistan's gross domestic product (GDP) to be about U.S.$295.3 billion in 2002, which translates into a per capita GDP of about U.S.$2,000. As is typical of many developing countries, Pakistan is burdened by a large external public debt, estimated at about U.S.$32.3 billion. Some 35 percent of the country's population is estimated to be living below the national poverty line. For 2002, the annual inflation rate was estimated at just under 4 percent, the unemployment rate at about 7.8 percent (with considerable additional underemployment), and the industrial production growth rate at some 2.4 percent.

Unusual for a developing country, Pakistan's economy is primarily service oriented, with the services sector accounting for 51 percent of GDP. Industry accounts for 25 percent, and agriculture the remaining 24 percent (CIA *World Factbook* 2003). However, with respect to the labor force, the three sectors of the economy account for 39, 17, and 44 percent of labor, respectively, which is possibly indicative of significant distortions in wage distributions. Furthermore, with respect to the services sector, a large number of Pakistanis are part of the labor force of several Middle East (mainly Persian Gulf) states, where they perform service-oriented work. The earnings of these workers contribute significantly to Pakistan's GDP as well as its foreign exchange reserves. However, to the country as a whole, these benefits are not necessarily reflected in the standards of living of these workers themselves. Pakistan's major industrial outputs comprise textiles and apparel, food processing, beverages, construction materials, paper products, and fertilizer (CIA *World Factbook* 2003). Although Pakistan is a net importer of oil, it produces sufficient natural gas to meet its current domestic needs. Fossil fuels account for some 69 percent of the country's electricity production (CIA *World Factbook* 2003).

Regional Geopolitics

Pakistan faces a very complex pattern of regional geopolitical relationships and rivalries. Since the country is situated astride three regional systems, south Asia, central Asia, and the Middle East, Pakistan affects and is affected by the geopolitics of all three regions. Furthermore, Pakistan is also affected by the geopolitical considerations of three more distant actors, China, Russia, and the United States, each with its own set of reasons for having an abiding interest in the politics of Pakistan.

Within the south Asia regional system, India clearly enjoys a dominant position (Blank 2003), which in turn is a source of great consternation for Pakistan given the history of conflict and rivalry between the two states. India's significant advantages over Pakistan in geographic size, population, resource base, and so forth drive that country's dominant geopolitical position. If third-party countries without a direct link to the India-Pakistan relationship are for any reason forced to choose between the two rivals, obviously they are more likely to choose friendship with the stronger rather than the weaker of the two actors. India's success in securing strong working relationships with several former Soviet central Asian republics in the face of contrary Pakistani lobbying efforts is testament to this reality. India is also able to significantly influence Pakistan's relationships with the other smaller states of south Asia. Even Bangladesh, a fellow Muslim south Asian

state, is wary of exceedingly close ties to Pakistan—the result of the post-Partition history between Pakistan and Bangladesh (formerly East Pakistan). Furthermore, the loss of East Pakistan/Bangladesh following the 1971 war also meant the loss of a gateway to closer geopolitical relationships with such proximal states as Bhutan, Myanmar (formerly Burma), and Thailand.

Regional geopolitical considerations in central Asia are obviously more recent phenomena, a product of the end of the Cold War and the collapse of the former Soviet Union. Afghanistan has traditionally been the transitional state between south and central Asia. The Soviet withdrawal from Afghanistan preceding the fall of the Soviet Union opened up Afghanistan, as well as newly independent republics further to the north, to Pakistani power plays. Unfortunately for Pakistan, those groups within Afghanistan most amenable to close ties to Pakistan—groups that subsequently coalesced into the recently ousted Taliban regime—were vigorously opposed by groups with close ties to other regional actors, most notably Tajikistan, Uzbekistan, Kyrgyzstan, Iran, and Russia. Therefore, Pakistan's strident efforts to create a pro-Pakistan regime in Afghanistan following the Soviet withdrawal from that country ran counter to the interests of other regional states with whom Pakistan also wished to generate close strategic relationships.

The fall of the Pakistani-supported Taliban regime in Afghanistan in 2001–2002 was a serious blow to Pakistan's efforts to create favorable geopolitical conditions for itself in the region. Although the new regime that has arisen in Afghanistan has expressed a desire to maintain a close friendship with Pakistan, it has also been very active in pursuing close relationships with all other regional states. Most importantly, the new Afghan government has established a good relationship with India, and India is playing an important role in the rebuilding of post-Taliban Afghan society. India has also further enhanced its relationships with Tajikistan and Uzbekistan, both countries having viewed India as an ally in their opposition to the old Taliban regime in Afghanistan (Gupta 2003).

The continuing post-Taliban instability in Afghanistan also affects Pakistani national security in more direct ways. Significant numbers of Taliban and al-Qaeda fighters continue to operate from the Afghanistan-Pakistan border areas that are home to tribal groups that straddle both countries. The presence of these fighters on Pakistani soil not only threatens to expand the ongoing U.S.-led war in Afghanistan across the international border into Pakistan, but also serves to generate domestic instability and violence within Pakistani society, especially within Pakistani villages and cities in the North-West Frontier Province, Balochistan, and the tribal areas where sympathy for the radical Islamic visions of the Taliban and al-Qaeda runs deep.

Turning to the Middle East, three countries are particularly important to any discussion of Pakistan's regional geopolitics: Iran, Saudi Arabia, and Israel. Although on the surface it may appear reasonable to assume that Iran and Pakistan would be the best of friends and allies, this is not quite so for a variety of reasons. First, the explanation for the bitter rivalry between the Iranian Islamic theocracy and the Afghan (Taliban) Islamic theocracy also explains the somewhat distant and cool relationship between Iran and Pakistan. Shi'a Iran is deeply suspicious of its Sunni neighbors, even when (or perhaps especially when) those states pursue radical (Sunni) Islamic ideologies similar to its own (i.e., Saudi Arabia, and Afghanistan under the Taliban). Therefore, Pakistan's unbridled support for the Taliban regime did not win Islamabad any friends in Tehran. Second, Iran is increasingly worried by the radicalization and identity consciousness being evoked within the Baloch minority on the Pakistani side of the Iran-Pakistan border. A similar Baloch minority exists on the Iranian side of the border, and Tehran greatly fears a spillover effect. Finally, Iran's close friendship with Russia and Russia's close friendship with India seem to have produced a "friend-of-my-friend" effect between Iran and India. Furthermore, India has much to offer an internationally isolated Iran in terms of economic, scientific, technological, and industrial (including military-industrial) cooperation—mutually beneficial ties with which Pakistan simply cannot compete in any meaningful way.

As a result of the combination of these factors, Iran and India enjoy a very cozy relationship, one that some Indian officials have actually described as an alliance (Ahrari 2003; Peimani 2003a; 2003b). To be fair, the Iranian government does emphasize that its relationship with India does not exist at the expense of Pakistan and that Iran values its ties to Pakistan, including their shared Islamic fraternity.

If India comes out ahead of Pakistan within the India-Pakistan-Iran triangular relationship, it may be safe to say that Pakistan similarly comes out ahead within the India-Pakistan-Saudi Arabia triangular relationship. Although such a conclusion may indeed be reasonably drawn, it is not, however, as easy to offer specific details substantiating this conclusion given the extreme secrecy with which the Saudi regime handles all of its geopolitical relationships. Pakistan receives a generous amount of financial assistance from Saudi Arabia, along with subsidized petroleum products. Some have argued that many Pakistani nationals serve in the armed forces of Saudi Arabia (and the armed forces of some of the other smaller Persian Gulf Arab states as well), in particular as combat pilots in the Royal Saudi Air Force (and perhaps also the United Arab Emirates [UAE] air force). Some have even suggested that Saudi Arabia and possibly the UAE have guaranteed military assistance to Pakistan in the event of another war with India in exchange for access to Pakistani nuclear warheads if these Arab states' survival is ever threatened.

Finally, with respect to Israel, India and Israel have in recent years emerged as strange bedfellows, underscoring the Machiavellian nature of regional geopolitics in this part of the world. Beginning in the 1960s and through much of the 1980s, India was a strong supporter of the Palestinian cause and a vocal critic of Israel, but has since established a strong strategic partnership with Israel. As a result of this partnership, India has received substantial amounts of advanced military technology from Israel, and the two countries routinely share terrorism-related intelligence. Pakistan is particularly troubled by this relationship because it believes that the two countries could some day decide to mount a joint military operation to preemptively neutralize Pakistan's nuclear forces and nuclear-related research and development facilities, along the lines of Israel's preemptive strike against Iraq's nuclear reactor facility in 1981. It is noteworthy that India's two closest counter-Pakistan strategic partners in the region appear to be Iran and Israel who, ironically, label each other as their gravest security concern.

China, Russia, and the United States affect Pakistan's geopolitical calculations in varied ways. China is, and has been for some years now, Pakistan's primary strategic ally. After having been a close Cold War ally of the United States, especially during much of the 1980s when Pakistan served as the primary conduit for U.S. support for the mujahidin battling the Soviet occupation of Afghanistan, Pakistan fell out of favor with Washington due to its continued pursuit of nuclear weapons. For China, Pakistan served two strategic purposes. First, Pakistan proved to be useful leverage against India given the historic border tensions and rivalry between the two Asian giants. From China's perspective, since India provided legitimacy and support for Tibetan separatists, China would—through Pakistan—do the same with respect to Kashmir. It should be noted that India recently recognized Tibet as an integral part of China and agreed not to support Tibetan nationalist aspirations in any form. Subsequently, China has begun to pressure Pakistan toward accommodation with India on the Kashmir issue. Second, Pakistan served as a useful gateway for China into the Islamic world and the Middle East. Pakistan's value in this regard has begun to diminish for China in recent years because of China's improving relationship with several former Soviet central Asian republics, particularly Kazakhstan and Kyrgyzstan.

With respect to the United States and Russia, the early geopolitical relationships with both Pakistan and India had more to do with the Cold War than with these south Asian states themselves. Pakistan aligned itself with the United States at an early stage in its short history, not because of any shared values or interests but because it needed quality armaments with which to match Indian military capabilities. The United States, in turn, wanted as many allied states as possible in the greater Middle East region where it constantly feared Soviet expansionism, and later wanted a frontline state to counter the Soviet presence in Afghanistan. Therefore, the U.S.-Pakistan relationship throughout the Cold War was based on each side's calculated security needs rather than true friendship, and as such proved to be a very inconsistent, seesaw relationship. India, although nominally nonaligned, received substantial arms and diplomatic support from the Soviet Union and often aligned itself with the Soviet Union on major international issues during the Cold War. Especially in the aftermath of the 1971 war with Pakistan, where the Soviet Union played a major role in the negotiations to bring the war to an end, India emerged as a major Soviet ally (though not a client state like most other Soviet allies), extending to the Soviet Union access to Indian ports, airfields, and transit rights, thereby making it feasible for the Soviet Union to expand its military reach into the Indian Ocean.

With the end of the Cold War and the collapse of the Soviet Union, and subsequently the Indian and Pakistani tit-for-tat nuclear tests in May 1998 and the events of September 11, 2001, the relationships among these four countries have evolved significantly. Russia and several other former Soviet republics have emerged anew as close friends of India, especially with respect to conventional arms and arms-technology transfers. However, the United States has also begun to establish a good working relationship with India, initially with respect to issues of trade and commercial technology transfers, but more recently with respect to regional and global security affairs. Moreover, the U.S.-Pakistan relationship has also received a new lease on life thanks to Pakistan's desperate need for economic and financial assistance and its central role in the U.S. global war on terrorism.

Conflict Past and Present

Conflict History

Pakistan's postindependence conflict history is almost entirely a history of conflict with India. Three full-blown wars have been fought, all with India, along with numerous minor border conflicts. The most serious of the border conflicts occurred in the Kargil area of Kashmir in the summer of 1999 when Pakistani-backed militants crossed in strength into the Indian side of the Line of Control and battled with Indian forces for some eight weeks before being driven back into Pakistan by Indian battlefield successes and severe international diplomatic pressures. Cross-border exchanges of fire between Indian and Pakistani military forces is a routine occurrence. However, minor border battles have not been confined to the border with India. Throughout the 1980s, during the years of the Soviet occupation, Pakistani and Soviet-supported Afghan forces engaged each other in several border skirmishes. On a few occasions, Pakistan actually succeeded in shooting down Afghan air force aircraft that ventured too close to or crossed the border between the two states. It is useful to note that the border between Pakistan and Afghanistan—the so-called Durand Line—has been disputed by Afghanistan since the creation of Pakistan in 1947, a holdover from

British attempts to conquer Afghanistan in the nineteenth century.

With respect to the three major wars to which Pakistan has been a party, two were centered on Kashmir while the third had to do with Indian intervention in a Pakistani civil war in the former East Pakistan (now Bangladesh). The First Kashmir War was fought from early October 1947 to January 1, 1949, when the UN Security Council brought the fighting to an end. Indian and Pakistani accounts of this and the other India-Pakistan wars vary considerably, but basic facts are discernable (Blood 1994).

Under the rules of Partition established by Britain, the "princely states" that had retained significant autonomy under British rule were theoretically free to accede to either India or Pakistan. The choice was clear and obvious for those princely states that were either overwhelmingly Hindu or Muslim, or which were geographically completely enclosed within the new Indian or Pakistani states. The princely state of Jammu and Kashmir (commonly referred to simply as Kashmir), with a Hindu maharaja, a Muslim-majority population, and long borders with both India and Pakistan, initially attempted to remain free of both states. This choice proved unpopular with segments of the Kashmiri population, who launched an insurgency against the maharaja's regime. When the insurgency expanded with Pakistani irregulars—tribesmen from the North-West Frontier Province and volunteers from the Pakistani army—crossing over the border to aid their Muslim compatriots in Kashmir, the maharaja requested military assistance from India. The price that India demanded for its aid was the accession of Kashmir to India, which the maharaja agreed to in late October 1947. Following the accession, In-

dian military forces entered Kashmir and were able to quickly crush the insurgency and reestablish control over all of Kashmir. Now fearing for its own territorial integrity, Pakistan committed its regular forces into combat in the summer of 1948. These forces performed quite well against Indian forces and were able to occupy about 30 percent of Kashmiri territory before a UN-brokered cease-fire went into effect on January 1, 1949.

The Second Kashmir War occurred from early 1965 through September 23, 1965, when another cease-fire was arranged by the UN Security Council. The prelude to war was a series of border skirmishes along the cease-fire line in Kashmir, as well as along the poorly demarcated border in the Rann of Kutch—the border area of the two states adjacent to the Indian Ocean coast. The Rann of Kutch disputes were quickly settled by mutual consent and with British arbitration, but the situation along the Kashmir line continued to worsen. By 1965, Pakistan correctly assessed that India was making good progress toward consolidating its political control over Indian-occupied parts of Kashmir. Fearing that any further delay in dealing with Kashmir would give India an irreversible advantage vis-à-vis the future of Kashmir, Pakistan sent infiltrators into Indian Kashmir in early spring of 1965 to organize new uprisings against Indian rule. These Pakistani efforts did not meet with much success within Indian-controlled parts of Kashmir. Nevertheless, fighting between Indian and Pakistani forces spread quickly during August and finally escalated into a full-scale war in early September 1965, when India launched a major offensive aimed at encircling the large Pakistani city of Lahore while Pakistan attacked India in the Chamb sector in southwestern Kashmir. The war proved inconclusive for both sides, with both countries having fought with limited military objectives in mind. At the time of the cease-fire on September 23, 1965, each side occupied small tracts of the other's territory, which were handed back with the signing of the Tashkent Declaration in January 1966 that formally ended the war.

The third India-Pakistan war, the Bangladesh War of 1971, is perhaps the easiest to understand yet the most complex as far as its continuing ramifications for India-Pakistan geopolitical relations. The first point that must be made about this war is that it was simultaneously an interstate war between India and Pakistan as well as an intrastate war between Punjabi-dominated West Pakistan and Bengali East Pakistan. At the intrastate level, political and social tensions between West Pakistan and the Bengali East had been steadily escalating throughout the 1960s, culminating in the East Wing's demands for representation in the National Assembly based on "one-person-one-vote" and proportional allocation of seats. Given the East Wing's advantage in population over the West Wing, a majority of seats in the National Assembly (169 of 313) would therefore be reserved for the people of the East Wing. Pakistan's first-ever truly open and free general election, held on December 7, 1970, resulted in the Awami League Party in East Pakistan sweeping 160 seats in the East without winning a single seat in West Pakistan. This meant that the Bengali-based Awami League had a clear majority of seats in the National Assembly and could rule Pakistan entirely on its own even though it had absolutely no support in West Pakistan. This outcome was anathema to the elites in West Pakistan who had dominated Pakistani politics and other key Pakistani institutions

such as the military officer corps since independence.

Efforts to form some sort of accommodationist government uniting East and West Pakistanis failed, and the ruling military government suspended the National Assembly and moved to impose martial law upon the country. This sparked widespread civil unrest in the East, and central government authority collapsed in East Pakistan. The Pakistani army's authoritarian attempts to restore order in the East—undertaken with egregious human rights violations—compelled Bengali nationalists to declare an independent Bangladesh with a government-in-exile in neighboring India. The ensuing civil war sent hundreds of thousands (some sources suggest millions) of refugees flooding into India.

At the interstate level, India saw Pakistan's troubles in the East as a golden opportunity to deliver a decisive blow to its archnemesis. The massive numbers of East Pakistani refugees within India's borders gave India all of the justification it needed to act, and on March 31, 1971, the Indian Parliament passed a resolution declaring India's support of the Bangladeshi freedom movement. The Mukti Bahini (Liberation Force), the independence movement's military forces, received equipment, training, and other assistance from India and soon launched a series of offensive operations inside East Pakistan aimed at fulfilling the goal of Bangladeshi independence. The Indian army also began conducting military movements and exercises along its borders with Pakistan. Certain that India was planning on attacking Pakistan in its moment of weakness, the Pakistani high command decided to strike preemptively against Indian forces along the northern and western borders and launched air strikes against India on December 3, 1971. The next day, India launched a massive, coordinated land-sea-air assault on East Pakistan. Pakistani forces in the east reeled under India's onslaught, and on December 16, 1971—a mere twelve days later—all Pakistani forces in the east surrendered to India.

In addition to the intrastate component of the Bangladesh War, two other major instances of internal conflict have occurred in Pakistan. Between 1973 and 1977, the Pakistani army carried out an extensive pacification campaign against the Baloch minority in the western area, resulting in several thousands of casualties on both sides. Although the region has remained fairly stable since the campaign, the potential for future problems clearly exists because the Baloch people feel increasingly threatened by the immigration of non-Baloch peoples into this sparsely populated province. Interestingly, it is alleged that both Afghanistan and the Soviet Union were involved in the unrest in Pakistani Balochistan during the mid-1970s.

Finally, the early to mid-1990s saw yet a third internal conflict occur, this one between two minority groups in Pakistan's Sindh Province, with the state finding itself caught in the middle of their dispute. Sindh had long been home to much of Pakistan's muhajir population (Muslims who had been displaced from various parts of India during Partition and their descendants), a minority in Sindh yet dominant in Sindh's political and economic life. The backlash against the dominance of the Urdu-speaking muhajirs compelled the majority (a majority in Sindh, though a small minority within all of Pakistan) Sindhis to organize nationalist political movements pushing for the establishment of an independent Sindhi homeland. The threat to national unity posed by the Sindhi nationalist movements, and the conviction that India was complicit in these recurring internal conflicts within Pakistan, combined to elicit a harsh response from Pakistani central authorities, with bloody clashes among Sindhis, muhajirs, and state authorities being commonplace through 1994 and 1995.

Current and Potential Military Confrontation

Singular external and internal security threats continue to dominate Pakistan's fears and politico-military calculations regarding its future survival. Externally, India remains—and is likely to remain for the foreseeable future—Pakistan's singular threat focus. The complex postindependence relationship between Pakistan and India is a good example of what scholars describe as an "enduring rivalry" (Diehl and Goertz 2000). From the Pakistani point of view, its post-Partition experiences with India drive its side of this rivalry. Although several experiences from the early years following Partition are important and relevant, the catastrophe that befell Pakistan as the result of the 1971 Bangladesh War is the ultimate driving force behind the rivalry today. That war is viewed by many Pakistanis—even after the passage of decades—as having been a deliberate and calculated act by India to set in motion a long-term campaign to undermine and eventually destroy Pakistan. The war itself resulted in major geostrategic losses for Pakistan, in that the country lost a significant amount of territory and about 60 percent of its population. For a country that was already considerably smaller than its rival (India) in terms of territory and population, these losses were monumental. Furthermore, Pakistan's armed forces suffered significant losses in manpower (some 9,000 soldiers killed and some 90,000 taken prisoner) and in military equipment as well. However, the psychological and symbolic losses for Pakistan have proven even more costly in the years since 1971.

As a result of the intense, enduring rivalry between Pakistan and India, plus such factors as the bulk of military forces for both sides being in close proximity, the nuclear dimension, and most importantly, the continuing tensions over and violence within Kashmir, it can be reasonably concluded that the likelihood of a third Kashmir war is rather high (Sathasivam and Shafqat 2003). Recent movements by the two rivals toward dialogue and compromise are both positive and welcome. However, both states will have to make fundamental changes in their respective national policies with respect to their mutual hostility before the high probability of war decreases in any appreciable way.

In addition to the possibility of Kashmir being a catalyst for yet another war with India, Pakistan also confronts the possibility of tension and conflict in the future along its border with Afghanistan. In the context of interstate war, the threat level along the Afghan border is very low. However, the extremely porous nature of this border contributes significantly to Pakistan's elevated internal security problem.

The essential internal threat faced by Pakistan stems from the rise of Islamic radicalism, particularly in Pakistan's tribal areas in the north and northwest, and the emergence of a "Kalashnikov culture"—the consequence of a society burdened by large numbers of unemployed or underemployed youth, well-armed with a variety of weapons and imbued with the belief that jihad and martyrdom are the only meaningful values in their lives. The prospect of Pakistan becoming a failed state is very real. Numerous radical groups, including Pakistan-based Kashmiri and Afghan groups, remain active within Pakistan and conduct a variety of acts of terrorism and sabotage on an almost daily basis. Some of these groups have even come close to successfully assassinating members of Pakistan's political leadership. If these groups ever succeed in carrying out a major attack against Pakistan's political establishment, its state institutions and civil society might collapse, and the country could descend into anarchy and warlordism—much like recent experiences in Somalia, Sierra Leone, or Afghanistan—but with the added dimension of unaccounted-for nuclear weapons, material, and technology.

Alliance Structure

Pakistan's formal alliances have all been exclusively at the behest of the United States. This relationship with the United States began with Pakistan's acceptance of an offer of military and economic assistance from the United States in 1953. The arrangement was subsequently formalized in 1954 when the United States persuaded Pakistan to enter into a security treaty with Turkey, a close Cold War ally of the United States. This treaty, the TurkoPakistan Pact, in combination with the Mutual Defense Assistance Agreement, which Pakistan signed in 1954, made it possible for the United States to channel significant military aid to Pakistan. The year 1954 also saw Pakistan joining the U.S.-led Southeast Asia Treaty Organization (SEATO), not because Pakistan perceived any threat from SEATO's primary target—China—but because it was a move that pleased Washington. The following year, 1955, witnessed the creation of the Baghdad Pact, yet another U.S.-inspired entente encompassing Iraq, Iran, Turkey, and Pakistan. When Iraq subsequently withdrew from the pact, this alliance was relaunched as the Central Treaty Organization (CENTO) in 1959.

At about this same time, Pakistan also agreed to the leasing of bases in Pakistan for U.S. intelligence and communications facilities, including U.S. U-2 reconnaissance flights over Soviet territory. However, given that India and not the Soviet Union was Pakistan's true concern, the government insisted on an additional bilateral agreement with the United States, the Agreement of Cooperation, signed in March 1959. Under the provisions of this agreement, Pakistan fully believed that it had formally secured the United States as a direct ally against India.

Although the United States continued to provide extensive military aid to Pakistan through 1965, the 1965 war with India marked a dramatic change in the U.S.-Pakistan relationship when the Johnson administration placed an arms embargo on Pakistan. The embargo remained in place through the 1971 Bangladesh War and was lifted only in 1975. Pakistan's bitterness over what it perceived to be U.S. betrayal during the traumatic 1971 war resulted in Pakistan's withdrawal from SEATO by 1973, and the fall of the shah of Iran brought about the collapse of CENTO in 1979. In recent years, in particular the post–September 11 era, the renewed and greatly increased cooperation between the United States and Pakistan appears to be formally based on the 1954 Mutual Defense Assistance Agreement.

Pakistan has also maintained informal defense arrangements with a few other powers. Following the 1965 war with India and also after the 1971 war in Bangladesh, China provided military hardware to Pakistan so that the country could reconstitute its depleted forces. No publicly recorded formal defense agreements were ever signed, but China emerged as a major arms supplier and strategic ally for Pakistan vis-à-vis India in the post-1965 period. In the Islamic world, Pakistan provided military advisers and instructors to many Middle East states beginning in the 1960s and secretively deployed a security force of roughly two combat divisions to Saudi Arabia in 1979 to help protect the Saudi regime during a period of internal unrest. The large deployment of combat forces reportedly ended in 1987, but it is believed that many Pakistani military advisers continue to serve in the armed forces of Saudi Arabia and the armed forces of the UAE as well.

Finally, Pakistan has entered into a limited nonaggression agreement with archrival India. Under the provisions of this 1991 agreement, each side agreed not to strike at the other's nuclear installations and in exchange to provide the other with an updated listing of all such installations on an annual basis (Shahid 2003). India continues to press Pakistan to enter into a "no-first-use" agreement with respect to nuclear weapons, while Pakistan continues to insist on a comprehensive mutual nonaggression treaty instead.

Size and Structure of the Military

Pakistan's military forces are organized into three service branches: the army, the navy, and the air force. Each service branch is headed by a chief of staff, the highest-ranking officer within that branch.

The service chiefs of staff and other general staff officers together form the Joint Chiefs of Staff Committee (JCSC), an organization tasked with coordinating and integrating the operations of the three service branches and with military strategic planning. The chairman of the JCSC, a staff officer separate from the three service chiefs, is the country's highest-ranking military officer and the principal military adviser to the president of Pakistan.

A new politico-military decision-making institution known as the National Security Council is expected to be established in the near future. It will be chaired by the president of Pakistan and will include the prime minister of Pakistan, the chairman of the Senate, the speaker of the National Assembly, the opposition leader of the National Assembly, the chief ministers of the country's four administrative provinces, the chairman of the JCSC, and the chiefs of staff of the three military service branches as its other members (*News International, Pakistan* 2004).

Pakistan maintains a sizable military force, weighted heavily toward the army and including numerous paramilitary forces. According to the most recent assessment by the International Institute for Strategic Studies (IISS) (2003), Pakistan possessed 620,000 active duty and 513,000 reserve military personnel in its armed forces. Of the active duty forces, 550,000 were in the army, 25,000 in the navy, and 45,000 in the air force. Additionally, large numbers of personnel serve with several paramilitary formations—185,000 in the National Guard, roughly 65,000 in the Interior Ministry's Frontier Corps, nearly 25,000–30,000 Pakistan Rangers (also under the Ministry of Interior), and about 12,000 in the Northern Light Infantry.

The Pakistani army is organized into nine corps headquarters and an area command. Major operational formations include 22 divisions (2 armored, 2 mechanized infantry, 17 infantry, and 1 artillery), 43 separate brigades (8 armored, 6 mechanized infantry, 8 infantry, 14 artillery and missile, and 7 engineer), 3 light antitank regiments, 4 special forces groups, and an air defense command. Major equipment holdings roughly include 2,450 main battle tanks, 1,250 armored personnel carriers, 1,700 artillery pieces and multiple rocket launchers, about 1,200 surface-to-air missiles, 19 attack helicopters, and more than 180 surface-to-surface missiles (including more than 100 nuclear-capable ballistic missiles). See Table 2 for additional details of Pakistan's arsenal of ballistic missiles. The best available information regarding

Table 2   Pakistan's Ballistic Missile Systems

System Name	System Status	Inventory	Range (km)	Fuel Type
Hatf-1/-1A	Operational	~80	80/100	Solid
Hatf-2 (Abdali)	Operational	Few	180	Solid
Hatf-3 (Ghaznavi)	Operational	~65	300	Solid
Hatf-4 (Shaheen I)	Operational	~20	750	Solid
Hatf-5 (Ghauri I)	Operational	~15	1,500	Liquid
Hatf-5A (Ghauri II)	Operational	~5	1,600–2,300	Liquid
Hatf-6 (Shaheen II)	In development	—	2,000–2,500	Solid
Hatf-7 (Tarmuk)	In development	—	550	Solid
Hatf-? (Ghauri III)	In development	—	2,500–3,000	Liquid

the peacetime deployment of the major operational formations of the Pakistani army is as follows:

- *I Corps (Army Reserve North)* at Mangla, with the 6th Armored, 17th Mechanized, and 35th Infantry Divisions
- *II Corps (Army Reserve South)* at Multan, with the 1st Armored, 14th Mechanized, and 2nd Artillery Divisions
- *IV Corps* at Lahore (Narowal-to-Sulemankie sector), with the 10th and 11th Infantry Divisions
- *V Corps* at Karachi, with the 16th and 18th Infantry Divisions
- *X Corps* at Rawalpindi, with the 12th, 19th, 23rd, and 25th Infantry Divisions
- *XI Corps (Army Reserve Center)* at Peshawar, with the 7th and 9th Infantry Divisions
- *XII Corps* at Quetta, with the 40th and 41st Infantry Divisions
- *XXX Corps* at Gujranwala (Jhelum-to-Narowal sector), with the 8th and 15th Infantry Divisions
- *XXXI Corps* at Pannu Aquil, with the 33rd and 37th Infantry Divisions
- *Force Command Northern Areas* at Gilgit, covering Dansum, Khapalu, Siari, and Skardu

The Pakistani navy includes the 1,200-strong marines and the 2,000-strong Maritime Security Agency. It operates from Karachi, Pakistan's only major port city, although two additional bases are being constructed at Gwadar and Ormara. The navy's order of battle includes seven diesel-electric attack submarines, eight frigates, and six missile craft. Naval aviation includes nine antisubmarine helicopters; six antiship missile-armed patrol aircraft are operated by the air force on behalf of the navy.

The Pakistani air force operates more than 400 combat aircraft in nineteen operational and operational conversion unit (OCU) squadrons. Additional squadrons serving such functions as transport, electronic warfare, search and rescue, and training are also part of the air force's order of battle. Furthermore, the air force also operates seven batteries of surface-to-air missiles to help defend its seven primary air bases. The best available information regarding deployment and type of aircraft flown by Pakistani air force combat squadrons is as follows:

- *Masroor Air Base:* No. 2 Squadron (F/FT-7P); No. 7 Squadron (Mirage III EA); No. 8 Squadron (Mirage V PA); and No. 22 OCU Squadron (Mirage III DA/DP, Mirage V PA/DPA)
- *Mianwali Air Base:* Nos. 18 OCU and 19 OCU Squadrons (F/FT-7P)
- *Minhas/Kamra Air Base:* No. 14 Squadron (F/FT-7P) and Nos. 15 and 25 Squadrons (Mirage V EF/DF)
- *Peshawar Air Base:* Nos. 16 and 26 Squadrons (A-5C, FT-6)
- *Rafiqui-Shorkot Air Base:* No. 5 Squadron (Mirage III EP/RP) and No. 20 Squadron (F/FT-7P)
- *Sargodha Air Base:* Nos. 9 and 11 OCU Squadrons (F-16A/B); Mirage and F-7 Squadrons of the Combat Commanders' School (Mirage III EA, F-7P)
- *Sumungli Air Base:* Nos. 17 and 23 Squadrons (F/FT-7PG)

The constitutional basis of the armed forces does allow for their use in a broad range of civil functions including domestic public service and economic development activities. The military services have often been called on to aid in natural disaster relief operations and support the civilian security forces (i.e., the police) during periods of communal or political unrest. Pakistan has also been quite willing to contribute its military forces to security operations in foreign countries, including the deployment of combat forces, advisers, and training instructors in several Middle East states from the mid-1960s onward. One notable deployment was in Saudi Arabia during the 1990–1991 crisis following Iraq's invasion of Kuwait, although Pakistani forces only served in Saudi Arabia in an internal security capacity and did not join in combat operations during the 1991 war against Iraq. Pakistan also routinely contributes military personnel to UN peacekeeping operations. In 2003, Pakistani troops served in UN operations in the Democratic Republic of Congo, East Timor, Georgia, Sierra Leone, and the Western Sahara (IISS 2003).

Budget

Throughout the years since Pakistan's founding, the armed forces have enjoyed relatively high levels of funding despite austere overall budgetary conditions. Successive Pakistani governments as well as the Pakistani public have demonstrated remarkably consistent support for high levels of military spending even though such spending was possible only at the expense of general social welfare. At the height of such spending during the 1950s, 1960s, and early 1970s, the military budget accounted for 50–60 percent of the overall annual national budget; however, the military's share of the overall budget has dropped to levels below 30 percent in more recent years. Pakistan's military budgets for the past three years, 2001 to 2003, were estimated by the IISS

(2003) at U.S.$2.1 billion, $2.5 billion, and $2.8 billion, respectively. IISS (2003) also estimated that Pakistan's actual defense expenditures for 2001 and 2002 were U.S.$2.5 billion and $2.7 billion, respectively, accounting for approximately 4 percent of annual GDP. These estimates are likely to be in variance with similar estimates by other authorities given the general consensus that significant portions of Pakistan's defense-related expenditures are not accounted for within its published annual budget figures. Such off-budget expenditures are said to include some procurement, research and development, intelligence, and nuclear weapons–related activities. As such, the variance in budgetary estimates for Pakistan from one estimating authority to the next could be quite large.

Although Pakistan has generally done well for itself in terms of spending its available resources to generate the best possible military capabilities, Pakistan's best is not as good as it ought to be because of three key considerations. First, although Pakistan has been willing to spend large proportions of its overall national budget on its military, these amounts, in absolute terms, are just not that high given the overall small size of Pakistan's revenue base. Pakistan is not particularly rich in natural or industrial resources, and its ability to efficiently gather revenue in the form of taxes has historically been notoriously poor. Second, given Pakistan's relatively low level of industrial and technological development and manufacturing capacity, it is incapable of producing a broad range of high-quality military hardware domestically and thus must import such systems. Such imports can be quite expensive and must be paid for in hard currency—currency that Pakistan does not possess in great quantities and that must also serve the purposes of servicing Pakistan's foreign debt and the importation of other essential commodities such as food, medicine, and energy. Finally, geopolitics also serves to constrain Pakistan's ability to equip itself with the best in military hardware. From Pakistan's perspective, the United States has proven itself to be an unreliable supplier of weapons, willing to transfer weapons to Pakistan whenever it needed Pakistan as a regional ally in securing its own interests but imposing embargoes at other times without consideration for Pakistan's security needs. Russia has also historically refused to provide Pakistan with armaments given its close strategic relationship with rival India. China has proven to be a reliable supplier for Pakistan, but Chinese weapons are clearly of inferior quality in comparison with U.S. or Russian systems.

Although Pakistan's domestic industries are not capable of producing an extensive range of high-quality weapon systems, domestic capabilities have done extremely well in providing maintenance and munitions for foreign-built systems (Cheema 1997; Sayigh 1997). This is reflected in the establishment of a Ministry of Defense Production in 1991. Limited exports of spare parts, munitions, and low-technology military hardware (basic pilot training aircraft, for example) have been provided to such countries as Bangladesh, Sri Lanka, and Iran, among others. However, in terms of research, development, and production, Pakistan has wisely focused its meager resources on a few key military capabilities, namely nuclear weapons and ballistic missiles. Given Pakistan's historical grievances toward and abiding fear of a much larger and more powerful India, perceived betrayal by allies in the past,

and inability to procure sufficient high-technology conventional forces, since the mid-1970s the development and possession of a nuclear deterrent force has been Pakistan's national obsession.

Sathasivam (2003) and others have recounted in detail the history of the race for nuclear weapons on the subcontinent leading up to the series of nuclear tests by both India and Pakistan in 1998. It is estimated that Pakistan now possesses an arsenal of perhaps fifty nuclear (fission) warheads. Delivery systems include dozens of indigenously produced and imported ballistic missiles (Hatf–3 Ghaznavi/Chinese M-11, Hatf–4 Shaheen I, and Hatf–5/–5A Ghauri I/II) and aircraft (U.S. F-16, French Mirage III/V, and Chinese A-5C). Additional ballistic missiles of greater sophistication and with increased ranges are claimed to be under development (Hatf–6 Shaheen II, Hatf–7 Tarmuk, and Hatf–? Ghauri III). Given Pakistan's precarious economic condition, and the severe constraints on its annual national budget that follow from that condition, Pakistan's only hope of being able to keep up with India with respect to the strategic rivalry between the two states has rested on its development and deployment of (nuclear-armed) ballistic missile systems (see Table 2). Such systems provide Pakistan with a significant strategic military capability at a relatively low cost and therefore are viewed by many in Pakistan as the nation's great equalizer in the otherwise unequal, enduring rivalry with India.

Civil-Military Relations/The Role of the Military in Domestic Politics

In a country deeply divided by ethnic and tribal loyalties and in the absence of other strong national institutions, the

Pakistani military has been viewed by many Pakistanis as perhaps the only truly national institution, capable of eliciting loyalty, credibility, and respect from across the social spectrum. As such, the military has played either an indirect or a direct role in the governing of the country from its early days (*BBC News Online* 1999b; Ali 2003).

The prestige of and public respect for the military was established immediately after national independence, and especially during the First Kashmir War, when the Pakistani public came to view the military as the savior and protector of an independent Pakistan standing valiantly against the imperial ambitions of India, its larger and more powerful neighbor. Thus, during the early years of Pakistan's history, the military largely stayed above national politics and focused its energies on defending the nation's borders and maintaining national unity (by moving decisively against Baloch tribes seeking an independent Baloch homeland, for example). Furthermore, the well-organized and well-funded military bureaucracy was very effective in bolstering the functioning of the country's civilian bureaucracy.

However, following the transformation of Pakistan into a constitutional republic in 1956, the country witnessed increased domestic instability and economic malaise, finally leading the civilian president to abrogate the constitution and share executive power with the army high command in October 1958. This arrangement lasted only a few weeks, after which the chief of the army staff, General Muhammad Ayub Khan, deposed the civilian political leadership and assumed all executive powers. Thus began the era of direct military participation in Pakistan's political life. Ayub Khan's focus on domestic development and stability seemed to sat-

isfy the public, and martial law was lifted in 1962, although the military continue to run the country. This era of stability ended in 1965 with widespread public dissatisfaction over the outcome of the Second Kashmir War with India. Public political unrest continued to escalate, culminating in 1969 when Ayub Khan was replaced as president by the sitting army chief, General Agha Muhammad Yahya Khan, who reimposed martial law. However, the Yahya Khan era did not last long. He in turn was forced to resign in disgrace following the disastrous 1971 Bangladesh War that resulted in the loss of East Pakistan.

Following Yahya Khan's resignation, another brief period of civilian rule lasted until 1977 when widespread rioting broke out after the incumbent prime minister's election victory was challenged by his political opposition. Prime Minister Zulfikar Ali Bhutto was overthrown by General Mohammad Zia ul-Haq, the army chief of staff, and Pakistan returned to martial law. Zia maintained martial law until 1985, when he allowed highly limited elections to take place for a civilian government, although he continued to maintain ultimate executive authority. This arrangement collapsed in 1988, and Zia dissolved the National Assembly and all four provincial assemblies. However, Zia's mysterious death in an air crash that year moved the country toward open elections and a return to democracy.

Pakistan remained under civilian rule until October 1999, when the sitting army chief of staff, General Pervez Musharraf, organized a coup against the government of Prime Minister Nawaz Sharif (see Sidebar 1). Although Musharraf has acquired sweeping executive powers for himself and engineered his continued hold on those powers through 2007, he did allow limited parliamentary elections in 2002, resulting in the naming of a civilian prime minister and cabinet to handle the day-to-day conduct of governmental functions. Furthermore, unlike in past periods of military rule, Musharraf has not imposed martial law upon Pakistan, and he appears to command at least some amount of public support. He has vowed to relinquish his dual role as chief of the army by the end of 2004, and he was instrumental in promoting the proposed National Security Council, a new executive institution that was established in 2004. It is arguable that this new institution is a means of formalizing military oversight of future civilian governments, especially with respect to issues of national security and unity. The establishment of this formal politico-military institution may be an attempt to break Pakistan's pattern of periods of civilian rule followed by periods of direct military rule, a way of thinking that borrows from the experiences of civil-military relations in Turkey over the past two decades.

Terrorism

The problem of terrorism is a very serious concern for Pakistan on two fronts. First, Pakistan is confronted with continuing domestic unrest and instability because of the use of political violence and terrorism by various Pakistani tribal, ethnic, and sectarian groups against each other. As noted previously, the widespread civil unrest in Sindh Province during the 1990s was the result of violent conflict between the Sindhi and muhajir communities, with the Pakistani government caught in the middle. Similar communal uprisings have also occasionally

---

Sidebar 1   The 1999 Military Coup in Pakistan

The coup against Prime Minister Nawaz Sharif in October 1999 was prompted by the cumulative effect of several factors. By mid-1999, the domestic political and economic climate had become so calamitous for Sharif that members of his own party were beginning to conspire against him. Pressured from all sides, Sharif decided to act preemptively and dismiss General Musharraf, the army chief of staff, to try to head off any potential threat to the prime minister's government while reinvigorating his fading political legitimacy.

Sharif's machinations collapsed, however, when senior military officers he'd been counting on for support turned against him and instead threw their lot in with Musharraf—who then successfully turned the tables on Sharif. Ironically, Sharif had appointed Musharraf army chief of staff over other more senior generals because he was convinced that Musharraf—a muhajir within the Punjabi-dominated officer corps—could never amass enough political support to launch a successful coup against him.

Source
BBC News Online. 1999b. *Pakistan's Coup: Why the Army Acted.* October 13. http://news.bbc.co.uk/low/english/world/south_asia/newsid_473000/473297.stm.

occurred in Balochistan and the tribal areas of the northwest. More recently, acts of extreme violence and terrorism between Pakistan's Sunni majority and Shi'a minority have grown to alarming levels, and the government has taken action to proscribe and crackdown on the following four major militant Islamic groups (*BBC News Online* 2003):

- *Sipah-e-Sahaba:* A radical Sunni group particularly active in Punjab Province and the city of Karachi; very supportive of the former Taliban regime in Afghanistan.
- *Lashkar-e-Jhangvi:* A breakaway faction of the Sipah-e-Sahaba and even more extreme; believed to be aligned with the al-Qaeda network.
- *Tanzeem-e-Nifaz-e-Shariat-e-Mohammadi:* Another radical Sunni group operating in the northwest tribal regions and aligned with the Saudi Wahhabi school of thought; fought with the Taliban against U.S.-led forces during the 2001 war in Afghanistan.
- *Tehrik-e-Jafria:* The main Shi'a group in Pakistan; founded at the same time as the Islamic revolution in neighboring Iran and drawing its spiritual guidance from that revolution.

The sectarian violence between Sunni and Shi'a within Pakistan has been exacerbated by the rise of Islamic radicalism in neighboring Afghanistan. Many Afghan radical groups that fought the Soviet occupation operated from Pakistan, and the successful drive to power by the Taliban (an amalgamation of several of these groups) after the Soviet withdrawal was aided by support from like-minded Pakistani Sunnis and agencies of the Pakistani government including the notorious Directorate for Inter-Services Intelligence. Support for Afghanistan's radical Sunnis in turn has served to radicalize Pakistani Sunnis. Even now, following the defeat of the Taliban regime in Afghanistan in 2001, the Pakistani government admits that remnants of the Taliban and of al-Qaeda are hiding out in and operating from Pakistani territory, particularly the tribal areas of northwest Pakistan.

Pakistan's second terrorism-related problem arises from its support for the ongoing armed rebellion in Indian-controlled parts of Kashmir. Pakistan claims it provides only political, diplomatic, and moral support, while India alleges material and even direct military support for rebel groups. Many of the groups active in carrying out attacks in Indian Kashmir are thought to have bases in Pakistan, and at least some of the fighters belonging to these groups are thought to be non-Kashmiris (Pakistanis and others). Although acts of violence and terrorism perpetrated by these groups have largely been confined to Indian Kashmir, the December 13, 2001, attack by one of these groups on the Indian Parliament in New Delhi almost resulted in another India-Pakistan war, this time with both states armed with nuclear weapons. Four major Pakistan-connected groups fighting Indian rule in Kashmir are (*BBC News Online* 2000):

- *Hizbul Mujahidin:* Active since the beginning of the insurgency against India and composed mostly of Kashmiri fighters
- *Lashkar-e-Toyeba:* A radical Sunni group with many non-Kashmiri fighters
- *Harkat-ul-Mujahidin:* Believed to be a true international force, with

many Pakistanis, Afghans, and even some Arabs

- *Jaish-e-Mohammad:* A radical Sunni group with possible ties to the al-Qaeda network

Relationship with the United States

The best way to describe the relationship between Pakistan and the United States is as a marriage of convenience. During the 1950s and the 1960s, the United States was almost single-mindedly focused on securing alliances with as many countries in the greater Middle East region as possible, and Pakistan received its share of U.S. attention. Pakistan entered into a series of U.S.-inspired alliance relationships and received large amounts of financial and material aid from the United States in return (see the Alliance Structure section). However, the imposition of arms embargoes during the 1965 and 1971 wars, and the withdrawal of economic aid in April 1979, engendered considerable bitterness in many Pakistanis toward the United States.

The U.S.-Pakistan relationship witnessed a tremendous revival during the years of the Soviet occupation of Afghanistan (1979–1989), with many billions of dollars in U.S. military and economic aid being transferred to Pakistan. The end of the Soviet occupation and the reemergence of the issue of Pakistan's nuclear weapons program brought an end to the revitalized relations, and the first Bush administration cut off aid to Pakistan again in 1990. The period from 1990 to late 2001 was one of cold estrangement for the two states. For example, although Pakistan agreed to send several thousand troops to Saudi Arabia during the 1990–1991 crisis with Iraq, it refused to join in the actual war, and many Pakistanis, including the chief of staff of the army, publicly professed support for the Iraqi position on the crisis. In 1998, during the period following India's nuclear tests when the U.S. administration was attempting to find a way to keep Pakistan from doing the same, Pakistan was quite brazen and unapologetic in its categorical rejection of U.S. entreaties for restraint (Sathasivam 2003). Clearly U.S. attempts to use sanctions, embargoes, and other such coercive strategies to force a change in Pakistan's nuclear weapons development policy were a colossal failure, serving only to strengthen Pakistan's resolve to avoid dependence on any other country for its national security needs (Hewett 1998).

The U.S.-Pakistani relationship has improved dramatically in the aftermath of the September 11, 2001, attacks on the United States and the subsequent U.S.-led war against the Taliban regime in Afghanistan. The United States desperately needed Pakistan's cooperation in order to effectively conduct the war. U.S. tactical aircraft and cruise missiles had to cross through Pakistani airspace on their way to targets in Afghanistan, and temporary bases were needed in Pakistan from which special operations, search and rescue, and logistical forces could stage into the theater. In the period since the end of the war, the United States has counted on Pakistani cooperation in tracking down terrorist operatives and Islamic fighters who are hiding among Pakistan's 150 million inhabitants, many of whom are very sympathetic to the radical Islamic cause. In return, Pakistan has begun to receive significant amounts of economic (and soon also military) assistance from the United States and, importantly, greater international legitimacy for its military government. Perhaps most significantly from

Pakistan's point of view, the United States has now emerged as a major player in attempting to bring about a resolution to the conflict between Pakistan and India over the Kashmir question.

The Future

Given the incredibly delicate and unstable domestic and regional geopolitical circumstances that confront Pakistan at present, any attempts to describe what the future holds for Pakistan—even in the very near term, let alone the long term—are fraught with intellectual peril. In very broad and general terms, it is perhaps possible to draw the following conclusions. If the level of tension between Pakistan and India remains high, there is a strong probability that Kashmir will spark a new war between the two states, a war that might engulf other states and that might result in the use of nuclear weapons (see Sidebar 2). If some accommodation is reached with India on the Kashmir question, such that Pakistan can turn its undivided attention and resources inward, tremendous improvements are possible for the people of Pakistan in terms of their quality of life. Finally, regardless of external considerations (including Kashmir), if Pakistan is unable to reverse the rising tide of Islamic radicalism and communalism within its society, in particular among its youth, Pakistan faces the very real prospect of becoming the world's next failed state, an outcome that would be disastrous not only for the people of Pakistan but also for the people of the region and perhaps the world at large.

Sidebar 2   The Potential Consequences of an India-Pakistan Nuclear War

What might the consequences be if India and Pakistan ever fight a nuclear war? Both U.S. and Asian researchers have concluded that even a "limited" nuclear exchange between the two rivals—five warheads detonated over major Indian cities and five over major Pakistani cities—would result in a minimum of 3 million people being killed, and an additional 1.5 million would suffer serious injuries. These calculations do not even take into account the additional number of people who would suffer the long-term consequences of radioactive fallout.

Other simulations have determined that a simple tit-for-tat exchange targeting just a single city in each country would result in some 250,000 immediate fatalities. On the other end of the range of possibilities, a "worst-case" Pentagon study assesses that a full-blown exchange would kill 9 million to 12 million people, and would severely injure an additional 2 million to 7 million. Once again, these numbers account for only the immediate casualties.

Sources

Edwards, Rob. 2002. *Three Million Would Die in 'Limited' Nuclear War over Kashmir.* *NewScientist.com news service,* May 24. http://www.newscientist.com/article.ns?id=dn2326.

Sands, David R. 2002. *Scenario of Nuke Strikes Weighed. Washington Times,* May 28. http://www.washtimes.com/world/20020528-18740032.htm.

Shanker, Thom. 2002. *12 Million Could Die at Once in an India-Pakistan Nuclear War.* New York Times, May 27. http://www.nytimes.com/2002/05/27/international/asia/27NUKE.html.

References, Recommended Readings, and Websites

Books

Ahmed, Samina, and David Cortright. 1998. "Pakistani Public Opinion and Nuclear Weapons Policy." In *Pakistan and the Bomb: Public Opinion and Nuclear Options*, S. Ahmed and D. Cortright, eds. Notre Dame, IN: University of Notre Dame Press.

Amin, Shahid M. 2000. *Pakistan's Foreign Policy: A Reappraisal*. Oxford, UK: Oxford University Press.

Arnett, Eric. 1997. "Military Research and Development in Southern Asia: Limited Capabilities Despite Impressive Resources." In *Military Capacity and the Risk of War: China, India, Pakistan and Iran*, E. Arnett, ed. Oxford, UK: Oxford University Press (for the Stockholm International Peace Research Institute).

Asghar Khan, Muhammad. 1983. *Generals in Politics: Pakistan, 1958–1982*. New Delhi: Vikas.

Baxter, Craig. 1991. "The United States and Pakistan: The Zia Era and the Afghan Connection." In *Friendly Tyrants: An American Dilemma*, D. Pipes and A. Garfinkle, eds. New York: St. Martin's Press.

Binder, Leonard. 1986. "Islam, Ethnicity, and the State in Pakistan: An Overview." In *The State, Religion, and Ethnic Politics: Afghanistan, Iran, and Pakistan*, A. Banuazizi and M. Weiner, eds. Syracuse, NY: Syracuse University Press.

Burke, S. M., and Lawrence Ziring. 1990. *Pakistan's Foreign Policy: An Historical Analysis*. Rev. 2d ed. Karachi: Oxford University Press.

Buzan, Barry, and Gowher Rizvi. 1986. *South Asian Insecurity and the Great Powers*. New York: St. Martin's Press.

Cheema, Pervaiz Iqbal. 1990. *Pakistan's Defence Policy, 1947–58*. Basingstoke, UK: Macmillan.

———. 1997. "Arms Procurement in Pakistan: Balancing the Needs for Quality, Self-Reliance and Diversity of Supply." In *Military Capacity and the Risk of War: China, India, Pakistan and Iran*, E. Arnett, ed. Oxford, UK: Oxford University Press (for the Stockholm International Peace Research Institute).

Cohen, Stephen P. 1984. *The Pakistan Army*. Berkeley: University of California Press.

———. 1999. "The United States, India, and Pakistan: Retrospect and Prospect." In *India and Pakistan: The First Fifty Years*, S. S. Harrison, P. H. Kreisberg, and D. Kux, eds. Cambridge, UK: Cambridge University Press (for the Woodrow Wilson International Center for Scholars).

Diehl, Paul F., and Gary Goertz. 2000. *War and Peace in International Rivalry*. Ann Arbor: University of Michigan Press.

Ganguly, Sumit. 1990. *The Origins of War in South Asia: Indo–Pakistan Conflicts since 1947*. Boulder, CO: Westview.

Harrison, Selig S., and Geoffrey Kemp. 1993. *India and America after the Cold War*. Washington, DC: Carnegie Endowment for International Peace Press.

Husain, Ross Masood. 1997. "Threat Perception and Military Planning in Pakistan: The Impact of Technology, Doctrine and Arms Control." In *Military Capacity and the Risk of War: China, India, Pakistan and Iran*, E. Arnett, ed. Oxford, UK: Oxford University Press (for the Stockholm International Peace Research Institute).

International Institute for Strategic Studies (IISS). 2003. *The Military Balance 2003/2004* (annual yearbook). Oxford, UK: Oxford University Press (for the International Institute for Strategic Studies).

Ispahani, Mahnaz. 1990. *Pakistan: The Dimensions of Insecurity*. London: Brassey's (for the International Institute for Strategic Studies).

Kennedy, Charles H. 1993. "Managing Ethnic Conflict: The Case of Pakistan." In *The Territorial Management of Ethnic Conflict*, Regions and Regionalism Series, No. 2. J. Coakley, ed. Portland, OR: Frank Cass.

Kux, Dennis. 2001. *The United States and Pakistan 1947–2000: Disenchanted Allies*. Baltimore, MD: Johns Hopkins University Press (for the Woodrow Wilson International Center for Scholars).

LaPorte, Robert, Jr. 1999. "Pakistan: A Nation Still in the Making." In *India and Pakistan: The First Fifty Years*, S. S. Harrison, P. H. Kreisberg, and

D. Kux, eds. Cambridge, UK: Cambridge University Press (for the Woodrow Wilson International Center for Scholars).

McMahon, Robert J. 1994. *The Cold War on the Periphery: The United States, India, and Pakistan.* New York: Columbia University Press.

Rizvi, Hasan-Askari. 1993. *Pakistan and the Geostrategic Environment: A Study of Foreign Policy.* New York: St. Martin's Press.

Rose, Leo E., and Kamal Matinuddin. 1989. *Beyond Afghanistan: The Emerging U.S.–Pakistan Relations.* Berkeley, CA: Institute of East Asia Studies Press.

Sathasivam, Kanishkan. 2003. "'No Other Choice': Pakistan's Decision to Test the Bomb." In *Integrating Cognitive and Rational Theories of Foreign Policy Decision Making,* A. Mintz, ed. New York: Palgrave Macmillan.

Sathasivam, Kanishkan, and Sahar Shafqat. 2003. "In India's Shadow: The Evolution of Pakistan's Security Policy." In *Conflict in Asia: Korea, China–Taiwan, and India–Pakistan.* U. Heo and S. A. Horowitz, eds. Westport, CT: Praeger.

Sayigh, Yezid. 1997. "Arms Production in Iran and Pakistan: The Limits of Self-Reliance." In *Military Capacity and the Risk of War: China, India, Pakistan and Iran,* E. Arnett, ed. Oxford, UK: Oxford University Press (for the Stockholm International Peace Research Institute).

Sisson, Richard, and Leo E. Rose. 1990. *War and Secession: Pakistan, India, and the Creation of Bangladesh.* Berkeley: University of California Press.

Tahir-Kheli, Shirin R. 1982. *The United States and Pakistan: The Evolution of an Influence Relationship.* New York: Praeger.

———. 1997. *India, Pakistan, and the United States: Breaking with the Past.* New York: Council on Foreign Relations Press.

Thornton, Thomas P. 1999. "Pakistan: Fifty Years of Insecurity." In *India and Pakistan: The First Fifty Years,* S. S. Harrison, P. H. Kreisberg, and D. Kux, eds. Cambridge, UK: Cambridge University Press (for the Woodrow Wilson International Center for Scholars).

Vertzberger, Yaacov. 1983. *The Enduring Entente: Sino-Pakistan Relations, 1960–80.* New York: Praeger.

Wirsing, Robert G. 1991. *Pakistan's Security under Zia, 1977–1988: The Policy Imperatives of a Peripheral Asian State.* New York: St. Martin's Press.

Wriggins, W. Howard. 1977. "The Balancing Process in Pakistan's Foreign Policy." In *Pakistan: The Long View.* L. Ziring, R. Braibanti, and W. H. Wriggins, eds. Durham, NC: Duke University Press.

Articles/Newspapers

Ahrari, Ehsan. 2003. "As India and Iran Snuggle, Pakistan Feels the Chill." *Asia Times Online,* February 11. http://www.atimes.com/atimes/South_Asia/EB11Df01.html.

Ali, Mahmud. 2003. "The Rise of Pakistan's Army." *BBC News Online,* December 24. http://news.bbc.co.uk/1/hi/world/south_asia/3227709.stm.

BBC News Online. 1999a. "Pakistan's Army and Its History of Politics." October 12. http://news.bbc.co.uk/hi/english/world/south_asia/newsid_472000/472953.stm.

———. 1999b. "Pakistan's Coup: Why the Army Acted." October 13. http://news.bbc.co.uk/low/english/world/south_asia/newsid_473000/473297.stm.

———. 2000. "Who are the Kashmir Militants?" August 10. http://news.bbc.co.uk/1/hi/world/south_asia/1719612.stm.

———. 2003. "Pakistan's Militant Islamic Groups." October 7. http://news.bbc.co.uk/1/hi/world/south_asia/3170970.stm.

Blank, Stephen. 2003. "India's Grand Strategic Vision Gets Grander." *Asia Times Online,* December 25. http://www.atimes.com/atimes/South_Asia/EL25Df09.html.

Canfield, Robert L. 1992. "Restructuring in Greater Central Asia: Changing Political Configurations." *Asian Survey* 32 (October):875–887.

Edwards, Rob. 2002. "Three Million Would Die in 'Limited' Nuclear War over Kashmir." *NewScientist.com news service.* May 24, 2002. http://www.newscientist.com/article.ns?id=dn2326.

Gupta, Shishir. 2003. "Foothold in Central Asia: India Gets Own Military Base."

Indian Express (Internet Edition).
November 13. http://www.indianexpress.
com/full_story.php?content_id=35229.

Hewett, Jennifer. 1998. "Analysis: Search
for a Carrot to Replace Stick That Does
Not Work." *Sydney Morning Herald*
(Internet Edition). June 2. http://www.
smh.com.au/news/9806/02/world/
world3.html.

Jillani, Anees. 1991. "Pakistan and
CENTO: An Historical Analysis."
*Journal of South Asian and Middle
Eastern Studies* 15 (Fall):40–53.

Nasr, Seyyed Vali Reza. 1992.
"Democracy and the Crisis of
Governability in Pakistan." *Asian
Survey* 32 (June):521–37.

News International, Pakistan (Internet
Edition). 2004. "Federal Cabinet
Approves Draft National Security Bill,
2004." January 28. http://www.jang.
com.pk/thenews/jan2004-daily/
28-01-2004/main/update.shtml.

Peimani, Hooman. 2003a. "India and Iran:
Renewed Energy." *Asia Times Online.*
May 22. http://www.atimes.com/
atimes/South_Asia/EE22Df01.html.

———. 2003b. "Iran Takes a Step Closer
to India." *Asia Times Online.* January
18.http://www.atimes.com/atimes/
Middle_East/EA18Ak01.html.

Rizvi, Hasan-Askari. 1989. "The Legacy of
Military Rule in Pakistan." *Survival* 31
(May–June):255–68.

Sands, David R. 2002. "Scenario of Nuke
Strikes Weighed." *Washington Times,*
May 28. http://www.washtimes.com/
world/20020528-18740032.htm.

Shahid, Zia Iqbal. 2003. "India, Pakistan
Set to Exchange Lists of Nuclear
Installations." *News International,
Pakistan* (Internet Edition). December
31. http://www.jang.com.pk/thenews/
dec2003-daily/31-12-2003/main/
update.shtml.

Shanker, Thom. 2002. "12 Million Could
Die at Once in an India-Pakistan
Nuclear War." *New York Times.* May
27. http://www.nytimes.com/2002/05/
27/international/asia/27NUKE.html.

Syed, Anwar H. 1988. "Political Parties
and the Nationality Question in
Pakistan." *Journal of South Asian and
Middle Eastern Studies* 12 (Fall):42–75.

Thornton, Thomas P. 1989.
"U.S.–Pakistan Relations." *Foreign
Affairs* 68 (Summer):142–59.

Websites

AsiaSource. *AsiaPROFILES: Pakistan.*
From the Internet website of
AsiaSource—A Resource of the Asia
Society. http://www.asiasource.org/
profiles/.

BBC News. *Country Profile: Pakistan.*
From the Internet website of the British
Broadcasting Corporation. http://news.
bbc.co.uk.

Blood, Peter, ed. 1994. *Pakistan: A
Country Study.* From the Internet
website of the Library of Congress,
Federal Research Division. http://
lcweb2.loc.gov/frd/cs/pktoc.html.

Central Intelligence Agency (CIA). 2003.
World Factbook: Pakistan. From the
Internet website of the Central
Intelligence Agency. http://www.odci.
gov/cia/publications/factbook/.

Correlates of War (COW) 2. *COW Formal
Interstate Alliance Data Set,
1816–2000 (v3.03).* From the Internet
website of the Correlates of War 2
Project. http://cow2.la.psu.edu.

———. *COW Inter-State War Data,
1816–1997 (v3.0).* From the Internet
website of the Correlates of War 2
Project. http://cow2.la.psu.edu.

———. *COW Intra-State War Data,
1816–1997 (v3.0).* From the Internet
website of the Correlates of War 2
Project. http://cow2.la.psu.edu.

Defence Journal [Pakistan]: http://www.
defencejournal.com.

Federation of American Scientists (FAS):
http://www.fas.org.

GlobalSecurity–Pakistan: http://www.
globalsecurity.org/military/world/
pakistan/index.htm.

Government of Pakistan: http://www.pak.
gov.pk/public/government.html.

Institute of Strategic Studies, Islamabad
(ISSI): http://www.issi.org.pk.

IUCN-Pakistan. *Climate of Pakistan.*
From the Internet website of the World
Conservation Union, Education Unit,
IUCN Pakistan: http://edu.iucnp.org/
edu/climateofpakistan.htm.

Ministry of Foreign Affairs of Pakistan:
http://pakistan.gov.pk/foreignaffairs-
ministry/index.jsp.

PakistaniDefence: http://www.
pakistanidefence.com.

Permanent Mission of Pakistan to the
United Nations: http://www.un.int/
pakistan.

Paraguay

Daniel S. Morey

Geography and History

Paraguay is landlocked and located between two of the most powerful South American states, Argentina and Brazil. Having no sea access has limited Paraguay's ability to trade internationally and has been a source of dispute with its powerful neighbors. Paraguay is rather small, covering 157,047 sq. miles (about the size of California). The land is divided by the Rio Paraguay into the Paranena (eastern region) and the Chaco (western region). The Chaco region comprises over 60 percent of the total area of Paraguay and is a marshy plain. Although the Chaco is an uninviting location, it is home to most of Paraguay's natural resources, including oil. The Paranena is a mixture of grassy plains, woodland, and tropical forests.

The vast majority of Paraguay's 6 million plus residents live in the Paranena, which is also where most of the country's major cities are located. Paraguay is a very homogeneous society with 95 percent of the people being of mixed Spanish and Guarani Indian descent. Further, roughly 90 percent of the population is Catholic (Bureau of Western Hemisphere Affairs 2003). Despite its lack of economic development, Paraguay has enjoyed success in education; it is estimated that as of 2003, Paraguay had a 94 percent literacy rate (compared to 86 percent for Brazil) CIA *World Factbook* 2004).

In the 1530s the area that is now Paraguay was part of a large province, including Uruguay, eastern Bolivia, and most of Argentina, under Spanish control. Before this time little is known of Paraguay or its indigenous people, the Guarani, because of the extreme difficulty in reaching the area. After different bureaucratic reorganizations, the area of Paraguay came under the control of the Viceroyalty of the Plate, which was headquartered in modern-day Argentina (Leuchars 2002, 1–2). The Paraguayans resented being under Argentine control, and during this time a desire for independence arose among the people, along with a deep animosity for Argentina. This animosity helps explain the conflictual relationship between the two states immediately following independence (Leuchars 2002, 2).

After the invasion of Spain by Napoleon in 1808, Spain lost the ability to control its empire. Many states in South America declared independence including Argentina and Paraguay. However, Argentina desired to continue its rule over Paraguay and dispatched an army to conquer the country. Despite its military advantage, Argentina was defeated by the Paraguayans (English 1984, 343). Along with freeing Paraguay from Argentine interference, the defeat of Argentina ended Spanish rule in Paraguay.

Paraguay achieved independence from Spain on May 14, 1811, initially led by Dr. Jose Gaspar Rodriquea de Francia and General Fulgencio Yegros. Over the next five years Francia gained political power, culminating in his being named dictator for life in 1816. This marked the beginning of Paraguay's long experience with dictatorial rule. Francia desired to create a society without class distinctions and severely limited contact with neighboring states, which retarded Paraguay's economic development. For the next 176 years Paraguay was primarily controlled by one dictatorial leader after another, with short periods of democracy, until 1989 when General Alfredo Stroessner was removed from office in a coup led by General Andres Rodriguez. After the coup, Rodriguez was elected to the presidency and began efforts to reform Paraguay. The reform movement culminated in a new constitution in 1992 that limited the powers of the president, and in 1993 Carlos Wasmosy was elected as the first civilian head of government in more than forty years. While shaky, the constitutional republic that began with the 1992 constitution has survived.

Paraguay's political struggles have been one of the country's major hindrances to economic growth. The isolation of the Francia years allowed for very little international trade and slowed the development of export industries. Continued political instability and widespread corruption combine to limit economic growth and foreign investment in Paraguay. Paraguay does not have a firm economic base, and the informal sector—the re-export of consumer goods (with a large underground element)—is the largest industry. Paraguay is predominantly an agricultural-based economy with a large number of subsistence farmers and suffers from high unemployment. In 2002 the gross domestic product (GDP) was $5.6 billion, a 2.2 percent decrease from the previous year (Bureau of Western Hemisphere Affairs 2003).

Table 1   Paraguay: Key Statistics

Type of government	Constitutional republic
Population (millions)	6.04 (2003)
Religion	Catholic 90%, Mennonite, and other Protestant
Main industries	Informal sector, sugar, cement, textiles
Main security threats	Instability in rural region where Argentina, Brazil, and Paraguay converge (smuggling, drugs, Islamic militants)
Defense spending (% GDP)	1.1% (2002)
Size of military (thousands)	18.6 (2002)
Number of civil wars since 1945	1
Number of interstate wars since 1945	0

Sources

CIA *World Factbook*. 2004. http://www.cia.gov/cia/publications/factbook/ (accessed February 18, 2004).
International Institute for Strategic Studies (IISS). 2002. *The Military Balance 20020–2003*. Oxford, UK: Oxford University Press.
Sarkees, Meredith Reid. 2000. "The Correlates of War Data on War: An Update to 1997." *Conflict Management and Peace Science* 18, no. 1:123–144.

Regional Geopolitics

Although Paraguay has been plagued by external and internal threats for most of its existence, it has lately enjoyed relative peace. Paraguay faces no imminent external threat. Regional relations have been strained in recent years over economic relations, specifically the status of Paraguay in the Southern Cone Common Market (MERCOSUR), but none of these disagreements have taken on a militarized nature. Further, Paraguay is isolated from the area's only regional fighting, located in Colombia. Thus, the probability of direct conflict with a neighboring state or conflict spilling over into Paraguay is very low at this time.

Internally Paraguay still faces many challenges associated with democratic consolidation and the maintenance of law and order in all of its territory. Although Paraguay has not had a full-scale civil war since 1947, its governance has been plagued by a large number of coups or attempted coups. The most recent major challenge came in 1996 when President Wasmosy ordered General Lino Oviedo to step down as commander of the Paraguayan army over Oviedo's interference in internal politics. Oviedo retaliated by threatening to kill Wasmosy and moved Paraguay to the brink of civil war. Oviedo did eventually step down and was later convicted of attempting a coup. His conviction was later pardoned by President Cubas (elected in 1998), which started another crisis that ended with Cubas and Oviedo fleeing the country under suspicion of having assassinated the vice president. However, according to the U.S. State Department, in recent years the military has been withdrawing from the political realm, resulting in increased stability. Although civilian-military relations have improved, there have been growing efforts to destabilize the government in other areas. In January 2004, President Nicanor Duarte Frutos delayed his return to Paraguay from vacation due to threats against him. Although it is not clear where these threats originated, reports indicate they may have stemmed from business leaders and government officials upset with Frutos's crusade against corruption. Both of these examples show Paraguay is making progress but still does not have a consolidated and secure domestic political structure. A successful assassination attempt or continued economic difficulties could push Paraguay back into domestic instability.

Finally, Paraguay faces a potentially severe problem in the Tri-Border Region. The Tri-Border Region is a rough and secluded area where Paraguay, Brazil, and Argentina all join (near the Paraguayan town of Ciudad del Este). The Tri-Border Region is known as a lawless area where drug trafficking and smuggling flourish (Mendel 2000). Recently the area has gained notoriety because of its high number of Muslim immigrants and the activities of many terror groups including Hezbollah (see Terrorism section). If this region were to become a major recruiting and training ground for organized terror groups, it would pose a major challenge to Paraguay's security forces and in the end could destabilize not only Paraguay but large portions of Brazil and Argentina.

Conflict Past and Present
Conflict History
Paraguay has been involved in two major foreign wars since gaining independence in 1811. The first—the War of the Triple Alliance—occurred in 1864, and the second—the Chaco War—occurred in

1932. Along with these two major conflicts, Paraguay has been involved in a large number of disputes with its neighbors. Relations between Argentina and Paraguay have been particularly conflictual as Paraguay has felt its sovereignty threatened by Argentina.

Starting in the 1840s Paraguay began having frequent militarized international disputes with both Argentina and Brazil, who share land borders with Paraguay and are more powerful states. Over the next twenty years the conflicts grew more intense, particularly between Paraguay and Argentina, culminating in the War of the Triple Alliance (1864–1870).

The War of the Triple Alliance began with Brazilian intervention in Uruguayan domestic politics that prompted Paraguay to declare war on Brazil. President Francis Solan Lopez launched the war to defend the local balance of power and as an opportunity for self-aggrandizement (OnWar.com). Shortly after war was declared, Brazil and Argentina formed an alliance with the new Uruguayan government (installed by Brazil), and all three attacked Paraguay. Despite having the largest army in the region (estimated at 50,000 members), Paraguay was soon vastly outnumbered and suffered a series of defeats (Loveman 1999, 49). The war ended in 1870 when President Lopez was killed and the three victors established an interim government in Paraguay. The fighting and a cholera epidemic combined to devastate Paraguay. In total, Paraguay lost around 300,000 of its 500,000 prewar population, and only an estimated 28,000 males survived (English 1984, 343). Paraguay remained under occupation until 1876 and was militarily weak long into the future.

Although the War of the Triple Alliance devastated Paraguay, it did not end the conflict with its neighbors, particularly its rival Argentina. Starting in 1911, Argentina and Paraguay were once again involved in militarized disputes. In the late 1920s, Paraguay again began to have disputes with Brazil. Although these disputes did not reach the level of open war, they did involve threats of force and in many cases military mobilizations and clashes (Sarkees 2000). The relations between Paraguay and Brazil became more calm in the early 1930s, mainly due to Paraguay's increasing trouble with its northeastern neighbor, Bolivia. Having started in 1886, conflict between Paraguay and Bolivia over control of the Chaco region (western Paraguay) intensified during the 1920s and culminated in war between the two states.

The Chaco War (1932–1935) marked Paraguay's second major war. Bolivia, motivated by a belief that the Chaco region contained oil reserves, invaded Paraguay in 1932, capturing fortifications along the border. The start of the war looked bleak for the Paraguayan army as they were outnumbered by a better-trained and -equipped Bolivian force. Despite these disadvantages the Paraguayans smashed the Bolivian army in the Chaco, mainly due to better morale (defending the homeland) and superior knowledge of the terrain. Because of poor leadership, however, Paraguay was not able to achieve an early victory, and after an ill-advised cease-fire, which allowed the Bolivians to reorganize, the war continued until 1935 when a multinational effort was made to negotiate an end to hostilities. While the Chaco War was fought between two Third World countries, it drew a substantial amount of international attention and had an important, if indirect, impact on American politics (see Sidebar 1). Although Bolivia did gain some territory, the majority of the disputed region was retained by Paraguay, who emerged as the nominal victor despite high losses (OnWar.com).

Sidebar 1   International Impact

In an effort to stop the fighting between Paraguay and Bolivia during the Chaco War, the U.S. Congress granted the president the right to stop all weapons sales to either country. President Roosevelt used the new authority and authorized an arms embargo on both nations. Shortly after the embargo went into effect, the U.S. government charged the Curtiss-Wright Corporation with violating the law by shipping machine guns to Bolivia. The Curtiss-Wright Corporation challenged the constitutionality of the law that gave the president the power to stop arms shipments and the case reached the U.S. Supreme Court. The Court's ruling found in favor of the government, determining that the president had very broad powers granted to him in the area of foreign affairs. This ruling expanded the power of the presidency greatly, and has given the president almost uncontested control over American foreign policy.

Source
Alder, David Gray. 1988. "The Constitution and Presidential Warmaking: The Enduring Debate." *Political Science Quarterly* 103, no. 1:1–36.

Bolivia and Paraguay continued to have disputes through the 1930s, including military mobilizations and small clashes the year after the Chaco War ended (Sarkees 2000). However, these declined over time, and Paraguay, partially distracted by domestic divisions, enjoyed peaceful relations with its neighbors for the next twenty years. Paraguay declared war on the Axis powers during World War II, but not until 1945. The delay was mainly due to the pro-Axis feelings of then-president General Higinio Morinigo.

In 1947, parties on the political left joined forces to attempt to remove General Morinigo from power. A fierce battle erupted as a large portion of the officer corps joined the rebels, but the bulk of the army remained loyal to Morinigo. During the conflict, Lt. Col. Alfredo Stroessner distinguished himself by destroying a strategic rebel-held neighborhood and defeating naval attacks against the capital (OnWar.com). These victories laid the groundwork for Stroessner to later gain power. The civil war had the effect of reducing Paraguay to single-party rule and decreased the number of political and military elite (OnWar.com), concentrating power in a small group.

In 1959, the rivalry with Argentina began to heat up with military clashes along the border. However, at the conclusion of an armed engagement in 1962, relations between Paraguay and Argentina calmed significantly. In fact, since the early 1960s, Paraguay has not been involved in any militarized dispute with any of its neighbors. Although Paraguay has not enjoyed calm relations either internally or externally, it has managed to avoid any large-scale conflict for over forty years.

Current and Potential Military Confrontation

In the near future, conflict for Paraguay does not seem likely. The rivalry with Argentina has remained dormant since their last clash in 1962, and Paraguay has not been involved in a militarized dispute with its other neighbors since before 1962. Further, Paraguay and its neighbors have increased economic relations through MERCOSUR, an agreement established with the Treaty of Asunción (1991). Although the MERCOSUR agreement has caused diplomatic disputes between its members, which at one time escalated to the point that Paraguay considered withdrawing, it seems that the parties have resolved their disputes with a supplemental agreement signed in 2002. Further, current Paraguayan President Nicanor Duarte Frutos (elected in 2003) has pushed for closer relations with neighboring states, particularly Brazil and Argentina ("Winning Respect" 2004), Paraguay's two largest trading partners.

Internally, the prospects for conflict are also low, but several important issues could change this outlook. First, civil-military relations seem to have stabilized following the failed effort of General Oviedo to remove former President Wasmosy in 1996. This incident seems to have reinforced civilian control of the military as outlined in the 1992 constitution. There was an effort in 2000 to overthrow the government when a small group of soldiers using armored personnel carriers (APCs) tried to seize control of government buildings in the capital of Asunción. However, this effort was quickly subdued, lasting only about six hours, as the people and the rest of the military supported the government (Thomas 2004). Taken together, these incidents demonstrate that Paraguay is still not a consolidated democracy; however, the reaction of the people and the majority of the military clearly show a preference for civilian rule.

The preference for civilian rule could decline if Paraguay continues its dismal economic record. Not only has Paraguay not managed any economic growth, it has actually taken a step backward with GDP falling by almost 3 percent in 2002 (CIA *World Factbook* 2004). If the economy continues to struggle, it could reduce the legitimacy of the current democratic regime and increase pressure for a change. With Paraguay's long history of authoritarian regimes and the clear desire of some individuals to be installed as ruler, this is a serious source of potential conflict.

The largest potential source of future conflict for Paraguay comes from terrorism and terror groups located inside of Paraguay. Although no terror group is currently working to overthrow or destabilize the country, there are many groups, including Hezbollah and Hamas, that have bases and operatives inside Paraguay (see Terrorism section). Terror camps and operatives inside Paraguay have received increased attention from the United States after September 11, 2001, and the war in Afghanistan, with the United States encouraging action against these groups. If Paraguay moves against these terror elements it could lead to a long and widespread conflict. It is unclear if the Paraguayan military is up to the task of combating these forces, even in conjunction with Argentina and Brazil, who share jurisdiction over the area where the terror groups have concentrated. The terrain and the nature of the enemy make a long guerilla-style war likely, and such a conflict could be a long-term destabilizing force inside of Paraguay.

Alliance Structure

Since gaining its independence, Paraguay has not been involved in many alliances. Most of Paraguay's alliance ties have come from large multinational agreements with the United States as the central actor, a pattern familiar in most Latin American states.

Paraguay's only bilateral treaty was with Argentina between 1856 and 1962. Although both sides pledged neutrality with respect to third-party wars, the alliance could not be sustained due to the rivalry between the two states. This treaty marked Paraguay's only alliance until the 1930s, mainly due to Paraguay's frequent disagreements with its neighbors (Gibler and Sarkees 2004).

Starting in 1936, the United States began organizing an alliance structure for the Western Hemisphere. This started with an entente between the United States and most countries in Latin America, including Paraguay. The 1936 entente was soon replaced by a short-lived defensive alliance in 1945 (Gibler and Sarkees 2004). After the first all-Americas defensive alliance, the United States and most of the Latin American states formed a second defensive alliance known as the Rio Pact in August 1947. This alliance was formed early in the Cold War and was designed to meet the U.S. need to keep the Soviet Union out of the Western Hemisphere. This treaty has served as the U.S. basis for hemispheric security and is Paraguay's only current alliance commitment.

The Rio Pact is a defensive alliance targeting any aggression. The body must vote with a two-thirds majority to bring the treaty into effect, with each state free to make its own choice regarding active involvement. An important component of the alliance is that it calls for nonintervention against other allied powers, which in theory should eliminate intraregional conflict. Finally, the Rio Pact helped lead to the creation of the Organization of American States (OAS), which governs relations in Latin America.

Size and Structure of the Military

Size and Structure

The armed forces of Paraguay are some of the smallest in South America and are dwarfed by the forces of its three neighbors. Active forces in Paraguay total 18,600 troops (excluding the paramilitary national police) compared to 69,900 for Argentina, 287,600 for Brazil, and 31,500 for Bolivia (International Institute for Strategic Studies [IISS] 2002). Conscripts, who serve between twelve months and two years, depending on branch of service, form a majority of active forces, 11,000 in total (IISS 2002, 186). Having such a large number of conscripts lowers the professionalism and effectiveness of the armed forces. Further, since the army's primary job under the Stroessner regime was to maintain internal control, the army's ability to conduct regular combat operations is questionable.

Supporting the active military force is a 14,800-member national police force, of which 4,000 are conscripts (IISS 2002, 187). This force serves as a reserve for the army and performs national policing duties. Along with the military, the national police were highly politicized under the Stroessner regime and played active roles in various coup attempts. Supplementing the active military and national police are 164,500 reserve troops (IISS 2002, 186). After finishing their term of service in the active forces, soldiers are required to serve an additional nine years in the reserves, ten years as part of the national guard, and then serve in the territorial guard until they reach the age of forty-five (English 1984, 345).

Although this is a substantial number of troops, they do not exist as an organized body and are seen as a paper army (especially the territorial guards).

The army is the largest branch of the Paraguayan military with 14,900 soldiers (10,400 conscripts). The army is divided over six military regions with most troops stationed in the first region surrounding the capital of Asunción. Five of the military regions are on the eastern side of the Paraguay River with the entire western half of the country falling under one command. The presidential guard, specifically charged with protecting the president, is composed of an infantry, military police, and artillery battalion (IISS 2002, 186). Along with little training, the army is not well equipped. There is no standard rifle or side arm for soldiers, and units often have soldiers carrying a mixture of weapons from M-1s to M-16s, along with older weapons in some

units. Table 2 provides a partial list of the major military equipment Paraguay possesses. Much of its equipment is World War II–era surplus that has been given to Paraguay by various countries (mainly Brazil and Argentina). Further, the equipment the army does have is often a mixture from many different countries, making an odd collection of nonintegrated weapon systems.

The navy has 2,000 active duty personnel; of these 900 are marines and 100 are in naval aviation. Since Paraguay is a landlocked country, most of the navy's responsibility is patrolling inland rivers. This being the case, the navy does not possess any capital ships and employs ten river patrol boats of various classes along with an assortment of smaller crafts (IISS 2002, 186). Along with the army, the navy is being reduced in size; this includes the decommissioning of one of the navy's largest patrol boats, which has been

Table 2 Major Military Equipment (Partial List)

Armor	12 M-4A3 Sherman medium tanks
	8 M-8 armored cars
	30 EE-9 Cascavel armored cars
	10 EE-11 Urutu APCs
Artillery	6 Vickers 6-inch coast guns
	15 M-101 105 mm
	20 Model 1927/1934 75mm
Air force	8 F-5E Fighters
	4 F-5F Fighters
	3 HB-350 Helicopters
	4 Bell 47G Helicopters

Sources

Hanratty, Dennis M., and Sandra W. Meditz, eds. 1990. *Paraguay: A Country Study*. 5th ed. Washington, DC: U.S. Government Printing Office.

International Institute for Strategic Studies (IISS). 2002. *The Military Balance 2002–2003*. Oxford: Oxford University Press.

Stockholm International Peace Research Institute (SIPRI). 2002. *SIPRI Yearbook 2002: Armaments, Disarmament and International Security*. Oxford, UK: Oxford University Press.

Stockholm International Peace Research Institute (SIPRI). 2003. *SIPRI Yearbook 2003: Armaments, Disarmament and International Security*. Oxford, UK: Oxford University Press.

Stockholm International Peace Research Institute (SIPRI). 2004. *SIPRI Yearbook 2004: Armaments, Disarmament and International Security*. Oxford, UK: Oxford University Press.

turned into a floating museum. The marines are divided into four battalions and include 200 conscripts.

The Paraguayan air force is the smallest of the three branches with only 1,700 members, 600 of which are conscripts. The air force has twenty-eight total combat aircraft, most of which are used as training craft instead of for active patrols. The air force also operates about fourteen helicopters, none of which are armed, and various other support and training aircraft. To facilitate troop transportation, the air force has one squadron of transports that includes five C-47s and three DC-6Bs along with other transport craft (IISS 2002, 187). Its small size and limited number of combat aircraft restricts the air force's capability as a combat unit (see Table 2). However, the air force can play a significant role in reconnaissance, especially over the sparsely populated Chaco region and in troop deployments.

The Paraguayan constitution stipulates that the commander-in-chief of the military is the president and that this duty cannot be deferred to another individual. Along with overall command of the military, the president is also in command of the Presidential Guard Regiment, which is outside the normal military command structure and answers only to the president. Under the president is the armed forces general staff, headed by a general officer, which controls all three branches of the military. Each of the three branches maintains separate command staffs. Further, due to its size, the army is divided into three corps: support, logistics, and military instruction. After the overthrow of the Stroessner regime, the army corps were reorganized, with the first corps becoming the most powerful with three cavalry divisions and given responsibility for

strategic frontiers with Brazil and Argentina. The second corps was placed in command of two infantry divisions and the third corps three infantry divisions. Further, a detached divisional zone was created around the capital, manned by the first infantry division under the control of the commander-in-chief (Martini and Lezcano 1997, 68).

The military of Paraguay has not been involved in any external fighting since the end of the Chaco War with Bolivia (1936). However, there were minor border skirmishes for a number of years after the war. By and large, the Paraguayan military's main function for the past fifty years has been internal control, specifically under Stroessner who employed the military as a control tool. With the end of the Stroessner regime the role of the military in internal policing has been reduced. Also during the Stroessner regime, and continuing today, the military has a large role in developmental projects. Specifically the engineering battalions have been responsible for building roads, schools, churches, and bridges, as well as carrying out antimosquito efforts. The signal corps provides radio and telephone service to rural areas, and the air force and navy transport goods to isolated communities. The medical corps also plays a leading role in providing medical services for secluded regions (Keegan 1979).

Paraguay currently has soldiers serving in two UN missions. There are seventeen Paraguayan members on the UN observer mission in the Democratic Republic of Congo and two observers attached to the UN mission in Ethiopia and Eritrea (Stockholm International Peace Research Institute [SIPRI] 2002, 132; IISS 2002, 187). Although these are not large contingents, they do provide valuable external contacts for Paraguayan military members, which should aid recent efforts to improve military professionalism and efficiency.

Budget
In 2001 Paraguay spent U.S.$78 million on defense, down from $90 million the year before (IISS 2002, 313). How this money is allocated is unclear as Paraguay is not traditionally forthcoming with such information. It is known that the army, as the largest branch, receives the majority of the funds. Further, a large amount of these funds are allocated to civil action projects that leave little money for military operations (Hanratty and Meditz 1990, 218). The low (and decreasing) amount of spending on the military has left the Paraguayan army with obsolete equipment, most of which has been given to Paraguay by third parties.

With virtually no internal arms industry, Paraguay is completely dependent on equipment from outside sources. Most equipment is made by the United States but transferred from third parties, mainly Brazil and Argentina. The most recent major acquisition came in 1998 when Paraguay acquired five F-5E fighters from Taiwan (IISS 2002, 316). Although this expanded the Paraguayan fighter force to twelve (all versions of the F-5), the gain is tempered by the fact that the F-5E is a 1970s-era craft and not a truly modern fighter plane.

Civil-Military Relations/The Role of the Military in Domestic Politics
The military has always played a significant role in Paraguayan politics, a fact that does not seem likely to change in the near future. The military has long defined itself as the guardians of the state and has

used this special status as grounds for constant political intervention.

After the Chaco War the military, specifically the army, was divided between competing factions (as was civil society). The era between 1936 and 1945 was one of instability in Paraguay as the army was the force behind every change in leadership (Hanratty and Meditz 1990, 171). Between 1940 and 1947 there were twenty-seven separate rebellions involving parts of the military (Loveman 1999, 113). Finally, in 1954 Stroessner (who had previously defended the rule of dictator Federico Chaves) led a successful coup in which he took control of Paraguay.

During the Stroessner regime (1954–1989), the military formed one of the two main pillars of government support (along with the Colorado Party). During this time the army became a tool for internal repression. Officers who were not loyal to Stroessner were removed and were replaced by men who would support the regime. Stroessner personally headed the promotion board for all officers and based command assignments on political rather than military considerations (Hanratty and Meditz 1990, 172). Officers were rewarded for their loyalty and they formed the social and economic elite of the nation with most officers supplementing their income with outside enterprises, including smuggling, prostitution, and drug trafficking (Loveman 1999, 114).

Just as it had installed Stroessner in power, the military also removed him. In 1989 powerful members of the military and the Colorado Party were removed from power by a militant faction in the Colorado Party. Specifically, the militants attempted to remove General Rodriguez, the commander of the Paraguayan First Brigade, and his supporters. Instead of giving up command, General Rodriguez ordered his troops into action against Stroessner, including an attack on the Presidential Guard Regiment. After several hours of fighting, leaving roughly fifty dead, Stroessner surrendered and went into exile in Brazil (Roett and Sacks 1991, 131).

The leader of the coup, General Rodriguez, was placed in power and later won election as president. Rodriguez started the reform process that led to the new constitution in 1992. Although Rodriguez began the reform process, his goal was to liberalize the country in order to improve the economic situation, which the military believed necessary to ensure long-term security. However, once started, the changes took on a life of their own and led to a new democratically based constitution.

In 1993 Carlos Wasmosy was elected as the first civilian leader of Paraguay in almost forty years. The new constitution bars members of the military from holding political office or from being members of a political party; in fact, it bans the military from all political activity in an effort to remove the military's dominance from politics. Despite this, the military is still an important power in Paraguayan politics. Shortly after taking office, Wasmosy faced an attempted coup by General Lino Oviedo, but most of the army remained loyal and the attempt failed. However, the next president, Raul Cubas (Oviedo's political ally), pardoned Oviedo for the coup, touching off a domestic dispute when the supreme court ruled the pardon illegal. After being accused of assassinating Vice President Luis Maria Argana Ferraro, both Oviedo and Cubas fled the country.

As recently as 2000, President Luis Macchi, who took over Cubas's term, faced a military uprising as a small military unit using APCs attempted to seize control of government buildings in Asunción. The coup failed to gain popular support either in the military or the general population and was put down when units loyal to Macchi threatened to open fire on the APCs (Thomas 2004).

Even though the military has refused to aid recent efforts to overthrow the democratic government in Paraguay, this situation still shows the importance of the military. First, the repeated coup attempts show dissatisfaction inside the military with recent policy decisions, particularly anticorruption efforts. If widespread dissent should materialize, there are clearly forces inside the military willing to lead a return to the authoritarian past of Paraguay. Second, the army is clearly the protector of Paraguayan democracy. Without military support, the nation's democracy seems unable to maintain itself against attack. This situation provides the military with great leverage to negotiate policy with the democratic government, meaning that, at least for now, any changes in Paraguay must win approval from the military.

Terrorism

Paraguay could find itself on the front line of the war against terrorism. Although Paraguay does not harbor terror groups and does not have any home-grown terror organizations, the Tri-Border Region (eastern Paraguay) has become a breeding ground for terror groups and training camps. One expert has called the Tri-Border Region the world's new Libya, drawing terror groups from all across the political spectrum to train and trade information (Stern 2003). The Tri-Border Region has long been home to smuggling, theft, drug trafficking, and gunrunning. In recent years this has taken on a new dimension as connections have been made between this region and various terror organizations. There is evidence that a weapons-for-drugs connection has been made between the Colombian rebel group FARC (Revolutionary Armed Forces of Colombia) and entities in the Tri-Border Region. Further, the estimated 30,000 Arabs who live in the area have become a fundraising source for Middle Eastern terror groups (Mendel 2000, 53). Members of Hamas and Hezbollah are known to operate in the area, with several high-ranking members of Hezbollah arrested in this region (only to later escape).

Of more concern to the United States are claims from Paraguay that Osama bin Laden has been attempting to establish an al-Qaeda unit in the region (Mendel 2000, 55). Although there is no solid evidence connecting al-Qaeda to the Tri-Border Region, documents captured in Afghanistan describing the area have raised concerns. The lawless nature of the Tri-Border Region would provide a natural refuge for al-Qaeda and other terror groups that have lost their traditional sanctuaries due to the war against terrorism.

For the past several years Paraguay, Argentina, and Brazil have attempted to coordinate their law enforcement efforts in the Tri-Border Region, with only minimal success. Corruption is high in the area, particularly in Paraguay, which undercuts most efforts to reduce criminal activity. If terror groups do establish (or have established) themselves in the Tri-Border Region, it will take a considerable effort to eliminate them. Given Paraguay's small and ill-equipped forces, it seems unlikely that they would be able to secure their territory in the region without considerable outside assistance.

Relationship with the United States

Paraguayan-U.S. relations have oscillated over the almost two centuries since Paraguay's independence. Paraguay's small size, both economically and militarily, has made it difficult to attract sustained attention from the United States. Relations have been strained recently by concerns over human rights and drug trafficking.

The United States did not have much formal contact with Paraguay until 1845, when Francia's reign and his policy of isolation ended. When Carlos Lopez began to open Paraguay to the international community, the United States began low-level relations, with Edward Hopkins being appointed as a special agent to Paraguay. The relationship was rocky as Lopez and Hopkins did not get along, and the two states nearly went to war in 1854 when Paraguay fired on a U.S. naval vessel conducting research on the Parana River. Paraguay did eventually back down, paying reparations, but only after the United States sent nineteen ships and several thousand soldiers into Paraguayan waters (Roett and Sacks 1991, 145).

American President Hayes earned a special place in Paraguayan history by mediating a dispute between Paraguay and Argentina in 1877. Paraguay and Argentina were disputing ownership of parts of the Chaco (western Paraguay), and through U.S. efforts, Argentina rescinded its claim to the territory. In thanks to President Hayes, Paraguay named a city and one of its departments after him (Roett and Sacks 1991, 145). The United States was also a member of the peace negotiations between Paraguay and Bolivia to end the Chaco War; however, U.S. negotiators did not play a large role.

World War II complicated U.S.-Paraguayan relations as Paraguay adopted a pro-fascist policy. Contacts with both Germany and Italy increased, and Paraguay was the first South American country with a fascist party, to which many leading political figures belonged (Roett and Sacks 1991, 146–147). After the attack on Pearl Harbor and U.S. entrance into the war against the Axis powers, Paraguay broke official relations with Germany and Italy, but did not take actions against their holdings or agents in Paraguay. Despite unofficial fascist connections, the United States provided Paraguay with large amounts of aid during this time and worked hard to shift Paraguay away from pro-Axis Argentina and toward pro-ally Brazil. Despite these efforts, Paraguay refused to totally break with the fascist powers until Allied victory was assured, declaring war against the fascists only in 1945.

The start of the Cold War brought the United States and Paraguay close together, diplomatically driven by similar security interest, U.S. trade interest, and Paraguay's need for developmental assistance (Hanratty and Meditz 1990, 196). This was especially true under the Stroessner regime that was fiercely anti-communist and concerned with communist attempts to overthrow the regime. During this time Paraguay broke relations with Cuba after Castro came to power, voted with the United States regularly in the United Nations and the OAS, and even sent forces to Vietnam. In exchange for this support the United States provided Paraguay with foreign aid and military training.

In the mid- to late 1970s the relationship between Paraguay and the United States turned cooler as concerns over human rights abuses during the Stroessner regime became more prominent in Washington, especially with the election of President Carter (see Sidebar 2). No longer willing to overlook human rights abuses, the United States began to pressure Paraguay to make changes, stating more than once that government practice

---

Sidebar 2   Stroessner's Dictatorship

Alfredo Stroessner ruled Paraguay longer than any other leader, and left a legacy of abuse and corruption that still haunts Paraguay today. Stroessner took control in 1954 and, lacking widespread popular support, relied upon the military to suppress opposition to his regime and maintain power. Stroessner maintained a state of emergency (state of siege) in rural Paraguay until 1970, with only a short break in 1959, and in the capital of Asunción until 1987. Using the powers granted to him under the state of emergency, Stroessner allowed the military and security forces to terrorize and murder his opponents. Paraguayan civil society was brought under control by attacking labor unions, restricting freedom of the press, and limiting the powers of the Catholic Church. Stroessner held power until 1989, when his repressive measures came under repeated attack from the international community, forcing changes inside of Paraguay that Stroessner could not control.

Sources
Hanratty, Dennis M., and Sandra W. Meditz, eds. 1990. *Paraguay: A Country Study.* 5th ed. Washington, DC: U.S. Government Printing Office.
Sondrol, Paul C. 2000. "Paraguay: Precarious Democracy." In *Latin American Politics and Development,* Howard J. Wiarda and Harvey F. Kline, eds. Boulder, CO: Westview, pp. 312–330.

in Paraguay would have to change if relations between the two states were to improve (Hanratty and Meditz 1990, 197). The relationship was also altered by the fact that trade between the two nations had been declining for many years.

When Stroessner was removed from power, U.S.-Paraguayan relations improved as the new government, headed by General Rodriguez, began a process of liberalization that ended in a new democratic constitution. The new government received high-ranking U.S. officials for state visits and received increased aid (Sondrol 2000, 328). Although relations improved, there was still wide concern in the United States over drug trafficking in Paraguay, including possible illegal activity by members of the military and government officials. In 1998, these concerns led the United States to give Paraguay a failing grade on antidrug efforts (for the second time).

In the aftermath of the September 11, 2001, terror attacks on the United States, Paraguay, like most Latin American states, has not been a high priority for U.S. diplomatic attentions. The problem is even more acute for Paraguay because it is such a small state and unable to provide significant resources for the war on terrorism.

The Future

Currently the military is in a process of contraction that will continue for the next several years, including a reduction in military budget and personnel. This reduction reflects the economic difficulties Paraguay has faced in recent years as well as the lack of a significant external security threat. At this time there is little chance of a conflict arising between Paraguay and one of its neighbors that

would progress to the point of a military engagement. Disagreements between Paraguay and its neighbors have been confined to economics and how to proceed with economic integration under MERCOSUR. The budget reduction should also allow Paraguay to remove elements from the military that would be prone to intervene in domestic politics.

Although continuing the process of military contraction seems likely, this could change based on events in the Tri-Border Region. Should substantive terror links be found, particularly to al-Qaeda, the military could quickly move from contraction to expansion. If the Tri-Border Region becomes a front in the global war on terror, it seems likely that the United States would provide all three bordering states with military assistance and training to allow them to gain control over the area. Even if U.S. troops are brought in to conduct combat operations, commitments in other locations will mean that U.S. troops will need support from Paraguay and its neighbors. This could mean a significant increase in military budgets, personnel, and considerable improvement in equipment. This scenario would also entail redefining the primary military mission from one of external defense to counterinsurgency. Such a shift would necessitate a major reorganization of the military, with more emphasis on rapid deployment and special forces.

References, Recommended Readings, and Websites

Books
English, Adrian J. 1984. *Armed Forces of Latin America: Their Histories, Development, Present Strength and Military Potential.* London: Jane's Publishing Company.
Farcau, Bruce W. 1996. *The Chaco War: Bolivia and Paraguay, 1932–1935.* Westport, CT: Praeger.

Hanratty, Dennis M., and Sandra W. Meditz, eds. 1990. *Paraguay: A Country Study.* 5th ed. Washington, DC: U.S. Government Printing Office.

International Institute for Strategic Studies (IISS). 2002. *The Military Balance 2002–2003.* Oxford, UK: Oxford University Press.

Keegan, John. 1979. *World Armies.* New York: Facts on File.

Lambert, Peter, and Andrew Nickson, eds. 1997. *The Transition of Democracy in Paraguay.* New York: St. Martin's Press.

Leuchars, Chris. 2002. *To the Bitter End: Paraguay and the War of the Triple Alliance.* Portsmouth, NH: Greenwood Publishing Group.

Lewis, Paul H. 1980. *Paraguay under Stroessner.* Chapel Hill: University of North Carolina Press.

Loveman, Brian. 1999. *For la Patria: Politics and the Armed Forces in Latin America.* Wilmington, DE: Scholarly Resources.

Martini, Carlos, and Carlos Maria Lezcano. 1997. "The Armed Forces." In *The Transition to Democracy in Paraguay.* Peter Lambert and Andrew Nickson, eds. New York: St. Martin's Press, pp. 65–71.

Roett, Riordan, and Richard Scott Sacks. 1991. *Paraguay: The Personalist Legacy.* Boulder, CO: Westview.

Sondrol, Paul C. 2000. "Paraguay: Precarious Democracy." In *Latin American Politics and Development,* Howard J. Wiarda and Harvey F. Kline, eds. Boulder, CO: Westview, pp. 312–330.

Stockholm International Peace Research Institute (SIPRI). 2002. *SIPRI Yearbook 2002: Armaments, Disarmament and International Security.* Oxford, UK: Oxford University Press.

Thomas, J. 2004. *A History of Paraguay.* Unpublished manuscript.

Whigham, Thomas L. 2002. *The Paraguayan War: Causes and Early Conduct.* Lincoln: University of Nebraska Press.

Articles/Newspapers

Bureau of Western Hemisphere Affairs, United States Department of State. "Background Note: Paraguay." http://www.state.gov/r/pa/ei/bgn/1841.htm (accessed February 18, 2004).

Castaneda, Forge. 2003. "Latin America, the Forgotten Relative." *Foreign Affairs* 82, no. 3:67–81.

Gibler, Douglas M., and Meredith Sarkees. 2004. "Measuring Alliances: the Correlates of War Formal Interstate Alliance Data Set, 1816–2000." *Journal of Peace Research* 41, no. 2:211–222.

Hudson, Rex. 2003. "Terrorist and Organized Crime Groups in the Tri-Border Area (TBA) of South America." Federal Research Division, Library of Congress. http://www .loc.gov /rr/frd/ pdf-files/TerrOrgCrime_TBA.pdf.

Mendel, William H. 2000. "Paraguay's Ciudad del Este and the New Centers of Gravity." *Military Review,* March–April:51–57.

Nickson, Andrew R. 1988. "Tyranny and Longevity: Stroessner's Paraguay." *Third World Quarterly* 10, no. 1:237–259.

OnWar.com. "Chaco War 1932–1935." http://onwar.com/aced/nation/pat/paraguay/ fchaco1932.htm (accessed February 18, 2004).

———. "Paraguayan Civil War 1947." http://onwar.com/aced/nation/pat/paraguay/fparaguay1947.htm (accessed February 18, 2004).

———. "War of the Triple Alliance 1864–1870." http://onwar.com/aced/nation/pat/paraguay/ftriple1864.htm (accessed February 18, 2004).

Sarkees, Meredith Reid. 2000. "The Correlates of War Data on War: An Update to 1997." *Conflict Management and Peace Science* 18, no. 1:123–144.

Shifter, Michael. 2001. "United States-Latin American Relations: Preparing for the Handover." *Current History,* February:51–57.

Stern, Jessica. 2003. "The Protean Enemy." *Foreign Affairs* 82, no. 4:27–34.

"Winning Respect: Something Stirs in a Backward Country." *The Economist* 370, no. 8357:31–32.

Websites

American Embassy in Paraguay: http://asuncion.usembassy.gov/.

CIA *World Factbook:* http://www.odci.gov/cia/publications/factbook/geos/pa.html (accessed February 18, 2004).

Constitution of Paraguay (English): http://www.oefre.unibe.ch/law/icl/pa00000_.html.

Government of Paraguay: http://www. paraguaygobierno.gov.py.

Internet Resources for Latin America: http://lib.nmsu.edu/subject/bord/ laguia/.

Latin American Network Information Center: http://lanic.utexas.edu/ la/sa/paraguay/.

National Police of Paraguay: http://www. policia.gov.py/historia.htm.

University of Illinois, Chicago: http:// dosfan.lib.uic.edu/ERC/bgnotes/wha/ paraguay9005.html.

U.S. Department of State Background Notes: http://www.state.gov/r/pa/ei/ bgn/1841.htm.

Washington Post Paraguay News: http:// www.washingtonpost.com/wp-dyn/ world/americas/southamerica/ paraguay/.

Philippines

Rodelio Cruz Manacsa

Geography and History

The Republic of the Philippines is an archipelago located between the South China Sea and the Pacific Ocean. It is composed of around 7,100 islands, with a total land area of nearly 300,000 sq. km. However, only 880 of these islands are inhabited, with a majority of the people living on the 11 largest islands. Currently, the country has around 80 million inhabitants (91.5 percent Christian Malays, 4 percent Muslims, and 1.5 percent Chinese).

The Philippines traverses Southeast Asia's main water bodies and shipping lanes. It has a tropical marine climate, with only two seasons: wet and dry. Because the terrain is very mountainous, there is considerable regional variation in the seasons. Rain comes to the western side of the country from June to late September, while the eastern side gets most of its rainfall from November to March. The mean annual sea-level temperature rarely falls below 27°C (80°F) (Demaine 2004, 949).

The Philippines was a Spanish colony from 1565 to 1898, the year the Philippine revolution broke out (Carino 1988). The United States obtained legal ownership of the islands in 1898 through the Treaty of Paris that ended the Spanish-American War, but had to fight a fierce Filipino uprising from 1899 to 1902. The United States voluntarily transferred sovereignty to the Filipinos on July 4, 1946. The Philippines had a political system similar to the United States until Ferdinand Marcos placed the entire country under martial law in 1972. In 1986, a civilian-military uprising (called the "People Power Revolution") dismantled the dictatorship. Democratic institutions were reestablished by Corazon Aquino (1986–1992) and consolidated by Fidel V. Ramos (1992–1998). The constitutional foundations of the Philippines were shaken by the military withdrawal of support from Joseph Estrada that forced him to abdicate the presidency (1998–2001) and two failed coups against Gloria Macapagal-Arroyo (2001–2004).

The Philippine economy is based on light industries, agriculture, and a very strong services sector (Hodgkinson 2004). In 2002, its gross domestic product (GDP) was estimated at U.S.$356 billion (purchasing power parity) and a per capita GDP of U.S.$4,600. Exports from the Philippines (mostly electronic equipment, machinery, and garments) were valued at U.S.$35.1 billion, while its imports totaled U.S.$33.5 billion. Its main trading partners are the United States, Japan, and the European Union. The Philippines has an external debt of U.S.$60.3 billion (*World Almanac* 2004).

Table 1 Philippines: Key Statistics

Type of government	Presidential democracy
Population (millions)	80 (2003)
Religion	Roman Catholic 83%; Protestant 9%; Islam 5% (2003)
Main industries	Electronics, pharmaceuticals, textiles, wood products, chemicals, food processing (2003)
Main security threats	Secessionist movement in Mindanao, communist insurgency, territorial dispute in the Spratlys
Defense spending (% of GDP)	.9 (2003)
Size of military (thousands)	106 (2002)
Number of civil wars since 1945	3
Number of interstate wars since 1945	2

Sources

Central Intelligence Agency. 2003. *World Factbook: Philippines.* http://www.odci.gov/cia/publications/factbook/print/rp.html (accessed February 27, 2004).

International Institute for Strategic Studies (IISS). 2003. *The Military Balance 2003–2004.* London: IISS and Oxford University Press.

Correlates of War 2. 2004. http://cow2.la.psu.edu/ (accessed February 27, 2004).

World Almanac. 2004. "Philippines." *World Almanac Book of Facts.* New York: World Almanac Books.

Regional Geopolitics

The Southeast Asian region lives under the security umbrella of the United States, the looming military hegemony of China, and the economic influence of Japan. The stability of the region mostly depends on the relational dynamics of these powers (Wah 2003, 9). After 2001, the region gained salience as a critical point for global security when it was revealed that groups linked with al-Qaeda have utilized some countries in the area (notably Indonesia and the Philippines) as training grounds for their activities. There is strong evidence that armed groups like the Abu Sayyaf Group (ASG),

---

Sidebar 1   The "People Power" Revolution

In 1986, after a tumultuous election, military forces formerly affiliated with then-Philippine strongman Ferdinand Marcos initiated a coup that was eventually neutralized. The rebels took their last stand in one of the military headquarters. Inspired by Catholic prelate Jaime Cardinal Sin and then-presidential candidate Corazon Aquino, however, the soldiers were shielded from state forces by civilian supporters. Dwindling domestic and international support drove Marcos into exile after several days. This is a fine case of the people saving the military.

Sources

Reid, Robert, and Eileen Guerrero. 1995. *Corazon Aquino and the Brushfire Revolution.* Baton Rouge: Louisiana State University Press.

Santiago, Angela Stuart. 1995. *1986: Chronology of a Revolution.* Manila: Foundation for Worldwide People Power.

the Moro Islamic Liberation Front (MILF), and the Jemaah Islamiyah (JI) have been funded and trained by al-Qaeda (Abuza 2003; Schweitzer and Shay 2003).

However, governments in the region have been mostly recalcitrant to cooperate and coordinate their efforts to combat terrorism even after the violent assault on the World Trade Center (Gunaratna 2003). Most of these responses were bilateral agreements to exchange information and to jointly patrol borders. It was only after the murderous terrorist attack by the JI in Bali, Indonesia, on October 12, 2002, did the states in the region come to a stark realization of the need to coordinate their efforts in a more extensive and institutionalized manner. This led to the creation of the Southeast Asian Regional Center for Counter-Terrorism in Kuala Lumpur.

The Spratly Islands archipelago also remains an area critical to the stability of the region. It is a long stretch of shoals, islets, and reefs that lie between 4° to 11°30' north latitude and 109°30' east longitude in the South China Sea (Tolin 2002). The total area is around 5 sq. km. It has a large continental shelf and is a very fertile area for fishing. It is strategically located near several primary shipping lanes. Most importantly, the Spratly Islands also have potential oil and gas reserves (Catley and Keliat 1997). Thus, ownership of the islands is of vital importance to the contending states for economic and strategic reasons, making this dispute extremely volatile. The contending parties are the People's Republic of China (China), Vietnam, the Philippines, Taiwan, Malaysia, and Brunei (see Table 2).

China, Taiwan, and Vietnam have the most extensive claims. China asserts territorial sovereignty over the entire Spratly Islands archipelago based on historical title and effective occupation. In 1992, the entire South China Sea and all the islands within it, including the Spratly Islands and the Paracels, were declared by the National People's Congress to be Chinese territory. The Taiwanese claim is similar to China's contention. Vietnam also claims the entire Spratly Islands archipelago and the Paracels based on historical right and cession (Valencia 1995).

The Philippines lays claim to only fifty-three islands and islets, mostly to the west of the Spratly Islands archipelago, which it calls the Kalayaan Island group (KIG). The Philippines' claim is based on discovery and effective occupation. The state avers that in 1947, the KIG was discovered by a Filipino seafarer, Tomas Cloma, who later ceded all his rights in favor of the Philippine government. In 1978, the islands were integrated into the Philippine province of Palawan through Presidential Decree No. 1596.

The contesting claims have been pursued vigorously, leading to armed skirmishes that threaten to escalate into higher levels of militarized confrontation. The Philippines has clashed with China over Mischief Reef, with Malaysia around Investigator Reef, and with Vietnam over Pigeon Reef. In 2002, the Philippines signed a Code of Conduct on the South China Sea with Brunei, Malaysia, China, and Vietnam. The document maintains the status quo over the disputed area and proposes the holding of certain measures (e.g., cooperation on marine life protection) to hopefully facilitate the creation of an environment that is less hostile and more conducive for negotiation.

Conflict Past and Present
Conflict History
After World War II, the Philippines was primarily involved in interstate conflicts

Table 2 Rival Claims on the Spratlys and Occupied Islands

Country	Basis of Claim	Islands Currently Occupied
Brunei	Doctrine on the Continental Shelf; EEZ principle	None
People's Republic of China (PROC)	Historical title; effective control	1. Cuarteron Reef 2. Fiery Cross Reef 3. First Thomas Shoal 4. Gaven Reef 5. Johnson South Reef 6. Konnan Reef 7. Ladd Reef 8. Len Dao Reef 9. Mischief Reef 10. Subi Reef
Malaysia	Doctrine on the Continental Shelf; EEZ principle	1. Ardasier & Dallas Reef 2. Louisa Reef 3. Mariveles Reef 4. Swallow Reef
Philippines	Principle of "Discovery"; EEZ principle	1. Commodore Reef 2. Flat Island 3. Lankiam Cay 4. Loaita Island 5. Nanshan Island 6. Northeast Cay 7. Thi Tu Island 8. West York Island
Republic of China (Taiwan)	Historical title	Itu Aba
Vietnam	Historical title, EEZ principle, cession	1. Allison Reef 2. Amboyna Cay 3. Barque Canada Reef 4. Central Reef 5. Cornwallis South Reef 6. Discovery Great Reef 7. East Reef 8. Grainger Reef 9. Nam Yit Island 10. Pearson Reef 11. Petley Reef 12. Pigeon Reef 13. Prince Consort Bank 14. Prince of Wales Bank 15. Rifleman Bank 16. San Cay 17. Sin Cowe Island 18. Southwest Cay 19. Spratly Island 20. Vanguard Reef 21. West Reef

Sources
Catley, Robert, and Makmur Keliat. 1997. *Spratlys and the Dispute in the South China Sea.* Aldershot, UK: Ashgate.
Van Dyke, Mark, and Noel Ludwig. 1999. *Sharing the Resources of the South China Sea.* The Hague: Kluwer Law International.

because of its support for the United States. It provided both manpower and logistical support to U.S. military operations in the Korean War (1950–1953) and the Vietnam War (1966–1973).

Within the Southeast Asian region, the Philippines was involved in a bitter territorial dispute with Malaysia over the island of Sabah. Sabah is the northern part of Borneo bordered by Sarawak in the southwest and Kalimantan in the south. It has a total land area of 76,115 sq. km. In 1704, the sultan of Brunei ceded Sabah to the sultan of Sulu as a sign of gratitude for the latter's help in quelling a rebellion. In 1878, the sultan of Sulu leased Sabah to the British North Borneo Company in exchange for providing military arms to resist Spanish colonizers. The agreement also stipulated that the company would pay the sultan an annual rental fee of 5,000 Malaysian ringgits or its equivalent in gold. Currently, the Malaysian government still continues to pay the fee to the heir of the sultanate of Sulu (Tan 2000).

When the Malaysian Federation was created in 1963, its territorial expanse included Sabah, much to the chagrin of the Philippine government. In 1968, Ferdinand Marcos authorized the secret training of military commandos, code-named Operation Jabidah, to foment a separatist rebellion in Sabah (Majul 1985). However, the covert operation was revealed when twenty-eight Muslim recruits were executed in Corregidor for refusing to be deployed to Sabah. In retaliation, Malaysia provided training to Muslim secessionists fighting to create an Islamic state on the Philippine island of Mindanao.

Philippine-Malaysian relations were so strained they threatened the very existence of the Association of Southeast Asian Nations (ASEAN) (Indorf 1984).

Presidents Aquino and Ramos requested legislation to formally drop the Sabah claim, but the Senate spurned their initiatives. Present actions of the Philippine government demonstrate that it is not yet willing to give up its claim. In 2001, the Philippines intervened in the Malaysian and Singaporean case over the ownership of the Ligitan and Sipadan islands at the International Court of Justice, contending that any judgment in the case should not prejudice the Philippines' claim to Sabah. Thus, this issue is likely to continue as a major irritant in Philippine-Malaysian relations.

Domestically, the Philippine state had faced several challenges to its internal sovereignty. In the 1950s, it was confronted with a peasant rebellion spearheaded by the Hukbong Mapagpalaya ng Bayan (Hukbalahap). The armed uprising was triggered by the depressing living conditions in the countryside and the seeming indifference of the state to the plight of the rural poor (Kerkvliet 1977). At the peak of the rebellion in 1951, the Hukbalahap had an estimated 11,000–15,000 adherents. The rebellion was eventually subdued in 1954 by a combination of relentless military pressure and by Hukbalahap mistakes. Atrocities perpetrated by the rebels were widely reported, wearing down support for the rural insurgency.

In 1968, Jose Maria Sison and a group of committed radicals re-established the Communist Party of the Philippines (CPP-NPA), beginning what is now the longest-running Maoist insurgency in Asia. The organization's goal was to dismantle the bourgeois, capitalist Philippine state that was beholden to the imperialist United States (Sison 1971). The CPP-NPA advocated an armed revolution patterned after the Maoist dictum of a protracted people's war: to penetrate and consolidate a potent rural base and encircle the cities from the countryside (Jones 1989). The Nationalist Democratic Front (NDF) was the group's political component and the New People's Army (NPA) was its armed wing. The NPA was formed by Bernabe Buscano, renowned in Philippine lore as "Commander Dante."

The CPP-NPA steadily grew in membership as disenchantment with martial law deepened. Starting as a ragtag group of insurgents in 1971, the movement had an estimated 22,500 members in 1986 and formidable influence over 20 percent of the Philippine villages (Dolan 2003a). However, the organization committed the strategic mistake of advocating a boycott of the 1986 special presidential elections. Because of this position, the insurgents had very little leverage to demand any meaningful role in the construction of the postauthoritarian political structure. In the 1990s, the CPP-NPA splintered into two groups: the Reaffirmists and the Rejectionists (Rocamora 1994). The Reaffirmist group was associated with the old vanguard of the party who still controlled revolutionary operations long distance from their base in Utrecht, The Netherlands. This faction of the communists contended that the only way for the group to survive and eventually emerge victorious was to remain committed to tested Maoist principles. The Rejectionists advocated a revolutionary strategy centered on action in urban areas. The division became absolute in 1992.

The legitimacy of the communist insurgency in the Philippines is steadily being eroded by two other factors. First, there is a growing disenchantment against the leaders who are living comfortably abroad while their cadres are suffering on the field. Second, internal purges of revisionist cadres further decimated the movement's membership.

The Philippine state has also confronted challenges to its internal sovereignty in Mindanao. The Jabidah Massacre of March 1968 triggered the mobilization for a separate Islamic state (Majul 1985; Jubair 1999). Twenty-eight Muslims were purportedly killed on Corregidor after resisting their deployment to Sabah as part of Marcos's plan to create an incident that would justify a military invasion. The Muslim recruits were later found dead (George 1980; Kamlian 1995).

In 1968, Nur Misuari, Salamat Hashim, and other young Muslim intellectuals founded the Moro National Liberation Front-Bangsa Moro Army (MNLF-BMA) with the aim of creating an independent state in Mindanao (Chalk 2002, 189). For the MNLF-BMA, the state had become a *gobirno a sarwang tao* (government of foreign people) keen on destroying the cultural identity of the Bangsa Moro (Philippine Muslim population) through assimilation. They rejected this policy as cultural genocide and characterized their struggle as a jihad (holy war).

The MNLF allied with the traditional Muslim elite, a strategy that proved detrimental to its cause in the long run (McKenna 1998; Molloy 1988). In the beginning, the traditional Moro clans supported the MNLF, but eventually found the Marcosian system of patronage more rewarding and aligned themselves with the state (Che Man 1990). Belief in the MNLF also slowly eroded among intellectuals as the movement proved incapable of producing any workable redistributive agenda (Molloy 1988, 69–70).

The MNLF tried to strengthen its political and military position by seeking monetary and logistical support from external sources such as Libya, Malaysia, and, eventually, the Organization of Islamic Conference (OIC). However, the OIC proved to be a conservative influence. Some states (e.g., Libya) publicly declared their support for the MNLF's call for an independent state, but some members expressed fears that support for its cause could become the precedent on how the OIC should deal with secession. For example, Indonesia had issues with Christians in West Papua, and Iraq has its Kurdish dilemma. Eventually, the OIC declared, "All political resolution to the GRP [Government of the Republic of the Philippines]-MNLF's dispute must be settled within the framework of Philippine sovereignty and territorial integrity" (Santos 2001, 67). There was subtle pressure on the MNLF to negotiate for a result other than separation (Balacuit 1994, 21).

In 1976, the Tripoli Agreement between the GRP and the MNLF reduced the dispute issue to regional autonomy. There were criticisms that the MNLF had "become reliant on and become subservient to the OIC" (Santos 2001, 62). Salamat Hashim eventually founded his own group, the Moro Islamic Liberation Front (MILF). The MILF has predicated its struggle for an Islamic state on Islamic renewal rather than on nationalist vision (Vitug and Gloria 2000). Currently, the MILF has an estimated 12,000–15,000 combatants.

Current and Potential Military Confrontation

The Philippines is still in a contentious situation with Malaysia over Sabah, but it has not assiduously pursued its territorial claim the past few years. The state has more vigorously advanced and protected its rights in the Spratly Islands archipelago where it has been recently involved in armed skirmishes with China and Vietnam over the island chain.

The Philippines only claims fifty-three islands and islets in the Spratly Islands, which it calls the Kalayaan Island group (KIG). These are the islands that are within the purview of its exclusive economic zone (EEZ) that is granted to the Philippines by international maritime law. The Philippines considers KIG as part of its territory, a distinct and separate municipality of the province of Palawan.

In 1999, the Philippines entered into a diplomatic row with China over structures that were being built by the Chinese, purportedly for the protection of its fishermen at Mischief Reef. The same year, the Philippines was involved in an imbroglio with Malaysia over the construction of facilities that could easily be converted into military use at Investigator Reef and Erica Reef. The dispute over the Spratly Islands would continue to be the Philippines' earnest external security concern in the next few years.

Sidebar 2   Communications in the Philippines

The Philippines is probably the text messaging capital of the world. There are around 15 million cellular phone users in the country (out of a population of 80 million) who are producing 150 to 200 million text messages a day. Because it is more expensive to have a landline connected than it is to buy a cell phone, the Filipinos simply leaped ahead into the digital millennium.

Source
Conde, Carlos. 2002. "Texting Is as Good as Calling for Filipinos." *International Herald Tribune*, April 28, 2003.

On the domestic front, the Philippine state is in the process of negotiating a permanent end of hostilities with both the CPP-NPA and the MILF. Support for the communist insurgency is in steady decline, and factionalism within its ranks has dissipated what remains of its military capability. The MILF suffered a major blow to its campaign to establish a separate Islamic state in Mindanao when its training camps and operational base (Camp Abubakar) was overrun by the Philippine military in 2000. The MILF has renewed its call for independence after a cessation of hostilities with the government in 2001. However, it would probably take a few more years of steady logistical buildup and recruitment before it could recover from its encounter with the Philippine military in 2000.

The most salient domestic threat to the Philippines would probably come from independent al-Qaeda cells and their Filipino counterparts in the region (Abuza 2003). The terrorist network's horizontal command structure and its nonreliance on a traditional base of operations have made it difficult for the military to eliminate the ASG and related organizations. In this regard, the 1998 Visiting Forces Agreement (VFA) and Mutual Logistic and Support Agreement (MLSA) pacts signed by the Philippines with the United States would greatly abet the ability of the armed forces to contain the terror threat.

Alliance Structure

The Philippines has relied almost exclusively on its defensive alliance with the United States for external security (Hedman 2001). The United States secured a ninety-nine-year lease for its military bases in the Philippines under the 1947 Military Bases Agreement (MBA). In return, the United States committed to fund and train the Philippine armed forces under the MBA's sister treaty, the Military Assistance Agreement (MSA). Finally, in 1952, the allies concluded a Mutual Defense Treaty (MDT), which bound the signatories to aid each other in case of an attack on their metropolitan areas, territories, armed forces, public forces, or aircraft in the Pacific. However, the U.S. government has stated that the MDT does not cover an attack on Philippine positions in the Spratly Islands archipelago (Niksh 2003b, 14).

Under a 1959 amendment, the MBA was made subject to review every five years. Eventually, in 1991, the Senate of the Philippines rejected a proposed extension. The termination of the MBA severely strained the security relations between the two countries (Dolan 2003a, 183). In 1998, the Philippines acceded to the VFA with the United States. This document laid down the provisions that will govern the status of U.S. military personnel during training exercises with their Filipino counterparts. The alliance was revitalized by the staunch Philippine support of the U.S. global war on terrorism. The Philippines has been part of the U.S. "coalition of the willing" in its military operations in Afghanistan and Iraq. In return for its support, it was designated a major non-NATO ally by the United States.

During the Cold War, the Philippines had involved itself in multilateral initiatives designed to secure the Southeast Asian region. In 1955, it was a founding member of the Southeast Asian Treaty Organization (SEATO) together with the United States, United Kingdom, France, Australia, New Zealand, Pakistan, and Thailand. The organization was envisioned to be a bulwark against the spread of communism in the Pacific, the regional equivalent of the North Atlantic Treaty Organization (NATO). However, the organization lost any sense of legitimacy when the United States undertook military operations against Vietnam without consulting or invoking SEATO's collective defense mechanisms.

In 1961, the Philippines, Thailand, and Malaysia formed the Association for Southeast Asia (ASA) in order to institutionalize efforts to cooperate on common socioeconomic and cultural concerns. ASA was eventually pushed aside by the territorial antagonism between Malaysia and the Philippines over Sabah and between Malaysia and Indonesia over Borneo. The same fate befell the MAPHILINDO, an organization formed by Malaysia, the Philippines, and Indonesia in 1963 (Indorf 1984).

In 1967, the Philippines was a founding member of ASEAN, arguably the region's most successful organization. Originally instituted to facilitate cooperation in socioeconomic and cultural concerns, ASEAN's scope eventually broadened to include security issues with the establishment of the ASEAN Regional Forum (ARF) in 1994. ARF brought together twenty-three countries: the ASEAN members (Brunei, Burma, Cambodia, Indonesia, Laos, Malaysia, the Philippines, Singapore, Thailand, and Vietnam), ASEAN dialogue partners (Australia, Canada, China, the European Union, India, Japan, New Zealand, South Korea, Russia, and the United States), and three other states: North Korea, Mongolia, and Papua New Guinea (observer status).

ARF was envisioned to be a forum for consultation that would eventually be endowed with the institutional capability for preventive diplomacy and conflict resolution (Leifer 1996). However, the organization has made very little impact in facilitating cooperation on the current fight against terror in the region primarily due to its cumbersome decision-making procedures and financial constraints.

Size and Structure of the Military
Size and Structure
As of 2003, the Armed Forces of the Republic of the Philippines (AFP) has an active, regular forces strength of 106,000 military personnel (International Institute for Strategic Studies [IISS] 2003). The AFP is subdivided into three major services: army, navy, and air force. There are an additional 131,000 reservists. The Philippine National Police (PNP) is a 44,000-person-strong contingent tasked with domestic law and order functions. The coastal area is secured by the coast guard (3,500 personnel).

Commonwealth Act 1 (National Defense Act of 1935) created the Philippine army, which originally comprised all land, sea, air, and national police forces. In 1947, it was reorganized into the AFP. The 1987 constitution enshrined the principle of civilian supremacy over the military (Art. II, Sec. 3). Thus, the president is de jure the commander-in-chief of the AFP. During grave crises, the president may convene the National Security Council (NSC) to help him/her formulate an effective course of action. When convened, the NSC is composed of all former presidents, the vice president, the AFP chief of staff, NSC director, the executive secretary, and the heads of the defense, foreign affairs, finance, and justice departments (Dolan 2003a).

The person directly responsible to the chief executive for security matters is the secretary of the department of national defense (SDND). The chief of staff heads the AFP and reports to the SDND. The AFP general headquarters is located at Camp Aguinaldo. The SDND is assisted by a vice chief of staff and a deputy chief of staff, the latter being the effective administrator of the AFP bureaucracy. There are three major services and six unified commands (Armed Forces of the Philippines 2002).

The Philippine army is headed by a commanding general and is based in Fort Bonifacio. It has the largest number of personnel (66,000 active and 100,000 reservists). Its major tactical divisions are its eight infantry divisions, supported by a light armor brigade, a special operations command, five engineering brigades, one construction battalion, and an intelligence and security group. The army's original mission was to secure the territorial integrity and external sovereignty of the archipelago, but has been largely deployed for counterinsurgency operations given the protective umbrella given by the United States to the Philippines under the 1952 MDT (Dolan 2003a).

Currently, the army's weaponry is more attuned for domestic operations rather than combating external threats. It has 65 tanks (Scorpion class), 85 armored infantry fighting vehicles, 370 armored personnel carriers, and 250 light and medium artillery (IISS 2003; Stockholm International Peace Research Institute [SIPRI] 2003).

The Philippine navy was organized in 1950. It has total personnel of 39,000 (24,000 active and 15,000 reservists). It is headed by a rear admiral, who in turn is assisted by vice and deputy flag officers in command. The navy's task is to secure the Philippines' maritime territory of 36,289 km, as well as its EEZ. The headquarters is located in Manila, with a key base in Cavite. Attached to the navy service are the Philippine marines.

The Philippine navy is currently suffering from a lack of reliable ships. It has one frigate (the *Rajah Humabon*), thirteen offshore patrol boats, eleven coastal patrol boats, and thirty-four inshore boats, but almost all of these are quite advanced in age. The navy has seven amphibious vessels (two U.S. F.S. Besson–class LSTs and five U.S. LST-1/511/542s) but no submarine or armed helicopters (IISS 2003).

The Philippine air force was created in 1947 with a mission to protect the state's territorial airspace. It is divided into five major commands: air defense, tactical operations, air logistics and support, air reserve, and air education and training. The air force is headed by a commanding general, who is usually a two-star general. Its headquarters is located in Villamor Air Base in Manila and it has five other major bases located on the outskirts of the capital.

The Philippine air force continues to rely on a fighter squadron of fourteen F-5s, which are of World War II vintage. It has three squadrons of armed helicopters (eighty-seven total) and one F-27M. The air force has four RT-33A-type attack helicopters and twenty OV-10 Bronco class helicopters. It has only three squadrons of transport helicopters (IISS 2003; SIPRI 2003).

Budget
The national defense sector share in the budget of the Philippines has been stable, constituting around 0.8 percent of the GDP from 1994 to 2003 (Congressional Planning and Budget Department [CPBD] 2004). It is the second-lowest budget for defense as percent of total expenditures in Southeast Asia, next only to Indonesia.

Most of the budget allotted for defense purposes is spent on personal services (75 percent), leaving very little resources remaining for maintenance and operating expenses. Only 0.03 percent of the budget allocation has been utilized for capital outlay from 1994 to 2003. This has contributed to the very low level of modernization in the armed forces' weaponry and other equipment. Upgrades in these areas are made possible by defense assistance from the United States, which totaled $623 million from 1990 to 2001 (CPBD 2004).

The Department of National Defense is comprised of six bureaus: the Office of the Secretary of National Defense, the AFP, the Government Arsenal, the National Defense College of the Philippines, the Office of Civil Defense, and the Philippine Veterans Affairs Office. The AFP usually receives the largest allocation, taking almost half of the annual budget, with the Philippine army receiving the largest share among the services. The rest of the AFP resources are divided among the Pension and Gratuity Fund, the General Headquarters, the Philippines' MNLF Integration Program, and other units (Department of Budget and Management 2004).

Civil-Military Relations/The Role of the Military in Domestic Politics

The Philippine military is a politicized genie that cannot be returned to its constitutional lamp. Military involvement in politics has become so endemic to Philippine political processes that the question is not "why?" but "how much?"

It has been contended that prior to 1972, the Philippines had a very professional military (Casper 1995). This means that the military had considerable expertise in the employment of the instruments of violence and had an ethos that recognizes the civilian supremacy over the military, as well as fidelity to the national interest rather than some sectoral agenda (Hernandez 1997, 44). The 1935 constitution explicitly prohibited the military from entering into any partisan political activity.

However, the military was given an expanded role beginning in the 1950s because of the Huk rebellion. The focus of the armed forces moved from the preservation of state sovereignty from external threats to internal security and socioeconomic development. It was contended that grassroots insurgency movements couldn't be eradicated by military force alone (Dolan 2003a, 65–66). The state must win the hearts and minds of the populace. Thus, the military was made to undergo programs that equipped them with the necessary managerial skills to run socioeconomic projects in conflict areas.

When Ferdinand Marcos placed the entire country under martial law, he turned the military into a personal force to maintain his grip on political leadership. The military was made to neutralize the opponents of the dictator, to enforce all his orders, and to depoliticize the citizenry (Bresnan 1987). It was tasked to do police functions in 1974 as well as the judicial function of passing judgment over the critics of the regime (military and civilian) through its military tribunals. The armed forces became a junior partner in governance (Hedman 2001). It was obliged to be loyal not to the institutions of civilian authority but to the very person of the despot.

In the 1980s, the armed forces were not only very politicized but also heavily factionalized (Magno, Quiros, and Ofreneo 1986). Conflict simmered between those at the top of the hierarchy and the more junior set of officers. Marcos rewarded the loyalty of his generals by keeping them in command positions beyond their retirement age (Hernandez 1985). This was the main grievance of the junior military officers who would later form the Reform Armed Forces Movement (RAM) in 1982 under the leadership of Gregorio Honasan. In 1986, this group would form the armed component of a civilian-military uprising (the People Power Revolution) that would drive Marcos and his cronies from power (Nemenzo 1986).

The administration of Corazon Aquino (1986–1992) tried to prod the military back to the barracks. The new constitution enshrined as a bedrock belief the supremacy of civilian authorities over the military (Art. II, Sec. 3) and prohibited the armed forces from engaging in any partisan political activity except to vote (Art. XVI, Sec. 5 [3]). In order to win the allegiance of the military, Aquino organized commissions to address the grievances of junior officers and regularized the promotion process (Brown 2004). However, there were elements within the military that expected to be given the same powerful influence they enjoyed under martial law. They believed that Aquino owed her presidency to their intervention and anticipated a major role in governance (Casper 1995).

Various segments of the armed forces, from Marcos loyalists to units associated with RAM, launched seven coup attempts against the administration of Corazon Aquino (Hedman 2001, 181–182). The most violent assault, in 1989, was nearly victorious in seizing state power until "persuasion flights" from U.S. jetfighters turned the tide of battle against the putschists (Davide et al. 1990). The flights were interpreted to mean U.S. support for the Aquino government and galvanized the Aquino defense forces against the rebels, who were eventually crushed.

Sidebar 3   The 1989 Coup D'état and "Persuasion Flights"

The bloodiest coup against the administration of Corazon Aquino was attempted on December 1, 1989. The rebels seized the national airport, attacked the army headquarters, and bombed the presidential palace grounds. With the political situation hanging in the balance, U.S. fighter jets suddenly appeared in the sky and flew over rebel bases, an action interpreted to be a gesture of support for Aquino. The tide of battle turned and the rebellion eventually was crushed. The fighter jets did not fire on the rebels or militarily aid the Aquino forces, thus their actions were simply called "persuasion flights." Jet power is persuasive indeed.

Sources
Davide, Hilario, Carolina Hernandez, Ricardo Romulo, Delfin Lazaro, and Christian Monsod. 1990. *Report of the Fact Finding Commission.* Makati, Philippines: Bookmark.
Dolan, Ronald. 2003a. "Philippines: A Country Study." In *The Philippines: Current Issues and Historical Background,* Harry Calit, ed. New York: Nova Publishers.

One of the staunch defenders of the Aquino administration, General Fidel V. Ramos, was elected to the presidency in 1992. Under his leadership, the military's involvement in politics was curtailed. However, Ramos appointed retired generals into civilian posts and was accused of militarizing the bureaucracy. In 1998, a popular movie-actor-turned-politician, Joseph Ejercito Estrada, was elected president of the Philippines.

On October 12, 2000, Estrada was implicated by a close friend, Luis Singson, of enriching himself through an illegal numbers game (*jueteng*) and other unlawful activities. After a consideration of the evidence, Estrada became the first Filipino president to be impeached by the House of Representatives and was tried by the Senate.

Things came to head on January 16, 2001, when the Senate voted 11–10 to keep key evidence from being used against Estrada (Doronila 2001). People massed into the streets at the same place where the first People Power Revolution transpired—the long stretch of *Epifanio de los Santos* Avenue (EDSA). On January 19, 2001, the chief of staff of the armed forces, General Angelo Reyes, joined the people at EDSA and announced the military's withdrawal of support from Estrada (Hedman 2001, 184). The elected vice president, Gloria Macapagal-Arroyo, was installed as successor. For a second time on the same site, the military decided the fate of the Philippine presidency (the uprising was called People Power Revolution II or EDSA *Dos*).

Ascending to the presidency because of military support, Macapagal-Arroyo's political standing was very precarious. She did her utmost best to keep the loyalty of the military by raising their salaries and respecting the seniority promotion system. However, politicians linked to Estrada have managed to convince segments in the military to attempt seizing state power. There were two armed putsches attempted against Macapagal-Arroyo (Teodoro 2003; Vanzi 2004), but both were decisively subdued. The administration became even more beholden to military support.

The military will continue to determine the outcomes of the Philippine political process as long as the political institutions are incapable of resolving bitter social disputes within the democratic framework (Alagappa 2001). Political actors should refrain from turning every policy disagreement into a constitutional crisis. Furthermore, the military often intervenes in polities with inept administrations (Huntington 1996; Trinkunas 1999). Thus, economic development borne out of proficient state governance can fortify popular support for democracy in the Philippines. Armed actions against effectively functioning governments are difficult to justify.

Terrorism

The focus of the campaign against global terror shifted to Southeast Asia when it gradually became evident that countries such as Indonesia and the Philippines have been deeply penetrated by terrorist organizations like al-Qaeda (Sahni 2003). Countries with weak intelligence systems, porous financial systems, and internal armed conflicts were utilized as bases for the recruitment and training of members, the funneling of funds to regional organizations, and the planning and testing of terrorist attacks.

There is now very strong evidence that the Philippines was an operational hub of al-Qaeda activities (Gunaratna 2002; Reeve 1999). Two of the organizations that have benefited from funding and training from Osama bin Laden's organization were the MILF and the ASG (Abuza 2003; Schweitzer and Shay 2003). It has been discovered by Philippine intelligence that some of the most violent terrorist attacks, such as the *Oplan Bojinka* (a plot to assassinate the Pope and to bomb eleven U.S. jetliners) were hatched in the Philippines (Clamor 2003; Ressa 2003).

The MILF became engaged with al-Qaeda when it sent 500–700 persons to train and fight for the mujahidin in Afghanistan. The experience was critical in the development of the military competency of the MILF. Bin Laden saw that the armed group was worthy of support and designated Mohammed Jamal Khalifa as his conduit in Mindanao (Abuza 2003). Fathur Rohman Al-Ghozi founded and trained the component within the MILF that was engaged in terrorist activities. Rohman Al-Ghozi was killed in 2003.

The ASG is the second armed group that is associated with al-Qaeda. It is one of the thirty-three organizations designated by the U.S. Department of State as engaged in terrorism. Founded by Ustadz Janjalani in 1991, the ASG gained notoriety for the kidnapping of foreigners and Filipinos in the Malaysian resort in Sipadan in 2000 and Dos Palmas in 2001. In both instances, considerable ransom was paid to the group (Ressa 2003). To date, the key leaders of ASG have been either killed or arrested by the Philippine military. Founder Ustadz Janjalani was killed in a shoot-out with the PNP in 1998. Ustadz's brother, Khadaffy, who succeeded him as leader, was gunned down in Lamitan in 2001. Abu Sabaya, the head of one of the groups that splintered from ASG, was slain in June 2002 by Filipino and U.S. troops. Finally, Ghalib Andang, the suspected mastermind of the Sipadan abductions, was arrested in Sulu in December 2003.

A third group, the CPP-NPA, was designated by the United States and its European allies as a terrorist organization primarily for its extortion and kidnap-for-ransom activities (U.S. Department of State 2001).

The Philippine government has adopted measures to coordinate the efforts of its various security agencies (Tolin 2002). However, the most critical quandary in this drive is the lack of sophisticated counterterrorist equipment of its military personnel. In this regard, the designation of the Philippines as a major non-NATO ally by the United States favorably positions the country to acquire military materials and antiterrorist training for its armed forces.

Relationship with the United States

The Philippines became a colony of the United States by virtue of the 1898 Treaty of Paris. The United States consolidated its hold over the archipelago by subduing the native forces in the Philippine-American War of 1899–1902 (Linn 2000). Eventually, a transitional mechanism—the Commonwealth government—was created through the Tydings-McDuffie Act of 1934. After World War II, the United States granted independence to the Philippines on July 4, 1946.

Several treaties linked the two economies after independence, though these agreements heavily favored U.S. interests (Dolan 2003a, 62–63). Currently, the United States is still the Philippines' foremost trading partner. In 2001, the Philippines exported U.S.$8.834 billion worth of goods to the United States, mostly semiconductor devices, computer peripherals, and garments. Its imports from the United States amounted to U.S.$4.988 billion (Hodgkinson 2004). Meanwhile, the Philippines was the United States' nineteenth-largest export market and its twentieth-largest supplier of goods in 2002. The United States has also been the Philippines' largest foreign investor. In 2002, U.S. investment in the country was estimated to be about $3.3 billion and constituted 22 percent of the Philippines' direct investment stock (U.S. Department of State 2003).

The Philippines has come to depend on the United States for the protection of its territorial integrity and political sovereignty. The United States was allowed to maintain its military bases in the Philippines under the 1947 MBA in exchange for commitments to train and fund the nascent Philippine armed forces under the MSA of 1947 and agreed under the 1952 MDT to come to the Philippines' aid in case of an armed attack. The Philippines fought with the United States in both the Korean and Vietnam wars.

In 1959, the MDT was amended in order to subject the agreement to five-year reviews. In 1991, the Upper House of the Philippines voted to reject a proposed extension. Consequently, U.S. aid to the Philippines gradually diminished as the United States looked for alternative arrangements to keep its military presence in the region (Caballero-Anthony 2003). In 1998, the Philippines concluded a VFA with the United States that provided the legal framework for joint military exercises and training of Filipino military personnel. In 2002, both countries entered into an MLSA that allowed the United States to pick up supplies from Manila for its military operations and to ask for logistical support from the Philippine armed forces, even for activities that lie outside the scope of the 1952 MDT, as long as it is mutually consented to by both states (Morada 2003).

The Philippines is an ardent supporter of the United States in its global war against terrorism and its military actions in the Persian Gulf, Afghanistan, and Iraq. The Philippines sent soldiers, police, and humanitarian workers to Iraq to be part of coalition peacekeeping forces. The Philippine-U.S. partnership against terrorism has intensified after it became evident that the Philippines had been penetrated by terrorist cells linked to al-Qaeda (Abuza 2003; Ressa 2003; U.S. Department of State 2003). Joint military exercises have been held annually in the southern part of the Philippines since 2001. Code-named Balikatan ("shoulder to shoulder"), the aim of the exercises were to develop the counterterrorist competency of the Philippine armed forces as well as to train Filipino military personnel on how to operate more sophisticated air and naval vessels. On May 20, 2003, the Philippines was designated by the United States as a major non-NATO ally, a designation that has been granted to other major U.S. security partners in the region such as Australia, Japan, and South Korea.

The Future

The Philippines is in the process of consolidating its democratic system after a series of events that polarized its society and necessitated instances of military intervention. Although the role of the military in politics has declined considerably in Asia (Alagappa 2001), the Philippines continues to be beset by military attempts at state seizure because of the inability of the political process to resolve the conflicting positions of political actors without fomenting a constitutional crisis. The cardinal challenge for the Philippine polity is to contain military interventionism through effective state governance.

Internally, the most salient security threat for the Philippines in the next few years will emanate from the actions of organizations linked with al-Qaeda and its regional network of terror. The MILF has renewed its demand for an independent Islamic state, and the military has yet to completely dismantle the remnants of the ASG in Mindanao.

There is a need for the Philippine government to invest heavily in supplying its military with more sophisticated counterterrorist equipment and to consolidate the efforts of its security agencies. However, the budget allocated for defense purposes had been at around 0.8 percent of the GDP for the past decade, and a dramatic increase in appropriation is unlikely in the future. Because of this, much of the upgrading of military equipment and competence would be sourced from military development packages from the United States, most likely resulting from the Philippines' designation as a major non-NATO ally.

Finally, the Philippines is expected to experience further challenges from rival claimants to the Spratly Islands archipelago. The Philippines would be hard-pressed to keep up with the military buildup of its competitors (Collins 2000; Valencia 1995) given the weakness of its economy and the traditional aversion of the state to invest in the armed forces. Seen in this light, the security umbrella provided by the United States has stunted the development of the Philippine armed forces, as the military was forced to develop competency in dealing with domestic rather than external threats. The Philippines will spend the next few years "playing catch up," pin-ning its hopes on the resilience of the Filipino nation and the munificence of Washington.

References, Recommended Readings, and Websites

Books

Abinales, Patricio. 2000. *Making Mindanao.* Quezon City, Philippines: ADMU Press.

Abuza, Zachary. 2003. *Militant Islam in Southeast Asia.* Boulder, CO: Lynne Rienner.

Alagappa, Muthiah, ed. 2001. *Coercion and Governance: The Declining Role of the Military in Asia.* Stanford, CA: Stanford University Press.

Baker, Richard, and Charles Morrison. 2002. "Regional Overview." In *Asia-Pacific Outlook 2002,* Christopher McNally and Charles Morrison, eds. Tokyo: Japan Center for International Exchange.

Bertrand, Jacques. 2003. "Good Governance and the Security of Ethnic Communities in Indonesia and the Philippines." In *Development and Security in Southeast Asia,* David Dewitt and Carolina Hernandez, eds. Aldershot, UK: Ashgate.

Bresnan, John, ed. 1987. *Crisis in the Philippines: The Marcos Era and Beyond.* Princeton, NJ: Princeton University Press.

Brown, Ian. 2004. "History-Philippines." In *The Far East and Australasia 2004.* New York: Europa Publications.

Caballero-Anthony, Mely. 2003. "The Winds of Change in the Philippines: Whither the Strong Republic?" In *Southeast Asian Affairs 2003.* Singapore: Institute of Southeast Asian Studies.

Calit, Henry, ed. 2003. *The Philippines: Current Issues and Historical Background.* New York: Nova Publishers.

Carino, Ledivina. 1988. "The Land and the People." In *Government and Politics of the Philippines,* Raul de Guzman and Mila Reforma, eds. Singapore: Oxford University Press.

Casper, Gretchen. 1995. *Fragile Democracies: The Legacies of Authoritarian Rule.* Pittsburgh: University of Pittsburgh Press.

Catley, Robert, and Makmur Keliat. 1997. *Spratlys and the Dispute in the South China Sea.* Aldershot, UK: Ashgate.

Chalk, Peter. 2002. "Militant Islamic Extension in the Southern Philippines." In *Islam in Asia,* Jason Isaacson and Colin Rubenstein, eds. New Brunswick, NJ: Transaction Press.

Che Man, W. K. 1990. *Muslim Separatism: The Moros of Southern Philippines and the Malays of Southern Thailand.* Quezon City, Philippines: ADMU Press.

Clamor, Ma. Concepcion. 2003. "The Philippine Response." In *Terrorism in the Asia-Pacific: Threat and Response,* Rohan Gunatartna, ed. Singapore: Eastern Universities Press.

Collins, Allan. 2000. *The Security Dilemmas of Southeast Asia.* New York: St. Martin's Press.

Davide, Hilario, Carolina Hernandez, Ricardo Romulo, Delfin Lazaro, and Christian Monsod. 1990. *Report of the Fact Finding Commission.* Makati, Philippines: Bookmark.

Demaine, Harvey. 2004. "Physical and Social Geography-Philippines." In *The Far East and Australasia 2004.* New York: Europa Publications.

Dolan, Ronald. 2003a. "Philippines: A Country Study." In *The Philippines: Current Issues and Historical Background,* Harry Calit, ed. New York: Nova Publishers.

———. 2003b. "The Philippines: Facts at a Glance." In *The Philippines: Current Issues and Historical Background,* Harry Calit, ed. New York: Nova Publishers.

Doronila, Amando. 2001. *The Fall of Joseph Estrada.* Pasig City, Philippines: Anvil Publications.

George, T. J. S. 1980. *Revolt in Mindanao: The Rise of Islam in Philippine Politics.* Kuala Lumpur, Malaysia: Oxford University Press.

Gunaratna, Rohan. 2002. *Inside Al Qaeda: Global Network of Terror.* New York: Berkley Books.

———. 2003. "Preface." In *Terrorism in Asia-Pacific.* Rohan Gunaratna, ed. Singapore: Eastern University Press.

Hedman, Eva-Lotta. 2001. "The Philippines: Not So Military, Not So Civil." In *Coercion and Governance:*

The Declining Role of the Military in Asia, Muthiah Alagappa, ed. Stanford, CA: Stanford University Press.

Hodgkinson, Edith. 2004. "Economy-Philippines." In *The Far East and Australasia 2004.* New York: Europa Publications.

Huntington, Samuel. 1996. "Reforming Civilian-Military Relations." In *Civil-Military Relations and Democracy,* Larry Diamond and Marc Plattner, eds. Baltimore, MD: Johns Hopkins University Press.

Indorf, Hans. 1984. *Impediments to Regionalism in Southeast Asia.* Singapore: Institute of Southeast Asian Studies.

Institute of Southeast Asian Studies. 2003. *Southeast Asian Affairs 2003.* Singapore: Institute of Southeast Asian Studies.

International Institute for Strategic Studies (IISS). 2003. *The Military Balance 2003–2004.* London: Oxford University Press.

Jones, Gregg. 1989. *Red Revolution.* Boulder, CO: Westview.

Jubair, Salah. 1999. *Bangsamoro: A Nation under Endless Tyranny.* Malaysia: Marin Press.

Kerkvliet, Benedict. 1977. *The Huk Rebellion.* Berkeley: University of California Press.

Layador, Rowena. 2002. "Philippines." In *Asia-Pacific Outlook 2002,* Christopher McNally and Charles Morrison, eds. Tokyo: Japan Center for International Exchange.

Leifer, Michael. 1996. *The ASEAN Regional Forum: Extending ASEAN's Model of Regional Security.* New York: Oxford University Press.

Linn, Brian McAllister. 2000. *The Philippine War 1899–1902.* Lawrence: University of Kansas Press.

Magno, Alexander, Conrado de Quiros, and Rene Ofreneo. 1986. *The February Revolution.* Quezon City, Philippines: Karrel Press.

Majul, Cesar. 1973. *Muslims in the Philippines.* Quezon City, Philippines: UP Press.

———. 1985. *Contemporary Muslim Movements in the Philippines.* Berkeley, CA: Mizan.

Marohomsalic, Nasser. 2001. *Aristocrats of the Malay Race: History of the*

Bangsa Moro in the Philippines. Marawi, Philippines: MSV Press.

McKenna, Thomas. 1998. *Muslims, Rulers and Rebels.* Berkeley: University of California Press.

Morada, Noel M. 2003. "Philippine American Security Relations after 11 September: Exploring the Mutuality of Interests in the Fight against International Terrorism." In *Southeast Asian Affairs 2003.* Singapore: Institute of Southeast Asian Studies.

Niksh, Larry. 2003a. "Abu Sayyaf: Target of Philippine-U.S. Anti-Terrorism Cooperation." In *The Philippines: Current Issues and Historical Background,* Harry Calit, ed. New York: Nova Publishers, pp. 3–10.

———. 2003b. "Philippine-U.S. Security Relations." In *The Philippines: Current Issues and Historical Background,* Harry Calit, ed. New York: Nova Publishers.

Reeve, Simon. 1999. *The New Jackals: Ramzi Yousef, Osama bin Laden and the Future of Terrorism.* Boston: Northeastern University Press.

Reid, Robert, and Eileen Guerrero. 1995. *Corazon Aquino and the Brushfire Revolution.* Baton Rouge: Louisiana State University Press.

Ressa, Maria. 2003. *Seeds of Terror: An Eyewitness Account of Al-Qaeda's Newest Center of Operations in Southeast Asia.* New York: Free Press.

Rocamora, Joel. 1994. *Breaking Through: The Struggle within the Communist Party of the Philippines.* Pasig, Philippines: Anvil.

Sahni, Ajai. 2003. "The Locus of Terror: Has the Gravity of Terrorism Shifted in Asia?" In *Terrorism in the Asia-Pacific: Threat and Response,* Rohan Gunatartna, ed. Singapore: Eastern Universities Press.

Santiago, Angela Stuart. 1995. *1986: Chronology of a Revolution.* Manila: Foundation for Worldwide People Power.

Santos, Soliman. 2001. *The Moro Islamic Challenge: Constitutional Rethinking of the Mindanao Peace Process.* Quezon City: University of the Philippines Press.

Schweitzer, Yoram, and Shaul Shay. 2003. *Globalization of Terror.* New Brunswick, NJ: Transaction Press.

Sison, Jose Maria. 1971. *Philippine Society and Revolution.* Hong Kong: Ta Kung Pao.

Stockholm International Peace Research Institute (SIPRI). 2003. *SIPRI Yearbook 2003.* New York: Oxford University Press.

Tan, Andrew. 2000. *Intra-ASEAN Tensions.* London: Royal Institute of International Affairs.

Timberman. David. 1992. *A Changeless Land.* Singapore: Institute of Southeast Asian Studies.

Valencia, Mark. 1995. *China and the South China Sea Disputes.* New York: Oxford University Press.

Van Dyke, Mark, and Noel Ludwig. 1997. *Sharing the Resources of the South China Sea.* The Hague: Kluwer Law International.

Vitug, Maritess Danguilan, and Glenda M. Gloria. 2000. *Under the Crescent Moon: Rebellion in Mindanao.* Quezon City, Philippines: Ateneo Center for Social Policy and Public Affairs and Institute for Popular Democracy.

Wah, Chin Kin. 2003. "Southeast Asia in 2002: From Bali to Iraq—Cooperating for Security." In *Southeast Asian Affairs 2003.* Singapore: Institute of Southeast Asian Studies.

World Almanac. 2004. "Philippines." *World Almanac Book of Facts.* New York: World Almanac Books.

Articles/Newpapers

Balacuit, Jimmy. 1994. "Muslim Rebellion in Southern Philippines Revisited." *Mindanao Forum* 9, no. 1:1–29.

Conde, Carlos. 2002. "Texting Is as Good as Calling for Filipinos." *International Herald Tribune,* April 28, 2003.

De Castro, Renato. 2000. "The Legality of the People's Republic of China's Claim to the Spratlys." *Philippine Political Science Journal* 21:27–56.

Hernandez, Carolina. 1985. "The Philippine Military and Civilian Control under Marcos and Beyond." *Third World Quarterly* 7:903–919.

———. 1997. "The Military and Constitutional Change: Problems and Prospects in a Redemocratized Philippines." *Public Policy* 1:42–61.

Kamlian, Jamail. 1995. "MNLF Identity and Attitudinal Perspectives." *Mindanao Forum* 10:1–28.

Macansantos, Rosello. 1996. "Building the Culture of Peace in Southern Philippines: Retrospect and Prospects." *Mindanao Forum* 11:47–60.

Molloy, Ivan. 1988. "Decline of MNLF in Southern Philippines." *Journal of Contemporary Asia* 18, no. 1:59–76.

Nemenzo, Francisco. 1986. "A Season of Coups: Military Intervention in Politics." *Diliman Review* 54:1–25.

Trinkunas, Harold. 1999. "Ensuring Democratic Civilian Control of the Armed Forces in Asia." *East West Center Occasional Papers* 1:1–29.

Websites

Armed Forces of the Philippines. 2002. *AFP Organization.* http://www.afp.mil.ph (accessed February 20, 2004).

Association of Southeast Asian Nations (ASEAN). 1992. *ASEAN Declaration of the South China Sea.* http://www.aseansec.org/3634.htm (accessed February 11, 2004).

———. 2001. *2001 ASEAN Declaration to Counter Terrorism.* http://www.aseansec.org/3638.htm (accessed February 8, 2004).

———. 2004. *ASEAN Overview.* http://www.aseansec.org/92.htm (accessed February 21, 2004).

Carlos, Clarita. 2001. *Challenges Facing Asia-Pacific Defense and Military Leaders in the 21st Century: Focus on Budgets.* http://www.defense.gov.au/adc/Conference_Papers/National%20Resources%2-Presentation.ppt (accessed February 16, 2004).

Central Intelligence Agency (CIA). 2003. *World Factbook: Philippines.* http://www.odci.gov/cia/publications/factbook/print/rp.html (accessed February16, 2004).

Congressional Planning and Budget Department. 2004. *An Analysis of the President's Budget for Fiscal Year 2003.* http://www.congress.gov.ph/download/12th/budget2003.pdf (accessed February 11, 2004).

Correlates of War 2. 2004. *Inter-State War Participants.* http://cow2.la.psu.edu (accessed February 11, 2004).

Department of Budget and Management. 2004. *Armed Forces of the Philippines: Appropriations 2003.* http://www.dbm.gov.ph/dbm_publications/nep_2004/bpms_files/DND-afp-ghq.txt (accessed February 8, 2004).

Flores, Rose Shiela. 2001. *The Challenge of a Constitutional Revision in Japan and Its Implications on Asian Security.* http://www.ncdp.edu.ph/ppapers/nppindex.htm (accessed February 27, 2004).

National Statistics Office. 2000. *Census 2000.* http://www.census.gov.ph (accessed February 11, 2004).

Official Website of the Republic of the Philippines: http://www.gov.ph

Philippine Air Force http://www.paf.mil.ph.

Philippine Army http://www.army.mil.ph.

Philippine Department of Finance: http://www.dof.gov.ph.

Philippine Department of Foreign Affairs: http://www.dfa.gov.ph.

Philippine Department of National Defense. 2004. *The National Internal Security Plan.* http://www.dnd.gov.ph/nisp.htm (accessed February 8, 2004).

Philippine National Statistics Office: http://www.census.gov.ph.

Philippine Navy http://www.navy.mil.ph.

Teodoro, Luis. 2003. *The Coup Next Time.* http://www.worldpress.org/Asia/1384.cfm (accessed February 27, 2004).

Tolin, Francisco. 2002. *Territorial Issues in the South China Sea.* http://www.ncdp.edu.ph/ppapers/nppindex.htm (accessed February 11, 2004).

U.S. Department of State. 2001. *Background Information on Terrorist Groups.* http://www.state.gov/s/ct/rls/pgtrpt/2000/2450.htm (accessed February 8, 2004).

———. 2003. *Background Note: Philippines.* http://www.state.gov/r/pa/ei/bgn/2794.htm (accessed March 26, 2004).

Vanzi, Sol Jose. 2004. *Military Coup Attempt Nipped in the Bud.* http://www.newsflash.org/2003/05/h1/h1019759.htm (accessed February 20, 2004).

Poland

Elizabeth P. Coughlan

Geography and History

Polish geography is dominated by broad open plains and lowlands rising to the Carpathian Mountains in the south, including the Tatry, Beskidy, and Sudety mountain ranges. The plains of central and northern Poland are drained to the north into the Baltic Sea by the Vistula and Oder river systems. With a territory of 312,685 sq. km and a population of almost 39 million, Poland is a significant medium-sized central European country. As a result of the Holocaust, border changes, and the expulsion of the German minorities after World War II, Poland is ethnically 98 percent Polish and 95 percent Roman Catholic. The climate is typically continental: temperate with cold, cloudy, moderately severe winters with frequent precipitation; mild summers with frequent showers and thundershowers (CIA *World Factbook* 2003).

The written history of Poland as a unified power begins with the establishment of the Piast Dynasty in 966 C.E., when Mieszko I accepted Catholic baptism and introduced scribes to his court. The contribution of the crown for the coronation of Mieszko's son, Bolesław, by Pope John XIX marked the acceptance of Poland into the realm of Christendom where it continued as a significant regional player until 1795, when it was partitioned among its neighbors, Austria, Prussia, and Russia. Militarily, Poland continued to be significant during the period between 1795 and 1918 as it was the site of many military uprisings, particularly against czarist rule. Poles flocked to fight with Napoleon during his campaigns against Austria and Russia and fought on both sides during World War I. At the end of World War I, the Poles lobbied successfully for the establishment of an independent Poland, which soon found itself at war with Lithuania and then with the Soviet Union. The war against the Soviet Union was part of Lenin's plan to start revolution in Germany and went badly for the Poles until the Battle of Warsaw, also referred to as the Miracle on the Vistula, which is seen as one of the important turning points in the history of Western society and pointed to by many Polish patriots as the second time that Poland had saved Western culture from an Eastern menace (the first being at the walls of Vienna in 1683).

This is an important point, as the Poles have always seen themselves as part of Western culture and often bristle at being referred to as eastern European. They are quick to point out that Poland is at the center of the continent, measured both north to south and east to west. Indeed, Poland is the great plain through which anyone seeking to control the continent must pass, which explains much of its

Table 1   Poland: Key Statistics

Type of government	Constitutional republic
Population (millions)	38.622 (2003)
Religion	Roman Catholic 95% (about 75% practicing), Eastern Orthodox, Protestant, and other 5%
Main industries	Machine building, iron and steel, coal mining, chemicals, shipbuilding, food processing, glass, beverages, textiles
Main security threats	Unrest in neighboring countries, nuclear terrorism
Defense spending (% GDP)	2.0% (2003)
Size of military (thousands)	147 (2003)
Number of civil wars since 1945	Pacification of noncommunist opposition lasted until 1948, martial law imposed 1981–1983
Number of interstate wars since 1945	0

Sources
Central Intelligence Agency Website. 2003. CIA *World Factbook.* http://www.cia.gov/cia/ publications/factbook/ (accessed February 20, 2004).
Polish Ministry of Defense Website. http://www.wp.mil.pl/start.php?page=1000000001 (accessed February 25, 2004).

hardship over the past century. Much of the fighting of both world wars took place on Polish soil, and during the Cold War, the Poles were host to multiple Soviet garrisons acting as the advance lines of defense for the Soviet Union. The modern Polish state was established on November 11, 1918. Poland was invaded and divided by Nazi Germany and the Soviet Union in 1939. The country suffered extraordinarily under both occupiers, losing the largest percentage of population of any participants in World War II and experiencing the destruction of 90 percent of the capital city of Warsaw as retribution for the Warsaw Uprising in August 1944. Liberated in 1945 by the Soviets, Poland came under increasing Soviet influence and pressure to establish a communist state. Although there was resistance on the part of the Home Army and ethnic Ukrainian groups, by 1948 the country was pacified and a Soviet-style government established. Poland was anchored in the Soviet camp as a major component of the Warsaw Treaty Organi-

zation (WTO) and the Council for Mutual Economic Assistance (COMECON). In spite of this, there were incidents of political unrest in 1956, 1968, 1970, and 1976, culminating with the crisis that the led to formation of the opposition group Solidarity in 1980–1981. Martial law was imposed in December 1981, ostensibly to prevent either civil war or Soviet invasion and pacification of this important western neighbor (see Table 2 for a chronology of events at this time).

Economically, the country limped along until 1989 when the communist government under General Wojciech Jaruzelski began negotiations with leaders of the outlawed Solidarity trade union. Those negotiations resulted in limited free elections in June 1989 and the appointment in August of the first noncommunist prime minister in the post–World War II era. Free presidential elections in 1990 led to the replacement of Jaruzelski by Solidarity-era hero Lech Wałęsa. A new constitution came into effect on October 16, 1997.

Table 2   Chronology of Events during the Solidarity Crisis

1980	July	Increase in meat prices causes protests and strikes across Poland
	August	80,000 workers take over Lenin Shipyards in Gdańsk; Lech Wałęsa heads negotiations for strikers demanding the establishment of a free trade union; Gierek resigns; party leadership reorganized; agreement reached on workers' rights to strike and to form independent trade unions
	September	Stanisław Kania named new party leader; independent trade union Solidarity is formed
	October	Solidarity legalized
	November	Warsaw Pact forces maneuver near Polish border
	December	Meat rationing, austerity plan introduced; strikes called off as Warsaw Pact troops mass on border
1981	February	General Wojciech Jaruzelski named prime minister, pleads for ninety days of social peace; students form an independent union
	March	Warsaw Pact maneuvers extended; strikes begin anew; United States and EEC extend aid to Poland, reschedule Polish debt payments; United States issues warning to USSR against interference in Poland; Solidarity activist accused of disrupting meeting at Bydgoszcz and was beaten
	April	Other Warsaw Pact governments criticize Polish reforms
	June	Ninth Extraordinary Party Congress meets, calls for change in party and society, generally well received
	September	Strikes continue; government warns of crackdown
	October	Solidarity pleads for unity; Jaruzelski replaces Kania as first secretary; Polish army deployed in regional and metropolitan operational groups in an attempt to keep the economy on line
	November	Strikes end; discussions begin between state and Solidarity
	December	Solidarity makes new demands for free elections, access to media, limiting of planned economy, threatens twenty-four-hour general strike for December 17
	December 13	Martial law is declared, Solidarity leaders are interned; strikes are crushed; eleven miners are killed at the Wujek Mine in Silesia; Military Council for National Salvation formed

The Republic of Poland is a weakly semipresidential system with a directly elected head of state and a council of ministers lead by the prime minister as head of government. The National Assembly is a bicameral legislature with an upper house or *Senat* consisting of 100 members elected from single-member districts on a provincial basis and a lower (and far more powerful) house or *Sejm* consisting of 460 members elected by proportional representation.

The main issue facing the postcommunist governments has been economic reform. Under the leadership of Prime Minister Tadeusz Mazowiecki, Poland implemented a program of "shock therapy" beginning on January 1, 1990. The idea was to rationalize and stabilize the economy as quickly as possible in order for restructuring to begin. Privatization of state-held assets was begun quickly but has proceeded in fits and starts. As might be expected, agriculture remains an important aspect of the Polish economy, providing employment for 27 percent of the population. However, a strong indicator of the issues endemic to the Polish economy is the fact that this sector also accounted for only 3.8 percent of the gross domestic product (GDP) in 2000 (CIA *World Factbook* 2003). Industry accounted for 35 percent, while services made up the other 61 percent. Under Soviet dominance following World War II, Poland was the only one of the central and eastern European countries whose agricultural sector remained largely in private hands. These small and inefficient landholdings were a source of stability during communism but now prove to be something of a stumbling block to both modernization of the Polish economy and full integration into the European Union (EU). Politically, the farmers are too important to ignore, but their political demands tend to run counter to the interests of the country as a whole. The agricultural sector is in sore need of reform, but this is a potentially explosive issue. It was not helped by the fact that Polish farmers stood to receive only 25 percent of the subsidy available to French farmers when Poland became a member of the EU in April 2004.

In general, the Polish economy suffers from two major problems: a low GDP (purchasing power parity, $9,700 [CIA *World Factbook* 2003]) and high unemployment (20 percent in February 2004 [Główny Urząd Statystyczny 2004]). Although the GDP is competitive by eastern European standards, it is lower than that of Poland's central European neighbors and very low compared to long-term EU members. Issues include restructuring health care, education, and pensions as well as the ongoing battle over privatization of state sectors. Poland's largest

export partners are Germany, 33 percent; Italy, 5.7 percent; France, 5 percent; the United Kingdom, 4.8 percent; and the Czech Republic, 4.3 percent (2002 figures). Exports have a total value of $32.4 billion free on board (2002 figure). Poland's main import partners are Germany, 29.9 percent; Italy, 8.1 percent; Russia, 7.4 percent; France, 7.2 percent; and the Netherlands, 5.3 percent (2002 figures). Imports have a total value of $43.4 billion free on board (2002 figure). External debt totals $64 billion (2002 figure) (CIA *World Factbook* 2003). However, to place these numbers somewhat in perspective, it might be helpful to know that although Germany is Poland's most important trade partner, Germany does less than 2 percent of its trading with Poland.

Regional Geopolitics

There have been enormous changes in the security situation facing Poland over the last fifteen years. After World War II, bordered to the east by the Soviet Union, to the south by Czechoslovakia, and to the west by the German Democratic Republic, Poland was firmly enmeshed in the WTO and bordered on all sides by ostensible allies. This situation changed radically in the early 1990s when the Soviet Union fell apart, the Czechs and Slovaks parted ways, and Germany reintegrated. Instead of three neighbors, Poland now has seven (the Federal Republic of Germany, the Czech Republic, Slovakia, Ukraine, Belarus, Lithuania, and the Russian Federation). Before 1989, the Poles were surrounded by allies; now Poland's eastern border constitutes the current front line of the North Atlantic Treaty Organization (NATO). This new situation has placed significant demands for change on the Polish military establishment. Beginning in 1990, the Poles reformulated their national security policy to reflect the uncertainties of the new geopolitical configuration. The Polish government has moved swiftly and expended considerable resources to bring the military into line with the requirements of participation in NATO, making it clear that Polish security in the twenty-first century could only be achieved in the context of a multinational military alliance.

This insistence has two sources: Germany and the Russian Federation. The lesson of Polish history has been that the country must be aligned with one neighbor or the other lest the two conspire against it. It is this reality that led the Mazowiecki government to drag its feet over calling for the removal of Soviet troops in 1990, when the Kohl government was refusing to guarantee the Oder-Neisse Line as the border between a newly unified Germany and Poland. It is also this reality that caused Poland to hesitate in drawing down its forces in the early 1990s when former Soviet troops withdrawn from East Germany and Poland were massed in Kaliningrad (the small chunk of Russian territory between Lithuania and Poland). Polish awareness that the Russians had more troops in Kaliningrad than the Poles had men under arms led to reluctance to begin immediate restructuring. As economic factors have caused the Russians to restructure, the Poles have been more willing to do so. Restructuring the military, in particular implementing a comprehensive system of civilian control, was also one of the basic prerequisites for NATO membership.

As the easternmost border of NATO, Poland has been careful to balance its role in regional affairs. The government has made a commitment to advocate for the security and economic needs of Poland's neighbors to the east, just as Germany advocated for Poland, along with Hungary and the Czech Republic. The Polish government maintains cordial relationships with Ukraine and Belarus while at the same time expressing concern about the political situations in both countries. The government also works on behalf of the Polish minority in Lithuania (a significant portion of the population of Vilnius is ethnically Polish) while respecting the sovereignty of Lithuania as an independent state.

Conflict Past and Present
Conflict History
Military conflict plays a prominent part in Polish history and in Polish national consciousness. The *hajnał,* a trumpet fanfare broadcast daily at noon across the country, commemorates the death of a Cracovian sentry brought down in the middle of his warning by Mongol invaders in 1241. However, as devastating as the Mongol raids were, they were worse for the unity of Kievan Rus to the east, and Poland was able to expand in power and territory at Russia's expense. The other early source of conflict were the Teutonic Knights, invited by Conrad of Mazovia to help quell the pagan Prussian tribes on the Baltic coast. Having accomplished that, they soon expanded their territory at Polish expense, claiming most of the coastland along the Baltic. At the same time, Poland was menaced from the south by Bohemia, whose princes were to control roughly two-thirds of Poland's territory by the end of the 1300s. A solution was sought in a political union with Lithuania that was to last four centuries.

Beginning with a devastating victory over the Teutonic Knights at the Battle of Grünwald in 1410, the Polish-Lithuanian Commonwealth enjoyed a long span as a dominant power in central Europe, coming to rule over the territory of Bohemia and Hungary as well. The decline of this dominance began with the Battle of Mohacs in 1526, which established the Ottoman Turks as a power in the southeastern quadrant of Europe.

By the time of the Treaty of Westphalia in 1638, Poland was entering an era of conflict and disaster referred to as the Deluge. An uprising by Ukrainian Cossacks opened the door for Russian predation on Polish territory at the same time Charles X of Sweden began a military drive to the south. The Poles were eventually able to drive the Swedes out, but the territorial losses to the Russians were not recovered, and ongoing battles with the Turks contributed to the decline of the Commonwealth as the modern era began. Victorious at the gates of Vienna in 1683, Poland failed miserably in the long-run task of protecting its territorial integrity from its neighbors. The main causes of this were not military, but rather two peculiar artifacts of the Polish-Lithuanian Commonwealth: the elected monarchy and the *liberum veto*, which allowed any member of the gentry to stand in the way of a law with which he disagreed.

Beginning in 1772, Poland was successively partitioned among its neighbors: Prussia, Russia, and Austria. The last partition was carried out in response to a military uprising in 1794 led by Tadeusz Kościusko, hero of the American War of Independence. Even though it ceased to exist as a unified political entity, Poland continued to have military significance in Europe, most particularly during the Napoleonic Wars. Napoleon established an independent Duchy of Warsaw, and the Poles enthusiastically supported his campaigns, believing that his success would result in renewed independence for the country. The lingering effects of the sentiments encouraged by Napoleon can be seen in the history of military revolts occurring in 1830, 1846, and 1863.

Polish romanticism kept the idea of an independent Poland alive, although there were disputes about how to best achieve such a thing. In the early twentieth century, there was a deep split between those who favored achieving autonomy through cooperation with the dominant countries and those who favored pursuing a more revolutionary strategy. World War I found a large number of Poles willing to throw their lot in with the occupiers against the other side. A total of 2 million Polish troops fought with the armies of the three occupying powers, and 450,000 died (Library of Congress, *Poland: A Country Study*). The outcome of the war was the collapse of Austria-Hungary, the diminishment of Germany, the withdrawal of Russia (occupied by its own revolutionary events), and the liberation of many of the peoples of central Europe, including the Poles.

Newly independent Poland's western, southern, and northern borders were dictated by the Treaty of Versailles. Its eastern borders were not determined until the Treaty of Riga (1921) ended the conflict between Poland and Lenin's Soviet Union. This treaty ended the conflict, but not the tension among Poland and its neighbors. Interwar Poland was 68 percent Polish, and the other populations tended to be viewed with hostility, as possible fifth columns. The terms of the Treaty of Versailles were a source of great irritation to the Germans, who viewed their losses in Silesia and along the Baltic coast with great resentment. Ultimately, this resentment led to the invasion of Poland in September 1939, signaling the beginning of World War II.

Germany invaded Poland on September 1, 1939, and the Soviets followed suit on September 17. Although the Poles were outnumbered and woefully underarmed, they managed to resist far longer than Hitler had foreseen. Both France and Britain declared war on Germany, but neither offered any effective help to the beleaguered Poland. There are myriad stories of military and civilian heroism including apocryphal tales of Polish cavalry fighting German panzers. Polish underground resistance continued throughout the war, inflicting serious casualties on Nazi forces. Poles able to escape to unoccupied Europe enlisted in the military as they were able and contributed significantly to the Allied effort. In particular, the Polish contribution to the Battle of Britain is noteworthy, with Polish pilots compiling the highest hit rate against Nazi aircraft.

Germany's invasion of the Soviet Union in 1941 changed things for the Poles in that those who had found themselves in Soviet-occupied territory in 1939 were now allowed to contribute to the war effort. Those who were able to arrive at the conscription point in time were evacuated through Iran as part of the Polish First Army under Władysław Anders. These forces played an important role in Africa and on the Italian front, particularly at the Battle of Monte Cassino. Those coming later were kept in the Soviet Union as part of the Polish Second Army under Zygmunt Berling and fought side by side with the Red Army on the Eastern Front. It was the formation of these two armies that first brought international attention to the fate of 15,000 Polish officers missing since September 1939. The discovery of a mass grave in the forests at Katyń confirmed the whereabouts of 4,000 of these officers. The Soviets insisted that they must have been murdered by the Nazis after 1942 (see Sidebar 1). The Nazis and independent observers claimed that the murders had been carried out earlier, while the territory was under Soviet control. Disputes over responsibility for this travesty were the immediate cause of the cessation of diplomatic relations between Stalin and the Polish government in exile, which allowed Stalin to create a provisional government dominated by Polish communists. (Documentation made available by Boris Yeltsin in 1991 proved that Stalin had ordered these murders. It also led to the location and examination of other graves associated with the incident.)

Sidebar 1   Katyń

The Soviet-allied Polish government censored all mention of the officers murdered at Katyń after 1948, but Poles kept the memory alive along with that of the Soviets' refusal to help during the Warsaw Uprising. The Soviet government's version pointed to the Germans as the villains, but Polish popular culture held Stalin responsible. The actual number killed (in excess of 12,000), and the fact that most of the officers were reservists, meant that the murders had eliminated a large segment of the Polish intelligentsia. A proper monument for the victims of Katyń was one of Solidarity's demands in 1981 and the issue continues to be a source of friction between the Polish and Russian governments.

More than any other country, Poland suffered enormous losses in World War II. Three million Polish Jews perished in the Holocaust, and almost as many Polish gentiles perished with them. One and a half million Polish citizens were sent to labor camps in the Soviet Union, and roughly 2.5 million were sent to camps in Germany. Poles were forcibly removed from their homes in territories occupied by both the Soviets and the Nazis. There was significant material damage done both as a result of the war and as retribution for Polish resistance to Nazi occupation. The Warsaw Uprising in 1944 resulted in the Germans' systematic depopulation and razing of the city. No sooner had the Germans finished than the Soviet military, which had been camped on the eastern bank of the Vistula River during the uprising, entered and "liberated" the city. Soviet failure to act sooner in the aid of Warsaw would be an ongoing source of friction between Poles and the Soviets. Although the Soviets argued that German bombardment of the eastern bank made it impossible to establish a bridgehead, Poles remained sure that the Red Army had purposely waited for the Germans to destroy the larger part of the pro-Allied Home Army before advancing on the city. Soon after the liberation of Warsaw, the Soviets supported the establishment of a provisional government by the Polish Workers' Party.

Poland was fully liberated from German occupation by March 1945. This liberation came at the price of a second occupation; however, for now the country was fully under control of the Red Army and its Polish ally, the communist-inspired Polish People's Army. The People's Army assisted in the liberation of the country and in the pacification of the countryside. The years immediately following World War II were characterized by frequent battles with "bandits" (as the resistant remnants of the Home Army were called) and nationalist Ukrainians in the southeast of the country. By 1948, however, the Polish United Worker's Party was firmly in control of the government, and Poland was on its way to becoming the Soviet Union's most important (if least trusted) ally to the west. Military conflicts after 1948 were confined to minor crises such as the strikes in 1956 and in 1970 when troops were called out to subdue workers protesting rising costs. In 1968, Polish troops participated in the pacification of the Prague Spring. In December 1981, a swift and mostly effective military operation imposed martial law on the entire country, putting an end to the Solidarity crisis, which began with the increase of meat prices in late July 1980 (see Sidebar 2).

Sidebar 2   Societal Confidence in the Military

It is worth noting that, in spite of the Polish military's role in imposing and maintaining communist rule in Poland during the Cold War, the military was one of the most trusted institutions in the country, and was consistently outranked only by the Catholic Church. In 2004, the military is the most trusted institution in the country, as it has been since the Catholic Church lost its leading position in the early 1990s.

Source
Centrum Badania Opinii Społecznej: http://www.cbos.com.pl/SPISKOM.POL/2004/K_036_04.PDF.

*Current and Potential
Military Confrontation*

Currently, Poland has neither military confrontations nor even the real potential of a classical military confrontation on its own territory. Always wary of both Germany and Russia, the Poles have worked to maintain positive relations with all of their neighbors. Suspicion of Germany, along with the experience of German military effectiveness, is one of the motivating factors for both NATO and EU membership, but it is certainly not the overwhelming reason why the Poles have sought these. Rather the Poles seek to assure their place as a European country in the center of the European continent. Somewhat ironically, Germany has been the most active supporter of Polish accession to both of these institutions.

Current Polish security doctrine identifies the following issues as key to Polish security: international terrorism, proliferation of weapons of mass destruction, the rise of unforeseen authoritarian regimes, the disintegration of current regimes (which intensifies the threat of both terrorism and uncontrolled weapons proliferation), natural and human induced ecological catastrophes, and international organized crime. These basic changes in Poland's security environment demand a significant change in Poland's security preparations. The goal of Poland's foreign policy is to construct an international situation that will be favorable to Polish security. Among the most important tasks in this area are ensuring the efficacy of alliance structures of which Poland is a member and the effectiveness of international institutions and international law. Poland seeks to maintain friendly relations with all alliance partners, especially those countries directly neighboring Poland. The government is committed to support of transformational processes in southern and eastern Europe, international environmental protection efforts, and promotion of democracy and respect of human rights (Biuro Bezpieczeństwa 2003).

Alliance Structure

After World War II, the Polish military was firmly embedded in the WTO. Under the plans of that organization, Polish forces were to act as the forward defense in case of an attack by NATO forces toward the east, in particular the former Soviet Union. For this reason, the Polish military was one of the largest in Europe. Although the WTO was touted as an alliance among equals, it was clearly dominated by the Soviet Union, something many Polish officers claim to have chafed under. The WTO was formally disbanded in June 1991, but had been a dead entity for about a year before that. Poland began lobbying for NATO membership as soon as it could, but was instead offered membership in the Partnership for Peace, formed in 1994. Poland saw this as a short-term solution, but made it clear that this would be an unacceptable long-term alternative to NATO membership.

Poland, along with Hungary and the Czech Republic, became a member of NATO in April 1999. EU membership was achieved in May 2004. Polish national security doctrine makes it clear that membership in these two alliances is fundamental to Polish security. NATO is seen as the basic platform for bilateral and multilateral cooperation in security and defense issues as well as the main pillar of political and military stability on the continent. Poland is active at all levels in NATO and has representatives in various commands and staffs, as well as liaison teams to other commands and to the rapid reaction corps. In the period just prior and just after NATO accession, the main task was to divide the armed forces into components similar to those already used by NATO armies. Alliance norms have been adopted at the unit level, and a Polish contribution to the reaction forces was prepared. In 2000, Poland was asked to take on responsibilities similar to those shouldered by countries like Germany and the United Kingdom.

Preparation of Polish military units is a process that has required structural changes as well as a significant financial commitment. This is a task to be completed over the long term. For the moment, seven brigades and battalions from the army, six vessels from the navy, and three squadrons from the air force are ready to act within the NATO framework and are considered part of the alliance's rapid reaction forces. Polish troops have supported NATO activities in Bosnia, Albania, and Kosovo. In 2003, Polish troops took responsibility for the security of an entire sector in Iraq.

In addition to its commitment to NATO, Poland is fully prepared to act within the framework of the Common Foreign and Security Policy of the EU. More than that, Poland sees EU membership as fundamental to creating the basis for a security that extends well beyond military affairs to embrace cultural and economic issues. EU membership will strengthen Poland's ability to meet the security needs of its citizens in all aspects of a broadened conception of security (Polish National Security Doctrine 2003).

Size and Structure of the Military

The total size of the Polish armed forces (147,841, according to the Ministry of Defense's 2004 budget) was below projections for 2004. In 1989, the Polish armed forces numbered some 350,000 men under arms. It was expected that by 2006, it would number 150,000. This smaller military is in line with the changed perception of Polish security. No longer on the front line of Soviet defense, Polish military strategists no longer foresee the need to employ massive force in conventional warfare across its broad plains. Instead, the size and structure of the military is based on the need for small, rapidly mobile units capable of responding to modern security threats and the need to be interoperational with other NATO forces. The armed forces are largely professional, with fewer than 10,000 troops drawn from compulsory service.

The Polish armed forces are divided unequally into four branches: the army (87,877 troops), the air force (31,147 troops), and much smaller navy and territorial defense units. The tasks of the Polish army are to (1) defend the territory of the country, (2) deflect any hostile invasion and recover lost territory, and (3) protect strategic regions and objectives, defend lines of communication, and maintain operational freedom. To this end, the army consists of three mechanized divisions, an armored cavalry division, eight mechanized brigades, six armored brigades, two artillery brigades, two antimine brigades, a storm brigade, an air cavalry brigade, a coastal defense brigade, a brigade of mountain riflemen, two logistical brigades, and twenty-four military regiments. Within the army are also special information, psychological operations, and logistical units (Military Internet Gazette 2004). The army is located primarily in Bydgoszcz (on the Baltic coast) and Katowice (in Silesia). The navy consists of two coastal defense fleets, a fleet of battleships, and an air brigade. The fleets are made up of battleships and associated floating and coastal units. Polish fleets are stationed at the military ports of Gdynia, Świnoujście, Kołobrzeg, and Hel. The Polish air force is organized in two tactical brigades, nine tactical squadrons, thirty-six special transport regiments, two transport and communications squadrons, and thirteen transport squadrons. The air force is concentrated in Warsaw.

The Polish military has long played an active role in UN peacekeeping operations. More than 40,000 Polish soldiers have served in more than forty-six UN, NATO, Organization for Security and Cooperation in Europe, and EU peacekeeping and humanitarian missions. Originally, Polish contingents specialized in providing logistics such as medical services and sanitation. However, with the United Nations' Protection Force in Macedonia (UNPROFOR) in 1992, Poland was requested for the first time to provide an operational battalion, which was later incorporated into the Nordic-Polish Brigade under NATO's Implementation Force in Bosnia (IFOR). Poland is one of the largest contributors of troops to UN peacekeeping operations, with as many as 2,200 troops deployed in over fifteen missions at one time (Ilnicki n.d.). Poland currently has 740 military and civilian personnel engaged in missions in Côte d'Ivoire, the western Sahara, the Democratic Republic of Congo, the Golan Heights, southern Lebanon, Ethiopia and Eritrea, Kosovo, Liberia, and Georgia. The bulk of Polish peacekeeping forces serve in the Middle East ("Contributors to United Nations . . ." 2003).

Budget
The total budget for national defense for 2004 is $4.3 billion. Of that, $4.1 billion are designated for the Department of Defense in the national budget, $37 million are spent by the Ministry of Science and Technology on military research, $8.5 million are spent by the Ministry of Foreign Affairs on military representatives and attachés, and $7.9 million are the result of privatization activities of the defense sector of the economy. The four main spending priorities are modernization of military equipment ($755 million), ensuring Poland's contributions to peacekeeping missions, fulfilling Poland's obligations to its allies, particularly in NATO, and completing the reorganization of military units. Within the Ministry of Defense's budget, $2.9 billion are designated for national defense. Of this, $1.4 billion or 50.3 percent are for the army, $579 million or 20.48 percent are for the air force, and $261 million or 9.24 percent are for the navy ("Polish Ministry of Defense Budget," 2004). Poland's military spends a little over 30 percent on salaries and somewhere between 15 and 20 percent on capital improvements every year.

Polish military technology is of a high level. This is necessary because of the requirement of interoperability with NATO. Poland's efforts to bring their personnel and weaponry up-to-date were a priority even before the invitation to join NATO was official. The Poles are in the process of modernizing their equipment and purchasing new equipment abroad. The Polish and U.S. governments came to an agreement in July 2003 for the sale of forty-eight F-16 fighters. These planes are worth $3.5 billion, but the agreement includes a ten-year loan and forty-three offset agreements worth about $7.5 billion. The offset agreements will affect several Polish arms and aviation companies, including WSK Rzeszów (where the Pratt and Whitney engines will be built for use in the F-16s). The offsets will hopefully allow the United States and other international investors to bridge the barrier created by Polish industry's limited capabilities for implementing new technologies (Szymczak 2003).

It is hoped that these offsets, along with the ongoing restructuring of the defense industry, will lead to the recovery of this sector of the economy. Once the seventh-largest arms exporter in the world, Poland lost much of its market with the collapse of the Soviet Union. This, combined with the "zero sum option" adopted by the Polish government, according to which Soviet receivables due for Polish arms deliveries were forgiven in return for acquisition of the infrastructure of Soviet bases on Polish territory, led many Polish arms manufacturers into bankruptcy. The 2002 restructuring program concentrates the remaining manufacturers into two groups—one for ammunition, armor, and rockets and the other for aviation—and slows down plans for privatization in this sector. This restructuring and the increased attention paid by the government to promoting arms sales are already having an effect. According to the Ministry of the Treasury, in 2003 the value of special exports exceeded $86 million, $55 million of which went to companies belonging to the Polish defense industry. The year 2003 also saw the conclusion of contracts for the supplies of arms and military equipment for the sum of $180 million ("Growth of Arms Industry Export" 2004).

The Polish arms industry benefits as well from the need of many countries possessing Soviet-built arms to modernize their equipment. India recently signed a contract for the modernization of its T-72 tanks, and Poland expects to be a top competitor for the contract to modernize the T-72 tanks and other Soviet-era equipment possessed by the Iraqi military. In addition, contracts for new equipment are starting to arrive from Asia. Malaysia, which has already made an advance payment, will pay nearly $400 million for the supply of forty-eight PT-91M tanks. It is ironic that a major arms supplier cannot make use of its own product, but agreements are being worked out for the licensing of NATO-member technology to Polish factories. In addition to the planes, the Polish government has also purchased armored personnel carriers from the Finnish company Patria. It is expected that these will be produced at a factory in Silesia.

Civil-Military Relations/The Role of the Military in Domestic Politics

Poland has a minor history of military involvement in politics. The democratic nature of the Second Republic came to an end in 1926 when Marshall Józef Piłsudski assumed power in a military coup. Piłsudski's government had elements of military rule but was essentially the personalist regime of a historically active political figure. After Piłsudski's death in 1935, however, the regime became more openly authoritarian, especially in regard to the large minority population.

The military was also an important component of the post–World War II government. Military personnel "aided" in the elections that led to the establishment of the communist government in 1947, and the military was an important instrument in dealing with political unrest, playing a significant role in the crises of 1956, 1968, 1970, and 1976. The Solidarity crisis of 1981 was brought to an end by the imposition of martial law and the establishment of a Council of National Salvation dominated by high-ranking military officers. General Wojciech Jaruzelski, who emerged from the collective government to take control during the crisis, remained as head of state until presidential elections in 1990 led to his replacement by Solidarity hero Lech Wałęsa.

Under Wałęsa, the military participated publicly and vociferously in the debate over the distribution of power in the Polish political system. The crux of the issue was the division of power between the directly elected president and the prime minister. The *Sejm* expressed a strong preference for a parliamentary system of government and indeed had been experiencing something similar to that during Jaruzelski's tenure as president. After August 1989, Jaruzelski had stayed largely on the sidelines rather than taking advantage of the considerable powers of the presidency under the Round Table Agreements. When Wałęsa became president, he attempted to exercise those powers, arguing that Poland should be a semipresidential system along the lines of France rather than parliamentary. One of the focal points of this argument was civilian control of the military. Parliament believed that the Council of Ministers should exercise control through the minister of defense, while Wałęsa argued that as commander-in-chief, the president should exercise control through key appointments such as the chief of the general staff. Under General Tadeusz Wilecki, the military joined this debate publicly (see Sidebar 3). The issue was ended, however, when Wałęsa lost the presidential election to Aleksander Kwaśniewski, who signed the law making the general staff responsible to the minister of defense.

This new law was seen by most parliamentarians as necessary to Poland's long-

---

Sidebar 3   The Drawsko Affair

The so-called Drawsko Affair occurred when officers at a dinner in Drawsko Pomorskie declared their allegiance to chief of staff General Tadeusz Wilecki, and requested that Defense Minister Piotr Kołodziejczyk step down. A parliamentary commission declared the incident to be military interference in politics and recommended that the officers involved be reprimanded, but Wałęsa forced Kołodziejczyk into retirement instead.

The incident contributed to the collapse of the Pawlak government and was part of the ongoing struggle between president and Parliament that ended with Kwaśniewski's election. For a more complete account of the incident, see Andrew Michta, "Civil-Military Relations in Poland after 1989: The Outer Limits of Change," in *Problems of Post-Communism* (March–April 1997), at p. 62.

---

term interests, including joining NATO and the EU. Poland is committed to maintaining a defense system strong enough to allow a swift and effective response to all potential external security threats. It is also committed to active participation in ongoing international stabilization and conflict prevention activities. At the same time, Poland takes its commitments to NATO and the EU seriously when it comes to maintaining pluralist democratic guarantees. As a result, the Polish constitution of 1997 clearly guarantees democratic civilian oversight of the military. The president of the republic and the Council of Ministers are the primary governmental organs responsible for ensuring the defense of the country. The constitution charges the president with protecting Poland's sovereignty and security as well as the integrity of its borders and territory. The president is aided in this task by the National Security Council. The president is commander-in-chief of the armed forces.

The Council of Ministers, and in particular the prime minister as head of government, is responsible for formulating and carrying out domestic and foreign policies that will ensure national security, as well as for the general formulation and direction of defense policies. These are formulated with the help of the Council of Ministers' committee on defense issues. It is expected that the president and the prime minister will cooperate in the formulation and implementation of defense policies. In peacetime, military affairs are directed by the Council of Ministers through the minister of defense and the Ministry of Defense.

The general staff is the basic planning organ of the combined Polish armed forces. The leadership of each branch is represented, and they are responsible for directing the peacetime activities of the four branches, as well as ensuring their preparation to act in times of war or military crisis. This system ensures that in case of a political or military crisis threatening Polish security, there would be no need for an extraordinary shift in the leadership structures of the defense system but rather the activation of certain additional crisis procedures.

In the case of war, if the *Sejm* is unable to meet, the president, working with the Council of Ministers, would undertake necessary legislative functions. During wartime, the president, prime minister, and any appointed member of the Council of Ministers form a Central National Defense Leadership. The supreme wartime leader of the military is appointed by the president on the advice of the prime minister. This person is fully responsible for all Polish armed forces not designated for integration into joint NATO forces. Any Polish troops participating in NATO joint forces are under the leadership of those forces during wartime.

Terrorism

Poland does not have a problem with terrorism, nor does the country harbor terrorists, but it is an active participant in the U.S. global war on terrorism. There appears to be some concern that Poland could become a target of the kind of terrorist acts seen in the United States and Indonesia because of its strong level of support for the U.S. program, including hosting a conference on combating terrorism in Warsaw on November 6, 2001. Polish troops have been the target of terrorists in their sector in occupied Iraq.

Relationship with the United States

Poland has long enjoyed a strong and positive relationship with the United States. Polish patriots Kazimierz Pułaski and Tadeusz Kościusko made significant contributions to the American War of Independence. Polish immigration to the United States was strong throughout the nineteenth and early twentieth centuries. These immigrants maintained strong ties to home and were active in lobbying for Polish independence, a call that found resonance and support from President Woodrow Wilson. Wilson's support for Polish independence is remembered with gratitude, and most Poles assumed that the United States would continue that support. The Yalta Accords of February 1945 came as something of a shock, because the agreement clearly allowed the Soviets to exert their influence in the area. Regardless of this, however, and in spite of an alliance structure that declared the United States to be Poland's enemy, the relationship between the two countries remained reasonably cordial throughout the Cold War. As many as 3 million Poles traveled to the United States during this period, often staying and working illegally so that they could go home and build houses with the dollars they earned. Cultural exchanges continued even during the period of martial law.

Since 1989, the relationship between the two countries has continued to improve, in fact to the point that some members of the EU were concerned about Poland's accession. The fear was that Poland is too close an ally of the United States and would act as a proxy, particularly on foreign policy and security issues. Polish intellectuals and the Polish government have both been criticized for not always remembering that Europe can be a more important ally in the long run than the United States (Osica 2001). Indeed, the Poles have a somewhat utopian attitude toward the United States and continue in their belief that they will be recognized as important allies and that the United States will take care of them. In the early 1990s, Polish intellectuals in Warsaw expressed confidence that that United States would rush in with monetary and military aid to make up for Yalta. The general belief was that Yalta had been a mistake instead of a coldly calculated trade-off (the Soviets were guaranteed influence in Polish affairs as well as a chunk of what had been Polish territory in return for their promise to join the war against Japan). Even though it is true that Polish public opinion is highly supportive of the United States, it

is unlikely that Polish politicians or military officials will forget that their true interests lie on their eastern and western borders. The Polish drive to join both NATO and EU stems from their relationships with Germany and the Russian Federation as well as from a desire to please the United States.

The Future

Poland has entered the twenty-first century as a stable democracy and valued member of NATO. Its entry into the EU in May 2004 completes the return to Europe. Although this transition has not been without enormous costs and burdens, these are prices the Poles have clearly been willing to pay. The government and population have been in agreement on these goals, insisting that NATO and EU membership are crucial to Polish well-being and security. The Poles have worked to meet the responsibilities and burdens of membership, especially in the area of security. Their willingness can be seen most clearly in the shouldering of responsibility for an entire sector of occupied Iraq.

Since Polish security has come to be identified with participation in the two major European alliances, it is a safe prediction that future expenditures, plans, and personnel changes will be carried out in the context of these alliances as Poland continues to discharge its obligations as a geographically crucial member of these regional defense structures. The Poles will have to learn to balance their interests between the United States and Europe when these two are in dispute, but it is unlikely that they will ever be forced to make a definitive choice. Indeed, the Poles are uniquely situated to act as arbitrator between the United

States and France or Germany when these are at odds with each other.

It is unclear whether Poland's eastern frontiers will form a shorter- or longer-term outer boundary of the Schengen countries. What is clear is that the Polish government is committed to the security of those boundaries while continuing to work with the country's eastern neighbors. The Poles have long seen themselves as a key to European security as well as a bridge between east and west. It is safe to say that they will continue to seek to position themselves to play that role as well as it can be played. Polish security efforts and decision making will continue to function within the context of the perspective that Poland must be strong and must have strong allies. Those who are critical of the Polish relationship with the United States fail to understand this truism of Polish national security: strength lies in standing with the strong.

References, Recommended Readings, and Websites

Books
Davies, Norman. 1972. *White Eagle, Red Star: the Polish-Soviet War, 1919–1920.* London: Macdonald.
———. 1982. *God's Playground, a History of Poland.* New York: Columbia University Press.
———. 1984. *Heart of Europe: A short History of Poland.* New York: Oxford University Press.
Malcher, George C. 1984. *Poland's Politicized Army: Communists in Uniform.* New York: Praeger.
Michta, Andrew. 1990. *Red Eagle: The Army in Polish Politics, 1944–1988.* Stanford, CA: Hoover Institute Press.
Orenstein, Mitchell A. 2001. *Out of the Red: Building Capitalism and Democracy in Post Communist Europe.* Ann Arbor: University of Michigan Press.
Szayna, Thomas S., and F. Stephen Larrabee. 1995. *East European Military Reform after the Cold War:*
Implications for the United States. Santa Monica, CA: RAND.
Terry, Sarah Meiklejohn. 1983. *Poland's Place in Europe: General Sikorski and the Origin of the Oder-Neisse Line, 1939–1943.* Princeton, NJ: Princeton University Press.
Wiatr, Jerzy. 1988 *The Soldier and the Nation: The Role of the Military in Polish Politics, 1918–1985.* Boulder, CO: Westview.

Articles
"Arms Industry: Two Holdings." 2002. *Economic Bulletin of the Polish Foreign Ministry* 34, no. 528, August 26. http://www.paiz.gov.pl/oldpai/biul_ekon/nr34_2002.html#top (accessed February 15, 2004).
Biuro Bezpieczeństwa Narodowego. 2003. "Strategia Bezpieczeństwa Narodowego Rzeczypospolitej Polskiej." (National Security Policy of the Republic of Poland). http://www.bbn.gov.pl/pl/dokument/strategia_bezpieczenstwa.html (accessed March 8, 2004).
"Contributors to United Nations Peacekeeping Operations. Monthly Summary of Contributors as of 31 December 2003." 2003. http://www.un.org/Depts/dpko/dpko/contributors/December2003Countrysummary.pdf (accessed February 20, 2004).
Coughlan, Elizabeth P. 1997. "The Changing Structure and Values of the Polish Military." In *To Sheathe the Sword: Civil-Military Relations and the Quest for Democracy,* John P. Lovell and David E. Albright, eds. Westport, CT: Greenwood Publishing Group.
———. 1998a. "Democratization and the Military in Poland: Establishing Democratic Civilian Control." In *The Military and Society in the Former Eastern Bloc,* Constantine Danopoulos and Daniel Zirker, eds. Boulder, CO: Westview.
———. 1998b. "Democratizing Civilian Control: The Polish Case." *Armed Forces and Society* 24, no. 4.
"Employment Aspects of Arms Industry Restructuring." 2003. *European Industrial Relations Observatory On-Line.* http://www.eiro.eurofound.eu.int/2003/09/feature/pl0309107f.html (accessed February 26, 2004).
"Growth of Arms Industry Export." 2004. *Economic Bulletin of the Polish Foreign*

Ministry 9, no. 607, March 1. http://www.msz.gov.pl/start.php (accessed March 3, 2004).

Herspring, Dale. 1981. "The Polish Military and the Policy Process." In *Background to Crisis: Policy and Politics in Gierek's Poland*, Maurice Simon and Roger Kanet, eds. Boulder, CO: Westview.

Ilnicki, Stanisław. "Polish Participation in UN Peacekeeping Missions and Researches in PTSD." http://skmponz. w.interia.pl/baereia.htm (accessed February 20, 2004).

Kochanowski, Franciszek. 2000. "Participation of the Polish Armed Forces in Peacekeeping Missions in the Nineties." *Polish Ministry of Foreign Affairs Yearbook.* http://www.msz.gov. pl/warecka/yearbook/2000/franciszek_ kochanowski_participation_of_the_ polish_armed_forces.html.

Komorowski, Bronisław. 2001. "Reforming Poland's Military." *NATO Review* 49, no. 2. http://www.nato.int/docu/ review/2001/0102–08.htm.

Korbonski, Andrzej. 1981. "The Dilemmas of Civil-Military Relations in Contemporary Poland: 1945–1981." *Armed Forces and Society* 8, no. 1.

———. 1988 "Civil-Military Relations in Poland between the Wars: 1918–1939." *Armed Forces and Society* 14, no. 2.

Latawski, Paul. "The Polish Armed Forces and Society." http://www.bris.ac.uk/ Depts/GRC/CMR/TCMRpercent20 Papers/polish.pdf.

Michta, Andrew. 1997. "Civil-Military Relations in Poland after 1989: The Outer Limits of Change." *Problems of Post-Communism*, March–April.

"Monthly Summary of Military and Civilian Police Contribution to United Nations Operations." 2004. http://www. un.org/Depts/dpko/dpko/contributors/ January2004Summary.pdf (accessed February 25, 2004).

Osica, Olaf. 2001. "Poland between America and Europe: Distorted Perspectives." *Yearbook of Polish Foreign Policy 2001.* http://msz.gov. pl/warecka/yearbook/2001/olaf_ osica_poland_between_america_and_ europe.html (accessed February 15, 2004).

Pisarski, Maciej. 2000. "Relations with the United States." *Yearbook of Polish Foreign Policy 2000.* http://msz.gov.pl/ warecka/yearbook/2000/maciej_pisarski_ relations_with_the_united_states.html (accessed February 15, 2004).

"Polish Ministry of Defense Budget for 2004." http://www.wp.mil.pl/auths/ 293/files/4033690ad9549_budzet2004. ppt (accessed March 8, 2004).

Sakson, Andrzej. 2000.. "Crisis or Normalcy? Reflections on Contemporary Polish-German Relations." *Yearbook of Polish Foreign Policy 2000.* http://msz. gov.pl/warecka/yearbook/2000/andrzej_ sakson_crisis_or_normalcy_reflections_ on_contemporary_polish_german_ relations.html (accessed February 15, 2004).

"Sales of Defense Industry Products." 2003. *Economic Bulletin of the Polish Foreign Ministry* 48, no. 594, December 1. http:// www.paiz.gov.pl/oldpai/biul_ekon/no48_ 2003.htm (accessed February 20, 2004).

Sennott, Charles. 2003. "Arms Deals Criticized as Corporate US Welfare." *The Boston Globe*, January 14. http:// www.commondreams.org/headlines03/ 0114–02.htm (accessed Feburary 28, 2004).

Szymczak, Robert. 2003. "Poland's Contract of the Century." *The Warsaw Voice.* http://www.warswvoice.pl/ view/2816 (accessed March 8, 2004).

Websites

Armed Poland (Polska Zbrojna): http:// www.polska-zbrojna.pl/.

Central Intelligence Agency Website. 2003. *World Factbook.* http://www. cia.gov/cia/publications/factbook/.

Główny Urząd Statystyczny (Main Bureau of Statistics of the Polish Government). http://www.stat.gov.pl/

Library of Congress. *Poland: A Country Study.* http://lcweb2.loc.gov/frd/cs/ pltoc.html.

Military Internet Gazette: http://www. army.mil.pl/strona_pl/glowna/ charakter/charakter.htm.

Polish Land Forces Website: http://www. army.mil.pl/strona_pl/glowna/home_pl. htm.

Polish Ministry of Defense Website: http://www.wp.mil.pl/start.php?page= 1000000001.

Polish Ministry of Foreign Affairs Economic Bulletin: http://www.msz. gov.pl/start.php?page=1030000001.

Portugal

Brandon C. Prins

Geography and History

Portugal is a small, maritime country that lies on the westernmost point of continental Europe, jutting out into the eastern Atlantic Ocean. With a total land area of approximately 92,000 sq. km, it is smaller in size than many states in the United States Mountainous in the north and east and largely flat with open plains in the south, Portugal goes from a temperate climate north of the Tejo estuary to a Mediterranean coastal climate in the southern Algarve region (Anderson 2000). Portugal's southern and westernmost districts border the Atlantic Ocean, giving Portugal 1,793 km of pristine coastline. On the east and north, Portugal abets its larger Iberian neighbor, Spain. No natural barrier separates the two countries, and yet surprisingly the territorial delimitation has remained largely unchanged for 800 years (Anderson 2000; McAlister 1984).

With a total population of 10.2 million (2003 estimate), Portugal ranks in the middle of the fifteen European Union (EU) nations. Such population figures have not translated into economic gain though. Portugal remains one of the poorest countries in western Europe. Only Greece ranks below Portugal in purchasing power parity (2001 figures) (Eurostat 2003), and in terms of overall human development, Portugal scores near the bottom of European nations. According to Eurostat, Portugal's gross domestic product (GDP) per capita of U.S.$16,059 in purchasing power parity (2001 figures) places it nearly 32 percent lower than the per capita income of the United Kingdom and 40 percent lower than The Netherlands. Further, the 2002 UN Human Development Index places Portugal twenty-eighth, even with Slovenia but behind both South Korea and Cyprus.

Still, Portugal has made significant progress since joining the European Community (EC) in 1986. Portugal's GDP per capita (in purchasing power parity) when it entered the EC was only 53 percent of the EC average. Today, it is closer to 80 percent (*The Economist* 2000b). Further, since joining the EC, successive democratically elected governments have liberalized the economy and sold off state-controlled industries, such as the financial and petroleum sectors, which had been nationalized following the 1974 military coup (Solsten 1993). Extensive economic aid from the EC has also helped finance infrastructure improvements, while foreign direct investment has quadrupled in the last fifteen years (Solsten 1993; *The Economist* 2003). Portugal's unemployment rate remains lower than many wealthier European countries, and its Internet and mobile telephone use have jumped dramatically (Eurostat 2003). Portugal also joined the European Monetary Union and began circulating the new currency on January 1, 2002.

Despite these remarkable economic achievements, Portugal struggles to keep pace with its EU partners (Corkill 2002). In 2002 and 2003, Portugal's GDP increased by less than the Organization for Economic Cooperation and Development average and its inflation remained higher. In part, this was a consequence of a spending binge by public authorities in the 1990s, and now these same officials are cutting spending to meet EU regulations (*The Economist*, 2000a). In 2001, Portugal violated the EU stability and growth pact limit with a budget deficit greater than 3 percent of its GDP. The EU Commission has been charged with punishing such transgressions, but as luck would have it, both Germany and France also violated the limits and the EU Council of Ministers has seen fit to allow these countries to slide (*The Economist* 2004a). Increasingly, Portugal faces tough competition from industries in central and eastern Europe (CIA *World Factbook* 2003), and as the EU expands eastward, Portugal may lose a substantial portion of its EU economic aid. However, with improvements in education, greater investment in research and development, a relatively young population, and continued access to new technology, Portugal remains on a path to catch up to the rest of Europe by 2020 (*The Economist* 2000b).

From the shores of this small Iberian country, European explorers first set sail to the far corners of the world. Prince Henry the Navigator, one of Portugal's most acclaimed mariners, looked out at the Atlantic from the white cliffs of Sagres in the early fifteenth century and effectively initiated Europe's age of exploration. A short time later (1497), Vasco da Gama, another Portuguese navigator, took Portugal (and Europe) around the Cape of Good Hope and then north to India, helping secure trade routes that would make Portugal a world power (see Sidebar 1). Unfortunately, this global empire also brought about Portugal's eventual diminishment. Colonies in Africa, Asia, and South America became increasingly costly to administer, and more critically, Portugal began to face imperial competition from the likes of Spain, Holland, and Great Britain.

Portugal capitalized on independence, favorable geography, and early colony acquisition. As part of the territorial fron-

---

Sidebar 1   Imperial Portugal

The Treaty of Tordesillas (1494) divided the world into Spanish and Portuguese zones of control. The line of demarcation at 46 degrees west latitude and 134 degrees east latitude gave the Portuguese monarchy claim to lands as far west as Brazil (which had not yet been discovered by Europeans) and as far east as the Spice Islands (Indonesia). Portugal then acquired one of the largest colonial empires in history. Beginning with the Madeira Islands in 1419, Portugal went on to seize territories in Africa, South America, India, China, and the South Pacific. On December 20, 1999, Portugal's last territorial possession (Macao) officially became a Special Administrative Region of China.

Sources
Birmingham, David. 1993. *A Concise History of Portugal.* Cambridge, UK: Cambridge University Press.
McAlister, Lyle N. 1984. *Spain and Portugal in the New World, 1492–1700.* Minneapolis: University of Minnesota Press.

tier during the Christian reconquest of the Iberian Peninsula from the Moors, the area of what would become the independent nation of Portugal featured prominently in many of the early battlefield successes. By the early thirteenth century the Moors had not only retreated to the Andalusia region of what is now southern Spain, but Portugal received both recognition from the Crown of Leon and the Catholic Church (Vincent and Stradling 1994; Birmingham 1993). Independence brought political stability. With stability came increased economic development. As Spain continued to fight the Moors, Portugal turned to the sea. A seafaring tradition serendipitously met technological advances in shipbuilding and navigation. The seaports of Lisbon and Oporto served as the launching points for caravel expeditions out into the Atlantic. A half-century head start on Spain put Portugal in the lead for wealth and global influence (McAlister 1984).

Portugal's first attempt at democracy began in 1910, making it only the second country on the European continent (after France) to institute a republican form of government (Birmingham 1993; Anderson 2000). However, after sixteen years of political instability and inefficiency, the military stepped in to ensure order and amend an increasingly corrupt public system (Solsten 1993). Only a few years later (1933) Antonio de Oliveira Salazar assumed control of the regime and inaugurated an authoritarian political system that abolished political parties, rigged elections, limited the press, and built a police force that crushed domestic opposition (Solsten 1993; Ferreira and Marshall 1986). As a result of ill health, Salazar relinquished control of the dictatorship in 1968 to Marcello José das Neves Caetano, but Caetano continued

the fascist policies of his predecessor. Even with the leadership change, the regime could not withstand disastrous colonial wars in Africa in the 1960s and early 1970s, and the military was compelled to step in once again to prevent its own destruction on battlefields in Angola, Mozambique, and Guinea-Bissau (Vincent and Stradling 1994). Two years of factional and frequently violent political competition followed the 1974 coup, but ended with the drafting of a new constitution and the adoption of a strong presidency in 1976 (Solsten 1993).

Given Portugal's previous experience with democracy and the legacy of authoritarianism, the successful consolidation of the Second Republic has been a remarkable achievement (Solsten 1993; Robinson 2002). Even with the economic shocks that rocked the country in the late 1970s and the collapse of multiple governing coalitions, Portuguese democracy seems to have muddled through. From 1975 to 1979, Portugal suffered through nine separate governments, only one of which survived longer than a year (Strøm 1990), and Portugal had to wait for more than a decade after the 1974 revolution for the first majority government to take office (Sousa 2002, 138). Despite continued economic weakness in the 1980s, the governing coalition adopted a series of constitutional amendments that reduced the authority of the president while strengthening the prime minister (Solsten 1993). According to Solsten (1993), "The presidency remained an essential governing institution, but the balance of political power had shifted to favor the cabinet and the legislature, as in most other Western democracies." Perhaps more importantly, Portugal's military began a slow march back to the barracks, and in the decade that followed, the size of the army

Table 1　Portugal: Key Statistics

Type of government	Parliamentary democracy
Population (millions)	10.2 (2003)
Religion	Roman Catholic 97% (2003)
Main industries	Textiles; wood pulp, paper, and cork; oil refining; chemicals; fish canning
Main security threats	Instability resulting from immigration from North Africa; drugs; terrorism
Defense spending (% GDP)	2.1% (2001)
Size of military (thousands)	44 (2001–2002)
Number of civil wars since 1945	0
Number of interstate wars since 1945	1 (Afghanistan 2001)
Number of extrasystemic wars since 1945	3 (Angola, Guinea-Bissau, Mozambique)

Sources

Central Intelligence Agency Website. 2005. CIA *World Factbook*. http://www.cia.gov/cia/
publications/factbook/ (accessed May 15, 2005).

Ghosn, Faten, Glenn Palmer, and Stuart Bremer. 2004. "The MID3 Data Set, 1993–2001:
Procedures, Coding Rules, and Description." *Conflict Management and Peace Science* 21,
no. 2:133–154.

International Institute for Strategic Studies (IISS). 2003. *The Military Balance 2003–2004*.
London: IISS and Oxford University Press.

Sarkees, Meredith Reid. 2000. "The Correlates of War Data on War: An Update to 1997."
Conflict Management and Peace Science 18, no. 1:123–144.

Stockholm International Peace Research Institute (SIPRI). 2003. *SIPRI Yearbook 2003:
Armaments, Disarmament and International Security*. London: Oxford University Press.

was reduced dramatically and civilian control was strengthened (Vincent and Stradling 1994).

The parliamentary democracy established with the constitution of 1976 allocates political power to a five-year popularly elected president, a prime minister selected by the president from the majority party (or majority coalition), and a unicameral legislature with 230 seats elected under a proportional representation system (Anderson 2000, 5). Despite an uncertain beginning, Portugal's democracy has continued to deepen and diffuse under the Second Republic (Robinson 2002). Since 1982, Freedom House has awarded Portugal the highest ranking on its measure of political freedom. With additional protections adopted in 1991 and increased liberalization of the media, Portugal has ranked for over a decade now equally high on Freedom House's measure of civil liberties (Freedom House 2003; Sousa 2002). Polity IV, another project aimed at measuring levels of democracy, maintains that Portugal has open and competitive elections for the executive, stable and enduring political participation, and strong legislative constraints on executive actions (Marshall and Jaggers 2000, 17–26). Further, Portugal's level of political corruption dropped by nearly 20 percent from 1995 to 2003. A score of 5.56 in 1995 placed Portugal slightly above Malaysia but below South Africa, while its 2003 score of 6.6 meant Portugal was more corrupt than France but less corrupt than either Cyprus or Taiwan. Despite allegations in 2002 regarding the mismanagement of public monies by Portugal's Socialist Party in power, businesspeople, country analysts, and local residents all considered Portugal's public sector less corrupt in 2003 than in previous years (Transparency International 2003).

Regional Geopolitics

Despite Portugal's geographic isolation from the heartland of Europe, it remains a European state buffeted by the security concerns confronting countries further north and east. With the breaching of the Berlin Wall in 1989 and the implosion of the Soviet state in 1991, European (and Portuguese) security changed fundamentally. For over half a century, superpower rivalry dominated European geopolitics as North Atlantic Treaty Organization (NATO) military forces anticipated a Warsaw Pact strike though the Fulda Gap. In this volatile environment, western European countries shared U.S. concerns regarding their own political stability and economic development, as well as the containment of Soviet power (Duffield 2001). U.S. troops on the ground in West Germany strengthened its deterrent pledge, while large infusions of the greenback helped stabilize economies and avert communist influence. Portugal, for example, received $229 million in U.S. economic and military assistance during the Marshall Plan period (1949–1952) (U.S. Agency for International Development 2003).

In the post–Cold War era, Europe faces challenges quite different than the ones that dominated discourse for forty-five years. With Russia and eastern Europe democratizing; western Europe stable, wealthy, and developed; and the United States a dominant power, attention has turned to economic integration, immigration, and terrorism (Bailes 1997). These new security issues invoke substantially different political interests compared with Cold War concerns over territorial integrity and military competition and, consequently, necessitate different foreign policy responses. Although territorial disputes have not been entirely eliminated from European geopolitics in the post–Cold War period, the absence of any real military threat and continued U.S. security guarantees have allowed EU states to dramatically reduce their military budgets, invest increasingly in social welfare programs, and focus on integration.

With ten states scheduled to join the EU on May 1, 2004, the political and economic stability of countries in eastern and central Europe, as well as the Balkans, represents a primary foreign policy concern of European leaders. Indeed, hopes of a peace dividend following the collapse of the Soviet Union were shattered by three years of warfare among the peoples of the former Yugoslavia. With the help of the United States and NATO, the religious and ethnic conflagration was eventually controlled, but only after tens of thousands had lost their lives and many more were left homeless as refugees. Although a precarious peace has held in Bosnia for the last eight years, the Dayton Peace Accords did not end violence in the Balkans. In 1998, only three years after the establishment of peace in Bosnia, Serbian military forces attempted to reassert control over Kosovo (Foyle 2002; Moskowitz and Lantis 2002). The United States once again stepped in to enforce order and Milosevic eventually backed down. However, the potential for renewed violence in the Balkans cannot be ignored by European leaders. The desire for a rapid reaction military force comprised of, and led by, Europeans alone is in part a reaction to the most recent Balkan wars. European governments have had to acknowledge their political and military weakness in failing to address such violence in their own backyard. Today, the EU administers the peacekeeping mission in Macedonia, but only after NATO agreed to supply the necessary equipment.

European governments also confront twin threats of terrorism and weapons proliferation. European police forces and intelligence agencies now work more closely with the United States and United Nations to monitor terrorist cells and prevent attacks (*The Economist* 2002). However, open borders across EU countries and Mediterranean shorelines too long to monitor effectively frustrate antiterrorist units. Plus, Europe's proximity to the Middle East and North Africa ensures relatively inexpensive passage from these politically charged and underdeveloped regions. Couple terrorism and open borders with illicit trade in weapons of mass destruction (WMD) and nightmare scenarios can easily be envisioned. In the last decade the United States has spent billions of dollars dismantling Soviet nuclear weapons, and Europe now recognizes the growing danger from Russia's WMD stockpiles, its deteriorating security situation, and the possible diffusion of weapons expertise (Allison 2004; *The Economist* 2001; *Business Week* 2001). Consequently, European governments now work more closely with the United States in monitoring and intercepting the proliferation of these deadly weapons (Feinstein and Slaughter 2004). Eight European governments, including Portugal, joined with the Bush administration in 2003 to cooperatively develop the political, economic, and military tools necessary to combat the spread of WMDs (Friedman 2003; U.S. Department of State 2003d).

Conflict Past and Present

Conflict History

Portugal emerged from Spanish domination in 1640. After sixty years of foreign rule, Portugal seized upon a Catalonian rebellion and an offer of aid from France to oust the Spanish garrison in Lisbon (Anderson 2000, 109). The new Bragança Dynasty immediately began securing allies against its aggressive Iberian neighbor. States such as Holland, France, and England agreed to align with Portugal to check further Spanish aggression on the peninsula. To secure such foreign support, Portugal offered lucrative trade deals. Even with the deterrent pledges of these European powers, war with Spain broke out in 1641. Almost immediately Spanish troops crossed the border near Olivença, and for the next twenty-five years, deadly combat continued along the border. Two events then changed the direction of the conflict. First, Charles II of England married Princess Catherine of Portugal and thereby solidified an alliance that would help ensure Portuguese sovereignty for the next 150 years. Second, Philip IV of Spain died in 1665 and his widow recognized the independence of Portugal (Anderson 2000, 118). Admittedly, Spain was distracted with events elsewhere. Thousands of Spanish troops were deployed in central Europe defending the Austrian branch of the Habsburg Dynasty in the Thirty Years' War (Brightwell 1982; Parker 1980).

Spanish attention turned away from Portugal after the death of another monarch (Carlos II) in 1700. The possible accession to the Spanish throne by a grandson of Louis XIV of France set off a frantic effort by most of the ruling houses of Europe to prevent the union of Bourbon France with the Spanish Empire. In the following War of Spanish Succession, Portugal joined England, the Netherlands, Denmark, and Prussia to balance the rising power of France on the European continent. The new Bourbon king of Spain declared war on Portugal in 1704, Spanish troops seized the Portuguese province of Beira and planned to move on Lisbon. English troops turned the tide and a combined army of English and Portuguese soldiers took Madrid in 1706 and replaced the Bourbon with an Austrian Habsburg. Unfortunately, the choice of an Austrian Habsburg to ascend the Spanish throne became problematic in 1709 after the Holy Roman emperor died, thus catapulting the new Habsburg king of Spain into the emperor's chair as well. The union of Austria and Spain was just as unacceptable as the union of France and Spain. Finally, the Treaty of Utrecht brought the War of Spanish Succession to an end in 1714, but only after a Bourbon was placed back on the Spanish throne and it was agreed by all interested parties that France and Spain would permanently remain separate crowns (Bromley 1971).

Following the War of Spanish Succession, Portugal managed to remain neutral in the European struggles that continued. However, the French Revolution and the rise of Napoleon drew Portugal back into questions of European security. As the armies of the French Republic pressed into Belgium and Germany, Portugal aligned with England and Spain to contest the rising revolutionary power of the new France. With Spain's defeat, Portugal found itself in an awkward position, appeasing enemies and allies alike to avoid invasion. The Peace of Amiens in 1802 brought the wars of the French Revolution to an end, but Napoleon then began his quest for European dominance. Until 1807 Portugal successfully avoided Napoleon's gaze and was one of the few European states to remain free of French control. Indeed, Napoleon's battlefield successes at Ulm, Austerlitz, and Jena secured most of Europe for France by 1806 (Liddle Hart 1991). Napoleon's attention then turned north across the channel, and a blockade was instituted to bring the English to their knees. However, Napoleon's ability to deny continental access to British goods broke down on the Iberian Peninsula as illicit trade continued through Lisbon and Oporto. To stop the leak, Napoleon sent a French army into Portugal and seized Lisbon in 1807. The royal family fled to Brazil, and Portuguese soldiers were conscripted to fight for France.

Napoleon's empire began to collapse on the peninsula only a year later. A Spanish insurgency against French rule emerged after Napoleon's brother was placed on the Spanish throne. To aid these nascent guerrilla groups, England sent General Arthur Wellesley and 26,000 redcoats to Portugal (Liddle Hart 1991). For two years, between 1809 and 1811, Napoleon sought to crush rising opposition on the Iberian Peninsula. English and Portuguese troops successfully defended Lisbon as English naval strength maintained crucial supply lines and French regulars faced a devastating insurgency campaign in the countryside (Keegan 1994). Starvation eventually defeated Napoleon's peninsula army as it failed to overcome defensive fortifications established around Lisbon (Liddle Hart 1991, 115). British, Portuguese, and Spanish troops then pushed the remnants of the French force back across the Pyrenees to Toulouse by 1814. The peninsula campaign cost Napoleon nearly 400,000 casualties and Portugal lay in ruins. Not only did combat ravage Portuguese infrastructure, but government revenue from trade also dropped precipitously and spending on the army led to financial devastation (Anderson 2000, 129).

With the defeat of Napoleon, Europe turned to industrialization, colony acquisition, and political repression. What interstate conflict did occur remained limited, and issues in contention were typically handled through active diplomacy by the major powers. Political leaders in the major ruling houses of Europe also were preoccupied with the growing number of groups seeking democratic reforms. Indeed, in 1829 Portugal found itself confronting political transformation as liberal groups sought to impose constitutional constraints on the monarchy. Conservatives (absolute monarchists) fought such changes, prompting a five-year civil war that resulted in nearly 20,000 deaths (Anderson 2000; Sarkees 2000). Even though clashes between conservatives, moderates, and liberals continued for the next half century, the conflict remained limited.

As the growing military might of Germany and Russia began to upset the geopolitical status quo toward the end of the nineteenth century, Portugal sought neutrality once again. However, its long-standing alliance with Britain and concerns over German intentions toward its African colonies eventually drew Portugal into World War I on the Allied side. Although skirmishes with German troops in southwest Africa in 1914 did not lead to war, the same was not true for the seizing of German merchant ships detained in Lisbon harbor at England's request in 1916 (Anderson 2000, 143). Germany and the Habsburg Empire immediately declared war on Portugal. Interestingly, Britain had attempted to appease both Portugal and Germany leading up to the war. A secret agreement signed in 1898 between the British and German governments agreed to carve up Portuguese colonies in Africa if Portugal failed to control them. Yet soon after this agreement, the British reaffirmed its commitment to the defense of Portugal and its colonies (Joll 1984). In the last two years of the conflict Portugal sent 40,000 troops to the western front (60,000 Portuguese troops also served in Mozambique). Over 7,000 died and nearly 14,000 more suffered grievous injuries fighting in the mud of Flanders (Solsten 1993).

Portugal did not fare well after the Great War. Political instability and economic underdevelopment continued unabated, and the depression that followed in the 1930s made matters even worse. As Europe marched toward war again, the newly constituted Salazar regime served all sides by facilitating the movement of war materiel and foodstuffs throughout Europe. German guns reached Franco's rebels in Spain by way of Lisbon, and tungsten from Portuguese mines was shipped to Germany, Italy, and Great Britain (Anderson 2000, 148). Portugal's colonies also helped provide food to Axis and Allied nations alike. As early as 1940, Salazar anticipated an Allied victory, and in 1943 the United States and Great Britain were granted air bases in the Azores (Solsten 1993). Although Portuguese troops did not actively participate in World War II battles, nearly 20,000 Portuguese citizens volunteered to fight alongside Franco in the Spanish civil war and 8,000 of them died (Ferreira and Marshall 1986).

After World War II, Portugal refused to relinquish control of its colonies despite pressure from the international community. In 1951 the Salazar regime took an even more radical move by passing a law defining its colonial holdings as overseas territories, and the media were prohibited from using the word "colony" (Ferreira and Marshall 1986). However, Portugal could not silence calls for independence and it no longer possessed the strength to suppress the emergence of liberation movements. Although in 1961 the Portuguese garrison in Goa gave up without much of a fight in the face of an overwhelming Indian force, Salazar was determined to contest attempts to overthrow Portuguese authority in its more lucrative African colonies.

Opposition to Portuguese rule began in Angola in March 1961. By 1964, insurgencies had also developed in Mozambique and Guinea-Bissau (see Table 2). To combat the guerrilla movements, the Salazar regime increased the size of the army from a mere 10,000 soldiers in 1964 to over 200,000 by 1972 (Ferreira and Marshall 1986). But the losses continued and resistance within the Portuguese military began to grow. Further, Soviet surface-to-air missiles were introduced into the conflicts in the early 1970s, and Portuguese pilots began to pay the price. For an army that had not seen active engagement since World War I, battles in Africa were dispiriting (Anderson 2000). Junior officers often served in one colony only to be transferred to another soon after a tour of duty had been completed. With thousands of casualties in each of the three African colonies over a ten-year period (and tens of thousands of African casualties), Portugal had little to show for its struggle. Indeed, when Guinea-Bissau declared independence in 1973, sixty countries recognized the new African state within a matter of weeks (Anderson 2002, 160). By 1975, Salazar's fascist regime had been toppled, and 500 years of Portuguese control in West Africa came to an end (see Sidebar 2).

Current and Potential Military Confrontation

Portugal faces few serious security risks today. The colonial wars have ended, dramatic reductions have occurred in the defense budget, and Portugal's attention remains fixed on European integration. Since 1975, Portugal has found itself in only three militarized interstate disputes and all three involved cooperation with U.S.-led actions: two in the Balkans contesting Serbian aggression (1998–2000)

Table 2   Portugal: African Possessions

Colony	Date of Colonization	Date of Independence	Colonial War Dates	Colonial War Fatalities
Madeira Islands	1419	Autonomous region of Portugal	—	—
Guinea-Bissau	1446	September 10, 1974	1962–1974	~15,000
Cape Verde Islands	1462	July 5, 1975	1962–1974	—
São Tomé & Príncipe	1485	July 12, 1975	—	—
Mozambique	1505	June 25, 1975	1964–1975	~30,000
Angola	1574	November 11, 1975	1961–1975	~55,000

Sources

Sarkees, Meredith Reid. 2000. "The Correlates of War Data on War: An Update to 1997." *Conflict Management and Peace Science* 18, no. 1:123–144.

Solsten, Eric, ed. 1993. *Portugal: A Country Study.* Library of Congress: Federal Research Division. http://lcweb2.loc.gov/frd/cs (accessed August 8, 2003).

Sidebar 2   The Carnation Revolution

After more than a decade of colonial conflict in Africa, opposition within the Portuguese military to the governing elite reached the critical stage. On April 25, 1974 at 12:25 A.M., army units across the country seized important government buildings, including the presidential palace. As soldiers marched into Lisbon—accompanied by tank columns—euphoric crowds greeted the military men with fresh flowers. Only one shot was fired in defense of the Salazar dictatorship as the Portuguese people celebrated both the end of the colonial wars and the beginning of democracy.

Source
Anderson, James M. 2000. *The History of Portugal.* Westport, CT: Greenwood Press.

and the U.S.-led war in Afghanistan to remove the Taliban regime and eradicate al-Qaeda terrorists. In the Kosovo air campaign, Portugal contributed seven F-16A-B fighter planes and one C-130 transport (Daalder and O'Hanlon 2000), while Portugal's contributions in Afghanistan were limited to a medical team and one C-130 cargo plane (Rumsfeld and Portes 2002). The Portuguese government also supported the U.S.-led war to overthrow the Baathist dictatorship in Iraq, and 128 Portuguese military police arrived in the southern Iraqi city of Nasariyah in November 2003 to participate in an international stabilization force.

The potential for future militarized confrontation remains limited. Portugal may accept supporting roles in UN-, NATO-, or U.S.-led efforts abroad, but only in unusual circumstances will Portuguese military units actively engage enemy forces. Closer to home, Portugal is at peace with its larger Iberian neighbor, Spain, and it is highly unlikely that the relationship will become militarized at any time in the near future. Although one existing territorial claim remains (Olivença) between Portugal and Spain going back to the Congress of Vienna in 1815, Portugal rarely invokes its rights over the disputed territory, and neither side has any interest in militarizing the issue.

Alliance Structure

Given its size, Portugal has historically faced threats from larger and more powerful European countries. To ensure sovereignty, Portugal has actively sought allies to help deter aggressive neighbors. In return for aid, Portugal has offered two prizes. First, port cities such as Lisbon and Oporto have opened their harbors to foreign merchant ships, while trading rights with Portugal's colonies also could be granted. Second, Portugal's geographic location on the southwest corner of the European continent has provided maritime states, such as Great Britain and the United States, a bridgehead to land troops and supplies for operations against potential European challengers.

The defensive alliance with England represents Portugal's most long-standing partnership. The Treaty of Windsor signed in 1386 professed eternal friendship and committed both sides to defensive aid if threatened by foreign aggression (Anderson 2000, 40–41). Since the fourteenth century the alliance between England and Portugal has been reaffirmed numerous times, including a twelve-year pact involving both France and Spain signed in 1834 (Bennett 1997; Gibler and

Sarkees forthcoming). The defensive alliance with Great Britain again was authorized in 1899 and theoretically remains in effect although NATO has now largely replaced this bilateral pact. Portugal's only other security commitment involves a neutrality agreement signed with Spain five months before the Nazi invasion of Poland (but after the Spanish civil war). This agreement (the Iberian pact) committed both Spain and Portugal to defend the peninsula and helped maintain the neutrality of both states during World War II.

Toward the end of World War II, Portugal foresaw the growing dominance of U.S. naval and airpower. Given its Atlantic coastline, the U.S. ability to resupply Portugal via its port facilities offered the greatest protection. However, joining NATO did not solely revolve around the perceived Soviet threat to western Europe. Indeed, Portugal's distance from what would have been U.S.-Soviet battlefields meant that even a USSR bent on territorial expansion would only remotely threaten Portuguese sovereignty. NATO rather allowed Portugal the ability to retain its colonial possessions while offering U.S. forces access to airfields and naval facilities. The geostrategic importance of the Azores bases, port facilities to resupply Europe from the south, and access to the Mediterranean via the Straits of Gibraltar all meant that the United States tolerated Portuguese policies in its colonies. NATO also provided a means by which the Salazar regime could acquire military armaments. But ultimately Portugal's African wars estranged it from NATO allies and prevented deeper integration into the NATO command structure.

Regime transition in the mid-1970s and democratic consolidation soon after that led to a greater role for Portuguese forces in the NATO alliance. Indeed, by 1980 Portugal not only resumed training exercises with NATO forces, but also began participating fully in the Nuclear Planning Group (Solsten 1993). The Iberian Atlantic Command (IBERLANT), a major subcommand of the Allied Command Atlantic (ACLANT), which was upgraded in 1971, was offered to Portugal in 1982. Although no permanent combat forces were assigned to IBERLANT during peacetime, the command remained strategically significant in connecting North America and Europe (Solsten 1993). With Spain's full integration into NATO's military command structure in 1999 and the streamlining of NATO structure that continued at Prague in 2003, ACLANT was abolished and all forces were placed under control of Allied Command Operations (ACO). Much of the command and control infrastructure for the southwest regional command of NATO-South has been relocated to Madrid, but Portugal remains important to the alliance and Lisbon was chosen in March 2004 to host the new joint headquarters, which represents one of three operational-level headquarters under ACO.

Size and Structure of the Military

Since the collapse of the Soviet empire in 1991, NATO has significantly reduced its standing forces. Troop commitments by European NATO states have been slashed 35 percent since 1992, while naval vessels and air force combat squadrons have witnessed reductions of 30 percent and 40 percent, respectively (NATO 2001). Of course, readiness levels have also correspondingly dropped over this time period. Portugal, like its NATO allies, has also seen fit to reduce the overall size of its military establishment. Recent Portuguese governments have increasingly allocated scarce public resources to social welfare and economic development projects. Total military personnel dropped 64 percent from 1994 to 2001, and today available military manpower hovers around only 44,000 soldiers (Stockholm International Peace Research Institute [SIPRI] 2003; Cordesman 2002; CIA *World Factbook* 2003).

The bureaucratic organization of the Portuguese military follows a common template. The three service commands (army, navy, and air force) report directly to their individual chiefs of staff, who all reside under the minister of defense. The president then serves as commander-in-chief. The three military services are divided into regional commands based on geographic location. All three branches have continent, Azores, and Madeira commands, although the army is further divided at home into north, central, south, and Lisbon regions. Portugal also deploys a small marine force housed within the navy.

The army fields the bulk of Portugal's uniformed personnel. Nearly 60 percent of Portugal's active armed forces reside in the army (25,000 soldiers). Portugal deploys only 7,500 air force personnel and 11,000 sailors (Cordesman 2002). Although Portugal does not field the smallest NATO contingent, its forces have not kept pace with the latest technological advancements in weapons systems and communications. In recent years, the United States has provided a small amount of military aid (approximately U.S.$800,000) to help modernize Portugal's small force. In terms of available military equipment, Portugal in 2001 reported 187 battle tanks (mostly U.S. Pattons), 370 AIFVs, 6 armored personnel carriers (APCs), and 134 artillery pieces. The air force maintains 101 total combat aircraft, with 51 fixed-wing planes, plus 5 armed helicopters, while the navy has 39 total ships, which includes 31 patrol boats, 6 frigates, and 2 submarines (Cordesman 2002).

Despite such a small force structure, Portugal has actively participated in recent NATO-, UN-, and U.S.-led peacekeeping operations. Portugal, in fact, volunteered one of the largest troop contributions to IFOR (the implementation force for the Dayton Peace Accords). One thousand soldiers from the Airborne Infantry Battalion deployed to Bosnia in 1995 to help prevent further sectarian violence. Additional Portuguese forces help disarm groups in Macedonia (now under EU control), and a battle group of 323 soldiers patrols northwest of Sarajevo. In Afghanistan, a Portuguese medical team operates under NATO authority, while Portuguese peacekeepers now patrol in southern Iraq and in the former Portuguese colony of East Timor. Small numbers of Portuguese soldiers further contribute to UN peacekeeping operations in Angola and Mozambique, while observers participate in UN missions in the western Sahara, Congo, Guatemala, and the Central Africa Republic (SIPRI 2003).

Budget

In recent years Portugal's defense establishment has contracted as budgets have been slashed to meet EU regulations. In 2002, Portugal allocated only U.S.$2.3 billion to its military. This represented less than 5 percent of total government expenditures and only 2.3 percent of Portugal's GDP. In both procurement and research and development, Portugal spends less than nearly all of its NATO allies. In 2001, Portugal allocated U.S.$366 million to weapons procurement and only $4 million to research and development. Spain, in contrast, spent over $1 billion on procurement and $174 million on research and development in the same year (Cordesman 2002).

Although Portugal historically has had a small domestic defense industry producing mostly ordinance and small arms, today Portugal hardly exports any weapons at all. Consequently, Portugal imports needed military equipment from abroad. The United States has transferred small numbers of F-16s, APCs, self-propelled artillery pieces, and ammunition, while states such as France, Spain, and Great Britain supply additional equipment (SIPRI 2003). Portugal also ratified the Nuclear Non-proliferation Treaty (NPT) and neither possesses nuclear weapons today nor had a program in the past to build them.

Civil-Military Relations/The Role of the Military in Domestic Politics

The Portuguese military has historically played an important role in civil affairs. During the nineteenth century, for example, military leaders generally opposed the return of a strong monarchy and consequently helped move the nation toward a republic (Anderson 2000; Solsten 1993). In fact, two years after the king and heir were murdered by republican activists in 1908, the military staged a revolt in Lisbon that eventually dismantled the 800-year-old monarchy and replaced it with only the second constitutional democracy on the European continent (Anderson 2000, 8). Political divisions prevented the early success of Portugal's first republic. Plus, a world soon consumed by trench warfare acerbated the economic and political difficulties faced by this nascent democracy. Soon, riots broke out in the

streets of Lisbon. Until the final overthrow of Portugal's first democracy in 1926, the military served a caretaker role as numerous governing coalitions collapsed and the assassination of political leaders became almost commonplace (Anderson 2000; Solsten 1993).

When the military dictatorship failed to revive an already weak economy, it sought help from economist Antonio de Oliveira Salazar at Coimbra University (Ferreira and Marshall, 1986). This economist began almost immediately to lay the groundwork for his own dictatorship, which was officially inaugurated with the adoption of a new constitution in 1933. Salazar managed the military well and kept it at bay for nearly thirty years. However, opposition to the dictatorship emerged during the colonial wars in the 1960s, culminating in a bloodless military coup in 1974 (the Carnation Revolution). The Portuguese military, in particular, resented being scapegoated for military failures in Goa and the African colonies. As the casualties mounted, junior officers within the military establishment began voicing frustration at the government's inept policies. Because organized dissent by the general population had been silenced by a brutal secret police force, opposition to the fascist regime emerged and grew within the military (Ferreira and Marshall, 1986). Finally, on April 25, 1974, military forces marched into Lisbon and occupied the city center. The military assumed control, but pledged to hold elections and transfer authority to civilian officials in short order. However, splits within the military emerged over its role in the new state, and a Council of Revolution was established by military leaders, which was to possess authority over both the executive and legislative branches of any new government. After radical elements in the military were finally purged in 1975, the military then agreed to elections and the official transfer of power to civilian authorities.

The constitution of 1976 preserved a special role for the military in ensuring stable, democratic governance. The Council of Revolution continued to advise civilian authorities on both foreign and domestic policy and actually retained a veto over parliamentary decision making. Civilian governments soon faced opposition from the council and support emerged for its dissolution. In 1982, constitutional amendments officially stripped the military of its role in the public policy process and relegated it to a pure advisory role on national security issues only (Ferreira and Marshall 1986; Anderson 2000). Despite losing formal institutional power, the military retained influence over civilian authorities for a number of years thereafter. However, this influence waned over the next decade, and by 1991 civilian control was strengthened by giving greater institutional power to the civilian minister of defense (Solsten 1993). Today, authority squarely resides in the civilian branches of the Portuguese republic.

Terrorism

During the Salazar dictatorship, state-sponsored repression prevented most forms of political dissent. However, in the years following the Carnation Revolution, political violence exploded, only to be silenced with the establishment of the Second Republic and the economic progress that began soon after. In 1974, for instance, Portugal experienced nine acts of violent political dissent, which included guerrilla wars, purges, riots, and government crises (Banks, Muller, and Overstreet 2002). The level of domestic political violence peaked in 1975 with twenty-two acts, but decreased in the following years as the Second Republic consolidated. Only ten and eight acts of violent political dissent were reported in 1976 and 1977, respectively (Banks, Muller, and Overstreet 2002). Today, few acts of political violence occur within Portugal. Civil society remains largely satisfied with both the current status quo and the direction of policy change. Plus, few foreign terrorist organizations view Portugal as a worthwhile target. From 1990–1999, only one political assassination occurred in Portugal (in 1990), while France suffered five and Spain six over the same time period (Banks, Muller, and Overstreet 2002).

Acts of terrorism have declined over the last decade, both worldwide and in Europe. From a high of 666 total terrorist incidents in 1987, the U.S. Department of State reported only 348 in 2001, with the vast majority occurring in Latin America and Asia (U.S. Department of State 2001). In western Europe, the number of incidents has also diminished significantly over the last decade. In 1995, 272 terrorist acts were reported, but this dropped to only 17 in 2001. Although Portugal has experienced few, if any, terrorist incidents in the last ten years, the attacks against New York and Washington, D.C., in 2001 propelled the issue to the forefront of even Portugal's policy agenda. In 2002, for instance, Portugal recommended to its European partners that a common security plan for addressing terrorist threats was urgently needed. As chair of the Organization for Security and Cooperation in Europe (OSCE), Portugal directed member states to attend to political and juridical limitations on combating terrorism. The new charter adopted by the OSCE in December 2002 committed member states to coordinate law enforcement and border security to more effectively disrupt terrorist networks. Further, member states agreed to confront the political, economic, and environmental sources of terrorism (OSCE 2002). To reinforce Portugal's commitment to eradicating this form of violent political dissent, Portugal hosted a world forum designed to explore further the underlying causes of terrorism. Portuguese Foreign Minister Antonio Martins da Cruz insisted on the opening day of the conference that the goal of the summit "should be not to prevent only acts of terrorism but also to prevent people from becoming terrorists" (*EU Business* 2003).

Portugal, like its Iberian neighbor, has been a strong supporter of the U.S. global war on terrorism. On March 16, 2003, Portugal's prime minister Jose Manuel Durao Barroso joined U.S. President George Bush, Britain's prime minister Tony Blair, and Spain's president Jose Maria Aznar to reaffirm their transatlantic alliance and commit themselves to "face and overcome the twin threats of the twenty-first century: terrorism and the spread of weapons of mass destruction." (U.S. Department of State 2003). Despite the absence of terrorist acts within Portugal, the Portuguese prime minister has recognized the continued threat terrorist groups pose even to his small and geographically remote country. To be sure, travel across the unprotected Atlantic tends to dissuade illegal immigrants and radical Islamists even though North Africa sits less than 200 km from Portuguese shores. Spain, France, Italy, and Greece all present easier targets for shore landings, and the Mediterranean

Sea offers a less dangerous ocean voyage for illicit smuggling operations. However, Barroso's concerns appear well founded. In January 2003 sixteen alleged members of an al-Qaeda cell were arrested next door in Barcelona, Spain, with explosives and other bomb-making materials (U.S. Department of State 2003b). With open borders across EU states, the presence of terrorist groups in any one country clearly poses a threat to others as well.

Relationship with the United States

Portugal's ties with the United States date back to the Washington administration. Formal relations opened in 1791 after Portugal became the first neutral country to recognize U.S. independence (U.S. Department of State 2003a). The bilateral relationship strengthened during and immediately after World War II as Portugal provided access to air bases and port facilities and later became a founding member of the NATO alliance. The Lajes Air Base on Terceira Island in the Azores provides a refueling stop for military transports crossing from the United States and Canada while additionally offering a landing site for antisubmarine aircraft working in the Atlantic (Solsten 1993). The air base still houses nearly 1,000 U.S. Air Force personnel and continues to serve as an important link between North America and Europe.

In 1951, the United States and Portugal formalized access to Lajes with a bilateral security pact. Nearly every U.S. president since Eisenhower has traveled to Terceira to reiterate the importance of the relationship and the air facility (Solsten 1993). Although the Portuguese government refused access to U.S. warplanes during the 1986 El Dorado Canyon operation against Libya, it was the only NATO country to allow the United States to resupply Israel from its air bases during the 1973 Yom Kippur War (Lesser 2000). Portugal also provided comprehensive access to the Lajes air base during the first Gulf War. Thirty-three tanker aircraft and over 600 U.S. Air Force personnel deployed to Lajes to support the massive airlift to the Persian Gulf. Despite downsizing after the Soviet collapse, the air facility at Lajes provided support for nearly every military operation in Europe, Africa, and Southeast Asia in the 1990s. The United States and Portugal reaffirmed the bilateral pact in June of 1995. According to the U.S. State Department (U.S. Department of State 2003a), "The Agreement on Cooperation and Defense provides for continued U.S. access to the Lajes Air Base in the Azores as well as cooperation in nonmilitary endeavors."

Since World War II, the United States has also provided significant economic and military assistance to Portugal. From 1946 to 2003 the U.S. government supplied the Portuguese government with over $2 billion dollars in grants and $1 billion in loans, which included funds for schools, housing, sanitation, disaster assistance, and military equipment (U.S. Agency for International Development 2003). Although the United States tended to look the other way when it came to Portugal's colonial wars in the 1960s and 1970s, the relationship improved markedly with Portugal's transition to democratic rule in 1976. Over the last twenty-eight years, political, economic, and cultural ties between the two countries have only gotten stronger. Bilateral trade in 2001 was estimated to be worth more than $2.8 billion dollars, which was nearly a 60 percent increase from 1994 (U.S. Department of State 2003a). More importantly, perhaps, the latest U.S. census estimates that 1.3 million people of Portuguese ancestry now live in the United States, while 20,000 Americans reside in Portugal (U.S. Department of State 2003a).

The Future

Portugal has moved from the center of international politics to the periphery over the last 600 years. The world no longer divides along lines established in Lisbon nor does the world's wealth flow through Portugal's ports. But increasingly this small nation on the tip of continental Europe is reasserting its identity and playing a useful role in Europe and the world. To be sure, the last thirty years have been particularly trying. From dictatorship to democracy, statism to free market, colonial conflict to peace and political stability, the changes since the end of the dictatorship have been both deep and diffuse. Portugal, though, has managed these complex transitions skillfully. Today, Portuguese democracy appears well established and the economy more diversified than in the past.

Still, Portugal faces many challenges. The economy remains in recession, unemployment has increased over 6 percent in the last year, and the government budget has fallen into the red (*The Economist* 2004b). According to the Eurobarometer (European Opinion Research Group 2003), the economy, crime, and drug trafficking represent the most important issues in Portugal, and while support for the EU remains high, it has dropped over fifteen percentage points in the last twelve years. Further, satisfaction with national democracy was lower in Portugal in 2003 than in any other EU country and dissatisfaction higher than all except Italy. Clearly, Portugal's rapid social, economic, and political development over the last thirty years has not come without costs.

However, Portugal appears increasingly confident and forward-looking. Five hundred years after rounding the tip of Africa, Portugal may not have the extensive empire it once commanded, but today it is firmly anchored in Europe, at peace with its neighbors, and prosperity seems within reach.

References, Recommended Readings, and Websites

Books

Anderson, James M. 2000. *The History of Portugal.* Westport, CT.: Greenwood Press.

Banks, Arthur S., Thomas C. Muller, and William R. Overstreet. 2002. *Political Handbook of the World.* Washington, DC: CQ Press.

Birmingham, David. 1993. *A Concise History of Portugal.* Cambridge, UK: Cambridge University Press.

Bromley, John S. 1971. *The New Cambridge Modern History, Vol. 6.* Cambridge, UK: Cambridge University Press.

Bruneau, Thomas C., and Alex Macleod. 1986. *Politics in Contemporary Portugal: Parties and the Consolidation of Democracy.* Boulder, CO: L. Rienner Publishers.

Central Intelligence Agency (CIA). 2003. *The World Factbook* 2003. http://www.cia.gov (accessed August 29, 2003).

Corkill, David. 2002. "Portugal's Changing Integration into the European and Global Economy." In *Contemporary Portugal: Dimensions of Economic and Political Change,* Stephen Syrett, ed. Aldershot, UK: Ashgate, pp. 25–46.

Daalder, Ivo H., and Michael E. O'Hanlon. 2000. *Winning Ugly: NATO's War to Save Kosovo.* Washington, DC: Brookings Institution Press.

Ferreira, Hugo Gil, and Michael W. Marshall. 1986. *Portugal's Revolution: Ten Years On.* Cambridge, UK: Cambridge University Press.

Foyle, Douglas C. 2002. "Public Opinion and Bosnia: Anticipating Disaster." In *Contemporary Cases in U.S. Foreign Policy: From Terrorism to Trade,* Ralph G. Carter, ed. Washington, DC: Congressional Quarterly Press.

Gallagher, Tom. 1983. *Portugal: A Twentieth-Century Interpretation.* Dover, NH: Manchester University Press.

Harsgor, Michael. 1976. *Portugal in Revolution.* Beverly Hills, CA: Sage Publications.

Joll, James. 1984. *The Origins of the First World War.* London: Longman.

Keegan, John. 1994. *A History of Warfare.* New York: Vintage Books.

Kennedy, Hugh N. 1996. *Muslim Spain and Portugal: A Political History of Al-Andalus.* London: Longman.

Lesser, Ian O. 2000. *NATO Looks South: New Challenges and New Strategies in the Mediterranean.* Santa Monica, CA: RAND Corporation.

Liddle Hart, B. H. 1991. *Strategy.* New York: Penguin Books.

Livermore, H. V. 1976. *A New History of Portugal.* Cambridge, UK: Cambridge University Press.

Mailer, Phil. 1977. *Portugal, the Impossible Revolution.* London: Solidarity.

McAlister, Lyle N. 1984. *Spain and Portugal in the New World, 1492–1700.* Minneapolis: University of Minnesota Press.

Moskowitz, Eric, and Jeffrey S. Lantis. 2002. "The War in Kosovo: Coercive Diplomacy." In *Contemporary Cases in U.S. Foreign Policy: From Terrorism to Trade,* Ralph G. Carter, ed. Washington, DC: Congressional Quarterly Press.

North Atlantic Treaty Organization (NATO). 2001. "NATO Handbook." http://www.nato.int (accessed February 19, 2004).

Parker, Geoffrey. 1980. *Europe in Crisis, 1598–1648.* Itaca, NY: Cornell University Press.

Robinson, Richard A. H. 2002. "National Political Change in Portugal, 1976–99." In *Contemporary Portugal: Dimensions of Economic and Political Change,* Stephen Syrett, ed. Aldershot, UK: Ashgate, pp. 179–196.

Sousa, Helen. 2002. "The Liberalization of Media and Communications in Portugal." In *Contemporary Portugal: Dimensions of Economic and Political Change,* Stephen Syrett, ed. Aldershot, UK: Ashgate, pp. 133–156.

Strøm, Kaare, 1990. *Minority Government and Majority Rule.* Cambridge, UK: Cambridge University Press.

Syrett, Stephen, ed. 2002. *Contemporary Portugal: Dimensions of Economic and Political Change.* Aldershot, UK: Ashgate.

Vincent, Mary, and R. A. Stradling. 1994. *Cultural Atlas of Spain and Portugal.* New York: Facts on File.

Wheeler, Douglas L. 1978. *Republican Portugal: A Political History, 1910–1926.* Madison: University of Wisconsin Press.

Articles/Newspapers

Allison, Graham. 2004. "How to Stop Nuclear Terror." *Foreign Affairs* 83, no. 1:64–73.

Bailes, Alyson. 1997. "Europe's Defense Challenge." *Foreign Affairs* 76, no. 1:15–20.

Bennett, D. Scott. 1997. "Testing Alternative Models of Alliance Duration, 1816–1984." *American Journal of Political Science* 41, no. 2:846–878.

Brightwell, Peter. 1982. "Spain, Bohemia, and Europe, 1619–1621." *European Studies Review* 12, no. 4:371–399.

Business Week. 2001. "Putin's Russia." November 12:66–76.

Cordesman, Anthony H. 2002. "Western Military Balance and Defense Efforts." Center for Strategic and International Studies. http://www.csis.org/burke/mb (accessed February 20, 2004).

Daniel M. Jones, Stuart A. Bremer, and J. David Singer. 1996. "Militarized Interstate Disputes, 1816–1992: Rationale, Coding Rules, and Empirical Patterns." *Conflict Management and Peace Science* 15, no. 2:163–213.

Duffield, John S. 2001. "Transatlantic Relations after the Cold War: Theory, Evidence, and the Future." *International Studies Perspectives* 2, no. 1:93–116.

The Economist. 2000a. "In the Club." November 30. http://www.economist.com. (accessed August 8, 2003).

———. 2000b. "Still Travelling Hopefully." November 30. http://www.economist.com. (accessed August 8, 2003).

———. 2001. "A Survey of Russia." July 21. http://www.economist.com (accessed January 12, 2004).

———. 2002. "Who Needs Whom?" March 7. http://www.economist.com. (accessed January 26, 2004).

———. 2004a. "Government by Judges." January 15. http://www.economist.com (accessed January 23, 2004).

———. 2004b. "Forecast." February 17. http://www.economist.com (accessed February 26, 2004).

EU Business. 2003. "World Gathering on Terrorism Closes in Portugal." September 2. http://www.eubusiness.com (accessed February 23, 2004).

European Opinion Research Group. 2003. "Standard Eurobarometer 59: Public Opinion in the European Union." Spring. http://europa.eu.int/comm/public_opinion/standard_en.htm. (accessed February 27, 2004).

Eurostat. Program of the European Union. 2003. "Key Indicators on Member States and Candidate Countries." http://europa.eu.int/comm/eurostat (accessed February 27, 2004).

Feinstein, Lee, and Anne-Marie Slaughter. 2004. "A Duty to Prevent." *Foreign Affairs* 83, no. 1:136–146.

Freedom House. 2003. "Freedom House Country Ratings." http://www.freedomhouse.org/ratings/index.htm (accessed February 27, 2004).

Friedman, Ben. 2003. "The Proliferation Security Initiative: The Legal Challenge." Global Security Institute: Bipartisan Security Group Policy Brief. http://www.gsinstitute.org/programs/bsg.shtml (accessed January 23, 2004).

Ghosn, Faten, and Scott Bennett. 2003. "Codebook for the Dyadic Militarized Interstate Incident Data, Version 3.0." http://cow2.la.psu.edu (accessed January 23, 2004).

Ghosn, Faten, and Glenn Palmer. 2003. "Codebook for the Militarized Interstate Dispute Data, Version 3.0." http://cow2.la.psu.edu (accessed January 23, 2004).

Ghosn, Faten, Glenn Palmer, and Stuart Bremer. 2004. "The MID3 Data Set, 1993–2001: Procedures, Coding Rules, and Description." *Conflict Management and Peace Science* 21, no. 2:133–154.

Gibler, Douglas M., and Meredith Sarkees. Forthcoming. "Measuring Alliances: The Correlates of War Formal Interstate Alliance Data Set, 1816–2000." *Journal of Peace Research* 41, no. 2:211–222.

International Institute for Strategic Studies (IISS). 2003. *The Military*

Balance 2003–2004. London: IISS and Oxford University Press." http://www.iiss.org (accessed January 23, 2004).

Marshall, Monty G., and Keith Jaggers. 2000. "POLITY IV Project: Political Regime Characteristics and Transitions, 1800–1999: Data Users Manual." http://www.bsos.umd.edu/cidcm/inscr/polity (accessed January 23, 2004).

Organization for Security and Cooperation in Europe (OSCE). 2002. Press Release. December 7. http://www.osce.org/cio/archive/portugal (accessed on February 23, 2004).

Rumsfeld, Donald, and Paulo Portes. 2002. "Policy Briefing." June 18. The United States Mission to the European Union. http://www.useu.be (accessed February 16, 2004).

Sarkees, Meredith Reid. 2000. "The Correlates of War Data on War: An Update to 1997." *Conflict Management and Peace Science* 18, no. 1:123–144.

Solsten, Eric, ed. 1993. "Portugal: A Country Study." Library of Congress, Federal Research Division. http://lcweb2.loc.gov/frd/cs (accessed August 8, 2003).

Stockholm International Peace Research Institute (SIPRI). 2003. "Facts on International Relations and Security Trends (FIRST)." http://first.sipri.org (accessed January 23, 2004).

Transparency International. 2003. "Global Corruption Report." http://www.globalcorruptionreport.org (accessed January 23, 2004).

United Nations. 2003. "Human Development Report." http://www.undp.org/hdr2003 (accessed February 17, 2004).

U.S. Agency for International Development. 2003. "U.S. Overseas Loans and Grants, Obligations and Loan Authorizations July 1, 1945–September 30, 2003." http://qesdb.cdie.org/gbk/index.html (accessed May 18, 2005).

U.S. Department of State. "Patterns of Global Terrorism 2001." http://www.state.gov/s/ct/rls/pgtrpt/2001/pdf (accessed February 26, 2004).

———. 2003a. "Bureau of European and Asian Affairs. Background Note: Portugal." November. http://www.state.gov/r/pa/ei/bgn/3208.htm (accessed February 26, 2004).

———. 2003b. "Bureau of European and Asian Affairs. Background Note: Spain." November. http://www.state.gov/r/pa/ei/bgn/2878.htm (accessed February 26, 2004).

———. 2003c. "Commitment to Transatlantic Solidarity: Statement of the United States, Britain, Spain, Portugal at Azores Meeting." March 16. http://usinfo.state.gov/topical/pol/terror (accessed February 23, 2004).

———. 2003d. "The Proliferation Security Initiative." September 15. http://www.state.gov/r/pa/ei/rls/24134.htm (accessed May 18, 2005).

Websites

Consulate of Portugal in the United States: http://www.webx.ca/consulado.new.bedford.eua/eng/main1e.htm.

Country Watch: http://www.countrywatch.com.

General Information: http://www.portugal.gov.pt/Portal/EN/Portugal.

Permanent Mission of Portugal to the United Nations: http://www.un.int/portugal.

Portugal and the EU: http://www.europa.eu.int/abc/governments/portugal/index_en.htm.

Portugal and the WTO: http://www.wto.org/english/thewto_e/countries_e/portugal_e.htm.

Portuguese Embassy in the United States: http://www.portugalemb.org.

Portuguese Government: http://www.portugal.gov.pt/Portal/EN.

Portuguese Ministry of Defense: http://www.mdn.gov.pt/primeira.asp.

Portuguese Ministry of Foreign Affairs: http://www.min-nestrangeiros.pt/mne.

Portuguese Parliament: http://www.parlamento.pt/ingles/index.html.

Portuguese Presidency: http://www.presidenciarepublica.pt/en/main.html.

Portuguese President: http://www.presidenciarepublica.pt/en/main.html.

Portuguese Prime Minister: http://www.portugal.gov.pt/Portal/EN/Primeiro_Ministro.

Portuguese Republic: http://www.presidenciarepublica.pt/en/main.html.

Russia

Tatyana A. Karaman

Geography and History

The Russian Federation (Russia, for short) is the world's largest country in terms of land size. It spreads over two continents—Europe and Asia—covering more than one-tenth of the world's land's surface, some 17,075,200 square kilometers (6,600,000 sq. mi.). Russia's borders comprise 20,139 kilometers of land borders and 37,653 kilometers of coastline. Altogether, Russia boarders fourteen countries: Azerbaijan, Belarus, China, Democratic People's Republic of Korea (North Korea), Estonia, Finland, Georgia, Kazakhstan, Latvia, Lithuania, Mongolia, Norway, Poland, and Ukraine. Its longest borders are with Kazakhstan (6,846 kilometers), China (3,645 kilometers), and Mongolia (3,441 kilometers); its shortest is with North Korea (19 kilometers). Three oceans—the Arctic, Atlantic, and Pacific—touch Russian shores.

The Urals and the Caucasus mountain range act as natural boundaries to separate Europe and Asia. The European part of Russia comprises the great East European Plains. Two of the largest lakes in Europe—Ladoga and Onega—also lie in the European part of Russia, not far from St. Petersburg. The Asian part of Russia lies west of the Urals and is comprised of the West Siberian Plains, the Central Siberian Plateau, and the varied terrain of the Pacific coastal region. The world's deepest lake, Lake Baikal, lies in the Asian part of Russia. Owing to its enormous territory, Russia's climate varies greatly, from subtropical areas in the southwest to frozen territories in the north. Asian Russia has a much harsher climate and less fertile soil than European Russia. Overall, 45 percent of Russia is forest, and only 10 percent is arable land.

Contemporary Russia evolved from the medieval state of Kievan Rus, founded in 882, by the Viking chieftain Oleg. The city of Kiev is located on the Dnieper River, and its favorable location enabled Kievan Rus to flourish, acting as a entrepôt for trade with the Byzantine Empire, western Europe, and Asia. Over time, the Viking state became an important power. In 989, Kievan Rus Prince Vladimir accepted Eastern Orthodox Christianity from Byzantium. By doing so, he brought Christianity to this part of the world, but changing trade routes and a series of nomadic invasions weakened the state. In 1240, the Mongols under Genghis Khan conquered Kievan Rus, and for the next 400 years, Russia was effectively a Mongolian vassal. It began to break free under the czars of Muscovy in the 1500s and was modernized under Peter the Great and Catherine the Great in the 1700s. Following a stormy century and defeat in World War I, Vladimir Lenin and the Bolsheviks established a communist state that lasted from

1917 until 1991. Today's Russian Federation was established in 1991.

Contemporary Russia is a democratic federation with eighty-nine regional units. The federal government is based on a constitution approved in 1993 and is composed of executive, legislative, and judicial branches. The head of government is the president, who is elected for a four-year term and can be reelected for one additional term. The president sets major principles of domestic and foreign policy and represents the country at home and abroad. Russia has a bicameral Parliament. Its upper house, the Federation Council, has 178 seats, with two representatives for each of the eighty-nine regional jurisdictions. The lower house, the State Duma, has 450 members elected for four-year terms. The head of the legislative branch of government is the prime minister. The prime minister appoints the government (cabinet) and administers policy according to the constitution, laws enacted by Parliament, and presidential decrees. The judicial branch of government

has three federal-level judicial bodies, the Constitutional Court, the Supreme Court, and the Superior Court of Arbitration. Judges are appointed by the president, but must be confirmed by the Federation Council.

Russia has a multiparty system with the ideological orientations of parties ranging from [liberal?] pro-Western to communist and nationalist. As a result of the 2003 parliamentary election, four parties obtained seats in the Duma. The pro-government United Russia Party mustered 37.57 percent of the vote. Some 22,779,279 people supported this party. About 7,648,000 people (12.61 percent) supported the Communist Party. The Liberal Democratic Party of Russia (LDPR) enjoyed the support of 6,944,000 voters (11.45 percent), while 5,470,000 voters (9.02 percent) supported the Rodina (motherland) bloc.

In addition to establishing democratic political institutions, the Russian Federation has continued to reform its economy, from the state-controlled Soviet style to a

Table 1   The Russian Federation: Key Statistics

Type of government	Democratic federation
Population (millions)	144.1 (2003)
Religion	Eastern Orthodox 94%, other 6%
Main industries	Energy (natural gas and oil), metals and metal manufactures, machine building, shipbuilding, machine tools.
Main security threats	Chechen separatist movement, terrorism
Defense spending (% GDP)	2.69 (2004)
Size of military (millions)	1.028 (2003)
Number of civil wars since 1945	1 (Chechen war 1994–1996)
Number of interstate wars since 1945	1 (Afghanistan)

Sources

Central Intelligence Agency Website. 2003. CIA *World Factbook*. http://www.cia.gov/cia/publications/factbook/ (accessed May 15, 2005).
Russian Ministry of Defence. 2004. http://www.mil.ru/.
World Bank. 2004. *The World Bank Group: Data & Statistics*. http://www.worldbank.org/data/.

more market-based system. During the 1990s, Russia underwent a rapid economic reform, often referred to as shock therapy, which led to hyperinflation, high levels of unemployment, and a rapid decline in the GDP. However, since 2000 the Russian economy has begun a slow recovery. The year 2003 was an especially successful one for Russia, which registered economic growth of 7.3 percent and a GDP of U.S.$434 billion. Inflation was kept to 10 percent, and a sizable surplus of 1.6 percent of GDP was created.

Conflict Past and Present

Conflict History

In 1480 Moscow, the chief principality of the Russians, finally ended more than two centuries of Mongolian domination and started to expand. By the end of the sixteenth century, Russia had conquered the Tatar (Mongol) states of Kazan, Astrakhan, and Sibir, opening the way to the Pacific Ocean. The most remarkable rise of Russia as a major European power took place under the rule of Peter the Great, who became czar in 1682. His military reforms led to the creation of professional military and naval forces. When Peter became czar, the Russian army was based on the recruitment of peasants led by village elders. The only professional units in the army were the Streltsy and the Cossacks, but their officers were mostly foreign born. In 1699, Peter the Great established a standing army and created two new elite regiments—the Preobrazhenskii and the Semeonovskii, which replaced the Streltsy unit, whose ranks Peter had purged. Beginning in 1705, any Russian male was eligible to be drafted and served in the army for twenty-five years. In addition to modernizing the army, Peter also created the Russian navy, which was originally stationed on the River Don.

Peter used his military forces to wage war against the Ottoman Empire, Persia, and Sweden. Known as the Great Northern War, the conflict with Sweden lasted twenty-one years and depopulated large areas of Russia. In 1709, the new Russian army won its first major victory at Poltava, and in 1714 the Russian navy defeated the Swedes off the Hangö Peninsula. As a result, Russia gained access to the Baltic Sea, acquired Finnish territory, and supplanted Sweden as the dominant power in the Baltic. Victorious over Sweden, Peter proclaimed the Russian Empire in 1721 and established St. Petersburg, a city on the Baltic Sea, as its new capital. Peter endowed his new "window on the West" with a major port and magnificent palaces.

After Peter's death in 1725, Russia faced a succession of weak leaders, until Catherine II ascended the throne in 1762. The German wife of Peter the Great's grandson, Peter III, Catherine quickly became a powerful ruler. Like Peter, she focused on both reform, inviting Cesare Beccaria to reform Russia's penal system, and military expansion. Catherine fought a series of wars with the Ottoman Empire and Poland, acquiring new territories in the south and west. Following the 1768–1774 war with the Ottoman Empire, Russia gained access to the Black Sea, and the Crimean Tatars broke free of Ottoman rule. In 1783, Catherine annexed Crimea, provoking another war with the Ottoman Empire. During this war, Russia expanded southward to the Dniester River. As a result of Russian victories in these wars, the Ottoman Empire ceased to be a serious threat to Russia and was forced to tolerate an increasing Russian influence over the Balkans.

Russia's westward expansion under Catherine II was the result of the partitioning of Poland among Russia, Prussia, and Austria. Through the 1772 partition of Polish territory, Russia acquired parts of Belorussia and Livonia. Poland subsequently initiated an extensive reform program, which included a democratic constitution that alarmed reactionary factions in both Poland and Russia. Using the danger of radicalism as an excuse, in 1793 Russia joined with Prussia and Austria to abrogate the Polish constitution and strip away more territory from Poland. This time Russia obtained most of Belorussia and Ukraine west of the Dnieper River. The 1793 partition led to an anti-Russian and anti-Prussian uprising in Poland, which ended with the third partition in 1795, wiping Poland off the map.

During the nineteenth century, Russia participated in two major conflicts, a victorious war against Napoleon and the devastating Crimean War. In June 1812 the French emperor Napoleon invaded Russia with his Grand Army of nearly 500,000 soldiers. Napoleon controlled most of continental Europe, and his invasion of Russia was an attempt to force Czar Alexander I to honor the terms of a treaty that Napoleon had imposed upon him four years earlier at Tilsit. Outnumbered, the Russians under Marshal Mikhail Kutuzov retreated, destroying crops and harassing the flanks of the Grand Army. By the end of the summer, Napoleon's supply lines could no longer supply his forces, and the scorched earth policy followed by Kutuzov left no local provisions for the Grand Army, whose fighting ability began to decline. Nevertheless, Napoleon continued to make steady progress toward Moscow. To prevent Moscow's occupation, Alexander I insisted on engaging the French army in

---

Sidebar 1   The Russian Army

Since the times of Peter the Great, theft has always been present in the Russian army. It has reached record proportions, however, during the period following the breakdown of the Soviet Union. According to the Ministry of Domestic Affairs, the value of the property stolen from the Russian army from 1990 to 2000 is estimated at 350 billion rubles (approximately U.S.$1.5 billion) with weapons and provisions being the most common object of theft. To combat this problem, criminal charges have been brought against suspected military personnel of all ranks. Nearly 100 Russian generals and admirals have been charged with theft and embezzlement of property of the Russian army. By the results of criminal investigations, additional serious thefts of weapons totaling U.S.$2 billion have been prevented.

Source
"News in Brief." 2002. *Komsomol'skaya Pravda*, August 16:2.

---

major battles at Smolensk (August 17, 1812) and at Borodino Field just seventy miles from Moscow (September 7, 1812). The latter battle cost the French losses comparable to those taken by the Russians. But Kutuzov realized that he could not defend Moscow, so he withdrew his forces, prompting the panic-stricken citizens of Moscow to flee the city. When Napoleon's army arrived on September 14, they found a city abandoned, burned, and bereft of supplies.

Although he had lost his capital and large swaths of Russia, Alexander I refused to surrender. Out of supplies and unable to win a decisive victory over Kutuzov's forces, Napoleon ordered his troops to begin a retreat home. Because Kutuzov's forces blocked the route south, the Grand Army—now seriously suffering from lack of food, severe cold, disease, and fatigue—had to retrace the long, devastated route of the invasion. Starting a 500-mile march to the west in mid-October, the exhausted imperial army found itself in the midst of an unusually early and especially cold winter. Temperatures soon dropped well below freezing, Cossacks attacked isolated units, and food was almost nonexistent. Only about 30,000 French soldiers survived the invasion and the retreat. Napoleon had lost his troops, his horses, his artillery, and any hope of holding his empire. Russia now emerged as a leading power, and in 1814 Russian troops entered Paris.

The immediate cause of the Crimean War (1853–1856) was the dispute between Russia and France over the right to protect Christian pilgrims and holy places in Palestine, then a part of the Ottoman Empire. Once it became clear that the French were likely to win the dispute, the Russian czar, Nicholas I, demanded the Turkish sultan grant Russia the right to protect the Orthodox Church's holy places and all Orthodox subjects of the sultan. When the sultan rejected this demand, the Russian army marched into Turkish territory in July 1853, and, in October 1853, Turkey declared war against Russia.

Afraid that Russia would defeat Turkey and become too powerful in the Balkans, Britain and France declared their alliance with Turkey against Russia in March 1854. That September, a joint British, French, and Turkish force laid siege to the Russian fortress of Sevastopol, which was located on the southwestern tip of the Crimean peninsula. In September 1855,

Sevastopol fell after a yearlong siege that exposed the Russian military as inferior to its Western rivals. But Nicholas I refused to end the war. Only after his death in March 1856 was the Treaty of Paris signed. The treaty forced Russia to give up all Turkish territories occupied during the war and to cease its efforts to protect the Orthodox subjects of the sultan. But the Turkish sultan also declared religious equality for all his subjects, including Christians.

During the first half of the twentieth century, the Russians lived through three international wars, two revolutions, foreign occupation, and a bloody civil war. The Russo-Japanese War (1904–1905) had its roots in the rivalry between Japan and Russia to establish spheres of influence in the Far East. At the time, Japan enjoyed the fruits of a severe treaty it imposed after defeating China in 1894–1895. According to the treaty, China ceded Japan a number of territories, including the island of Formosa (Taiwan) and Port Arthur (now Lüshun) at the tip of the Liao-tung Peninsula in southern Manchuria. But Russia also wanted Port Arthur to establish itself on the Pacific Ocean. So, after obtaining the support of Germany and France, Moscow pressed Japan to relinquish the strategically located Port Arthur. In 1898, Russia pressed China into granting it a lease for the city's port facilities and occupied the peninsula. Russia also concluded an alliance with China against Japan and gained rights to extend the Trans-Siberian Railroad across Chinese-held Manchuria to the Russian seaport of Vladivostok.

Korea now became a second point of rivalry between Russia and Japan. Both sides wished to gain control over the Korean peninsula, especially the Japanese, who saw it as a dagger pointed at the heart of Japan. After a period of tension, Russian and Japanese forces clashed. In 1901, the two countries opened negotiations. But Russia reneged on its promise to withdraw its troops from Manchuria, which Russia had occupied since the Boxer Rebellion in 1900, and so Japan decided to go to war. On February 8, 1904, Japan launched a surprise attack on Port Arthur. In March, the Japanese landed an army in Korea, and in May another Japanese army landed on the Liao-tung Peninsula, cutting off the Port Arthur garrison from the main body of Russian forces in Manchuria. Although Port Arthur's Russian commander surrendered the city to the Japanese on January 2, 1905, fighting continued on land and sea until the naval Battle of Tsushima of May 27–29, 1905, gave the Japanese the upper hand in the conflict.

The peace conference ending this conflict took place in August 1905 at Portsmouth, New Hampshire, with President Theodore Roosevelt serving as mediator. By the Treaty of Portsmouth, Japan gained control of the Liao-tung Peninsula, including Port Arthur and the South Manchurian Railroad, which led to Port Arthur, as well as half of Sakhalin Island. Russia agreed to evacuate southern Manchuria, which was restored to China, and Japan's control of Korea was recognized. Japan established itself as the dominant indigenous power in Asia and a potential threat to the Western powers, as well as to Russia.

Just as defeat in the Crimean War had led to reforms in Russia, so defeat in the Russo-Japanese war contributed to an already unstable situation in Russia. Heavy loss of life and treasure during the war was followed by the civil disturbances known as the Revolution of 1905. Faced with the revolution, the Russian czar Nicholas II issued the October Manifesto, which was the equivalent of a constitutional charter. The October Manifesto established a Russian Parliament, the Duma, and limited the czar's powers.

In 1914, Russia honored its treaty obligations to France and entered what would come to be known as the Great War on the side of the entente against the Central Powers. The war did not go well for Russia. In 1914 the Russian army was the largest in the world, counting almost 5 million soldiers. But it was cumbersome and had to guard a land frontier of more than 1,300 miles. Russia's poor roads and railways hampered the effective deployment of its forces, which were still short of artillery and rifles as a result of the war with Japan. Although the Russians enjoyed considerable success against the Austro-Hungarian army, they suffered heavy losses in East Prussia against the Germans. The czar's strategic mistakes increasingly discredited his government, and inflation and losses at the front led to political tension, strikes, and desertions. Food was in short supply, especially in the Russian capital. By late 1916 in Petrograd, renamed because St. Petersburg sounded too German, the city's inhabitants began the New Year by standing in long lines in front of food shops. In February 1917, bread riots broke out in Petrograd, which, combined with a collapse of Russia's forces at the front and a general lack of confidence in the czar, led Nicholas II to abdicate.

After the monarchy's collapse, a provisional government, headed by Prime Minister Aleksandr Kerensky, was created. However, Kerensky's government continued to wage war rather than sue for peace, and the political and economic crisis continued. On October 25, 1917, the Bolshevik wing of the Russian Social

Democratic Labor Party, which had split in 1903, overthrew the provisional government and established itself as the ruling party. Led by Vladimir Lenin, the coup provoked a civil war that lasted from 1918 through 1921. Fighting initially erupted between the revolutionary forces led by workers of Petrograd, who would form the core of the Red Army, and counterrevolutionary forces, which would become the White Armies, led by former officers of the czarist army. By early 1918, German troops were so close to Petrograd that Lenin's Bolshevik government moved the capital to Moscow, far from the front.

Confronted with an advancing German enemy and counterrevolutionary forces throughout Russia, the Bolshevik government agreed to a humiliating peace with Germany. By the 1918 Treaty of Brest-Litovsk, Russia lost many of its western territories. Angered at Russia's decision to conclude peace with Germany and alarmed at the ascension to power of Lenin's Bolsheviks, Britain, France, the United States, and Japan landed troops in Russia to support the White Armies. The Allies hoped that once the Bolshevik regime was overthrown and monarchy restored, Russia would resume its war with Germany. However, even after Germany was defeated in November 1918, Allied intervention in the Russian civil war against the communists continued.

By the end of 1920, a Bolshevik victory in the civil war seemed all but assured. Although in 1919 Soviet Russia had shrunk to the size of sixteenth-century Muscovy, the Red Army, led by the former Social Revolutionary Lev Trotsky, had the advantage of defending the heartland, with Moscow at its center. In contrast, the White Armies were divided geographically and without a clearly defined

command. Hopes of restoring the monarchy effectively ended when the Bolsheviks executed the imperial family in July 1918. The Allied governments, lacking support for intervention from their own war-weary citizenry, withdrew most of their forces by 1920, although Japan did not do so until 1922. As soon as the Allies had defeated Germany, Russia denounced the Treaty of Brest-Litovsk and established Soviet republics in Belorussia (January 1919), Ukraine (March 1919), Azerbaijan (April 1920), Armenia (November 1920), and Georgia (March 1921), thereby creating the Soviet Union. However, the Bolsheviks were not able to reoccupy Russia's Baltic and Polish territories. As a result, the independent states of Estonia, Latvia, and Lithuania were founded, and Finland and Poland were reborn.

The Soviet Union remained unchallenged from abroad for almost two decades. However, by the end of 1930, with Hitler's rise, the war with Germany was almost unavoidable. Nevertheless, in 1939, Joseph Stalin, who had gradually consolidated his hold on power after Lenin died in 1924, decided to cooperate with Hitler to realize territorial gains. On August 23, Germany and the USSR signed a nonaggression pact with secret protocols. On September 1, the German army invaded Poland and quickly advanced on Warsaw. On September 17, as German troops besieged the Polish capital, Soviet troops invaded Poland from the east, dividing the country according to the terms of the August pact. Stalin also demanded that Finland give up some of its territory for Russian military bases. When the Finnish government rejected Stalin's demand, Soviet forces invaded Finland, starting the Russo-Finish War. Although Soviet troops suffered a series of setbacks, by March 1940 they had ground down the Finnish army, and Finland surrendered and ceded its eastern territories to the USSR. The Soviet Union then invaded the Baltic States of Latvia, Lithuania, and Estonia and forced them to sign treaties allowing Soviet military bases on their territory. In April 1941, following bloody skirmishes between Soviets and Japanese on the border between Manchuria and Siberia, Moscow and Tokyo signed a nonaggression pact.

On June 22, 1941, Hitler attacked the Soviet Union in what the German General Staff had code-named Operation Barbarossa. Shortly afterward, Italy, Romania, Hungary, Slovakia, and Finland declared war on the Soviet Union. By September 1941, German troops had reached Leningrad (formerly Petrograd) and initiated a siege that would last until January 1944, a 900-day struggle, which became a symbol for Soviet resistance to German aggression. In October 1941, German forces passed Minsk and began to close on Moscow, leading the Russian government to evacuate to Kuibyshev (now Samara). Although German troops reached the outskirts of Moscow in December, reinforcements arrived from Siberia under the command of General Zhukov, and a series of Russian counterattacks forced the German army to retreat. The Soviets had also evacuated more than 1,300 factories to the Ural Mountains, along with 10 million workers. As a result, by early 1942, the Soviets were outproducing Germany in every major category of weaponry, from tanks and automatic weapons to aircraft and artillery. Current scholarship considers the failure of German troops to take Leningrad and Moscow in 1941 to have been the turning point of Germany's war with Russia, even though it was not until January 31, 1943, that Germany's defeat was assured with the Soviet victory at

Stalingrad. In the summer of 1942, a much-depleted German army mounted an attack meant to reach the Soviet oil fields at Baku. Stalingrad, named in honor of the Soviet leader and since renamed Volgograd, was considered both a strategic and a symbolic target. But German troops met strong Russian resistance. The battle over Stalingrad lasted for six months (August 19, 1942, to January 31, 1943) until the Soviet army under command of Georgy Zhukov encircled the 6th Army of General Field Marshal Friedrich von Paulus and forced him to surrender. In the battle for the city named after the Soviet leader, Soviet forces killed, captured, or dispersed 600,000 German troops, as well as 350,000 Romanians, 100,000 Hungarians, 100,000 Italians, and 30,000 Slovaks. Among the 107,800 German prisoners of war were twenty-four generals.

In December 1943, Stalin met with Roosevelt and Churchill at Tehran. They agreed that in June 1944 the Western Allies would invade France, and the Soviet Union would launch a new offensive attack from the east. During the late summer, the Soviet army liberated all of the Soviet territory and advanced toward German-occupied eastern European countries. On April 23, 1945, Soviet troops reached Berlin with more than a million men and 20,000 pieces of artillery. A few days later, Soviet troops advancing from the east met U.S. troops advancing from the west at the Elbe River. On May 2, 1945, Soviet troops completed the capture of Berlin, and all remaining German troops surrendered within a few days. The war in Europe was over. However, the war in the Pacific was still in progress. Honoring his promise to his allies, in August Stalin denounced his nonaggression pact with Japan and sent Soviet troops into Japanese-held Manchuria. Soviet historians maintain that this action helped to win the war in the Pacific, although U.S. historians tend to see it as a belated action by Stalin to ensure a Soviet presence in Asia.

The wartime losses of the people of the Soviet Union were enormous. More than 10 million soldiers died in combat or German POW camps, and 10 million civilians perished as well. Estimates of losses run as high as 25 million. More than 70,000 cities and villages were destroyed, and the Soviet economy was devastated, especially the Don-Bass Basin, the heart of Soviet industrial might before 1941, which was the scene of constant fighting. Nonetheless, much as Alexander I's army had ended the Napoleonic Wars as the most formidable army in Europe, so did the Soviet army in 1945 emerge as the most powerful military force on the continent at the end of World War II. Consequently, Britain, France, and the United States could not effectively contest Soviet control of territories that the Soviet army had occupied, and the Western powers couldn't effectively contest Soviet-backed seizures of power by communist parties in Eastern Europe. Instead, the United States and its Western Allies consolidated their own spheres of influence. What began as tension over which ally should control Italy and Poland eventually hardened into what ultimately was named the Cold War, a low-level conflict involving proxy wars and diplomacy, which lasted until 1989.

The Soviet Union was involved in several conflicts during the Cold War. Among the most significant was the use of force to quell rebellions in eastern Europe during the 1950s and in Afghanistan during the 1970s. By the mid-1950s, Soviet rule had become increasingly unpopular in Poland and Hungary. Popular uprisings first broke out in Poland, then a spontaneous revolu-

tion flared in Hungary, prompting Imre Nagy and other Hungarian communist leaders to attempt to establish a multiparty political system and to withdraw from the Warsaw Pact, a defensive alliance of the Soviet Union and eastern European countries founded in 1955. To prevent these changes, in November 1956 Nikita Khrushchev sent troops and tanks to Hungary to crush the revolution. This action demonstrated that Soviet leaders would not hesitate to use force to sustain communist rule in eastern Europe and showed as well that Western leaders, who had encouraged eastern Europeans to rebel, would not aid those who did. Consequently, there were no further uprisings in the region for the next decade.

When rebellion did come, it was peaceful, not violent. During the 1960s, the liberal faction of the Czechoslovakian Communist Party liberalized the country's regime, distanced themselves from the Soviet Union, and strengthened ties with the West. In response, the Soviet Union again used force. In 1968, Soviet and other Warsaw Pact troops entered Czechoslovakia and forced Alexander Dubček and his liberal collaborators from office. But Soviet repression was not as bloody as in 1956, largely because the challenge to their control had not been as violent. The Soviet Union's confirmation of its resolve to maintain its control over eastern Europe became known as the Brezhnev Doctrine and threatened to stymie liberalization movements in the region.

In addition to controlling eastern Europe, the Soviet Union tried to establish its influence over developing countries. During the 1970s, the Soviet Union helped to establish new communist or left-leaning governments in such countries as Angola, Ethiopia, Mozambique, and Nicaragua. In the Middle East, the

Soviet Union vied for influence by backing the Arabs in their dispute with Israel. But Soviet prestige among moderate Muslim states suffered in the 1980s when the Soviet Union sent its army into Afghanistan.

Russian military involvement in Afghanistan has a long history. In the eighteenth century, the Russians and British fought over this country, which eventually became a "buffer state" between the two powers, separating Russian Asia from British-ruled India for almost four decades. After gaining its independence in 1919, Afghanistan was a monarchy until the military took power in a 1973 coup. Once the monarchy was toppled, the country went through a series of coups, until communists seized power. To secure the new communist government, the Soviet Union sent in more than 100,000 troops. However, the majority of the Afghan population resisted both the Soviet troops and the new regime and waged a guerrilla war against them. The war continued until 1989, when Mikhail Gorbachev introduced perestroika and glasnost in the Soviet Union and brought Soviet troops home from Afghanistan.

Present Conflict

Since the collapse of the Soviet Union in 1991, the Russian Federation has struggled to preserve its territorial integrity, with Chechnya presenting a particularly vexing challenge to its efforts to do so. The Republic of Chechnya is located on the north slope of the Caucasus Mountains within 100 kilometers of the Caspian Sea. Russia acquired this territory during the 1818–1919 conquest of the Caucasus. In 1921 Chechnya became a part of the Mountain People's Republic, and in 1936 it became a part of the Chechen-Ingush Republic. After World War II, the republic was dismantled and many of its residents were deported to central Asia as punishment for having collaborated with the Germans. In 1957 the republic was reestablished.

Chechen territory is strategically vital to Russia for two reasons. First, access routes to both the Black Sea and the Caspian Sea go from the center of the federation through Chechnya. Second, vital Russian oil and gas pipeline connections with Kazakhstan and Azerbaijan run through Chechnya. In 1993, the Chechen government of Dzhokar Dudaev declared full independence. In response, in December 1994, the government of Russia sent three armored divisions, pro-Russian Chechen infantry, and internal security troops to crush the separatist movement. The objective was a quick victory followed by pacification and the reestablishment of a pro-Russian government. However, Russian troops encountered strong resistance from Chechen separatists. By 1995, Russian forces had gained control of many urban areas, including Chechnya's capital, Grozny, devastated by urban warfare. But Chechen separatists controlled much of the southern mountain territory and carried out a series of terrorist attacks in other parts of Russia. They mounted a number of hostage-taking attacks, including major actions in Budennovsk in southern Russia in June 1995 and in the Dagestani border town of Pervomayskoye in January 1996. The Pervomayskoye incident led to the complete destruction of the town and numerous civilian casualties. In 1996, Russian troops withdrew, conceding Chechnya de facto autonomy.

In 1997, the chief of staff of the Chechen forces, Aslan Maskhadov, was elected president. However, in 1999, Islamic militants gained power over the republic and established Islamic law. A series of terrorist attacks against Russia, including bombings of Moscow, took place, and Chechen forces again invaded neighboring Dagestan. In response, Russia bombed Chechnya, captured Grozny, and forced separatist guerrillas to retreat to mountains. From there, the rebels have continued to carry out attack, on Russian troops as well as terrorist attacks in Moscow and other major Russian cities. In 2003 Chechnya adopted a new constitution and Akhmad Kadyrov became president. Both the new constitution and the president gained approval of the Russian Federation.

Alliance Structure

During World War II, the Soviet Union joined the alliance with the United States and Britain against Germany, Italy, and Japan. Once the war had ended, the Soviet Union decided to create a buffer zone in eastern Europe to preclude another crippling attack, like those mounted by Germany in 1914 and 1941. By 1949 the Soviet Union had concluded twenty-year bilateral treaties of friendship, cooperation, and mutual assistance with Bulgaria, Czechoslovakia, Hungary, Poland, and Romania, which granted the Soviet Union rights to a continued military presence on their territory. In addition, a significant Soviet garrison (the Group of Soviet Forces) was stationed in eastern Germany. On May 14, 1955, the Soviet Union and Albania, Bulgaria, Czechoslovakia, Hungary, Poland, and Romania signed the multilateral Treaty of Friendship, Cooperation, and Mutual Assistance, which became known as the Warsaw Pact. The Soviet Union claimed that the creation of the Warsaw Pact was in direct response to the inclusion of the Federal Republic of Germany (West Germany) in NATO in 1955. The alliance lasted until March 31, 1991; it was officially dissolved at a meeting in Prague on July 1, 1991.

Since the Soviet Union's collapse, Russia has signed a number of bilateral and multilateral alliance treaties. Among those are entente agreements with France, Mongolia, and North Korea and neutrality and nonaggression pacts with Moldova, Ukraine, Belarus, Armenia, Georgia, Azerbaijan, Turkmenistan, Tajikistan, the Kyrgyz Republic, Uzbekistan, Kazakhstan, and China.

Size and Structure of the Military

The Russian Federation has inherited most of the military forces of the Soviet Union. Overall, the Russian military

Table 2   Soviet and Russian Casualties in Major Conflicts (Twentieth Century)

Conflict	Rival	Date	Total Casualties
Russo-Japanese War	Japan	1904–1905	125,000
WWI	The Central Powers	1914–1919	9,150,000
Soviet-Japanese Border War	Japan	1938–1939	4,000
WWII	The Axis Powers	1939–1945	22,000,000
Soviet-Afghan War	The Mujahiddin	1979–1989	25,000

Sources

Correlates of War Project: International and Civil War Data, University of Michigan. http://www.umich.edu/~cowproj.

Russian Ministry of Defense. 2004. http://www.mil.ru/.

count more that a million officers and enlisted personnel. Structurally, there are three branches—the navy, the air forces, and the ground forces. There are also three independent combat arms not subordinate to any of the three branches—airborne troops, strategic rocket forces, and military space forces. The Russian navy is still one of the most powerful forces afloat. It has a force of 171,500 officers and enlisted personnel deployed in the Northern Fleet, the Pacific Fleet, the Baltic Fleet, the Black Sea Fleet, and the Caspian flotilla. The navy operates about seventy-five warships of various types, including aircraft carriers, cruisers, destroyers, and frigates. In addition, it deploys around 240 submarines, including 14 operational nuclear-powered ballistic missile submarines. The Russian air forces have 186,600 officers and enlisted personnel and deploy more than 4,700 aircraft of various types, including strategic bombers, attack aircraft, and carrier-based aircraft.

The ground forces make up the largest branch of the Russian military forces. They are estimated to number approximately 670,000 officers and enlisted personnel. The ground forces are organized into eight military districts, one independent army, and two groups of forces. They include about seventy divisions, including armored divisions, motorized infantry divisions, and airborne divisions. The main armament of the ground forces consists of 19,000 main battle tanks, 20,000 artillery pieces, 600 surface-to-surface missiles with nuclear capability, and about 2,600 attack and transport helicopters.

Territorially, the ground forces are divided into eight military districts: the Northern, Moscow, Volga, North Caucasus, Ural, Siberian, Transbaikal, and Far Eastern districts. The Northern Military

---

Sidebar 2   Nuclear Force of Russia

Russia reserves the right of first use of nuclear weapons and its nuclear forces are an important part of its military. According to May 2004 statistics, Russia has approximately 8,000 nuclear warheads, 627 missile systems that can carry up to 2,429 nuclear warheads, 12 operational nuclear-powered ballistic missile submarines that can carry 672 nuclear warheads, 78 strategic aircrafts that can carry up to 852 long-range cruise missiles, and 897 strategic delivery platforms that can carry up to 3,953 nuclear warheads. The space tier of the Russian nuclear forces includes three early-warning satellite systems that transmit information in real time to the command center.

Sources
Russian Ministry of Defense. 2004. http://www.mil.ru/articles/article3665.shtml.
Stockholm International Peace Research Institute. 2003. *SIPRI Yearbook 2003: Armaments, Disarmament and International Security.* London: Oxford University Press.

District is the successor to the Soviet-era Leningrad Military District. The district includes the 6th Combined Arms Army, the 30th Army Corps, the 56th District Training Center, and several smaller units. One air army also is stationed in the district, but it appears to be subordinate to the Air Force High Command. The airborne division is stationed at Pskov. Formerly subordinate to the Ministry of Defense, it was reassigned for special combined duty in 1996.

The Moscow Military District is an anomaly in the command structure because it includes the national capital. It has special significance because of its proximity to the western border with Belarus and Ukraine, traditionally the routes followed by invaders from the west. The district's official troop strength includes the 1st and 22nd Combined Arms armies and the 20th Army Corps. Other forces within the Moscow District include the Moscow Air Defense District, one airborne brigade, and one brigade of special forces (spetsnaz) troops. The special forces brigade is directly subordinate to the Ministry of Defense.

The Volga Military District, headquartered at Samara, is an interior district that includes the 2nd Combined Arms Army, together with an airborne division that is operationally subordinate to the Ministry of Defense. The 2nd Combined Arms Army consists of the 16th and 90th Tank divisions. Also in the Volga District are the 27th Motorized Rifle Division and the 469th District Training Center, which are directly subordinate to the district commander.

The North Caucasus Military District, headquartered at Rostov-na-Donu, faces the former Soviet republics of Georgia, Armenia, and Azerbaijan. It includes the 58th Combined Arms Army and the 8th and 67th Army Corps. However, these are not powerful forces. The 8th Army Corps and the 58th Army each include only one motorized rifle division, and the 67th Army Corps has only reserve forces with no heavy equipment. The weakness of these units has helped motivate Russian proposals to renegotiate CFE (Conventional Armed Forces in Europe) Treaty limitations to allow additional forces along Russia's southern flank.

The Ural Military District lies south of the Northern District and east of the Ural Mountains, with the Siberian District to its east. The Ural District, whose headquarters is at Yekaterinburg, includes two tank divisions and two motorized rifle divisions. The Siberian Military District lies in the center of Asiatic Russia, with its headquarters in Novosibirsk. Its ground forces are organized into one corps of four motorized rifle divisions and one artillery regiment.

The Transbaikal Military District is headquartered in Chita. The district comprises three combined arms armies, totaling four tank divisions and six motorized rifle divisions. One tank division and one motorized rifle division are headquartered at district training centers that are believed to be directly subordinate to the district headquarters. One artillery division and two machine-gun artillery divisions deployed on the Chinese border also have district training center status.

The Far Eastern Military District, headquartered in Khabarovsk, includes four combined arms armies and one army corps. Among them, those units have three tank divisions and thirteen motorized rifle divisions, of which one tank division and two motorized rifle divisions have headquarters that serve as district training centers. One artillery division and five machine-gun artillery divisions are directly subordinate to district headquarters.

The president of the Russian Federation is the commander-in-chief, and executive authority over the military lies in the office of the president. The government (Council of Ministers) is responsible for maintaining the armed forces at the appropriate level of readiness. The State Duma exercises legislative authority through the government. Direct leadership of the armed forces is vested in the Ministry of Defense, and the General Staff exercises operational control.

The Ministry of Defense directs the armed services and all military activities on a daily basis. It is responsible for fielding, arming, and supplying the armed services, and in peacetime all territorial commands of the armed forces reported to it. The Ministry of Defense consists of the General Staff and a number of main and central directorates. The Ministry of Defense is managed by a collegium of three first deputy ministers, six deputy ministers, and a chief military inspector, who together form the principal staff and advisory board of the minister of defense.

The General Staff is a major link in the centralization of the Russian national command authority. It provides staff support and acts as the executive agency for the Supreme High Command. Similar to the Ministry of Defense, the General Staff is dominated by the ground forces. In wartime the General Staff would become the executive agent of the Supreme High Command, supervising the execution of military strategy and operations by subordinate commands. The General Staff would exercise direct control over the combat arms of the armed forces that operate strategic nuclear weapons and would coordinate the activities and missions of the armed services.

During the Soviet era, the military was a very conservative and influential institution determining the nation's prerogatives in both national security and foreign policy. However, once the Soviet Union collapsed, a new military doctrine became necessary. After long discussion, in 1993 Russia finally produced a military doctrine designed to fit a completely new set of global and domestic circumstances. Many of the priorities in the Soviet Union's national security doctrine—such as the capability to launch amphibious invasions in support of client states on the other side of the world—had no logical priority in the new Russian state. At the same time, the Russian military retained a strong role in the formation of a new national foreign policy, especially policy relating to the recently independent former Soviet states.

The new military doctrine defines the primary objective for the armed forces as the prevention, early termination, and containment of military conflict through employment of peacetime standing forces. The principal areas of concern are the territory and property of the Russian Federation, the areas contiguous to its borders, and the threat of nuclear attack by a foreign power. Military operations in Chechnya are justified under the paragraph on protection of the territory and property of the Russian Federation. Justification for a continued Russian military presence in the former central Asian republics derives from the paragraph on protection of areas contiguous to Russian borders, as well as provisions of the CIS treaty.

Budget

Prior to its collapse, the Soviet Union devoted between 15 and 17 percent of its annual gross national product to military spending. Until the early 1980s, Soviet defense expenditures rose between 4 and 7 percent per year. Subsequently, they slowed as the yearly growth in Soviet GNP slipped to about 3 percent. In 1988 military spending was a single line item in the state budget, totaling 21 billion rubles, or about U.S.$33 billion. During the 1990s, Russia's deteriorating economic situation negatively affected military spending, resulting in about a 5 percent cut from 1995 to 1999. In addition, throughout the 1990s, there were substantial differences between adopted military budgets and actual expenditures, reflecting shortfalls in government tax revenues.

Military spending continued to decline in 2001 and 2002. However, the 2004 national budget seemed to disrupt this pattern. National defense appropriations for 2004 exceed all other appropriations, accounting for 20.33 percent of the entire budget. Overall, the Russian armed forces will receive 411,472,653,400 rubles, or 2.69 percent of the entire Russian GDP, which is 66,947 million rubles more than the 2003 figure.

Civil-Military Relations/The Role of the Military in Domestic Politics

Prior to the Bolshevik revolution in 1917, the Russian monarchy exercised control over the military. During communist rule, civil-military relations were characterized by strong party control over the military. The leadership of the Communist Party determined under what circumstances and to what degree the military should be involved in politics, and the military strictly followed the party's directions. The military's compliance was ensured though politicizing the army and making the high command and officers members of the Communist Party. In addition, the institute of military-political commissars was established to monitor the day-to-day activity of officers and soldiers at all levels. Party control of the military was extremely efficient in preventing the military from any unregulated involvement in the foreign and domestic politics of the state. As a result, there has been not a single attempt by the military to take the power into its hands. Even when hundreds of officers were executed during periods of repression, the military did not attempt a coup.

However, this type of civil-military relations began to unravel once Mikhail Gorbachev started the process of liberal-

ization. The search for a new doctrine redefining the military's role in society began in the late 1980s, but before it could be completed, the Soviet Union disintegrated. As a result, the newly established Russian Federation had to reform its military and to redefine the principles of civil-military relations suitable to a democracy. This task was clearly complicated by the fact that the 1993 constitution of the Russian Federation failed to define the role of the armed forces in society.

Contemporary reforms of civil-military relations have focused on increasing civilian control of the military through the legislature and the Ministry of Defense, as well as on the increasing role of the president in defining the role of the military in politics. To ensure legislative oversight of the military, Russian Parliament has created several Duma committees dealing with issues of security and defense, including the Defense Committee and the Security Committee. In addition, legislators exercise a certain degree of control over the military through budget appropriations.

At the same time, presidential influence over the military has become more visible over the years. According to the constitution, the president of the Russian Federation appoints and dismisses all ministers, including the minister of defense. He also nominates the members of the Russian Security Council, which he chairs; approves the military doctrine of the Russian Federation; appoints and dismisses higher military commanders; and is the supreme commander of the armed forces. These constitutional provisions guarantee presidential domination in civil-military relations.

Appointing a civilian to the post of minister of defense became the most visible sign of establishing civilian control over the country's national security policy as well as a high degree of presidential influence over the institution. Early proposals that a civilian should be the minister of defense were made in 1991. However, it took ten years for the idea to be realized. In March 2001, President Vladimir Putin made a sweeping decision by appointing Sergei Ivanov the minister of defense and a woman, Lyubov Kudelina, to a senior defense ministry post formerly the domain of uniformed male officers.

Terrorism

Since the 1990s, terrorism has become one of the major concerns of the Russian Federation. Most of the terrorist attacks committed on Russian territory have been executed by the Chechen separatists or credited to them. The first significant terrorist act occurred in Budennovsk in 1995 when Chechen separatists under command of Basaev occupied this small town. During the attack, 129 people, including 18 policemen and 17 servicemen, were killed, and 415 citizens were wounded. More than 1,600 people were kept without food and water as hostages in the local hospital. The attack shocked the Russian people and demonstrated the vulnerability of the country to terrorist actions. In January 1996, Chechen separatists mounted another attack. This time they took hostage some 200 noncombatants in the Dagestani town of Pervomayskoye, eventually executing civilians and completely destroying the town. Since then, the toll of terrorist attacks has continued to grow, including shopping center, metro train, and apartment building bombings and hostage taking in the Russian capital, Moscow. Moscow's most dreadful terrorist attack occurred on Oc-

tober 23, 2002, when more than forty armed Chechen militants took hostage 800 Moscow theatergoers to demand an immediate end to all Russian military actions in Chechnya. More than 120 of the hostages—including one U.S. citizen—died from a narcotic gas used during the rescue operation.

Russia has sought to combat terrorism in a number of ways both overseas and at home. The country has participated in a number of G-7/P-8 ministerial conferences on counterterrorism, and the Russian security forces underwent a counterterrorist training. After the September 11 attack, President Putin was the first foreign leader to call President Bush and offer support. In the aftermath, the United States and Russia have established a close partnership to fight the common threat of terrorism. Within the framework of this partnership, Russia has opened its airspace for humanitarian missions, offered to share intelligence, and provided strong support for the anti-Taliban Northern Alliance in Afghanistan. In addition to the partnership with the United States, Russia has cooperated with the members of the European Union. At the November 2002 Summit, the EU and Russia reached agreement on a far-reaching framework for the fight against terrorism through more intensified cooperation. The framework sets out the shared values and commitments in the fight against terrorism and identifies a series of specific areas for future EU-Russia cooperation.

Relationship with the United States

Since the end of World War II, relations with the United States have occupied a central role in Soviet foreign policy. Both the Soviet Union and the United States emerged from the war as leading world powers. However, their wartime relationship deteriorated once the Soviet Union decided to establish its zone of control in eastern Europe. The relationships deteriorated further in the 1950s as the Soviet Union developed first a nuclear capability and then a nuclear strategy. At that point, the relations between the countries were reduced to the choice of mutual nuclear annihilation or continued hostility expressed in the diplomatic struggles and proxy wars of the Cold War era.

The Cuban Missile Crisis (October 1962) marked the climax of the Cold War in the sense that a nuclear war suddenly seemed imminent. The crisis started on October 16, 1962, when the United States discovered that the Soviet Union had installed medium- and intermediate-range ballistic missiles in Cuba. After considering various options, President John F. Kennedy decided to place a naval quarantine, or blockade, on Cuba to prevent further Soviet shipments of missiles. Once the blockade was established, the Soviet ships delivering missiles to Cuba chose not to attempt to force through it and instead returned to the Soviet Union. Subsequently, the leaders of the two nations reached an agreement. The Soviet Union promised to remove the missiles from Cuba, and the United States promised not to invade Cuba and to remove U.S. missiles from Turkey.

The 1970s witnessed a short period of detente in the relationship between the United States and the Soviet Union. In 1972, the countries concluded the Anti-Ballistic Missile Treaty (ABM Treaty). According to the treaty, both sides promised not to build antiballistic missile systems, which were supposed to intercept and destroy enemy missiles before they could reach their targets. It was assumed that building such a system would increase a likelihood of nuclear war, because it would allow a nation to survive a nuclear attack. Therefore, the ABM Treaty served as a sign of goodwill between the superpowers.

However, the period of detente ended once the Soviet Union invaded Afghanistan in December 1979. In response to the Soviet invasion, the United States organized a trade and cultural embargo against the Soviet Union, including the U.S. boycott of the 1980 summer Olympic Games in Moscow. The tension between the countries remained high until the mid-1980s when Mikhail Gorbachev came to power in the Soviet Union.

In 1985, U.S. President Ronald Reagan and the new Soviet leader began a series of annual summit meetings that resulted in the Intermediate-Range Nuclear Forces Treaty (INF Treaty, 1987) and a number of cultural exchange agreements. As a result, journalists from both sides gained access to everyday lives of presumed enemies, and a series of exchanges began between the public of the two nations, leading to the end of the Cold War. In July 1991, Presidents Gorbachev and George H. W. Bush declared a United States–Soviet strategic partnership signifying the formal end of the Cold War.

During the earlier 1990s, the Soviet Union, and then Russia, supported the United States on several international issues. In the UN Security Council, the Soviet Union and Russia supported sanctions and operations against Iraq before, during, and after the Iraqi invasion of Kuwait in 1990; called on the Democratic People's Republic of Korea (North Korea) to abide by safeguards of the International Atomic Energy Agency (IAEA); supported sending UN observers to conflict-ridden Georgia and Tajikistan; and supported UN economic sanctions against Serbia. The Soviet Union cosponsored Middle East peace talks that opened in October 1991.

With respect to strategic arms control, Russia continued cooperation with the United States established by the Soviet Union. In January 1993, Russian President Boris Yeltsin and U.S. President Bush signed the second Strategic Arms Reduction Treaty (START II). In addition, in September 1993, Russia acceded to the Missile Technology Control Regime, promising not to transfer sensitive missile technology to India.

However, in the mid-1990s, the newly established Russo-American friendship and cooperation ran into a series of problems. Among other things, Russia specifically opposed a NATO membership for central European and Baltic countries. In turn, the United States criticized Russian involvement in Georgia and Russia's insistence on selling nuclear reactor technology to Iran. Another blow to U.S.-Russia relations came in 1994 with the U.S. arrest of Aldrich Ames, a longtime Soviet and Russian spy. Nevertheless, many elements of bilateral cooperation, including most U.S. aid programs, continued.

After the September 11 attack, U.S.-Russia relations focused on a partnership to fight terrorism. But the partnership was strained by the unilateral U.S. decision to withdraw from the 1972 ABM Treaty. On May 24, 2002, Presidents George W. Bush and Vladimir Putin signed Strategic Offensive Reduction Treaty (SORT), under which the United States and Russia will reduce their strategic arsenals to 1,700–2,200 warheads each. Although the two sides have not agreed and appear unlikely to agree on specific counting rules, the Bush administration has made clear that it will reduce only warheads deployed on strategic de-

livery vehicles in active service, that is, "operationally deployed" warheads, and will not count warheads removed from service and placed in storage or warheads on delivery vehicles undergoing overhaul or repair.

The Future

Terrorism will probably continue to be the main concerns of Russian national security in the short term. This concern will unite Russia with the United States and European Community. So far, the partners managed to agree on a common agenda to fight terrorism, but reaching agreement on how to deal concretely with weapons of mass destruction has proven more difficult. Specifically, the future partnership among the United States, the European Community, and Russia will depend on their ability to develop a common stance with respect to nuclear programs of North Korea and Iran. Also, despite cooperation with NATO, it is unlikely that Russia will join the organization any time in the near future. Nevertheless, Russia will play an active role in defining European security through its involvement in the Organization for Security and Cooperation in Europe (OSCE).

References, Recommended Readings, and Websites

Books
Adams, Jan S. 1992. *A Foreign Policy in Transition: Moscow's Retreat from Central America and the Caribbean, 1985–1992.* Durham, NC: Duke University Press.
Adelman, Jonathon R. 1982. *Communist Armies in Politics.* Boulder, CO: Westview.
Avrich, Paul. 1972. *Russian Rebels, 1600–1800.* New York: Schocken.
Barylski, R. V. 1998. *The Soldier in Russian Politics: Duty, Dictatorship and Democracy under Gorbachev and*

Yeltsin. London: Transaction Publishers.

Billington, James H. 1966. *The Icon and the Axe: An Interpretive History of Russian Culture*. New York: Knopf.

Blackwell, William L. 1968. *The Beginnings of Russian Industrialization, 1800–1860*. Princeton, NJ: Princeton University Press.

Blank, Stephen. 1994. *The New Russia in the New Asia*. Carlisle Barracks, PA: U.S. Army War College Strategic Studies Institute.

Brusstar, James H., and Ellen Jones. 1995. *The Russian Military's Role in Politics.* (McNair Paper No. 34). Washington, DC: National Defense University Institute for National Strategic Studies.

Chew, Allen F. 1970. *An Atlas of Russian History: Eleven Centuries of Changing Borders*. New Haven, CT: Yale University Press.

Colton, Timothy J. 1979. *Commissars, Commanders, and Civilian Authority: The Structure of Soviet Military Politics*, London: Harvard University Press.

Curtiss, John Shelton. 1965. *The Russian Army under Nicholas I, 1825–1855.* Durham, NC: Duke University Press.

Dawisha, Karen, and Bruce Parrott. 1994. *Russia and the New States of Eurasia: The Politics of Upheaval*. Cambridge: Cambridge University Press.

De Madariagha, Isabel. 1981. *Russia in the Age of Catherine the Great*. New Haven, CT: Yale University Press.

Dmytryshyn, Basil. 1977. *A History of Russia*. Englewood Cliffs, NJ: Prentice-Hall.

Donnelly, Christopher. 1988. *Red Banner: The Soviet Military System in Peace and War*. Coulsden, Surrey: Janes Information Group.

Geyer, Dietrich. 1987. *Russian Imperialism: The Interaction of Domestic and Foreign Policy, 1860–1914*. Bruce Little, trans. New Haven, CT: Yale University Press.

Glantz, David M. 1992. *Soviet and Commonwealth Military Doctrine in Revolutionary Times*. Ft. Leavenworth, KS: Foreign Military Studies Office.

Grechko, Aleksander. 1977. *The Armed Forces of the Soviet Union*. Moscow: Progress.

Herspring, Dale R. 1996. *Russian Civil-Military Relations*, Bloomington: Indiana University Press.

Hosking, Geoffrey A. 1973. *The Russian Constitutional Experiment: Government and Duma, 1907–1914.* Cambridge: Cambridge University Press.

Jelavich, Barbara. 1964. *A Century of Russian Foreign Policy 1814–1914.* Philadelphia: Lippincott.

Keep, John L. H. 1963. *The Rise of Social Democracy in Russia*. Oxford, UK: Clarendon.

Kliuchevsky, Vasily. 1959. *A Course in Russian History, 4: Peter the Great*. Liliana Archibald, trans. New York: Knopf.

Lincoln, Bruce D. 1978. *Nicholas I: Emperor and Autocrat of All the Russians*. Bloomington: Indiana University Press.

MacKenzie, David, and Michael W. Curran. 1987. *A History of Russia and the Soviet Union*. Chicago: Dorsey Press.

Malozemoff, Andrew. 1958. *Russian Far Eastern Policy, 1881–1904.* Berkeley: University of California Press. Reprint, New York: Octagon, 1977.

Mandelbaum, Michael. 1991. *The Rise of Nations in the Soviet Union*. New York: Council on Foreign Relations Press.

Norretranders, Bjarne. 1964. *The Shaping of Czardom under Ivan Groznnyi*. Copenhagen. Reprint, London: Variorum, 1971.

Pelenski, Jaroslav. 1974. *Russia and Kazan: Conquest and Imperial Ideology, 1438–1560s*. The Hague: Mouton.

Rogger, Hans. 1987. *Russia in the Age of Modernization and Reform, 1881–1917.* London: Longman.

Saikal, Amin, and William Maley. 1995. "From Soviet to Russian Foreign Policy." In *Russia in Search of Its Future*, Amin Saikal and William Maley, eds. Cambridge: Cambridge University Press, pp.102–122.

Schwartz, Solomon H. 1967. *The Russian Revolution of 1905: The Workers' Movement and the Formation of Bolshevism and Menshevism*. Chicago: University of Chicago Press.

Sestanovich, Stephen. 1994. *Rethinking Russia's National Interests.* Washington, DC: Center for Strategic and International Studies.

Shevtsova, Lilia. 2003. *Putin's Russia.* Washington, DC: Carnegie Endowment for International Peace.

SIPRI Yearbook 2003. New York: Humanities Press.

Smith, Clarence J. 1946. *The Russian Struggle for World Power, 1914–1917: A Study of Russian Foreign Policy during World War I.* New York: Philosophical Society.

Taylor, Brian D. 2003. *Politics and the Russian Army: Civil-Military Relations, 1689–2000.* New York: Cambridge University Press.

Thaden, Edward C. 1981. *Russification of the Baltic Provinces and Finland, 1855–1914.* Princeton, NJ: Princeton University Press.

Vernadsky, George. 1954. *The Mongols and Russia.* New World Defense Almanac 2001–2002. New Haven, CT: Yale University Press.

Articles/Reports

Adams, Jan S. 1994. "Who Will Make Russia's Foreign Policy in 1994?" *RFE/RL Research Report* 3:36–40.

Alexandrovna, Olga. 1993. "Divergent Russian Foreign Policy Concepts." *Aussenpolitik* 4:363–372.

Allison, Roy. 1994. "Russian Peacekeeping: Capabilities and Doctrine." *Jane's Intelligence Review* 6:544–547.

Almquist, Peter. 1993. "Arms Producers Struggle to Survive as Defense Orders Shrink." *RFE/RL Research Report* 2:33–41.

Arbatov, Alexei G. 1993. "Russia's Foreign Policy Alternatives." *International Security* 18:5–43.

Barylski, Robert V. 1992. "The Soviet Military before and after the August Coup." *The Armed Forces & Society* 19, no. 1:27–45.

Bogaturov, Alexei D. 1993. "Russia in Northeast Asia." *Korea and World Affairs* 17:298–315.

Brzezinski, Zbigniew. 1994. "The Premature Partnership." *Foreign Affairs* 73, no. 2:67–82.

Crow, Suzanne. 1994. "Why Has Russian Foreign Policy Changed?" *RFE/RL Research Report* 3, no. 18:1–6.

Dick, Charles. 1994. "The Military Doctrine of the Russian Federation." *Jane's Intelligence Review* 6:1–12.

Handler, Joshua. 1995. "The Future of Russia's Strategic Forces." *Jane's Intelligence Review* 7:162–165.

Herspring, Dale R. 1995. "The Russian Military: Three Years On." *Communist and Post-Communist Studies* 28, no. 2:163–182.

———. 1999. "The Russian Military Faces 'Creeping Disintegration.'" *Demockratizatsiya: The Journal of Post-Soviet Democratization* 7, no. 4:580–596.

Hudson, George E. 1994. "Russia's Search for Identity in the Post-Cold-War World." *Mershon International Studies Review* 38:235–240.

Jones, Ellen, and James H. Brusstar. 1993. "Moscow's Emerging Security Decisionmaking System: The Role of the Security Council." *Journal of Slavic Military Studies* 6:345–374.

Jonson, Lena. 1994. "The Foreign Policy Debate in Russia: In Search of a National Interest." *Nationalities Papers* 1:175–193.

Kasatkin, Anatoliy. 1994. "Priorities and Other Components of Foreign Policy." *International Affairs* 12:79–86.

Kozyrev, Andrei. 1994. "The Lagging Partnership." *Foreign Affairs* 73, no. 3:59–71.

———. 1995. "Partnership or Cold Peace?" *Foreign Policy* 99:3–14.

Lepingwell, John W. R. 1993. "Restructuring the Russian Military." *RFE/RL Research Report* 2, no. 25:17–24.

———. 1994. "The Russian Military and Security Policy in the 'Near Abroad.'" *Survival* 36:70–92.

Lugar, Richard G. 1992. "Assessing the Soviet Union and Eastern Europe in the 1990s." *Problems of Communism* 41:76–80.

Lunev, Stanislav. 1996. "Future Changes in Russian Military Policy." *Prism* 2:1–5.

The Military Balance, 1993–1994. London: Brassey's, 1993.

The Military Balance, 1994–1995. London: Brassey's, 1994.

The Military Balance, 1995–1996. London: Brassey's, 1995.

The Military Balance, 1999–2000. London: Brassey's, 1999.

Olcott, Martha Brill. 1995. "Sovereignty and the 'Near Abroad.'" *Orbis* 39:353–367.

Oznobishchev, Sergei. 1996. "Russia Now Has Its Own 'National Security Policy.'" *Prism* 2:1–5.

Pushkov, Alexei K. 1993. "Letter from Eurasia: Russia and America—The Honeymoon's Over." *Foreign Policy* 93:76–90.

Slagle, James H. 1994. "New Russian Military Doctrine: Sign of the Times." *Parameters* 24:88–89.

Szporluk, Roman. 1993. "Belarus, Ukraine, and the Russian Question: A Comment." *Post-Soviet Affairs* 9:366–374.

———. 1994. "Soviet Domestic Foreign Policy: Universal Ideology and National Tradition." *Nationalities Papers* 22 (Spring):195–207.

Timmermann, Heinz. 1992. "Russian Foreign Policy under Yeltsin: Priority for Integration into the 'Community of Civilized States.'" *Journal of Communist Studies* 8:163–185.

Tolz, Vera. 1993. "Thorny Road toward Federalism in Russia." *RFE/RL Research Report* 2:1–8.

Webber, Mark. 1993. "The Emergence of the Foreign Policy of the Russian Federation." *Communist and Post-Communist Studies* 26:243–263.

Werner, Klaus. 1993. "Russia's Foreign Trade and the Economic Reforms." *Intereconomics* 28:144–152.

Wittag, Gerhard. 1994. "Moscow's Perception of NATO's Role." *Aussenpolitik* 2:123–133.

Yassman, Victor. 1993. "Five Different Perceptions on the Future of Russian Foreign Policy." *Demokratizatsiya* 4:84–95.

Zelikow, Philip. 1994. "Beyond Boris Yeltsin." *Foreign Affairs* 73, no. 1:44–55.

Websites

Central Intelligence Agency. *World Factbook. http://www.cia.gov.*

Russian Ministry of Defense. http://www.mil.ru/ (In Russian).

State Committee of the Russian Federation on Statistics: http://www.gks.ru/ (In Russian).

The World Bank of Russia Country Office. Russian Economic Report #7. 2004. http://www.worldbank.org.ru.

Saudi Arabia

Ronald R. Macintyre

Geography and History

Flying down the Persian Gulf (hereafter Gulf) one is impressed by the development of modern cities, airports, refineries, and petrochemical plants in Saudi Arabia and neighboring Gulf states. But it was only about seventy years ago that about 90 percent of the people in Saudi Arabia lived in humble villages or Bedouin encampments. Today, however, most live in modern cities and towns and invest heavily in modern technology and consumer goods. But behind the outward symbols of modernity, impressions can be deceptive. Look more closely at Saudi Arabian society and its religiously conservative Islamic face comes to light: a face that has been resistant to modernizing value change. Ninety percent of the population is Arab and 10 percent Afro-Asian. In religion the indigenous population is 100 percent Muslim. This includes between 5 and 10 percent Shiite Muslims, who are mainly found in the Al-Hasa region, also known as the Eastern Province of the kingdom. There are also about 6 million expatriates—mainly Asian and European—out of a population of 24.3 million in the kingdom (see Table 1).

Saudi Arabia is the largest and most powerful state in the Arabian Peninsula.

Table 1   Saudi Arabia: Key Statistics

Type of government	Traditional monarchy
Population (millions)	24.3
Religion	Islam 100% (2003)
Main industries	Oil
Main security threats	Maritime disputes with Kuwait and Iran, tribal resistance to boundary demarcation, regional instability from Gulf wars, internal Islamic extremism, ongoing tensions resulting from Arab-Israeli conflict
Defense spending (% GDP)	13 (2003)
Size of military (thousands)	200
Number of civil wars since 1945	0
Number of interstate wars since 1945	2

Sources

Central Intelligence Agency Website. 2005. CIA *World Factbook.* Saudi Arabia. http://www.cia.gov/cia/publications/factbook/ (accessed May 15, 2005).
International Institute for Strategic Studies (IISS). 2003. *The Military Balance 2003–2004.* London: IISS and Oxford University Press.

It is sometimes referred to as the "Kingdom," "Family Business," or the "House of Saud" (Al Saud). It makes up over 80 percent of the Arabian Peninsula, and with a land area of approximately 2.2 million square kilometers is roughly the size of western Europe or the United States east of the Mississippi. It is bounded in the north by Egypt, Israel, Jordan, and Iraq and on the east by the Gulf states of Kuwait, Bahrain, Qatar, the United Arab Emirates (UAE), and Oman; in the south Saudi Arabia (capital Riyadh) shares its longest frontier with a united Yemen (1990). Saudi Arabia is strategically located between Africa and mainland Asia, lying close to the Suez Canal, and has borders on both the Red Sea and the Persian Gulf (al-Farsy 1991, 1–2).

Saudi Arabia's increase in prominence since independence (1932) followed the discovery of commercial quantities of oil in 1938 by a consortium of U.S. oil companies, which formed the influential Arabian American Oil Company (ARAMCO). Since the mid-1970s Saudi Arabia has been a major oil player on the world stage. Its oil reserves amount to 25 percent of proven world oil reserves. Conservatively it can produce over 10 percent of the world's daily oil needs, and, most importantly, it has excess capacity to meet increasing world demands within the Organization of Petroleum Exporting Countries (OPEC 1960). In a world increasingly dependent on fossil fuel, Saudi Arabia's ability to produce oil at a reasonable price—and to meet shortfalls in global oil production—may be seen to be crucial to the development of its relationship with the United States and other industrialized countries. In 2004 Saudi Arabia was the largest oil exporter in the world and currently ranks only second to Canada in the list of oil exporting countries to the United States. To illustrate the magnitude of this: The United States imported 19 percent of its oil from Saudi Arabia, or 1.8 million barrels of oil per day, in the first eight months of 2003 (Country Analysis Briefs 2003).

Without oil Saudi Arabia would literally be a dead camel in the desert. Petroleum contributes 75 percent of the kingdom's budgetary revenues, 40 percent of its GDP, and 90 to 95 percent of government earnings. It is also rich in a number of metals (bauxite, copper, iron, lead, tin, zinc), including reserves of gold (al-Farsy 1991, 3). Industry accounts for 51.2 percent, agriculture 5 percent, and services 43.6 percent of GDP. Major export markets include the United States (18.6 percent), Japan (15.6 percent), and South Korea (10.1 percent). In imports the United States (11.2 percent), Japan (8.8 percent), and Germany (7.6 percent) are the major players (*World Factbook* 2003). But oil is only one determinant of Saudi Arabia's evolving lifestyle—Islam is the other.

Saudi Arabia's historical roots go back to the mid-eighteenth century and derive from a compact in 1744 between Muhammad ibn Saud (d. 1762), a clan leader of Diriyah in Najd (central Arabia in the vicinity of modern Riyadh), and Muhammad ibn Abd al-Wahhab (d. 1792), an itinerant religious sheikh from southern Najd. This compact remains as valid today as when it was first established and provides Saudi kings with the basis for legitimacy and authority within an approved framework of religious orthodoxy as determined by the religious leaders (ulama) (al-Rasheed 1996, 364).

Abd al-Wahhab was a follower of Ibn Taimiyya (d. 1328), an Islamic scholar who subscribed to the Hanbali school of Islamic jurisprudence, the most puritani-

Sidebar 1   Women in Saudi Arabia

Women in Saudi Arabia are still highly restricted in public life and must be veiled whenever they leave their homes. Segregation of the sexes is rigorously policed by the religious police, who operate as the regime's enforcer of public morals. Segregation is also extended to the workplace and government service. Within Saudi female society, women currently run banks, factories, publishing houses, and many other businesses and professions only for women, while social interaction with nonrelated males is only permitted at strictly regulated family occasions. Women are not permitted to drive cars and those who break this law might well be imprisoned. Saudis fear that free and open association of the sexes might lead to moral decline and the breakup of the family. The family is conceived to be the focal point of Saudi society.

cal and conservative of the recognized schools of Islamic jurisprudence. He believed in the oneness of God, or Allah (*tawhid*). For him anything other than a strictly literalist interpretation of the Quran (Muslim Bible) was deviation (*shirk*). His allotted goal was to purify and refine the religious beliefs of the Arabian Peninsula, which, he believed, had declined since the days of the Prophet Muhammad (d. 632 C.E.). He was opposed to innovation (*bida*) and the Islamic concept of interpretation (*ijtihad*) of the Quran. And he recognized the Quran and the Sunna (traditions of the Prophet Muhammad) as the foundation of Islamic law (sharia) (Schwartz 2002, 69–78).

Abd al-Wahhab was committed to a religious crusade against Islamic polytheists

(worshippers of saints, tombs, shrines) and Shiites, which he regarded as heretics. The only distinction that he recognized was between "true" Muslims and others. Followers of Abd al-Wahhab were known as Unitarians (*muwahhidun*) or Wahhabis. His descendants are known as the Al ash-Sheikh, a prominent family that has intermarried with the House of Saud to reinforce the Saudi-Wahhabi compact to the present day.

The Saudi-Wahhabi compact led to the emergence of an aggressively expansionist and highly intolerant religious brotherhood (*ikhwan*), which was committed to spiritual revival and/or holy war (jihad). However after the sack of the Shiite city of Karbala (1802) and the conquest and occupation of Mecca and Medina (1803), Saudi influence steadily declined, reaching rock bottom in 1891 when archrival Muhammad ibn Rashid of Jabal Shammar (northern Arabia) forced the leading Saudi family into exile in Kuwait. But under Abd al-Aziz ibn Saud (hereafter Abd al-Aziz) (d. 1953) Saudi fortunes changed once more. He began the reconquest of Najd in 1902 with the recapture of Riyadh, and by 1913 he had taken the Al-Hasa region from the Ottoman sultan. A treaty with Britain in 1915 recognized Abd al-Aziz's status as sultan of Najd and central Arabia. Encouragement by Britain enabled him to conquer Asir (southwest Arabia) and Jabal Shammar in the early 1920s and to overcome the Hashemite kingdom of the Hejaz (western Arabia) in 1926. Mecca and Medina were retaken in 1925 and Abd al-Aziz was crowned sultan of Najd and king of Hejaz in 1927. After crushing insurrections by dissident Wahhabis (1928-1930), he proclaimed himself king of Saudi Arabia in 1932 (Vassiliev 1998, 272–284).

At birth Saudi Arabia was a poor tribal kingdom with few economic resources, other than pearling and the pilgrimage (hajj). It was dominated by Britain in Aden, Kuwait, Iraq, and Transjordan, which curbed Wahhabi expansion in the 1920s and 1930s. For Abd al-Aziz the marriage bed was another means of "cementing" tribal alliances and consolidating conquests. In his lifetime it was estimated that he had 300 wives and many concubines and slave girls. He married into leading tribal families and had 45 sons and 217 daughters (al-Yassini 1985, 83; Hiro 1996, 1). His links with the Sudairi clan were especially strong. King Fahd (r. 1981–) is the most influential of seven full brothers—known as the "Sudairi seven"—who are the offspring of Abd al-Aziz and Hussa bint al-Sudairi (Bill and Springborg 2000, 132). Abd al-Aziz ran the kingdom like a gigantic personal household, appointing sons, relatives, and in-laws to prominent civil and military offices, including provincial governors. After his death in 1953 his sons became the future kings of Saudi Arabia: Saud (r. 1953–1964), Faisal (r. 1964–1975), Khalid (r. 1975–1982), and Fahd (r. 1982–). Crown Prince Abdullah took over as de facto ruler of the kingdom following the illness of King Fahd in 1995.

Regional Geopolitics

If Saudi Arabia were created on a wave of Wahhabi militancy, to what extent has this religio-political tradition influenced the kingdom's subsequent relations with its neighbors (see Table 2)?

Saudi Arabia's relations with Egypt, a predominantly Arab Islamic state, have had their ups and downs. In the 1950s radical Arab nationalism centered on Egypt, and Syria forced Saudi Arabia into the conservative bloc within the Arab world where, in the mid-1960s, it attempted to foster regional alignments based on Islamic solidarity. Between 1962 and 1967 Saudi Arabia undermined Egypt's attempt to set up a republican regime in North Yemen (Sana'a). In the aftermath of Israel's military defeat of Egypt and Arab armies in the Six Days' War (1967), Saudi Arabia reasserted its influence over Cairo with the offer of aid for postwar reconstruction. Saudi Arabia worked more closely with Egypt's pro-Western governments under presidents Sadat (1970–1981) and Mubarak (1981–) in terms of prosecution and/or resolution of the conflict with Israel, including the Palestine problem.

Within OPEC, Saudi Arabia imposed selective oil embargoes against the "friends" of Israel (mainly the United States) in support of Egypt and Syria in the October War (1973). Riyadh rejected Egypt's peace treaty with Israel (1979) and reluctantly supported its expulsion from the Arab League (1945) and the Islamic Conference Organization (ICO) (1970) between 1979 and 1987. In general Saudi Arabia and Egypt might be described as "moderates" within the Arab world, committed to a "dual state" solution to the Palestine problem (i.e., Israel and Palestine) within the current U.S. "road map" for peace.

Cairo and Riyadh share a common ally in the United States and have been instrumental in supporting U.S. efforts at peace mediation between Israel and the Palestinian Authority (1994). Since the 1970s Riyadh and Cairo have shared broadly similar views on regional security, including a commitment to foster opposition to international terrorism. But both remain implacably opposed to the U.S. failure to limit Israel's military

Table 2   Saudi Arabia: Conflict and Regional Geopolitics

Name of Conflict	Parties	Issues	Start	Intensity	Resolution
Saudi–Abu Dhabi & Oman (Buraimi dispute)	Saudi vs. pro-British Abu Dhabi & Omani forces	Territory, national power, resources (oil)	1952	3	Treaty (1974)
Saudi-Afghanistan (Soviet-Afghan War)	Pro-Saudi mujahidin vs. Soviet troops	Ideology (Islam), national power, international power	1979	4	Withdrawal of Soviet troops (1989)
Saudi-Egypt (civil war in Yemen)	Pro-Saudi monarchists vs. Egyptian republicans	Ideology, national power, inter-national power	1962	4	Egypt's with-drawal of forces (1967), internal factional agreement (1970)
Saudi-Iraq (Gulf War)	Saudi & US/UN multinational force vs. Iraq	Territory, national power, inter-national power, resources (oil)	1990–1991	5	UNSC Resolution 687 (1991)
Saudi-Iran (Iran-Iraq War)	Saudi-Iran (indirect engagement)	Ideology, national power, inter-national power, resources (oil)	1980	5	UNSC Resolution 598 (1988)
Saudi-Israel (Arab-Israeli conflict)	Saudi vs. Israel (indirect engagement)	Territory, national power, inter-national power, resources (oil)	1948	5	U.S. "road map" (2003) but no over-all settlement
Saudi-Kuwait (offshore islands)	Saudi vs. Kuwait	Territory, resources (oil)	1969	2	Demarcation agreement (2000)
Saudi-Qatar (border demarcation)	Saudi-Qatar	Territory, resources (oil)	1992	3	Demarcation agreement (2001)
Saudi–North Yemen (border war)	Saudi vs. North Yemeni tribal forces	Ideology (Islam), territory, national power	1933	4	Treaty of Taif (1934)
Saudi–North Yemen (civil war)	Saudi monarchists versus Yemeni republicans	Territory, ideology, (civil war in Yemen)	1962	4	Arab summit & internal agreement (1967)
Saudi–United Yemen (civil war)	Saudi & southern Yemeni secessionists vs. Yemen (Sana'a)	National power, international power	1994	3	Conflict peters out

Source

Adapted from Heidelberg Institute on International Conflict Research (HIIK). 2003. "Conflict Barometer 2003." 1: *latent conflict* (nonviolent clashing interests); 2: *manifest conflict* (demands, claims, and threats); 3: *crisis* (short-term brief violent clashes); 4: *severe crisis* (organized violent clashes); 5: *war* (systematic use of violent force).

excesses within the Occupied Palestinian Territory (OPT).

Saudi Arabia's relations with North Yemen (Sana'a), a small Arab Islamic state, are rooted in the tribal wars of the 1920s. Abd al-Aziz's *ikhwan* initially wanted to conquer all of Yemen but were restricted by the presence of European powers on the periphery of the Arabian Peninsula. The Treaty of Taif (1934) failed to resolve grievances of Yemeni border tribes, and resentment toward the Saudis has lingered to the present. While the ruling family in Yemen never lost its distrust of the Al Saud, it accepted military assistance from Riyadh after it was deposed in a pro-Egyptian republican coup in 1962. The ensuing civil war (1962–1967) escalated to include regional and major powers in a dangerous proxy war over Yemen. Despite attempts to find a political solution, the conflict largely petered out after Egypt's defeat by Israel in the Six Day's War (1967) and the withdrawal of Cairo's forces from Yemen (see Table 2).

Riyadh was fearful over the emergence of the pro-Marxist People's Democratic Republic of Yemen (PDRY) in the wake of Britain's departure from the South Arabian Federation in 1968. It encouraged factional differences between the two Yemens and engaged in some border clashes with PDRY forces, as it sought to neutralize strategic threats on its southern border. The hasty union of the two Yemens (1990) was viewed with caution in Riyadh and exacerbated by the fact that Sana'a had refused to condemn Saddam Hussein's occupation of Kuwait (1990). In retaliation Riyadh expelled close to 1 million Yemenis from Saudi Arabia. In addition Riyadh supported the southern secessionist movement in Yemen (1994) after a highly contentious general election in 1993. Subsequent relations between the two states have been adversely affected by lingering disputes over the Treaty of Taif (1934), border demarcation problems, and incursions by arms smugglers and al-Qaeda operatives in what remains a tense border region (see Table 2).

Saudi Arabia's current friendly relations with Jordan, a small Arab Islamic state, belie an earlier turbulent history. Jordan is currently ruled by a Hashemite king (Abdullah II) whose ancestors, the previous custodians of the Muslim holy places, were driven out of the Hejaz by Abd al-Aziz in the 1920s. In the 1950s Riyadh remained highly suspicious of the pro-British Hashemite states of Jordan and Iraq and their commitment to the unification of Greater Syria (Iraq, Jordan, Syria). After the military overthrow of the Iraqi ruler (Faisal II) in July 1958, Riyadh assumed a protective attitude toward Jordan. Considerable aid was provided for development projects after the Six Day's War (1967) and for limiting the movement of left-wing Palestinian forces to the Arabian Peninsula. Riyadh mediated between Jordan and the Palestine Liberation Organization (PLO) in the Jordanian civil war (1970–1971) and over the question of PLO "recognition" in 1974. But Amman's pro-Iraqi sympathies in the Gulf War (1991) angered Riyadh, which responded by terminating grants, removing oil price concessions, and restricting imports. In the 1990s relations improved as Amman detached itself from Iraq. But Riyadh continued to be concerned about the spread of anti-Saudi Islamic "reformist" ideas across the Jordanian border (Aburish 1996, 143).

The overthrow of the monarchy in Iraq (1958) led to the emergence of secular military nationalist and Baathist regimes (i.e., Saddam Husein) in the 1960s and a subsequent downturn in relations with Riyadh. This was exacerbated by Iraq's treaty of friendship with the Soviet Union (1972) and its support for radical anti-Western organizations in the Gulf and southern Arabia. Riyadh provided generous aid to Saddam Hussein in his war against Iran (1980–1988), as it feared the spread of militant Iranian Shiite forces on the Arabian side of the Gulf, and especially during the hajj. But in 1990 the tables turned once more. Riyadh joined the U.S.-led multinational force in 1991 to eject Saddam Hussein from Kuwait because he posed a threat to Saudi security (see Table 2).

In the 1990s Riyadh reluctantly supported UNSC sanctions against Iraq (1991–2003) and enforcement of British and American "no-fly zones" over Iraq. While Riyadh welcomed the overthrow of Saddam Hussein, it opposed the use of its bases by the United States for an attack on Iraq (2003), perhaps fearing a backlash from anti-U.S. critics of the regime. Saudi-Iraqi relations remain tense and unpredictable in the aftermath of the U.S. invasion of Iraq in March 2003.

Saudi Arabia's relations with Iran, a Persian Islamic Shiite state, have had a checkered history. Riyadh and Tehran were generally opposed to the centers of radical Arab nationalism and in the mid-1960s cautiously explored cooperation based on an Islamic solidarity pact. Sharing a common patron in the United States led to both countries seeking to counter the spread of anti-Western forces in the Gulf and in southern Arabia in the 1960s and 1970s. In the 1970s the shah increasingly saw himself as the "policeman" of the Gulf, a role encouraged by the United States. This concerned Riyadh because of the shah's occupation of three UAE islands (Abu Musa and the Tunbs) in the highly strategic Straits of Hormuz and his claim to Bahrain (1971). The emergence of a militant Shiite Islamic regime in Tehran (1979) also exacerbated ideological and nationalist rivalries between Riyadh and Tehran, heightened by the outbreak of the Iraq-Iran War (1980–1988) (see Table 2). In the 1990s the regional balance of power changed once more following the defeat of Saddam Hussein's forces in the Gulf War (1991). Since the late 1990s Riyadh and Tehran have attempted to build bridges for greater regional cooperation, notwithstanding the unresolved dispute over the three islands at the entrance to the Gulf. While rapprochement brought strategic benefits for both states in the Gulf, it may also have raised concerns in Washington that Iran's clerics might seek to undermine Riyadh's alliance with the United States.

Saudi Arabia and Israel, a Jewish state, represent diametrically different positions on almost every regional issue and in particular the Palestine question. Riyadh followed the Arab League (1945) in opposition to Israel, asserting that there could be no peace without full redress of Arab demands for the liberation of Palestine and the withdrawal of Israel from "all" Arab land occupied in the Six Day's War. This position evolved into the "dual state" solution, proposed by King Fahd (1981), reiterated by Crown Prince Abdullah (2003), and currently the policy of the UNSC and the Arab League. This policy is also reflected in the U.S. "road map" for peace (2003).

Riyadh has generally refrained from "direct" Arab military confrontation with Israel (1948, 1956, 1967, 1973, and 1982). However Saudi diplomacy has worked indirectly to fund frontline Arab states and the Palestinians in the conflict with Israel (see Table 2). Riyadh used its considerable influence within OPEC (1973–1974) through price hikes and production cutbacks to punish the "friends" of Israel, especially the United States. In addition, it pressured the international community to comply with UNSC Resolutions 242 (1967) and 338 (1973), linking Israel's withdrawal from occupied Arab territories to secure and recognized frontiers for peace (Milton-Edwards and Hinccliffe 2004, 17).

In theory Saudi-Israel relations do not officially exist. Riyadh will not recognize Israel until it withdraws from "all" occupied Arab land and permits the establishment of a Palestinian state in the OPT, including East Jerusalem. Riyadh also discourages smaller Gulf sheikhdoms from engaging in commercial relations with Israel. Riyadh and Tel Aviv "talk" to each other through their common interlocutor, the United States. Israel's close and enduring friendship with Washington has repeatedly strained Saudi-U.S. relations, especially in the area of arms procurement. Washington has sometimes limited the sale of sophisticated aircraft and weapons to Riyadh, fearing that these might be used against Israel. Not only has this undermined the confidence of Riyadh in the U.S. alliance, it has enabled Wahhabi opponents to berate the regime over its increasing dependence on the United States, a close and enduring ally of Israel (see Terrorism below).

Riyadh provides generous aid to the Palestinian Authority for the OPT and to Islamic Palestinian organizations such as Hamas and Islamic Jihad in their struggle to liberate Palestine. Aid disbursement also enables Riyadh to regulate and/or control political interference from radical Islamic groups in the affairs of the king-

dom. While Riyadh supports the cause of the Palestinians, there have been times when relations have become strained. Riyadh suspended aid to the PLO following its perceived sympathy for Saddam Hussein's occupation of Kuwait in August 1990. But following a subsequent improvement in relations, Riyadh pledged $250 million out of a target of $1 billion to assist with Palestinian reconstruction in the wake of the second intifada (uprising) in the OPT in September 2000 (Peterson 2002, 24).

In the early nineteenth century Saudi-Wahhabi *ikhwan* roamed far and wide across the Arabian Peninsula, occupying territories that were later to become independent Arab Islamic sheikhdoms such as Oman, UAE, Qatar, Bahrain, and Kuwait. Not surprisingly historical claims over territory continued to linger and in some cases fester. In the late 1940s ARAMCO encouraged Saudi Arabia to expand its territorial claims and interests in the largely undemarcated region of the Buraimi Oasis, a large fertile depression in the southeast corner of the Arabian Peninsula, where there was likely to be oil (Halliday 1974, 281). In 1952 disputed ownership of the Buraimi Oasis led to conflict between Saudi Arabia and the British protectorates of Abu Dhabi (later part of the UAE) and Oman (see Table 2). Attempts at international arbitration failed, and in 1955 pro-British tribal forces ejected a small occupying Saudi force from the oasis. The Buraimi dispute also briefly strained Anglo-American relations and pushed Riyadh toward Egypt in the mid-1950s. It was not until 1972 that an agreement delineated the border in the Buraimi Oasis in favor of the UAE and Oman. In a separate border agreement (1974) Saudi Arabia recognized the UAE and in return was allocated income from the Shaybah-

Zarrarah oil field in the disputed border area between the UAE and Qatar (Seddiq 2001).

Saudi Arabia's relations with Kuwait were determined by the Treaty of Uqair (1922), which delimited the land border and set up a neutral zone to facilitate migration of border tribes and sharing of resources. The border was further demarcated in 1969 but it did not extend to offshore islands, which led to increasing unrest over the need to delimit offshore oil concessions. In 2000 an accord gave Kuwait sovereignty over the islands of Umm al-Mardim and Quruh, while undersea gas reserves would continue to be shared by both countries (Seddiq 2001).

Saudi Arabia's relations with Qatar have been adversely affected by border disputes (see Table 2). In 1965 the border demarcation line ran from Duhat as-Salwa to Khwar Udaid, adjoining the border with Abu Dhabi. However Riyadh claimed that it was the only country with the right to have a common land border with Qatar. In 1992 there were clashes between Saudi Arabia and Qatar over border delineation, leading to the deaths of two Qatari border guards. Following mediation by Egypt's president Husni Mubarak in 1999, a new border delineation agreement was signed in 2001. However relations between these two oil-rich states have continued to suffer as a result of Qatar-based al-Jazeera TV's critical coverage of the Saudi regime, personal differences between the ruling elites, and Qatar's desire to strengthen military co-operation with the United States in the wake of the rundown of its bases in Saudi Arabia (2003).

Saudi Arabia's relations with Bahrain in recent years have generally been proper. However Bahrain, with its relatively large Shiite population, posed major security concerns for Riyadh in the 1970s and 1980s, given Iran's historic claims to the island state. Bahrain's growing importance as a banking and commercial center has been welcomed by Riyadh while its relatively "liberal" social policies have served as a certain "release" for many Saudis, who regularly visit the island now joined by causeway to the Saudi mainland.

With the exception of the militant Wahhabi or jihadist phase (1933–1934), and the Afghan-Soviet War (see Conflict Past and Present below), Saudi Arabia's regional geopolitics have been influenced largely by pragmatic territorial disputes, nationalist rivalries, ideological issues, and an ongoing quest for resources, especially oil (see Table 2). Islamic solidarity or brotherhood, though a factor, does not appear to have rated very highly in this equation. While undoubtedly government aid and charitable disbursements to Islamic states and jihadist organizations (Hamas, Islamic Jihad, al-Qaeda) may have influenced Riyadh's foreign, defense, and covert intelligence policies (see Terrorism below), pragmatic state nationalism seems to have been the main driving force in Saudi Arabia's regional geopolitics since independence in 1932 (see Table 2).

Conflict Past and Present

Conflict History

In the space of seventy years Saudi Arabia evolved from a tribalized state with limited capabilities to one that presided over a major oil crisis (1973–1974) involving the international community. Riyadh has a crucial role to play in world politics in the wake of September 11, 2001. As we have seen, Saudi-Wahhabi aggressiveness in the 1930s was moderated by the need to ensure regime survival, especially during the period of radical Arab nationalism in the 1950s and 1960s and regional Cold War (see Table 2). The interaction of regime survival and strategic necessity evolved within the framework of a broadening alliance with the United States, influencing the policies of the kingdom to the present (see Relationship with the United States below).

Current and Potential Military Confrontation

In December 1979 Riyadh was deeply concerned by the Soviet occupation of Afghanistan, which had come within striking distance of the Gulf oil fields. Pressed by Wahhabi militants to "reform" in the wake of the seizure of the Grand Mosque in Mecca (November 1979), Riyadh welcomed the opportunity to become involved in an anti-Soviet Islamic resistance movement assembling in Pakistan (1980). After all, it would be under the aegis of the CIA and Pakistan's Inter-Service Intelligence (ISI), whose aim was to undermine the Soviet occupation of Afghanistan.

Between 1982 and 1992 about 35,000 Muslim radicals from 43 Islamic countries joined the ranks of the "holy warriors" (mujahidin) in Afghanistan. Tens of thousands also came to study in hundreds of new religious schools (madrassah) funded by Saudi Arabia and Pakistan along the Afghan border. These would permit the spread of Wahhabi religious values and encourage recruitment for the mujahidin. Overall more than 100,000 Muslim radicals in Afghanistan were "exposed" to Wahhabi jihadist ideals. In the 1990s "graduates" from these schools would serve as recruits for many radical Islamic jihadist organizations, including al-Qaeda and the Taliban (lit. "religious students") regime in Afghanistan (1996–2001). Along the Afghan-Pakistan border

the Islamic resistance was largely controlled and directed by the CIA and the ISI. It received state-of-the-art military technology and satellite intelligence from the CIA/United States. Between 1983 and 1987 "covert" arms transfers to Afghanistan increased annually from 10,000 to 67,000 tons. The total cost of the operation, which finally "broke the back" of the Soviet Union in 1989, was estimated at between $3 billion and $6 billion. Riyadh's contribution to this was over $1 billion.

Osama bin Laden (b. 1957) was one of the first volunteers to join the ranks of the mujahidin. He came from a wealthy Saudi construction family in Jiddah, which had very close links to the Al Saud. Bin Laden and Saudi intelligence chief Prince Turki bin Faisal were also on friendly terms, and most likely bin Laden served as the "eyes and ears" of Saudi intelligence in Afghanistan. In 1984 bin Laden took over the Arab Service Bureau (Maktab al-Khidamat) set up by the ISI to funnel money, arms, and fighters to the Islamic resistance. Ironically he also set up recruitment offices in Detroit and Brooklyn with the approval of Saudi intelligence. Bin Laden recruited about 4,000 Saudis, collected considerable sums of money from wealthy Saudi citizens, and developed relations with radical mujahidin leaders in Afghanistan. With the end of the war in sight, he took over al-Qaeda (the Base) in 1988 to channel the energies of the mujahidin into new Islamic causes (Gunaratna 2002, 2).

Following the Soviet withdrawal from Afghanistan (1989), bin Laden returned to Saudi Arabia. But he soon became disenchanted with the large buildup of U.S. and allied forces in the kingdom—the custodian of Islam's most holy places—as a prelude to the Gulf War (1991). He would soon part company with Riyadh on this issue and, with recent military experience in Afghanistan, launch a violent "career" in international terrorism (see Terrorism below).

Alliance Structure

Regionally, Saudi Arabia is a member of the Arab League (1945), the Islamic Conference Organization (ICO) (1970), and the Gulf Cooperation Council (GCC) (1981). It also has an important economic and military "alliance" with the United States (see Relationship with the United States below).

The Arab League is basically committed to inter-Arab cooperation. In 1950 its members signed a treaty of joint defense and economic cooperation to provide protection to member states against Israel's aggression (al-Farsy 1991, 279–281). Saudi Arabia's role within the Arab League has been consistent, cautious, and conservative. This has extended to mediation in inter-Arab state and/or factional disputes, especially over Lebanon (1975–1989), and on matters relating to Israel. Since 1981 Riyadh has upheld a "dual state" solution to the Palestine problem, reaffirmed by the Beirut Arab summit in 2002.

The ICO was created after an arson attack on the al-Aqsa mosque in Jerusalem in 1969, which outraged the Islamic world. Saudi Arabia has been the main financial backer of ICO, whose secretariat is in Jiddah. The ICO is a pan-Islamic organization open to all Muslim states. Its charter is based on Islamic solidarity, including social, cultural, and economic cooperation between Islamic states. In addition, it is firmly committed to the protection of the Islamic holy places, especially in Jerusalem. The ICO supports the Palestinian struggle against Israel and seeks a just solution to the Palestine problem. It has also served as a forum to resolve and/or narrow differences between Islamic states (al-Farsy 1991, 295–296).

Sidebar 2   Saudi Charities

Official Saudi charities, such as the Haramain Foundation, have received considerable government funding for the disseminating of Wahhabi religious values, including the building of mosques, schools, and cultural centers worldwide. It is estimated that aid disbursements from Saudi government "charitable" and private sources between 1975 and 2004 amounted to more than U.S.$50 billion. A good deal of Saudi-Wahhabi "aid" has been spent legitimately on religious and educational institutions in the United States, which has a Muslim population of over 6 million. If only a small amount of these charitable funds were to find its way into the hands of Islamic extremists, it might be deemed to be a princely sum.

The GCC (1981)—Saudi Arabia, Kuwait, Qatar, Bahrain, UAE, and Oman—was formed in response to the Islamic revolution in Iran (1979), the seizure of the Grand mosque in Mecca (1979) by Islamic militants, and the outbreak of the Iran-Iraq War (1980). It seeks to work for closer economic, cultural, and political cooperation as a basis for enhanced regional security (see Table 2). In the 1980s the establishment of a "peninsula shield force" at the Saudi base at Hafar al-Batin near King Khalid city was intended to serve as the forerunner of a more unified response to Gulf security. However, a number of difficulties interposed to slow down the process. Above all, there is an inherent size imbalance between Saudi Arabia and its five smaller allies. Saudi Arabia has a population of 24.3 million while the total populations of the other five combined is about 10.6 million (2004); its defense expenditure in 2002 was $22.2 billion compared to $11 billion for the others. Riyadh's armed forces number about 200,000 compared to 147,000 for the rest of the GCC (IISS 2003). From its inception the GCC has reflected an unequal power relationship, undermining unanimity of purpose between Riyadh and the smaller sheikhdoms (U.S. Arms Clients Profiles 2002).

Size and Structure of the Military
Size and Structure
In the Saudi military tradition the king is commander-in-chief of the armed forces. His overall powers are considerable if he has the support of leading princes and senior Wahhabi clerics (ulama). Since 1962 Prince Sultan bin Abd al-Aziz, minister of defense and aviation, has exercised operational control and supervision over the Royal Saudi Armed Forces, including the navy, air force, and Air Defense Force. Over the same period, the Saudi Arabian National Guard (SANG), a parallel force for the defense of the regime, has been under the control of Crown Prince Abdullah bin Abd al-Aziz. The total personnel of the four services, plus SANG and the ministry of the interior's paramilitary forces under Prince Nayef bin Abd al-Aziz, was approximately 200,000 (2003). Numerically, this is a relatively small force compared to potential enemy states like Iran, which has an armed force of 540,000 (IISS 2003, 109–112). It is believed that the Al

Saud prefer relatively small and highly equipped armed forces, linked to the U.S. alliance, to minimize any threat to regime survival (Aburish 1996, 184).

Saudi Arabia's regular army of 75,000 comprises three armored brigades, five mechanized brigades, one Royal Guard, eight artillery battalions, and several army aviation commands (2003). Despite the addition of a number of units and increased mobility achieved during the 1970s and 1980s, the army's personnel complement has expanded only moderately since the buildup was launched in the late 1960s. Perceived or imagined threats along the borders (see Table 2), and surplus revenues from oil exports in the 1970s, provided the means to spend lavishly on infrastructure and advanced equipment systems, including the purchase of M-1A2 Ahrams tanks, Bradley armored vehicles, and heavy artillery pieces (IISS 2003, 120–121).

The regular army has been deployed in a number of strategically situated military cities built in the 1970s and 1980s. These include: Khamis Mushayt in the southwest close to the border with Yemen; Tabuk in the northwest protecting routes leading from Jordan, Israel, and Syria; and Assad military city at Al-Kharj in the southeast close to the capital Riyadh, where the national armaments industry is also located. The largest of the military cities is King Khalid, situated close to the border with Kuwait and Iraq, protecting the strategic Trans-Arabian Pipeline (Tapline) and the road connecting Dammam with Jordan. These cities have been designed to maximize regime defense until, hopefully, external assistance arrives to secure the country and the oil fields. They are also sufficiently far enough away from Riyadh so as not to threaten or intimidate the central government (Aburish 1996, 185).

SANG comprises 75,000 men, plus 25,000 part-time tribal levies. It has three mechanized brigades and five infantry brigades and is mainly equipped with light weapons and armored vehicles for internal security. SANG is a direct descendant of the *ikhwan*, Abd al-Aziz's tribal army. The chain of command of SANG is completely separate from regular military channels, as is its communication system. Commanders of major units report directly to Crown Prince Abdullah.

In the early 1960s SANG was set up as a parallel army to ensure regime survival. It is based in Riyadh, Dhahran, Taif, and Jiddah and is entrusted with protecting the royal family (Aburish 1996, 185). Its continued existence, however, was also a matter of tribal and family politics. Crown Prince Abdullah is considered the head of the Shammar branch of the Al Saud, a rival source of power to the Sudairi branch that dominates the regular armed forces (2004). Family checks and balances might also be seen to be an inherent part of the Saudi military system. Training SANG became the responsibility of the Vinnell Corporation of the United States in 1975 (Library of Congress 1992).

SANG currently has three mechanized brigades, four armored brigades provided with light armored personnel carriers (APCs), antitank guided weapons, and 105mm and 155mm towed howitzers. The second component of SANG is under the command of local tribal chiefs and is organized into five infantry brigades comprising sons of local chiefs or veterans of the *ikhwan* forces. In addition, there are 15,000 paramilitary forces under the control of Prince Nayef (IISS 2003, 121).

Saudi Arabia's navy was formed as an adjunct of the army in 1957 and functioned as a separate force from 1969 (Peterson 2002, 28). It has to patrol coastal sea-lanes, which carry vast amounts of oil to foreign ports through the highly strategic Straits of Hormuz. It comprises a force of 15,000, including 3,000 marines, equipped with 14 frigates (some with guided missiles), corvettes, missile and patrol craft, minesweepers, amphibious craft and attack helicopters (IISS 2003, 121).

The Saudi air force has held pride of place in the kingdom since its inception in the 1950s. Strategically, it was assumed that the most likely attacks on the kingdom would be launched by air across the Red Sea, the Gulf, or the northern or southern deserts. Air defense would be of crucial importance. The development of the air force relied mostly on British and U.S. assistance, beginning with the provision of fighters in the 1950s and 1960s. In 2004 the air force had 16,000 personnel and 294 modern combat aircraft (F-5B, F-5E, F-15, and British Tornados) in four fighter squadrons, with surface-to-air missile capabilities (e.g., Sidewinders), plus assorted transport, electronic jamming, and tanker aircraft. In addition, there were Air Defense Forces of 16,000, armed with Hawk and other surface-to-air missiles (IISS 2003, 121).

Budget

Since 1990 Saudi Arabia has been America's "top customer" for military weapons (U.S. Arms Clients Profiles 2002). Britain also secured large contracts between 1986 and 1989 for Tornado aircraft and minesweepers. Between 1988 and 2003 Saudi Arabia's defense expenditure amounted to $287 billion (IISS 1989, 2003). In 2003 defense expenditure amounted to 13 percent of GDP, which was a significant decline from the high of 19.5 percent in 1985. In comparison defense spending for Israel amounts to 9.7 percent, Iran 4. 6 percent, and the United States 3.3 percent of current GDP (IISS 2003).

In 1975 Riyadh may have tried to buy a nuclear reactor from China. It supported Pakistan's nuclear program and contributed $5 billion to Iraq's nuclear weapons program between 1985 and 1990. It also "congratulated" Pakistan on the explosion of its first nuclear bomb in 1998, notwithstanding the fact that Riyadh had signed the Nuclear Non-Proliferation Treaty in 1988. Riyadh might still be interested in acquiring nuclear weapons as a means of deterring Iran's nuclear ambitions and filling a strategic gap in the event of a critical breakdown of relations with Washington (Henderson 2003b).

In terms of the top five arms importing countries in 1999, Saudi Arabia rated first followed by Turkey, Japan, China-Taiwan, and Britain (U.S. Department of State 2003). In 2003 Saudi Arabia had dropped to ninth overall, reflecting reduced revenues from oil and more pressure on government spending on key services like health, education, social welfare, and job creation programs. Between 1995 and 2003 U.S. arms sales to Saudi Arabia amounted to about 35 percent of Riyadh's total arms imports (IISS 1995/2003).

Civil-Military Relations and the Role of the Military in Domestic Politics

Within Saudi Arabia the king is head of state, leading sheikh (tribal leader), custodian of the two holy places of Mecca and Medina (*haramain*), and commander-in-chief of the armed forces. The fusion of these roles, in theory, does not permit any leeway for military and civilian societies to operate as entirely separate entities in the kingdom. Military officers are subjects of the king under God, with obligations to fulfill common ideals, which derive from the Quran and the sharia. In theory Islamic militants might attempt to redress the problems of secular modernizing society through pressure on the king for religious reforms. Evidence of this was found in the abortive seizure of the Grand mosque in Mecca in November 1979 by tribal elements and militant Wahhabis. But it would be a widely unpopular and irreligious act for military officers to challenge the existing Saudi-Wahhabi system of government without decrees (fatwas) from respected senior religious leaders such as the state-appointed mufti.

The Saudi regime normally appoints reliable family members to leading positions in government, the armed forces, and security services. Most senior officers have been recruited from Najd, the home base of the Al Saud. The military also plays a significant but indirect political role by bolstering national cohesion and development. Civilian authorities have the power to appoint and remove troublesome military officers (U.S. Department of State 1998). This authority has been exercised on occasions during and since the Gulf War (1991). SANG draws its recruits from tribal confederations and serves as an important means by which the royal family secures and maintains the loyalty of the tribes and the security of the oil fields. SANG is also responsible for the protection of the holy cities of Mecca and Medina, a role centering on the domestic and international legitimacy of the Al Saud.

Terrorism

The Gulf War (1991) literally blew the lid off the Saudi religio-political "kettle." Liberal and secular factions took advantage of the large U.S. and allied presence in the kingdom to press for "democratic" reform, while Wahhabi religious elements believed that King Fahd had drifted too far away from the principles of the Saudi-Wahhabi compact (al-Rasheed 1996, 359–371). It was the first serious challenge to the regime since the seizure of the Grand mosque in 1979 (Fandy 1999, 49–60; Viorst 1996, 95). In London the exiled Committee for the Defense of Legitimate Rights (CDLR) (1993) and the Movement for Islamic Reform in Arabia (MIRA) (1996), with links to bin Laden, accused the Al Saud of religious deviation, abuse of human rights, mismanagement of the economy, and "illegal" association with the United States and Israel. They saw themselves as the "official" Islamic opposition, arguing that it was the duty of all true Muslims to struggle through jihad to achieve their religious objectives inside and outside of the kingdom (Fandy 1999, 115–147). Between 2000 and 2004 pressure on the regime's credibility by hard-line Wahhabi clerics marked a serious blow to its prestige (Doran 2004, 44).

Increasing dissatisfaction with the Saudi regime can also be correlated with growing Islamic militancy inside and outside the borders of Saudi Arabia (see Table 3).

Between 1992 and 2004 al-Qaeda terrorist attacks against Americans were fairly evenly divided between military and civilian targets (see Table 3). However attacks on civilian, or "soft," targets became more common after 1998, reflecting a broadening of bin Laden's war with the United States and the West. The most significant terrorist operation by far has been September 11, 2001 (see Table 3). This had a profound effect upon the United States and the wider international community, while it revealed glaring gaps in U.S. security (U.S. Congress 2002, 2004). The fact that fifteen out of nineteen al-Qaeda hijackers were Saudis immediately put the spotlight on bin Laden and Saudi Arabia. While deeply concerned about the turn of events, the Bush administration tended to play down the Saudi "connection" with regard to September 11. Citing grounds of national security, Bush removed twenty-eight pages of intelligence analysis from a joint House-Senate report (2002) that is believed to have established links between "official" Saudi charities (e.g., Haramain Foundation) and the September 11 hijackers (U.S. Congress 2002; Henderson 2003a). Riyadh strongly rejected such allegations, suggesting that "someone" was trying to drive a "wedge" between the United States and Saudi Arabia. A more recent report largely exonerated the Saudi regime of complicity in the events of September 11 (U.S. Congress 2004, 317). However, the United States sought firm assurances from Riyadh that it would exercise greater control over the distribution of charitable funds to terrorist organizations and broaden its political process by way of power sharing and greater respect for human rights. The change of emphasis in the 2004 report may have been designed to "cushion" the Saudi alliance in the aftermath of the U.S. invasion of Iraq (March 2003). Indeed a reliable and secure Saudi regime would be of inestimable value to U.S. strategic interests in Iraq and the wider Gulf region.

Within Saudi Arabia the impact of September 11 has been equally far-reaching.

Table 3   Terrorist Attacks against Americans

Place and Year	Targets	Number Killed	Number Injured	Responsibility
Yemen (Aden) 19 December 1992	U.S. soldiers, bomb attacks	2 non-American civilians		al-Qaeda
New York 26 February 1993	World Trade Center bombed	6 civilians	1,000	al-Qaeda
Somalia (Mogadishu) 3 October 1993	U.S. helicopter shot down	18 U.S. soldiers		al-Qaeda
Saudi (Riyadh) 13 November 1995	OPM/U.S. SANG bombed*	7 U.S. soldiers	42	al-Qaeda suspected
Saudi (Dhahran) 25 June 1996	Khobar Towers, U.S. military housing complex bombed	19 U.S. soldiers	500	Saudi Hizballah (Iranian Shiite)
Kenya (Nairobi) and Tanzania (Dar es Salaam) 7 August 1998	U.S. embassies bombed	12 U.S. civilians; 212 local Africans	4,000	al-Qaeda
Yemen (Aden Harbor) 12 October 2000	USS *Cole* suicide attack	17 U.S. soldiers	39	al-Qaeda
New York, Washington, Pennsylvania, 11 September 2001	World Trade Center, Pentagon & rural Pennsylvania, aircraft suicide attacks	2,995, mainly U.S. civilians	thousands injured and traumatized	al-Qaeda
Saudi Arabia (Riyadh) 12 May 2003	Housing compounds for westerners, suicide attacks	10 Americans; 35 other civilians	200	al-Qaeda
Saudi Arabia (Yanbu) 1 May 2004	Office of Western oil company bombed	2 U.S. civilians; 5 other civilians	28	al-Qaeda
Saudi Arabia (Khobar) 29 May 2004	Housing compounds of oil workers bombed	1 American; 16 other civilians	some injuries	al-Qaeda

* Office of Program Manager, U.S. training mission, SANG.

Sources

Gunaratna, Rohan. 2002. *Inside Al Qaeda: Global Network of Terror.* Melbourne: Scribe Publications.
U.S. Congress. 2002. *Report of the Joint Inquiry into Terrorist Attacks on September 11, 2001 by the House Permanent Select Committee on Intelligence and Senate Select Committee on Intelligence.* http://www.gpoaccess.gov/serialset/creports/911.html (accessed August 20, 2004).
———. 2004. *The 9/11 Report of the National Commission on Terrorist Attacks upon the United States.* http://www.9-11commission.gov/ (accessed August 20, 2004).

Opinion polls in 2002 showed, for example, that only 12 percent of the Saudi population had a favorable opinion of the United States. And in 2003 the bottom had fallen out of support for the United States in most of the Muslim world (U.S. Congress 2004, 375). September 11 further exacerbated existing factional divi-sions within the kingdom, leading to the outbreak of violence on a much larger scale in Riyadh, Yanbu, and Khobar between 2003 and 2004 (see Table 3). Militant Wahhabis (*muwahhidun*) seemed to incline more openly toward bin Laden and al-Qaeda, opposing policies of liberal reform identified with the imposition of secular U.S./Western values (Doran 2004, 36–37). Official government "appeasement" of the United States was firmly denounced by Wahhabi clerics and directed against so-called Americanizers within the Al Saud—namely Crown Prince Abdullah (SANG) and Prince Sultan (defense minister). Rival centers of power always inherent within the fragmented Saudi political system played either the U.S. or Wahhabi "card" to suit their own political ambitions. Prince Nayef (interior minister), who had aggressively persecuted Islamic militants in the 1990s, now found allies in the ranks of the militant Wahhabi clerics. They were useful for keeping reformers in check (Doran 2004, 40) and, with succession to the Saudi throne in mind, might serve to neutralize the power base of his pro-American half brothers Abdullah and Sultan, now in their eighties. The game of Saudi musical chairs might be expected to continue in terms of the quest for personal power, regime domination, and ultimately the survival of the Al Saud.

As we have seen, "terrorism" in Saudi Arabia grew out of the concept of Islamic religious struggle (jihad), which was politicized by Islamic militants (e.g., CDLR, MIRA) in the 1990s and 2000s. Lacking a political process in which to express their dissent, they were increasingly forced into religious conflict with the Al Saud and its close ally, the United States. September 11 might well have been conceived by bin Laden in Afghanistan and hatched in Hamburg, but it was rooted in financial support, religious sentiment, and political ideology in Saudi Arabia. A complex symbiotic relationship still exists between bin Laden and the Al Saud, even if outward appearances seem to suggest that they are bitter enemies.

Relationship with the United States

Although currently battered and bruised in the wake of September 11, Saudi-U.S. relations evolved from the discovery of oil in the late 1930s. As the full extent of Saudi Arabia's oil fields became known, Washington assumed more direct responsibility for the security of the kingdom. In 1943 President F. D. Roosevelt declared that the defense of Saudi Arabia was of vital interest to the United States and dispatched the first military mission to the kingdom. U.S. army engineers constructed an airfield at Dhahran (Eastern Province) in 1946 and other military facilities soon after (al-Farsy 1991, 285).

In 1945 Abd al-Aziz and Roosevelt cemented formal ties aboard the USS *Quincy* in the Suez Canal. In 1947 Truman reassured Abd al-Aziz that the United States was committed to the security and political independence of Saudi Arabia. This commitment became the basis for the 1951 mutual defense agreement, which provided military equipment and training for Saudi armed forces. In 1969 Nixon called upon regional "surrogates" such as Saudi Arabia and Iran to counter the spread of anti-Western forces in the Gulf region, which might interfere with the free movement of oil tankers to and from Gulf ports. In the wake of the Soviet invasion of Afghanistan (1979), Carter stated that any threat to the Persian Gulf would be deemed to be a threat to the United States. He proposed the setting up of a Rapid Deployment Force and an increased U.S. naval presence in the Gulf. And in 1982 Reagan declared that an attack on Saudi Arabia and the oil fields of the Gulf would be considered an attack on the United States

In the post–Gulf War period Bush and Clinton (1991–2001) were primarily

Sidebar 3   Saudi Arabia: A Major Player

Having 25 percent of proven world oil reserves, Saudi Arabia is a major player in the oil market. Within OPEC, Riyadh generally has been a price moderate. It has been able to play this role because of Saudi Arabia's enormous reserves of oil, relatively low production costs, spare capacity to meet shortfalls in world oil production, and its political commitment to stay friendly with major Western industrial powers, including the United States. Riyadh's ability to control and regulate OPEC price excesses has undoubtedly strengthened its alliance with the United States and especially after September 11. Disruption of Saudi oil production by al-Qaeda terrorists could have disastrous economic consequences for all oil-consuming nations. At a time of relatively high oil prices Saudi Arabia's role in the global economy must take on added significance.

committed to "dual containment" of Iraq and Iran, with increasing strategic reliance on Saudi Arabia and the GCC (Chubin and Tripp 1996). In contrast the G. W. Bush administration (2001) has adopted a much more "assertive" unilateralist approach, especially in the wake of September 11, with emphasis on "preventive" war and a "crusade" against global terrorism (Hirsh 2002).

Saudi-U.S. relations have undoubtedly suffered as a result of Washington's long and enduring friendship with Israel. Pro-Jewish/Zionist lobbies in the United States are closely linked to the White House and political establishment and operate as an extension of Israel's political, economic, and security interests, es-

pecially during a presidential year. In contrast Saudi Arabia's influence in the United States is primarily economic and linked to oil and investments of around 7 percent of the U.S. economy. And while economically Riyadh has a good deal of political clout, it lacks the overall organization capability of pro-Israeli lobbies to significantly impact on U.S. foreign policy. As seen from Riyadh, U.S. Middle East policies tend to be unbalanced and prone to uphold Israel's security needs and interests at the expense of Muslims—and especially the Palestinians.

Since September 11 Saudi-U.S. relations have visibly cooled despite efforts by both sides to preserve their long-standing and mutually profitable alliance. While this might be motivated by powerful commercial and strategic considerations, the depth of understanding between the two nations currently remains shallow and subject to mutual accusations of cultural bias and prejudice. Muslims in the United States feel that September 11 has opened up an almighty chasm between U.S. security and the mosque. This has impacted negatively on social discourse between Muslims and non-Muslims. In Saudi Arabia the U.S. image everywhere rates very low, while al-Qaeda operatives continue to terrorize U.S. and foreign nationals into leaving the kingdom (2004). Anti-U.S. reaction has also forced Washington to withdraw most of its military personnel from the kingdom to neighboring Qatar in the aftermath of its widely unpopular invasion of Iraq (2003). Attempts by the Bush administration to foster ideals of "political democracy" as a means of resolving Saudi Arabia's internal problems have been diplomatically interpreted as yet another example of American interference and cultural imperialism. If in the short term there is gloom, what about the future?

The Future

During the latter part of the twentieth century Saudi Arabia evolved from a largely tribalized society to one with a relatively high level of economic growth but with limited "capacity" for real political development (Bill and Springborg 2000, 10). What Saudi Arabia lacks today is a viable political culture to meet the expectations of a society that is seeking to become a modern nation-state, with current expectations of power sharing. Educational textbooks are often Wahhabi based, religiously myopic, and obscure and serve as a weak platform for student development in the modern world (Doumato 2003, 245). There is no civil society in the kingdom that might serve as a framework for political discourse between the government, dominated by the Al Saud, its Wahhabi allies, and wider society. Wahhabism is openly antithetical to "political democracy" (at least in its American form) and remains firmly anchored in the ideals of its eighteenth-century founder, Muhammad ibn Abd al-Wahhab. This extremely conservative Islamic approach seems to run counter to the kingdom's needs for greater popular participation in government if it is to cope with the complexities of a postmodern society within an expanding global economy, including membership in the World Trade Organization (WTO), and to define its security needs in the twenty-first century.

One face of Saudi Arabia today seeks "reform," including an elected national assembly *(majlis)*, abolition of the powers of the oppressive religious police *(mutawwiyin)*, and the removal of discrimination against women and minorities (Shiites) in association with UN conventions of which Saudi Arabia is a signatory. The other face inclines toward a "reformist" Islamic government—or theocracy—requiring the government to purify religious values and stamp out all heresies that have appeared within the kingdom due to the laxness of the Al Saud and its close and "unhealthy" association with the United States. Of course, there are many shades of meaning and changing factional alignments within these two camps based on differing interpretations of Saudi-Wahhabi society and its agenda for the future.

If it is to survive, Saudi Arabia will need to resolve serious religio-political factional divisions associated with regime legitimacy. If these are not channeled into a viable institutional framework for the resolution of internal conflict, turbulence and unrest will continue to undermine the political process and may impact negatively on oil production. This would be catastrophic for the future of the U.S. alliance and, of course, the global economy reliant on Saudi oil. Major political concessions will have to be made by the regime by way of power sharing—but in what direction? The present stand of the regime is to drift back and forth under pressure from different domestic factions and the United States in the hope that regime survival might be assured, and bin Laden will go away! But in the end it might simply be staving off the inevitable confrontation that could blow the kingdom apart.

References, Recommended Readings, and Websites

Books
Aburish, Saïd. 1996. *The Rise, Corruption and Coming Fall of the House of Saud.* New York: St Martin's Griffin.

al-Farsy, Fouad. 1991. *Modernity and Tradition: The Saudi Equation*. London: Kegan Paul.

al-Yassini, Ayman. 1985. *Religion and State in the Kingdom of Saudi Arabia*. Boulder: Westview.

Bill, James, and Robert Springborg. 2000. *Politics in the Middle East*. 5th ed. New York: Longman.

Fandy, Mamoun. 1999. *Saudi Arabia and Political Dissent*. New York: Palgrave.

Gunaratna, Rohan. 2002. *Inside Al Qaeda: Global Network of Terror*. Melbourne: Scribe Publications.

Halliday, Fred. 1974. *Arabia without Sultans*. Penguin Books.

Hiro, Dilip. 1996. *Dictionary of the Middle East*. London: Macmillan.

Macintyre, Ronald. 1981."Saudi Arabia." In *The Politics of Islamic Reassertion*, Mohammad Ayoob, ed., London: Croom Helm.

Milton-Edwards, Beverley, and Peter Hincliffe. 2004. *Conflicts in the Middle East*. 2d ed. London: Routledge.

Schwartz, Stephen. 2002. *The Two Faces of Islam: The House of Sa'ud from Tradition to Terror*. New York: Doubleday.

Vassiliev, Alexei. 1998. *The History of Saudi Arabia*. London: Saqi Books.

Articles

al-Rasheed, Madawi. 1996. "God, King and the Nation: The Rhetoric of Politics in Saudi Arabia in the 1990s." *Middle East Journal* 50, no. 3:359–371.

Brisard, Jean-Charles. 2002. "Terrorism Financing: Roots of Saudi Terrorism Financing." Report prepared for the president of the Security Council, New York, December 19.

Chubin, Shahram, and Charles Tripp. 1996. "Iran–Saudi Arabia Relations and Regional Order." *Adelphi Paper* 304. London: The International Institute for Strategic Studies.

Dekmejian, Hrair. 1998. "Saudi Arabia's Consultative Council." *Middle East Journal* 52, no. 2:204–218.

Doran, Michael. 2004. "The Saudi Paradox." *Foreign Affairs* 82, no. 1:35–51.

Doumato, Eleanor. 2003. "Manning the Barricades: Islam According to Saudi Arabia's School Texts." *Middle East Journal* 57, no. 2:231–247.

Hardy, Roger. 2004. "Saudi Arabia between Violence and Reform." *Middle East International*, no. 717 (January 23): 27–28.

Heidelberg Institute on International Conflict Research (HIIK), 2d rev. ed. 2003. "Conflict Barometer 2003." 12th Annual Conflict Analysis.

Hirsh, Michael. 2002. "Bush and the World." *Foreign Affairs* 81, no. 5:19–43.

International Institute for Strategic Studies (IISS) 1989. *The Military Balance 1989–90*. London: IISS.

———. 2002. "Saudi Arabia in Transition." *Strategic Survey* 2001–2002. London: Oxford University Press.

———. 2003. *The Military Balance 2003–2004*. London: Oxford University Press.

Peterson. J. E. 2002. "Saudi Arabia and the Illusion of Security." *Adelphi Paper* 348. London: Oxford University Press for International Institute for Strategic Studies.

Viorst, Milton. 1996. "The Storm and the Citadel." *Foreign Affairs* 75, no. 1:93–107.

Websites

Central Intelligence Agency. 2003. *World Factbook—Saudi Arabia*. http://www.cia.gov/cia/publications/factbook/geos/sa.html (accessed March 20, 2004).

Country Analysis Briefs. 2003. Saudi Arabia. http://www.eia.doe.gov/emeu/cabs/saudi.html (accessed June 1, 2004).

Henderson, Simon. 2003a. *The September 11 Congressional Report: A Sea Change in US-Saudi Relations. Policy Watch*, no. 777 (July). http://www.washingtoninstitute.org/watch/policywatch/policywatch2003/777.htm (accessed August 18, 2004).

———. 2003b. *Towards a Saudi Nuclear Option: the Saudi-Pakistan Summit. Policy Watch*, no. 793 (October 16). http://www.washingtoninstitute.org/watch/policywatch/policywatch2003/793.htm (accessed August 18, 2004).

Library of Congress. 1992. *Country Studies—Saudi Arabia*. http://lcweb2.loc.gov/frd/cs/satoc.html (accessed March 20, 2004).

Saudi Arabia News Net: http://www.saudiarabianews.net/ (accessed March 20, 2004).

Saudi-US Relations. 2004. *Information Newsletter.* http://www.Saudi-us-relations.org/Fact_Sheets/Timeline Terrorism.html (accessed August 22, 2004).

Seddiq, Ramin. 2001. *Border Disputes on the Arabian Peninsula. Policy Watch* 525 (March 15). http://www.washingtoninstitute.org/watch/policywatch/policywatch2001/525.html (accessed February 2, 2004).

U.S. *Arms Clients Profiles 2002. Saudi Arabia.* http://www.fas.org/asmp/profiles/saudi_arabia.htm (accessed March 20, 2004).

U.S. Congress. 2002. *Report of the Joint Inquiry into Terrorist Attacks on September 11, 2001 by the House Permanent Select Committee on Intelligence and Senate Select Committee on Intelligence.* http://www.gpoaccess.gov/serialset/creports/911.html (accessed August 20, 2004).

———. 2004. *The 9/11 Report of the National Commission on Terrorist Attacks upon the United States.* http://www.9-11commission.gov/ (accessed August 20, 2004).

U.S. Department of State. 2002. *Country Reports on Human Rights Practices—Saudi Arabia.* http://www.state.gov/g/drl/rls/hrrpt (accessed March 20, 2004).

———. 2003. *Military Expenditures and Arms Transfers 1999–2000: Fact Sheet* (February 6). http://www.state.gov/r/pa/prs/ps/2003/17447 (accessed February 22, 2004.

South Africa

Trevor Rubenzer

Geography and History

Occupying the southernmost area of the African continent, South African topography is dominated by a large plateau with a narrow coastal plain in the southeast. The climate of South Africa is primarily subtropical, and approximately 12 percent of the land is arable. One of the major geostrategic issues for South Africa is the lack of a navigable river, resulting in a dependence on road and rail for transportation purposes. As a result, South Africa has more than 350,000 kilometers of highway, of which more than 70,000 kilometers are paved (Van Buren 2002, 979). In addition, the country possesses 22,298 kilometers of rail, including a commuter rail system that is quite well developed by regional standards. South Africa also enjoys the most well-developed communication system in Africa, with approximately 5 million telephone landlines and 9.2 million cellular subscribers.

South Africa gained independence from the United Kingdom on May 31, 1910, as the Union of South Africa. In October 1960 South Africa adopted a republic form of government as the result of a successful referendum. The current head of state and head of government is Thabo Mbeki, elected in June 1999. The head of state is elected indirectly by the National Assembly and may be removed constitutionally via a no-confidence vote or impeachment. The South African constitution, which entered into force in 1997, formally enumerates the rights of all citizens, regardless of race. The legislature is bicameral, with each province represented at the subnational level.

Moderate levels of growth characterize the postapartheid economy in South Africa. Although the economy grew at a dynamic pace in the 1960s, growth has slowed to around 3 percent a year. Extreme poverty, one legacy of the unequal distribution of wealth during the apartheid era, continues to be a problem, with 50 percent of the population falling below the poverty line. In addition, whites, who constitute approximately 13 percent of the population, earn about 54 percent of the income. Gross domestic product (GDP) per capita is approximately U.S.$3,000 (Van Buren 2002, 975–976).

The South African economy is quite diverse by regional standards, with an extensive service sector and a large industrial and mining base. The country is the world's largest producer of platinum and gold. Manufacturing is the strongest overall sector in the economy. Metalworking and automobile assembly are two of the main industries. The textile industry is well developed, but has suffered from both external competition and illegal imports. Multilateral economic sanctions imposed as a result of apartheid had the

Table 1   South Africa: Key Statistics

Type of government	Republic
Population (millions)	42.8 (2003)
Religion	Christian 68% (2003)
Main industries	Mining, metalworking (2003)
Main security threats	Overall regional instability
Defense spending (%GDP)	1.7% (2002)
Size of military (thousands)	63.4 (2000)
Number of civil wars since 1945	0
Number of interstate wars since 1945	0

Sources

Central Intelligence Agency Website. 2003. CIA *World Factbook.* http://www.cia.gov/cia/ publications/factbook/ (accessed December 15, 2003).

Stockholm International Peace Research Institute (SIPRI). 2003. *SIPRI Yearbook 2003: Armaments, Disarmament and International Security.* London: Oxford University Press.

unintended side effect of stimulating many domestic industries, including petrochemicals. The industrial production growth rate in 2002 was 3 percent.

South Africa's population in 2003 was estimated at 42,768,678. This estimate accounts for increased mortality as a result of the AIDS epidemic, as well as the undercounting of certain ethnic groups. Approximately 5 million South Africans are currently infected with the HIV/ AIDS virus. The population growth rate is 0.01 percent as of 2003, with a fertility rate of 2.24 children born for each woman. Approximately 68 percent of South Africans are Christians, whereas about 2 percent are Muslims and 1.5 percent are Hindu (including the majority of the Indian population).

Regional Geopolitics

During the apartheid era, South Africa was one of the primary sources of regional instability in southern Africa. The end of the Soviet threat, accompanied by the beginning of majority rule in South Africa, has created a set of regional security concerns that are more similar to those of other African states. Although the South African Department of Defense sees no short- or medium-term external threat to security, the government is concerned about the prospect of regional instability and its impact on the security situation within the country (South African Department of Defense 2002b). The Ministry of Foreign Affairs has identified several states where stability is a concern, including Angola, the Democratic Republic of the Congo (DRC), Lesotho and Zimbabwe (South African Department of Foreign Affairs 2003, 6–11). This entry will discuss each of these regional security concerns in turn.

South African security concerns with regard to Angola relate to overall regional stability. With the decades-long civil war in Angola formally ended, the prospects for a lasting peace are uncertain. Even though its victory in the war has placed the government in a position to consolidate peace, the demobilization of rebels from the União Nacional Para a Independência Total de Angola (UNITA) resulted in unemployment for thousands of soldiers. In addition, food shortages abound in the demobilized areas, with hundreds of thousands claiming to face starvation. If the needs of the demobilized UNITA members are not met, the renewal of violence might once again become a viable alternative.

South Africa is quite cognizant of the ramifications of food shortages for Angolan stability. As a result, the South African government has been an important donor of food and other supplies to the Angolan government. In addition, South Africa lends its technical and logistical support to the removal of antipersonnel land mines, which are a major obstacle to renewed economic and agricultural activity. It appears at this point that exhaustion from decades of civil war has created at least some basis for peace, although it is unclear how durable the peace will be.

South Africa is also concerned with the prospects for lasting peace in the Democratic Republic of the Congo (DRC). South Africa played a major role in brokering a peace agreement between the various factions in the civil war, including the Global and Inclusive Agreement on the Transition in the DRC, which was signed in South Africa in December 2002. As part of this agreement, Joseph Kabilia was named leader of an all-party transitional government in July 2003. On January 13, 2004, President Mbeki became the first South African head of state to visit the DRC in an official capacity. The visit was designed both to lend legitimacy to the continuing peace process and to lay the groundwork for future economic cooperation. The DRC possesses some of the most promising mineral and energy resources in the world, an opportunity known to the only state in the region currently capable of recovering many of them.

Many barriers to a lasting peace remain in the wake of a five-year conflict that claimed the lives of as many as 3 million people. Both the physical and agricultural infrastructure was largely destroyed in a war that at one point involved troops from several states, including Burundi, Rwanda, Uganda, Angola, Namibia, and Zimbabwe. In addition, as many as nine rebel groups operated in the DRC at one point in the conflict. Some of these groups provided opposition to Laurent Kabilia, and others used the DRC as a convenient base for operations into other states in the region. For example, UNITA maintained bases in the DRC for use in attacks against the Angolan government. The same can be said of Hutu rebels and their relationship with Burundi.

As in Angola, one of the primary threats to peace is disease and starvation in the wake of war. Fighting continues as remnants of various rebel groups and other armed forces battle for access to resources. Many groups with no enemy left to fight have taken to seizing crops from local farmers, since they are no longer compensated as soldiers. However, it appears that some integration efforts have enjoyed success, because many former rebels have been provided with government jobs and a role in the peace process. In addition, Rwanda and Burundi have reached accommodations with rebel leaders that have permitted the withdrawal of rebel and government troops from the DRC. An organization referred to as the Third Party Verification Mechanism (TPVM) was created in 2002 to monitor the implementation of the peace agreement. As the head of the African Union (successor to the Organization of African Unity) at the time of the agreement that created the TPVM, South Africa has played a leading role in verifying the withdrawal of foreign troops. South Africa also maintains more than 1,300 troops in the DRC as part of the UN peacekeeping operation in the country.

Given the fact that it lies within South Africa, the overall stability of Lesotho is of critical importance to the government. South Africa, Botswana, and Zimbabwe put down a coup attempt in Lesotho in 1995. South Africa and Botswana intervened again in September 1998 in order to prevent a second coup attempt from succeeding. South Africa was part of the observer group that lent legitimacy to the general elections that took place in Lesotho in May 2002. The elections were declared free and fair, and the RSA has been consistent in its attempts to consolidate democracy, including the mobilization of the international donor community in order to promote economic development in the country.

Overall political instability and the violence surrounding land reform in Zimbabwe are a major security concern for South Africa. In 1997, Zimbabwe's president Mugabe declared that white farmers in the country would no longer have the right to compensation for territory seized as part of the land reform efforts in the country. This led to an increase in often-violent seizures of territory from white farmers. The nature of land reform in Zimbabwe is thus both a source of political instability and a point of major stress between the country and the international donor and lending communities. Zimbabwe's direct support of the Kabila regime in the DRC was also a source of instability in the country prior to the withdrawal of forces in 2002.

Although it is unlikely that conflict will spread from Zimbabwe to South Africa, the nature of land reform is a source of concern for white farmers who fear for their property and security. The failure of the Mbeki government to firmly renounce the policy is a further cause for concern. The official policy of the South African government is one of *constructive bilateral engagement.* However, there is some ambiguity as to what is meant by the term. South Africa has moved to provide food aid to Zimbabwe in an effort to alleviate the impact of land reform on agricultural production. In addition, the government declared land seizures illegal in 2001. However, violence over land reform does occur in South Africa, and Mbeki's refusal to directly condemn the means of land reform in Zimbabwe could continue to be a source of potential instability.

Conflict Past and Present
Conflict History

Since the conclusion of World War II, South Africa has participated in one intrastate war (Angola) and one extrastate war (Namibia). South Africa has not experienced its own civil war, and it has not participated in a traditional interstate conflict. The purpose of this section is to provide an overview of each episode in the context of South Africa's apartheid-era security concerns. South Africa's interest and involvement in the civil war in Angola can be traced to three primary security goals. These include the destabilization of the "front-line" states opposed to minority rule; acting against the threat posed by the African National Congress (ANC), which operated in part from Angola; and countering Soviet influence in the region. The convergence of these interests in the case of Angola makes understanding the nature of the conflict critical to knowledge of South African security policies during the apartheid era.

When Angola became independent from Portugal in 1975, four primary political actors fought for dominance of the new state. The Movimento Popular de Libertacao de Angola (MPLA) had a leftist orientation and tended to represent intellectuals around the capital city of Luanda as well as those who were of mixed European and African descent. The Frente Nacional de Libertacao de Angola (FNLA) primarily represented the interests of the northern areas of Angola. The FNLA was originally favored by the United States in the civil war. UNITA, mentioned earlier, claimed to represent the Ovimbundu people, who constitute the majority of Angolans. UNITA and its leader Jonas Savimbi were favored by the South Africans in the civil war. The Frente para a Libertacao do Enclave de Cabinda (FLEC), as its name indicates, favored separation for the enclave of Cabinda.

As a result both of the presence of Cuban troops acting on behalf of the Soviets and ANC bases in and around the capital city, South Africa began a campaign of active support of UNITA. The South African army created bases for UNITA in the province of Cuando-Cubango. In addition, the air force provided close support directly to Savimbi in order to help protect him from government forces. The MPLA had gained the advantage early in the conflict as a result of superior organization and Soviet support, forcing UNITA to fight a guerrilla war. In addition, South Africa regularly conducted operations in Angola, including the famous Operation Protea in 1981 in which South Africa made its deepest penetration into Angolan territory. By 1986, the United States began to support UNITA as well. The result was an intense conflict primarily between the MPLA and UNITA, with seemingly unlimited resources fueling the conflict.

Concerned about Soviet activities in the region, South Africa initiated negotiations that were intended to tie the removal of Cuban troops from Angola to Namibian independence and a South African withdrawal from Angola. However, South Africa violated the terms of this and other agreements and continued to make incursions into Angola both in support of UNITA and in order to hunt Namibian rebels. Finally, in 1988, an accord was signed among Angola, Cuba, and South Africa. South Africa agreed to cease incursions into Angola and curtail UNITA support in exchange for a Cuban withdrawal and the departure of the ANC from Angola. The UN Security Council established the UN Angola Verification Mission (UNAVEM) to monitor the withdrawal of Cuban troops (Garztecki 2002, 36). UNAVEM began to exercise its mandate in January 1989. Although regional agreement did not result in an end to fighting in Angola, it served as the termination point for direct South African intervention in the country.

In addition to its involvement in the civil war in Angola, South Africa participated directly in the Namibian conflict. Primary South African involvement in Namibia began during World War I, when the RSA occupied what was then the German colony of South West Africa. The League of Nations, which intended to establish a system of trusteeship over non-self-governing territories before its collapse, granted South Africa a mandate to administer the territory. Given the RSA's policies on minority rule, it is not surprising that the first movements toward self-government in what was to become Namibia were granted to whites. After the International Court of Justice (ICJ) failed to issue a fully substantive ruling on the legality of South African control of the territory, the UN General Assembly voted to terminate the South African mandate and assume direct administration of the territory (Saunders 2003, 727). In 1968, the UN decided to rename the territory, choosing the name Namibia. In 1971, the ICJ did rule that South African administration of Namibia was illegal. The ruling also established that the South West Africa People's Organization (SWAPO) was the legitimate representative of the Namibian People. SWAPO was founded in 1960 and became in part an armed resistance movement in northern Namibia.

The conflict in Namibia is closely tied to the conflict in Angola. When the MPLA gained the advantage in Angola, it backed SWAPO in its calls for independence. More importantly, MPLA actions in Angola provided a base outside of Namibia for the armed wing of SWAPO, the People's Liberation Army of Namibia (PLAN), to conduct activities within Namibia. This, in turn, led to repeated South African incursions into Angola in order to track down and engage the rebels. South Africa also increased its counterinsurgency activities within Namibia, eventually pushing the bulk of SWAPO forces back into Angola. However, South Africa's efforts to eliminate SWAPO were thwarted both by Angolan support, and after 1971, support from the Soviet Union. However, by the mid-1980s, Namibia remained firmly in South African hands, with SWAPO military power cut by more than half by the RSA's commitment of more than 25,000 troops to the conflict (Rotberg 1985, 140). In 1985, South Africa unilaterally installed a transitional government in Namibia, with a constitution that maintained dependence on the RSA for internal and external security. The document and the government were re-nounced by SWAPO, which pledged continued armed insurrection via the PLAN until a final resolution of the dispute. The Democratic Turnhalle Alliance (DTA), a conservative grouping of ethnic groups offering the only alternative to SWAPO, suffered severe legitimacy problems based on corruption and ties to South Africa. For its part, South Africa was also guilty of several human rights abuses within SWAPO-controlled territory.

In 1988, as part of the agreement to end South African and Cuban involvement in Angola, South Africa agreed in principle to Namibian independence. A year later, SWAPO gained victory in UN-supervised elections. When Namibia gained formal independence in 1990, Sam Nujoma became the president. The final contentious issue between South Africa and Namibia was control of Walvis Bay, a strategic area originally controlled by the British. South Africa retained control of Walvis Bay until 1994, when it agreed to turn over the territory to Namibia. Although the conflict in Namibia was not as costly in terms of human life as that in Angola, the war did result in thousands of deaths and tens of thousands of refugees and displaced persons.

It is clear from both of the previously discussed conflicts that the major security concern of South Africa during the apartheid era was Soviet influence via its Cuban proxy in southern Africa. Without Soviet assistance, there was no credible threat to South Africa within the region. As a result, even before the formal end of apartheid, South Africa was willing to make political concessions, including the introduction of unfriendly governments on its borders, in exchange for the end of direct Cuban assistance in southern Africa. U.S. interests in preventing the spread of communism also played a role, as did the demonstrated superiority of Soviet armor used by the Cubans in Angola.

One of South Africa's primary security policies during the apartheid era was the destabilization of unfriendly neighboring states. The Front-Line States of Angola, Botswana, Mozambique, Tanzania, Zambia, and Zimbabwe were a group of countries dedicated to the end of apartheid and to protecting themselves from domination by South Africa. Having treated the conflict in Angola, it is possible to discuss in general terms South African conflict, both economic and military, with this group of states. Since South Africa's economic domination of southern Africa was a salient feature of its security policy in the apartheid era, it is prudent to begin there.

During the 1970s and 1980s, South Africa was the only major food exporter in the region. It also provided the major source of electricity to several states, including Mozambique, Lesotho, Namibia, Swaziland, and Zimbabwe. South Africa often used its economic power to both punish and reward states, depending on the nature of their policies toward the RSA. This was enabled by the fact that the Front-Line States were dependent on South Africa for access to goods and transport routes (Maasdorp 1985, 106–110). Conversely, South Africa was not dependent on imports from the rest of southern Africa. South Africa used its economic power to support the Unilateral Declaration of Independence in Rhodesia (now Zimbabwe) when the state was economically isolated by sanctions. The government also used the threat of trade retaliation to make the economic sanctions placed on South Africa more porous.

For its part, the rest of southern Africa did attempt to decrease its economic dependence on the RSA. This is the primary reason that the Southern African Development Coordinating Conference (SADCC) was formed. One of the primary goals of the SADCC was to provide transportation linkages between southern African states in order to decrease dependence on South African transport networks. Conversely, the goal of South Africa was to increase regional integration in a manner conducive to economic dominance. Zaire (now the DRC) and Zambia, for example, were dependent on existing South African infrastructure in order to secure exports to the West. In the end, the SADCC failed to limit the economic control of South Africa in part because of RSA economic subversion techniques and in part because the economic resources needed to provide for a regional integration alternative were not forthcoming from the donor community in the amount required to provide a credible alternative to South African dominance.

South Africa also provided direct and indirect military support in order to destabilize the Front-Line States. In Mozambique, South Africa supported the rebel group Renamo in response to Mozambique's support of sanctions against Rhodesia and its support of the ANC. South Africa also used the conflict in Mozambique in an attempt to cut off Zimbabwe's access to the sea as an outlet for its exports. This in turn caused Zimbabwe to support the government in Mozambique. In Botswana, the South African government recruited members of the Basarwa ethnic group to fight in Namibia against SWAPO. Although South Africa and Botswana never engaged in a declared war, they did exchange fire across their mutual boarder. South Africa also raided ANC bases in Botswana, resulting in civilian death. At the time of the 1987 general elections in

South Africa, the government threatened each of the Front-Line States with invasion if they allowed the ANC to disrupt the electoral process from their territories. Overall, South African military policy toward the rest of southern Africa was destabilization, with occasional support of rebel groups and even less frequent cross-border raids on ANC strongholds.

The final apartheid-era conflict worth noting is that between the minority government of the RSA and the ANC. Although it is true that an entire constellation of groups formed within South Africa in order to oppose the government, the ANC is both the most recognizable and salient of these groups. The ANC was formed in 1912 in part in response to the native reserve policy of the South African government. The basis of the native reserve policy was to isolate the various nonwhite ethnic groups in South Africa into homelands that would be granted "independence" but remain in practice completely dependent on the government. The RSA would use a system of "tribal chieftains" to maintain and administer the homelands. This would enable more effective control of the majority population.

The principal initial method used by the ANC was civil disobedience. However, in response to the Sharpeville massacre in 1961, the ANC, along with an antiapartheid group consisting of whites, formed a military organization called Umkhonto we Sizwe (Spear of the Nation). The MK, as the Spear group was also called, focused its efforts on attacking white property without endangering civilians (Saunders 2002b, 966). Nelson Mandela, the leader of the ANC, was arrested in 1962 and sentenced to life in prison two years later on charges of sabotage. In response to the arrest of Mandela,

the ANC stepped up its military campaigns, at times claiming the lives of white South Africans.

In 1976, membership in the MK swelled in response to the Soweto massacre. Soweto was a group of segregated townships to the southwest of the capital. The government opened fire on a group of students assembled to protest the imposition of Afrikaans as an official language of instructions in the schools. The ANC used the situation to recruit members into the resistance. Attacks on white property and civilian casualties increased. It was during this time that the number of ANC bases in countries such as Angola and Mozambique greatly increased.

The South African government responded to the escalation in violence by altering the balance between the military and the police. P. W. Botha, who became prime minister in 1978, granted more powers to the armed forces. This enabled more effective government control of anti-ANC activities. Botha also moved toward the adoption of a new constitution that would provide some level of participation for blacks, coloreds, and Indians (the three nonwhite classifications used in the country). However, power would remain firmly vested with the white population.

In response to the new constitution, a series of township revolts took place in conjunction with strikes by a group of labor unions allied with the ANC. During the township revolts, there were also numerous clashes between the ANC and the rival Inkatha movement, led by Mangosuthu Buthelezi. The government responded to the revolts by declaring a state of emergency in the townships. The state of emergency was later extended to the entire country. During this time, ANC military activities continued, with increased economic pressure placed on the government as a result of multilateral economic sanctions.

The beginning of the end for apartheid and the conflict between the government and the ANC occurred in 1987 when a group of members of the Afrikaner community met with ANC leaders in Senegal. In 1989, F. W. de Klerk replaced Botha as National Party leader. Both de Klerk and Botha met with Nelson Mandela, and in 1990 Mandela was released from prison. Even though violence continued, in part because of government exploitation of the ANC and the Inkatha supporters, the process initiated by de Klerk ultimately led to a new constitution in the first real democratic election in South African history.

Current and Potential
Military Confrontation

With the end of apartheid, and the prior removal of Soviet influence, South Africa's external security situation has improved. Neither the military nor the government anticipates an external threat to the state any time in the near future. Both before and after the 1994 elections, there was a great deal of fear that either Zulu separatism or white reactionary sentiment would result in internal instability in the new democracy. However, the Inkatha Freedom Party's (IFP) decision to drop demands for a weak central government and the reformation of the National Party, along with Mandela's reconciliation skills, have decreased these fears. In addition, the 1999 elections seemed to mark a move toward the center both by the IFP and the National Party (known now as the Democratic Party). In the 1999 elections, the ANC fell one seat short of securing the two-thirds majority necessary to unilat-

erally amend the constitution. In spite of these gains, it is possible that either of the ANC's two principal rivals could become dissatisfied with the government. At present, however, it appears that South Africa enjoys a high level of internal stability, especially by regional standards. Military confrontation between South Africa and its neighbors appears unlikely as well.

Another potential threat to South African internal stability is the AIDS virus. Not only does AIDS have an adverse impact on the economy, but the military is adversely impacted as well. AIDS affects at least 25 percent of the military, with costs both in terms of military service and economic resources. Since this situation is common in Africa, the AIDS epidemic does not place South Africa at a strategic disadvantage relative to its neighbors. However, the demands placed on the military by the virus could lead to the diversion of resources away from modernization programs vital to long-term security.

Alliance Structure

South Africa has participated in two alliances since 1945. The first of these was initiated by South Africa in 1982 with the Kingdom of Swaziland. In a secret agreement reached between the two countries, Swaziland would receive land concessions in exchange for a supportive policy with regard to the ANC. Even though the land transfer did not occur, Swaziland did undertake a mass set of deportations of ANC members beginning in that year. This served to cut off a route through which ANC military operations could be conducted via bases in Mozambique. South Africa was able to arrest or kill several key members of the ANC as a result of this alliance. In spite of tensions between the two states over the issue of the absolute monarchy in Swaziland, the alliance continues.

The second alliance was between South Africa and Mozambique and lasted from 1984 through 1992. In 1984, the two countries agreed to a nonaggression treaty as a result of South African pressure on Mozambique via Renamo. In essence, Mozambique agreed to prevent the ANC from operating on its territory in exchange for an end to South African support of Renamo (Cravinho 2002, 701). Once the South African government recognized the existence of the ANC as a legitimate political entity, the need for a formal alliance no longer existed.

Size and Structure of the Military
The total size of active forces within the South African National Defense Force (SANDF) as of the year 2000 stood at approximately 63,400 (South African Statistics 2002). In addition, the reserve force of the SANDF stands at approximately 87,400. The army is the largest branch of the military, with about 43,000 active members. The air force consists of 9,640 active members, and the navy has just over 5,000 members. Finally, the medical corps of the SANDF, which is very well developed by African standards, contains 5,290 members.

Even before the elections that resulted in the formal inauguration of majority rule in South Africa, the bureaucratic structure of the military was undergoing fundamental changes that reflected a desire to enforce the civilian control of the military that is an essential part of any democracy. As a result of the reorganization, the minister of defense, a civilian, is responsible for basic control of the military. The minister of defense is advised by a secretary of defense on overall defense policy issues and by the chief of the SANDF on operational matters. As a result of the need for integration of the majority into the military, an Equal Opportunities Directorate was created within the Defense Secretariat in order to manage this process. Procurement issues are now placed under the civilian portion of the defense bureaucracy in order to separate these issues from operational decision making. The chief of each branch of the military reports to the chief of the SANDF, who in turn reports to the minister of defense.

In 1996 the South African government drafted *The White Paper on National Defense for the Republic of South Africa* to serve as a template for the continued reorganization of the military (Nathan 1998, 42–43). The *White Paper* states that the SANDF is subordinate to both the Parliament and the executive. In addition, military planning would take place within the context of South Africa's overall development strategy. As a result, cuts in military spending were to be diverted to activities designed to stimulate growth and decrease inequality. To the extent that the military was to play a role in the development of South Africa, the focus would be on increasing the international competitiveness of the arms industry. One of the offshoots of the *White Paper* was the adoption in 1999 of a Code of Conduct for Uniformed Members of the Department of Defense. The code requires military personnel to respect civilian control, treat civilians with respect regardless of ethnic background, and obey the basic dictates of the Geneva Conventions. Given the previous blend between military and policing operations, as well as the history of human rights abuses within South Africa, the code of conduct was viewed as an important step toward the development of a professional military.

The reorganization of the military bureaucracy was facilitated by a series of compromises reached during negotiations prior to the end of apartheid between members of the old South African Defense Force (SADF) and members of the African National Congress (ANC). One of these compromises resulted in the naming of a SANDF chief from the ranks of the SADF. Although this decision did not reflect the demographic reality present in South Africa, the move did serve to placate those within SADF who might have otherwise more actively resisted the transition to democracy.

Since South Africa has developed what it considers a fully defensive posture in the postapartheid era, most military deployments are a part of regional and international peacekeeping and observer missions. Participation in peacekeeping is one of many ways that South Africa has attempted to assert its leadership in African affairs (see Sidebar 1 for more details). As of December 2003, South Africa had approximately 1,400 troops participating in UN missions, the bulk of these serving in the mission within the DRC. South Africa also contributes to UN missions in Ethiopia/Eritrea and Liberia. In addition, South Africa provided 750 troops to the Protection and Support Detachment in Burundi, which was designed to ensure the safe return of political exiles. South Africa also contributes troops to the African Union observer mission in the Comoros.

Within South Africa, the 7th Division of the army is the principal battle-ready force. It is deployed in the Pretoria/Johannesburg area. Two other divisions at lower levels of readiness are located in Durban (the 8th Division) and Cape

---

Sidebar 1   South Africa's Role on the African Continent

As the most dynamic military and economic power on a comparatively weak continent, South Africa uses many means to assert its leadership. South Africa was the first country to contribute to the Organization of African Unity (now African Union) Peace Fund. Most contributions came from sources within the developed world. In addition to its role in troop contribution, South Africa also provides technical and logistical assistance where it is sorely needed in African peacekeeping missions. South Africa hopes to cement its role as Africa's leader by securing a permanent seat, with veto power, on the United Nations Security Council. Other African challengers, however, including Egypt and Nigeria, have a similar goal. Any expansion of the Security Council will ultimately require the approval of the current permanent members—an event that is not likely in the near future.

Source
South Africa Department of Foreign Affairs Website. 2004. http://www.dfa.gov.za (accessed May 23, 2005).

Town (the 9th Division). Budget constraints prevent the SANDF from maintaining a higher level of readiness, especially considering the demands of peacekeeping deployments. South Africa also maintains four regional commands. The central command is located in Pretoria and also covers the northwestern provinces. The northern command is located in Pietersburg, and the eastern command is headquartered in Durban. Port Elizabeth is the headquarters of the southern command, which also patrols a coastal area. Finally, the western command is located in Cape Town and covers the Western and Northern Cape Provinces (*Jane's World Armies* 2000, 663). The army also maintains a border patrol, whose mission is to prevent arms smuggling into South Africa and to support the police in their patrol efforts.

Budget

One of the primary goals of the SANDF enumerated in the 1996 *White Paper* was to provide an "affordable" defense, based on more carefully enumerated priorities (Nathan 1998). Military expenditures as a percentage of GDP have declined significantly in the postapartheid era. In 1989, military expenditure accounted for approximately 4.1 percent of GDP (Batchelor and Willett 1998, 25). As of 2001, the figure had fallen to 1.6 percent (SIPRI 2003). Military expenditures in constant

dollars have also decreased since the end of apartheid, amounting to about 2.2 billion in constant U.S. dollars as of 2002. This figure is up from the low point of 1.6 billion in constant U.S. dollars set in 1999. Table 2 summarizes South African military expenditures as a percentage of GDP.

The total defense budget in 2003 was just less than 19 billion rand. Landward defense makes up about 3.5 billion rand of this total, and air defense accounts for just over 2 billion rand of total defense expenditure. Maritime defense accounts for just under 1 billion rand of the defense budget, and the military health figure has increased to more than 1.2 billion rand in part as a result of the increased cost of confronting the AIDS epidemic in the military. The largest portion of the defense budget is the Special Defense Account to which 7.7 billion rand was di-

Table 2   South Africa: Military Expenditures as a Percentage of Gross Domestic Product (1989–2002)

1989	4.1%
1990	3.8%
1991	3.2%
1992	2.9%
1993	2.5%
1994	2.6%
1995	2.2%
1996	1.8%
1997	1.6%
1998	1.5%
1999	1.3%
2000	1.5%
2001	1.6%
2002	1.6%
2003	1.7%

Sources

Batchelor, Peter, and Susan Willett. 1998. *Disarmament and Defense: Industrial Adjustment in South Africa*. Oxford, UK: Oxford University Press.

Central Intelligence Agency Website. 2003. CIA *World Factbook*. http://www.cia.gov/cia/publications/factbook/ (accessed December 15, 2003).

Stockholm International Peace Research Institute (SIPRI). 2003. *SIPRI Yearbook 2003: Armaments, Disarmament and International Security*. London: Oxford University Press.

rected. Total personnel expenditure accounted for 35 percent of the total expenditure. Although detailed research and development spending data is not as current as other spending data, the Department of Defense acknowledges that research and development spending has decreased significantly over the last decade (South African Department of Defense 2002b). Of course, the decision by South Africa to abandon the nuclear option after having previously developed a usable weapon has resulted in cost savings.

South Africa without doubt possesses some of the most sophisticated military equipment and forces in Africa. The army possesses three active mobilized infantry battalions, one tank regiment, one artillery regiment, nine light infantry regiments, and one parachuting infantry battalion (South African Department of Defense 2002a). The air force consists of twenty-eight fighter aircraft, twenty recon aircraft, twelve combat helicopters, and eighty-eight medium or light helicopters. Although once the only African state to possess nuclear weapons, the country has renounced the nuclear option and subjected its nuclear program to full-scope safeguards by the International Atomic Energy Agency (IAEA). South Africa remains the only state to indigenously develop a nuclear weapon and later abandon its nuclear program. As such, the country remains a model for nuclear disarmament efforts in other regions (see Sidebar 2).

Although South Africa accounts for less than 1 percent of the global arms trade, it is a significant arms exporter within Africa. South Africa has provided arms exports to Rwanda, Burundi, and Uganda and has been a source of arms for Algeria. Given budget constraints within South Africa, one of the major policy

Sidebar 2 The South African Nuclear Weapons Program

The South African nuclear weapons program began in 1969, when the government began researching the feasibility of peaceful nuclear explosions for use in mining operations. By the mid- to late 1970s, the government decided that nuclear explosive devices would be part of the overall strategy of military deterrence. Though it was widely known both within the United States and the Soviet Union that South Africa was developing nuclear weapons, the exact nature and stage of development was uncertain. It was not until 1982 that South Africa produced its first deliverable nuclear weapon. As the apartheid system began to crumble in the late 1980s, however, South Africa decided to abandon its program. To provide confidence and transparency in the nuclear disarmament process, South Africa signed a full-scope safeguards agreement with the International Atomic Energy Agency in the early 1990s. By the time South Africa completed the transition to majority rule in 1994, its nuclear weapons had been completely dismantled.

Source
Center for Nonproliferation Website. 1999. *South Africa's Nuclear Weapons Program: An Annotated Chronology, 1969–1994.* http://www.cns.miis.edu (accessed December 20, 2003).

goals of the government has been to increase revenues from the international sale of armaments. Part of the Growth Employment and Redistribution (GEAR) strategy in South Africa is to successfully transition the arms industry from an import substitution to an export-oriented base. South Africa manufactures a diverse set of products, including artillery, armor, and attack helicopters. However, the end of apartheid and the opening of South Africa to external competition in the domestic market has been a source of declining revenue for the arms industry. In spite of these losses, Denel, the major manufacturer of equipment, remains one of the 100 largest armaments producers in the world.

Civil-Military Relations/The Role of the Military in Domestic Politics

South Africa does not have the same history of military coups present in many developing states. However, the military has historically played a significant role in the South African political process. Even after apartheid was abolished, an agreement was necessary to maintain a strong white presence in the military. The historical role of the military in politics is best understood, however, as a blurring of the line between domestic and military law enforcement.

Compared with other stages of South African history, the initial phases of apartheid were perhaps the least repressive. Although repression was common, the police, who were in control of internal law enforcement, carried it out more sporadically. In 1963, however, the use of ethnic homelands to restrict movement and force resettlement required an increased level of repression. The Bureau of State Security (BOSS) was formed to centralize security functions. In 1978, the BOSS was abolished and the armed forces in effect took control of internal security under the auspices of the State Security Council. The result was the marginalization of party politics in favor of centralized control. In the process, the armed forces gained increased influence on the government. Botha became a president in the new system, a change that gave both he and the military further powers in terms of declaring states of emergency. The military used its political power both to increase military spending and to use the means necessary to prevent rebellion. It is during this period that the use of torture and summary execution as control tactics are broadly reported.

In spite of the fact that whites remain overrepresented in the military, many steps have been taken in the postapartheid era to decrease the influence in the political process. The power of the military is constitutionally subverted to the civilian leadership as was previously mentioned. This was made possible by reconciliation and reassurance that the military would not become the instrument of majority repression. The military has become professional within the new bureaucracy, whereas policing functions are now actually carried out by the police. For its part, the military appears to be accepting its reduced role in politics without much resistance. To be sure, there have been critics who have argued, with some merit, that the military has used its influence to gain funding for armaments that violate the spirit of the 1996 *White Paper*. However, the charges of military influence in the budget allocation process are common in many states where the technology exists to pursue more ambitious projects.

Terrorism

South Africa has not been threatened by terrorism, and it is not known to be harboring terrorists. However, there are elements of South African foreign policy that are at odds with U.S. interests on the issue. There are also areas of cooperation.

With regard to the Taliban, and al-Qaeda, South Africa has taken the financial and political restrictions called for by UN resolutions. South Africa, since it is a transit point for some illicit drugs, shares information with the international community through Interpol regarding monies from the sale of drugs or arms that could be diverted to terrorist activity. South Africa participated in 2002 in the establishment of a regional terrorism database where information and intelligence concerning terrorism in southern Africa can be accessed (South African Department of Foreign Affairs 2003, 18–19).

Although South Africa's policies on terrorism are not hostile toward the United States, there are some areas of conflict. For example, whereas the United States considers suicide bombings by Palestinians within Israel as terrorist acts, South Africa considers the entire situation within the region as falling under the definition of a "legitimate act of self-determination." As such, it has upheld the African Union and Non-aligned Movement (NAM) policy of separating acts of national self-determination and liberation from acts of terrorism. South Africa has also expressed its conviction that the war on terrorism should not take place at the expense of human rights. South Africa recognized Yassir Arafat as the legitimate leader of the Palestinian Authority. It should be noted, however, that South Africa's policies are consistent with those of the NAM, a natural development given the end of apartheid and the extent of African membership in the organization.

Relationship with the United States

Although U.S. relations with South Africa were strained by apartheid, the fact remains that, during the Cold War, South Africa was a key anticommunist player in southern Africa. As a result, U.S. policy toward the Republic of South Africa (RSA) during the apartheid era tended to be more reactive to certain events within the state. In 1960, in response to the Sharpeville massacre, the United States declared its first public condemnation of South African policies at the UN General Assembly. In 1963, the United States voted in favor of a UN resolution imposing an arms embargo on the country. However, the United States soon decided that the embargo was not consistent with its interest in containing communism. In order to maintain its interests in the region, the United States pushed for strategic exceptions to the embargo, including allowances for the sale of helicopters, air-to-air missiles, and submarine torpedoes. These exceptions were advanced as necessary elements in South Africa's efforts to resist external threats to its security. This was another way of saying that the arms embargo should not stand as an impediment to South Africa's fight against communism. Although the United States voted for the second arms embargo in 1976, South Africa continued to receive military equipment and technology from the United States.

The United States also played a large role in South Africa's development of a nuclear weapon. Although the United States did not officially approve of the RSA's decision to develop nuclear weapons, the United States did participate in the transfer of critical dual-use technologies to South Africa. In addition, many of South Africa's top nuclear scientists received training in the United States. When Soviet intelligence confirmed the existence of a nuclear test facility in the RSA, the Carter administration warned the country not to use the facility. South Africa ultimately abandoned its nuclear program in the early 1990s.

In 1986, the U.S. Congress passed the Antiapartheid Act, overriding a veto from President Ronald Reagan. Reagan was concerned that the sanctions called for in the act were too severe and would place South Africa under more communist pressure. As a result, the portions of the act calling for international cooperation were never implemented, although divestment in South Africa did occur on the part of many U.S. firms. The import of South African iron and steel as well as agricultural products was also a part of the 1986 act. U.S. sanctions, combined with European and broader economic sanctions and pressure, did play a role in the end of apartheid. The exact magnitude of this role is unclear, however, given the success of South African import substitution, the porous nature of the sanctions, and South African wealth in natural resources such as gold and diamonds.

With the end of apartheid and the Cold War, U.S.–South African relations have for the most part been positive. Strains do exist over South Africa's policy of nonalignment. The nonaligned policy permits South Africa to maintain relations with countries such as Syria, and South Africa has exported arms to that country against U.S. wishes. In addition, the United States has made it clear that it desires South Africa to be "less friendly" with states that do not uphold fundamental human rights. Specifically, the United States would like South Africa to be more proactive on the issue of democracy in Zimbabwe. On the trade front, the South African decision to allow the import of inexpensive drugs from foreign sources has created tension with the United States, which is concerned about the protection of intellectual property rights.

In spite of divergence on these issues, South Africa and the United States enjoy a high level of cooperation on security-related and other issues. The U.S.–South Africa Binational Commission was established in 1995 to engender cooperation on a variety of issues, including crime prevention and the training of legal professionals in South Africa. As the undisputed economic and political power of southern Africa, South Africa is a key partner with the United States in securing stability in the region. The United States has also provided assistance to the South African government for dealing with the AIDS epidemic.

The Future

Over the next five to ten years, we can expect to see the SANDF continue its efforts to become more equipped to deal with the current security situation in southern Africa. This will include developing increased mobility, with less focus on the type of armaments needed to respond to the Soviet/Cuban threat. As a result, we should expect less of an emphasis on armor and continued development of rapid-response technology, including advances in troop mobility. The development of attack helicopters will continue as the budget permits.

In terms of the defense budget, the spending floor was reached in 1999 (both in real and percentage terms) and will probably not be seen again. However, it is equally unlikely that spending will return to apartheid-era levels in excess of 4 percent. One area of the defense budget that is likely to grow is that of the medical corps, which assists in dealing with the AIDS epidemic. AIDS will continue to cost the military dearly, in personnel hours, medical expenses, and long-term care, until the virus is successfully brought under control.

As the country strives to reconcile budgetary and security concerns, South Africa will continue to be concerned with regional instability in southern Africa. The government has already decided to divert resources used to station troops at home toward increasing the number of South African soldiers participating in regional and international peacekeeping. This does involve additional expenditures, since South African peacekeepers receive an additional stipend. South Africa will continue to promote increased regional security, including the development of regional stand by forces, such as the one currently under negotiation within the African Union. The problem of course is that because South Africa is the most developed country in the region, it will continue for the short and medium term to shoulder most of the financial obligation for these innovations. South Africa possesses the resources necessary to meet these challenges, but eventually it will need more regional burden sharing in order to ensure its own stability.

References, Recommended Readings, and Websites

Books

Batchelor, Peter, and Susan Willett. 1998. *Disarmament and Defense: Industrial Adjustment in South Africa*. Oxford, UK: Oxford University Press.

Brown, Richard. 2002. "Zimbabwe: Recent History." In *Africa South of the Sahara*, Katharine Murison, ed. London: Europa Publications, pp. 1170–1176.

Byrnes, Rita M., ed. 1997. *South Africa: A Country Study*. Washington, DC: Library of Congress Federal Research Division.

Christopher, A. J. 1994. *The Atlas of Apartheid*. New York: Routledge.

Cravinho, João Gomes. 2002. "Mozambique: Recent History." In *Africa South of the Sahara*, Katharine Murison, ed. London: Europa Publications Ltd., pp. 700–702.

Garztecki, Marek. 2002. "Angola: Recent History." In *Africa South of the Sahara*, Katharine Murison, ed. London: Europa Publications, pp. 34–40.

Gastrow, Peter. 1995. *Bargaining for Peace: South Africa and the National Peace Accord*. Washington, DC: United States Institute of Peace Press.

Guelke, Adrian. 1999. *South Africa in Transition: The Misunderstood Miracle*. New York: Tauris Academic Studies.

Hutcheson, A. MacGregor. 2002. "South Africa: Physical and Social Geography." In *Africa South of the Sahara*, Katharine Murison, ed. London: Europa Publications, pp. 964–965.

Jane's World Armies. 2000. Alexandria, VA: Jane's Information Group.

Landgren, Signe. 1996. *Embargo Disimplemented: South Africa's Military Industry*. Oxford, UK: Oxford University Press.

Maasdorp, Gavin G. 1985. "Squaring Up to Economic Dominance: Regional Patterns." In *South Africa and Its Neighbors: Regional Security and Self Interest*, R. Rotberg et al., eds. Lexington, MA: Lexington Books, pp. 91–136.

Mokoena, Kenneth, ed. 1993. *South Africa and the United States: The Declassified History*. New York: New Press.

Nathan, Laurie. 1998. "The 1996 Defense White Paper: An Agenda for State Demilitarization?" In *From Defense to Development: Redirecting Military Resources in South Africa*, Jacklyn Cock and Penny Mckenzie, eds. Ottawa, ON: International Development Research Centre, pp. 41–59.

Rotberg, Robert. 1985. "South Africa and the Soviet Union: A Struggle for Primacy." In *South Africa and Its Neighbors: Regional Security and Self Interest*, R. Rotberg et al., eds. Lexington, MA: Lexington Books, pp. 55–68.

———. 2002. "South Africa Statistical Survey." In *Africa South of the Sahara*,

Katharine Murison, ed. London: Europa Publications, p. 1003

Saunders, Christopher. 2002a. "Botswana: Recent History." In *Africa South of the Sahara*, Katharine Murison, ed. London: Europa Publications, pp. 81–84.

———. 2002b. "South Africa: Recent History." In *Africa South of the Sahara*, Katharine Murison, ed. London: Europa Publications, pp. 965–975.

Seegers, Annette. 1996. *The Military in the Making of Modern South Africa*. New York: I. B. Tauris.

Shea, Dorothy C. 2000. *The South African Truth Commission: The Politics of Reconciliation*. Washington, DC: United States Institute of Peace Press.

Simon, David, ed. 1998. *South Africa in Southern Africa: Reconfiguring the Region*. Athens: Ohio University Press.

Stockholm International Peace Research Institute. 2003. "Military Expenditure." *SIPRI Yearbook 2003: Armaments, Disarmament and International Security*. New York: Humanities Press.

Van Buren, Linda. 2002. "South Africa: Economy." In *Africa South of the Sahara*, Katharine Murison, ed. London: Europa Publications, pp. 975–981.

Zacarias, Agostinho. 1999. *Security and the State in Southern Africa*. New York: I. B. Tauris.

Articles

Gibler, Douglas M., and Meredity Starkees. Forthcoming. "Measuring Alliances: The Correlates of War Formal Interstate Alliance Data Set, 1816–2000." *Journal of Peace Research*.

Howe, Herbert M. 1994. "The South African Defense Force and Political Reform." *The Journal of Modern African Studies* 32, no. 1:29–51.

Jaster, Robert S. 1983. "A Regional Security Role for Africa's Front-Line States: Experience and Prospects." *Adelphi Papers* 180:19–27.

Luckham, Robin. 1994. "The Military, Militarization and Democratization in Africa: A Survey of Literature and Issues." *African Studies Review* 37, no. 2:13–75.

Sarkees, Meredith Reid. 2000. "The Correlates of War Data on War: An Update to 1997." *Conflict Management and Peace Science* 18, no. 1:123–144.

Websites

African Union Website: http://www.africa-union.org.

Barletta, Michael, and Christina Ellington. 1999. *South Africa's Nuclear Weapons Program*. Center for Nonproliferation Studies http://www.cns.miis.edu/research/safrica/chron.htm

Central Intelligence Agency. *World Factbook*. http://www.cia.gov.

Official Web Page of the South African Government: http://www.gov.za.

South African Broadcast Corporation: http://www.sabcnews.com.

South African Department of Defense. 2000. *Code of Conduct for Uniformed Members of the SANDF*. http://www.mil.za.

———. 2002a. *Annual Report: 2002/2003*. http://www.mil.za/Articles&Papers/AnnualReports/AnnualReport2002_2003/AnnualReport03.pdf.

———. 2002b. *Strategic Plan for 2002/03*. http://www.mil.za

South African Department of Foreign Affairs. 2003. *South Africa's International Relations 2002/03*. http://www.dfa.gov.za.

South African Ministry of Defense. 2002. *Address by the Minister of Defense-Mosiuoa Lekota at the Media Conference at Milpark Holiday Inn, Johannesburg, 16 July 2002*. http://www.mil.za.

South African Statistics. http://www.statssa.gov.za.

South Korea

Jung-Yeop Woo

Geography and History

South Korea is located on the southern half of the Korean peninsula, which is on the northeastern section of Asia. The peninsula is roughly 1,100 kilometers north to south, or roughly the distance of the U.S. state of California. The peninsula and the islands lie between 33°06′40″N and 43°00′39″N parallels and 124°11′00″E and 131°52′42″E meridians. Korea is similar in latitude to the Iberian Peninsula and Greece. The total area of the peninsula is approximately 222,154 square kilometers, roughly the same size as Britain or the U.S. state of Minnesota. South Korea makes up 45 percent of the peninsula at 99,392 square kilometers, with North Korea occupying the remaining 122,762 square kilometers. Alone, South Korea is roughly the size of Portugal or Hungary, slightly larger than the U.S. state of Indiana.

The original border distinguishing the two Koreas was the 38th parallel. Following the Korean War, the Demilitarized Zone (DMZ) became the boundary. The DMZ is a 4,000-meter-wide strip of land along the cease-fire line from the east to west coasts, a distance of 241 kilometers. The Korean peninsula shares a border with Russia and China to the north, formed by the Amnokgang (Yalu) and Duman-gang (Tumen) rivers. To the east of the peninsula lies Japan approximately 200 kilometers across the East Sea (Sea of Japan). To the west, is the Korean Bay in the north and the Yellow Sea in the south, across which is China, approximately 200 kilometers away. The Korean peninsula is relatively stable geologically with no active volcanoes and no strong earthquakes, unlike much of the rest of the Pacific Rim.

Sidebar 1   South Korea and Broadband

The broadband penetration rate for South Korea is four times higher than for the United States, sixty times higher than for the United Kingdom, and twice that for Canada. The Republic of Korea leads the way in broadband penetration, and had approximately 21 broadband subscribers for every 100 inhabitants in 2002. Hong Kong (China) ranks second in the world with nearly 15 broadband subscribers per 100 inhabitants, and Canada ranks third with slightly more than 11 broadband subscribers per 100 inhabitants.

Source
ITU World Telecommunication Indicators Database. 2003. *Number of Global Broadband Subscribers Grows 72% in 2002 Republic of Korea, Hong Kong (China) and Canada Top the List.* http://www.itu.int/newsarchive/press_releases/2003/25.html (accessed May 14, 2005).

Korea's population is extremely homogeneous ethnically and linguistically. Besides a small Chinese community of around 23,000, nearly all Koreans share a similar cultural and linguistic heritage. All Koreans speak and write the same Korean language, contributing to a sense of national identity. South Korea has a population of 47 million, making it one of the most densely populated nations on earth. South Korea's population has grown rapidly since 1948, when the nation was first established. However, in recent years its growth rate has slowed to resemble that of other industrialized nations. The rapid industrialization and urbanization of South Korea in the 1960s and 1970s led to heavy migration of rural inhabitants into the cities, in particular Seoul, which has resulted in very heavily populated metropolitan areas.

According to government statistics, 42.6 percent of South Koreans in 1999 professed membership in a religious community. Freedom of religion is guaranteed in the South Korean constitution. About 20 percent of the population is Buddhist, 16 percent Protestant, 5 percent Catholic, 1 percent Confucian, and 0.6 percent other. Korea is part of a sphere of Buddhist and Confucian influence with Japan and China who exchanged culture often through Korea.

Korea was colonized by Japan between 1910 and 1945. On August 8, 1945, the Soviet Union honored its World War II agreements with the United States and declared war on Japan, launching an attack on Japanese-held territory in Manchuria and Korea. Following the dropping of atomic bombs on Hiroshima and Nagasaki on August 6 and 9 by the United States, Japan surrendered on August 15, 1945.

In December 1943 at the Cairo Conference, the Allies had agreed to strip Japan of its colonies acquired since 1894. The United States, China, and Great Britain agreed to a free and independent Korea. In its declaration of war on Japan, the Soviets also agreed to this principle. Still, no precise formula had been agreed to between Roosevelt and Stalin for governing the newly independent Korea. Landing of Soviet forces forced the hand of the United States, and on August 15, 1945, fearing Soviet control of the entire Korean peninsula by the Soviets, U.S. President Harry Truman proposed the division of Korea to Joseph Stalin, who agreed one day later to the proposal.

South Korea is one of East Asia's Four Dragons. Its economic growth in recent decades has been remarkable. Only thirty years ago, GDP per capita was similar to the poorest countries in Asia and Africa. Today South Korea's GDP per capita is seven times India's, thirteen times North Korea's, and comparable to some smaller European Union nations. Success has been marked by strong business-government relations, including measures such as direct credit, import restrictions, industry sponsorship, and a strong labor effort. Promotion of raw material imports and technology at the expense of consumer goods and investment over consumption are hallmarks of South Korea's economic policy. The government's role in pursuing "export-led" strategy is considered crucial in economic development in South Korea. Despite the 1997 Asian financial crisis, South Korea recovered financial stability in 1999. The next challenge for Seoul is to maintain the current pace of growth in South Korea's economy.

Since its inception as a republic, South Korea's government has functioned almost exclusively as a presidential system. Within this system, three primary branches share power: the legislative, executive, and judiciary. The Constitutional Court and the National Election Commission also share in governing responsibilities.

The legislature is the unicameral National Assembly, consisting of 299 representatives serving four-year terms. The National Assembly is organized into individual members, presiding officers, the plenary, sixteen standing committees, negotiation groups, and supporting administration. The legislature is empow-ered to inspect the executive, approve appointments of prime minister and director of the Board of Inspection and Audit, impeach officials, and recommend to the president the removal of executive officials.

Sixteen provincial and thirty-four municipal-level local governments exist, but they are considered part of the executive branch and therefore are controlled by the central government. On July 1, 1995, direct, popular elections returned for local chief executives, granting some degree of local autonomy. Prior to this, the central government simply appointed local chief executives. Local government autonomy is still relatively limited compared with that in most developed countries. Virtually all major policies, including those specifying local government functions, taxation, resident welfare and services, and personnel management, cannot be determined solely by the local government.

Geopolitics

Since there are no formidable land or sea barriers along its borders and it occupies a central position among East Asian nations, the Korean peninsula has served as

Table 1   Republic of Korea: Key Statistics

Type of government	Republic (presidential system)
Population (millions)	48 (July 2003 est.)
Religion	Buddhist (20%), Christian (17%)
Main industries	Electronics, automobiles, chemicals
Main security threats	North Korea
Defense spending (% GDP)	2.8% (2001)
Size of military (thousands)	600
Number of civil wars since 1945	0
Number of interstate wars since 1945	1

Sources
Central Intelligence Agency Website. 2005. CIA *World Factbook.* http://www.cia.gov/cia/publications/factbook/ (accessed May 15, 2005).
Korea National Statistical Office: http://www.nso.go.kr/eng/.

a cultural bridge between the mainland and the Japanese archipelago. Korea contributed greatly to the development of Japan by transmitting both Indian Buddhist and Chinese Confucian culture, art, and religion.

At the same time, Korea's exposed geographical position left it vulnerable to invasion by its stronger neighbors. In the late nineteenth century, Korea became the focus of intense competition among imperialist nations such as China, Russia, and Japan. In 1910, Japan annexed Korea and instituted colonial rule, bringing the Chosun Dynasty to an end and with it traditional Korea. National liberation occurred in 1945 but was soon followed by territorial division. The Republic of Korea (ROK) in the south has a democratic government, and the Democratic People's Republic of Korea (DPRK) in the north is ruled by a communist regime. Since then, the Korean peninsula has inevitably been a strategically important place in world politics.

Ever since Russia (former Soviet Union) occupied the northern part of the Korean peninsula after World War II and helped North Korea in the Korean War, the relationship between South Korea and Russia seemed irreconcilable. The crucial turning point was made by President Roh Tae-woo's so-called Nordpolitik, or northern policy. President Roh aggressively pursued better relations with the socialist countries including the Soviet Union, which recognized South Korea in 1990, and the People's Republic of China, which recognized South Korea in 1992. This policy of Nordpolitik also appeared to move north-south relations on the peninsula into a new phase of negotiations between the prime ministers of the DPRK and the ROK. Through this policy, South Korea has sought to exploit

the opportunities emanating from the end of the Cold War and develop close relations with those nations holding influence on North Korea. Designed not to isolate the north, South Korea brought about better relationships with those states that had previously been aligned with North Korea in an effort to alter their partisan attitude toward the peninsular struggle.

In 1991, Seoul agreed to extend $3 billion in loans to Moscow. The origin of Roh's Nordpolitik dates back to 1973 when the so-called June 23 Declaration was issued under the principle of improving ties, even with communist countries, as long as they refrained from taking an unfriendly posture toward Seoul. President Roh's diplomatic initiative was crystallized in the July 7 Declaration of 1990, under which Seoul reaffirmed its will to normalize diplomatic relations with the Soviet Union and China, while offering to help North Korea improve ties with Seoul's allies. The declaration, in essence, meant that Seoul would seek to ensure stability on the Korean peninsula through a "cross-recognition" of the two Koreas by outside powers.

As the Soviet Empire was dissolved, Russia lost its status in Asian politics as well as in world politics. Russia will seek a balanced relationship with the two Koreas by separating politics and economics. According to Joo (2001), Russia will continue to be in a neutral position between South Korea and North Korea on political issues, particularly inter-Korean affairs. On certain international matters, such as U.S.-led UN sanctions against North Korea over nuclear weapons and missile issues, Russia is likely to exercise a veto power. Russia, however, will continue to unequivocally support nuclear nonproliferation on the Korean peninsula and champion a peaceful and diplomatic solution to the Korean question. However, as far as economic and military relations are concerned, Seoul is by far a more important partner to Russia than is Pyongyang, the capitol of the DPRK. Therefore, Russia will continue to lean heavily toward Seoul for economic and military cooperation, because it hopes that Seoul can help Russia develop its economy. Moscow wants to boost its prestige and influence on the Korean peninsula by promoting its role as an objective mediator and by leading a multilateral security mechanism in northeast Asia.

China has been a great influence on Korea historically. After World War II, with the communist victory in the Chinese civil war, it was natural that newly established People's Republic of China (China) recognized North Korea as the sole legitimate state on the Korean peninsula. As Scalapino (2001) noted, China's leaders saw the unity of Korea under an anticommunist government and its alliance with the United States as its greatest threat to security. Ever since, China and North Korea have been in a close relationship in both politics and economy.

It was in 1992 that South Korea and China normalized their relations. China discarded its pro–North Korean posture and strongly established a two-Korea policy. This move was not merely a pragmatic accommodation to recently changed circumstances around the Korean peninsula (Lee 1998). This normalization was conceived as a necessary step toward peace on the Korean peninsula. President Roh emphasized that the ultimate goal of his Nordpolitik was to secure peace on the Korean peninsula by inducing North Korea to open up to South Korea. It was an indispensable measure to build relations with China and other socialist nations. In the economic arena, the change in relationship between the two states cannot be overstated. China's changing economic interests in the Korean peninsula have been reflected in this process of diplomatic relations.

Although China's military policy seems not to be substantially changed compared with the conspicuous shift in its economic and diplomatic relations with Korea, China's current two-Korea policy has begun to erode its alliance system with North Korea. Although China will maintain its military ties with North Korea, it is not likely that China will extend an unconditional military commitment to North Korea.

According to Scalapino (1997), it is clear that China would not desire a reunified Korea under Seoul's command. That would push South Korea to the Chinese border, and China has some 700,000 Chinese Koreans on its side of the Yalu River. Korean nationalism might be rekindled in that group. Again, this would be conceived as major threat to China, as it was in the Korean War. Thus, China's perceived interests are strongly in the maintenance of two Korean states. Chinese policymakers do not favor any radical changes on the Korean peninsula.

The relationship between Korea and Japan can be depicted as "so near, and yet so far." In other words, even though they are geographically close, there exists a wide chasm in terms of national emotions as a result of historical experience. The Korean people have not yet forgotten thirty-six years of Japanese colonial rule over the Korean peninsula. Even though there has been a great deal of progress such as jointly hosting the 2002 Korea-Japan World Cup soccer games, emotional distance is revealed on issues such as disagreement on the name of the sea separating them, which the Japanese call the Sea of Japan and the Koreans call the East Sea. Also territorial disputes over Tokdo have been another source of emotional tension between Korea and Japan.

However, in terms of politics, economy, and international security, the relationship between Korea and Japan has undergone significant changes. Since the normalization of relations in 1965, Japan has been the second-largest trading partner of South Korea.

According to Koh (1998), there are two things that enable continued security cooperation between South Korea and Japan. Those are a shared ally and a common source of threat. The shared ally is the United States, and the common source of threat is North Korea. Koh also said that the emergence of a crisis surrounding North Korea's nuclear weapons threat strengthened the relationship between South Korea and Japan.

However, when it comes to the reunification of the two Koreas, the interests of Korea and Japan are very different. Armacost and Pyle (2001) contend that even though Japanese cooperation with the United States is essential, because the nature of reunification is so uncertain in its implications for Japan's interests, Japanese policymakers might prefer a continuation of the status quo of the Korean peninsula.

Cossa (2000) noted that the strategic partnership among the United States, Japan, and South Korea would serve the national security interests of all three nations as well as the broader cause of peace and stability in northeast Asia.

The relationship between South Korea and North Korea in the 1950s and 1960s was dominated by extreme antagonism, without compromise or dialogue. Until

1960, the First Republic led by Syngman Rhee adhered to the principle of unification by force to regain sovereignty in the northern area. Despite the global trend toward dismantling Cold War structure since the late 1980s, North and South Korea have been trapped in a vicious cycle of mutual distrust, negation, and protracted military confrontation. In dealing with North Korea, President Roh Taewoo first applied an engagement policy in his determination to build reconciliation and cooperation with the north, while at the same time reducing military tensions on the Korean peninsula. This engagement policy toward the north was continued through President Kim Young-sam. President Kim Dae-jung has embarked on the so-called Sunshine Policy to seek reconciliation with the north through the donation of aid, increased trade, and reuniting families that were separated in 1953. It is expected that there will continue to be greater progress in inter-Korea relations. President Kim Dae-jung won the Nobel Peace Prize for contributing to peace on the Korean peninsula.

However, the current crisis over North Korea's nuclear threat has brought world attention to the Korean peninsula. It was in 1993 that North Korea said it had excluded itself from the Nuclear Nonproliferation Treaty amid suspicions that it was developing nuclear weapons. Since then, North Korea's nuclear threat has been the major source of threats to world security as well as to South Korean security. North Korea's resumption of its nuclear weapons program has set its neighbors and much of the rest of the world on edge. Five nations—the United States, China, Russia, Japan, and South Korea—are now piling the pressure on North Korea to curb its nuclear ambitions. Pyongyang has said it wants a formal nonaggression treaty with the United States before it makes any move.

Although the historic summit was instrumental for reviving and expanding economic, social, and cultural exchanges between the two nations, it failed to produce concrete measures to resolve security problems surrounding the Korean peninsula. Moon (2001) contends that in order to ensure stability, both Koreas should more actively engage in negotiations on inter-Korean tension reduction, confidence-building measures, and arms control. At the same time, issues of weapons of mass destruction and missiles should be resolved. There must also be new discourses on the status of U.S. forces in South Korea in particular and the ROK-U.S. alliance in general. Otherwise, U.S. forces in South Korea could become another major barrier to peace-making and peace building in Korea. In view of this, transforming the armistice treaty into a viable inter-Korean peace treaty and forging a peaceful reunification of Korea could take a much longer time than expected. Heo and Horowitz (2003) contended that it is necessary for Seoul to form a new cooperative framework with Washington in approaching North Korea to make the Sunshine Policy more effective.

Conflict Past and Present

At a speech at the National Press Club in Washington in January 1950, then U.S. Secretary of State Dean Acheson stressed UN protection for places beyond the U.S. "defensive perimeter." The intention of this speech was to alert communist mainland China that the United States would not act militarily to prevent an invasion of Taiwan and that there was no need to launch an attack on Chiang Kai-

shek's nationalist government there. However, the speech also seemed to indicate that the United States would not act to protect South Korea from attack by its northern neighbor. This combined with the 1948 South Korean elections and the 1949 U.S. military withdrawal from the peninsula indicated a lack of desire to repel an invasion by North Korea. It was viewed within the United States as unlikely that the Soviet Union would allow such an attack to take place.

On June 25, 1950, North Korea crossed the 38th parallel and attempted to unify the peninsula by quick and decisive force, believing a response from the United States and its allies would be slow or non-existent. According to MacDonald (1996), Kim Il-sung seemed unaware that the United States would not stand to lose South Korea to communism. However, by the end of June, the United Nations had created an international force under the command of U.S. Army General Douglas MacArthur to defend South Korea. As shown in Table 2, sixteen countries had sent their combatants to the Korean peninsula.

After UN forces defeated North Korea, the UN General Assembly supported a U.S. proposal to occupy the north until elections could be held for a unified government.

This proposal would not be carried out, as the rapid advance of UN troops into North Korea brought China into a supporting role for the north. The combined North Korean and Chinese forces pushed the UN back south of Seoul before a UN counteroffensive finally moved the front lines back to the 38th parallel in March 1951.

In June 1951, the Soviet representative to the United Nations proposed cease-fire talks. These negotiations went on for two

Table 2   UN Forces Casualties in Korean War

	Killed in Action	Wounded	Missing in Action	Total
Australia	291	1,240	39	1,570
Belgium/Luxembourg	97	350	5	452
Britain	710	2,278	1,263	4,251
Canada	291	1,072	21	1,384
Colombia	140	452	65	657
Ethiopia	120	536	—	656
France	288	818	18	1,124
Greece	169	543	2	714
Netherlands	111	589	4	704
New Zealand	34	80	—	114
Philippines	92	299	57	448
South Africa	20	—	16	36
Thailand	114	794	5	913
Turkey	717	2,246	107	3,070
United States	54,246	103,284	8,177	165,707

Source
Korea Institute for Military History Compilation: http://www.imhc.mil.kr/.

years, while fighting continued in Korea. An armistice would not be reached until July 1953, between the UN commander and the combined forces of the North Korean People's Army and the Chinese People's Volunteers. South Korean president Rhee disagreed with the armistice and unilaterally released 28,000 prisoners in an attempt to prevent the agreement from being finalized. The United States responded to Rhee's disagreement by offering a mutual defense treaty, U.S.$1 billion in economic aid over three years, and equipment for a twenty-division army. Rhee allowed the agreement, but South Korea never signed the armistice. As such, the Korean War has technically never ended and the Armistice Agreement of 1953 is the longest cease-fire in history.

In the Vietnam War, South Korea dispatched its two divisions. In spite of fierce controversies in South Korea, President Park acceded to the U.S. request for support of its military force in Vietnam. Two South Korean divisions served there from 1965 to 1971. The South Korean government sent forces to ensure economic advantage and maintenance of U.S. strategic support afterward.

Since 1991, attention has focused on the implications of North Korea's drive to develop nuclear weapons. Potential nuclear crisis is the most important security issue in the Korean peninsula. According to Heo and Horowitz (2003), since George W. Bush took office, the situation on the Korean peninsula has changed. Contrary to the Clinton administration, which relied on economic and food aid to stop North Korea from developing nuclear weapons and long-range missiles, the Bush administration has employed a hard-line policy toward North Korea. This change has led the South Korean government to be concerned about potential discord between the United States and South Korea with respect to North Korean policy. In December 2002, North

Korea ended the eight-year-old freeze on its nuclear program by expelling inspectors and reopening its plutonium production facilities. North Korea's resumption of its nuclear weapons program has caused concern among its neighbors and much of the rest of the world.

Alliance Structure

The U.S.-ROK alliance was established during the Korean War and formalized by the U.S.-ROK Mutual Defense Treaty after the war, on October 1, 1953. Under this treaty, the United States and South Korea agreed on six articles, reaffirming their desire to declare publicly and formally their common determination to defend themselves against external armed attack in the Pacific area.

According to Article 4, "The Republic of Korea grants, and the United States of America accepts, the right to dispose United States land, air and sea forces in and about the territory of the Republic of Korea as determined by mutual agreement," the essence of this treaty calls for the two nations to maintain a strong military alliance. Based on this agreement, the United States dispatched combat units to the Korean peninsula and combined forces with the combat units of South Korea. The two governments established a combined command structure that assumed the primary role of preventing North Korea from initiating another war on the Korean peninsula.

Size and Structure of the Military

This section is based on the Ministry of National Defense White Paper 2000. The ROK army is the central component of South Korea's national defense strategy. During peacetime, its primary objective is to deter war, and in times of war it is called upon to win ground combat missions.

The army consists of 560,000 troops organized into eleven corps, forty-nine divisions, and nineteen brigades. These groups are then divided into the ROK Army Headquarters, three Field Army Commands, the Aviations Operations Command, the Special Warfare Command, and units developed to support each command. Army equipment includes 2,400 armored vehicles, 2,360 tanks, and 5,180 pieces of field artillery. Every command is made up of several corps, divisions, and brigades.

The First and Third Field Army Commands are given the task of defending the region between the Military Demarcation Line and Seoul. Responding to the risks of surprise attacks or high-speed mobile warfare being launched by North Korea, troops from these commands are deployed along major routes between Seoul and North Korea.

Defense of the nation's rear area, including the coastline, is the responsibility of the Second Field Army. The central assignment of this command is to repel any North Korean invasion by land, sea, or air and in the case of successful North Korean infiltration to destroy the invading forces. The primary tasks used to achieve these goals include guarding the coastline, defending major facilities and sea lines of communication, and managing reserve forces and material for wartime mobilization.

The Aviation Operations Command consists of various kinds of helicopters, which can provide ground forces with fire support, airlift, and reconnaissance support and move into the rear of the enemy to conduct fire support and air strikes. This command is organized into one aviation brigade and a number of battalions.

Several brigades make up the Special Warfare Command, whose primary responsibilities include collecting intelligence, locating enemy targets, and carrying out a variety of other tasks.

Maintaining the security of Seoul and protecting the city's infrastructure is the responsibility of the Capital Defense Command, made up of several divisions.

The CBR (chemical, biological, and radiological) Defense Command includes the Chemical Defense Research Institute, one reconnaissance battalion, and one decontamination battalion. The CBR Defense Command is charged with conducting research and evaluating chemical warfare-related issues, as well as supporting CBR operations.

An artillery unit is assigned to each field army, corps command, and division. These units provide fire support for ground forces attached to them. Various artillery, targeting equipment, fire control systems, and high-tech weapons make these units highly capable and proficient.

During peacetime the ROK navy upholds national sovereignty, protects maritime rights, supports foreign policy, deters war, and enhances national prestige. In wartime, the navy ensures control over the sea in order to maintain the safety of maritime activities and the ability to make surprise landings on the enemy's rear and flanks.

Sixty-seven thousand troops, including marines, make up the navy, which is divided into the ROK Navy Headquarters, Operations Command, Marine Corps Headquarters, and various support units. The navy operates 190 vessels, which include submarines as well as 70 aircraft.

The ROK Navy Operations Command controls three fleets based in the East Sea, Yellow Sea, and Korean Straits. Each fleet is made up of destroyers, escorts, patrol battleships, high-speed boats, and other vessels. In order to conduct major naval component operations, including antisubmarine warfare, mine operations, landing, salvage, and special operations, Operations Command has its own vessels and aircraft.

Two divisions and one brigade make up Marine Corps Headquarters. Marines are focused on amphibious landing operations and have at their disposal a wide range of landing equipment. This includes amphibious tanks and their own fire support.

The primary mission of the air force during wartime is to gain air superiority in order to prevent enemy forces gaining access to South Korean airspace. Further, it is expected to destroy targets central to enemy capability and also to give air support to ground and naval forces.

The ROK air force is made up of Air Force Headquarters, Operations Command, and support commands. Headquarters directly controls the Air Defense Artillery Command as well as the Aircraft Control and Warning Wing. Nine tactical fighter wings are under the direction of Operations Command. The Training Command also operates one training wing.

Sixty-three thousand troops make up the air force, together with more than 800 aircraft, including KF-16 fighters.

Air operations are under the command of the Theater Air Control Center (TACC). Aircraft are capable of carrying precision-guided munitions and long-range air-to-air missiles. Further, these aircraft are capable of air support operations.

The Local Reserve Forces Establishment Law was enacted in 1961. In January 1968, North Korean operatives attempted an assault on the Blue House (presidential residence). In response, in April 1968, the first reserve forces were created.

Reservists receive regular training during peacetime. During wartime they are expected to become supplementary manpower for creating additional units, reinforcing current units, or replacing combat losses.

All individuals completing military service must remain in the reserves for eight years. There are currently 3.04 million such reservists in South Korea.

In October 1953, the ROK-U.S. Mutual Defense Treaty was completed. Since then, the U.S. Forces in Korea (USFK) have remained a presence on the peninsula.

USFK consists of the Eighth U.S. Army (EUSA), U.S. Naval Forces Korea, U.S. Air Forces Korea, U.S. Marine Forces Korea, and Special Operations Command Korea. USFK is directed by the commander of the United Nations command (UNC)/Combined Forces Command (CFC).

The Eighth U.S. Army is made up of 140 M1A1 tanks, 170 Bradley armored vehicles, 30 155-mm self-propelled howitzers, 70 AH-64 helicopters, 30 MRLs, and a number of surface-to-surface and surface-to-air missiles.

U.S. Air Forces Korea consists of roughly 100 aircraft, consisting of advanced fighters, intelligence-collecting and reconnaissance aircraft, as well as transport aircraft. U.S. Air Forces Korea can be augmented by the Seventh Fleet and the Seventh Air Force Command, substantially increasing their capability.

U.S. Naval Forces Korea, U.S. Marine Forces Korea, and Special Operations Command Korea maintain a limited presence on the peninsula during peacetime. However, they can be substantially augmented by the U.S. Pacific Command in the event of war.

Approximately 690,000 troops make up U.S. augmentation forces comprising army divisions, carrier battle groups, tactical fighter wings, and marine expeditionary forces. These forces are located on Okinawa and the U.S. mainland.

Three types of augmentation capability exist: Flexible Deterrence Options (FDOs), Force Module Packages (FMPs), and Time-Phased Forces Deployment Data (TPFDD). These are executed when requested by the commander of CFC and ordered by the U.S. Joint Chiefs of Staff.

FDOs are set to be used when war is imminent. They can be deployed according to political, economic, diplomatic, and military options.

FMPs augment combat and combat support units requiring support early in a war if FDOs should fail.

Both FDOs and FMPs are included in TPFDD. This option includes planning the deployment of key troops in case of the outbreak of war. TPFDD includes in-place forces, already deployed; preplanned forces for time-phased deployment; and on-call forces that could be deployed when appropriate.

Budget

South Korea's defense budget for the year 2001 was about 15.4 trillion won, amounting to 15.5 percent of the total state budget and 2.8 percent of GDP. For the five years previous, the average growth rate of the defense budget was 4.8 percent.

Civil-Military Relations/The Role of the Military in Domestic Politics

South Korea's government was dominated by the military from 1961 through 1987. Civil-military relations provide an important framework for understanding South Korean politics in the second half of the twentieth century. Yung Myung Kim (1998) argues that structural factors play into the structure of civil-military relations. If a gap exists between civilian and military institutions, and civil society is weak and unorganized compared with the military, then intervention by the military can be expected. However, if civil society is strong and well organized, it could likely challenge military domination and facilitate military withdrawal.

Yung Myung Kim also notes that international structure plays an important role in the relationship between civilian and military interests. During the Cold War, the ideological struggle between the communist Soviet Union and the capitalist United States led to possible military intervention in order to prevent perceived communist subversion. In contrast, the end of the Cold War and such ideological rivalries means the perceived threat has changed, allowing for military withdrawal from politics.

The first coup took place on May 16, 1961, involving nearly 3,600 troops led by Major General Park Chung-hee and Lieutenant Colonel Kim Jong-pil. The military was well regarded by most of the public, as they were a symbol of national security. Thirty-two officers were designated as the Supreme Council for National Reconstruction, which abolished the legislature, suspended the constitution, and ruled directly for two years. Political freedoms were suppressed for a number of years. The new government moved to build the economy. Under U.S. pressure, they created a new constitution, which passed a popular referendum in 1963, and an elected civilian government headed by Park Chung-hee took office in January 1964. According to Yung Myung Kim, the coup of 1961 was a historical turning point, which temporarily stopped political struggles among the diverse forces that sought to fulfill different objectives of nation building in the newly independent country. In this struggle, the military's alternative-capitalist industrialization, combined with authoritarian control-gained supremacy, dominated Korean society for some time.

After nearly losing a presidential election to challenger Kim Dae-jung in 1971, Park Chung-hee declared a state of emergency in 1972 and conducted a coup d'état from within. This coup led to a more authoritarian Fourth Republic under the Yushin (Revitalization) constitution. The new constitution granted the president broad powers to rule by decree, which Park took every advantage of in order to control political activity. Kim Chae-kyu, the head of the Korea Central Information Agency (KCIA), demanded moderation of Park's new regime, and in October 1979 Kim killed President Park. Choi Kyu-ha, the prime minister at that time, became acting president as stipulated by the Yushin constitution.

Prime Minister Choi Kyu-ha took over as interim president and then as president with the approval of the electoral college. Martial law was declared the night Park Chung-hee was assassinated, and an investigation was begun by the ROK Army Security Command. Army Security commander Major General Chun Doo-hwan emerged as the center of military power. On December 12, 1979, he and his supporters attacked martial law headquarters and the Ministry of National Defense. Effectively, Chun took over control of the military establishment. From then on, although Choi was officially president, Chun was, in reality, the autocratic ruler of South Korea.

In April 1980, Chun took over control of the directorship of the KCIA, which intensified the feeling that he would attempt to take total control of the country. Student demonstrations already taking place grew, and Chun declared full martial law on May 17, 1980. He canceled the National Assembly session and arrested a number of leading dissidents, including Kim Dae-jung.

Kim's arrest sparked demonstrations among students in Kim's home region of South Cholla Province. The incident in Kwangju permanently tarnished Chun's public image. Three months after the uprising he took over as interim president from Choi Kyu-ha. Two months later another new constitution was created, ushering in the Fifth Republic. This led to the end of martial law and the reorganization of civilian politics. Chun was named president for a seven-year term by the electoral college. Military backing of the government continued. This centralized government effectively continued South Korea's economic expansion, making military rule more acceptable to the people. An increase in political freedom did occur, with opposition parties winning one-third of the National Assembly in 1985.

Despite Chun's claims that he wished to be South Korea's first president to leave office through constitutional means, it became clear that he and the military would not relinquish control. Their grip on power tightened when they decided to support former general and coup leader Roh Tae-woo. Popular opposition led to a constitutional amendment allowing direct presidential elections, but the opposition split its votes and Roh won with a plurality of 36.6 percent of the votes. His presidency lasted from 1988 to 1992 and fostered the growth of democracy in South Korea, culminating in the inclusion of opposition candidates in the ruling Democratic Justice Party and in the election in 1992 of Roh's successor and longtime opposition leader, Kim Young-sam.

Roh had broken with Chun, but his government was not a strictly civilian one. The military was loyal to him, but still hostile to opposition parties. Voting by soldiers was frequently rigged in the 1992 National Assembly elections to favor ruling party candidates.

The election of Kim Young-sam in 1992 marked the first direct election of a civilian president in South Korea's history. The democratic process was further expanded creating free and fair local and general elections for the first time in the country's history. Following Kim's inauguration, the inner circle of top military officers that had held top government posts were removed, and real civilian control of the military occurred in which the military took orders from the president, but respected opposition parties as well.

Since the democratization process began, the chance of military reintervention in politics appears to have become more remote in South Korea. Politics in South Korea are now managed through a civilian-led liberal democratic procedure in which elections and public opinion are significant.

Terrorism

South Korea is a mostly stable nation from both an ethnic and a religious point of view, thereby avoiding internal terrorist threats from those sources. However, the North Korean government has made a number of violent attempts toward South Korea in the years since the Korean War.

Commando raids have taken place consistently along the DMZ, occasionally escalating into artillery battles. Such raids topped off in 1968 with more than 600 reported infiltrations by North Korean agents, including one in which agents attempted an attack on the Blue House in Seoul. The arrival of more than 120 commandos on South Korea's east coast also occurred in 1968. In 1969, nearly 400 agents were involved in more than 150 infiltration attempts. In both 1970 and 1974, North Korean agents attempted to assassinate President Park. The 1974 attempt ended in the murder of Mrs. Park.

The mid-1970s through the early 1980s saw infiltration attempts mostly carried out by heavily armed reconnaissance teams, which were generally unsuccessful. Following a brief set of sea infiltration attempts in the 1980s, North Korea began to prefer inserting agents from third countries. This preceded an aborted attempt to recruit Canadian criminals to assassinate then President Chun Doo Hwan in 1982. This was followed by a 1983 assassination attempt in Rangoon, which killed seventeen South Korean officials and four Burmese dignitaries as well. In 1987, North Korea broke from its pattern of targeting government officials, in particular the president, when it destroyed a Korean Air airliner, killing 115 people.

More recently, in 1996 a North Korean submarine came aground along South Korea's East Sea coast. Eleven of the twenty-six crew members killed themselves, and the rest were killed by South Korean troops during a manhunt targeting them. In 2002, a North Korean navy vessel sank a South Korean patrol boat, killing at least four sailors.

Relationship with the United States

The relationship between South Korea and the United States involves a wide range of security, economic, and political concerns. The United States has remained committed to maintaining peace on the Korean peninsula since the Korean War. This commitment is widely seen as vital to the peace and stability of northeast Asia as well as of the Korean peninsula. Therefore, the United States has been the central concern of Korean diplomacy because of the U.S. role in Korean national security and its importance as a market and source of investment capital.

In the 1954 U.S.-ROK Mutual Defense Treaty, the United States agreed to help the Republic of Korea defend itself against external aggression. In support of this commitment, the United States currently maintains approximately 37,000 service personnel in Korea, including the army's Second Infantry Division and several air force tactical squadrons. To coordinate operations between these units and the 650,000-strong Korean armed forces, a Combined Forces Command (CFC) was established in 1978. The head of the CFC also serves as commander of the United Nations Command (UNC) and the U.S. Forces in Korea (USFK). South Korea has agreed to pay a larger portion of USFK's stationing costs and to promote changes in the CFC command structure. On December 1, 1994, peacetime operational control authority over all South Korean military units still under U.S. operational control was transferred to the South Korean armed forces.

U.S. economic assistance to South Korea, from 1945 to 2002, totaled more than $6 billion; most economic aid ended in the mid-1970s, as South Korea reached higher levels of economic development. U.S. military aid, from 1945 to 2002, totaled more than $8.8 billion.

As Korea's economy has developed, trade has become an increasingly important aspect of the U.S.-Korea relationship.

The United States seeks to improve access to Korea's expanding market and to increase investment opportunities for U.S. business. The United States is South Korea's largest trading partner and largest export market. South Korea is the seventh-largest U.S. trading partner.

During the administration of President Rhee (1948–1960), Korea's foreign policy was almost exclusively concerned with maximizing its benefits through its special relationship with the United States. This relationship was inevitable, because South Korea was primarily helped by the United States in establishing the republic and was saved from a total collapse in the course of the Korean War (1950–1953) by the U.S.-initiated, UN-sponsored rescue operation. The United States was South Korea's principal source of international support in every aspect. Since 1953, South Korea has depended almost entirely on the presence of U.S. troops in Korea and on its air and naval protection to deter North Korea from launching another armed invasion.

From the U.S. perspective, South Korea was considered as a critical forward base in northeast Asia for containing the Soviet Union while protecting the free world. At the same time, to South Korea, the United States was its most reliable patron in the process of building a free and democratic country, while it protected itself from North Korea's military threats.

Declining South Korean fears of a North Korean invasion and the inter-Korean talks have produced a growing debate in South Korea over U.S. military presence. Growing numbers of South Koreans, especially among younger generations, seek a reduction of U.S. military forces. Incidents between U.S. military personnel and South Korean civilians have necessitated ROK-U.S. negotiations on several such issues.

The Future

As Eberstadt and Ellings (2001) state, "The Korean peninsula's eventual political future—in terms of both internal domestic arrangements and the sort of regional order in which Korea finds itself embedded—remains at this juncture highly uncertain" (p. 315). They also contend that the pivotal question on the Korean peninsula is the future of North Korea.

According to Heo and Horowitz (2003), because of North Korea's nuclear program and long-range missiles, the United States does not want to be excluded from the scene. Other great powers' interests are also involved in this regard. Seoul needs to take advantage of these international actors in dealing with North Korea.

In addition to dealing with international actors, if the reunification of the two Koreas occurs in the near future, it could be the most important source of turmoil in world politics. According to Lee (2001), all four great powers in the Pacific region favor the status quo over radical peninsular changes. Moreover, the overlap of their concerns and interests about maintaining Korean security is now considerable. Thus, South Korea should also form a cooperative framework with those great powers whose interests are not congruent with those of the Korean people.

The ultimate disposition of North Korea will shape the entire East Asian regional order, and the disposition of this troublesome, failing state lies in the hands of South Korea, the United States, China, Japan, and Russia. Therefore, South Korea's future will depend on how it induces change in North Korea and how effectively it deals with the great powers, especially the United States, concerning that change.

References, Recommended Readings, and Websites

Books

Armacost, Michael H., and Kenneth B. Pyle. 2001. "Japan and the Unification of Korea: Challenges for U.S. Policy Coordination." In *Korea's Future and the Great Powers*, Nicholas Eberstadt and Richard J. Ellings, eds. Seattle: University of Washington Press, pp. 125–163.

Armstrong, Charles K. 1997. "The Politics of Transition in North and South Korea." In *Korea Briefing: Toward Reunification*, David R. McCaron, ed. New York: M. E. Sharpe, pp. 5–24.

Eberstadt, Nicholas, and Richard J. Ellings. 2001. "Assessing Interests and Objectives of Major Actors in the Korean Drama." In *Korea's Future and the Great Powers*, Nicholas Eberstadt and Richard J. Ellings, eds. Seattle: University of Washington Press, pp. 315–342.

Heo, Uk, and Shale A. Horowitz. 2003. *Conflict in Asia: Korea, China-Taiwan, and India-Pakistan*. Westport, CT: Praeger.

Joo, Seung-ho, and Tae-hwan Kwak. 2001. *Korea in the 21st Century*. Huntington, NY: Nova Science.

Kim, Yung Myung. 1998. "Pattern of Military Rule and Prospects for Democracy in South Korea." In *The Military and Democracy in Asia and the Pacific*, R. J. May and Viberto Selochan, eds. Bathurst, Australia: Hurst, pp. 119–131.

Koh, B. C. 1998. "Japan and Korea." In *The Korean Peninsula and the Major Powers*, Bae Ho Hahn and Chae-Jin Lee, eds. Seoul: Sejong Institute, pp. 33–68.

Lee, Chae-Jin. 1998. "The Evolution of China's Two-Korea Policy." In *The Korean Peninsula and the Major Powers*, Bae Ho Hahn and Chae-Jin Lee, eds. Seoul: Sejong Institute, pp. 115–146.

———. 2001. "Conflict and Cooperation: The Pacific Powers and Korea." In *Korea's Future and the Great Powers*, Nicholas Eberstadt and Richard J.

Ellings, eds. Seattle: University of Washington Press, pp. 51–87.

MacDonald, Donald Stone. 1996. *The Koreans: Contemporary Politics and Society*. Boulder, CO: Westview.

Noland, Marcus. 2000. *Avoiding the Apocalypse*. Washington, DC: Institute for International Economics.

Oberdorfer, Don. 1997. *The Two Koreas*. Reading, MA: Addison-Wesley.

Scalapino, Robert A. 2001. "China and Korean Reunification—A Neighbor's Concerns." In *Korea's Future and the Great Powers*, Nicholas Eberstadt and Richard J. Ellings, eds. Seattle: University of Washington Press, pp. 107–124.

Articles

Cossa, Ralph A. 2000. "U.S.-ROK-Japan: Why a 'Virtual Alliance' Makes Sense. *The Korean Journal of Defense Analysis* 7, no. 1:67–86.

Joo, Seung-ho. 2001. "Russia and Korea: The Summit and After." *The Korean Journal of Defense Analysis* 8:103–127.

Moon, Chung-In. 2001. "Security Pragmatics for the Korean Peninsula," prepared for presentation at the workshop on East Asian Regional Security Futures. Nautilus Institute and Fudan University, March 3–4.

Scalapino, Robert A. 1997. "Foreign Policy for a New Administration." In Chibong Hahm, Robert A. Scalapino, and David Steinberg in *AsianUpdate*, http://www.asiasociety.org/publications/update_elections.html#Foreign (accessed January 2004).

Websites

Asia Society Publications: http://www.asiasociety.org/publications/index.html.

Korea Herald—English Newspaper: http://www.koreaherald.co.kr/index.asp.

Korea Ministry of Foreign Affairs and Trade: http://www.mofat.go.kr.

Korea Ministry of National Defense: http://www.mnd.go.kr.

Korea National Intelligence Service: http://www.nis.go.kr/eng/indes.shtml.

Korea National Statistical Office: http://www.nso.go.kr.

Korean Overseas Information Services: http://www.korea.net.

Korean Peninsula Energy Development Organization: http://www.kedo.org.

Spain

Kyle Wilson

Geography and History

Spain's defense policy emanates from the policy of the North Atlantic Treaty Organization (NATO). Although Spain is an important member of the alliance, Spain makes military decisions based on the interests of the alliance. Gradually, the European Union has become a second pole of Spain's focus, evidenced by Spain's participation in the Eurofighter and A-400 military transport programs. Overall, Spain's continued military improvement has made it an increasingly important partner on international security issues.

Geographically, Spain occupies about four-fifths of the Iberian Peninsula with the remainder belonging to Portugal. Spain also possesses the Balearic Islands in the Mediterranean Sea, the Canary Islands in the Atlantic Ocean, and the Spanish cities of Ceuta and Melilla in Morocco. Spain lies southwest of France on the Iberian Peninsula, covering 507,782 square kilometers, or slightly more than twice the size of Oregon. The Pyrenees Mountains cover the border area between France and Spain. Much of Spain is covered by rugged, hilly, plateaus, and it has hot summers and cold winters, which are more temperate than other parts of western Europe. With an estimated population of 40.2 million, Spain represents one of the largest states in Europe.

Economically, Spain has a GDP (PPP) of U.S.$850.7 billion, which amounts to a per capita of U.S.$21,200. Its economy consists of agriculture 4 percent, industry 31 percent, and services 65 percent (2000 est.). Spain's agricultural products include grain, vegetables, olives, wine grapes, sugar beets, citrus, beef, pork, poultry, dairy products, and fish. Spain's industries include textiles and apparel (including footwear), food and beverages, metals and metal manufactures, chemicals, shipbuilding, automobiles, machine tools, and tourism. Exports are valued at $122.2 billion f.o.b. (2002 est.) and comprise machinery, motor vehicles, foodstuffs, and other consumer goods. Spain's main trading partners for exports are France 19 percent, Germany 11.4 percent, United Kingdom 9.6 percent, Portugal 9.5 percent, Italy 9.3 percent, and the United States 4.6 percent (2002). Imports are valued at $156.6 billion f.o.b. (2002 est.) and comprise machinery and equipment, fuels, chemicals, semifinished goods, foodstuffs, and consumer goods (1997). Spain's main trading partners for imports are France 17 percent, Germany 16.5 percent, Italy 8.6 percent, United Kingdom 6.4 percent, and The Netherlands 4.8 percent (2002). With a $34.4 billion trade deficit and being a donor of $1.33 billion in Official Development Assistance (ODA) (1999), Spain does

Table 1 Spain: Key Statistics

Type of government	Parliamentary monarchy
Population (millions)	40.2 (July 2003 est.)
Religion	Roman Catholic 94%, other 6%
Main industries	Textiles and apparel (including footwear), food and beverages, metals and metal manufactures, chemicals, shipbuilding, automobiles, machine tools, tourism
Main security threats	Basque separatist movement, terrorism
Defense spending (% GDP)	1.20% (2003)
Size of military (thousands)	135
Number of civil wars since 1945	0
Number of interstate wars since 1945	1

Sources

Central Intelligence Agency Website. 2003. CIA *World Factbook.* http://www.cia.gov/cia/publications/factbook/ (accessed May 15, 2005).

Eriksson, Mikael, Peter Wallensteen, and Margareta Sollenberg. 2003. "Armed Conflict 1989–2002." *Journal of Peace Research* 40:593–607.

North Atlantic Treaty Organization. Press Release 146. http://www.nato.int/docu/pr/2003/p03-146e.htm (accessed May 27, 2005).

Soltsen, Eric, and Sandra W. Meditz, eds. 1988. *Spain: A Country Study.* Washington, DC: GPO for the Library of Congress.

not have a powerful economy in relation to European standards; however, it is an important economic force compared with the rest of the world (*World Factbook* 2003, *Europa* 2003, 3796).

Spanish hegemony in the sixteenth and seventeenth centuries has gradually declined over time to a point where Spain, although an important member of the European Union (EU), United Nations (UN), and NATO, does not have a military structure comparable to that of the United States or China. With this gradual decline, Spanish identity has had to adapt to its fall from major power status to an important component of a strong military organization. Despite losing its supremacy Spain as reinvented itself over the last decade to increase its stature within NATO, and by being a staunch supporter of the policies of the United States, especially in Iraq, it has gained favor with the sole remaining superpower. Spain, situated on the Iberian Peninsula, has existed as an independent entity since 1492 when King Ferdinand and Queen Isabella eradicated the last vestiges of Moorish control over the peninsula. Since that time Spain has been an integral part of the transformation of Europe and the West into the dominant region on the planet. At one time no state was more powerful than Spain, which once possessed an empire that spanned the globe, most notably in Latin America. However, the Spanish Empire's hegemony slowly receded, and Spain now controls little territory outside the Iberian Peninsula. Spain is a constitutional monarchy led by King Juan Carlos since November 22, 1975. He is the head of state, commander-in-chief of the armed forces, and head of the Supreme Council of Defense. Jose Luis Rodriguez Zapatero is the head of government and president. In addition to the head of state and government, Spain has a bicameral legislature (*Cortes Generales*), of which the head of government is a member. The two houses consist of a 259-seat Senate (*el Senado*) and a 350-seat Congress of Deputies (*Congreso de los Diputados*). The highest court in Spain is the Supreme Court. The major religion in Spain is Roman Catholicism; however, the constitution does not recognize an official state religion.

Regional Geopolitics

Spain is a member of the European Union and the United Nations and accepts the purposes and principles espoused in the Charter of the United Nations. European integration has minimized regional threats to Spain's sovereignty. However, owing to Spain's proximity to North Africa, domestic and international terrorism are regional geopolitical security concerns that Spain must address. Spain continues to consider the Spanish cities of Ceuta and Melilla as important to its territorial integrity, despite their location in Morocco. Spain also considers Gibraltar as an integral component of Spain; however, it has rejected the use of force to regain this territory. Relations between Spain and the United Kingdom are cordial, because it is in both countries' interests to continue their relations in NATO, the EU, and the United Nations. As a member of NATO, Spain has had to deal with new and challenging missions outside of its borders. With NATO's decision to participate in military operations in Afghanistan, Spain deals not only with regional geopolitical issues but also with international geopolitical issues. Furthermore, NATO operates within the Balkans. With the expansion of the European Union and NATO, regional geopolitical situations have expanded as well. With tens of thousands of troops in the Balkans, there is the opportunity for the conflict to spread throughout the region. However, with the amount of political and economic capital spent in the area, the likelihood of conflict reigniting remains low. The campaigns in Kosovo and the Balkans have proven that ethnic and religious conflicts are still possible in Europe. Finally, Spain has provided more than 1,000 combat troops to Iraq to assist the multinational operation (Taglibabue 2003, A13). This involvement could cause Spain to be more of a target for terrorists, domestic and international, which could cause increased pressures for Spain to withdraw from multilateral missions. Another issue that has caused concern among the Atlantic Alliance is the European Union's proposed rapid reaction force. The United States firmly believes that such a force would weaken the NATO Alliance by taking away important resources that could be put toward NATO missions. However, Europe believes it is necessary to have such a force to ensure that it can operate an independent foreign policy, especially in light of the disagreement over the use of force in Iraq (Johnson 2003). Spain believes that Europe should have such a rapid reaction force; however, they want to ensure that it does not weaken the NATO Alliance. In fact, they believe that such a force would strengthen the alliance, because the European NATO members would have to increase military spending to create a force that the United States supports. Spain is located in a complex geopolitical region, especially in light of the debate over the appropriate use of military force. To this point Spain has accepted U.S. policies in Iraq, a position that will be debated throughout this region for the foreseeable future.

Conflict Past and Present

Conflict History

As an important member of the European community since the fifteenth century, Spain has endured several conflicts that have formed Spain into the state it is today. Although humans have resided on the Iberian Peninsula for millennia, Spain's entry into the international system was realized after the removal of the Muslim presence on the peninsula. As Ferdinand and Isabella returned to the throne presiding over a united Spain, Spain began to take its place as the major power of the period. The War of Spanish Succession weakened Spain and allowed other European states to rise to higher levels of dominance in the regional and international systems. The war was caused by a dispute between Philip V and Charles of Austria over who would succeed to the throne. Philip V was installed to the throne; however, Charles of Austria's supporters (England and The Netherlands) began a land invasion into Spain. A coalition of French and Catalans defended Spain from the invasion and were able to repel the invaders, keeping them from capturing Madrid. However, Catalonia was lost in the bid to defend Madrid. The war also became a civil war as Britain made peace with France, splitting the coalition between France and Catalonia. Catalonia continued its resistance, despite Britain's withdrawal from the area. Eventually, the Catalonian resistance failed and their homeland was devastated. Philip V went on to take Barcelona in a long siege (1713–1714), sealing their fate. An uneasy peace was reached through the Treaty of Utrecht, where concessions were made that still affect international relations today. Spain agreed to a Bourbon succession in Spain, as long as there was never a united Crown in Spain and France.

Spanish possessions in The Netherlands and Italy were ceded to the Austrian Empire, whereas Gibraltar and Minorca came under the control of Great Britain. Furthermore, Spain was forced to make trade concessions with Great Britain in the New World. Fortunately, for Spain, it was able to come out of the war intact and unified; however, its position within Europe declined (Soltsen and Meditz, 1988, 21).

At the end of the nineteenth century the Spanish Empire was still widespread, including Cuba, Puerto Rico, the Philippines, and several African possessions. However, over time the military might of the Spanish Empire declined, while the power of the United States grew, especially in Latin America. Many Spaniards had emigrated to the Spanish possession in Latin America, forming a large middle class in Cuba, which supported close ties with Spain. In Cuba, uprisings against the colonial policies were sporadic at first; however, they grew especially after 1868 in size and scope. Publicly, Spain proclaimed that it would take any and all actions to protect its empire. The uprisings continued to grow in the 1890s to a point where open rebellion broke out into hostilities between the independence movement and Spain. As a democratic state, the United States supported the independence movement over the colonial oppression that Spain inflicted on its colonies. Owing to U.S. support, Spain had to send substantial military resources to control the situation. Under the leadership of General Valerio Weyler, the Spanish military began to crack down on the independence movement. Reports of oppression by the Spaniards in Cuba created a public outcry in the United States, which mobilized public opinion in favor of war with Spain. The mysterious explosion of the USS *Maine* in Havana harbor sealed Spain's fate, as the United States declared war in April 1898. Spanish military forces were ill prepared to defend themselves against the superior U.S. military. Spain's antiquated naval forces fared no better than the Spanish military, and within two weeks' time Spain surrendered. In September 1898 Spain ceded control over Cuba, Puerto Rico, and the Philippines to the United States. This would be the last loss by the Spanish Empire, because its possessions nearly evaporated after its loss to the United States. With the loss of its territory and the lack of European support, Spain's loss represents the end of the Spanish Empire (Soltsen and Meditz, 1988, 30–31).

During World War I Spain maintained its neutrality and thus emerged without the catastrophic effects that the other European powers had to endure. However, the Spanish civil war erupted in 1936, a battle between the Nationalists and the Republicans, and took a tremendous toll on the Spanish state. At the heart of this dispute lay great divisions among the government, the military, and the people as to whether Spain should be a monarchy, republic, or authoritarian government and as to what type of economic system should prevail; fascism, socialism, or some other type. Within this dispute, a small coalition of monarchists and fascists strived to reinstate King Alfonso XIII with the army's cooperation. Calvo Sotelo led the coalition; however, before being able to realize the coalition's goal Sotelo was murdered in July 1936 in what many thought was an attempt to end the movement toward reinstating the monarchy. The army reacted to this event with a *pronunciamento* that led to the full break with the Republicans. Open fighting began in the cities; however, in Madrid and Barcelona, the urban police and the worker's militias were able to put down the military revolts. Although there were attempts at peace, the army and the leftists rejected attempts at compromise. General Emelio Mola (Nationalists) was successful in maintaining control over the territory surrounding Burgos (north-central Spain). The Nationalists were also successful in the Carlist strongholds of Navarro and Aragon and in North Africa where the Spanish armies in Morocco, led by the young General Franco, supported the Nationalist cause. These troops were elite and easily seized control of Spain's North African empire. Early in the war Germany and Italy came to the aid of the Nationalists by transporting Franco and his troops into Andalusia. Franco went on to take over the major cities in the south before moving north to join forces with Mola near Burgos. Upon joining forces, a junta (governing group/council) was formed at Burgos and was immediately recognized by Germany and Italy. In October 1936 Franco was named head of state, leading the Nationalists in a borderline fascist government. Now that they formed a cohesive political and military unit the goal of the Nationalists was to separate Madrid from Catalonia, a firmly Republican region; Valencia; and Marcia. However, the Republicans were able to hold Madrid for more than three years. Another front of the war was in the Basque region where Asturias and Vizcaya wanted autonomy, fighting without support from Madrid against Franco. In October 1937, Franco was successful, and the Basque region came under Nationalist control. This front was the only area that changed hands until July 1938. At this time the Nationalists were able to break through to the Mediterranean south of Barcelona. Throughout the war the Nationalists generally held the agriculture areas, whereas the Republicans held the industrial areas. Republican military forces were not professionally trained, which weakened their ability to operate in an offensive manner. Although many in the army remained loyal, there were also many members of the air force and navy on the Republican side. These forces were not involved earlier in the war, because the workers' militias and organized armed political units conducted much of the early fighting.

Many countries intervened in the Spanish civil war. The former Union of Soviet Socialist Republics (USSR) provided advisers, logistical experts, field grade officers, and arms and munitions early in the war. Foreign volunteers comprised a large component of the Republican ranks, including 2,000 Americans, part of the so-called International Brigade. France gave artillery and aircraft, and Mexico also assisted. For the Republicans, this external assistance was extremely important because domestic production of military-related goods came to an abrupt end as the war continued. The strength of the Nationalist forces was the regular army, including the elite units from Morocco (Foreign Legion). When these elite units were coupled with the effective Carlist troops, these two groups were considered the backbone of the Nationalist military movement. Nationalist forces also relied on foreign intervention, as Italy and Germany actively supported their movement. Italy sent 50,000 troops (mostly conscripts), including air and naval units. Germany sent the Condor Legion, made infamous by the bombing of Guernica. Each country also supplied large amounts of armor and artillery.

As the interventions by foreign forces escalated, the European powers began to worry about the Spanish civil war spreading throughout Europe. Therefore, a group of countries, including France, Germany, the United Kingdom, and Italy, called for a nonintervention commission. This commission formed at the Lyon Conference in 1936, where France and the United Kingdom proclaimed that they did not want the war to spread and therefore a mechanism should be created where a public agreement could be reached for all foreign interventions to cease. Although France and the United Kingdom abided by the agreement, Germany and Italy continued their support for the Nationalists, and the USSR never signed the agreement, so it was free to continue its support for the Republicans. Barcelona fell in January 1939; Valencia, the temporary capital, fell in March 1939; and finally on the last day of March 1939 Madrid surrendered, ending the civil war. It is estimated that 600,000 died and several hundred thousand more were displaced (Soltsen and Meditz 1988, 31–40). Spain did not participate directly in World War II; however, it began the war as a sympathizer to the Axis powers, but switched sides to ensure that it was on the prevailing side of the war in an attempt to gain favor for the postwar era.

Current and Potential Military Confrontation

Spain has an enduring rivalry with the United Kingdom over the enclave of Gibraltar. This rivalry extends back to the early eighteenth century when the combined naval forces of England and Holland occupied the enclave in the War of Spanish Succession. At the conclusion of this war in the Treaty of Utrecht (Article 10), England was granted sovereignty over the enclave. However, according to Spain, the treaty only governed the Rock of Gibraltar, not the Isthmus of Gibraltar, which the United Kingdom also occupies (Soltsen and Meditz 1988, 269–272). Spain believes that it is in their best interest to negotiate the transfer of sovereignty over Gibraltar from the United Kingdom to Spain peacefully. Spain believes that the negotiation should be on a global basis rather than a bilateral basis to ensure that the purposes and principles of the United Nations are upheld. Spain recognizes that only through cooperation and negotiation can the situation in Gibraltar finally be resolved (Spanish Mission to the United Nations 2004).

Spain also has an enduring rivalry with Morocco over the Spanish cities of Ceuta and Melilla. Although their relationship remains cordial, it is also very intense. The intensity stems from the contentious issues of immigration policy, use of fishing grounds, and the question of sovereignty over Ceuta and Melilla. Recently, Moroccans occupied a rocky island off the coast of Ceuta, Isla de Pereguil (Daly 2002a, A2). This led to a tense standoff between the Moroccans and Spanish authorities. Morocco insisted that it had maintained sovereignty over the island since independence. Negotiations did not succeed at first; therefore, Spain sent navy patrol boats to the island to remove the Moroccans from the island. The removal succeeded without incident. Spain reoccupied the island; however, in subsequent negotiations mediated by the United States, it was agreed that Morocco and Spain would revert to the status quo. Spain would maintain sovereignty, but would not maintain any permanent presence on the island (Daly 2002b, A4). Part of the complexity involved in the relationship between Spain and Morocco over the islands is the status of Gibraltar. Morocco sees Spain's irredentist claim as a means to offset the United Kingdom's possession of both the Rock and Isthmus of Gibraltar. Therefore, although the issue of Gibraltar remains a bilateral one with multilateral attention, Morocco would like to solve both problems at the same time, bringing the situation to a mutually beneficial conclusion.

Alliance Structure

Spain is a member of the North Atlantic Treaty Organization (NATO). Spain joined the alliance in 1982 despite initial apprehension about joining NATO; however, world events gradually guided Spain into a closer relationship, not only with Europe, but also the non-European members of NATO (United States and Canada). Owing to Spain's strategic location in the Iberian Peninsula, NATO proponents in Spain stressed that Spain would be welcomed into NATO and that nonmembership could lead to attacks on Spain from NATO's enemies. The proponents also emphasized that Spain's military could benefit from the additional spending that would be required to meet NATO's standards while creating the foundation for a more professional military with fewer aspirations for power within or as the government. Finally, the proponents argued that the Spanish military leaders would focus less on reactionary policies and more on the common defense of its NATO allies. The main opponents to Spanish membership in NATO, the socialists and communists, countered these arguments. They believed that Spanish membership would lead to a heightening of tensions between East and West, creating a fait accompli where Spain would trigger a conflict. Furthermore, they believed that NATO membership would offer little to Spain, since some of Spain's most pressing foreign policy issues were the enclaves of Ceuta and Melilla and the United Kingdom's colony of Gibraltar. Ceuta and Melilla were outside the NATO area at that time, and many believed that NATO would support the British position on Gibraltar. Finally, many people in Spain were resentful of the United States, the main supporter of France. Spain's leadership believed that NATO membership would expedite integration into the European Community, and with the government's support the *Cortes* approved membership in December 1981. Spain officially became the sixteenth member of NATO, the first since West Germany, in May 1982 (Soltsen and Meditz 1988, 263–265).

Despite the government's support, promises were made to hold a referendum on Spain's membership in NATO. When a new socialist government came to power in October 1982, the referendum gained further support; however, this government felt it in their best interest to delay the referendum. Over time the government began to realize the benefits of NATO membership, and despite strong Spanish sentiment for neutrality, the government began to gradually support NATO membership to fortify its ties with the European Union. The referendum finally occurred on March 2, 1986, with the government supporting it on economic grounds. Although polls before the referendum showed overwhelming support for neutrality, NATO membership was approved by a margin of 52.6 percent to 39.8 percent with a 60 percent voter turnout. With this victory Spain remained the sixteenth member of NATO (Soltsen and Meditz 1988, 263–265).

It was agreed that Spanish integration would progress in stages. Spain would first have membership in the political committees, then integration in the alliance military activities. Spain also had several con-

ditions in being a member of NATO. First, Spain would not be incorporated in the integrated military structure. Second, there would be a ban on the installation, the storage, and the introduction of nuclear weapons on Spanish territory. This condition was directly related to the incident where a U.S. B-52 bomber collided with a KC-135 refueling plane and dropped three thermonuclear weapons on Spanish territory and one in Spanish territorial waters. Third, there would be a progressive reduction in U.S. presence in Spain. In addition to these conditions, Spain would remain a full member of the North Atlantic Council and its subsidiary organs. It would have an observer status on the Nuclear Planning Group and be a full member on the Military Committee. Spain would be able to appoint military representatives for liaison with the NATO military commands and participate in the logistical coordination, development of common equipment and material, and civil protection measures. Finally, Spain would participate in the integrated communications system and nominate candidates for the NATO secretariat and the International Military Staff. After joining under these strict conditions Spain was flexible on some conditions when it offered to coordinate national military missions with those of NATO, especially in the sea between the Balearic Islands and the Canaries. Furthermore, Spanish forces were to be commanded only by Spanish officers, they were not to be dispatched outside of Spain for long periods, and Spain's air defense system was to be integrated with that of France and Italy (Soltsen and Meditz 1988, 263–265).

Overall, current Spanish military doctrine in regard to NATO and other military operations for international organization requires an armed force that can project power throughout Spain and the world. With this international outlook Spain has mobilized its military budget and industrial complex toward the production/training of units that can perform well outside of Spain. Programs like the F-100 Frigate, the A400 Transport plane, the Eurofighter, and the Leopard Tank are focused on meeting this goal. Spain's worldview definitely puts priority in its European ties, not only for economic purposes but also for security issues. Although Spain does clearly prefer European ties, it looks at NATO as a means of providing the security cooperation that Europe needs to move on to a European first security policy.

Size and Structure of the Military

Size and Structure

As of August 2002, the Spanish military had a total strength of 177,950 people. (See Table 2 for a graphical representation.) Although this number does not match the NATO figures, definitional differences explain the variance. Of this number the army comprised 118,800, the navy comprised 26,950 (5,600 marines), and the air force comprised 22,750. The service did not designate 9,450. The Civil Guard comprised 72,600 additional people. Spanish law ended conscription in 2000 as part of the professionalization process; however, it was later determined that military service of nine months was to remain compulsory until December 2002, and the process was scheduled to be completed in 2003 (*Europa* 2003, 3807).

The Spanish military is organized under the civilian leadership of the president of the government. He makes all decisions about war and peace with the approval of the legislature and the king.

Under the president is the minister of defense, also a civilian. The minister of defense oversees the Joint Chiefs of Staff, headed by a chairman. Each branch of the military, army, navy, and air force has a chief of staff who oversees the day-to-day operations of their respective branches. The minister of defense exercises delegated powers from the president of the government with regard to arranging, coordinating, and directing the military administration. His title corresponds to the government he supervises, the state of the administration, and operational efficiency of the armed forces, and he exercises the regulatory power and discipline that the laws assign to him. Moreover, his other competencies are in the material of military politics, in the administration of resources, economic and financial programs, and personal politics of the armed forces. The higher direction of the questions of national defense count on the assistance of the National Defense Council. Its composition is expressive of the fullness and complexity of the matter. Members include the president, vice presidents, minister of defense, defense chief of staff, the chiefs of staff of the army, navy, and air force, and other experts invited by the president. The defense chief of staff has the military authority over that which the Ministry of Defense orders and coordinates and directs the actions of the armed forces in the fulfillment of the missions derived from the strategic plans and of those others that might arise in situations of crisis or that the government charges to the armed forces. The defense chief of staff is the commander for the joint command of the armed forces, who besides the exercise of the leading strategy of the operations, assumes the chain of command of the land forces, naval forces, and air forces that might be

Table 2   Armed Forces Average Annual Strength

Year	Spain	United States	France	Germany	United Kingdom
1980	356	2,050	572	490	330
1985	314	2,244	560	495	334
1990	263	2,181	548	545	308
1995	210	1,620	502	352	233
1999	155	1,486	420	331	218
2000	144	1,483	394	319	218
2001	151	1,487	366	306	215
2002	135	1,506	355	295	214
2003 (est.)	135	1,496	350	285	214

Source

North Atlantic Treaty Organization. 2003. Press Release 146. http://www.nato.int/docu/pr/
2003/p03-146e.htm (accessed May 27, 2005).

assigned for carrying out the corresponding operations. The defense chief of staff acts under the supervision of the Ministry of Defense while creating an adequate operational organization for the fulfillment of all missions. When developing exercises, the defense chief of staff will either command the mission or designate a commander to act on his behalf (Ministry of Defense—Spain 2004).

The commanders of the operational commands of the army, navy, and air force are, respectively, the chiefs of staff of the army, navy, and air force. As such they depend directly on the commander of the Joint Command of the Armed Forces in all that is concerned with planning, leading, and executing of the operations and the development of the exercises that they are responsible for. Within their principal functions is to advise the commander of the Joint Command of the Armed Forces. In all their commitments, and particularly in the relations with their specific areas, they are to elaborate the operation plans that might be assigned to them and to conduct the operations that might be entrusted to them (Ministry of Defense—Spain 2004).

As of December 31, 2003, Spain contributes a total of twenty-three people to UN peacekeeping missions. This includes thirteen civilian police, six military observers, and four troops (United Nations 2004). Spain has been involved in several peacekeeping missions, not only through the United Nations, but also through the European Union, NATO, the Organization for Security and Cooperation in Europe (OSCE), and independent humanitarian missions. Spain has participated in UN missions throughout Africa, Latin America, Europe, and Asia. These include missions in Ethiopia/Eritrea, Rwanda, Angola, the Democratic Republic of the Congo, Namibia, Mozambique, Western Sahara, Guatemala, Central America, El Salvador, Haiti, the Former Yugoslavia, Bosnia, Albania, Kosovo, Iraq, and Afghanistan. Spain also participates in peacekeeping missions under the auspices of the OSCE, which usually take the form of missions to enforce democratic elections or peace initiatives where conflict is not active. Missions that Spain has participated in under the auspices of the OSCE include those in

Moldova, Kosovo, Croatia, Chechnya, Georgia, and Azerbaijan. Spain has also participated in peace missions under the auspices of the European Union. These missions have been centered on the former Yugoslavia. Spain also participates independently in many humanitarian missions. These include relief missions for the earthquake in Turkey, the floods in Mozambique, the aftermath of Hurricane Mitch in Central America, and in Afghanistan. Overall, Spain is an active participant in peacekeeping and humanitarian missions under the auspices of international organizations (Ministry of Defense—Spain 2004).

In operations with its allies, including operations with NATO, OSCE, and the European Union, Spain has set out its goals for operational capabilities. Spain

will work to develop capabilities "on a joint level, by establishing and using a headquarters along with the necessary structures and systems, the Spanish Armed Forces should be able to: (1) plan, conduct and sustain national defense operations, (2) plan and coordinate our specific contribution to international or multinational organizations for collective defense and crisis response missions, by conducting the necessary activities in order to project, control, sustain and recover the forces involved, and (3) plan, coordinate and provide host nation support for Allied forces operating in or passing through our territory" (Bland 2003, 191–193). Since it joined NATO, Spain's capabilities have generally increased as defense spending has been focused on the skills necessary to operate within these

---

Sidebar 1   Spain's Bloody Election (2004)

From staunch supporter of the United States to advocate of multilateralism explains the rapid transition Spain encountered as the party of Anzar fell to the party of Zapatero. The transition from conservatism to socialism did not receive the overwhelming attention from the global media because it meant the end to Anzar's conservative policies, but instead because it showed that the Spanish people not only opposed the war in Iraq but also opposed being a target of international terrorism. The terrorist bombings that killed nearly 200 Spaniards on their morning commute on the eve of national elections shocked the people of Spain into awareness that there were costs to Spain's activist foreign policy.

Although Spaniards first looked to the domestic terrorism (Basque) it was soon realized that international terrorism (al-Qaeda) was the source. In the future, this event may be remembered as a turning point in the war in Iraq and, by extension, the war on terrorism due to its monumental implications in the affairs of a democratic, sovereign state. Zapatero's election promise to remove Spain's 1,300 troops from Iraq was immediately implemented causing an immediate concern to the U.S. coalition. Spain's decision was soon matched by another country, the Dominican Republic, which removed its troops as well. Spain's history books may always remember this election; however, it has yet to be decided if history will look at these events as a stand against unilateralism or a defeat to international terrorism.

Source
CNN.com. 2004. *Massacre in Madrid*. July 17. http://www.cnn.com/SPECIALS/2004/madrid.bombing/ (accessed May 14, 2005).

organizations. Also, Spain has benefited from joint agreements with its allies for coproduction within Spain of several weapons systems.

Spain has set out specific goals for each of its military branches. For the army Spain has set the priority of defending the homeland from invasion; however, because there are few threats to the sovereignty and territorial integrity of Spain, it has also moved beyond territorial defense and on to force projection to conflict zones around the world. Specifically, "Land forces must protect the national territory and maintain a forward presence in extrapeninsular Spanish territories. In addition, though not simultaneously, they must have the capability to: (1) participate in the full spectrum of crisis response missions for an indefinite period of time, in two theatres distant from each other and from national territory, rapidly deploying one Brigade in each of them, with the necessary combat and logistics support; or two Brigades and the required combat and logistics support in one single theatre with a Division Headquarters capable of commanding a multinational force, and (2) participate in the full spectrum of collective defense and crisis response missions for a continuous period not longer than six months, rapidly deploying an Army Corps level Headquarters capable of activating a multinational Land Command Component, and a Division with the required combat and logistics support in a theatre far removed from national territory" (Bland 2003, 191–193). These priorities combined with Spain's military modernization/professionalization program attempt to combat the weaknesses that Spain's army has suffered from throughout its post–World War II history.

Geographically the army is divided into four peninsular military regions, located in the northwest, in the Pirenaica (northeast) region, the south, and the central, and four extrapeninsular military zones, located in the Balearic Islands, the Canary Islands, Ceuta, and Melilla (Ministry of Defense—Spain 2004). The army is divided into a permanent force comprising a Maneuvers Force, area defense forces, and specific forces for joint action and mobilized reserves comprising mobilized defense forces. The Maneuvers Force has several components, including one mechanized division with three brigades (one armored and two mechanized), a rapid reaction force of three brigades (one light infantry paratroop brigade, one light infantry brigade, and one air transportable light infantry brigade), one mountain brigade, one cavalry brigade, one signals brigade, and others that include a field artillery command, an engineering command, a support logistics command, the air mobile forces of the army, and small regiments for antiair artillery, electronic warfare, intelligence, and nuclear, chemical, and biological weapons. The area defense forces defend specific areas that include the Canaries, the Balearic Islands, Ceuta, and Melilla. All report to the army chief of staff. Specific Forces for Joint Action conduct tasks such as the defense and control of the coasts, the air defense of the national territory, and running the Joint Systems for Telecommunications and Electronic Warfare. The Specific Forces for Joint Action are composed of the joint Artillery Command of the Estrecho (literally means narrow) Coast, the Anti-Aircraft Artillery Command, and the Communications Command. All report to the army chief of staff. The Mobile Defense Forces are used when overwhelming force is required—a level of force superior to that of the standing army. It includes a light infantry brigade

Sidebar 2   Spain's Nuclear Weapons

On January 17, 1966, Spain acquired four nuclear weapons from the United States; unfortunately these weapons were an unintended consequence of the Spanish-American alliance. The incident occurred when an American B-52 collided with a KC-135 tanker during a refueling operation. Two nuclear weapons were damaged, scattering radioactive materials over the fields of Palomares, Spain; and while one landed intact, the other landed twelve miles off the coast. The United States spent millions of dollars on recovery and cleanup efforts. These efforts included a fleet of ships, divers, cleanup and removal of radioactive particles, and a monetary settlement with the people of Palomares, Spain. This event marked the beginning of a gradual decline in the number of U.S. personnel in Spain. Although Spain eventually would become a member of the North Atlantic Treaty Organization, this event permanently impacted the Spaniard people's opinion on weapons of mass destruction.

Sources
Maydew, Randall C. 1997. *America's Lost H-Bomb! Palomares, Spain, 1966.* Manhattan, KS: Sunflower University Press.
Soltsen, Eric, and Sandra W. Meditz, eds. 1988. *Spain: A Country Study.* Washington, DC: GPO for the Library of Congress.

As one of the largest navies in Europe, the Spanish Armada, as it is called in Spain, is tasked with defending some of the most strategic sea-lanes in the world. As such, the "Naval forces should ensure the defense and control of waters under national sovereignty, and participate in the full spectrum of collective defense and crisis response missions in scenarios far removed from the national territory by making the following efforts simultaneously: (1) leading a Naval Component capable of integrating multinational naval forces, providing an aero-naval Projection Group based on an aircraft carrier, with the required escorts and support ships, and an amphibious component with the capacity to project a Marines Brigade; that should be sufficient to constitute an expeditionary force operational for two months in any of the maritime areas of interest, within a radius of 3600 miles, participate in operations at two theatres separate and distant from each other, providing two escorts to each of them continuously, (2) permanently maintain two mine counter measures vessels as part of a multinational mine-clearing force, with the capability to lead it, and (3) simultaneously maintain two submarines operating in two theatres, one distant and the other close" (Bland 2003, 191–193). These priorities compare similarly with other NATO naval forces, and to accomplish these missions Spain has made substantial investments into the F-100 Frigate to accompany its naval task forces in accomplishing their missions. An important example of Spain's navy operating outside territorial waters is its leadership of a naval group off the Horn of Africa used to interdict terrorists and other criminals (Shanker 2002, A1). This important task in the global "War on Terrorism" demonstrates the importance of the

and smaller units that deal with combat support. Overall, the army also has support units for land force support, a Command for Training and Doctrine, a Personnel Command, a Logistics Support Command, and an Inspector General for Mobilization (Ministry of Defense—Spain 2004).

Spanish navy and its ability to accomplish difficult missions outside its usual area of operations.

The Spanish navy divides its operations into four maritime zones. These zones include Cantabrico in the north, Estrecho in the south, Mediterraneo in the east, and Canarias in the Atlantic Ocean surrounding the Canary Islands. Spain has four main naval bases: in Ferrol in the Cantabrico maritime zone, Cadiz (consists of Rota and San Fernando) in the Estrecho maritime zone, Cartagena in the Mediterranean maritime zone, and Las Palmas in the Canary maritime zone. Spain also has a fifth zone, the Central Jurisdiction, which is a landlocked region surrounding Madrid that deals with defense-related issues and logistic support and houses the central organs of the navy. The main component of the navy is its fleet, which consists of five components: the Projection Group of the Fleet, the Third Navy, the Submarine Fleet, the Escort Fleet, and the Naval Air Squadron. The Projection Group is based in Rota (Cadiz) and is composed of an aircraft carrier, landing ships, and assault ships. Its purpose is to project naval power inland. The Third Navy is the marine infantry of the fleet, and it includes combat troops and support personnel, who allow it to conduct amphibious assaults and land combat. Based in Cartagena, the Submarine Fleet protects the fleet under the water and coordinates tactics and logistics. Spain possesses eight submarines, four Delfin class and four Galerna class. There are three escort fleets, one each at Rota, Ferral, and Cartagena. Spain has forty-one Santa Maria class frigates at Rota, thirty-one Baleares class frigates at Ferral, and twenty-one Descubierta class corvettes (corbetas) at Cartagena. Finally, the Naval Air Fleet has seven squadrons of planes and helicopters that support naval operations throughout Spanish waters and the world (Ministry of Defense—Spain 2004).

Like the other branches the air force is designed to be able to project power throughout the NATO theater of operations as well as outside the NATO area. It is with this doctrine that Spanish "Air forces should guarantee an integrated national air defense and participate in the full spectrum of collective defense and crisis response missions for an indefinite period of time in scenarios far removed from the national territory. To meet these conditions and lead efforts if necessary, the following is required: (1) to develop operations in two theatres, deploying a multirole combat aircraft squadron to each, with the required air transport means, combat and logistical support; while contributing with support means in a third theatre, (2) to collaborate in strategic air transport, sustainment and logistical support of forces deployed far or near, carrying out air-transport combat actions if necessary. The deployment of forces must be sufficient to permit the transport of a fighter Squadron and a light Tactical Group with its respective support to 3700 km distance within six days, and (3) to contribute to NATO's European Integrated Air Defense System (NATINADS), with air defense means and an Integrated Air Command and Control System fully compatible with the ACCS-NATO; guaranteeing surveillance, control and defense of our air space and reinforcing the Integrated Airborne Warning and Control System through participation in the NAEW Force" (Bland 2003, 191–193). To assist in meeting these priorities Spain is working with its European allies to design and manufacture the Eurofighter to ensure that Europe does not need to rely on the United States for air superiority fighters. To ensure that Europe has adequate airlift capabilities so it does not have to rely on the United States, Spain is also involved in the A-400 project that will give Europe the ability to project force independently of the United States.

The Spanish air force consists of a general headquarters, the air force itself, and force support. In general, the general headquarters supports the operations of the chief of staff of the air force. The air force itself is divided into air commands that include commands in the Central, Estrecho, Levante, and Canaries regions, including a new combat command. Spain has five main air bases, located in Zaragoza, Torrejon, Albacete, Moron, and Gando. The air force has some 500 planes that are divided into various squadrons, functional criteria, and type of air operations. Functionally, the air force is divided into the Principle Defense Forces, Reaction Forces, and Auxiliary Forces. Operationally, the air force is divided into Air Combat Units, Combat Air Support Units, and Auxiliary Air Units. In regard to the combat units Spain has nine squadrons (six in the Principle Defense Force and three in the Reaction Force). These squadrons mainly consist of fighter jets like the F-18 and the Mirage F-1 and maritime patrol craft like the P-3 Orion. Within the combat units are also air surveillance squadrons with radar and communications to protect the combat units. The Combat Support Units have fifteen squadrons (twelve in the Principle Defense Force and three in the Reaction Force). Planes within the Air Support Combat Units include the following: F-18 Hornet, RF-4 Phantom, Boeing 707, C-212 Aviocar, C-235, C-130 Hércules, Falcon 20, Cessna Citation V, and the Fokker 27 Maritime. These units also include helicopters like the AS-330 Puma and the AS-332 Superpuma. Within these units are smaller units like an airborne rapid reaction force, deployment air support, and mobile air controllers. Also, the air force has an air rescue service for rescuing downed airmen. Finally, the air force has a variety of auxiliary units (sixteen squadrons with a variety of aircraft) that support the other air force units (Ministry of Defense—Spain 2004).

Budget

In the 2003 budget the Spanish armed forces laid out three main objectives. These include the following: (1) culminate the implementation and consolidation of the professional armed forces model, (2) develop and consolidate the international dimension of defense, and (3) continue the process of investment in the armed forces. The 2003 budget for the Spanish military increased by 2.48 percent to 6.479 billion euros, of which 3.742 billion euros was for personnel (57.8 percent) and 2.654 billion euros was for equipment (42.2 percent). Spending on personnel decreased by 0.2 percent, whereas spending on equipment increased by that amount as a percentage of the total spending. (See Table 3 for a graphical representation.) Since 1995 overall military spending has increased from 5.207 billion euros to its current level of 6.479 billion euros, a 24.4 percent increase over nine years. In the same period, spending on personnel increased from 2.784 billion euros to 3.742 billion euros, from 53.5 percent of the budget to 57.8 percent of the budget.

In the general categories of modernization of the armed forces—maintenance of armament and materials, research and development, and other investment—the

Table 3   Defense Expenditures as Percent of Gross Domestic Product

	Spain	United States	France	Germany	United Kingdom
1980–1984 avg.	2.3	5.6	4	3.3	5.2
1985–1989 avg.	2.1	6	3.8	3	4.5
1990–1994 avg.	1.6	4.7	3.4	2.1	3.7
1995–1999 avg.	1.4	3.3	2.9	1.6	2.7
1999	1.3	3	2.7	1.5	2.5
2000	1.2	3.1	2.6	1.5	2.5
2001	1.2	3.1	2.5	1.5	2.5
2002	1.2	3.4	2.5	1.5	2.4
2003 (est.)	1.2	3.5	2.6	1.4	2.4

Source

North Atlantic Treaty Organization. 2003. Press Release 146. http://www.nato.int/docu/
pr/2003/p03-146e.htm (accessed May 27, 2005).

Spanish military increased its spending in 2003 marginally over 2002. For instance, Spain has seen a 2.9 percent increase in modernization, a 0.8 percent decrease in maintenance, no change in research and development, and a 6.2 percent increase in other investments. These categories accounted for 1.629 billion euros in 2003, whereas in 2002 they accounted for 1.607 billion euros, a 0.01 percent increase. Spain's most popular weapons systems, the F-100 frigate, the A-400 military transport plane, the Eurofighter, and the Leopard tank, accounted for 684 million Euros out of more than 1 billion Euros in spending on specific weapons systems. Spain's use of its physical assets in coordination with its process of professionalization of its human resources reflects Spain's intention to invest in its armed forces in preparation for the challenges of the twenty-first century (Ministry of Defense—Spain 2004).

Civil-Military Relations/The Role of the Military in Domestic Politics

When General Francisco Franco y Bahamonde came to power after winning the civil war of 1936–1939, Spain was characterized by repressive authoritarian rule. Although this authoritarianism led to stability, it did not promote human rights. Gradually, over General Franco's rule, he brought back the democratic institutions that Spain possessed before the civil war, including the monarchy, representative legislature, and independent courts. From this history of military involvement in politics Spain has moved to dismantle the role of the military in politics. Strong protections exist within the constitution for the role of the military, for which politics is not included. In the last decade, the transition from a conscript army to a professional army shows that Spain has become more comfortable that the military will refrain from politics.

Spain's constitution clearly defines the role of the military in a manner consistent with the democratic principles of Spanish society. The armed forces are charged with the defense of the homeland against all aggressors, foreign or domestic. In keeping with this theme the armed forces are to guarantee the unity, sovereignty, independence, territorial integrity, and the constitutional order of Spanish society. Furthermore, the armed forces are to protect the lives of the population and the interests of the country in domestic and foreign relations. To this effect, the armed forces are to act in harmony with the civilian institutions of the state. The constitution goes on to clearly state that the national defense is the responsibility of the state, and Spaniards have the right and duty to come to the national defense of the state. In general, Spain shall promote peaceful coexistence with its fellow states while protecting its people (Ministry of Defense—Spain 2004).

Spain's history of military interventions in politics creates an air of distrust; however, it has been several years since the military has exceeded its position in relation to the civilian leadership. As a modern, democratic state in Europe, Spain continues to keep a clear delineation between civilian and military leadership, without which Spain could not move forward as a member of the European Union. If current reforms continue, old animosities will fade away and the Spanish military will rise in stature within Spanish society.

Terrorism

Spain continues to address domestic terrorism from the Basque region. Euskadi ta Askatasuna (ETA), also know as Basque Fatherland and Liberty, continues to profess its intention to remove the yoke of Spanish imperialism. On a yearly basis, ETA uses car bombs, threats on politicians, and other forms of terrorist acts to realize their goal of independence. The Basque question remains an important issue in Spain as terrorist attacks continue. Founded in 1959, ETA continues to strive for its goal of independence. Although Spain offers the Basque region a large degree of autonomy, ETA continues to fight to maintain its cultural, historical, and linguistic independence from Spain. Owing to the rising disgust of ETA's tactics, the people of the Basque region have begun to look for an organization that can represent the peaceful aspirations of the Basque people (*Europa* 2003, 3802–3805).

Spain has offered strong support for the global "War on Terrorism." Since September 11, 2001, Spain has committed thousands of troops to the campaigns in Afghanistan and Iraq. This includes 1,200 soldiers for Afghanistan, plus air assets and a medical unit. Spain also contributes naval assets in the Horn of Africa regions to interdict possible terrorist vessels and was instrumental in halting a freighter carrying Scud missiles to Yemen. In the financial world, Spain has worked with its global partners in disrupting the finances of terrorist organizations. Furthermore, Spain works with its global partners in bringing terrorists to justice through their legal system. Spain is party to all twelve international conventions and protocols relating to terrorism (U.S. Embassy: Spain 2004).

After the terrorist attacks of September 11, 2001, the United Nations Security Council passed resolution 1373, which required member states under Chapter VII of the Charter of the United Nations to take necessary steps to eradicate terrorism. In operative clause 6, the Security Council created a Counter-Terrorism Committee to monitor the implementation of resolution 1373. Also, within the same clause the Security Council required that member states report to the committee on steps that they have made to implement the resolution. Since this resolution passed, member states have submitted at least three updates that provide a detailed overview of the actions member states have made in the fight against international terrorism (UN Security Council 2001a).

Spain submitted its first report in December 2001 with subsequent reports in July 2002 and June 2003. Having dealt with domestic terrorism for years, Spain had many of the important legal instruments for dealing with terrorism already in place. Spanish laws are in place to deal with all aspects of terrorism, including all areas that are covered by the twelve conventions on international terrorism, which Spain has acceded. Spain looks at the issue of international terrorism with the same determination that it addresses domestic terrorism. As such, Spain has taken steps to ensure that weapons or explosive materials do not end up in the hands of terrorists through strong licensing regulations on all such materials. In the field of cooperation Spain participates in the Schengen, Europol, and Interpol Agreements to ensure rapid exchange of information. Spain has also signed numerous bilateral agreements for cooperation in dealing with crime that includes terrorism. Some of the steps include the following: collaboration with other countries; transfer of information on terrorist groups and their activities; exchange of information through liaison officers in and from other countries; exchange of techniques and experiences with other services involved in combating terrorism, including training programs and participation of experts; exchange of information at bilateral or multilateral meetings on techniques and methods for the forgery of identity papers, passports, visas, residence papers, and other documents; and the exchange of information and analyses with a view to assessing terrorist threats. On the issue of safe haven for terrorists, Spanish law precludes granting asylum to terrorists, and because the concept of terrorism in Spanish law is very broad, its legislation can be considered a strong deterrent to terrorists seeking refuge in Spain. Spanish law also forbids the launching of terrorist attacks from Spanish territory. To prevent such actions Spain has conducted a number of major operations, including joint operations with Italy and other European Union members. These missions have succeeded in breaking up the Varesse group, the Meliani group (with ties to al-Qaeda), a cell of Grupo Salafista para el Predicacion y el Combate, as well as major raids against individual al-Qaeda members. Spain's specific legal penalties for being convicted of terrorist acts are steeper than those for regular crimes. For instance, murder would result in a sentence of fifteen to twenty years, whereas murder in connection with terrorist activities would result in a sentence of twenty to thirty years. Persons suspected of committing terrorist crimes might also receive special treatment when being detained, including lengthening the time a suspect can be held without being charged, the ability to hold terrorist suspects incommunicado with a court order, the ability to pursue terrorist suspects into domiciles without search warrants, and the ability to eavesdrop when ordered by the minister of the Interior. Additional measures are also in place to assist international terrorist investigations. These include Spain's membership in the European Convention on the Suppression of Terrorism and bilateral agreements, including those with Italy, Bulgaria, Hungary, Slovakia, Russia, Poland, China, and Ukraine. Spain cooperates in terrorist extraditions within the framework of the Council of Europe Convention on Extradition and two European conventions of 1995 and 1996 as well as several bilateral treaties on extradition. Overall, Spain addresses the issues described above by participating in an ongoing exchange of information among international entities, including states, organizations, and police agencies. The movement of terrorists has also been addressed by strengthening security in airplanes and airports and at Spain's borders and ports, continuing investigations to discover illegal border crossings, performing selective searches of people who are believed to be or are suspected of being terrorists, and strengthening cooperation with its fellow European Union members. Since September 11, 2001, Spain has participated in the strengthening of the Europol structures for combating terrorism; meetings of the chiefs of antiterrorism units within the European Union; preparation, in the framework of the European Union, of a list of terrorist organizations; and the promotion of the creation of joint investigation teams in the European Union. Overall, Spain has strong institutions in place for the fight against terrorism that were forged in its battle with ETA. As a strong member of the international community Spain has integrated itself into the institutions that are best able to fight terrorism and will continue to be a strong ally in the war on terrorism (UN Security Council, 2001b, 2002, 2003).

Relationship with the United States

Spain and the United States have had a long and complicated relationship. As mentioned earlier, the United States and Spain fought a war in the late nineteenth century that eliminated the majority of Spain's empire, and in the 1930s the United States did not intervene in Spain's civil war. Even during the war the U.S. government considered Franco a fascist dictator. After World War II the groundwork for the current relationship was formed, because Dwight Eisenhower embraced Franco and brought military and economic assistance to Spain. Upon the presentation of this aid, the United States received basing rights within Spain, and the isolation Spain had endured after World War II ended. Animosity still existed between the Spanish people and the United States because of their belief that the United States had enabled the dictatorial rule of Franco. After Franco's death in 1975 the United States supported Spain's liberalization and the crowning of Juan Carlos as king. At this point the bilateral agreement between the United States and Spain was expanded to a full Treaty of Friendship and Cooperation in 1976. The United States focused its attention on urging Spain to integrate more fully into the international system, especially their joining NATO. Spain was not immediately interested in joining NATO, but eventually did so with reservations (Soltsen and Meditz 1988, 265–267).

During the lead-up to the war in Iraq, Spain possessed a seat on the UN Security Council, where the United States made its case for the international community to take up arms against the dictator in Iraq. Throughout this process the United States could count on Spanish support, with Spain sponsoring Security Council resolutions supporting the use of force. Spain also supports the military campaign with its own soldiers, in a supporting role under the leadership of fellow NATO member Poland. U.S. military presence in Spain, as of mid-2002, totaled 2,190, of which 1,760 were naval forces and 260 were air forces (*Europa* 2003, 3807).

Spain and the United States have shared common interests, especially on security matters, since the beginning of the Cold War. Although Spain was not a member of NATO, Spanish-American relations thrived on bilateral levels. Several accords were signed to promote a U.S. military presence in Spain as well as to extend U.S. financial support for the modernization of the Spanish military. This cooperation, continued under the 1989 Agreement on Defense Cooperation, goes beyond the agreements set forth in the North Atlantic Charter. On January 11, 2001, Spain and the United States signed a joint declaration focused on improving cooperation on six important issues: political consultation, defense, economics and finance, science and technology, culture, and combating new threats and security. Although military cooperation remains an important mutual concern, Spain and the United States also cooperate on other matters, including scientific missions. The U.S. National Aeronautics and Space Administration (NASA) and the Spanish National Institute for Aerospace Technology (INTA) work together on the Madrid Deep Space Communications Complex, which supports exploration of the earth's orbit and solar system (most recently used for communications in the Mars Rover missions). This complex is part of NASA's deep space network, which conducts tracking and data acquisition tasks. Spain and the United States also have cultural and education exchanges, including a binational Fulbright program for advanced college students and professors. Overall, the relations between Spain and the United States are strong, and in the wake of the war in Iraq and the operations in Afghanistan, the United States can rely on Spain's strong support (U.S. Department of State 2004).

The Future

Spain's continued close relationship with the United States will put it in a comparable situation to that of the United Kingdom, making it a bridge between the United States and Europe. Being a member of not only the European Union but also the European Monetary Union gives Spain an advantage over the United Kingdom in inter-U.S.-European monetary negotiations, because Spain has a seat on the European Central Bank board. Close relations with the United States could strain Spain's relationship with European countries, especially in regard to Europe's stated policy of creating a European rapid reaction force. Spain continues to profess its support for such an initiative, although the United States remains skeptical because it could reduce Europe's reliance on NATO for defense policy. Thus, there is a possibility that Spain might find itself torn between European defense policy and North Atlantic defense policy, making it necessary to either create a delicate balance between the two or declare support for one or the other. Doing either could cause great strain in Spain's two most important relationships.

Spain's decision to create a professional military will pay dividends in the future as the men and women become more capable militarily while operating throughout the world. By participating in NATO, Spain will be able to conduct a foreign policy outside its actual military strength. Although Spain professes a modest foreign policy guided by the purposes and principles of the United Nations, its actions in regard to military affairs put it in a position to project force throughout the world when it is a part of NATO action. If Spain continues to invest in new weapons systems like the A-400 transport plane, the new versions of the Leopard Tank, the

F-100 Frigate, and the Eurofighter, it will have a fully professional, fully equipped military that can perform missions throughout the world. These investments will allow Spain to overcome the weaknesses it suffered throughout the Cold War period. As long as Spain continues on this path, the Spanish armed forces will rise into the elite ranks of European military forces.

On March 11, 2004, the direction of Spanish politics was violently altered. The terrorist attack on the Madrid train system jolted the international community, bringing the world to the stunning realization that terrorism can strike in any place at any time, despite heightened security. The death of nearly 200 Spaniards on the eve of national elections impacted the campaign of Popular Party candidate Mariano Rajoy. Prime Minister Jose Maria Anzar had anointed Rajoy as the next leader of Spain, and many expected an easy victory. After evidence began to mount that the attack might have been carried out by elements of al-Qaeda, along with Anzar's unpopular decision to contribute nearly 1,300 troops to the war in Iraq without an explicit UN resolution, the Spanish people decided that they could no longer support Aznar's pro-U.S., conservative policies and elected Jose Luis Rodriquez Zapatero, the leader of the Socialist Party. Upon claiming victory, the socialists began a process that changed many of the policies that the previous government had supported. Although the socialists proclaimed their determination to fight terrorism, they also proclaimed that they would remove the Spanish contingent from Iraq unless the United Nations played a greater role and passed an appropriate Security Council resolution. The terrorist attacks contributed to the downfall of the Popular Party and changed the path that Spain might have followed in the future, moving more toward France and Germany and away from the United States. This would have a distinct impact on the war on terrorism and international relations in general.

References, Recommended Readings, and Websites

Books

Alvarez-Junco, José, and Adrian Shubert, eds. 2000. *Spanish History since 1808.* New York: Oxford University Press.

Balfour, Sebastian, and Paul Preston, eds. 1999. *Spain and the Great Powers in the Twentieth Century.* New York: Routledge.

Bennett, Richard. 2001. *Fighting Forces.* Hauppauge, NY: Barron's Educational Series.

Bland, David. 2003. *Strategic Defense Review.* Madrid: Government of Spain.

Esdaile, Charles J. 2000. *Spain in the Liberal Age: From Constitution to Civil War, 1808–1939.* Oxford: Blackwell.

Europa World Yearbook, Volume 2. 2003. London: Europa Publications.

Gold, Peter. 2000. *Europe or Africa? A Contemporary Study of the Spanish North African Enclaves of Ceuta and Melilla.* Liverpool, UK: Liverpool University Press.

Maxwell, Kenneth, ed. 1991. *Spanish Foreign and Defense Policy.* Boulder, CO: Westview.

Soltsen, Eric, and Sandra W. Meditz, eds. 1988. *Spain: A Country Study.* Washington, DC: GPO for the Library of Congress.

Treverton, Gregory F. 1986. *Spain: Domestic Politics and Security Policy.* London: International Institute for Strategic Studies.

Articles/Newspapers

Cardenas, Sonia C. 1996. "The Contested Territories of Ceuta and Melilla." *Mediterranean Quarterly* 7:118.

Coates, Crispin. 2000. "Spanish Defence Policy: Eurocorps and NATO Reform." *Mediterranean Politics* 5:170–189.

Daly, Emma. 2002a. "Europeans Urge Morocco to Withdraw from Spanish Island." *New York Times,* July 15:A2.

————. 2002b. "Spain and Morocco Reach Deal to Vacate Uninhabited Islet." *New York Times,* July 23:A4.

Eriksson, Mikael, Peter Wallensteen, and Margareta Sollenberg. 2003. "Armed Conflict 1989–2002." *Journal of Peace Research* 40:593–607.

Johnson, Ed. 2003. "In Show of Unity, Blair and Chirac Agree on Plans for European Rapid-Reaction Force." *Associated Press,* November 24.

Sahagun, Felipe. 2000. "Spain and the United States: Military Primacy." *Mediterranean Politics* 5:148–169.

Shanker, Thom. 2002. "Scud Missiles Found on Ship of North Korea." *New York Times,* December 11:A1.

Taglibabue, John. 2003. "A Region Inflamed: Madrid: Losses in Iraq Won't Alter Spain's Policy, Leader Says." *The New York Times,* December 1:A13.

UN Security Council. 2001a. S/RES/1373 (2001), September 28.

————.2001b. S/2001/1246, December 26.

————. 2002. S/2002/778, July 19.

————. 2003. S/2003/628, June 9.

Websites

A400M Military Transport: http://www.airbusmilitary.com/home.html.

http://www.globalsecurity.org/military/world/europe/fla.htm.

Central Intelligence Agency. *World Factbook.* http://www.odci.gov/cia/publications/factbook/index.html.

————. *The World Fact Book—Spain.* http://www.odci.gov/cia/publications/factbook/geos/sp.html (accessed February 5, 2004).

Eurofighter: http://eurofighter.com/.

European Institute for Security Studies: http://www.iss-eu.org/.

European Union: http://europa.eu.int/index_en.htm.

F-100 Frigate: http://www.globalsecurity.org/military/world/europe/f–100.htm.

Head of Government: Spain: http://www.la-moncloa.es/.

Leopard 2 Main Battle Tank: http://www.globalsecurity.org/military/world/europe/leopard2.htm.

http://www.army-technology.com/projects/leopard/index.html.

Ministry of Defense—Spain. http://www.mde.es.

————. "Air Force: Organic Structure." http://www.mde.es/mde/fuerzas/aiestruc.htm (accessed February 5, 2004).

————. "Army: Organic Structure." http://www.mde.es/mde/fuerzas/testruct.htm (accessed February 5, 2004).

————. "Army: Regions and Military Zones." http://www.mde.es/mde/fuerzas/tzonas.htm (accessed February 5, 2004).

————. "Defense in the Constitution." http://www.mde.es/mde/organiza/organ1.htm (accessed February 5, 2004).

————. "Ministry of Defense Budget 2003." http://www.mde.es/mde/presup/2003/PRESUPUESTOS%202003.pdf (accessed February 5, 2004).

————. "Navy: Organic Structure." http://www.mde.es/mde/fuerzas/arestruc.htm (accessed February 5, 2004).

————. "Peace Missions." http://www.mde.es/mde/mision/mision.htm (accessed February 5, 2004).

Ministry of External Affairs: Spain: http://www.mae.es/.

North Atlantic Treaty Organization: http://www.nato.int.

————. "Table 6: Armed Forces—Annual Average Strength." http://www.nato.int/docu/pr/2003/table6.pdf (accessed February 5, 2004).

Permanent Mission of Spain to the United Nations: http://www.spainun.org/pages/home.cfm.

Spanish Mission to the United Nations. "Statement by the Representative of Spain, Roman Oyarzun, at the Committee of the 24 on Gibraltar." http://www.spainun.org/pages/viewfull.cfm?ElementID=2034 (accessed January 6, 2004).

United Nations. "Contributors of United Nations Peacekeeping Missions." http://www.un.org/Depts/dpko/dpko/contributors/December2003Countrysummary.pdf (accessed February 5, 2004).

U.S. Department of State. "Background Note: Spain." http://www.state.gov/r/pa/ei/bgn/2878.htm (accessed February 5, 2004).

U.S. Embassy: Spain. "2002 Patterns of Global Terrorism: Spain." http://www.embusa.es/terrorspainen.html (accessed February 5, 2004).

Switzerland

Kyle A. Joyce

Geography and History

Switzerland is a landlocked country in central Europe, covering approximately 16,000 square miles. Switzerland shares borders with Germany in the northwest, Austria and the principality of Liechtenstein in the east, Italy in the southeast, and France in the west. A mountainous country, Switzerland features the Alps in the south and the Jura Mountain range in the northwest. These expansive mountains and their foothills account for approximately 60 percent of the country's total surface area. The high alpine regions also mark the beginning of two of Europe's major rivers: the Rhine and the Rhone. Switzerland also contains several large lakes, including Geneva, Constance, Neuchâtel, Lucerne, Maggiore, and Zürich. In addition to mountains and lakes, farmland does exist; approximately 11 percent of the country is suitable for farming. Although weather conditions vary considerably with altitude, in general Switzerland's climate is temperate. The winter months are cold and cloudy with frequent rain and snow, and the summer months are warm with some humidity and occasional rain (Central Intelligence Agency 2003).

Switzerland has a population of approximately 7.3 million and a population growth rate of approximately 0.2 percent (Central Intelligence Agency 2003). Two-thirds of all citizens are between the ages of fifteen and sixty-four. The largest cities are Zürich (339,000 inhabitants), Basel (171,000), Geneva (173,000), the federal capital, Berne (124,000), and Lausanne (114,000) (Central Intelligence Agency 2003).

Switzerland has high levels of political, cultural, and religious diversity. No single language, religion, or ethnicity binds the country together. Specifically, Switzerland has four main ethnic groups: German (65 percent), French (18 percent), Italian (10 percent), and Romansch (1 percent). Other ethnic groups make up 6 percent of the population.

Corresponding with these main ethnic groups, Switzerland has four official languages: German (63.7 percent), French (19.2 percent), Italian (7.6 percent), and Romansch (0.6 percent). Other languages account for the remaining 8.9 percent. There are two dominant religions in Switzerland: Roman Catholic (46.1 percent) and Protestant (40 percent), with the other 13.9 percent of the population divided among other Christian denominations or other religions, mainly Judaism and Islam, or having no religious faith.

In 1291 Switzerland obtained independence when three ruling families signed a charter pledging mutual support to one another. This charter formed the Swiss Federation and permitted autonomous administration and judicial rule. Following a brief civil war in 1848, Switzerland became a federal republic when the twenty-five individual cantons formed a confederation.

Switzerland's political institutions are often held to be unique among nations because of their particular ruling structure. Switzerland is a pluralist country embedded within a strong federal system. The federal government is composed of twenty-six individual cantons, which can also be thought of as individual states. Twenty-five cantons joined together in 1848 to form the Swiss Confederation. In 1979, another canton was added, bringing the total number of cantons to twenty-six. Of the twenty-six cantons, there are twenty full cantons and six half cantons. Each canton has its own constitution, Parliament, and judiciary.

The federal system has three levels of political institutions: federal, cantonal, and local. The first level is the federation or confederation, the responsibilities of which are provided by the Swiss constitution, which was updated in 1999. One of the tasks entrusted to the federation is that of foreign and security policy. The federation contains executive, legislative, and judicial branches. The executive branch is run by the Federal Council, which consists of seven members who are elected annually by the legislature. All members of the Federal Council have equal weight. The president of the Confederation is the chairman of the Federal Council, and the presidency rotates annually among the seven members of the Federal Council. Thus, there is no publicly elected president. Beginning in 2004, the seven members of the Federal Council included one Christian Democrat, two Social Democrats, two Free Democrats, and two representatives of the Swiss People's Party.

The legislative branch is bicameral and contains the National Council and the Council of States, both of which are endowed with equal powers. The National Council consists of 200 members elected every four years in accordance with proportional representation, with each member representing approximately 35,000 citizens. Each canton constitutes an elec-

Table 1   Switzerland: Key Statistics

Type of government	Federal republic
Population (millions)	7.3 (2003)
Religions	Roman Catholic 46% (1990), Protestant 40% (1990)
Main industries	Machinery, chemicals, watches, textiles, precision instruments
Main security threats	None
Defense spending (% GDP)	0.01 (2001)
Size of military (thousands)	524 (2004)
Number of civil wars since 1945	0
Number of interstate wars since 1945	0

Sources

Central Intelligence Agency Website. 2003. CIA *World Factbook.* http://www.cia.gov/cia/publications/factbook/geos/sz/html (accessed February 7, 2004).

Ghosn, Faten, and Glenn Palmer. 2003. *Codebook for the Militarized Interstate Dispute Data, Version 3.0.* http://cow2.la.psu.edu (accessed February 4, 2004).

United States Department of State. 2004. *Background Note: Switzerland.* http://www.state.gov/r/pa/ei/bgn/3431.htm (accessed February 17, 2004).

toral constituency and elects at least one member regardless of the size of its population. The Council of States has forty-six members, with each full canton sending two members and each half canton sending one member. Members representing the cantons are also elected for four-year terms. At the local level, all cantons are divided into approximately 3,000 local municipalities. Within each municipality, decisions are made either through a local parliament or, in most cases, through direct democracy.

At the federal level, the judiciary consists of a single court, the federal supreme court, with judges elected for six-year terms by the Federal Assembly (Central Intelligence Agency 2003). Switzerland also has special military and administrative courts. The administration of justice is primarily handled by individual cantons.

Switzerland is a direct democracy. All Swiss men and women over the age of eighteen are allowed to vote on federal matters such as a revision of the constitution or approval of a treaty. Swiss foreign policy depends on the expression of the will of Swiss citizens through referendums on important foreign policy questions (see Sidebar 1). In this way, the institution of direct democracy has important foreign policy implications. In order for a referendum to pass it must be accepted by a majority of the people as well as a majority of the cantons (twelve out of twenty-three), with the twenty full cantons each receiving one vote and the six half cantons receiving one-half of a vote. This system of direct democracy facilitates the government's role of managing the country, rather than influencing the specific path it should follow. The critical responsibility of directing the country to move in one direction or an-

other (or to maintain the status quo) resides firmly in the hands of the Swiss citizens themselves.

Sidebar 1   Switzerland and the United Nations

Switzerland is a direct democracy and, thus, Swiss foreign policy is heavily influenced by the expression of the Swiss people through referendums on important foreign policy questions. For a referendum to pass, it must be accepted by a majority of the people as well as by a majority of the cantons. In March 2002, for example, a referendum on membership in the United Nations was held, with 54.6 percent of Swiss citizens voting in favor of the referendum and 45.4 percent voting against the referendum. In addition, the referendum needed the support of a majority of the cantons, which was achieved when twelve cantons passed the referendum. The successful vote on the referendum made Switzerland the first country to join the United Nations based on a popular referendum.

Source
Swiss Embassy–Washington, D.C.: http://www.eda.admin.ch/washington_emb/e/home.html (accessed February 12, 2004).

Switzerland has a workforce of approximately 4 million, with 4.2 percent of the country's population working in agriculture and forestry, 25.6 percent in industry and business, and 70.2 percent in services and government (United States Department of State 2004). The main industries of Switzerland include machinery, chemicals, watches, textiles, and precision instruments. Switzerland's agricultural products include grains, fruits, vegetables, meat, and eggs. In the service sector, banking, insurance, and tourism are dominant.

Switzerland has a stable modern market economy with low unemployment and inflation. In 2002, the estimated national unemployment rate was 1.9 percent, and the estimated rate of inflation rate was 0.5 percent (Central Intelligence Agency 2003). Switzerland has a skilled labor force, and its per capita gross domestic product (GDP) is larger than that of most European countries. At $34,428, Switzerland's GDP per capita measures only slightly below that of the United States, at $35,867 (Swiss Embassy–Washington, D.C. 2004). In 2002, Switzerland's GDP was $233.4 billion, with a growth rate of 0.1 percent (Central Intelligence Agency 2003).

As a landlocked state with access to few natural resources, Switzerland is dependent on both its trade and its financial relations with numerous other countries. In 2002, Switzerland's imports totaled approximately $94.4 billion (Central Intelligence Agency 2003). Switzerland's main import partners are Germany (27.4 percent), France (11.4 percent), Italy (9.7 percent), the United States (8.5 percent), Russia (5.8 percent), the United Kingdom (5.4 percent), Austria (4.6 percent), and The Netherlands (4.1 percent). The main import commodities are machinery, chemicals, vehicles, metals, agricultural products, and textiles. In 2002, Switzerland's exports totaled approximately $100.3 billion (Central Intelligence Agency 2003). Switzerland's main export partners are Germany (19.2 percent), the United States (10.2 percent), Italy (9.6 percent), France (8.9 percent), and the United Kingdom (7.7 percent). The main export commodities are machinery, chemicals, metals, watches, and agricultural products. In addition to maintaining healthy bilateral trade and financial relationships, Switzerland participates in several international economic organizations, including the Organization for Economic Cooperation and Development (OECD), the European Free Trade Association (EFTA), the World Bank, the International Monetary Fund (IMF), and the World Trade Organization (WTO).

Regional Geopolitics

As a result of being surrounded by large countries, throughout Swiss history the primary goal of Swiss foreign and security policy has been to avoid being drawn into external armed conflicts. The way in which Switzerland has traditionally achieved this goal has been its longstanding commitment to a policy of permanent neutrality. In terms of regional geopolitics, Switzerland's primary concern is the increasing political, economic, and military integration of Europe.

Despite the important role of neutrality, Switzerland's foreign and security policy is based on a belief in not only the necessity of cooperation, but also in the importance of international and regional institutions playing essential roles in resolving conflict and promoting peace. As a way to complement its defense capability, Switzerland actively participates in regional organizations, including the Organization for Security and Cooperation in Europe (OSCE), the North Atlantic Treaty Organization's (NATO) Partnership for Peace, and the Euro-Atlantic Partnership Council.

Switzerland was admitted to the OSCE in 1973. Membership in the OSCE provides Switzerland the opportunity to confer with Europe as well as with Canada and the United States on issues of international security. Under the auspices of the OSCE, Switzerland participates in peace-building operations throughout the world, particularly in southeast Europe.

In recent years, the European Union (EU) has become an important actor in the international community. Over the past decade, the EU has focused its energy on expanding its influence by increasing the number of its member states, completing its single market, introducing the euro, integrating the security policies of its members, and expanding its peace-keeping operations. The EU has also centralized its foreign and security policy through the Common Foreign and Security Policy (CFSP) established by the Treaty of Maastricht (1992) and the development of the European Security and Defense Policy (ESDP). In addition to these efforts by the EU, other European security organizations have undergone important changes. Of particular note have been the enlargement of NATO and the development of the Partnership for Peace, as well as the expansion of the OSCE.

As a result of its geographic location and history, Switzerland and member countries of the EU share close political, cultural, and economic ties. However, despite the intimate bonds between Switzerland and the EU, Switzerland is a member of neither the EU nor the European Economic Area (EEA). In 2001, an initiative that would have allowed the Swiss federal government to begin negotiations regarding potential entry into the EU was rejected by the Swiss people and cantons, primarily because the preconditions for entry into the union that had been set out by the federal government were not met. A list of recent votes on EU integration is found in the table below.

Despite the failure of the initiative to join the EU, in the short term the Swiss government continues to implement the seven bilateral agreements signed by the EU and Switzerland in 1999 in the areas of free movement of persons, overland transport, air transport, agriculture, research, and technical barriers to trade and procurement. The signing of these agreements allowed Switzerland to stabilize bilateral relations in important areas. Moreover, these agreements strengthened the Swiss economy. Further bilateral negotiations are ongoing in ten new areas, including improved market access for agricultural products, the environment, and regulating the taxation of pensions of former EU employees who are residing in Switzerland (Federal Department of Foreign Affairs 2000b).

Table 2   Switzerland: Referendums on EU Integration 1972–2001

Year	Referendum	Yes	No	Voter Turnout
1972	EFTA Membership	72.5%	27.5%	52%
1992	EEA Membership	49.7%	50.3%	78%
1997	EU Candidature	25.9%	74.1%	35%
2000	Bilateral Treaties with EU	67.2%	32.8%	48%
2001	EU Candidature	23.2%	76.8%	55%

Source
Initiative and Referendum Institute Europe. 2004. http://www.iri-europe.org/resources/ referendums.php (accessed August 1, 2004).

The long-term goal of the federal government is to enter the EU with the belief that Switzerland's interests would be better protected as a member of the EU than outside it. The federal government has set three primary preconditions for membership. First, Switzerland would like to assess the impact of the seven bilateral agreements signed in 1999. Second, issues relating to the effect of membership on Swiss political institutions need to be clarified. In particular, an assessment must be made regarding the impact that joining the EU would have on federalism, direct democracy, finance legislation, agricultural policy, migration policy, economic and monetary policy, and foreign and security policy. Third, and perhaps most importantly, there must be sufficient domestic support for entry (Federal Department of Foreign Affairs 2000b). The last referendum held on EU candidature only received support from 23.2 percent of the population.

Some Swiss citizens view Switzerland's nonmembership in the EU as being costly to the nation, both financially and politically. For example, on the financial side, Switzerland engages in large projects deemed to be of national importance, projects that are paid for by Swiss taxpayers. One such expensive project is the network of north-south railroad tunnels currently under construction. One Swiss scholar noted that, "the project serves the European Union more than Switzerland . . . and if Switzerland were a member of the Union, there is a possibility that such infrastructural undertakings would (at least in part) be financed by all Europeans" (Gabriel 2003, 17). With respect to the political costs, the rising power of the EU permits the union to be a major player in world affairs. Decisions are made by members of the EU on numerous issues, including security policy. Most of these decisions affect countries across the entire continent, including Switzerland. Not participating in the EU means that Switzerland does not participate in decisions that affect its economic and security policies. It is possible that remaining absent from important regional institutions, such as the EU, puts Swiss security at risk.

The rejection of communist rule and subsequent independence of the states of central and eastern Europe enhanced Swiss security. Switzerland contributes substantial financial resources to assist in the transformation of these central and eastern European states. In the past decade, the Balkans posed the primary security concern facing Switzerland. The disintegration of Yugoslavia through armed conflict was an important security event for Switzerland. Not only was Switzerland geographically proximate to the conflict, but also many members of ethnic groups in the former Yugoslavia now reside in Switzerland. As a result, Switzerland provided substantial humanitarian aid and assistance to refugees. The stabilization of southeastern Europe will remain one of the largest future challenges for Europe as a whole, and for Switzerland in particular.

Conflict Past and Present
Conflict History
Swiss foreign policy is anchored by two pillars: neutrality and sovereignty. As a permanently neutral entity, Switzerland has never participated in armed conflict with another country. This traditional stance of neutrality has played a significant role in allowing Switzerland to maintain its internal and external security (see Sidebar 2).

Sidebar 2   Switzerland and Permanent Neutrality

As a permanent neutral, Switzerland has never participated in armed conflict with another country. Swiss interpretation of neutrality has evolved over time, however, allowing Switzerland to participate in economic and military sanctions, as long as these sanctions are determined not to be in violation of international law.

Although the Swiss conception of neutrality has developed over time, its status as a permanent neutral has allowed Switzerland to ensure it external and internal security by avoiding military conflict with other countries. Switzerland's neutral status makes it highly unlikely that Switzerland will be involved in any military conflicts in the foreseeable future.

Although Switzerland remained neutral in both world wars, there was a difference in each war with regard to the unification of the country. During World War I, Switzerland was divided, with the German Swiss supporting the Kaiser and the French Swiss supporting the Associated Powers (Gabriel 2003). Thus, Swiss neutrality during World War I not only saved Switzerland from paying the costs of war but probably also prevented an internal crisis from emerging. During World War II, the Swiss public was united behind neutrality, and following the war a belief resided among the Swiss population that neutrality had again saved their country from the destruction of war. This public perception strengthened Switzerland's commitment to the practice of neutrality (Gabriel 2003).

Switzerland has only experienced one internal conflict during which militarized action occurred. In 1848 tensions between the conservative Catholic cantons, desiring to retain the status quo, and the Protestant liberal-radical cantons, seeking a centralized nation-state, escalated, and a brief civil war was fought. The war ended with the capitulation of the conservative cantons and the formation of a federal state.

Current and Potential Military Confrontation

At the moment, Switzerland is not threatened by the possibility of any military conflicts. Despite the fact that Switzerland does not participate in the EU and is not a full member of NATO, Switzerland still benefits from Europe's collective security structure. Furthermore, Switzerland simply does not have any historic rivalries that could threaten the security of the country. Most notably, Switzerland's neutral status makes the possibility that Switzerland will participate in any military conflicts in the foreseeable future highly unlikely.

Alliance Structure

The cornerstone of Swiss foreign and security policy is neutrality. Neutrality strongly affects the ability of Switzerland to form alliances. At the Congress of Vienna in 1815, Switzerland was recognized as a permanent neutral. Under the prescribed conditions of a permanent neutral, Switzerland does not need to declare neutrality on the eve of war but rather is always committed to neutrality, including during times of peace. Switzerland's neutrality has had a "political dimension preceding the outbreak of war and a legal dimension when war occurred" (Gabriel 2003, 7).

The legal dimension of Swiss neutrality emanates from the international laws of neutrality, which were codified at the Hague Convention Respecting the Rights and Duties of Neutral Powers and Persons in Case of War on Land (Hague V) and in Naval War (Hague XIII) in 1907. This convention laid out the rights and duties of neutral powers as follows: "When war breaks out among sovereign states, these conventions make it legal for states wishing to stay apart to declare neutrality, a status involving certain rights and duties. Among other things a neutral has to declare its neutrality publicly, must prevent the misuse of its territory by the warring parties and has the right to carry on free trade with all sides. Because this body of rights and duties can be claimed by any states when war breaks out, it is identified as occasional neutrality" (Gabriel 2003, 7). In 1815, Switzerland adopted a more restrictive type of neutrality, known as permanent neutrality, a status that reflects Switzerland's desire to remain neutral during periods of peace.

The political dimension of Swiss neutrality involves institutional precautions designed to prevent risking the country's neutral status. Thus, Switzerland will not enter into any obligation or military arrangement that could be interpreted as an alliance. However, Switzerland's commitment to forgo forming alliance partnerships pertains only to preventive alliances and not to reactive alliances. This does not mean that Switzerland will never form a preventive alliance. The important determination of whether a preventive alliance needs to be formed depends on the perceived nature of a threat. A minor threat to Swiss sovereignty does not warrant the formation of a preventive alliance; however, a major threat to Swiss sovereignty could necessitate the planning of a preventive alliance. For example, during World War I and World II secret contacts occurred pertaining to the formation of a potential preventive alliance (Gabriel 2003).

The political aspect of neutrality is flexible, being adaptable to the current international environment, particularly when peace and international security are threatened. For example, as a member of the League of Nations, Switzerland participated in international economic sanctions between the two world wars against states in violation of international law but did not participate in international sanctions during the Cold War. However, the end of the Cold War marked a change in the Swiss practice of neutrality. International and regional institutions were increasingly viewed as the frameworks in which global and regional problems needed to be addressed. In this context, nonparticipation in important institutions, such as the United Nations (UN) and the EU, could threaten Switzerland's security and independence. Only through international and regional cooperation would Switzerland's primary foreign policy objectives be achieved, including the preservation and promotion of security and peace, the promotion of social cohesion, the promotion of prosperity, the preservation of the environment, and the promotion of human rights, democracy, and the rule of law (Federal Department of Foreign Affairs 2000b).

In accordance with these changes in the political environment, Switzerland's *Report of Neutrality* (1993) signaled a shift in the practice of Swiss neutrality. Following the publication of this report, Switzerland strengthened its international commitments and cooperation with the international community. For example, since the 1990s, Switzerland has participated in all economic sanction regimes authorized by the United Nations including those aimed against Yugoslavia (1991–2001), Libya (1992–2003), Haiti (1993–1994), Sierra Leone (1997), Angola/Unita (1998), Afghanistan/Taliban (2000), and Liberia (2001). The Swiss view was that neutrality was not incompatible with participation in UN coercive measures such as economic sanctions. Participation in economic sanctions was compatible with the law of neutrality, because the law of neutrality does not include economic measures. "Participation in these coercive measures . . . indicated a change of policy in that it was the first time since WWII that Switzerland openly and fully participated" (Federal Department of Foreign Affairs 2000a, 4). Recently, Switzerland has also participated in sanctions imposed by the EU and OSCE, including those leveled against Yugoslavia (1998) and Myanmar (2000).

The *Report of Neutrality* (1993) also signaled a change in Switzerland's stance on military sanctions. The report indicated that participation in UN military sanctions was compatible with neutrality so long as the measures were congruent with international law. As a result, beginning in 1993, Switzerland authorized the use of its national territory by foreign military forces for overflights and transit rights in support of peace operations authorized by the UN. Switzerland has granted overflight permits for military surveillance aircraft for UN protection forces in Yugoslavia and the OSCE mission in Kosovo, as well as overflights and transit rights for missions in Bosnia-Herzegovina and Kosovo. The current view in Switzerland is that neutrality law does not apply in cases of measures taken by the UN. This view is based on the notion that neutrality cannot exist between the international community, acting for its part as a single unit, and a state engaging in violations of international law.

As a result of the current view on neutrality, Switzerland joined NATO's Partnership for Peace in 1996. The Partnership for Peace allows states, such as Switzerland, to develop closer cooperation with NATO member states without joining NATO officially. Specifically, this partnership enables Switzerland to work closely with NATO's member states without violating Swiss neutrality. The Partnership for Peace program, which is only political in nature, does not require the same obligation on the part of its members that is outlined in Article 5 of the NATO treaty, requiring member states to potentially respond with armed force to an attack against another member. Additionally, as a member of NATO's Partnership for Peace, Switzerland subsequently joined the Euro-Atlantic Partnership Council.

Switzerland has maintained a permanent observer mission to the UN since 1948 and has participated in most UN specialized agencies; however, following a successful referendum, Switzerland became a full member of the United Nations in March 2002. Switzerland is the first country to join the UN based on a popular referendum (United States Department of State 2004). Switzerland has stated that it will not participate in any peace enforcement operations but will participate in peacekeeping operations. In addition, Switzerland has arranged for the disposal of Swiss civilian and military experts to the UN. Within the confines of the UN, Switzerland has taken a particular interest in issues concerning disarmament and arms control, nonproliferation, averting terrorist attacks, and preventing the spread of weapons of mass destruction.

The conflicts that arose in the Balkans during the 1990s illustrate the applicability of Swiss neutrality in the current international environment, particularly given the changing view of neutrality compared with how it was practiced during the Cold War. During the Kosovo conflict in 1999, NATO conducted air strikes without the explicit authorization of the UN. As a result, Switzerland refused to allow NATO aircraft to enter Swiss airspace. However, Switzerland did participate in the arms embargo and most of the EU sanctions against Yugoslavia.

Although Swiss neutrality prevents the formation of alliances, a series of treaties signed following World War I between Switzerland and Liechtenstein led Switzerland to assume the responsibility for the diplomatic representation of Liechtenstein, the regulation of its customs, and protection of its borders (United States Department of State 2004).

Size and Structure of the Military

At the center of Swiss foreign policy is the idea of autonomous national defense, or armed neutrality. The cornerstone of the Swiss military system is the militia army, which in turn is also based on the notion of armed neutrality.

Under the Swiss constitution every male is required to perform military service for at least 300 days. The military reform plan, Army XXI, which began in January 2004, reduced the number of required days of military service from 300 to 260 days. Women are not required to do military service but are accepted on a voluntary basis and are now permitted to serve in all units, including combat service. For males, there are fifteen weeks compulsory recruit training at age nineteen to twenty, followed by ten refresher training courses of three weeks each over a twenty-two-year period between ages twenty and forty-two (International Institute for Strategic Studies 2003–2004, 81). A new class of military personnel called "single-term conscripts" will fulfill the total required time of military service at one time, serving 300 consecutive days of active duty.

Under the Army XXI reform plan, Switzerland is reducing the size of its army from 320,400 to 140,000 personnel, which includes 80,000 reserves. To counter these reductions there will be an increase in the number of professional personnel from 3,500 to 4,500. As a result of the militia system, there are almost no full-time active combat units; however, full mobilization is possible within seventy-two hours (United States Department of State 2004). The overall concept for defense presented in Army XXI prescribes that the militia system of defense will remain central to Swiss defense planning. Switzerland is also considering moving away from its traditional self-defense posture and establishing a second force designed to meet some of NATO's compatibility requirements (International Institute for Strategic Studies 2003–2004, 34).

The chief of the armed forces is responsible for strategic military command and development of the armed forces and reports to the head of the Ministry of Defense. The chief of the armed forces directs the Land Force, Air Force, Senior Cadre Training Organization, Armed Forces Logistics Organization, Central Command Support Organization, and the Information Technology (IT) directorate. The chief of the armed forces is assisted by the Armed Forces Planning Staff and the Armed Forces Joint Staff. The Armed Forces Planning Staff is responsible for ensuring the overall development of the defense department, the two armed services, management of the defense budget, and development of the overall military framework provided by Swiss security policy. The Armed Forces Joint Staff has command at the operational level.

The land and air forces are each led by an overall commander who holds the primary responsibility in terms of training, operations, and logistics. The Senior Cadre Training Organization provides the training for all military personnel. The Armed Forces Logistics Organization is responsible for all logistical services, one of which is the procurement and introduction of new weapons systems. The Central Command Support Organization is responsible for ensuring that the command function is operational and also provides the permanent organizational environment for supporting the command function. The IT directorate provides information technology services for the entire department.

Switzerland will participate in peacekeeping operations with a UN or OSCE mandate but will not participate in peace enforcement operations. Switzerland has participated in peace missions abroad since 1953 when ninety-six army personnel were sent to Korea to supervise the armistice. There are currently five military personnel serving in Korea. Beginning in 1989, Switzerland began deploying medical units to run field hospitals in several countries in Africa, including the Western Sahara and Namibia. Military observers have also served in the Middle East, Georgia, the Democratic Republic of the Congo, and Ethiopia/Eritrea.

Recently, Switzerland has increased its role in peacekeeping operations. Switzerland supported the OSCE peacekeeping mission in Bosnia-Herzegovina beginning in 1996 by sending an unarmed logistical unit. Since 1999, the Swiss army has also participated in the NATO-led protection force in Kosovo. In June 2001, a vote approved armed troops of the Swiss armed forces to participate in operations abroad under an OSCE or UN mandate. Currently an armed military unit is stationed in Kosovo under NATO command.

Budget
Between 1992 and 2002, Swiss military expenditure declined from $3.9 billion to $2.6 billion. Military expenditure as a percentage of GDP also declined from 1.8 percent in 1992 to 1.1 percent in 2001 (Stockholm Peace Research Institute 2003).

The Swiss armed forces are equipped with tanks, armored personnel carriers, fighter aircraft, and transport helicopters. Switzerland also has air-to-air missiles, antitank missiles, and surface-to-air missiles.

Switzerland is both an importer and exporter of military hardware. Switzerland imports fighter aircraft, armored personnel carriers, armed infantry fighting vehicles, and helicopters. Switzerland primarily imports military equipment from the United States, Israel, Canada, France, the United Kingdom, Germany, and Spain.

Civil-Military Relations/The Role of the Military in Domestic Politics

Civil-military relations in Switzerland are harmonious. The amicable relationship between the civilian government and the military is a result of Swiss political institutions. Direct democracy places civil-military relations entirely in the hands of Swiss citizens, who vote on important foreign policy issues, putting the role of the military at the behest of the ordinary population. As noted in the previous section, all male citizens are required to perform military service. The militia system functions with few professional soldiers and relies on the Swiss public to function. In addition, members of local, cantonal, and federal governments serve in the militia. Thus, the political institutions of Switzerland only allow the military to play a small role in domestic politics. If there is any role of the military in domestic politics, it is for the politicians to govern and all citizens to perform their military responsibility as provided by the Swiss constitution.

Terrorism

Switzerland does not have a terrorist problem and is not known to harbor terrorists; however, its banking secrecy laws create the potential for abuse by terrorist groups. Banking secrecy refers to the obligation that banks undertake not to disclose information regarding the affairs of their customers to others. Such secrecy not only ensures the financial privacy of individuals but also makes the banking sector susceptible to exploitation. Although Switzerland will maintain banking secrecy, the government has taken a number of steps to ensure that its financial institutions are not used for financing terrorist attacks. At the international level, Switzerland has signed a number of bilateral treaties on international mutual assistance and extradition. Switzerland has also taken a number of steps to protect against terrorist activity at the domestic level. One step has been to institute the spontaneous transmission of information and evidence that can be used by foreign authorities in investigations outside Switzerland. Switzerland can also freeze bank accounts as soon as a foreign authority requests international

mutual assistance. In addition, Swiss banks are required to report suspicious transactions related to organized crime and terrorism. These measures allow Switzerland to block financial transaction that might benefit terrorist organizations and prevent the abuse of the Swiss financial sector.

After the terrorist attacks on the United States on September 11, 2001, Switzerland came under pressure from the United States in the area of banking, specifically with regard to Swiss banking secrecy laws. In a statement before the UN General Assembly following the attacks, Switzerland's permanent observer to the UN stated, "There is no such thing as banking secrecy when it comes to the fight against terrorism" (Staehelin and Jenö 2001). Switzerland is party to multilateral and regional instruments to counter terrorism. Switzerland is a participant in all twelve UN conventions on combating terrorism, ten of which have been ratified. As mentioned previously, Switzerland works hard to avoid the abuse of its financial system by terrorist organizations or related individuals. The assets of more than 200 individuals or companies with suspected links to international terrorism have been frozen. In addition, Swiss officials have blocked eighty-two bank accounts containing $28 million in connection with the international investigations (*International Herald Tribune* 2004).

It is unclear whether Swiss financial institutions were used by al-Qaeda prior to the attacks of September 11, 2001. Investigations do indicate that several hijackers in the attacks might have passed through Switzerland and that senior leaders of al-Qaeda might have used Swiss cell phones in their communications (*International Herald Tribune* 2004).

Relationship with the United States

Switzerland maintains a strong relationship with the United States, but several issues have arisen between the two countries that have occasionally strained their interactions. This strain is due in large part to discrepancies between the two countries' conceptions of the obligations of a neutral country during war (Gabriel 2003). The dualistic or asymmetric nature of Swiss foreign policy, which is defined as an absence from international political organizations but a strong presence in foreign markets, led Switzerland to support the move toward trade liberalization led by the United States. Switzerland is a landlocked country with few natural resources and is highly dependent on international trade. The United States is the second-largest importer (10.2 percent) of Swiss goods and is the largest foreign investor in Switzerland. In addition, the United States is the primary benefactor of Swiss foreign investment.

In the realm of security affairs, however, Switzerland and the United States have experienced several clashes concerning neutral free trade. As described previously, during times of war a neutral country has the right to continue trading with all sides. The ability or desire of the Swiss to continue trade with Nazi Germany during World War II was unacceptable to the United States. In 1943, the United States put pressure on all neutrals to end all commercial and financial transactions with Nazi Germany. For Switzerland to have chosen to succumb to U.S. pressure would have been a violation of neutral law, at least according to the Swiss interpretation. During the war the United States embarked on a campaign of economic warfare against both the Axis powers and neutral countries, including Switzerland. One example of this warfare was the freezing of all neutral assets on U.S. soil. Pressure from the United States increased, and in 1946 the Swiss reluctantly signed the Washington Agreement, which concerned the restitution of Germany's monetary and gold assets (von Castelmur 1992).

During the Korean War, under intense pressure from the United States, Switzerland signed the Hotz-Linder Agreement in 1951. This agreement stipulated that Switzerland would adopt three control lists that limited certain categories of strategic exports. This was a secret agreement, and the details were not revealed until the end of the Cold War. In the 1980s, during the Reagan administration, economic sanctions were tightened, and although no documents exist, there is the belief that a second Hotz-Linder Agreement was signed.

At the end of the Cold War, restituting Jewish assets that had remained dormant in Swiss bank accounts became a central issue between Switzerland and the United States. This issue goes back to the Washington Agreement and is connected with German assets transferred to Swiss bank accounts during World War II. Following World War II, the United States, along with France and the United Kingdom, demanded that Switzerland transfer the assets to the Allied Control Council. This matter did not surface until the end of the Cold War and was brought on by the restrictive handling of individual Jewish claims by Swiss banks.

Switzerland has introduced initiatives, including the Humanitarian Fund, the Independent Commission of Experts (Bergier Commission), and the Claims Resolution Tribunal, to examine its role before, during, and after World War II. These initiatives examined assets moved to Switzerland by victims and members of the Nazi regime and compensated Holocaust survivors. The Humanitarian Fund distributed a substantial amount of money to approximately 312,000 Holocaust survivors in need. The Claims Resolution Tribunal was established to arbitrate claims of 5,570 dormant accounts in Swiss banks belonging to Holocaust victims and victims of Nazi persecution. Currently, $79 million has been distributed.

With respect to the threat of international terrorism, in September 2002 the United States and Switzerland signed the Anti-Terrorism Law Enforcement Agreement, which provides for law enforcement agents from both countries who are working on terrorist financing investigations to share information regarding the attacks of September 11, 2001, and related ongoing investigations (United States Department of State 2002).

The Future

Swiss foreign and security policy has undergone a gradual change, as indicated by recent votes to join the United Nations and allow the Swiss military to participate in operations abroad. These changes are examples of the country's reconceptualization of the role of a neutral state. Although Switzerland will maintain its neutral status in the future, it appears that other goals have been identified and pursued, specifically the five goals outlined in the Foreign Policy Report 2000, namely, the peaceful coexistence of nations, respect for human rights and promotion of democracy, preservation of natural resources, alleviation of poverty, and the protection of the interests of the Swiss economy abroad (Federal Department of Foreign Affairs 2000b). These goals, coupled with neutrality, are what will allow Switzerland to preserve its sovereignty. One notable future

challenge for the military will be the implementation of Army Plan XXI, which outlines major changes concerning the militia system, autonomous self-defense, and armed neutrality.

A second major challenge facing Switzerland in the future arises in connection with the increasing integration of Europe. As countries of central and eastern Europe join the EU, Switzerland will need to examine closely the costs of remaining outside the EU. It is becoming increasingly likely that Swiss politicians will attempt to convince Swiss citizens that neutrality is compatible with membership in the EU. Yet there are probably more important implications for membership than neutrality, especially given the unique nature of Swiss political institutions, particularly the role of direct democracy.

Overall, the future of Swiss foreign and security policy is positive. There are no main internal or external threats, and it is highly unlikely that Switzerland will become involved in a militarized conflict with another state in the international system. The future of Swiss security policy depends on the will of Swiss citizens who must decide how far Switzerland will go in the participation of international and regional organizations.

References, Recommended Readings, and Websites

Books
Charnley, Joy, and Malcolm Pender, eds. 1999. *Switzerland and War.* Bern: Peter Lang.
Chevallaz, Georges-André. 2001. *The Challenge of Neutrality: Diplomacy and the Defense of Switzerland.* Translated by Harvey Fergusson II. Lanham, MD: Lexington Books.
Gabriel, Jürg Martin, and Thomas Fischer, eds. 2003. *Swiss Foreign Policy, 1945–2002.* New York: Palgrave Macmillan.

Halbrook, Stephen P. 1998. *Target Switzerland: Swiss Armed Neutrality in World War II.* New York: Sarpedon.

Hilty, Donald P., ed. 2001. *Retrospectives on Switzerland in World War Two.* Rockport, ME: Picton Press.

Kobach, Kris W. 1993. *The Referendum: Direct Democracy in Switzerland.* Aldershot: Dartmouth Publishing.

Kreis, George, ed. 2000. *Switzerland and the Second World War.* London: Frank Cass.

Meier, Heinz K. 1970. *Friendship under Stress: US-Swiss Relations 1900–1950.* Bern: Verlag Herbert Lang.

Milivojevic, Marko, and Pierre Maurer, eds. 1989. *Switzerland's Defense and Foreign Policy.* Oxford, UK: Berg.

———. 1990. *Swiss Neutrality and Security: Armed Forces, National Defense and Foreign Policy.* Oxford, UK: Berg.

Urner, Klaus. 2001. *Let's Swallow Switzerland: Hitler's Plans against the Swiss Confederation.* Translated by Lotti N. Eichhorn. Lanham, MD: Lexington Books.

Articles/Newspapers

Fanzun, Jon A. 2003. "Swiss Human Rights Policy: From Reluctance to Normalcy." In *Swiss Foreign Policy 1945–2002,* Jürg Martin Gabriel and Thomas Fischer, eds. New York: Palgrave Macmillian, pp. 127–158.

Federal Department of Foreign Affairs. 1993. *White Paper on Neutrality.* http://www.eda.admin.ch/eda/e/home/recent/rep/neutral/neut93.Par.0002.UpFile.pdf/rp_931129_neut1993_e.pdf (accessed February 18, 2004).

———. 2000a. *Swiss Neutrality in Practice-Current Aspects.* http://www.eda.admin.ch/eda/e/home/recent/rep/neutral/neut00.Par.0002.UpFile.pdf/rp_931129_neut2000_e.pdf (accessed February 4, 2004).

———. 2000b. *Presence and Cooperation: Safeguarding Switzerland's Interests in an Integrating World.* http://www.eda.admin.ch/eda/e/home/recent/rep/forpol.Par.0003.UpFile.pdf/rp_001113_foreignpol_e.pdf (accessed February 1, 2004).

Gabriel, Jürg Martin. 1998. *Swiss Neutrality and the 'American Century': Two Conflicting Worldviews.* http://www.cis.ethz.ch/gabriel/docs/Publications/res_pap/14_Switzerland%20and%20the%20American%20Century.pdf (accessed January 25, 2004).

———. 2000. *Switzerland and the European Union.* http://www.cis.ethz.ch/gabriel/docs/Publications/res_pap/33_EU-CH.pdf (accessed January 25, 2004).

———. 2003. "The Price of Political Uniqueness: Swiss Foreign Policy in a Changing World." In *Swiss Foreign Policy, 1945–2002,* Jürg Martin Gabriel and Thomas Fischer, eds. New York: Palgrave Macmillan, pp. 1–22.

Gabriel, Jürg Martin, and Jon A. Fanzun. 2003a. *The Asymmetries of Swiss Foreign Policy.* http://www.cis.ethz.ch/gabriel/docs/Publications/res_pap/42%20Asymmetrie.pdf (accessed January 25, 2004).

———. 2003b. *Swiss Foreign Policy: An Overview.* http://www.cis.ethz.ch/gabriel/docs/Publications/res_pap/43%20Foreign%20Policy%20Overview.pdf (accessed January 25, 2004).

Ghosn, Faten, and Glenn Palmer. 2003. *Codebook for the Militarized Interstate Dispute Data, Version 3.0.* http://cow2.la.psu.edu (accessed February 4, 2004).

International Herald Tribune. 2004. *Swiss Arrest 8 Terror Suspects.* http://www.iht.com/ihtsearch.php?id=124492&owner=(AP,%20AFP)&date=20010210010000 (accessed February 10, 2004).

International Institute for Strategic Studies. 2003–2004. *The Military Balance.* http://www3.oup.co.uk/milbal/hdb/Volume_103/Issue_01/ (accessed January 31, 2004).

Staehelin, H. E., and Ambassador C. A. Jenö. 2001. "Measures to Eliminate International Terrorism." October 5. Fifty-Sixth General Assembly of the United Nations.

United States Department of State. 2002. *U.S., Switzerland Sign Anti-Terrorism Law Enforcement Agreement.* September 4. http://usinfo.state.gov/topical/pol/terror/02090407.htm (accessed February 10, 2004).

von Castelmur, L. 1992. *The Washington Agreement of 1946 and Relations between Switzerland and the Allies after the Second World War.* http://www.ess.uwe.ac.uk/genocide/appropriation15.htm (accessed February 2, 2004).

Websites

Avalon Project. 1907. *Laws of War: Rights and Duties of Neutral Powers and Persons in Case of War on Land (Hague V)* http://www.yale.edu/lawweb/avalon/lawofwar/hague05.htm (accessed February 14, 2004).

———. 1907. *Laws of War: Rights and Duties of Neutral Powers in Naval War (Hague XIII).* http://www.yale.edu/lawweb/avalon/lawofwar/hague13.htm (accessed February 14, 2004).

Central Intelligence Agency. 2003. *World Factbook.* http://www.cia.gov/cia/publications/factbook/geos/sz.html (accessed February 7, 2004).

Federal Department of Defense, Civil Protection and Sports (DDPS): http://www.vbs-ddps.ch/internet/vbs/en/home.html.

Federal Department of Foreign Affairs (DFA): http://www.eda.admin.ch/eda/e/home.html.

Initiative and Referendum Institute Europe. 2004. http://www.iri-europe.org/resources/referendums.php (accessed August 1, 2004).

Stockholm Peace Research Institute. 2003. *The SIPRI Military Expenditure Database.* http://first.sipri.org/non_first/result_milex.php?send (accessed February 15, 2004).

Swiss Embassy–Washington, D.C.: http://www.eda.admin.ch/washington_emb/e/home.html (accessed February 12, 2004).

The Swiss Parliament: http://www.parlament.ch/e/homepage.htm.

United States Department of State. 2004. *Background Note: Switzerland.* http://www.state.gov/r/pa/ei/bgn/3431.htm (accessed February 17, 2004).

Syria

Dong-hun Kim and Daniel S. Morey

Geography and History

Syria is about the size of North Dakota at 185,180 square kilometers and is primarily semiarid and desert plateau with hot dry summers and mild rainy winters; however, there is a narrow coastal plain on the Mediterranean Coast (CIA *World Factbook*). The coastal plain is very fertile, because mountains enclose it and capture moisture from the air moving off the ocean, creating around forty inches of rainfall annually in the higher elevations (Devlin 1983, 15–16). The large rainfall totals provide excellent farming areas and have attracted a large population to the coastal region. Rainfall drops off as the distance from the coast increases, and the land becomes more arid until the Euphrates River is reached.

Syria first became an independent state in 1920 as the Arab Kingdom of Syria, with Faisal as king. The Arab Kingdom of Syria only lasted a few months and was occupied by France. The Arab Republic of Syria was established on April 17, 1946. Syria received its independence as an outgrowth of World War II. When France fell to Germany in 1940, Syria came under the control of the French Vichy government. In 1941 British and Free French forces occupied the country to remove its resources from the Axis powers. After the war, France sought to reestablish Syria as a colony, and Syria was still under French

control stemming from a League of Nations mandate. However, nationalistic pressures were too high in Syria, and the French were forced to relinquish their mandate and leave Syria. A republican government was established after the French departure, but it was unable to control internal strife.

The early years of Syrian government were chaotic, with coups and countercoups occurring regularly. This was also a time of frequent external conflict, because Syria was involved in clashes with Israel starting with the 1948 war. In 1947 the Baath Party was founded, with a goal of Arab unity, desiring to unite all or most Arabs under a single state. The Baath Party has been the dominant political party in Syria since its establishment.

In 1950 oil reserves were discovered in Syria, providing a needed source of revenue. During the 1950s Syria began introducing social policies with agrarian reform, social insurance, and labor laws. In 1958 Syria and Egypt joined to form the United Arab Republic (UAR); the short-lived republic merged the two states into one entity. However, most of the power was in the hands of Egypt as the larger partner, which created a great deal of frustration and unhappiness in Syria. As a result of this uneven merger Syria broke away from the United Arab Republic in 1961. During this same time Syria began to base its economic development on Soviet-style five-year plans.

Syria's first constitution was adopted in 1963, providing many forms of democratic participation. In the same year these rights were suspended, because the government at the time declared a state of emergency and imposed martial law, which is still in force today. In 1964 Syria socialized its economy with most major industries coming under state control. Designed to increase economic growth, it had the opposite effect.

The 1970s saw an important change in Syria's domestic politics, when Hafiz al-Assad, then defense minister, led a bloodless coup and seized power. Under Assad's rule the constant coups ended, providing needed stability through authoritarian rule. In 1972 Assad became president and merged the Baath Party with other leftist parties to form the National Progressive Front, with the Baath Party as the dominant member. In 1973 Syria's second constitution was adopted, which gave broad powers to the president. Because Syria has remained under martial law, the democratic practices enshrined in the second constitution have never really been employed. In 1978 Syria finished constructing a dam on the Euphrates River that provided hydroelectric power and improved irrigation for eastern Syria. The completion of this large project is a point of national pride.

In the early 1980s Syria backed Iran in the Iran-Iraq War, which isolated Syria from its Arab neighbors. Syria's concern over the balance of power with Iraq, a state under Baath Party rule, outweighed Arab solidarity (Iranians are predominantly Persian, not Arab). Backing Iran forced Syria to close its oil pipeline with Iraq and reduced trade with Arab neighbors, both of which had a negative effect on the Syrian economy. Also in 1980, Syria signed a twenty-year agreement with the Soviet Union for the supply of weapons. The economy worsened when a major drought struck Syria in 1989.

The 1990s began with a dispute with Turkey over Turkish hydro projects up-river on the Euphrates. The Turkish projects diminish the amount of water flow-

Table 1   Syria: Key Statistics

Type of government	Republic (under martial law since 1963)
Population (millions)	17.5 million (2002)
Religion	Sunni Muslim 74%; Alawi, Druze, and other Muslim sects 16%
Main industries	Petroleum, textiles
Main security threats	Conflict with Israel over Golan Heights, Syria's alleged support of terrorists, Lebanon, and conflict with Turkey over hydro projects on Euphrates
Defense spending (% GDP)	5.9% (2000)
Size of military (thousands)	319 (2002)
Number of civil wars since 1945	1
Number of interstate wars since 1945	5

Sources

Central Intelligence Agency Website. 2004. CIA *World Factbook*. http://www.cia.gov/cia/publications/factbook/ (accessed February 28, 2004).

International Institute for Strategic Studies (IISS). 2002. *The Military Balance 2002–2003*. London: IISS and Oxford University Press.

ing to the Syrian dam, reducing the amount of electricity and the amount of water for irrigation projects in Syria. This is an open point of dispute between the two nations today. Syria ended its years of isolation during the 1990s starting with the opposition of the Iraqi invasion of Kuwait. The active Syrian support against Iraq improved Syria's standing with Arab states and the Western powers. Following the Gulf War, Syria received increased foreign aid and investments that helped its struggling economy improve. Also during this time Syria began to de-emphasize socialism in the economy, allowing a small private sector and increased foreign investment. The improved relations with Arab neighbors and the West came at an ideal time for Syria, because they lost their primary international backer when the Soviet Union collapsed in 1991.

Syria is technically a republic under its current constitution, adopted March 13, 1973. Although the framework of democracy exists in Syria, the state has been under military control since 1963 when a state of emergency was declared based on the fear of Israel and terror threats (radicals, Iraqi, and Lebanese) (Bureau of Near Eastern Affairs 2004). Under the state of emergency, the government is able to oppress all challenges to its authority.

Syria has both a president and a prime minister. Bashar al-Assad was elected president in July 2000, replacing his father Hafiz al-Assad, who had been president since 1970 (see Sidebar 1). Although there are presidential elections every seven years, competition is limited by the ruling government, and in essence, Bashar al-Assad inherited the presidency. The president is given extensive power in Syria, including the right to appoint ministers, declare war, issue laws, and appoint civil-

ian and military officials, with only minor legislative checks. The current prime minister is Muhammed Naji al-Utri, elected September 2003. Syria has a unicameral legislative body, People's Council, with 250 members. The majority party is the National Progressive Front, which comprises various socialist and communist parties. However, the majority party

---

Sidebar 1   Bashar al-Assad

Bashar al-Assad, the current president of Syria, is the son of Hafiz al-Assad who died in 2000 after thirty years as dictator. The day after Hafiz's death, Bashar was nominated as the sole candidate for the presidency at the age of thirty-four. After the nomination, a constitutional amendment was passed lowering the minimum age requirement of the presidency from forty to thirty-four. In July 2000, Bashar received 97.29 percent of all votes and was elected president of Syria.

Bashar specialized in ophthalmology at the Tishrin Military Hospital in Damascus and pursued further study in London until his brother Basil, who was to take power, died in 1994. Bashar raised the hopes for liberalization in Syria at his succession due to his passion for the freedom of expression and his campaign against corruption. But, as of 2004, political and economic reforms have gone nowhere, and Syria remains where Hafiz left it.

Sources
Bureau of Near Eastern Affairs, United States Department of State. 2004. *Background Note: Syria.* July 23. http://www.state.gov/r/pa/ei/bgn/3580.htm (accessed May 14, 2005).
Simon, Steven, and Jonathan Stevenson. 2004. "The Road to Damascus." *Foreign Affairs* 83, no. 3:110–118.

of the National Progressive Front, and the ruling party of Syria, is the Baath Party. The constitution has institutionalized Baath leadership and made Syria a single-party state, while at the same time maintaining a facade of party competition.

Although the government of Syria stresses nationalism and unity, striving for what they call secular Arabism, religion plays an important part in everyday affairs (Bureau of Near Eastern Affairs 2004). Even though there is no official religion, the constitution does state that the president must be a Muslim. The judicial system is established upon Muslim principles, but minority religions maintain their own courts. In Syria, Sunni Muslims comprise the vast majority, about 74 percent. Alawis are the next-largest group; they are a Shiite sect believing in divine incarnation and the divinity of Ali, which makes them heretics in the Muslim world. Although the Alawi are a small minority compared with the Sunni, they hold most of the powerful positions in government and the military, with their most powerful member being President Assad. The Christian population is the second-largest religious minority in Syria, about 10 percent, with the majority of these being orthodox. Druze, who mix elements of Shiite, Christian, and pagan beliefs, are the third-largest religious minority. The rest of the population are either Shiite or Arabic Jews (Collelo 1988, 84–100; CIA *World Factbook*). Despite the religious diversity in Syria, there are few religious clashes, because the religious groups tend to be geographically concentrated and the government stresses Arabism over internal divisions.

Syria has a population of just over 17.5 million (2002) with a growth rate of about 3 percent a year. Just over 90 percent are ethnically Arab, with the rest mainly being Kurdish. State-run schools educate most children in Syria, because the government seized private religious schools, but even with this heavy national government involvement in education, the literacy rate in Syria is only 76.9 percent (CIA *World Factbook*). As population growth continues to outpace economic growth, this number will not improve in the near future.

Although the Syrian economy benefits from its position along trade routes, it has not performed well. Its average growth rate was slightly above 2.5 percent during the 1980s, reaching a high mark of 3.6 percent in 2002. However, the recent war in Iraq and the "War on Terrorism" are expected to drive the growth rate back down (CIA *World Factbook*). Economic development in Syria has been hampered by state ownership of most industries, a drain of resources to the conflict with Israel and the occupation of Lebanon, and rapid population growth. Further, Syria's support of Iran in the Iran-Iraq War harmed its export business, particularly with its neighbors who support Iraq. However, Syria's support of the UN coalition against Iraq in 1991 brought back many of its trade opportunities and enhanced trade and investment ties with western Europe. Syria's main industries are petroleum, textiles, and food processing. Exporting petroleum is one of Syria's largest income sources, providing approximately $3 billion annually. Syria also has a large amount of hydroelectrical power from stations on the Euphrates River; however, as indicated previously, production has been limited by Turkish hydro projects upriver. The long-term growth of the Syrian economy is limited by the availability of water, which is aggravated by rapid population growth and water pollution (CIA *World Factbook*). The Syrian economy also struggles under an international debt of an estimated $16 billion; its largest creditors are Russia, Iran, and the World Bank. This massive debt limits Syria's ability to borrow money in order to modernize equipment or conduct needed civil projects to help improve economic growth.

Regional Geopolitics

In modern times the term "Middle East" has become synonymous with conflict and uncertainty. Although positive steps have been taken lately, the Middle East will continue to be an unstable region where military conflict could erupt on short notice.

The two major sources of conflict and instability in the region are the Israel-Palestinian dispute and the continued internal fighting after the fall of Iraq to U.S. forces. The Israel-Palestinian dispute continues to escalate, and there seems to be little hope of a quick end to the second *Intifada* that started in 2000. With most Arab countries supporting the Palestinians, this conflict is always at risk of widening. Attacks from terrorist groups based in Lebanon and Israeli retaliations are prime examples of this point. The conflict over the final settlement between Israel and the Palestinians could widen to include any number of groups and states. Although open war between Israel and its neighbors is slight, the use of state-sponsored terrorist groups as proxies threatens regional stability.

The second major concern is the internal fighting that continues in Iraq after the fall of Saddam Hussein. Although the fighting in Iraq has not spread to bordering states, it is a constant fear. If a long-term conflict establishes itself in Iraq, it could be a major challenge for regional peace, especially given the fact that Iraq borders many key states in the region, Iran, Syria, and Saudi Arabia, to name a few. If Iraq descends into anarchy, similar to Lebanon in the 1970s and 1980s, the results could be disastrous for the region. If, on the other hand, Iraq can be pacified and a civilian Iraqi government established, Iraq could serve as a regional anchor for peace and democratization in the region.

Relations between the United States and regional states could also play an important role in the prospects for war or peace in the region. The current U.S.-Iranian standoff over possible nuclear weapons production by Iran could serve to increase tensions and the possibility of another U.S.-led war in the Middle East. This possibility seems remote, especially given recent moderate steps taken by Iran ("Is a Pax Americana . . ." 2004, 1). However, if Iran adopts more hard-line policies, U.S.-Iranian relations could lead to increased regional discord or conflict. U.S.-Syrian relations are also a possible source of instability and conflict in the region. Although Syria was careful to not openly back Iraq during recent fighting, there is concern that there were clandestine shipments of weapons of mass destruction from Iraq to Syria before the U.S. invasion. Further, Syria has a long history of supporting terrorism, which could lead to conflict. However, recent moves by Syria to reduce tensions with the United States and their recent suggestion to reinitiate talks with Israel are good signs.

A final concern for the region is the continued high, and increasing, levels of spending on arms. Most states in the region, including all the major nations, have continued to build up their domestic arsenals. Egypt, Syria, Israel, and Iran have all implemented large increases in spending, with Iran seeing a 26 percent increase in 2001 (SIPRI 2002, 247). Much of the recent spending spree can be attributed to higher oil prices, allowing the oil-producing states to increase state budgets, with the military being the beneficiaries of these increases. Along with increasing the size of forces in the region, recent spending has been used for improving (modernizing) the forces the states have at their disposal (see International Institute for Strategic Studies 2002, 283–286 for recent acquisitions). If the recent arms-racing behavior is not checked, it could lead directly to regional instability and conflict, as states become more apprehensive about the power their neighbors possess.

Conflict Past and Present

Conflict History

Syria's history has been marked with almost constant fighting, either external or internal. Two years after independence Syria invaded the new state of Israel along with Egyptian, Lebanese, Iraqi, Transjordanian, and Palestinian forces. The Syrian-led and -supported Liberation army conducted most of the combat operations carried out by Syrian forces. The Liberation army was an irregular fighting force drawn from multiple nationalities, but all of the officers came from the Syrian army (Ma'oz 1995, 17–18). This force was hastily assembled before the war and was not well equipped, which limited its effectiveness. Troops from the regular Syrian army did conduct limited operations, mainly in the north of Israel, but these were minor engagements. Although Syria only lost 1,000 men in the war, the performance of the army proved to be a major disappointment. Along with poor training, supplies, and intelli-

gence (Mo'az 1995, 19), the army suffered from poor leadership. Army officers at the time owed their promotions to Baath Party loyalty instead of merit (Keegan 1979, 687); thus, they were not well trained in tactics and could not lead their men effectively. The Arab armies were also constrained by infighting.

The years following the 1948 war were often violent, both within Syria and with its neighbors. Although open war was avoided, the 1950s were marked with militarized disputes with most of Syria's neighbors. In the early 1950s the focus was Israel and threats to use force (and low-level uses of force on the border). However, starting in 1955 Syrian relations with Turkey began to deteriorate, and there were often border skirmishes, some of which became intense. Syria also had minor disputes with Iraq and Jordan during this time. Starting in the early 1960s, Syria also began to have militarized disputes with Lebanon, as well as continued disputes with Turkey and Jordan (Sarkees 2000).

Clashes between Israel and Syria intensified during the 1960s, with each attacking targets inside the other state's borders. In April 1967 Syrian and Israeli air forces fought a lopsided battle in which Syria lost six MiG fighters without destroying any Israeli craft (OnWar.com). Syria feared that Israel would follow up this victory with a ground assault and began a military buildup. Egypt also began a military buildup in the Sinai and ordered that United Nations (UN) forces be removed from Egyptian territory (Stoessinger 2001, 167). Jordan and Iraq later joined Egypt and Syria in a military alliance. After ordering the UN forces out, Gamal Nasser placed a blockade on shipping in the Strait of Tiran, which was Israel's link to sea trade. On June 5 Israel preemptively struck the

Arab armies arrayed against them, driving the Arab armies back on three different fronts. The Israeli strike was led by air attacks that destroyed most of the Arab airpower, including fifty Syrian craft (OnWar.com). The air attacks were followed by a ground invasion, and without air support the Arab armies were crushed, including the Syrian forces. As they did in the 1948 war, the Syrian army performed poorly, again owing to limited equipment and poor leadership. In some cases soldiers fought hard only to be abandoned by their officers (Keegan 1979, 687).

Syria's next military engagement came in 1970, aimed at its Arab neighbor, Jordan. For many years pressure had been building in Jordan between the Palestinian Liberation Organization (PLO) fighters (fedayeen) and the government of Jordon under King Hussein. The PLO had become so strong inside of Jordan that they almost composed a separate state there. The PLO began operations to remove Hussein, including an attempted assassination (Collelo 1988, 241). In August 1970 Hussein began an offensive to remove the PLO influence from Jordan, which culminated in heavy fighting in September. With the PLO in a perilous position, Syria sent a division of troops, including 200 tanks, to intervene on behalf of the PLO (OnWar.com). However, opinion inside of Syria was split over the intervention, causing the Syrian troops to go into battle without air support. The Syrian division was badly beaten and soon retreated with 3,000 dead and more than half of its tanks destroyed.

Yom Kippur 1973 was the next major action for the Syrian army. Failure to resolve the issue of captured territory from the 1967 war was the direct cause of the Yom Kippur War. Syria and Egypt launched a surprise attack to win back the disputed territory on an overly confident Israeli army (Trautman). Although Egypt attacked from the Sinai region, Syria swept into the Golan Heights, with a ten-to-one initial advantage (1,100 Syrian tanks to 157 for Israel) and initially won victory. Since the 1967 war Syria had expanded its forces and formed a professional, Soviet-trained officer corps. Syria had also improved the technology of its army, greatly aided by Soviet financing (Keegan 1979, 688–689). Both of these increased the effectiveness of the Syrian forces. However, four days later the tide had turned in favor of Israel, partially owing to the fact that Syria could not keep their troops supplied even with emergency Soviet aid, and the Syrian forces were beaten back by repeated counterattacks (Trautman). Later, the Israeli army invaded Syria and surrounded the Egyptian Third Army in Sinai, which brought the superpowers in to stop the fighting. When the fighting stopped, Syria had lost 5,000 men and more than 800 tanks had been destroyed (Keegan 1979, 688–689). Although these losses were severe for Syria, Soviet aid quickly replaced them, allowing Syria to conduct a low-scale war of attrition with Israel in the Golan region through 1974.

For the next several years the Syrian army was not engaged in any major battles. However, they were involved in border disputes with Iraq in 1975–1976. In 1976 the Syrian army moved into Lebanon, beginning a long-term military commitment. Syria had long had an interest in Lebanon, wanting to bring territory lost during the French colonial period back under Syrian control. Further, Syria had long-standing economic and military interest in Lebanon. In 1975 fighting broke out between Palestinian forces in Lebanon and Christian Militiamen, eventually evolving into open civil war. Syria quickly intervened to try to end the fight through diplomacy. Although they were negotiating with both sides, they were supplying the PLO forces with arms and ammunition (Avi-Ran 1991, 19). As fighting intensified, Syria became more engaged and negotiated an agreement that would provide Muslims in Lebanon with increased political power. They also sent troops to back the PLO and their leftist allies in Lebanon. Finally, in July 1976, Syria switched sides, as the PLO and its allies rejected the Syrian-supported settlement. Syria began coordinated attacks with Christian Militia forces and defeated the PLO and their allies (Avi-Ran 1991, 23). Even though the Syrian forces did not initially fare well in the fighting (Keegan 1979, 689), they did manage to marshal their forces and gain dominance in Lebanon.

Since the end of the civil war Syria has maintained a large troop presence in Lebanon and has control over most of the country. However, fighting did not stop, and the Syrian forces in Lebanon (about 30,000) have been the targets of attacks by various groups, including Christian Militias and Arabs who want Syria out of Lebanon. The Syrians were unable to crush the Christian Militias because of U.S. and Israeli backing of these groups. The continued fighting has been a substantial drain on Syria's military and economic resources. In 1989 an agreement was reached between the major powers in Lebanon and Syria regarding the governance of Lebanon and a Syrian withdrawal. The Taif Agreement maintained Christian rule in Lebanon but provided increased power for Muslims; it also called for Syria to redeploy their troops toward the Bekaa (Al Biqa) Valley (Prados 2003, 4; Thorne 2004, 10) within two years. Following the completion of the

talks, General Michel Aoun, leader of the Lebanese Army Militia, refused to support the new government, wanting more power for Muslims in Lebanon. This led to a short but intense fight between his forces and Christian Militiamen backed by Syria (OnWar.com). When the time came Syria did not, however, remove or redeploy its troops, their main reason being that Israel maintained troops in the south of Lebanon. However, after the Israeli withdrawal, pressure increased on Syria to fulfill its agreement to withdraw both by the international community and by forces inside of Lebanon (Thorne 2004, 10). Recently, there has been some effort by Syria to remove or redeploy its troops; however, there are currently still between 15,000 and 20,000 Syrian soldiers in Lebanon and outside of the Bekaa Valley (Prados 2003, 4; Thorne 2004, 10).

Along with the occupation of Lebanon, Syria has had continued militarized disputes with many of its neighbors through the 1980s, 1990s, and into the new century. Iraq and Syria have engaged in military posturing along their borders as the two rival Baath parties struggled for dominance (Iraq was governed by a faction of the Baath Party until the fall of Saddam Hussein in 2003). Syria has also engaged in disputes with Jordan and Turkey over boundaries and access to water. These disputes have often broken into local fighting, particularly in the early 1990s, when Syria fought engagements against both Jordan and Iraq (Sarkees 2000). Syria also deployed a small force joining the U.S.-led liberation of Kuwait during the Gulf War. Although Syria has often fought with its Arab neighbors, the majority of its military activity has been directed against Israel. Border clashes have taken place frequently between the two states (at least one a year since 1993), particularly along areas they both hold in Lebanon. As recently as October 2003, Israeli warplanes attacked targets south of Damascus, claiming they were terrorist training centers responsible for attacks inside of Israel. Also during the U.S.-led war against Iraq, Syrian forces were mobilized toward their border with Iraq to provide security. So although the Syrian army has not been engaged in an open war since 1973 (Yom Kippur), the army has been in frequent engagements with neighbors and deployed in force in Lebanon.

Although Syria has experienced many coups, only one true civil war has occurred since its independence. Starting around 1965, Sunni fundamentalists began to resist Alawi domination of the government. Even though there were different factions involved in this effort, the group was collectively named the Muslim Brotherhood. Starting in the early 1980s, conflict increased dramatically and President Assad viewed the brotherhood as a threat, especially since they received aid from Jordan. During this time the Muslim Brotherhood attacked regime members, killing hundreds of midlevel party members, members of the security forces, and Soviet advisers in Syria. In 1980 there was a full-scale insurgency in the city of Aleppo put down by government forces. In 1982 the Muslim Brotherhood staged another revolt in Hama. This uprising was crushed by the military, with part of the city leveled and 10,000 to 25,000 people killed. This uprising led to the outlawing of the Muslim Brotherhood and increased activity by the government to destroy the organization, resulting in several hundred more deaths. In 1985 the Muslim Brotherhood staged its final revolt, again seizing part of Hama. The army responded with troops, tanks, and artillery, destroying large parts of the town. In the end, another 10,000 to 25,000 people were killed, including around 1,000 soldiers (OnWar.com).

Current and Potential Military Confrontation

At this time there is little chance of Syria starting a large-scale conflict with any of its neighbors. Troop commitments in Lebanon comprise a large part of their army and would need to be redeployed before any large action could take place. Even though there is little chance of Syria starting an engagement, there are four sources of potential conflict. First, although Syria has recently showed interest in reopening negotiations with Israel, there is always danger of increased fighting along the border. If Syria allows Hezbollah to start high-scale operations against Israel again, the probability of a Syrian-Israeli conflict will increase. The probability of an all-out war is slim at this point, given the Israeli military advantage. However, if peace talks do not start, or break down, continued border conflict is likely.

The second source of potential conflict is Lebanon. Lebanese opinion has turned against continued Syrian occupation, especially on such a large scale (Thorne 2004, 10). There have been attacks by groups inside of Lebanon wanting Syria out, and if Syria refuses to leave, there is a high probability of more attacks on Syrian targets.

A third potential source of conflict is instability in Iraq. If Iraq falls into anarchy, especially after a U.S. pullout, there is a strong chance that conflict could cross the border into Syria.

The final source of potential conflict comes from the United States as related to Syrian ties to terrorist groups. As discussed elsewhere in this entry, Syria is known to have connections with many terrorist groups, which makes Syria a possible target in the "War on Terrorism." The concern over weapons of mass destruction (WMD) having been shipped to Syria from Iraq during the recent war does not help matters. Overall there is a low probability of U.S. Syrian conflict over this issue taking place. Syria has taken steps to limit the activity of Hezbollah, and an invasion of Syria would strain U.S. forces, which are already spread thin. However, if Syria does not limit its contact with terrorist groups or is found to be supporting attacks against U.S. interests, there is a possibility of a minor conflict, most likely a U.S. bombing campaign. The most likely outcome would be an accommodation between Syria and the United States, especially if Syria and Israel can come to peace.

Alliance Structure

After gaining independence in 1945, Syria joined other Arab states in the war against Israel (1948–1949) as a member of the League of Arab States. In 1955, Syria, with Egypt, entered into an alliance with the Soviet Union, partly to balance the British-led Baghdad Pact that included Iraq, Iran, Turkey, and Pakistan. Syria also briefly joined with Egypt to form the UAR from 1958 to 1961.

During the 1970s and 1980s, Syria tightened its relationship with the Soviet Union. Before the 1970s, Egypt was the primary ally of the Soviets in the Middle East. Once Anwar Sadat came to power in Egypt, however, Egyptian-Soviet relations became hostile. At this point, Syria became the primary ally of the Soviets in the Middle East (Quilliam 1999, 127).

Syria received most of its arms from the Soviet Union, and there was a large Soviet military presence in Syria until the late 1980s. In 1980, Syria signed the Treaty of Friendship and Cooperation with the Soviet Union, which formalized the relations (Collelo 1988). Syria, however, was not a Soviet proxy, and the Syrian leaders had little affinity with communism. The relationship was based on the strategic value each state lent to the other (Quilliam 1999, 128).

The rapprochement between the Soviets and the United States, and the collapse of the Soviet Union, drastically changed Syrian foreign policy. Syria turned to the Gulf Arab states and Egypt when the Soviet Union recognized the state of Israel and started to reduce military and economic supports to Syria. In 1989, Syria ended its opposition to Egypt and reestablished full diplomatic relations with it. In 1990–1991, Syria joined other Arab states in the U.S-led coalition against Iraq.

In the region, Syria essentially engaged in geopolitical balancing (Hinnebusch 2003, 213). Syria continues to maintain a close relationship with Iran, because Syria supported Iran during the Iran-Iraq War. Iraq, under Saddam Hussein, was a major rival for regional leadership and a potential military threat. Syria supported Iran in the hope of Iraq being weakened, despite the fact that there was no ideological affinity between Syria and Iran's Islamic fundamentalism, which most Gulf Arab states fear. This policy toward Iran, however, isolated Syria in the region, because most of the Gulf Arab states supported Iraq. In 1990, the Gulf War provided a great opportunity for Syria to escape the isolation. It was Syria's chance not only to cut Iraq down but also to reestablish its relations with other Gulf Arab states and the United States in the post-Soviet era (Rubin 2002, 99). Subsequently, Syria joined the other Arab states in the U.S.-led coalition against Iraq in 1990–1991.

From the late 1990s, however, Syria improved its relations with Iraq for "strategic rent" that provided Syria with cheap oil and an ally for Iraq in the region (Simon and Stevenson 2004, 113). Syria has established diplomatic relations and expanded trade relations with Iraq since 1997. Although bilateral trade ended in 2003, it was near $1 billion in 2001. The relations with Turkey also improved when Syria agreed to expel leaders of a dissident Turkish group, the Kurdistan Labor Party (PKK), in 1998. Syria's trade with Turkey increased from almost nothing to $1 billion in 2001 (Prados 2002, 5). In 2004, Bashar al-Assad made an official visit to Turkey. It was the first time in history for Syria's head of state to visit Turkey officially.

As of 2003, Syria has once again become relatively isolated, because its self-proclaimed role as the vanguard of Arab nationalism lost support owing to the U.S. intrusion into the Middle East and the fracturing of Arab alliances. Syria is a member of several international organizations, including the League of Arab States and the Organization of the Islamic Conference (OIC). Syria also served as a nonpermanent member of the UN Security Council from 2001 to 2003.

Size and Structure of the Military
Size and Structure
Syria maintained approximately 400,000 active troops throughout the 1980s and 1990s. As of 2002, Syrian armed forces totaled 319,000 with 354,000 reservists (IISS, 2002). Syrian command structure is

headed by the president, who is the supreme commander of the armed forces. The deputy prime minister acts as minister of defense and deputy commander-in-chief of the armed forces.

The army is the dominant force in Syria with the majority of military manpower, approximately 215,000 regulars, and is better equipped than the air force and navy. As of 2003, the Syrian army has seven armored divisions, and each has three armored brigades, one mechanized brigade, and one artillery regiment. In general, a division has around 8,000 men, and each armored brigade has around ninety-three main battle tanks and thirty other armored fighting vehicles. The Syrian army also has three mechanized divisions; each division has two armored brigades, two mechanized brigades, and one artillery regiment. Each division typically has about 11,000 men, and a typical mechanized brigade has forty main battle tanks and ninety other fighting vehicles. In addition, there is one Republican Guard division, with three armored brigades, one mechanized brigade, and one artillery regiment (IISS 2002, 117).

Syria's army has a total of 4,700 Soviet-built tanks, including 1,700 relatively modern T-72s. In recent years, Syria's army has modernized its antitank weapons capability. It has 200 modern man-portable Milans, 150 modern AT-4 Spigots, and 200 AT-5 Sprandrel antitank guided weapons with third-generation guidance systems. Syria also has 480 multiple rocket launchers (MRL), including 200 Type 63 107-mm Chinese weapons and 280 BM-21 Soviet bloc weapons (IISS 2002, 118; Cordesman 2002, 99). Syria also has a missile program obtaining FROG 7s in 1972 and the Scud B missile as early as 1974. As of 2002, Syria had a force of 18 FROG-7, 18 SS-21, and 26 Scud B and Scud C surface-to-surface missile units (Shoham 2002; IISS 2002, 118).

The Syrian air force is generally divided into an air force and Air Defense command. The air force has about 40,000 men and 611 combat aircraft. In general, Syria has been unable to modernize its combat aircraft. According to the International Institute for Strategic Studies (IISS), Syria only has 20 Su-24s and 20 MiG-29s as truly modern fighters (2002, 118). Most are MiG-21 and MiG-23 fighters that have limited air-to-air combat capability. Syrian Air Defense Command has 60,000 personnel separate from the air force. The Air Defense Command, however, has a large number of old Soviet-bloc systems, including SA-2s, SA-3s, SA-5s, SA-6s, and SA-8s. Syria is trying to modernize its system to include modern heavy surface-to-air missile systems such as the U.S. Patriots and Russia's S-300 or S-400 systems (Cordesman 2002, 129). As of 2002, the S-300 system has been on order. Syria also maintains a small 4,000-man navy. Syria's principal surface ships include two Petya III class frigates that are equipped with torpedo tubes and rocket launchers (IISS 2002, 118). The primary mission of the navy is the defense of Syria's ports at Lattakia and Tartus, coastal surveillance, and defense (Cordesman 2002, 140).

In addition to conventional weapon systems, Syria reportedly has WMD capabilities. Syria has made considerable progress in acquiring WMDs since the 1970s. Syria considers WMDs, especially chemical weapons, as a way of countering Israel and as means of maintaining its relative status to regional rivals (Pincus 2003). Syria has not signed the Chemical Weapons Convention and reportedly has nerve gases like sarin and VX (Cordesman 2002, 545).

It is reported, however, that Syria remains dependent on external sources for key elements, including precursor chemicals and production equipment (Prados 2003, 9). On nuclear capability, Syria has one small Chinese-supplied thirty-kilowatt nuclear research reactor, which is under International Atomic Energy Agency (IAEA) safeguards (Cordesman 2002, 539). Syria is party to the Treaty of the Non-Proliferation of Nuclear Weapons (NPT).

About 25,000 to 35,000 Syrian army troops have been stationed in northeastern and central Lebanon since 1976. Syria's troop presence in Lebanon, however, has been reduced in recent years to 18,000 in 2002 (IISS 2002, 118). As of 2002, the United Nations Disengagement Observation Force (UNDOF) remains in the Golan Heights, which is a part of Syria. UNDOF was established after the 1973 Yom Kippur War to maintain the cease-fire between Israel and Syria and to supervise the disengagement of Israeli and Syrian forces. UNDOF has totaled 1,037 troops, including 363 from Austria, 189 from Canada, 30 from Japan, 357 from Poland, 97 from Slovakia, and 1 from Sweden (SIPRI 2002).

Budget
Syrian defense expenditures have shrunk from $5,266 million in constant 2000 U.S. dollars in 1985 to $1,884 million in 2001 and also from 16.2 percent of GDP in 1985 to 10.8 percent in 2001 (IISS 2002). Arms import also have shrunk drastically from $2,278 million in 1985 to around $70 million in 2000. During the Cold War, Syria was able to increase their arms owing to a combination of aid from the Gulf Arab states and arms from the Soviet Union and the Warsaw Pact. Yet the breakup of the Soviet Union, which was the principal source of credit for the Syrian military, has slowed Syria's ability

to improve its forces. As of 2001, debt to Russia was estimated as approaching $11 billion, and Russia effectively halted credit to Syria (Prados 2003, 9). Russia has also cut back on scheduled deliveries and has refused new orders that are not paid in cash because Syria has defaulted on past loans (Cordesman 2002, 337). Aid from Arab states is in a similar situation. Although Syria did receive aid in the amount of almost $1 billion at the time of the Gulf War, it has received little aid after 1991 from the Gulf Arab states.

Syria is currently experiencing continued military spending and arms import problems. As a consequence, Syria has had only limited improvement in its military equipment since 1990. Financial problems have forced Syria to make shifts in strategy and procurement efforts to emphasizing the procurement of long-range ballistic missiles and WMDs as a relatively low-cost means to offset regional rivals (Cordesman 2002, 346).

Civil-Military Relations/Role of the Military in Domestic Politics

The military has played an important role in the social and political history of Syria. After the declaration of independence in 1946, Syrian politics were marked by a series of coups, until 1970, when Hafiz al-Assad assumed power by a bloodless military coup. In 1949, General Husni al-Zaim's coup marked the first military intervention in politics in Syria, which was followed by the second coup, led by Sami al-Hinnawi five months later. After the coup, Hinnawi announced the military's retirement from politics and returned Syrian government to civilian control. In December 1949, however, Colonel Adib Shishakli committed the third coup by accusing Hinnawi of conspiring with

Iraq (Seale 1986, 86). Shishakli did not instantly assume full power after the overthrow of Hinnawi. It was after his second coup in 1951 that the military publicly assumed power. Shishakli exercised military dictatorship by banning all political parties and legislating by decree until February 1954 (Seale 1986, 118). Although there was fierce civilian opposition to dictatorship, it was once again the military that overthrew Shishakli. Upon coming to power, Shishakli attempted to restore the army to a normal position in order to legitimize his regime. He trimmed the military's privileges and powers, which was resented by most of the military officers outside his entourage (Seale 1986, 142). In the face of revolt, Shishakli left the country and resigned as president on February 25, 1954.

In September 1961, Syria again experienced a military coup by those who were unsatisfied with the UAR. Syria seceded from the UAR after the coup and reestablished itself as the Syrian Arab Republic. This coup brought out all the conflicts among the diverse political groups in Syria once again. From 1961 to 1970, Syria had several coups and countercoups among various political factions. In November 1970, however, Syria ended its history of coups when a former air force commander and then Defense Minister Hafiz al-Assad seized control through a bloodless military coup by ousting the civilian wing of the Baath Party. Hafiz al-Assad exercised uncontested authority through his control of the Baath Party, the armed forces, and the intelligence apparatus until he died in June 2000 (Prados 2003, 1). Bashar al-Assad, an eye doctor and colonel in the Syrian army, succeeded his father, Hafiz, in a smooth transfer of power in July 2000.

Since independence in 1949, the military has been the main political force in

Syria. Although Syria exhibits forms of a democratic system, the president has almost absolute authority, based on the army's loyalty. The president and his aides in the military and security services make most decisions in the government (Bureau of Near Eastern Affairs 2004). Except during the first three years of independence, the head of government has been a military officer. Syria has operated under martial law since 1963, which was justified by the state of war with Israel and the continuing threat posed by terrorist groups.

Terrorism

Attention to Syria's terrorist connection grew in the early to mid-1980s, and since then Syria has regularly appeared on the U.S. government's list of states sponsoring terrorism. Syria has not been directly implicated in a terrorist attack since Syrian intelligence aided a failed effort to bomb an El Al plane (Israeli Airlines) in 1986. However, Syria does provide financial and material support to many terrorist organizations, including Ahmad Jibril's Popular Front for the Liberation of Palestine—General Command, Palestine Islamic Jihad, Abu Musa's Fatah-the-Intifada, George Habash's Popular Front for the Liberation of Palestine, Hamas (Islamic Resistance Movement), and Hezbollah (see Sidebar 2) (U.S. Department of State 2002). Syria allows many of these groups to maintain offices in Damascus, which Syria claims are for political activities only, and Syria allows Iranian supplies and weapons to cross its border to Hezbollah forces (Prados 2003, 10). Further, Syria allows training bases on its soil and in areas it controls in Lebanon, particularly the Bekaa Valley region. However, Syria claims that it does not

aid any terrorist groups, claiming that Hezbollah and other groups offer legitimate resistance against Israel.

Of these groups, Syria has the strongest link and the most control over Hezbollah, which Syria provides with free rein over sections of Lebanon, disarming rival factions, along with weapons and logistical support. Syria has great influence with Hezbollah and can veto attacks by

---

Sidebar 2　Hezbollah—Party of God

While 9-11 has focused attention on al-Qaeda, many terror experts feel Hezbollah is the true terror threat in the world today. Founded in 1982 after the Israeli invasion of Lebanon, Hezbollah has three primary objectives: the destruction of Israel, the liberation of Jerusalem, and the establishment of an Islamic state in Lebanon. To achieve these goals Hezbollah employs terror tactics such as kidnappings, bombings, and highjackings, along with more direct military engagements with the Israeli army.

Along with attacks on Israel, Hezbollah is responsible for bombing the U.S. Marine barracks in Beirut, highjacking TWA Flight 847, and the 1996 Khobar Towers bombing. Along with its terror activities, Hezbollah is active in the social and political life of Lebanon, running schools and hospitals and holding twelve seats in Lebanon's parliament. These political and social activities provide Hezbollah with a degree of legitimacy and a large pool of supporters that relies upon the services that Hezbollah provides.

Source
Byman, Daniel. 2003. "Should Hezbollah Be Next?" *Foreign Affairs* 82, no. 6:54–66.

the group and employ them in attacks to forward Syrian policy (Byman 2003, 61). Prior to the September 11, 2001, attacks on the United States, Hezbollah was responsible for more American deaths than any other terrorist group. Some of their major attacks include: the 1983 bombing of the marine barracks in Beirut, the hijacking of TWA Flight 847 in 1985, the 1992 bombing of the Israeli Embassy in Argentina, and the capture of three Israeli soldiers and the kidnapping of one civilian in 2000 (U.S. Department of State 2002). In recent years Syria has restrained Hezbollah activities, particularly attacks aimed at the United States. Specifically, Hezbollah has not targeted the United States directly since the 1996 bombing of the Khobar Towers, in which the group played some part. The relationship between Syria and Hezbollah is Syria's closest tie to terrorism and causes strained relations with many other states.

Syria has maintained a long-standing policy of not allowing strikes against Western targets to originate from inside Syria's borders. Syria has been seen as aiding the global "War on Terrorism" by providing information on al-Qaeda operatives and operations repeatedly over the past several years. Syria views al-Qaeda as a threat to its security, specifically because of the religious beliefs of al-Qaeda's leaders. Syria also expelled a Kurdish terrorist group (the PKK) after an agreement with Turkey not to support attacks against it. Support for the war against al-Qaeda has not weakened Syria's support for other terrorist groups, such as Hezbollah.

Along with being a sponsor of terrorism, Syria is occasionally the target of terrorist attacks. Most of these attacks originate in Lebanon and are aimed at removing Syrian forces and influence from Lebanon. Although some of these attacks have taken place inside of Syria, most are targeted at Syrian forces inside of Lebanon.

Relationship with the United States

Although the United States and Syria have worked together in areas of mutual interests in recent years, Syria continues to have serious differences with the United States in areas such as international terrorism, WMDs, and human rights. The United States and Syria resumed their relationship in 1974, which had been severed after the Arab-Israeli War in 1967, following the success of the Syrian-Israeli disengagement agreement. In December 1984, however, the two nations engaged in near warfare, which marked the first U.S.-Syrian armed conflict. In 1986, the United States withdrew its ambassador to Syria for a year in response to Syria's involvement in international terrorism (Collelo 1988).

During the 1990s, the relationship warmed somewhat. During the late 1980s, Syria's international ally, the Soviet Union, started to signal its plan to normalize relations with Israel and to stop supporting Syria politically and militarily (Seale and Butler 1996, 32). Syria's relationship with the Soviet Union was based on Syria's intention to counterweight the U.S.-Israeli relationship, whereas the Soviets wanted to limit U.S. influence in the region (Seale and Butler 1996, 33). When the Soviet Union collapsed in 1990–1991, Syria approached the United States to improve relations. Syria participated in the U.S.-led UN coalition in the Gulf War by dispatching 18,000 troops and 300 tanks (Abrahms 2003). Syria also participated in the several U.S.-sponsored bilateral peace talks with Israel. The relations improved further when Syria made efforts to secure the release of Western hostages held in

Lebanon and its lifting travel restrictions and real estate control on the Syrian Jewish community in 1992.

After September 11, 2001, Syria generally condemned the terrorist attacks on civilians and vital centers in the United States. Yet the United States and Syria disagree on organizations such as Hezbollah, which is described as a terrorist organization by the United States. Syria continues to argue that there is a distinction between terrorism and resistance to foreign occupation (Prados 2002, 9). Syria also disagreed with the United States on the war against Iraq in 2003. As a non-permanent member of the UN Security Council, Syria expressed opposition to the use of military force against Iraq while urging Iraq to comply with UN Security Council resolutions. After the United States and its allies launched Operation Iraqi Freedom on March 19, 2003, Syria called for withdrawal of foreign occupation forces as soon as possible from Iraqi territory.

From 1950 to 1979, the United States has provided a total of $627.5 million in aid to Syria, including $34 million in development assistance, $438 million in economic support, $155.4 million in food assistance, and $61,000 in military training assistance (Prados 2002, 11). Since 1981, however, the United States has provided no aid to Syria owing to a variety of legislative provisions and executive directives that prohibit U.S. aid to Syria and restrict bilateral trade (see Table 2). Syria has been on the U.S. list of state sponsors of terrorism since the list's inception in 1979 and subject to penalties, including export sanctions and ineligibility to receive U.S. aid. As of 2003, the Department of Commerce lists thirty-one categories of exports requiring a validated license for shipment to Syria, including most vehicles, computer equipment, and other high-technology goods (Prados 2003, 14).

The United States imported $112.4 million worth of goods, mainly mineral oils and fuels, apparel, and spices from Syria in 2002, and exported $219 million, mainly cereals, appliances, and tobacco. As of 2001, Syria owed the United States $237.8 million, mainly in loans from the U.S Agency for International Development remaining from the time when Syria received U.S. aid, and $138.8 million of interest in arrears (Prados 2003, 14).

Table 2   U.S Legislation with Sanctions Applicable to Syria

The International Security Assistance and Arms Export Control Act of 1976
The Export Administration Act of 1979
The Omnibus Budget Reconciliation Act of 1986
The Omnibus Diplomatic Security and Antiterrorism Act of 1986
The Anti-Terrorism and Arms Export Control Amendments Act of 1989
The Anti-Economic Discrimination Act of 1994
The Antiterrorism and Effective Death Penalty Act of 1996
The Consolidated Appropriations Act of 2003
The Syria Accountability and Lebanese Sovereignty Restoration Act of 2003

Sources

Prados, Alfred B. 2002. *Syria: U.S. Relations and Bilateral Issues.* Washington DC: Congressional Research Service.

———. 2003. *Syria: U.S. Relations and Bilateral Issues.* Washington DC: Congressional Research Service.

As of 2003, Syria maintains an unfriendly relationship with the United States. Since April 2003, the United States has warned Syria repeatedly to withdraw support of terrorism and resistance from Iraq ("From Baghdad to Damascus" 2003). In October 2003, Israeli aircraft attacked near the Syrian capital, Damascus, which was Israel's first direct attack on Syria since the war of 1973 as they reacted to a Palestinian suicide bomb. The Bush administration endorsed Israel's right to self-defense and called for restraint on all sides but reiterated previous warnings to Syria to cease support of terrorist organizations and other activities that are in discord with U.S. interests (Myre 2003). In 1973, former president of Syria Hafiz al-Assad said to Henry Kissinger that "there can be no peace in the Middle East without Syria." The United States also recognizes the importance of Syria in Middle Eastern politics, but the debate continues within the current U.S. administration and Congress over the best way to obtain Syrian cooperation in Middle Eastern affairs (Prados 2003, 16).

The Future

Syria is at a crossroads regarding its security. Recent attempts to restart negotiations with Israel, if fruitful, would eliminate the largest security risk Syria faces. If a long-term peace agreement could be reached, the likelihood of Syria being involved in a major military conflict within the next ten years would be greatly reduced. Failure to reach such an agreement would mean a continuation of the sporadic confrontation between the two states. Syria is also at an important juncture regarding its support of terrorism. If Syria maintains its support of terrorist organizations, such as Hezbollah, they could find themselves as a target in the "War on Terrorism." However, Syria's recent actions make this possibility slim.

The military in Syria will not be significantly reduced, and its budget will not be cut in the near future. Syria will continue its attempts to upgrade its military equipment by procuring modern technology from Russia and the West. Because most of their current equipment is Russian made, it is critical that Syria be able to gain access to more Russian-made equipment to avoid compatibility problems in their weapons systems. However, the excessive amount of debt Syria already owes Russia has limited their ability to make new purchases. In 1999 Syria began talks with Russia to arrange for the sale of advanced weapons systems, but the status of these sales is still unclear (Cordesman 2002, 348). Further, slow, or negative, growth in the Syrian economy represents a significant liability to its modernization.

References, Recommended Readings, and Websites

Books

Avi-Ran, Reuven. 1991. *The Syrian Involvement in Lebanon since 1975.* Boulder, CO: Westview.

Collelo, Thomas, ed. 1988. *Syria: A Country Study.* Washington, DC: U.S. Government Printing Office.

Cordesman, Anthony H. 2002. *Peace and War: The Arab-Israeli Military Balance Enters the 21st Century.* Westport, CT: Praeger.

Devlin, John F. 1983. *Syria: Modern State in an Ancient Land.* Boulder, CO: Westview.

Hinnebusch, Raymond. 2003. *The International Politics of the Middle East.* Manchester, UK: Manchester University Press.

International Institute for Strategic Studies (IISS). 2002. *The Military Balance 2002–2003.* London: IISS and Oxford University Press.

Kalawoun, Nasser M. 2000. *The Struggle for Lebanon: A Modern History of Lebanese-Egyptian Relations.* London: I. B. Tauris.

Keegan, John. 1979. *World Armies.* New York: Facts on File.

Kienle, Eberhard. 1990. *Ba'th v. Ba'th: The Conflict between Syria and Iraq 1968–1989.* London: I. B. Tauris.

Ma'oz, Moshe. 1995. *Syria and Israel: From War to Peacemaking.* Oxford, UK: Clarendon Press.

Maoz, Zeev, ed. 1997. *Regional Security in the Middle East: Past Present and Future.* London: Frank Cass.

Quilliam, Neil. 1999. *Syria and the New World Order.* London: Garnet Publishing.

Rubin, Barry. 2002. *The Tragedy of the Middle East.* Cambridge: Cambridge University Press.

Seale, Patrick. 1986. *The Struggle for Syria: A Study of Post-War Arab Politics 1945–1958.* New Haven, CT: Yale University Press.

SIPRI. 2002. *SIPRI Yearbook 2002: Armaments, Disarmament and International Security.* Oxford, UK: Oxford University Press.

Stoessinger, John. 2001. *Why Nations Go to War.* Boston: Bedford-St. Martin's.

Articles/Newspapers

Abrahms, Max. 2003. "When Rogues Defy Reason: Bashar's Syria." *Middle East Quarterly* 10, no. 4, http://meforum.org/article/562 (accessed July 24, 2004).

Blanford, Nicholas. "In U.S. 'War on Terror,' Syria Is Foe—and Friend." http://www. csmonitor.com/2002/0514/p01s04-wome.html (accessed February 28, 2004).

Bureau of Near Eastern Affairs, United States Department of State. "Background Note: Syria." http://www.state.gov/www/background_notes/syria_0499_bgn.html (accessed February 28, 2004).

Byman, Daniel. 2003. "Should Hezbollah Be Next?" *Foreign Affairs* 82, no. 6:54–66.

CIA *World Factbook,* "Syria." http://www.cia.gov/cia/publications/factbook/goes/sy.html (accessed February 28, 2004).

"From Baghdad to Damascus." 2003. *Economist* 367, no. 8320:10.

Gibler, Douglas M., and Meredith Sarkees. 2004. "Measuring Alliances: The Correlates of War Formal Interstate Alliance Data Set, 1816–2000." *Journal of Peace Research* 41, no. 2:211–222.

Hosenball, Mark, Stefan Theil, and Rachel Thurneysen-Lukow. 2004. "The Syrian Connection." *Newsweek* 143, no. 4:36–37.

"Is a Pax Americana in the Offing?" 2004. *Economist* 370, no. 8358:38–39.

McKay, Jeff. "U.S. War on Terror May Spread to Syria, Report Says." http://www.cnsnews.com/ViewForeignBureaus.asp?Page=/ForeignBureaus/archive/200401/FOR20040123b.html (accesssed February 28, 2004).

Myre, Greg. 2003. "The Mideast Turmoil: The White House, Bush Tells Israel It Has the Right to Defend Itself." *New York Times,* October 7:A13.

OnWar.com. "Aoun Mutiny in Lebanon 1990."http://www.onwar.com/aced/nation /sat/syria/flebanon1990.htm (accessed February 28, 2004).

———. "Black September in Jordan 1970–1971." http://www.onwar.com /aced/nation/sat/syria/fblacksept1970.htm (accessed February 28, 2004).

———. "Muslim Brotherhood in Syria 1965–1985." http://www.onwar.com/aced/nation/sat/syria/fsyria1965.htm (accessed February 28, 2004).

———. "The Six Day War 1967" http://www.onwar.com/aced/nation/sat/syria/f6day1967.htm (accessed February 28, 2004).

———. "Yom Kippur War 1963" http://www.onwar.com/aced/nation/sat/syria/fyomkippur1973.htm (accessed February 28, 2004).

Pincus, Walter. 2003. "Syria Built Arsenal as 'Equalizer.'" *The Washington Post,* April 17:A30.

"Powell, Gul Discuss Cyprus, Iraq, Syria, Terrorism, Middle East," http://www.usembassy-israel.org.il/publish/press/2004/january/012904.html (accessed February 28, 2004).

Prados, Alfred B. 2002. *Syria: U.S. Relations and Bilateral Issues.* Washington DC: Congressional Research Service.

———. 2003. *Syria: U.S. Relations and Bilateral Issues.* Washington DC: Congressional Research Service.

Sarkees, Meredith Reid. 2000. "The Correlates of War Data on War: An Update to 1997." *Conflict Management and Peace Science* 18, no. 1:123–144.

Seale, Patrick, and Linda Butler. 1996. "Asad's Regional Strategy and the Challenge from Netanyahu." *Journal of Palestine Studies* 26, no. 1:27–41.

Shoham, Dany. 2002. "Poisoned Missiles: Syria's Doomsday Deterrent." *Middle East Quarterly* 9, no. 4. http//www. meforum.org/article/510 (accessed July 25, 2004).

Simon, Steven, and Jonathan Stevenson. 2004. "The Road to Damascus." *Foreign Affairs* 83, no. 3:110–118.

Thorne, John. 2004. "Lebanese Chafe under Syria's Quiet Occupation." *Christian Science Monitor*, January 8:10.

Trautman, Robin. "The Yum Kippur War 1973." http://campus.northpark.edu / history/Webchron/MiddleEast/ YomKippurWar.html (accessed February 28, 2004).

U.S. Department of State. 2002. "Patterns of Global Terrorism 2002." http://www. state.gov/s/ct/rls/pgtrpt/2002/pdf/ (accessed February 28, 2004).

Websites
Center for Middle East and Jewish Studies http://www.columbia.edu/cu/lweb/ indiv/mideast/cuvlm/Syria.html.

Central Intelligence Agency. *World Factbook*. http://www.cia.gov.

Constitution of Syria: http://www.oefre. unibe.ch/law/icl/sy00000_.htm.

Heads of State: http://www.terra.es/ personal2/monolith/syria.htm.

Syrian Embassy to the United States: http://www.syrianembassy.us/.

Syrian News: http://www.washingtonpost. com/wp-dyn/world/mideast/neareast/ syria/.

United States Embassy in Syria: http:// usembassy.state.gov/damascus/.

Taiwan

Hans Stockton

Geography and History

The jurisdiction of the Republic of China (ROC) has been restricted to the primary islands of Taiwan, Qinmen, Matsu, and Penghu since 1949. Although the republican government was founded in mainland China on January 12, 1912, communist Chinese forces forced it off the mainland by 1949. Since the founding of the People's Republic of China (PRC) on October 2, 1949, two governments have claimed sovereignty over the Chinese state: the PRC in Beijing and the ROC in Taipei. This feud has since periodically flared up to the point of military clashes, endangering regional security and trade and calling on the United States to threaten military intervention to preserve the peaceful status quo. Since 1949, there have been five crisis events of particular note.

The ROC has assumed the status of "quasi state" since it lost the China seat in the United Nations in 1971. As of the end of 2003, the ROC enjoys formal diplomatic relations with twenty-seven states: fourteen states in Latin America (Belize, Costa Rica, Dominica, Dominican Republic, El Salvador, Grenada, Guatemala, Haiti, Honduras, Nicaragua, Panama, Paraguay, St. Christopher and Nevis, and St. Vincent and the Grenadines), eight states in Africa (Burkina Faso, Chad, Gambia, Liberia, Malawi, São Tomé and Principe, Senegal, and Swaziland), four states in Oceania (Republic of the Marshall Islands, the Republic of Palau, the Solomon Islands, and Tuvalu), and an embassy in the Holy See.

The island of Taiwan, also known as Formosa, named by Portuguese sailors in the 1540s "*Ilha Formosa*" (Beautiful Island), is the smallest province of the Republic of China and the only province under the direct jurisdiction of the ROC government. It is located between 21 53'50" and 25 18'20"N latitude and 120 01'00" and 121' 5915:E longitude. At its widest and longest points, the island is 144 kilometers and 394 kilometers, respectively. Total landmass is equivalent to the U.S. states of Maryland and Delaware combined. Although encompassing a total of 36,000 square kilometers, approximately one-third of the island is mountainous. The western coastal region is at sea level or below. Taiwan's climate is oceanic and subtropical monsoon. Temperatures and rainfall are quite similar to that of the southeastern portion of the U.S. state of Texas.

Owing to Taiwan's topography, its 22.51 million inhabitants are concentrated in the western coastal counties. Although the national average population density is 622 people per square kilometer, portions of the western counties reach a density as high as 5,000 people per square kilometer. The most densely populated areas are the southern city of Kao-hsiung City (9,827 sq.

km) and the capital city, Taipei (9,720 sq. km). Taiwan's population growth rate dropped below 1 percent by the mid-1990s. This combined with increasing life span has presented Taiwan with demographic challenges similar to those faced by the industrialized economies of western Europe.

Upon the retreat of the republican government to Taiwan in 1949, ROC president Chiang Kai-shek continued single-party rule within a hard authoritarian regime. The regime party, the Nationalist Party (KMT), continued its claim of sovereignty over the entirety of China and promised to forcefully retake the mainland from the Chinese Communist Party (CCP). This claim remained vociferous through the 1970s, but has faded in the face of strategic and geopolitical realities.

During the 1950s and 1960s, the authoritarian police state was so severe that these decades are referred to as the White Terror. Upon his death in 1975, Chiang's son, Chiang Ching-kuo, ascended to the dual positions of KMT chairman and ROC president. He began a program of liberalization that was completed by his successor, Lee Teng-hui. Lee came to power in 1988 and won the ROC's first direct presidential election in 1996.

By 1992, Taiwan experienced democratic transition with its first legislative election (referred to as the renewal election) restricted to candidates representing a constituency in Taiwan. The second direct presidential election in 2000 is viewed as the point of consolidation. Former President Lee is responsible for setting the stage for Taiwan's consolidation, completed with the election of the country's first opposition party president, Chen Shui-bian, in 2000.

Political party affiliation on Taiwan (since liberalization) has been substantially determined by the key ethnic divide on the island. Those living on Taiwan before the 1949 KMT exodus from the mainland have been referred to as *bensheng ren* or "province born" people. Those arriving on Taiwan from the mainland in 1949 have been referred to as *waisheng ren* or "outside province born" people. Although originally greeted as liberators from Japanese rule, the arrival of KMT troops after World War II quickly

Table 1   Republic of China on Taiwan: Key Statistics

Type of government	Republic
Population (millions)	22.51 (2002)
Religion	Buddhist, Confucian, and Taoist 93%, Christian 4.5%, other 2.5%
Main industries	Electrical machinery/mechanical appliances (2002)
Main security threats	PRC threat of military force
Defense spending (% GDP)	2.16 (2002)
Size of military (thousands)	380 (2002)
Number of civil wars since 1945	1
Number of interstate wars since 1945	0

Sources
Central Intelligence Agency Website. 2003. CIA *World Factbook.* http://www.cia.gov/cia/publications/factbook/ (accessed May 15, 2005).
Government Information Office (ROC). 2003. *Republic of China Yearbook.* Los Angeles: Kwang Hwa Publishing.

turned to occupation. The arrival of more than 1 million mainland refugees and the mainland-oriented KMT regime created an enduring divide between the extant Taiwanese population and those having their immediate origins on the mainland. The KMT was criticized for decades for treating Taiwan with a "motel mentality" because the island was seen as only a temporary home for the ROC government until the mainland could be retaken. Development and state resources were devoted to creating a fortress of Taiwan from which to launch liberation of the mainland from the CCP. As well, the mainlander KMT elites that fled to the island dominated political power.

Those individuals retaining strong familial and cultural ties to the mainland tend to prefer unification between Taiwan and the mainland. In 2003, this group composed about 10 percent of the island's population. Those identifying as "Taiwanese" or expressing an identification as "both Chinese and Taiwanese" generally divide the remainder of the population. Such statistics are important for Taiwan's security because the ever-growing move away from Chinese identification has emboldened political elites to also distance themselves from an outright policy of unification. Such "foot dragging" frequently prompts bellicose statements from Beijing.

With the onset of the Korean War, Taiwan gained prominence in U.S. foreign policy because of the staunch anticommunism of the KMT and the island's geopolitical value. Although President Truman rejected the ROC offer of three divisions for the fight in Korea, the United States brought Taiwan under its security umbrella, provided considerable aid in capital and technology, and pro-

vided generous access to the U.S. market. These resources would spur the ignition of the ROC's import-substitution industrialization policies by the 1960s.

Taiwan's economic development coincided with that of three other newly industrializing economies (NIE): Singapore, Hong Kong, and South Korea. Collectively, this group was heralded in the 1990s as the Four Mini-Dragons. In 1952, Taiwan's GNP per capita was just under U.S.$200. By 2003, GNP per capita was approximately U.S.$13,000 (Council for Economic Planning and Development 2003; hereafter CEPD). Industrialization, fed by an export-based economy, resulted in an average annual GDP rate of growth of 9.8 percent between 1965 and 1980. This rate dropped to 7.9 percent in the 1980s and 6.6 percent for the 1990s. The GNP growth rate through the third quarter of 2004 was 4.83 percent.

Taiwan's industrialization strategy differed from that of Japan's and South Korea's reliance on conglomerates, *keiretsu* and *chaebol*, respectively. Although the national government maintained monopolies on strategic sectors such as transportation, communications, and alcohol and tobacco into the twenty-first century, it relied primarily on small and medium-sized enterprises (SME) as engines of growth. State planning and promotion directed enterprises toward manufacturing and trade-related activities, although this has now been redirected toward the development of an internationally competitive service sector. The breakdown of GDP by sector for 2002 was agriculture (1.9 percent), industry (31 percent), and services (67 percent). The breakdown of employment by sector for 2002 was agriculture (7 percent), industry (27 percent), and services (66 percent) (Asian Development Bank 2003).

Taiwan's leading countries of imports in 2001 were the United States (17.1 percent), Japan (24.1 percent), and ASEAN (Association of Southeast Asian Nations) states (14.9 percent). Leading markets for exports were the United States (22.5 percent), Hong Kong (21.9 percent), and Europe (16.1 percent). Leading sources of inward investment in 2001 were the United States (18.3 percent), Japan (13.4 percent), and The Netherlands (10.3 percent) (Government Information Office 2003; hereafter GIO).

Regional Geopolitics

Regional security in East Asia continues to cycle through periods of stability and hostility. The two major ongoing conflicts are Cold War leftovers, the divisions of Korea and China. By 2004, mistrust and antagonism between communist regimes in Pyongyang and Beijing and democratic regimes in Seoul and Taipei continue to flare up to the point of minor clashes of commando units in Korea and large-scale military maneuvers and gesturing in the Taiwan Strait. All sides see the presence of U.S. military forces in Korea, Japan, and the Philippines as an essential ingredient for maintaining regional security.

Given the absence of a peace treaty between the Beijing and Taipei governments, the two entities are still technically at war, although mostly dedicated to peaceful resolution of the Taiwan question. Because the conflict is a civil war, it is still considered an "internal matter" by both regimes. Moves (perceived or real) on Taipei away from reunification with the mainland have, however, resulted in frequent reminders by Beijing that the PRC retains the right to use force to prevent the permanent division of the mother-

land. Although the PRC has gone to war with neighbors India and Vietnam, created a puppet government in Cambodia, and constantly flexes its military muscle at Taiwan, the PRC does not currently evoke fear as an expansionist and militarily destabilizing power. For example, through 2004, the PRC has exercised "responsible" regional politics by bringing North Korea to the six-power table to negotiate the dismantling of its nuclear arms program.

In addition to the tensions on the Korean peninsula and Taiwan Strait, a conflict that holds potential for military escalation is that of states' sovereignty over the Spratly Islands. Located in the South China Sea within a triangle that connects Ho Chi Min City, Brunei, and Manila, the 100 or so islands are positioned within strategic shipping lanes and are believed to hold considerable oil and gas reserves. Exclusive possession of the islands is currently claimed by the PRC, Taiwan, and Vietnam. Portions of the island chain are claimed by Malaysia and the Philippines. The PRC, Malaysia, the Philippines, and Vietnam maintain armed garrisons in the chain. Taiwan maintains a coast guard station on the key island of Taiping Island. Brunei claims sovereignty to some of the islands, but has no outposts. All of the parties (excluding Taiwan) signed the nonbinding "Declaration on the Conduct of Parties in the South China Sea" in 2002.

Given formal and informal alliance structures, close geographic proximity, and the natural animosities of the actors involved, the prospects for these conflicts to spill over are considerable. Although it is doubtful that any non-U.S. actor would unilaterally intervene militarily on behalf of Taiwan, the disruption of trade and finance resulting from a military clash would have global ramifications. A PRC attack on Taiwan would raise the very real possibility of an interstate war between the United States and PRC. The escalation of tensions and military preparation by U.S.-allied East Asian states would call for North Korean "defensive" mobilization, with corresponding calls by Pyongyang to aid a fellow regime. It can also be argued, however, that one of the key reasons for the PRC not attacking Taiwan is that the mainland and Taiwan are leading trade and investment partners with each other.

The PRC position on "one China" is expressed in white papers of 1993 and 2000. As well, former PRC President Jiang Zemin spelled out the mainland's stance in his "Eight-Point Offer" to Taiwan on January 30, 1995. The PRC is committed to pursuing peaceful reunification, but does not rule out the use of force; promoting exchange of people, economics, and culture between the two sides; initiating direct trade, air, postal, and shipping direct links; and negotiation possible only under one China.

Conflict Past and Present

Conflict History

The most immediate root of fifty years of conflict between Beijing and Taipei was the Chinese civil war, 1945–1949, between communist forces led by Mao Tse-tung and the Nationalist regime of the Republic of China under the leadership of Chiang Kai-shek. Having lost the civil war, the Nationalists evacuated Canton on October 13, 1949, and established a new ROC capital in Taipei on December 7, 1949. The very real specter of a final military resolution to the civil war lasted through the first two decades of division, with there being three primary crisis events. A form of detente then lasted until the fourth crisis event (Taiwan Strait crisis of 1995–1996) and then again until and after the fifth crisis event (summer 1999). A direct ground clash of large-scale forces and loss of territory resulting from military confrontation has not occurred since 1955. Militarization of the conflict has most often taken the form of the shelling of offshore islands, testing and placement of missiles, and rhetoric.

The first Taiwan Strait crisis occurred between August 1954 and April 1955. Fearing encirclement resulting from the creation of the Southeast Asia Security Organization (September 8, 1954) and U.S. interference in its bid to unify China under the CCP, Beijing reaffirmed its right to unify China by forcefully taking Taiwan. On September 3, 1954, the mainland began an artillery bombardment of the Taipei-claimed islands of Quemoy and Matsu. The ROC responded with air strikes on coastal positions in Fujian Province. The United States sent its Seventh Fleet to the Strait area and appealed to the United Nations (no resolutions or action taken). Shelling continued as the United States and ROC signed the U.S.-Taiwan Defense Pact on December 2, 1954. This led to ground assaults on Quemoy, Matsu, and Tachen by PLA forces.

By January 1955, PRC forces had invaded and taken the island of Tachen. With considerable U.S. assistance, the islands of Quemoy and Matsu were fortified sufficiently by the end of March 1955 to rebuff PLA advances. Convinced of U.S. commitment to Taiwan's security and declining prospects of a successful PRC invasion of Taiwan, Beijing and Washington, D.C., negotiated a settlement without the participation of the ROC government. Important outcomes of this crisis were (1) U.S. commitment to active and armed defense of the ROC and (2) fortification of Quemoy and Matsu, which provided for long-term defense.

The second Taiwan Strait crisis occurred between July and October 1958. Within the context of escalating Cold War tensions and the PRC's uncertainty about Soviet and U.S. commitments in East Asia, the leadership in Beijing initiated an arms buildup across from Taiwan by mid-July 1958. After meeting with Nikita Khrushchev in Beijing from July 31 to August 3, Mao ordered the bombardment of Quemoy and Matsu on August 23. With Taiwan mobilizing to defend and striking back, the United States once again sent the Seventh Fleet to the Straits area. In response, Beijing extended its maritime boundary outward by twelve miles, effectively blockading Quemoy and Matsu. The United States ignored the new boundaries and continued to supply these islands. This was the first major crisis over Taiwan in which the United States announced the possible use of nuclear weapons if Quemoy were invaded.

This U.S. escalation resulted in a Soviet threat to come to the aid of the PRC should it be directly attacked by U.S. forces. Russia, however, did not become an active participant in this crisis. U.S.-PRC negotiations began on September 14, and U.S.–ROC negotiations concluded on October 23. Important outcomes of this crisis were (1) Soviet denouncement of PRC use of force to liberate Taiwan, (2) public threat by the United States to use nuclear force to maintain Taiwan's sovereignty, (3) U.S. denouncement of ROC use of force to liberate the mainland, and (4) acknowledgment by the United States that Quemoy and Matsu were closely related to the defense of Taiwan.

The third Taiwan Strait crisis occurred from April to June 1962. At the beginning

---

Sidebar 1   Taiwan and Sovereignty

The issue of sovereignty of Taiwan is complex and often debated. Although the Ming and Qing dynasties recognized the island as falling within China's sphere of influence, it was not until 1885 that the Qing court agreed to incorporate the island as a province of the Chinese state. Ten years later, Taiwan was ceded to Japan after China's defeat in the Sino-Japanese War and Taiwan remained a colony of the Japanese until 1945. The Nationalist government of the Republic of China claimed Taiwan after World War II, but the Potsdam Conference, Cairo Declaration, and San Francisco Peace Treaty all were vague in their treatment of Taiwan's ownership. The Nationalist government would enjoy de facto jurisdiction of the Chinese state until its defeat in 1949 by the Chinese Communist Party. By the time that the People's Republic of China was founded in October 1949, the Nationalist regime had been reconstituted on Taiwan and recognized by most of the world as a continuation of the Republic of China. Thus, in its history, Taiwan has been directly incorporated into a mainland government for only fourteen years, and never was ruled by the Chinese Communist Party.

Source
Cohen, Marc, and Emma Teng. 1990. *Let Taiwan Be Taiwan*. Washington, DC: Center for Taiwan International Relations.

---

of 1962, the Nationalist regime escalated its public rhetoric on the forced unification of China under the ROC. A series of speeches by Chiang Kai-shek and other senior KMT officials created greater fears on the mainland (and in the United States) of imminent military action by ROC forces against Beijing. A series of domestic policy moves on Taiwan dealing with increased taxes and conscription laws provided tangibility to these threats. The PRC responded with an arms buildup in Fujian Province by June 1962.

At meetings with PRC representatives on June 23, U.S. officials assured Beijing that it would not support offensive actions by Taiwan. U.S. policy was to defend Taiwan, with peaceful relations the paramount goal. President John F. Kennedy reiterated this stance on June 27, effectively ending this crisis. Important outcomes of this crisis were (1) U.S. opposition to military resolution of the Cross Strait conflict in principle and (2) U.S. opposition to ROC use of force in particular.

The fourth Taiwan Strait crisis occurred between May 1995 and March 1996. This crisis was triggered by the issuance of a tourist visa by the United States to ROC President Lee Teng-hui. Lee had been invited to deliver a speech to his alma mater at Cornell University. Since the termination of formal diplomatic relations between the ROC and the United States in 1979, high-level contacts between U.S. and ROC officials had been forbidden. Despite earlier statements by the U.S. government that President Lee would not be allowed to visit the United States, a visa was issued on May 22, 1995. This was met with vigorous criticism by the PRC and was held to be in violation of the "Three Communiqués" that are the basis of U.S.-PRC relations.

President Lee spent his three days in the United States meeting with U.S. congressmen and senators and publicly remarked that the status quo of Taiwan's international legal status was becoming increasingly untenable. As president of

the ROC and chairman of the ruling party, Lee was constitutionally and politically restricted to a national goal of unification with the mainland. His public comments on unification with the mainland were, by this time, pessimistic, and his focus was more on consolidating ROC sovereignty over Taiwan rather than political reintegration with the mainland. The Beijing leadership was increasingly hostile to this stance.

From July 21 to July 26, 1995, the PRC responded with missile tests in the East China Sea and heightened rhetoric of a forced unification with Taiwan. President Lee's response was a series of public comments decrying the pressure placed on Taiwan by "external forces." The United States intervened in the crisis in December 1995 by sending the USS *Nimitz* to the Taiwan Strait. By early 1996, the PRC once again initiated an arms buildup in Fujian Province and military exercises just twenty-five miles west of Taiwan. At this point, the crisis triggered by Lee's trip to the United States blended into a second crisis related to the ROC's first direct presidential election. Because Lee was viewed by the mainland as a separatist, and the leading opposition candidate represented a party founded in the desire for Taiwanese independence, the PRC continued its arms buildup and military exercises as a way to intimidate voters on Taiwan to vote for a third-party candidate who was running on a platform of Chinese reunification.

On March 8, 12, and 18, the PRC launched three separate military exercises off the coast of Taiwan. The United States sent carrier battle groups to the area during this period to maintain the peace. On March 23, 1996, Lee won the election with 54 percent of the popular vote. The PRC de-escalated after the election, although political tensions remained high. Important outcomes of this crisis were (1) proof of U.S. military commitment to Taiwan's defense and (2) PRC-attempted intimidation of ROC voters backfired, leading to Lee's overwhelming victory.

The most recent crisis in the Taiwan Strait occurred in the month of July 1999. This fifth and latest crisis was initiated by President Lee's comments during a radio interview with the German Broadcasting Company Deutsche Welle on July 9. During the interview, Lee commented that Taiwan and the government in Beijing have a "special state-to-state relationship." Beijing took this to be an outright declaration by Lee that Taiwan was its own state, independent of the mainland. Military mobilization and a fierce rhetoric campaign were initiated by Beijing. PLA and IDF forces patrolled the dividing line in the strait, but no clashes occurred. The crisis ended on July 20, when President Lee offered further "elaboration" on his earlier comments. Lee indicated that he was simply voicing the reality that both sides are separately governed. Important outcomes of this crisis were (1) PRC commitment to military intervention to contain Taiwan and (2) confirmation of limited diplomatic space for Taiwan to operate.

Current and Potential Military Confrontation

As of early 2004, the potential for military confrontation between the ROC and PRC is minimal. Given their highly integrated economies and the desire on both sides to deal with more immediate political and economic problems at home, military conflict is an increasingly distant prospect. Additionally, the ascendance of PRC President Hu Jin-tao has introduced a more moderate approach to Taiwan. Although the PRC maintains its right to resort to force, President Hu has sought to portray Taiwan as an aggressor that refuses to negotiate with Beijing. To prevent separatist forces on Taiwan from pursuing independence, the PRC had stationed more than 300 missile batteries across from Taiwan by the end of 2003, with 50 to be added each year.

The campaigning leading up to the presidential elections on Taiwan on March 20, 2004, raised the issue of Taiwan's international legal status and its relationship with the mainland. Candidates have traditionally used this issue to mobilize supporters. Some of the more extreme predictions date a possible clash in 2008 when the world's attention will be trained in Beijing with the Olympic Games. The ROC government, it is argued, might assume that the world's attention would prevent a mainland attack in retaliation of an independence declaration.

Although elections are always a time of tension between Beijing and Taipei, the March 2004 election held a new element: that of two national referenda items to be voted on the same day. The presidential election resulted in the incumbent, Chen Shui-bian, winning just under 51 percent of the vote and the challenger, Lien Chan, winning just over 49 percent of the vote. The election results were bitterly contested by Lien, who felt that the assassination attempt on Chen and his vice president, Annette Lu, created a sympathy vote that allowed Chen to squeak by with his bare majority in the two-man race. A new law legalizing referenda was passed by the ROC legislature in the last days of November 2003. Although President Chen pushed for a version that would have allowed for a national vote on Taiwan's legal status, the version passed allowed for this only as a "defensive action" possible only if a PRC attack was imminent. The PRC reaction was hostile, and promises of invasion were voiced by leading PLA officials if Taiwan made moves toward breaking away from China.

Sidebar 2 National and Cultural Identity of Taiwan

Until the 1990s, a debate on the issue of cultural and national identity on Taiwan was, for the most part, illegal. As one way to secure its legitimacy after defeat in the Chinese civil war, the Nationalist Party (KMT) held itself as the protector and symbol of "high Chinese culture." During the first decades of its exile to Taiwan, the KMT implemented cultural programs on Taiwan to re-Sinicize the population after fifty years of Japanese colonial rule. The development of a national culture and identity akin to "Taiwanese," rather than "Chinese," was actively resisted by the KMT. Growing out of Taiwan's democratization movement in the 1970s and 1980s, a vigorous and divisive debate has now ensued as to whether "Taiwanese" is a national rather than provincial or local identity. Public surveys have revealed a dramatic decline in people identifying themselves as Chinese (less than 10 percent in October 2003). With a rise in local identification, the People's Republic of China fears increased prospects that this will lead to a declaration by Taipei of permanent, political separation from the Chinese state.

Source

Stockton, Hans. 2002. "National Identity on Taiwan: Causes and Consequences for Political Reunification." *American Journal of Chinese Studies* 9, no. 2:155–178.

The two original referendum questions related to China removing its missiles located across from Taiwan and renouncing the use of force. Neither action, of course, would be possible for the PRC, and the escalating tensions moved U.S. President George W. Bush to voice strong opposition to such referendum items during his meetings with PRC Premier Wen on December 9. On January 16, 2004, President Chen sought to diminish the firestorm by announcing two newly worded referendum items. The referendum items asked Taiwan's voters to support (1) peaceful resolution of the conflict with the mainland and (2) whether the ROC government should engage in new negotiations with the mainland. Both referendum items were defeated due to the fact that a majority of voters failed to cast a vote in the referendum ballot. While only 45 percent of voters participated in the referendum balloting, more than 95 percent approved both items.

Alliance Structure

As mentioned previously, the Republic of China holds formal diplomatic relations with only twenty-seven states. As a result of its loss of the UN China seat in 1971 and almost complete diplomatic isolation, the ROC has been excluded from most international governmental organizations (IGOs). When ROC membership is accepted, such as in the World Trade Organization, it is qualified under the pseudonym "Chinese Taipei" or as observer status. The ROC is a member of neither multilateral nor bilateral security treaties.

Size and Structure of the Military

The Republic of China maintains an active, regular forces strength of approximately 380,000 personnel. Of this number, 300,000 people serve in the four primary branches of the army (190,000), navy (50,000, including approximately 30,000 marines), air force (50,000), and military police (10,000). There are an additional 15,000 servicemen under the Combined Logistics Command and Reserves Command. Registered reservists number about 3.48 million (GIO 2003, 131). The number of persons on Taiwan (ages fifteen to forty-nine) fit for military service is 5,019,268 (CIA 2003).

The Ministry of Defense has been implementing a wide-reaching reform of the armed forces under the Ten-Year Troop Reduction Project (with first-stage completion in 2003) in pursuit of a more streamlined and integrated forces arrangement. This process has resulted in "streamlined organizations and more cost-effective measures by de-centralizing organizations, shortening the chain of command, accelerating reaction times, and promoting increased efficiency. Management and processing have shortened process flow times, fostered the creativity of lower-level units and individuals, and eliminated outdated approaches" (GIO 2003, 130).

National defense policy is premised on three goals. The first goal is the prevention of war and conflicts through sustainable defense and deterrence. The second goal is the maintenance of stability in the Taiwan Strait through dialogue, exchange of information, transparency, and mutual understanding. The third goal is the defense of national territory through military preparedness, effective deterrence, and resolute defense.

The Strategic Conceptual Framework of ROC national defense is "effective deterrence, resolute defense." At the onset of a war with the mainland, defense is premised on adopting "superior air and naval operations, selecting advantageous airspace and waters, to defeat incoming enemies in stages so as to ensure national security" (Ministry of National Defense 2002, 71; hereafter MND). Effective deterrence is predicated on achieving seven primary goals: (1) early warning system; (2) efficient and capable joint operations; (3) enhanced offensive, defensive, information, and electronic capabilities; (4) air superiority and naval dominance; (5) the launch of instant operations; (6) strong mobilization capacity; and (7) forcing the enemy "into a status of 'bewildering uncertainty to win and heavy casualties'" (MND 2002, 72).

The Strategic Conceptual Framework for national defense is implemented in a seven-point vision statement. These points are (1) seizing information superiority and early warning capability, (2) coordination of intelligence operations, (3) limiting amphibious assault through air and naval superiority and annihilating the enemy at landing areas through joint operations, (4) conducting all-out mobilization and strengthening of reserves, (5) unifying logistics, (6) refining organization, and (7) improving education and recruiting talented personnel.

The army's mission is twofold: to "defend state territory and to ensure the integrity of sovereignty" (MND 2002). During peacetime, the mission is dedicated to defending posts of strategic significance on Taiwan and its offshore areas. Upon the command of the president, the army also renders regional disaster relief.

GHQ Army commands the Army Corps, Defense Command, Aviation and Special Warfare Command, Army Logistics Command, Air-Defense Missile Command, Division Commands, Armored Brigades, Armored Infantry Brigades, Motorized Rifle Brigades, Infantry Brigades, Airborne Cavalry Brigades, Special Warfare Brigades, and Testing and Measuring Center.

The primary weapons systems employed by the army are: AH-1W attack helicopters, OH-58D scout helicopters, M-48H and M-60A-3 tanks, portable Stinger surface-to-air missiles, Chaparral self-propelled air defense missiles, M-109A-5 self-propelled howitzers, Sky Bow air defense missiles, and Patriot air defense systems. As of 2004, there were four Patriot batteries defending the airspace of Taipei.

The navy's mission is dedicated to maintaining superiority in the Taiwan Strait and maintaining the safe passage of sea lines of communication (SLOC). The navy conducts reconnaissance and patrolling, supplies offshore islands, and escorts ships in peacetime. Falling under the umbrella of the navy, the marine corps' mission is to defend navy bases and appointed offshore islands in peacetime while engaging in combat mission in wartime (GIO 2003).

GHQ Navy commands the Naval Fleet Command, Chinese Marine Corps Command, the Education, Training and Doctrine Development Command, Navy Logistics Command, Destroyer Fleet, Frigate Fleet, Submarine Fleet, Mine Fleet, Service Fleet, Amphibious Fleet, Fast Attack Boat Force (missile), Naval Aviation Force, Land-Based Missile Force, Surveillance and Communication System Command, Base Command, Marine Corps Brigade, Oceanic Survey Bureau, and Oceanic Development Center.

The primary weapons systems of the navy are: missile frigates, missile destroyers, missile corvettes, missile fast attack craft, minesweeping (laying) vessels, submarines, fixed-wing ASW aircraft, ASW helicopters, amphibious ships, and landing vehicles. The navy has recently complemented its forces with Lafayette class, Chengkung class, Knox class, and Chinchiang class ships.

The mission of the air force is to defend airspace, assist in the preservation of naval superiority through joint operations with the navy and army, and to ultimately maintain national sovereignty. Its peacetime mission emphasizes military preparedness and protection of ROC airspace.

GHQ Air Force commands the Air Combat Command, Air Force Logistics Command, Air Defense and Garrison Command, Education, Training and Doctrine Developing Command, Base Command, Tactical Fighter Wing, Combined Wing, Air Tactical Control Wing, Communications and ATC Wing, and Weather Wing. The primary weapons systems of the air force are: domestically built IDF fighter jets, F-16s, Mirage 2000-5 fighters, and Maverick, Sidewinder, and Sky Sword II missiles.

As stated in the ROC *Yearbook* 2003, ROC armed forces goals for 2004 are to (1) develop a low-altitude fire control radar system based on the existing radar structure to improve the air defense capabilities of important garrisons and field units; (2) develop infrared reconnaissance and tracking system, which can be integrated with weapon systems to give fighter aircraft, naval vessels, and armored vehicles the all-weather combat capabilities; (3) develop materials and apply stealth technologies for fighter aircraft to reduce radar detection; (4) upgrade unmanned aerial vehicles (UAV) based on previous R&D to obtain real-time intelligence; and (5) rely on UAVs to strengthen the ROC Armed Forces C4ISR and intelligence-gathering capacities.

Budget
As illustrated in Table 2, as a portion of overall government spending, military expenditures have declined over the last decade. Gradual annual decline accelerated with a drop from 22.7 percent of central government spending in 1999 to 18.03 percent in 2000 (MND 2002). The defense budget in FY 2002 was approximately U.S.$7.6 billion, down from U.S.$8.26 billion in FY 2001.

Table 3 provides a budget breakdown based on component (service) and category. As expressed above, the doctrine of the armed forces emphasizes integration and information. This is supported in the distribution of spending in the FY 2002 budget, with combined logistics and electronic and information warfare enjoying significant resources.

Table 2   Proportion of Military Budgets in Total Government, GNP, and Classified Spending—Taiwan

	Year					
Percentage Expenditure by Type	*1993*	*1995*	*1997*	*1999*	*2001*	*2002*
% Central Government Budget	25.32	24.51	22.51	22.70	16.48	17.19
% GNP	4.72	3.69	3.33	3.14	2.76	2.16
% Military Budget Classified	61.17	36.92	35.70	29.73	20.67	17.93

Source
Ministry of National Defense (ROC). 2002. *National Defense Report*. Taipei: Ministry of National Defense.

Table 3   Breakdown of Defense Budget by Component and Category (Taiwan, FY 2002)

Component	*Percentage*	*Category*	*Percentage*
Organic units	48.66	Electronic & Info. Warfare	32.39
Combined logistics	11.99	Combat Readiness Support	14.38
Army	11.04	Air Def. Battle Equip.	11.31
Air force	10.65	Maritime Def. Battle Equip.	9.85
Navy	7.78	Replenishment	9.21
Joint staffs	4.90	Educ. & Training Facilities	7.31
CSIST	3.52	Def. Counter-Measure Equip.	6.98
Nat. Defense Univ.	.58	Combat Readiness Work	3.36
Reserves	.40	Basic Living Facilities	3.10
Military police	.36	Anti-Landing Combat Equip.	2.11
NMD HQs	.12		

Source
Ministry of National Defense (ROC). 2002. *National Defense Report*. Taipei: Ministry of National Defense.

On an annual average, approximately one-eighth to one-sixth of ROC military expenditures are dedicated to the purchase of arms transfers from the United States. From 1993 to 1996, the ROC purchased U.S.$4.6 billion in material. From 1997 to 2000, the ROC purchased approximately U.S.$7.6 billion in material. The procurement for FY 2003 was U.S.$3.2 billion alone, with priority placed on modernizing air force and navy capabilities. Procurements planned for 2004 and 2005 were held up, as the ROC legislature was unable to pass a special procurement law that would free up to U.S.$4 billion.

Sidebar 3   Arms Transfers to Taiwan

The continuation of American arms transfers to Taiwan after derecognition of the Republic of China (ROC) in December 1978 was justified in the Taiwan Relations Act (TRA), signed into law on April 10, 1979. This was immensely unpopular with the Chinese Communist Party (CCP) leadership even prior to the TRA being enacted into law and continues to annually provoke criticism from Beijing. Prior to the TRA, even leaving the Senate Foreign Relations Committee, then PRC Vice Premier Deng Xiaoping noted that the continuation of arms transfers to Taiwan was unacceptable and that the PRC would reserve the right to forcefully reincorporate Taiwan into the PRC. Two and a half decades later, Beijing's objections and language have remained unchanged.

Source
Clough, Ralph N. 1999. *Cooperation or Conflict in the Taiwan Strait.* New York: Rowman & Littlefield.

Emphasis has been placed on acquiring the Pave Paws Radar, Patriot Advanced Capability (PAC-3) missiles, upgrading PAC-2 missiles already deployed, Kidd-Class destroyers, and a host of domestically produced capabilities. In November 2003, the United States delivered 120 AIM 120 missiles purchased by Taiwan in 2000, but has deferred the sale of Aegis Control System, M1A2 Abrams tanks, Joint Direct Attack Munitions (JDAM), and HARM antiradiation missiles (GIO 2003; MND 2002).

Civil-Military Relations/The Role of the Military in Domestic Politics

The ROC constitution states in Article 138 that "the Army, Navy, and Air Force of the nation shall rise above personal, regional, and party affiliations and shall be loyal to the State and love and protect the people." Article 139 stipulates "no political party and no individual shall make use of armed forces as an instrument in the struggle for political power." Article 140 precludes joint positions in the military and civil office.

Numerous mission statements of the ROC armed forces emphasize subordination to civilian control and integration into national goals of consolidating democracy on Taiwan. Of seven national defense priorities, the seventh stipulates that the armed forces shall support the goal of "realizing democracy to protect human rights and develop a clean and effective government with sound systems" (MND 2002, 66). There have been no coups launched against the ROC government on Taiwan.

There was some speculation that the armed forces would not accept the authority of the ROC's first non-KMT president, Chen Shui-bian, elected in 2000.

Given the new president's party platform of Taiwan's independence, there was minor concern that the armed forces would launch a preemptive action to prevent Taiwan's independence. This has not been a major issue since 2000.

Terrorism

Terrorism is not a problem on Taiwan.

Relationship with the United States

Since the Nationalist government's establishment on the mainland in 1912 up to the termination of diplomatic relations in December 1978, the United States recognized the Nationalist government as the legal sovereign of the Chinese state. Although forced to retreat to Taiwan in 1949, the ROC maintained the China seat in the United Nations until October 1971. As a culmination of U.S. normalization of relations with the communist government in Beijing, President Jimmy Carter switched U.S. diplomatic recognition to the PRC in December 1978. In response to this, pro-Taiwan forces in the U.S. Congress pushed through the Taiwan Relations Act (TRA).

A domestic law, the TRA has governed U.S. relations with Taiwan since its enactment on April 10, 1979. The TRA was the U.S. Congress's effort to maintain unofficial "normal" security and economic relations with Taiwan. Important U.S. treaties and laws regarding its position toward Taiwan have been spelled out in the Joint U.S.-China "Shanghai" Communiqué (February 27, 1972), Joint Communiqué on the Establishment of Diplomatic Relations (January 1, 1979), and the U.S.-PRC Joint Communiqué (August 17, 1982).

The TRA specifies that it is U.S. policy "to provide Taiwan with arms of a defensive character" and "to maintain the capacity of the United States to resist any resort to force or other forms of coercion" that are deemed to threaten Taiwan's security, society, or economic system. With regard to security relations, section 3(a) states that "the United States will make available to Taiwan such defense articles and defense services in such quantity as may be necessary to enable Taiwan to maintain a sufficient self-defense capability."

The TRA also specifies a congressional role in decision making on security assistance for Taiwan. Section 3(b) stipulates integrated decision making between the president and Congress for the determination of the type and quantity of defense articles and services. This section also directs that "such determination of Taiwan's defense needs shall include review by United States military authorities in connection with recommendations to the President and the Congress." Until 2001, this process was initiated by an annual request for arms transfers by Taipei. President Bush has since changed the timing to an "as needed" basis.

The TRA established the American Institute in Taiwan (AIT), a nonprofit (nongovernmental) organization, to handle U.S. relations with Taiwan. Under the auspices of the Departments of Defense and State, and the National Security Council, the AIT implements U.S. policy preferences.

The United States has favored a policy of strategic ambiguity with regard to just how committed it is to the defense of Taiwan and under what conditions it will intervene. Clearly, a unilateral move by Beijing or Taipei is unacceptable to the United States. This includes a PRC attack and unilateral declaration on Taiwan of independence. The United States has preferred to avoid having to lean to one side or the other, seeking engagement with the PRC while promoting peaceful interactions in the Taiwan Strait. Some recent exceptions are under the Clinton administration (PRC leaning) and under the early years of George W. Bush's presidency (Taiwan leaning) with President Bush remarking during his first month in office that the United States would do "whatever it takes" to defend Taiwan from a PRC attack.

The Future

The future of ROC security hinges entirely on its relationship with the mainland and the United States. The only military threat suffered by Taiwan is that of the PRC, and the ROC's only security guarantor is the United States. The most recent crisis episodes have been sparked by statements and actions on Taiwan deemed hostile to Beijing's preference for unification with Taiwan. The most recent period of elevated tension occurred in the run-up to the March 20, 2004, presidential election on Taiwan. The incumbent administration of Chen Shui-bian and his Democratic Progressive Party placed two referenda items up for consideration in November 2003. As originally worded, the items called for the PRC to renounce the use of force and to withdraw the 496 short-range ballistic missiles from across Taiwan. After an international uproar over what were deemed provocative acts by the Chen administration, the items were reworded to ask the people on Taiwan if the government should purchase more antimissile weaponry and whether it should engage in peace talks with the PRC. The day before national balloting, President Chen and Vice President Annette Lu suffered minor wounds in a failed assassination attempt in Chen's hometown of Tainan.

President Chen won reelection with just over 50.1 percent of the vote in a two-candidate race. The referendum failed to garner the 50 percent voter turnout threshold and thus failed consideration. On election-day evening, the opposition party called for a recount and nullification of the election. One week after the election, the PRC announced that it was keeping a serious eye on events in Taiwan and would be gravely concerned should political turmoil result in upheaval. The level of rhetoric from Beijing remained escalated through the first four months after Chen's reelection.

In their bid to regain the presidency, the KMT candidates promised a more conciliatory approach to the mainland that might have reduced tensions, but did not lead to any near-term resolution of the Taiwan question. The DPP plans on pursuing a major round of constitutional redrafting in 2006. Party leaders indicated that the constitutional articles dealing with the name of the country, national flag, anthem, and territory would be considered for revision. These actions alone or together have prompted Beijing to threaten ultimate military force to prevent Taiwan from abandoning the Chinese state.

Unofficial military relations between Taiwan and the United States have improved considerably under the administration of President George W. Bush, and the administration has pushed the envelope for quantity of arms sales and approved technologies to Taiwan. The United States and Taiwan plan joint war games in 2006, and President Chen has promised to keep the pressure on the opposition majority in the legislature to approve special budgets to purchase more

U.S. arms and technology. This also has been a sore point for Beijing, which views increases in arms transfers to Taiwan as a pro-Taiwan–United States stance and interference in its domestic politics. Some fear a preemptive strike by the PRC should Taiwan's national defense capabilities continue to improve. Until Beijing develops sufficient amphibious assault capabilities, an invasion of Taiwan is highly unlikely. The most likely near-term scenario would be a blockade of Taiwan and remote bombardment of the island's strategic centers in and around Taipei, Taichung, Hsinchu, and Kaohsiung.

The ROC will continue to seek superiority in air, naval, and electronic warfare capabilities, and budgets will continue to reflect these priorities. Examples of e-warfare projects under development on Taiwan are a VHG/UHG frequency-hopping communications network, stand-off electronic countermeasures for jamming ground-based air defense radar, and improved computer and e-mail security systems (GIO 2003). The purchase of the AEGIS combat system and expansion of the submarine fleet and improved fighter munitions are also future priorities.

References, Recommended Readings, and Websites

Books

Asian Development Bank. 2003. *Key Indicators*. Manila: Asian Development Bank.

Central Intelligence Agency (U.S.). 2003. *World Factbook*. Washington, DC: Central Intelligence Agency.

Chang, Paris. 1992. "The Changing Nature of Taiwan's Politics." In *Taiwan: Beyond the Economic Miracle*, Dennis F. Simon and Michael Y. M. Kau, eds. New York: M. E. Sharpe, pp. 25–42.

Chao, Chien-min. 2002. "The Republic of China's Foreign Relations under President Lee Teng-hui: A Balance Sheet." In *Assessing the Lee Teng-hui Legacy in Taiwan's Politics: Democratic Consolidation and External Relations*, Bruce J. Dickson and Chien-min Chao, eds. New York: M. E. Sharpe, pp. 177–217.

Cheng, Tun-jen, and Yun-han Chu. 2002. "State-Business Relations in South Korea and Taiwan." In *Emerging Market Democracies: East Asia and Latin America*, Laurence Whitehead, ed. Baltimore, MD: Johns Hopkins University Press, pp. 31–62.

Cheng, Tun-jen, and Chia-lung Lin. 1999. "Taiwan: A Long Decade of Democratic Transition." In *Driven by Growth: Political Change in the Asia-Pacific Region*, James Morley, ed. New York: M. E. Sharpe, pp. 224–254.

Clough, Ralph N. 1999. *Cooperation or Conflict in the Taiwan Strait*. New York: Rowman & Littlefield.

Cohen, Marc, and Emma Teng. 1990. *Let Taiwan Be Taiwan*. Washington, DC: Center for Taiwan International Relations.

Cossa, Ralph. 2000. "The U.S. Asia-Pacific Security Strategy for the Twenty-First Century." In *The Security Environment in the Asia-Pacific*, Hung-mao Tien and Tun-jen Cheng, eds. New York: M. E. Sharpe, pp. 36–51.

Council for Economic Planning and Development (ROC). 2003. *Taiwan Statistical Data Book*. Taipei: Council for Economic Planning and Development.

Dickson, Bruce J. 2002. "Taiwan's Challenges to U.S. Foreign Policy." In *Assessing the Lee Teng-hui Legacy in Taiwan's Politics: Democratic Consolidation and External Relations*, Bruce J. Dickson and Chien-min Chao, eds. New York: M. E. Sharpe, pp. 264–286.

Government Information Office (ROC). 2003. *Republic of China Yearbook*. Los Angeles: Kwang Hwa Publishing.

Heo, Uk, and Shale Horowitz. 2002. *Conflict in Asia: Korea, China-Taiwan, and India-Pakistan*. Westport, CT: Greenwood.

Huang, Chi, and Samuel S. G. Wu. 1995. "Inherited Rivalry: A Chronology." In *Inherited Rivalry: Conflict across the Taiwan Straits*, Tun-jen Cheng, C. Huang, and S. S. G. Wu, eds. Boulder, CO: Lyne Rienner Publishers, pp. 227–260.

Islam, Iyanatul, and Anis Chowdhury. 1997. *Asia-Pacific Economies.* New York: Routledge.

Kau, Michael Y. M. 2002. "The Challenge of Cross-Strait Relations: The Strategic Implications of the Missile Crisis." In *The Security Environment in the Asia-Pacific*, Hung-mao Tien and Tun-jen Cheng, eds. New York: M. E. Sharpe, pp. 241–258.

Lin, Wen-cheng, and Cheng-yi Lin. 2002. "National Defense and the Changing Security Environment." In *Assessing the Lee Teng-hui Legacy in Taiwan's Politics: Democratic Consolidation and External Relations*, Bruce J. Dickson and Chien-min Chao, eds. New York: M. E. Sharpe, pp. 241–263.

Ministry of National Defense (ROC). 2002. *National Defense Report.* Taipei: Ministry of National Defense.

Rigger, Shelley. 1999. *Politics in Taiwan: Voting for Democracy.* New York: Routledge.

Rubenstein, Murray. 1999. "Taiwan's Socio-Economic Modernization 1971–1996." In *Taiwan: A New History*, Murray Rubenstein, ed. New York: M. E. Sharpe, pp. 366–402.

Sheng, Li-jun. 2001. *China's Dilemma: The Taiwan Issue.* New York: I. B. Tauris.

———. 2002. *China and Taiwan: Cross-Strait Relations under Chen Shui-bian.* New York: Zed Books.

Stockton, Hans. 2002. "National Identity on Taiwan: Causes and Consequences for Political Reunification." *American Journal of Chinese Studies* 9, no. 2:155–178.

Tien, Hung-mao. 1989. *The Great Transition: Political and Social Change in the Republic of China.* Taipei: SMC Publishing.

Van Ness, Peter. 2000. "Globalization and Security in East Asia." In *East Asia and Globalization*, Samuel Kim, ed. New York: Rowman & Littlefield, pp. 255–276.

Articles

Department of Defense (U.S.). 1999. "White Paper Regarding Taiwan's Safety and Security." Washington, DC: Department of Defense.

Kan, Shirley. 2003. "Taiwan: Major U.S. Arms Sales Since 1990." Washington, DC: Congressional Research Service.

Websites

Asian Development Bank: http://www.adb.org.

Congressional Research Service (USA): http://www.ncseonline.org/NLE/CRS/.

Government Information Office (ROC): http://www.gio.gov.tw

Mainland Affairs Council: http:// www.mac.gov.tw.

Ministry of National Defense (in Mandarin only): http://www.mnd.gov.tw.

Taiwan Affairs Council: http://www.chinataiwan.org/webportal/portal.po?UID=DWV1_WOUID_URL_5023959.

Taiwan Security Research: http://www.taiwansecurity.org.

World Factbook: http://www.cia.gov/cia/publications/factbook/index.html.

Thailand

Kihong Eom and Dong-Yoon Lee

Geography and History

Located in the center of Southeast Asia, Thailand is approximately 200,000 square miles (514,000 kilometers), slightly more than twice the size of Wyoming. The Kingdom of Thailand borders with Laos and Cambodia to the east, Malaysia to the south, and Burma to the west. In addition, it is linked to islands of Southeast Asia by a narrow isthmus. It is composed of seventy-six provinces, and its capital city is Bangkok. The country comprises a central plain, Khorat Plateau in the east, and mountains elsewhere, with 32.88 percent arable land. In addition to the rainy and dry seasons, Thailand also has tropical monsoons. These articulated seasons facilitate agriculture, especially rice, and although the significance of the manufacturing and service industry has increased after industrialization in the 1970s and 1980s, agricultural products remain the major source of income. Thailand's GDP was $445.8 billion and $7,000 on a per capita basis in 2002 (CIA 2003).

In 2003, Thailand had a population of approximately 64 million people. Seventy-five percent of the population is Thai, and 14 percent is Chinese. There is another minority group, "hill tribes," who are primarily immigrants residing in the northern mountains. In terms of religion, 95 percent are Buddhists and 4 percent are Muslim. In the thirteenth century of the Sukhothai

Table 1 Thailand: Key Statistics

Type of government	Constitutional monarchy
Population (millions)	65 million (2005)
Religion	Buddhism 94.6%, Muslim 4.6%, Christianity 0.7%, Hinduism 0.1%, other 0.1% (2000)
Main industries	Agriculture, tourism, textiles, and garments
Main security threats	Border conflicts engaged with Cambodia, Laos, and Burma, although the number of combats has decreased
Defense spending (% per GDP)	1.8% (FY 2003)
Size of military (thousands)	530
Number of civil wars since 1945	0
Number of interstate wars since 1945	0

Source

Central Intelligence Agency. 2005. *CIA World Factbook 2005* (accessed July 26, 2005).
Stockholm International Peace Research Institute. 2003. *The SIPRI Military Expenditure Database.* http://projects.sipri.org/milex.html (accessed December 8, 2003).

Kingdom, Buddhism was introduced in Thailand and became a national religion. Thailand adopted *Hinayana* Buddhism, which emphasizes discipline and emancipation, instead of *Mahayani* Buddhism, which emphasizes evangelical work. Today, Thailand has approximately 34,000 temples and 300,000 monks. The constitution even states the importance of Buddhism in politics: the king should be Buddhist and a guardian of Buddhism. As such, Buddhism is a central force in Thailand (see Sidebar 4 for further detail). The Muslim minority, who are ethnically and religiously different from the majority of Thai society, are centered in the south on the Malaysian border. From the 1960s to 1970s, they attempted to become independent, yet the strong assimilation policy of the Thai government in the 1980s caused the independent movement to fade.

Thailand was the only country in Southeast Asia to remain autonomous during the colonial period, although the history of Thailand is marked with competition,

---

Sidebar 1   Vicious Circle of Thai Politics

Thailand was the only country in Southeast Asia to remain autonomous during the colonial period. A series of military coups d'état and the subsequent military governments, however, led to the institutionalization of the military involvement in the political process. The new military government dissolved the Assembly and called the New Assembly. By running and electing themselves in the following elections, the new military government established their regime.
Such civil-military relation in Thailand is called a "vicious circle of Thai politics."

---

conflicts, and wars with neighboring countries. Thailand has also experienced a series of foreign security threats and military coups d'état. The Buddhist Kingdom of Sukhothai (1257–1350) founded the first country of Thailand in the region of Sukhothai and established the kingdom in the mid-thirteenth century. The Sukhothai Kingdom aggressively expanded its territory toward the east, and the successor, the Ayuthaya Kingdom (1350–1767), continued the expansion policy of the Sukhothai. In the late fifteenth century, the Ayuthaya Kingdom conquered the Angkor Kingdom in the region of Cambodia and built the Great Empire in Southeast Asia. Yet, the Ayuthaya Kingdom, which was the longest kingdom in the history of Thailand, suffered from two major defeats by the Burmese in the mid-sixteenth and eighteenth centuries. After these defeats, the Ayuthaya Kingdom was taken over by the Burmese Kingdom, which was then replaced by the Kingdom of Thonburi in 1767. In 1782, the Chakri Dynasty became the reigning kingdom in Thailand after the collapse of the Thonburi Kingdom. The current king, Bhumibol Adulyadej (Rama IX), is a successor of the Chakri Dynasty.

Thailand has been a constitutional monarchy system since 1932. Formally, the king is a chief of state, yet the prime mister is the de facto head of administration. The Thai congress is bicameral, consisting of the Senate and the House of Representatives, and members of congress serve four years. Members of the Senate were recommended by the prime minister and appointed by the king until the 1997 constitutional amendment; now members of the Senate are elected by a popular vote, just as are members of the House. The major parties are the Thai Rak Thai Party, Democrat Party,

New Aspiration Party, Thai Nation Party, and National Development Party. The Thai Rak Thai Party has been in power since the 2001 House elections.

King Mongut (Rama IV, 1851–1868) and King Chulalongkorn (Rama V, 1868–1910) took the initiative to build a modern military in the late nineteenth century when Thailand was an absolute monarchy and made frequent contacts with European countries. The nature of the military and civil-military relationship changed after the coup d'état led by military and bureaucratic elites in 1932. An absolute monarchy was replaced with a constitutional monarchy, where the king is a symbol rather than the person in power. The influence of the military was significant not only in foreign relations, but also in the domestic political process. Despite the strenuous student-led movement and the first democratization in 1973, the influence of the military was evident where domestic and foreign security issues were at stake (e.g., border conflict, drugs, and terrorism). After the Cold War, however, the rationale for a strong military regime lost ground, and the influence of the military faded away. After the 1992 democratic transition and the 1997 "People's Constitution," the role of the military has been limited to foreign security, drug, and terrorism issues.

Regional Geopolitics

After World War II, the world faced a new type of conflict, the Cold War. Newly independent countries in Southeast Asia bogged down in the tension between the United States and the USSR. The tension was especially evident in Thailand, because the country connects continental countries with island countries. Thailand, therefore, became an important place to resist the expansion of communism into Malaysia and Indonesia, especially when China and Indo-Chinese countries became communist (Fineman 1997). With the help of the United States and other Western countries, the Thai government pursued a strong anticommunism policy and played a central role to establish the Southeast Asian Treaty Organization (SEATO) in 1954. Its goal was the containment of communism in the region.

Geopolitically, Thailand was in a strategic place to contain communism in the region from the 1950s to the end of the Cold War. Since the 1950s, the increasing communization in the region, especially in neighboring Indo-Chinese countries, augmented security concerns and in turn provided the rationale for the continuance of a strong military-authoritative regime. In the 1970s, the security threats peaked after the communization of Vietnam. During the period of the Vietnam War, the Thai government kept a close alliance with the United States and thus allowed the United States to use military bases in Thailand to send combat troops into Vietnam. After the establishment of "semidemocracy" in the 1980s, Thailand became stabilized from outside security threats. However, a series of military coups d'état continued up to the 1990s. As a result of the 1992 democratic transition and the 1997 "People's Constitution," the vicious cycle of military coups came to an end. Today, Thailand faces a new type of a security threat—terrorism.

With the demise of the Cold War, Thailand employed its geoeconomic advantage and economic capacity to facilitate economic openness and cooperation with neighboring communist countries. In particular, by investing in a development plan for the Mekong River, the main river in Southeast Asia, Thailand has enhanced economic cooperation with Vietnam, Laos, Cambodia, and Burma. In addition, the Thai government takes a central part in the Association of Southeast Asian Nations (ASEAN), thereby connecting continental countries with island countries. Thailand has become a central part of the region's economic development.

Conflict Past and Present

Conflict History

The conflict history of Thailand began in the late 1930s. Phibun Songkram, the leader of the 1932 coup d'état and a military major, nominated himself prime minister and announced that the national ideology "Pan-Thai Nationalism" should be pursued in 1938 (see Sidebar 3 for further detail). In addition to this, he adopted a military expansion policy. The purpose of the Pan-Thai nationalism was to build a national community in the region and expand the national identity of Thailand into the region (Girling 1981, 11). The Thai military government claimed that Thailand has sovereignty over the west of Laos and Cambodia, the Shan Province in Burma, and the north of Malaysia (Chai-Anan 1982; Prudhisan 1992). During World War II, Thailand allied with Japan and attacked Cambodia, Laos, and Burma, countries that France and England had authority over. However, in the end of 1944 when Japan was close to defeat, the Phibun government abdicated power, leaving the responsibility of the alliance to Japan. The following Pridi Panomyong government decided to secede from the Axis and joined the Allied forces. As such, Thailand escaped from war crimes. After returning the secured territory to Laos and Cambodia, Thailand became a member of the United Nations.

Since World War II, Thailand has had a strong alliance with the United States and other Western countries. When the Korean War began in 1950, Thailand entered the war immediately as one of the sixteen allied members of the United Nations and sent a brigade of infantry troops. In addition, in the late 1960s and the 1970s when communist countries increased the level of security threats in the region, Thailand called up a militia and engaged in an internal war in Laos with the United States. The Thai government also allowed the United States to use military bases and sent out more than 11,000 soldiers to Vietnam, including air force personnel. Thailand also waged a Vietnam-U.S. maritime operation against North Vietnam (Cooper 1995). The end of the Vietnam War and the retreat of the United States created security concerns in the region. The invasion of Cambodia by Vietnam increased Thailand's concerns about communization. In addition, the influx of Cambodian refugees into Thailand generated military conflicts near the Laotian and Cambodian borders. In response, Thailand enhanced alliances with the United States and other Western countries and entered into a diplomatic relationship with communist China in 1975.

In the late 1980s, the Thai government changed the direction of its foreign policy, especially toward Indo-Chinese countries. Thailand ceased to be hostile toward communist countries in the region and tried to avoid a direct conflict with them. In addition, the Thai government put forth an effort to end a Cambodian civil war through strong engagement and mediation. As a result, in October 1991 the Cambodian Peace Treaty was signed by the Cambodian parties, including representatives of nineteen nations.

*Current and Potential
Military Confrontation*

Currently, there is no major and imminent security threat against Thailand. After the Vietnam War, Thailand solidified a military alliance with the United States, yet the Thai government has also used its geoeconomical location to enhance economic cooperation with Vietnam, Laos, Cambodia, and Burma. Since 1988, the Chatichai Choonhavan and subsequent governments have emphasized the increase of economic cooperation with Indo-Chinese countries and the decrease of military tension in the region.

There are, however, a couple of potential security threats. First, the border between Burma and Thailand is a hot spot between the Karen tribe and the Burmese government. Attempts to place the Karen tribe under a federalism system led to the Karen tribe's resisting the Burmese government. The resistance movement of the Karen tribe frequently took place on the border of Burma and Thailand. Initially, Thailand publicly assisted the resistance movement; however, the Thai government stopped providing the assistance for the Karen tribe after a change in foreign policy. Even though the number of combats has decreased, a civil conflict between the Karen tribe and the Burmese government continues to be a security concern for Thailand. Second, border disputes remain between Cambodia, Laos, Burma, and Thailand because the borderlines were not drawn as part of the treaty among the parties, but instead were the consequence of French colonization. For example, when a Thai actress was alleged to have announced the sovereignty of Siem Reap, the embassy of Thailand in Cambodia was attacked and a national emergency ensued in Thailand.

Alliance Structure

The traditional foreign policy of Thailand is known to be flexible, dubbed a bamboo policy (IDEA 2001). Thailand has used major powers for its security and national interests. Considering that Thailand is a minor power in the region, the bamboo policy proved to be a realistic and pragmatic way to sustain sovereignty during the colonization period and the Cold War. This policy remains unaltered and has become the current foreign policy in Thailand during the post–Cold War, although the emphasis of Thai foreign policy shifted from a military to an economic aspect.

During World War I, Thailand officially joined in an alliance with and dispatched an expeditionary army for England, France, and Russia. As such, Thailand became a victorious country after the war and a member of the League of Nations. During World War II, however, Thailand strained its relationship with the United States and other Western countries, because the government in power sought "Pan-Thai Nationalism" and joined with the Axis countries. After the retirement of Phibun Songkram near the end of World War II, the new government decided to cooperate with the Allied forces and became a member of the United Nations.

Since World War II, the Thai government has concluded an entente cordiale with eight countries: the United States, the United Kingdom, France, Japan, Pakistan, the Philippines, Australia, and New Zealand. As Indo-Chinese countries rapidly communized in the 1960s and 1970s, the military relationship between the United States and Thailand was established. The United States provided economic and military assistance for Thailand so that communism might be contained (Girling 1981). The Sarit Thanarat government (1957 to 1963) and the succeeding government, the Thanom Kittikachorn government (1963 to 1973), pursued a strong anticommunism policy when communist countries increased their activities in the region. Although the U.S. troops left from this region after the Vietnam War, the Thai government has kept a close military relationship with the United States through SEATO and the Thanat-Rusk announcement of March 1962, which confirmed the effectiveness of a defense alliance. The annual training of joint maritime operations in the Gulf of Thailand also shows the close relationship between the United States and Thailand.

Thailand has kept a friendly relationship with neighboring communist countries as well. The Thai government entered into a diplomatic relationship with China when Indo-Chinese countries became communist, such as when Cambodia became a communist country after the Vietnam War ended. Thailand also purchased T-69 tanks, field artillery, and warships from China with a military modernization plan, and China became the first country to supply artillery to Thailand. Even though Taiwanese president Li Teng-hui's February 1994 private visit to Thailand strained Thailand's relationship with China, the two countries were back to having a close relationship after a twenty-year celebration of a peace treaty and amity between China and Thailand.

Since the Cold War, the Thai government has emphasized economic aspects of foreign policy over military aspects. Under a slogan "Transforming the Battlefield into the Market Place," the Chatichai Choonhavan government attempts to enhance economic cooperation and a friendly diplomatic relationship with communist Indo-Chinese countries (Buszynski 1994). Military cooperation and an alliance with the United States remain significant factors of foreign affairs, especially when neighboring Indo-Chinese governments are politically and economically unstable and provide security threats to Thailand. In addition, as reflected in the September 11, 2001, bombings in the United States and the bombing in Bali, Indonesia, terrorism has become a new security threat in this region.

Thailand also maintains a close relationship with members of the ASEAN regional forum. Although the Cold War made the Thai government play a minimal role in the regional forum, Thailand is one of the founders of the ASEAN regional forum and continuously makes an effort to achieve regional stability and economic cooperation through it. As ideological tension has been reduced since the Cold War, Thailand has accelerated its role in the forum by increasing economic cooperation with and investing in neighboring countries, especially communist Indo-Chinese countries.

Size and Structure of the Military

The military in Thailand consists of the Royal Thai Army, Royal Thai Navy, and Royal Thai Air Force. The size of active military power was 306,000 in 2003, and the size of military manpower, including national guards and reserves, was 17,904,298 in 2003 (CIA 2003; IISS 1970–2001). The conscription system is mandatory, under which a person who picks a white ticket from among black or white tickets serves two years in the military. The probability of picking a white ticket is 1 in 5. In theory, the monarch commands the military; in reality, the prime minister has authority over the military (see Sidebar 2 for further detail).

The Royal Thai Army consists of four regional army headquarters, two cavalry divisions, three armored infantry divisions, and an armored cavalry regiment with three air-mobile companies (IISS 2001, 210–211). The army has four reserve infantry divisions. The army has 190,000 members, including 70,000 conscripts. Because Thailand is surrounded by seas, the navy is a critical part of the military. The size of the active navy is 68,000, including 1,700 naval aviation personnel, 18,000 marines, 7,000 coastal defense personnel, and 27,000 conscripts. It is equipped with thirteen principal surface combatants, eighty-eight patrol and coastal combatants, and nine amphibious crafts. The number of personnel for the naval aviation is 1,700, including 300 conscripts equipped with several aircraft, helicopters, and missiles. Marines make up the largest component of the Royal Thai Navy. They are under a single command with two infantry regiments and one artillery regiment. Finally, the air force has the fewest personnel. The Royal Thai Air Force consists of 48,000 (with no conscripts) people, divided among four air divisions and one flying training school, and has 194 combat aircraft. It is interesting that the air force does not have an armed helicopter.

The number of military personnel has increased over the years. Beginning with 175,000 in 1970, the number increased to 234,000 in 1980, 283,000 in 1990, and 301,000 in 2000 (Werner 2000). The number of military personnel increases in proportion to the population, which has generally been on the incline over the years. Looking at the ratio of military personnel per thousand people is a good way to assess the trend in numbers of military personnel. The ratio of military personnel per thousand people represents the size of military personnel as a proportion of the population at a particular time. For example, in 1973, the ratio was 5.87 military personnel per thousand people, which was the highest ratio between 1946 and 2001. This ratio is calculated by dividing the 1973 population (39,693,000) by 1,000 (39,693,000 ÷ 1,000 = 39,693) and dividing the resulting number into the number of military personnel in that year (233,000) (233,000 ÷ 39,693 = 5.87).

The middle of the 1950s and the 1960s are the two times when the military grew most rapidly. After Phibun's takeover in 1947, the government resumed military expansion under the idea of "Pan-Thai Nationalism." The ratio was 2.24 military personnel per thousand people in 1950 and increased to 3.86 per thousand people in 1959. In the 1960s when Indo-Chinese countries became communist, Thailand increased its ratio of military to civilian personnel to 4.25 per thousand in 1965 and 4.81 per thousand in 1970, with the military and economic help of the United States. The enhancement was mostly focused on the north and northeast borders, neighboring with Laos and Cambodia (Lissak 1976, 92–93). After the

1992 democratic transition, however, the importance of the military was reduced.

Paramilitary force is a good indicator of the level of suppression in a country, because it typically indicates the degree of internal control a country has over its citizenry. The active paramilitary force of Thailand is 113,000, which is the second-largest military group in the country (IISS 2001, 211–212). The "National Security Volunteer Corps" makes up the largest proportion of paramilitary forces, followed by the border patrol police. There are 20,000 hunter soldiers (*Thahan Phran* in Thai), 50,000 principal police (including 500 special action forces), 2,500 paramilitary marine police, and 500 aviation police.

The high number of paramilitary personnel per thousand people in the 1970s reflects the elevated suppression that resulted from a series of military coups d'état. The paramilitary force per thousand was 0.88 in 1970, increased to 1.58 in 1975, and fell slightly to 1.41 in 1979 (IISS 1970–2001). Following an enormous fluctuation in the 1980s, when a series of military coups occurred, paramilitary personnel has declined since 1997, suggesting that the government has reduced its level of suppression. The paramilitary personnel was 1.44 per thousand people, and that number fluctuated between 1.40 in 1992, 1.37 in 1994, 1.55 in 1996, 1.18 in 1998, and 1.16 in 2000. With the exception of the slight increase in 1996, there is a clear, though gradual, downward trend in the level of Thailand's paramilitary forces.

The Thai government has sent some troops abroad, mostly for peacekeeping cooperation with the United Nations (IISS 1970–2001, 211). Six observation units are in East Timor, six are in Iraq and Kuwait, and five are in Sierra Leone, representing a total of 372 soldiers. On the other hand, the Thai government also allows some foreign military forces to be stationed in Thailand, including Singapore, which has one training camp, and the United States, with forty air force personnel, thirty navy personnel, and twenty-eight U.S. Marine Corps personnel.

Budget

Thailand devotes $1.4 billion to defense spending, which amounted to 1.4 percent of the GDP in 2001 (CIA 2003). Defense spending includes expenditures on current and retired military and civilian personnel, operations and maintenance, procurement, military research and development, military construction, and military aid (Stockholm International Peace Research Institute 2003). From 1941 to 1944, defense spending was 33 percent of the total budget, and the figure was 40 percent from 1944 to 1946. Up to the mid-1980s, the figure was more than 20 percent (Chai-Anan 1982; Fineman 1997). After democratization in 1992, however, the popularly elected government reduced the size of the defense budget (Funston 2001, 349) from 2.3 percent of the GDP in 1990 to 2.1 percent in 1995 and to 1.5 percent in 2000 (Stockholm International Peace Research Institute 2003). This downward trend is likely to continue in the future (Buszynski 1994).

Civil-Military Relations/The Role of the Military in Domestic Politics

The civil-military relations in Thailand are characterized as a "vicious circle of Thai politics" (see Sidebar 1 for further detail). A series of military coups d'état and the subsequent military governments led to the institutionalization of the military involvement in the political process (Chai-Anan 1982; Lissak 1976).

Table 2   Vicious Circle of Coup D'états

Period	Leader(s) of Coup D'état	Consequence(s)
1932	Phibun Songkram and the "People's Party"	Change of the absolute monarchy into the constitutional monarchy
1947	Sarit Thanarat, Phao Sriyanon, and Phibun Songkram	Establishment of a triumvirate authoritative regime
1957	Sarit Thanarat and his military faction	Pursuance of "authoritative development," which emphasizes an economic development over a democracy
1976–1978	Prem Tinsulanond and his military factions	Establishment of "semidemocracy," in which the power of government should be shared by the military, civilians, and the king
1991	The Class-5 group	Reestablishment of a strong military government emphasizing the increase of the political role of the military

The new military government dissolved the Assembly and created the New Assembly. By running and electing themselves in the following elections, the new military government established their regime. The history of military coups is summarized in Table 2.

The first military coup d'état in 1932 resulted in the change of the absolute monarchy to a constitutional monarchy (Girling 1981). The first coup was initiated by younger military personnel and technocrats, who were affiliated with the People's Party (*Khana Rassadorn* in Thai). The People's Party was founded by twenty-three army officers and twenty-four technocrats in 1927 in Paris, France. There were three factions of People's Party veterans centering around Major Phahon Phonphayuhasena, civil technocrats centering around Pridi Panomyong, and the young military members centering around Major Phibun Songkram. The second group pursued the realization of socialism, whereas the third group emphasized militarism (Narong 1996, 105–109). The Phibun faction seized power in 1938 and legitimated the government through the emphasis of strong nationalism. After winning against France in an Indo-Chinese dispute and securing the middle and south of Laos and the Battambang and Siem Reap regions of Cambodia, the Phibun government enjoyed great popularity among the people. Once the government allied with the Japanese stationed in Thailand, however, the Phibun government

---

Sidebar 3   Pan-Thai Nationalism

Phibun Songkram announced the national ideology "Pan-Thai Nationalism" in 1938. The purpose of the Pan-Thai Nationalism was to expand the national identity of Thailand into the region. As such, the Thai military government claimed that Thailand has sovereignty over the west of Laos and Cambodia, the Shan province in Burma, and the north of Malaysia during the 1940s.

was alienated from the people. The People's Party was split in half, and the second in power, Pridi Panomyong, formed an underground organization, "Free Thai" (*Seri Thai* in Thai), which was linked to the United States and the United Kingdom and protested against the alliance with Japan.

When Japan's defeat became obvious at the end of World War II, the Pridi government took power from the Phibun government. The leader of the former government, Phibun Songkram, retired from politics and left the responsibility of the alliance to Japan. Despite the strong involvement of the military in politics, party politics began and civilian politicians were appointed to the secretary of the ministry. However, the good days were to be short-lived, because economic depression and political and social disorders stirred up another military coup d'état. When King Ananda Mahidol (Rama VIII) was mysteriously killed, the military used his death as an excuse for the military coup d'état of 1947. After this coup, a triumvirate authoritative regime was established, centering on a military faction with Sarit Thanarat, a police faction with Phao Sriyanon, and a faction with the returning Phibun Songkram. Phibun Songkram mediated interactions between Sarit Thanarat and Phao Sriyanon. This triumvirate regime came to an end when Sarit Thanarat and his faction initiated a bloodless coup d'état in September 1957. As Phao Sriyanon and his followers were about to win a majority of the parliamentary seats in February 1957, Sarit Thanarat and his faction carried out another coup d'état and expelled the factions of Phao Sriyanon and Phibun Songkram.

The Sarit government enhanced the legitimacy of the government by increasing the status of the king. When a constitutional monarchy was adopted, the status of the king was reduced to that of a figurehead. Emphasizing the trinity of King, Buddhism, and Nation, the Sarit government showed loyalty to the king and in turn became popular among the people. After improving the relationship with the king, the Sarit government pressed for an economic growth plan under the slogan "Revolution and Development" and advocated political stability in the country for the sake of economic development. In addition, with economic and military aid from the United States, the Sarit government continued to pursue authoritative development, and Sarit's successor, Thanom Kittikachorn, followed suit. In a series of elections, the Sarit government enjoyed a majority status and continued to pursue an economic development plan at the expense of the civilian society.

Civilians in Thailand had another opportunity to change civil-military relations. In the late 1960s, the civilians in Thailand began to protest against the military authoritarian regime. When the Thanom government attempted to amend the constitution to increase military control over civilian society, students and intellectuals led an antiauthoritarian move-

---

Sidebar 4   Buddhist Thailand

In the thirteenth century, Buddhism was introduced in Thailand by the Sukhothai Kingdom and became a national religion. Currently, 95 percent of the population are Buddhists. The constitution states the importance of Buddhism in politics: the king should be Buddhist and a guardian of Buddhism.

ment, which peaked in 1973. This movement, called "Challenge from Society," led to the country's first democratization. This opportunity for change was lost, however, because of political immaturity and the threat of communism (Yos 1989). As U.S. troops left the region after the Vietnam War, Thailand was threatened by neighboring countries, which were rapidly becoming communized. The threat was aggravated from the inside as well, especially because communism had begun to spread to some of the Thai people. Domestically, interest groups expressed their voices, and the efforts of political groups to channel these diverse voices into one political system were not successful. For example, there were 1,333 strikes and 322 protests from 1973 to 1976 (Morell and Chai-Anan 1981, 251; Cooper 1995, 230).

After a series of military coups d'état in 1976, 1977, and 1978, Prem Tinsulanond established a "semidemocracy," wherein the power of the government was to be shared by the military, civilians, and the king (Neher 1988, 201; Yos 1989, 86–87). The Prem government continued to be in power as the political freedom of the people was kept to a minimum and the privilege of civilian politicians to express their ideological opinions was limited. The disruption of the regime began from the inside, however. The Prem regime was composed of three factions: Young Tucks, the Class-5 group, and the Democratic Soldiers (Suchit 1996, 47). The Young Tucks continuously initiated coups for overriding the Prem regime, although the first two coups failed because of a lack of support from the other factions.

With the 1988 general elections, the Prem government was replaced with the Chatichai government. As the Chatichai government pursued a series of policies against military interests, the Class-5 group initiated another coup and took over the Chatichai government. The semidemocracy, therefore, was replaced with a strong military government in 1991, emphasizing again the increase of the political role of the military. Under the interim government of Anand Panyarachoon, the military government attempted to achieve its legitimacy through general elections in March 1992. This attempt resurrected the spirit of civic movement, however, and provided another opportunity to improve the civilian-military relationship. A series of protests against the military government led the king to officially urge the military government to resign.

After the 1992 democratization, the newly elected Chuan Leekpai appointed a retired general, not a military officer in active service, as secretary of defense and made a series of military reforms (e.g., a modernization of weaponry and a reorganization of military offices). In addition, the military stayed strictly within its base, although in 1995 and 1996 some government officials were reported to have been corrupt, and Thailand experienced an economic crisis in 1997. Considering that the military had previously taken advantage of such situations to initiate military coups, it seems that the military has changed its behavior and is less likely to interfere with politics in the near future. All in all, the civilian-military relationship is in the process of changing from military dominance to civilian dominance in Thailand. Today, the military focuses on the duties related to national security, such as border control, illegal immigration, drug trafficking, and illegal weaponry.

Terrorism

Terrorism has not been a major threat in Thailand, but the level of alert has increased. There were a couple of protests against the military government in the past, but the level of threats was minimal. For example, in the 1960s and 1970s, some hill tribes in the north cooperated with communists and formed an opposition to the military authority. Furthermore, a small fraction of the Muslims in the south attempted to gain independence from Thailand. These attempts failed, and they never represented a major threat in Thailand.

The Thai Muslim resistance formed from the early 1960s to the 1970s, with organizations such as the Pattani United Liberation Organization, the National Liberation Front of the Pattani, and the National Revolution Front. Most of the organizations camped in the jungle by the borderline and waged resistance against the Thai government. Since the 1980s, however, the Thai government has pursued an assimilation policy through the education and economic improvement of the Thai Muslims. As a result, only a few organizations intermittently are involved in somewhat threatening activities, and most Muslim organizations engage only in nonthreatening activities (Fineman 1997). Although the number of Muslims has increased, the proportion in the population is still insignificant (3.8 percent in 2003), and a majority of Muslims are conservatively congregating in the south of Thailand. The resistance of the Thai Muslims, therefore, is not likely to be a major security threat in Thailand in the foreseeable future.

On the other hand, the increasing activity of terrorists in neighboring countries is a growing concern for the Thai government. Indonesia, the Philippines, and Malaysia are known to be active grounds for terrorism. The September 11, 2001, event in the United States and the bombing at a Bali nightclub in Indonesia added to government concerns about terrorism. In particular, the Thai government put out a special alert on terrorist activities after it was reported that some extreme Muslim organizations linked to al-Qaeda have used Southeast Asian countries as bases for their activities. As a part of the antiterrorism program, the Thai government has investigated some Muslim organizations alleged to be sponsored by Jemaah Islamiyah and al-Qaeda.

Relationship with the United States

Thailand has a long history with the United States. Thailand established a diplomatic relationship with the United States in 1833, twenty-one years before the Treaty of Kanagawa was signed by Japan and the United States. On May 1, 1856, Townsend Harris, a U.S. envoy, and King Mongut (Rama IV) cosigned a Treaty of Amity, Commerce, and Navigation, which provided the United States rights of extraterritoriality. After joining a charter member of the League of Nations, Norman Davis, as acting secretary of state in Thailand, signed a new treaty with the United States to replace the unequal treaty of 1856. The U.S. Senate, President Warren G. Harding, and King Vajiravudh (Rama VI) ratified this treaty in 1920. The Thailand-U.S. treaty of 1920 became an example for revision of the unequal treaties with Western countries.

In the early part of World War II, Thailand had allied with Japan and declared war against the United States and the Allied forces. The Thailand-U.S. relationship was the worst when the Phibun government attacked Burma, which was under British protectorate, and Laos and Cambodia, which were under French protectorate. At the end of World War II, Phibun Songkram assumed responsibility for the alliance of Japan and retired from politics. The new government led by Pridi Panomyong seceded from the Axis countries and joined the Allied forces.

During the Cold War, however, an increased security threat to Thailand from communist countries and the U.S. containment policy in the region made the United States and Thailand close partners. Thailand was faced with the expansion of communism, especially among Indo-Chinese countries (Yos 1989). When Phibun Songkram reclaimed power, he pursued a strong anticommunism policy and dispatched troops in the Korean War to fight communists. With a strong anticommunism policy, the United States gave economic and military assistance to Thailand (Girling 1981). The United States provided economic aid in the amount of $650 million from 1950 to 1970 and military aid in the amount of $935.9 million from 1951 to 1971 (Fineman 1997). In return, Thailand assisted with secret operations by the CIA in Burma and Laos and allowed the United States to use a military base (Lissak 1976; Fineman 1997). During the Vietnam War, Thailand sent army personnel, including air forces, and waged a joint maritime military operation with the United States in the Gulf of Thailand.

The end of the Cold War and the 1991 military coup d'état led by General Suchinda Kraprayoon marked the beginning of a short estrangement. The United States and the European Union expressed their regret regarding the military coup and the newly appointed prime minister, who was allegedly associated with cocaine trafficking in the north of Thailand.

With the restoration of a constitutional regime, the United States imposed economic sanctions against Thailand and stopped economic and military assistance (Elliott, Schott, Hufbauer, and Oegg 2004; Saitip 1995, 220). However, the Thailand–U.S. relationship returned to normal when Thailand played a mediator role between Cambodia and the United States and helped to improve the relationship between Vietnam and the United States. Since September 11, 2001, Thailand has been cooperating with the United States on an antiterrorism policy in the region. For example, the Thai government has dispatched a peacekeeping force of about 400 soldiers to Iraq and has exchanged information on antiterrorism activities with the United States. In addition, the United States and Thailand work closely together to follow the movement of some Southeast Asian terrorist organizations sponsored by al-Qaeda that are based in the south of Thailand and the Philippines.

The Future

Since the Cold War and the relaxation of regional security threats, Thailand has taken on a new role in the Southeast Asia region. Thailand's foreign policy has shifted from military competition to economic cooperation with neighboring countries. This trend has been more evident since recovering from an economic crisis in 2002. The Thai government uses its geoeconomic advantage to bring back Southeast Asian countries, including communist countries, to the regional economic cooperation forum. For example, Thailand persuaded Burma, Cambodia, and Laos to join the ASEAN and has bridged continental and island countries. Thailand held a summit meeting of the

Asia-Pacific Economic Cooperation in 2003. In addition, when Indonesia, a leading country in the region, suffered economic hardship as a result of an East Asian financial crisis, Thailand was called upon to play a major role in the region, especially in ASEAN. Recently, Thailand was heavily involved in the negotiation of a Free Trade Area as well as an expansion plan for ASEAN to include Korea, China, and Japan, called "ASEAN Plus 3." Furthermore, in responding to the increasing concerns of drugs and terrorism, the Thai government has enhanced its cooperation with neighboring countries and the United States.

With respect to civilian-military relations, the influence of the military on the political processes in Thailand has been significantly reduced. Although most Thai people respect the defense role of the military, they do not wish for the military to be involved in domestic politics; as a result of their exclusion from politics, professionalism has grown in the military. The modernization project of the military, furthermore, makes the organization more efficient and increases its military capability. The role of the military is and will be limited to foreign security issues and terrorism in the future.

References, Recommended Readings, and Websites

Books

Alagappa, Muthiah, ed. 2001. *Military Professionalism in Asia: Conceptual and Empirical Perspectives*. Honolulu, HI: East-West Center.

Bunbongkarn, Suchit. 1987. *The Military in Thai Politics, 1981–86*. Singapore: Institute of Southeast Asian Studies.

Chai-Anan, Samudavanija. 1982. *The Thai Young Turks*. Singapore: Institute of Southeast Asian Studies.

Chee, Stephen. 1989. "Thailand: A Stable Semi-Democracy." In *Democracy in Developing Countries: Asia*, Larry Diamond, Juan J. Linz, and Seymour Martin Lipset, eds. Boulder, CO: Lynne Rienner Publishers.

Chee, Stephen, ed. 1991. *Leadership and Security in Southeast Asia: Institutional Aspects*. Singapore: Institute of Southeast Asian Studies.

Colbert, Evelyn. 1977. *Southeast Asia in International Politics, 1941–1956*. Ithaca, NY: Cornell University Press.

Cooper, Donald F. 1995. *Thailand: Dictatorship and Democracy?* London: Minerva Press.

Darling, Frank C. 1965. *Thailand and the United States*. Washington, DC: Public Affairs Press.

Dhiravegin, Likhit. 1992. *Demi Democracy: The Evolution of the Thai Political System*. Singapore: Time Academic Press.

Djiwabdono, J. Soedjiati, and Yong Mun Cheong, eds. 1988. *Soldiers and Stability in Southeast Asia*. Singapore: Institute of Southeast Asian Studies.

Elliott, Kimberly Ann, Jeffrey J. Schott, Gary Clyde Hufbauer, and Barbara Oegg. 2004. *Economic Sanctions Reconsidered*. Washington, DC: Institute for International Economics.

Fineman, Daniel. 1997. *A Special Relationship: The United States and Military Government in Thailand, 1947–1958*. Honolulu: University of Hawaii Press.

Funston, John. 2001. "Thailand: Reform Politics." In *Government and Politics in Southeast Asia*, John Funston, ed. Singapore: Institute of Southeast Asian Studies.

Girling, John L. S. 1981. *Thailand: Society and Politics*. Ithaca, NY: Cornell University Press.

Hewison, Kevin, ed. 1997. *Political Change in Thailand: Democracy and Participation*. New York: Routledge.

International Institute for Democracy and Electoral Assistance (IDEA). 2001. *Challenges to Democratization in Burma: Perspectives on Multilateral and Bilateral Responses*. Stockholm, Sweden: International Institute for Democracy and Electoral Assistance.

International Institute for Strategic Studies. 1970–2001. *The Military Balance*. London: International Institute for Strategic Studies.

Lissak, Moshe. 1976. *Military Roles in Modernization: Civil-Military*

Relations in Thailand and Burma. Beverly Hills, CA: Sage Publications.

Morell, David, and Samudavanija Chai-Anan. 1981. *Political Conflict in Thailand: Reform, Reaction, Revolution.* Cambridge: Oelgeschlager, Gunn and Hain Publishers.

Narong, Sinsawasdi. 1996. *Kan-muang thai: Kan-wikhro chungchitawithaya [Thai Politics: An Analysis of Psychological Method].* Bangkok: Oriental Sakula.

Prudhisan, Jumbala. 1992. *Nation-Building and Democratization in Thailand: A Political History.* Bangkok: Social Research Institute, Chulalongkorn University.

Randolph, R. Sean. 1986. *The United States and Thailand: Alliance Dynamics, 1950–1985.* Berkeley, CA: Institute of East Asian Studies.

Saitip, Sukatipan. 1995. "Thailand: The Evolution of Legitimacy." In *Political Legitimacy in Southeast Asia: The Quest for Moral Authority,* Muthiah Alagappa, ed. Stanford, CA: Stanford University Press.

Suchit, Bunbongkarn. 1996. *Thailand: State of the Nation.* Singapore: Institute of Southeast Asian Studies.

Yos, Santasombat. 1989. "Leadership and Security in Modern Thai Politics." In *Leadership Perceptions and National Security: The Southeast Asian Experience,* Mohammed Ayoob and Samudavanija Chai-Anan, eds. Singapore: Institute of Southeast Asian Studies.

Articles/Newspapers
Bennett, D. Scott, and Allan Stam. 2000. "EUGene: A Conceptual Manual." *International Interactions* 26:179–204.

Buszynski, Leszek. 1994. "Thailand's Foreign Policy: Management of a Regional Vision." *Asian Survey* 34:721–737.

Central Intelligence Agency. 2003. *CIA World Factbook 2003* (accessed December 8, 2003).

Neher, Clark D. 1988. "Thailand in 1987: Semi-Successful Semi-Democracy." *Asian Survey* 28:192–201.

Stockholm International Peace Research Institute. 2003. *The SIPRI Military Expenditure Database.* http://projects.sipri.org/milex.html (accessed December 8, 2003).

Werner, Suzanne. 2000. "The Effects of Political Similarity on the Onset of Militarized Disputes, 1816–1985." *Political Research Quarterly* 53:343–374.

Websites
Central Intelligence Agency. CIA *World Factbook:* http://www.cia.gov/cia/publications/factbook/geos/th.html

Country Studies/Area Handbook Series published by the Library of U.S. Congress: http://countrystudies.us/thailand/.

Institute of Southeast Asian Studies: http://www.iseas.edu.sg/.

Ministry of Defense: http://www.mod.go.th/eng_mod/.

Royal Thai Air Force: http://www.rtaf.mi.th/eng/index.html.

Royal Thai Army (Thai): http://www.rta.mi.th/.

Royal Thai Government: http://www.thaigov.go.th/index-eng.htm.

Royal Thai Navy: http://www.navy.mi.th/newwww/eindex.php.

Thai Military Researchers: http://www1.mod.go.th/etmr/index1.html.

Thai Parliament: http://www.parliament.go.th/files/mainpage.htm.

Turkey

Peter Finn

Geography and History

The Republic of Turkey occupies a territory spanning two continents and sits astride a narrow waterway linking two seas. The Asian portion of Turkey, called the Anatolian peninsula, or Asia Minor, constitutes most of the country's land area; it is separated from the European portion (Thrace) by the Bosporus and Dardanelles straits and the Sea of Marmara, which together link the Black and Mediterranean seas. Turkey borders eight countries, namely (in order of decreasing border length), Syria, Iran, Iraq, Armenia, Georgia, Bulgaria, Greece, and Azerbaijan. Turkey's land area is 780,580 square kilometers (301,304 square miles)—slightly larger than the state of Texas. Its elevation ranges from sea level at the Mediterranean shore to 5,166 meters (16,949 feet) at Turkey's highest peak, Agri Dagi (Mount Ararat, the legendary resting place of Noah's Ark according to Judeo-Christian scripture), near Turkey's border with Iran.

The Anatolian peninsula is a high central plateau ringed by craggy mountains. In the north, the Pontus, or North Anatolian Mountains, run parallel to the Black Sea and restrict coastal access to a few passes. The Taurus Mountains in the south run parallel to the coast of the Mediterranean and extend down to the sea. Both ranges converge to form a natural border with Turkey's eastern neighbors. Central Anatolia is an elevated plateau characterized by arid steppes. Although this region's riparian lands are cultivated, the dominant steppe lands are used for grazing. The areas in the west, bordering the Marmara and Aegean seas, are the most populated and economically developed in the country, where rolling plains comprise most of Turkey's agrarian land.

Turkey has abundant freshwater from alluvium-rich rivers originating in its central highlands and mountains. The Tigris and Euphrates rivers, which converge in Iraq and empty into the Persian Gulf, both have their headwaters in Turkey. Turkey has capitalized on its water resources by damming both rivers for irrigation and hydroelectric power; and because these rivers are a critical freshwater supply to Iraq and Syria, their dams are an unresolved source of contention (Metz 1996, 316).

Although most Mediterranean countries share similar weather conditions, the Turkish peninsula's old name of Asia Minor is appropriate in terms of climate—it has climatic diversity that would be expected of much larger, continent-sized, landmasses. The climate ranges from the typical Mediterranean near the coasts to seasonal temperature extremes on the interior steps (occasioned by the rain-shadow

Table 1   Turkey: Key Statistics

Type of government	Republican, parliamentary democracy
Population (millions)	69.6 (2005 est.)
Religion	Islam 99.8% (mostly Sunni, though a significant, distinctly Turkish Shia minority, the Alevi, abounds)
Main industries	Textiles, food processing, automotive manufacturing, mining (coal, chromite, copper, boron), steel, petroleum, construction, lumber, paper
Main security threats	Regional instability, foreign and domestic terrorism, internal instability
Defense spending (% GDP)	5.3% (FY 2003)
Size of military (thousands)	514 (2004)
Number of civil wars since 1945	1
Number of interstate wars since 1945	1

Sources
Central Intelligence Agency Website. 2005. CIA *World Factbook*. http://www.cia.gov/cia/ publications/factbook/ (accessed May 29, 2005).
International Institute for Strategic Studies (IISS). 2003. *The Military Balance 2003–2004*. London: IISS and Oxford University Press.

effect of central Turkey's high, encircling mountain ranges).

Turkey's population is about 69 million, of which approximately 80 percent are ethnic Turks and 20 percent are Kurds, although these are only estimates, because the Kurdish population's size is not precisely known. Turkey's inhabitants are predominantly Sunni Muslim, with a negligible 0.2 percent combined Christian and Jewish minority. About one-third of Turkey's Muslims represent a (notionally) Shia sect called the Alevi. (See Sidebar 1: The Alevi: Turkey's Distinct Islamic Sect.) Turkish is the country's official language, although Kurdish, Armenian, Arabic, and Greek are also spoken.

Turkey has well-developed agriculture and light industry, leading the world in hard-shell nut, fig, and apricot production and placing in the global top seven producers of vegetables, tobacco, wheat, and cotton. Turkey is a leading nation in the production of finished textiles and

leather garments, with textile exports accounting for 37 percent of industrial exports. Fine, handmade, Turkish carpets are another significant, and nationally distinct, export (The Republic of Turkey, American Embassy).

Turkey's GDP is 509 billion, with a per capita GDP of $7,400. Services account for 58.5 percent of Turkey's GNP, followed by industry at 29.8 percent, and agriculture at 11.7 percent (CIA *World Factbook* 2005)

Contemporary Turkey is situated in a rich historical context spanning hundreds of years. To the extent such a distinction is possible—or even appropriate— Turkey's modern history began in the late nineteenth century, with the emergence of Turkish nationalism and Western liberal political thinking. Most of these ideas came to Turkey by way of students, many of them military, who had studied in Europe. Although some advances in Ottoman government were made—like constitutional government and parlia-

Sidebar 1 The Alevi: Turkey's Distinct Islamic Sect

While Turkey's religious constitution is often considered only in terms of being predominantly Islamic with a Sunni majority, a distinct, and unacknowledged, Shia minority abounds. Because of past persecution and resulting distrust, the Alevi generally keep their faith secret; as such, little is known about their beliefs or numbers (estimates range from one-quarter to one-third of the population). Alevism is syncretistic, nondogmatic philosophy influenced by Christianity, Zoroastrianism, and Buddhism and involves a mystical component rooted in the Turk's ancient tribal shamanism. The Alevi practice an intuitive faith rooted more in custom and practices than in theology. Many of their unique practices run counter to the five pillars of Islam: prayer is performed when inspired to, rather than at appointed times; no pilgrimage or fasts are performed; worship is not performed in mosques; in addition, alcohol is consumed as part of religious ceremonies, where men and women worship together; and sharia is not strictly observed. As the Alevi are suspicious of central authority in matters of faith, they endorse a secular Turkish state. Vicious persecution of the Alevi in the late 1970s was one factor occasioning the 1980 coup.

Source
Cornell, Erik. 2001. *Turkey in the 21st Century: Opportunities Challenges, Threats.* Richmond, Surrey: Curzon Press.

The Ottoman Empire was drawn into World War I by Germany; although the two countries shared common enemies—primarily Russia, but also Russian allies Britain and France. Beset on four fronts, with antiquated equipment and poor leadership, the Ottomans fared poorly throughout the war, their only major victory against allied forces being a vigorous defense of Port Gallipoli. The Ottoman Empire imploded, and its Anatolian heartland was occupied by allied forces.

With the old Ottoman sultanate virtually stripped of power and Anatolia under foreign occupation, Turkish nationalism emerged anew under the leadership of Mustafa Kemal. Mustafa Kemal, an outspoken nationalist even before the war, was now a national hero, the Ottoman Empire's only undefeated general who commanded Gallipoli's defense and later led a counteroffensive that repulsed Russia's advance into Anatolia. Mustafa Kemal helped win the war of independence, which followed the nationalists claiming sovereignty (described in the Conflict Past and Present section), then he resigned from the military to head Turkey's government and forge modern Turkey in his image.

Mustafa Kemal was committed to Westernizing Turkey politically, socially, and technologically—often at the cost of pervasive cultural institutions. Turkey's language was converted to a roman script, laws and penal codes were enacted on European models, female suffrage was instituted, the caliphate was abolished, education was secularized, the wearing of the fez (a modernized form of the turban, thus having religious connotations) was banned in public, and so on. Turkey's Western integration would remain an enduring theme of the country's foreign and domestic policy.

mentary representation of all Ottoman *millets*—infighting between authoritarian nationalists, liberals, and Islamic traditionalists weakened reforms.

Turkey remained neutral during World War II, but afterward actively sought participation in the international arena. Multiparty politics began in 1946, and the newly registered Democratic Party (DP) made rapid gains against the Republican People's Party (Cumhuriyet Halk Partisi—CHP). As the DP increased its power, it also became increasingly undemocratic—pushing through legislation limiting press access and government criticism. Finally, the DP tried to gain control of the general staff itself by influencing the appointment process, which led to a military coup in 1960 (all coups are described in the Civil-Military Relations section).

Turkey took a resolutely pro-Western stance during the Cold War, benefiting greatly from aid under the Truman Doctrine and Marshall Plan and by admittance to NATO and other treaty organizations, although dialogue between Ankara and the West was marred by disputes with Greece over Cyprus in 1964 and 1967 (described in the Conflict Past and Present section).

Turkey's economy was devastated following the 1973 oil embargo and continued to decline throughout the decade. By 1977 inflation had reached 50 percent and unemployment 30 percent (Metz 1996, 56–58). The Turkish lira was devalued twice, and the government sought to increase industrial production by increasing subsidies, although the resulting increase in debt was proportionally higher. These problems, coupled with emerging Kurdish separatism, led to a second full-blooded military coup in 1980.

Throughout the 1980s Turkey worked to revitalize its stagnant economy and institute political reforms aimed at ensuring future stability. Relations with Greece, while still tumultuous, improved as both countries made efforts to accommodate each other. The Soviet Union's collapse brought Turkey's strategic importance to the West into question, a question Turkey tried to resolve in its favor by participating in operation Desert Shield/Storm (1990–1991). The 1980s also saw a dramatic increase in terrorism and a Kurdish insurrection. The insurrection was ended at the close of the twentieth century, but the specter of foreign and domestic terrorism would haunt Turkey into the new millennium.

Regional Geopolitics

Turkey is situated at the nexus of three conflict-torn regions: the Balkans, the Caucasus, and the Middle East. Turkey shares not only a geographical proximity with these areas, but also (to varying degrees) their ethnicity, language, and religion, as well as a collective historical memory of Ottoman dominion. Turkey sees its fate as intertwined with those of its neighbors and takes a proactive interest in promoting peace and cooperation with and between its surrounding states. The reasons for instability in each of these regions are manifold and complex, and often exist in a historical context stretching back hundreds of years.

The Balkans is a region of latent ethnic and religious strife—kept in check only by the presence of one empire or another (be it the Ottomans, the Soviets, or Marshal Tito). Although the region's association with Turkey is primarily religious, Turkey's secularity makes this a weak connection, and in many Balkan states, the memory of Ottoman rule makes Turkey's involvement in the region controversial, as was the case during NATO's Kosovo operations. In addition, conflicts here do not involve transborder issues, as in the Caucasus or the Middle East, thus

Turkey faces little risk of conflicts spilling over or being drawn into them. Turkey's interests in the Balkans are primarily economic; the region is seen as a viable market for Turkish goods. In spite of the Balkans' volatility, Turkey remains relatively insulated, its efforts to promote peace in the region a moral and economic imperative.

The Caucasus' ethnic, territorial, and religious disputes are no less complex than those of the Balkans and are exacerbated by Russian, Turkish, and, to a lesser extent, U.S. attempts to influence the region's events. Turkey has strong ethnic ties to Azerbaijan, and both have described their relationship as "two nations, one people." Turkey and Azerbaijan share a pronounced (historical) animosity toward Armenia, which has pushed Armenia closer to Russia, whereas Georgia cautiously supports Turkey.

The possibility of a future war between Azerbaijan and Armenia still exists, as does the possibility that Turkey might get dragged into the war in support of Azerbaijan. Azerbaijan also has complex disputes with Iran over control of the Caspian Sea's littoral waters—and the oil that lies beneath them. An example of this relationship occurred in 2001 when Iranian gunboats began harassing Azeri oil exploration vessels operating in the southern Caspian Sea. Turkey responded with a strongly worded letter to Tehran—which coincided with the deployment of a Turkish F-5 fighter squadron to Baku, ostensibly for an aerial demonstration commemorating Azerbaijan's independence (Radu 2003, 72).

However, the possibility of Turkey intervening on behalf of Azerbaijan must be balanced by its limited participation in Azerbaijan's war with Armenia (1991–1994)—which Azerbaijan can be said to have lost. At the time Turkey was probably more concerned that its actions might escalate Russian involvement on behalf of Armenia or lead to a long-term commitment of troops. Turkey also acknowledges the instability of Azerbaijan itself, its government regularly convulsed by coups and attempted coups.

Russia does not welcome any action by Turkey, or other parties, to make political inroads into the Caucasus, which Russia considers its "backyard." Turkey is already Azerbaijan's and Georgia's leading trade partner, and Turkey offers the possibility of opening trade routes—particularly for oil exports—which Russia once controlled. Russia has a significant military presence in its border regions with the Caucasus and maintains signals intelligence (SIGINT) facilities in Armenia and Azerbaijan (under lease from the respective governments); but as long as Turkey makes no overtly threatening action in the region, Russia will likely refrain from forcibly pressing its complaints.

The Middle East is by far Turkey's most unstable front. Although Turkey recently has had modest success cultivating congenial relations with states in the Caucasus and the Balkans, it has been less successful finding friendship in the Middle East. Turkey has territorial disputes with Syria (described in the next section), on which neither side is willing to compromise, and a deep mutual suspicion—stemming from antithetical political philosophies—clouds Iranian-Turkish relations. Turkey's relationship with Iraq is dominated by one concern—the millions of Kurds in northern Iraq and their implications for Turkey's own problems with Kurdish separatism.

Turkey's frantic diplomatic efforts to avoid the U.S.-led war in Iraq (Operation

Iraqi Freedom) were motivated primarily by its desire to avert the instability that a regime change could bring—instability that could lead to the establishment of a Kurdish state, thus escalating Kurdish separatist ambitions in Turkey and possibly reigniting the Kurdish insurgency that ravaged Turkey for much of the 1990s. For this reason Turkey's foreign policy is emphatic that Iraq's territorial integrity be preserved and that a strong government be established, with broad popular support, to ensure the country's future stability and integrity.

Kurdish separatism is an intractable issue that Turkey shares with many of its neighbors. The Kurds are distributed among a number of states: Turkey (12 million), Iran (6 million), Iraq (4 million), and Syria (fewer than 1 million), with smaller concentrations inhabiting Armenia and Azerbaijan. Although the Kurds are a linguistically distinct people, inhabiting a largely contiguous area of land, their political aspirations are complex. Much of Kurdish society is organized around hierarchical clans who control their lands in a largely feudal arrangement. Disputes between these clans are common and frequently take on the character of bloody feuds. So although the Kurds are ethnically homogeneous (the source of their nationalism), they are socially heterogeneous, with clan loyalty often overriding loyalty to any greater Kurdish nation. This has led others (Cornell) to accurately characterize Kurdish nationalism as akin to Arab nationalism in the early twentieth century. To further complicate matters the PKK, the militant-political voice of Kurdish nationalism (whose activities are described in the Terrorism section), espouses a Marxist-Leninist ideology that understandably disdains both Turkish hegemony in "Kurdistan" and the Kurds'

own feudalistic social arrangement. Naturally many Kurdish tribal leaders oppose the PKK's ideology and are thus reluctant to support it.

Turkey's constitution lists the state's territorial integrity as one of three "irrevocable" constitutional articles and thus will make no concessions with respect to an independent Kurdish state, convincing the PKK that armed insurrection was their only hope. After nearly a decade of fighting and terrorism, however, the PKK was no closer to its goal. If any solution exists to the Kurdish question it will likely only come about with a more cohesive Kurdish political unity.

Conflict Past and Present

Although Turkey itself has not fought an interstate war since its War of Independence (1919–1920), it is a frequent (and enthusiastic) participant in UN and NATO operations and has nearly gone to war with Greece on more than one occasion. But although Turkey maintains a high readiness for war and the second-largest force contribution to NATO (after the United States), the country's foreign policy is characteristically pragmatic and peace oriented. Turkey has consistently sought diplomatic solutions to achieving stability in its region of the world.

Following the Mudros Armistice in 1918, which ended the Ottoman Empire's involvement in World War I, the Ottoman territories of Anatolia and Thrace were occupied by British, French, Russian, and Greek forces. Previously latent Turkish nationalist forces quickly rallied around the charismatic leadership of the Ottoman marshal Mustafa Kemal. Mustafa Kemal emerged as the only undefeated Ottoman general, a national hero who had blunted the allied assault on Gallipoli—still widely considered to be the British military's most humiliating defeat. In 1919, the nationalists established a national assembly in Ankara and abolished the Ottoman sultanate, proclaiming sovereignty over the Turkish nation and Mustafa Kemal president. In response, and under allied instruction, Greek armies moved from Thrace into southwest Anatolia and began advancing on the new capital. Greek forces advanced to within eighty kilometers (fifty miles) of Ankara, were Mustafa Kemal took personal command of the army and decisively defeated the Greeks in a twenty-day battle. Their forces exhausted, and their supply lines overextended, the Greeks were driven back into Thrace. The allies, acknowledging the viability of the new Turkish state, withdrew from Anatolia in 1922.

In the interwar years, Mustafa Kemal worked to consolidate power and implement a sweeping platform of radical social, economic, religious, and political reforms. So that he could focus his attentions on domestic matters, Mustafa Kemal (who took the surname Atatürk, "father [of the] Turk[s]") negotiated neutrality and nonaggression treaties with Turkey's neighbors, summarizing Turkish foreign policy as "peace at home, peace abroad." (Atatürk's foreign policy is explicated in the Alliance Structure section.)

Atatürk died in 1938, and his successor, İsmet İnönü, faithfully continued Atatürk's policy of neutrality, which he exercised with great integrity. During World War II, İnönü staunchly resisted pressure from Germany to allow military vessels through the straits and overflights of Turkish territory. Turkey finally entered the war on the side of the Allies in early 1945, as a largely symbolic gesture to ensure its participation in the war's aftermath.

Turkey was among the fifty-one original members of the United Nations when the first general assembly convened in August 1945, and its commitment to that organization would be tested five years later in the Korean War. Turkey was among the first UN members to send troops to Korea, dispatching an infantry brigade (4,500 troops) to the theater under UN command before the war's outbreak. By the time the war was over, 25,000 Turkish troops had served in Korea. The Turkish brigade became distinguished for its valor after sustaining the heaviest proportional casualty rate (more than 10 percent) of any UN force (Zürcher 1993, 246). Turkey's contribution to Korea did not go unnoticed by members of the newly formed North Atlantic Treaty Organization (NATO), who admitted Turkey to the alliance in 1952.

By far the most serious, and controversial, intervention in Turkey's history was the Cyprus crisis. The issue began in 1964 when Cypriot president Archbishop Makarios attempted to change the island's constitution and limit its ethnic Turkish minority's autonomy. Several Turkish villages in Cyprus were besieged, and during the ensuing violence, massacres of ethnic Turks were reported. Turkish president İnönü threatened a military invasion of the island, and the air force made a show of force by flying low-level runs over the island, although the threatened invasion did not occur. U.S. President Lyndon Johnson sent a letter to President İnönü, warning him that if Turkey's invasion provoked a Soviet response, the United States and NATO would not come to Turkey's aid. The letter also forbade Turkey from using U.S.-supplied materiel (which constituted the vast majority of Turkey's equipment) in any action against Cyprus.

The crisis subsided until 1967 when, following a coup d'état in Greece, Greece's military junta began encouraging ethnic Greek Cypriots to unite the island with mainland Greece—a doctrine known as enosis. Turkish threats against Greece ensued, and war was narrowly avoided when the junta quelled its enosis rhetoric.

Finally in 1974, Cypriot national guardsmen instigated a coup against Makarios in the name of enosis. Turkey, now under the leadership of President Bülent Eçevit, first sought a multilateral solution, inviting Britain (Cyprus's former imperial ruler) and Greece to join Turkey in restoring constitutional government in Cyprus. When no consensus was reached, Turkey unilaterally invaded northern Cyprus. In what the Turkish government termed *bariş harekâti* (or "peace operations"), 40,000 troops and 200 tanks were deployed to Cyprus with the declared purpose of protecting the island's ethnic Turkish minority (Zürcher 1993, 290). Turkish forces successfully gained control of the north (about 40 percent of the island) before a cease-fire was declared. Turkey subsequently reduced its forces to 30,000 troops (with reinforcements available by air from the Turkish mainland on short notice). The island was partitioned with the Republic of Northern Cyprus (RNC) established in the north (although the RNC is only recognized by Turkey). Population exchanges, either voluntary or coerced, have homogenized the respective partitions.

Cyprus is not one of Turkey's most pressing security issues, but Turkey's presence on the island—and the animosity this induces from Greece—complicates its involvement in NATO and its admission into the European Union.

After the Soviet Union's collapse, certain individuals in Turkey (although not the general public) were concerned with continuing their strategic partnership with the United States. So when Iraq invaded Kuwait in August 1990, Turkish president Turgut Özal became one of the most outspoken opponents of the occupation and an early supporter of the U.S.-led UN coalition. Özal believed that Turkish coalition assistance might force the door open for Turkey's EU membership—just as İnönü's military commitment to Korea forty years before had opened the door to NATO.

Özal gave the United States access to Turkey's strategic İncirlik air base in southeast Anatolia, putting Turkey at risk from Iraqi air and missile attacks. Although such attacks never occurred, a serious problem arose as Kurdish refugees from a failed insurrection in northern Iraq fled into Iran and attempted to flee across the border into Turkey. In response to the impending refugee crisis, Turkey formed a plan to establish a security zone in northern Iraq; thus the Iraqi air force would be prevented from attacking the Kurds, while relief operations could be organized. Although the Gulf War cost Turkey more than $6 billion, Özal's anticipated political gains never came about.

Syria and Turkey have several unresolved disputes, because of which Turkey's relations with Syria have been the coolest of those among its Arab neighbors. Syria claims the Turkish province of Hatay on the Syrian-Turkish border. Under France's League of Nations mandate following World War I, it was given control of Syria and Lebanon from 1920 to 1946 (Lebanon gained its independence in 1943). France ceded the Hatay region to Turkey in 1939 after a plebiscite, violating its League of Nations mandate. Thus, Syria considers this an illegal transfer of territory, although Turkey will make no concessions—Turkey's territorial integrity being one of three "irrevocable," unamendable articles of its constitution and a cornerstone of its foreign policy.

Of greater concern are Turkey's hydrological projects in southeast Anatolia. Dams along the Euphrates River restrict Syria's freshwater supply, thus frustrating Syrian efforts to expand agriculture along the Euphrates. Syria also has a history of supporting anti-Turkish forces from Armenian terrorists to Kurdish guerrillas, and this support seems to be linked to progress or regress in Syria's ongoing water negotiations with Turkey. In spite of these troubles, however, Syria's inferior military is kept occupied by its enduring rivalry with Israel, and so lacks the force with which to press its complaints.

Iran and Turkey share a mutual ideological disharmony. Iran, an Islamic theocracy, views Turkey's secularity as an affront to its interpretation of Islam; Turkey views Iran's Islamic republic as a threat to its secularity, which is strongly associated with Turkey's national character. Turkey backed Azerbaijan in its war with Armenia, and the two nations are ethnically and linguistically similar; Iran finds the prospect of a pro-Turkey Azerbaijan on its northern border threatening.

Greco-Turkish relations have steadily improved in recent decades, but disputes still remain. Greece seeks to apply the UN Convention on the Law of the Sea, passed in 1994, to its 2,000 islands in the Aegean Sea. The convention extends a country's territorial waters from six to twelve nautical miles, and if observed would give Greece control of nearly 70 percent of the Aegean. Turkey refuses to acknowledge the convention as applied by Greece, its shipping and aircraft regularly violating the twelve-mile limit.

Turkey has fought a long battle with domestic and (to a limited degree) foreign terrorism. These issues will be dealt with in the Terrorism section.

Alliance Structure

Throughout Turkey's early history (from its independence through World War II), its foreign policy was consistent with Atatürk's original goal of "peace at home, peace abroad." Atatürk's aim was to preserve the fledgling Turkish state's security during the process of internal nation building then under way. As a result, Turkey toiled, and succeeded, in cultivating amicable relations with most of its neighbors. Turkey's first alliance was through a mutual defense treaty signed with Afghanistan in 1921, although defense commitments were rare in the early days of Turkish foreign policy. Not wanting to see his young country drawn into a foreign war, most of Atatürk's early treaties were neutrality or nonaggression pacts. Turkey signed a major friendship and neutrality treaty with the Soviet Union in 1925. By 1933, Turkey had negotiated nonaggression or neutrality treaties with most of its Balkan and Middle Eastern neighbors, including Iran, Italy, Hungary, Bulgaria, France (then a regional imperial power), Greece, Romania, and Yugoslavia. In 1939, the Soviet Union unilaterally abrogated its nonaggression pact with Turkey and signed a similar agreement with Germany. Feeling threatened on all sides, Ankara negotiated a mutual defense treaty with France and the United Kingdom, although France's rapid fall to Germany left Turkey unable to uphold its end of the treaty and thus it remained neutral for the course of the war.

The Baghdad Pact (1955) began as a military alliance among Turkey, Britain, Iran, and Iraq. The pact became CENTO, the Central Treaty Organization, in 1958 when Iraq withdrew from the treaty following a successful coup; the United States joined the remaining treaty members that same year, and the Baghdad Pact became CENTO. CENTO formed part of the chain of alliances "containing" the Soviet Union and was affiliated with NATO to its west and SEATO (Southeast Asian Treaty Organization) to the east. Turkey played an important role in linking NATO and CENTO, whose headquarters was in Ankara. CENTO's members, however, lacked the confidence in each other to share communication ciphers and other military details vital for integrating their forces. As a result, CENTO remained a weak organization until it was finally dissolved in 1979, following the Iranian revolution.

Since the close of World War II, Ankara has aspired to bring itself closer to the West—particularly in terms of military relations that would give Turkey much needed aid and security against the Soviet Union. Almost immediately after NATO's founding in 1948, the Turkish government began inquiring about its prospects for joining the alliance. Turkey finally became a full member of NATO in 1952, after stubborn opposition from Norway and Denmark subsided (the two countries contending that Turkey was neither "North Atlantic" nor, at the time, "democratic"). NATO remains Turkey's most significant military alliance, to which it contributes the largest military force after the United States.

Turkey views NATO as a constructive means to improve relations and cooperation among the nations of Europe through increased interaction and military cooperation. Turkey endorses NATO's enlargement to include Bulgaria, Romania, Slovenia, Slovakia, Estonia, Lithuania, and Latvia and NATO's "Mediterranean dialogue" to improve the alliance's relations with several North African states and the Levant states.

Turkey was an important member of the Iran-Iraq Military Observer Group (UNIIMOG) during the Iran-Iraq War and later in the Iraq-Kuwait Observer Mission (UNIKOM). Turkey contributed 300 troops to UN operations in Somalia and commanded the operation for more than a year. Turkey also contributed to the UN observer missions in Georgia and East Timor. Excepting the United States, more Turkish soldiers have sacrificed their lives under the UN flag than any other nation.

Turkey sees itself as having a vested interest in the peace and security of its region. For this reason, Turkey has recently undertaken its own security initiatives with its surrounding states. Two examples of these are, in the Balkans, the Multinational Peace Force of South East Europe (MPFSEE) and, in the Black Sea, Black Sea Naval Cooperation Task Force (BLACKSEAFOR).

MPFSEE originated from a Turkish proposal in 1997 for a multinational military task force of Balkan states. The purpose of MPFSEE is to foster open and friendly relations among its members, as well as to provide security for the region and develop interoperability among the members' individual military forces. Turkey, Albania, Bulgaria, Greece, Italy, Macedonia, and Romania contribute forces to the group, whose command and headquarters rotate among the members. The United States participates in MPFSEE as an observer. MPFSEE became operational in May 2001, with its first headquarters in Bulgaria. MPFSEE is available to NATO for conflict prevention and peaceful support missions if mandated by the UN.

BLACKSEAFOR was signed in 2001 between Turkey and her former Cold War enemies Bulgaria, Georgia, Romania, the Russian Federation, and Ukraine—all littoral Black Sea states (Iran is conspicuously absent). BLACKSEAFOR's objectives are similar to those of MPFSEE and entail fostering openness among the signatory states through developing interoperability of naval forces on the Black Sea. Its missions include environmental protection, search and rescue, smuggling interdiction, humanitarian assistance, and mine warfare. Unlike MPFSEE, BLACKSEAFOR is a stand-alone alliance, having no affiliation with NATO or the UN.

Size and Structure of the Military

Turkey's military is unique not only because of its political role (described in the next section), but for its social role as well. Turkish society is pervaded with military values and traditions, and military service, particularly commission, affords great social respect. Turks view the military as the protector of not only Turkey's borders, but also of the Kemalist political ideology, which, although its interpretations vary, most Turks agree is an integral part of their national identity. (See Sidebar 2: The Six Arrows of Kemalism.)

Turkish society tends to be authoritarian, patriarchal, and hierarchal, although these tendencies are more a product of Turkey's cultural tradition than political constitution. Group interest tends to suppress individualism, because Turks are inculcated to identify themselves as members of a greater Turkish nation, rather than unitary individuals (Jenkins 2001, 11). The military is viewed as synonymous with the Turkish nation, a pure

---

Sidebar 2   The Six Arrows of Kemalism

Turkey's ideological tradition is as much a part of the state as is its ethnic constitution—Atatürk's revolution being as much for an idea of the state as for a greater Turkish nation. Although Turkey's political and social character is becoming increasingly liberal, embracing greater diversity of opinion, and accepting greater decent, the traditions of Kemalism still pervade Turkish society, and are considered by many as essential to it.

Attatürk's conception of the state embraced six principles that have come to be known as the "Six Arrows of Kemalism." These principles are republicanism, nationalism, populism, reformism, etatism, and secularism. Republicanism established the Turkish state as a republic, governed by the people and their representatives rather than a single ruler. Populism established that all Turkish citizens would be members of the Turkish state and equal participants in it, thus dissolving the old Ottoman *millet* system whereby distinct ethnic groups were afforded general autonomy. Reformism was the means through which Turkey would be modernized and westernized by sweeping away many of its traditional social and political institutions. Etatism (statism) established the government's central role in planning Turkey's economy, partly for the sake of efficient modernization and partly to deny excessive foreign economic influence.

Source
Glazer, Steven A., and Helen C. Metz, eds. 1996. "Historical Setting." In *Turkey: A Country Study.* 5th ed. Washington, DC: Library of Congress, pp. 37–38.

expression of its values and national identity and the defender of those values. Most importantly, the military views its role as not merely defending Turkey's national interests from foreign enemies, but preserving the ideological values of Kemalism from internal threats as well. Kemalist ideology engenders the Turkish military, particularly its officer corps, with a unique sense of purpose and responsibility.

The Turkish armed forces (TAF) are commanded by the Turkish general staff (TGS). The TGS is headed by the chief of staff, who is the commander of each individual branch of the military. Although traditionally a member of the army, the chief of staff might also wear the uniforms of the air force and the navy, because each falls under his command. The TGS is theoretically subordinate to the Prime Ministry, although in practice the chief of staff ranks below the prime minister and above the minister of defense (Jenkins 2001, 22). The TGS, like its U.S. analogue, comprises a number of joint chiefs (J-Chiefs) (seven, in Turkey's case), each responsible for their own department within the military.

In addition to the army, navy, and air force, Turkey has two paramilitary branches. One is the gendarmerie, which is responsible for internal security in the countryside. The other is the coast guard, which is responsible for the security and safety of Turkey's coastal waters and harbors. During peacetime, both the gendarmerie and the coast guard fall under the command of the Ministry of Internal Affairs.

The Turkish army (or the TLF—Turkish Land Forces) is the largest branch of the military, which, at 402,000 men and women, constitutes four-fifths of Turkey's active duty personnel. The army's mission

throughout the Cold War was primarily one of static defense (against a potential Soviet sweep into Asia Minor), with divisions and regiments serving as the principal organizational units. During the 1991 Persian Gulf War, Turkey deployed 120,000 troops to the frontier with Iraq and discovered serious problems in the army's ability to undertake large-scale redeployments on short notice. As a result, in 1992 the army underwent a drastic restructuring, shifting its organization to a more flexible structure centered around corps and brigades. Turkey's current (2005) organization stands at three infantry divisions, nine corps, and forty-four brigades, of which seventeen are mechanized infantry, fourteen are armor, nine are infantry, and four are commandos. Of these forty-four brigades, each mechanized infantry brigade consists of four battalions, one armored, two mechanized, and one artillery. The armor brigade consists of six battalions, two armored, two mechanized, and two infantry. The infantry brigades are composed of four infantry battalions and one artillery battalion. The four commando brigades are composed of four commando battalions each. Four aviation regiments are also divided among the commands.

Turkey is divided into four military sectors, each with a corresponding army. The First Army is headquartered in İstanbul and deployed in Thrace (the European portion of Turkey west of the straits) and is responsible for the defense of that province and the straits themselves. The Second Army is headquartered in Malatya, in southeastern Anatolia, for defense against Syria, Iraq, and Iran. The Third Army is headquartered in the northeastern city Erzincan and defends Turkey's borders with Georgia, Armenia, and Azerbaijan; however, the bulk of the

Third Army's armor, mechanized, and commando forces are deployed in central Anatolia to rapidly reinforce brigades in any other sector. Finally, the Fourth Army (or Aegean Army) is headquartered in İzmir and defends the Aegean coast. The Fourth Army is Turkey's most recent army, formed in 1970 during tensions with Greece over Cyprus. It is now primarily used for training elements of the other three armies. Only the first three armies may come under NATO command. The Turkish army is capable of conducting four simultaneous, battalion-sized, peacekeeping operations anywhere in the world, with air force support, and is capable of foreign-deploying up to 50,000 troops on short notice to support NATO operations (*The Military Balance 2003–2004*).

Available armor platforms range from the antiquated M-48 (2,876), to the slightly less antiquated M-60 (932), to the more respectable Leopard (397). Although the M-48 and M-60 are both evolutions of U.S. World War II designs, Turkey is in the process of modernizing the fire control systems on both platforms. Moreover, because the TLF's mission is primarily defensive, these systems are probably quite adequate—especially considering their large numbers and Turkey's capable air support. The TLF is equipped with a host of modern artillery systems, including the U.S. MLRS (12).

Turkey's navy is well trained, well equipped, and the foremost Levantine naval power, with 52,750 active duty personnel (including 3,100 marines). Its mission is to defend Turkish waters in the Mediterranean, Aegean, and Black seas—especially the straits. Its officers take great pride in the long tradition of Ottoman sea power and have a high level of professionalism. The navy's forces consist primarily of frigates, submarines, and fast attack craft. (Turkey's superannuated, World War II vintage U.S. destroyers have been completely phased out.) Turkey has twenty principal surface combatants, of which the most capable are seven U.S. O. H. Perry (Turkish *Gaziantep* class) and eight German MEKO Type 200 and modified Type 200 (Turkish *Yavus* and *Barbaros* class) frigates. Both ship classes mount Harpoon antiship missiles, Sea Sparrow, or Standard surface-to-air missiles (SAM), four-inch and five-inch guns, respectively, and Sea Zenith or Phalanx CIWSs. Twenty-one fast attack craft, used for patrol and coastal defense, also mount Harpoon or Penguin missiles and four-inch guns. Turkey's submarine fleet is undergoing modernization, as older (again, U.S., World War II era) Tang class boats are replaced with German Type 209 diesel-electric vessels capable of launching Harpoon missiles and Tigerfish heavyweight torpedoes. A mine warfare fleet of one mine-layer and twenty-three minesweepers have a responsibility (under NATO) to seal the Black Sea if needed. Three of Turkey's first MEKO frigates and two Type 209 submarines were assembled in Turkey from prefabricated components, with the newest MEKO platforms built entirely in Turkish naval yards (Sharpe 2003).

Turkey has an amphibious warfare capability centered around nine high-capacity LSTs and fifty-nine smaller LCTs and LCMs. One marine regiment (3,100 troops), consisting of three marine battalions and one artillery battalion (eighteen guns), comprises Turkey's naval infantry.

The Turkish air force is a vital aspect of Turkey's defense, and at 60,100 personnel is Turkey's second-largest military branch. The air force is equipped and trained to provide close air support to land forces in the event of an invasion, as well as to secure air superiority to allow safe mobility and logistical support to Turkish land and naval forces.

The air force is organized into two tactical air forces that operate roughly east and west of the thirty-fifth meridian and are responsible for defending the corresponding army sectors. Each tactical air force is organized into fourteen fighter/ ground attack squadrons (which are attached to NATO), six fighter squadrons, four transport squadrons, and two reconnaissance squadrons. One antisubmarine warfare (ASW) squadron operates with the First Tactical Air Force in western Anatolia.

Turkey operates a force of 483 combat aircraft, consisting of U.S.-built F-4s and F-5s and Turkish-built, U.S.-designed F-16C/Ds. (Turkey's 224 multi-role F-16s are the largest force of such aircraft outside the United States.) Long-range missions are possible through Turkey's fleet of seven KC-135R tankers. Fighter aircraft are equipped with advanced U.S. weapons systems, including AIM-7 Sparrow and AIM-120 AMRAAM air-to-air missiles and AGM-65 Maverick, AGM-88 HARM, and AGM-142 Popeye guided air-to-surface missiles. Laser-guided bomb kits are also available.

The air force is responsible for ground-based air defense as well. Four SAM squadrons of ninety-two conventionally armed Nike Hercules missiles and two squadrons of eighty-six British Rapier missiles defend major Turkish cities. The Nike Hercules is an obsolete technology incapable of missile defense, and because Turkey is within range of missile attacks from Syria, Iran, Russia, and (previously) Iraq, this is a concern. Turkey's NATO membership provides a strong deterrent to missile attack, and during the past two conflicts in Iraq, other NATO members have sent U.S. Patriot missile batteries to Turkey to shore up its defenses, but many government and military officials seek a less dependent solution to Turkey's missile vulnerability.

At $6.5 billion, Turkey ranks thirteenth in military spending globally, its defense spending accounting for 1 percent of the world's total. Defense spending equals about 5 percent of Turkey's GDP. As Turkey's relations with its neighbors improve, it will be possible to reduce defense spending—a significant peace dividend, considering that of all NATO members, only Greece spends a higher percentage of their budget on the military. Turkey is currently pursuing an initiative begun in 2000 to reduce its military's size, while increasing its mobility and firepower. In 2003, 45 percent of Turkey's budget was devoted to personnel expenditures, 31 percent to equipment, and 6 percent to infrastructure (*SIPRI Yearbook 2003*).

Turkey has one major indigenous arms manufacturer (although many Turkish companies contribute to military projects). Ranked eighty-seventh among the world's top 100 defense firms in terms of sales, Makina ve Kimya Endüstrisi Kurumu (MKEK) is a nationally owned company that produces small arms, ordinance, and ammunition (of foreign and domestic design) and explosives for the Turkish military and foreign clients. MKEK also manufactures light machinery, fabrication materials, and chemicals for the civilian market.

Turkey is a major recipient of U.S. arms exports, and because Turkey's economy is much weaker than those of other NATO allies, the United States extended loans and grants to Turkey for procuring U.S. weapons. Grant money (which was often higher than 50 percent of imports) was cut by Congress in 1993, and direct loans were increased until 1998 when all aid was cut (by then, Congress considered Turkey to be economically strong enough to provide for its own defense). But Turkey still receives heavily discounted surplus equipment from the United States (Federation of American Scientists). As evidenced previously, Turkey is allowed to purchase many advanced weapons systems from the United States, although some are still politically sensitive. For example, a recent order of AH-1 Super Cobra attack helicopters (which could be used to put down Kurdish uprisings) is currently pending revision by Congress.

The bulk of Turkey's foreign deployments are 36,000 troops with assorted armor and artillery in northern Cyprus. At the time of this writing, however, Turkey is negotiating a historic unification of Cyprus that would significantly reduce (and possibly end) Turkey's presence on the island. Battalion-sized forces are currently deployed on peacekeeping missions in Afghanistan, Bosnia, Serbia, and Montenegro.

Civil-Military Relations/The Role of the Military in Domestic Politics

Turkey is probably the only constitutional democracy where the military overthrow of legitimately elected governments is interpreted as a constitutional right, and, at times, an institutional duty. Since the end of single-party rule in 1946, elements of the military have instigated no fewer than four direct interventions against the elected government—twice through coups d'état (1960 and 1980) and twice through pressure and tacit coercion (1971 and 1997). In both the 1960 and 1980 coups, civilian power was subse-

quently restored after the military had addressed their complaints (Jenkins 2001, 35). The objective of these interventions was never to supplant the existing civilian government, but to affect certain changes in its policies or membership that the military perceived as a threat to the Turkish republic. This underscores the basic trend in Turkey's civil-military relations—that they are ideological in nature and usually not directed against issues of public policy or the economy. The military's role is defending Turkey's territory and republic, but it tends to interpret this mission very broadly, extending it to include internal threats to the doctrine of Kemalism, as the military interprets it.

Turkey held its first open, multiparty, election in 1950. Adnan Menderes of the Democratic Party became Turkey's first prime minister and held that position until he was overthrown ten years later. During its tenure, the Menderes government, and Menderes in particular, became increasingly authoritarian, attempting to control Turkey's military command by purging the TGS and frequently interfering with promotions and appointments. Criticisms against the government were met with increasingly strict censuring of the press. Finally, in 1960, officers representing the three branches of the military instigated a coup against the Menderes government. Menderes and two of his ministers were subsequently hanged. The 1960 coup was a haphazard affair that caused deep divisions in the military. The officers who planned the coup had few plans of what to do in its aftermath. Disagreements about how the junta should proceed in restoring civilian power led to power struggles that resulted in two attempted countercoups by military factions in 1961 and 1962.

In 1971 the military offered an ultimatum to then President Suleyman Demirel—either the government resign or the military would once again take power. Demirel's government immediately resigned. Unlike the action in 1960, the 1971 ultimatum was the end result of an escalating series of threats by the military, as Turkey's political climate deteriorated. By the late 1960s severe economic problems and runaway political violence between leftists and nationalists had brought Turkey to the brink of civil war. The violence finally led to martial law being declared in İstanbul, but the TGS resisted the notion of the military being used to support a broadly unpopular government. In July 1970, the air force submitted a platform of socioeconomic reforms it wanted implemented, still optimistic the problems could be dealt with by the civilian government. The military also made repeated warnings to the government and the Turkish people of the necessity for reform.

Instead of setting up a junta to rule the country, as in 1960, the military's role after Demirel was one of guidance and mediation among Turkey's various political parties. Reforms were made and censures were imposed upon various extremists on both ends of the political spectrum; but like the 1960 coup the 1971 intervention failed to lay the foundation of a strong government or internal stability.

The 1970s witnessed further instability, including the Kurdish nationalist movements, revived right-left violence, and the emergence of fervent political Islam. In September 1980, the military seized power, declared a state of emergency, dissolved the Parliament, and suspended all political parties. Having learned from both previous interventions, the 1980 coup was meticulously planned, had clear political goals, and the officer corps remained united. The military junta remained in power until 1983, and free elections were not held until 1987, the military using this time to reconstruct the political system. Turkey's constitution was revised, and political parties were restricted. Ironically, one reform was to begin teaching Islam in public schools; the intent of this was to guard against atheistic communism, although it resulted in radical Islam reawakening with a vengeance in the 1990s.

Political Islam's rise in the 1990s led to the creation of Turkey's first Islamist-controlled government in 1996. For advocates of secularism, one of the cornerstones of Kemalist ideology (of which the military is the most outspoken proponent and constitutionally declared defender), nearly eighty years of political tradition seemed in crisis. Members of the TGS had, once again, learned from their previous interventions and understood the political danger of confronting the Islamists too directly. Instead the military employed the complex system of formal and informal methods at its disposal to force the government from power, while minimizing confrontation (Jenkins 2001, 56).

After the 1971 intervention, and particularly the 1980 coup, many observers believed the military's role in politics was over, but as long as the military continues to define its role in ideological terms, and as long as political elements hostile to this ideology persist, interventions will continue.

Terrorism

Historically, Turkey's most persistent terrorist threat came from the Kurdistan

Workers Party (PKK), a Marxist-Leninist insurgent group founded in 1974 with the intent of carving out a democratic Kurdish state in southeast Anatolia. Between 1984 and 1999 the PKK carried out guerrilla activities in rural areas of southeast Turkey and eventually expanded to urban terrorism, which included attacks against Turkish targets in foreign countries. The scope of PKK's targets has changed over time. Initially, PKK activities were directed against local Turkish officials and security forces, but in the early 1990s its operations expanded to attacks against Turkish industrial targets in Europe and Turkey's tourism industry through kidnapping foreigners and bombing tourist attractions (United States Department of State). Because of its Marxist-Leninist, revolutionary ideology, the PKK also opposes the traditional clan hierarchies that constitute the social fabric of many Kurdish communities and the Islamic faith that animates Kurdish life; as such the PKK should not be seen as representing the wishes of Kurdish people as a whole, for it is antithetical to some of the cultural institutions that give the Kurdish nation its unique character. Nevertheless, although the PKK is opposed by many Kurds, it has sought to encourage antagonism between clansmen and Turks, because this furthers its separatist goals (Cornell 2001, 123).

In 1999 Turkish agents captured PKK chairman Abdullah Öcalan. Later that year, while in captivity, Öcalan called for a "peace initiative," ordering the PKK to refrain from violence and to resolve Kurdish grievances by opening a political dialogue with Ankara. Öcalan's initiative was accepted by members of the PKK, and at their 2002 party conference the PKK changed their party's name to the Kurdistan Freedom and Democracy Congress (KADEK) and proclaimed a commitment to nonviolence in support of Kurdish rights. Even though the proceedings were welcomed by Ankara, the government is quick to point out that the PKK's armed branch (the People's Defense Force) did not surrender their weapons, and no PKK members have surrendered to face Turkish justice. KADEK defended this by claiming a need for self-defense. Whatever their intentions, by retaining their arms, KADEK retained the capability to resume violent activities—and periodically threatened to do so. In an attempt to reestablish itself as a peaceful organization, KADEK changed its name again in 2003, this time to Kongra-Gel (KGK), although it has been associated with at least one terrorist attack since then. (See Table 2: Casualties Resulting from PKK Terrorism and Insurgency 1984–1998 for a statistical history of Turkey's bloody struggle with the PKK.) Kongra-Gel changed its name back to PKK in early 2004 and resumed its guerrilla war and terrorist activities against the Turkish state, ending the tenuous five-year ceasefire. By March 2005 the Turkish military had begun attacking PKK bases in northern Iraq.

Over the years state sponsors of the PKK have included Syria, Iraq, and Iran; the organization also conducts fund-raising activities in Europe where it has many sympathizers. According to the Turkish government, the PKK augments its income through organized crime that includes drug trafficking, arms smuggling, and extortion. The PKK presently has between 4,000 and 5,000 armed members, about 500 of whom are in Turkey, 500 in Iran, and about 4,000 in northern Iraq (United States Department of State).

(Turkish) Hizballah, or the Hizballah-Contra, is a Sunni Islamic organization—unrelated to Lebanese Hizballah—seeking

Table 2 Casualties Resulting from PKK Terrorism and Insurgency 1984–1998

Year	Major terrorist attacks	Civilians killed in major attacks	Civilians wounded in major attacks	Civilians killed in other actions	Turkish security forces killed[†]	Terrorists and insurgents killed[‡]	Public and private facilities damaged	Public and private facilities destroyed
1984	n/a	n/a	n/a	20	24	11	0	0
1985	n/a	n/a	n/a	82	67	100	1	3
1986	n/a	n/a	n/a	74	43	64	7	3
1987	4	37	3	237	62	107	13	13
1988	2	38	0	81	50	103	13	22
1989	1	24	0	136	153	165	44	44
1990	0	0	0	178	169	350	12	17
1991	1	11	18	170	264	356	26	46
1992	3	70	59	761	755	1,055	185	160
1993	6	176	37	1,218	671	1,699	255	263
1994	1	5	13	1,082	1,093	4,114	134	239
1995	4	48	9	1,085	584	2,292	36	25
1996	4	35	23	*1,000	*400	n/a	14	65
1997	2	11	19	*800	*300	n/a	60	92
1998	4	16	123	*600	*200	n/a	8	25
Total	32	471	304	7,524	4,835	10,416	808	1,017

* Precise data for these years is unavailable.
† Includes military, police, and village guards.
‡ Includes terrorists killed in suicide bombings.

Source

Turkish Ministry of Foreign Affairs Website. 2003. http://www.mfa.gav.tr/MFA/ForeignPolicy/ Mainissues/Terrorism (accessed June 1, 2005).

an independent Islamic state in southeastern Turkey. The group formed in the late 1980s, originally in response to PKK aggression against Muslims in the region. As Hizballah-Contra's activities were initially directed against the PKK, the group was tolerated by Turkish authorities. In the mid- to late 1990s, the group expanded its operations to include bombings against bars, liquor stores, nightclubs, brothels, and other establishments it considered un-Islamic. In the late 1990s (Turkish), Hizballah kidnapped and assassinated nearly seventy Turkish and Kurdish businessmen and journalists, culminating in the assassination of a Turkish police chief in 2001 (United States Department of State). (Turkish) Hizballah's shift in target-

ing from the PKK to the Turkish state coincided with the PKK's decline and eventual cease-fire with Ankara. (Turkish) Hizballah is considered dormant, having conducted no operations since 2001, and was removed from the State Department's *Patterns of Global Terrorism* in 2003—its members possibly assimilating into other terror organizations with similar agendas.

Turkey's most extreme indigenous terrorist organization is the Revolutionary People's Liberation Party/Front (DHKP/C). The DHKP/C is a political organization "party" with a militant wing "front" that espouses a Marxist-Leninist ideology and is vehemently opposed to the United States, NATO, and the Turkish establishment. Since its founding in the late 1980s the DHKP/C has carried out numerous kidnappings, assassinations, and suicide bombings of both domestic and foreign interests (United States Department of State). DHKP/C's targets include retired Turkish military officials, U.S. military and diplomatic personnel, and prominent Turkish businessmen. The DHKP/C is of unknown size and is believed to raise funds through armed robbery and extortion in Turkey and abroad.

The full scope of al-Qaeda's presence in Turkey is largely unknown. The group carried out suicide bombings of two synagogues and the British consulate in İstanbul in November 2003. The following month, Turkish security forces arrested members of the al-Qaeda cell who had perpetrated the bombings, but the presence of other al-Qaeda cells in Turkey cannot be ruled out. Al-Qaeda was also implicated in a bus bombing in June 2004. Turkey is, at least philosophically, an attractive al-Qaeda target; its secular, liberally aspiring government (in the context of an Islamic population) is ideologically offensive. In the eyes of al-Qaeda and other fundamentalists, Turkey stands as a vindication of how Western-style liberalism will subvert Islam's true practice by alienating its tenets from public life, thus introducing Christianity's chaotic (false) division between the sacred and secular.

Several other terrorist organizations carry out fund-raising and logistical operations in Turkey in support of activities carried out elsewhere. These groups include the Islamic International Peace Keeping Brigade (IIPB), which supports Chechen guerrillas.

Turkey's counterterrorism activities began earnestly in response to PKK violence during the 1980s. In the aftermath of the September 11, 2001, attacks, the range and scope of Turkey's counterter-

rorism project increased. Ambitious security operations undertaken since late 2001 can be credited with decreased activity from (Turkish) Hizballah, DHKP/C, and others—and by Turkey's rapid arrest of al-Qaeda members.

Relationship with the United States

Turkey's relationship with the United States has ebbed and flowed with Turkey's importance to U.S. security interests. Prior to Turkey's independence in 1927, and up to World War II, U.S. interest in Turkey was largely economic in nature and limited to the commerce of a few specialized products like tobacco, currants, and handmade carpets. Turkey's strategic importance to the United States—and U.S. importance to Turkey—expanded dramatically during World War II and its aftermath.

Turkey maintained good relations with the USSR, until Stalin signed a nonaggression pact with Hitler in 1939 and renounced a similar pact made with Turkey in 1925. Feeling pressured on all its borders, Turkey signed a mutual defense treaty in 1939 with Britain and France, although France's subsequent fall to Germany made it impossible—in the minds of Turkey's leaders—to fulfill its commitments under the treaty. Throughout World War II, Turkey maintained de facto neutrality.

In spite of its staggering losses during World War II, the Soviet Union emerged as a world power, augmented by its hegemony over eastern Europe. The USSR was an ideological and military threat to both the United States and Turkey. Soviet strategists understood the strategic value of Turkey's geography. Situated almost as a bridge between the Soviet satellite Bulgaria and the USSR's border along Georgia, Armenia, and Azerbaijan, Turkey controlled access to the Black Sea—a virtual Soviet lake—and could provide the USSR with a warm-water seaport, an enduring goal of Russian, and subsequently Soviet, foreign policy since Peter the Great. Pressure from the Soviets for territorial concessions along Turkey's northeastern border, and a Soviet naval base in the straits, drove Turkey closer to the West, and it joined the Council of Europe in 1939 and NATO in 1952. As the strategic maxim goes, "my opponent's best move is my best move," and thus, just as Soviet planners had taken an interest in Turkey, so did those in the United States. The same aspects of Turkey's geography that made it a Soviet interest made it a vital link in the emerging theory of "containment" developed by George Kennen and other U.S. policymakers in the late 1940s. The territory's advantages to the United States were many. Turkey's position allowed for surveillance over the Soviet Black Sea fleet's movements and allowed for the interdiction of these forces if war broke out. Medium-range bombers and ballistic and cruise missiles could attack the vital western heartland of the Soviet Union without overflying eastern Europe, and Turkey's close proximity to the Soviet Union made it an excellent location for SIGINT and other espionage activities (indeed many of the CIA's U-2 overflights of Soviet territory—including the disastrous and last such mission— were based in Turkey).

Turkey demonstrated its commitment to the United Nations and Western democracy through its participation in the Korean War. Turkey contributed the third-largest contingent of forces and in the course of the conflict sustained the highest proportional casualty rate of any UN participant. Throughout the 1950s Turkey's military and economic relationship with the United States increased, in spite of Turkey's transition to civilian government and the 1960 coup. During the first Lebanese civil war, the U.S. Marines that landed in Lebanon did so from bases in Turkey.

Two events during the 1960s, however, would begin to force Turkey and the United States apart. The first was the general relaxing of tensions between East and West following the Cuban missile crisis. Under an agreement between John F. Kennedy and Nikita Khrushchev, a squadron of Jupiter missiles (sixty) based in Turkey were removed in exchange for Soviet removal of offensive missiles in Cuba. Although the Jupiter missiles were obsolete (and scheduled to be removed anyway), the Turkish public viewed this as an act of betrayal—diminishing Turkey's strategic importance and increasing its vulnerability.

The second event to strain the U.S.-Turkey relationship was the Cyprus crisis. In 1964 massacres of ethnic Turkish Cypriots by Greek Cypriots in favor of Cyprus's annexation by Greece were reported. Turkey threatened to intervene on behalf of the ethnic Turks in Cyprus but was warned in a letter from U.S. President Lyndon Johnson that should the Soviets oppose Turkey's intervention and enter the conflict against them, the United States would probably not come to Turkey's assistance. The so-called Johnson Letter provoked widespread resentment of the United States in Turkish public opinion, which persisted throughout the 1960s. When Turkey finally did intervene in Cyprus in 1974 (following a Greek-sponsored coup attempt on the island), the United States countered with a trade embargo that lasted until 1978, which further strained U.S.-Turkish relations. As relations with the United States deteriorated, changes in Soviet policy gave Turkey the opportunity and incentive to improve relations with the USSR. Turkey eased its restriction on aircraft carriers transiting the straits, which allowed the Soviets to deploy their Kiev class aviation ships with the Black Sea fleet. U.S. opposition to Turkey's Cyprus intervention inflamed anti-U.S. leftist parties that had formed in Turkey following the government's civilianization in 1950. However, the suppression of these elements in the 1980 coup and the Soviet invasion of Afghanistan in 1979 gave Turkey reason and opportunity to renew its relationship with the United States.

Considering that U.S.-Turkish relations throughout the Cold War were predominantly military, and driven by the shared security interests of both countries, it would seem the relationship would also dissolve along with the Soviet Union. But, although the USSR's demise heralded a drastic redistribution of the global balance of power, the *pattern* of power, the distribution of power as a function of geography, was less affected. Turkey's strategic value had always been in some way a function of its geography, and Turkey remained a significant Levantine power in its own right, the strong southern flank of NATO, and a vanguard of Western secularism and democracy on the threshold of the Middle East. Although the Soviet Union's demise reduced the risk of superpower confrontation, it created power vacuums in areas of previous Soviet influence. Turkey's geography enabled it to project power over the unstable regions of the Balkans, Caucasus, and the Middle East.

Turkey's value in the scheme of U.S. foreign policy was demonstrated through its support in the 1991 Persian Gulf War—and it proved vital to enforcing the northern no-fly zone over Iraq. Turkey also made valuable commitments to operations in Kosovo.

After the events of September 11, 2001, Turkey provided landing and overflight support in Operation Enduring Freedom against Afghanistan's Taliban regime. Turkey also provided military personnel to U.S. CENTCOM headquarters to assist in managing the operation, and it took over ISAF operations in Afghanistan in 2002.

The present rift between the United States and Turkey over Turkish refusal to participate in Operation Iraqi Freedom is just another depression in a long relationship that has seen both highs and lows. Turkey and the United States have many ideological similarities and many overlapping security concerns and share a history of close cooperation. These factors, and Turkey's new importance to Iraq's stability, ensure that the present falling-out will have little long-term effect on future cooperation. For more on the relationship between Turkey, the United States, and Israel, see Sidebar 3: The Phantom Alliance.

The Future

Overall, Turkey's security situation is at its highest point in the country's eighty-year history, and its future prospects look positive. Turkey's tireless efforts to promote stability in its surrounding volatile regions are finally starting to take effect—paying peace dividends in the form of improved economic relationships, military cooperation, and relaxed security postures. Turkey's own security initiatives, independent of the UN and NATO, indicate that Turkey is assuming an important

---

Sidebar 3   The Phantom Alliance

While Turkey, the United States, and Israel share no formal security obligations, it has been speculated that there is a "phantom alliance" between the three countries. It is a special relationship of accommodation that has evolved slowly over several decades; and while its formation was measured and discrete, its existence is increasingly difficult to deny.

Turkey and Israel share many similarities that include a familiar political culture, a progressive western orientation, and—perhaps most importantly—common enemies. Israel and the United States have military technology and expertise that benefit Turkey who, in turn, supplies airspace for training Israeli pilots and air bases for the United States. Turkey's position is also advantageous for intelligence collection against Syria and Iraq, which also benefits both its partners. The level of intelligence sharing between the three is unknown, but speculation abounds that Israeli intelligence was responsible for tracking down Kurdistan Workers Party (PKK) leader Abdullah Öcalan.

In 1997, Turkey and Israel signed a historic free trade agreement, with trade volume currently exceeding $1.3 billion. Disagreements over US use of Turkish facilities during Operation Iraqi Freedom have done nothing to discredit the Phantom Alliance—and only underscore its phantasmal nature.

Sources

Blanche, Ed. 1999. "'The Phantom Alliance:' Turkish-Israeli Cooperation Is Changing the Regions Balance of Power." *Jane's Defence Weekly,* March 10.

Safire, William. 1999. "The Phantom Alliance." *New York Times,* February 4:A27.

---

leadership role—and in a geographic region of great strategic significance. At the time of this writing, Turkey was scheduled to begin EU accession talks in October 2005, which means Turkey could join the Union possibly as early as 2014. While obstacles still remain, like the unification of Cyprus and the so-called Armenian allegations, Turkey will likely gain admission to the EU if the country continues its enduring project of Westernization.

Turkey's military is currently undergoing extensive modernization, which will increase its firepower and mobility while decreasing its size and cost. As the country develops expertise in manufacturing its own weapons and platforms, it will be able to decrease its dependence on the West, which should quell some domestic dissent and improve Turkey's leadership

in the region. Ballistic missile defense remains a concern, and Turkey will have to update its aging air defense system soon. When it does, the logical course would be to deploy new Western systems with ABM capability like the U.S. Patriot. Through Turkey's emerging partnership with Israel, Turkey might be able to procure the Israeli Arrow missile system, which is a dedicated, mature ABM designed to counter the same missile threats faced by Turkey.

In spite of recent attacks by Al-Qaeda, terrorism incidents were diminishing overall by 2005. Turkey remains a vital strategic partner with the United States in its war against terrorism, with both countries benefiting from the other's unique expertise. However, Kurdish separatism, and the violence it tends to evoke, remains an intractable issue that will not be resolved soon. The tenuous peace shared by Turkey and the PKK since 1999 was finally shattered in early 2004. The PKK, not satisfied with the government's concessions to Kurds, renounced a political solution and reinitiated their guerrilla war. Turkish attacks against PKK bases in northern Iraq garnered international condemnation—and while Turkey implored the U.S. to use its forces in Iraq against the PKK, the United States was too preoccupied containing Iraq's own insurgency. At present the PKK's survival depends on its Iraqi bases, so its fate is tied to how events unfold in Iraq.

Although NATO remains a cornerstone alliance and a vital link in Turkey's relationship to the West (and shared fate with Europe), Turkey has become strong enough to organize its own broad military alliances. Turkey's MPFSEE and BLACKSEAFOR could be vehicles for future NATO expansion, as the member countries develop the skills and technologies for joint military operations under Turkey's guidance.

Turkey's relationship with the United States has cooled since disputes over Turkey's involvement (or lack thereof) in Operation Iraqi Freedom, but geography does not change, and Turkey's unique location will make it a continued asset to U.S. foreign policy. Turkey's importance to the United States in its fight against terrorism, and the two countries shared stake in Iraq's future stability, will ensure the continuance of their decades-long partnership.

References, Recommended Readings, and Websites

Books

Athanassopoulou, Ekavi. 1999. *Turkey–Anglo-American Security Interests 1945–1952: The First Enlargement of NATO*. London: Frank Cass.

Beckett, Ian F. W. 1999. *Encyclopedia of Guerrilla Warfare*. Santa Barbara, CA: ABC-CLIO.

Beeley, Brian W. 2002. *Turkish Transformation: New Century New Challenges*. Cambridgeshire, UK: Eothen Press.

Bozdağlıoğlu, Yücel. 2003. *Turkish Foreign Policy and Turkish Identity: A Constructionist Approach*. New York: Routledge.

Cornell, Erik. 2001. *Turkey in the 21st Century: Opportunities Challenges, Threats*. Richmond, Surrey: Curzon Press.

Dilek, Barlas. 1998. *Etatism and Diplomacy in Turkey: Economic and Foreign Policy Strategies in an Uncertain World, 1929–1939*. Leiden, Netherlands: Brill.

Dodd, Clement H., ed. 1999. *Cyprus the Need for New Perspectives*. Cambridgeshire, UK: Eothen Press.

Fuller, Graham E. 1993. *From Eastern Europe to Western China: The Growing Role of Turkey in the World and Its Implications for Western Interests*. Santa Monica, CA: RAND.

Henze, Paul B. 1996. *Turkey and Armenia: Past Problems and Future Prospects*. Santa Monica, CA: RAND.

Ismael, Tareq Y., and Mustafa Aydin. 2003. *Turkey's Foreign Policy in the 21st Century: A Changing Role in World Politics*. Aldershot, UK: Ashgate Publishing Limited.

Jenkins, Gareth. 2001. *Context and Circumstance: The Turkish Military and Politics*. Oxford, UK: Oxford University Press.

Kinzer, Stephen. 2001. *Crescent and Star: Turkey between Two Worlds*. New York: Farrar, Straus and Giroux.

Kramer, Heinz. 2000. *A Changing Turkey: The Challenge to Europe and the United States*. Washington, DC: Brookings Institution.

Lewis, Bernard. 2002. *The Emergence of Modern Turkey*. 3d ed. New York: Oxford University Press.

Metz, Helen C., ed. 1996. *Turkey: A Country Study*. 5th ed. Washington, DC: Library of Congress.

Ministry of Foreign Affairs, Ankara. 1998. *PKK Terrorism*. Ankara.

The Military Balance 2003–2004. 2004. Oxford: Oxford University Press.

Radu, Michael S., ed. 2003. *Contemporary Issues in Turkey's Foreign Relations: Dangerous Neighborhood.* New Brunswick, NJ: Transaction.

Rubin, Barry, and Metin Heper, eds. 2002. *Political Parties in Turkey.* London: Frank Cass.

Rubinstein, Alvin Z., and Oles M. Smolansky, eds. 1995. *Regional Rivalries in the New Eurasia: Russia, Turkey, and Iran.* Armonk, NY: M. E. Sharpe.

Shankland, David, ed. 1999. *The Turkish Republic at Seventy-Five Years: Progress-Development-Change.* Cambridgeshire, UK: Eothen Press.

Sharpe, Capt. Richard, ed. 2003. *Jane's Fighting Ships 2002–03.* Alexandria, VA: Jane's Information Group.

SIPRI Yearbook 2003. New York: Humanities Press.

Uslu, Nasuh. 2003. *The Turkish-American Relationship between 1947 and 2003: The History of a Distinctive Alliance.* New York: Nova Science.

Yavus, Hakan H. 2003. *Islamic Political Identity in Turkey.* Oxford, UK: Oxford University Press.

Zürcher, Erik J. 1993. *Turkey: A Modern History.* London: I. B. Tauris.

Websites

Center for Strategic and International Studies. Turkey Project: http://www.csis.org/turkey/index.htm.

Central Intelligence Agency. The *World Factbook.* http://www.cia.gov/cia/publications/factbook/.

Federation of American Scientists: http://www.fas.org.

The North Atlantic Treaty Organization: http://www.nato.int.

The Republic of Turkey, American Embassy: http://www.turkishembassy.org.

The Republic of Turkey, Ministry of Foreign Affairs (English): http://www.mfa.gov.tr/.

The Republic of Turkey, National Intelligence Organization (MIT) (English/Türkiçe): http://www.mit.gov.tr/english/main.html.

Turkish Defense Network: http://www.turkishdefense.net.

Turkish General Staff (TGS) (English): http://www.tsk.mil.tr/index_eng.htm.

Turkish Land Forces (English): http://www.kkk.tsk.mil.tr/01anaEN.asp.

United States Department of State. *Patterns of Global Terrorism.* http://www.state.gov/s/ct/rls/pgtrpt/.

United Kingdom

Eben J. Christensen

Geography and History

The United Kingdom has long enjoyed its geographic position as the only major European power that is an island. The United Kingdom comprises approximately 93,300 square miles (241,590 square kilometers), about the size of Oregon State. The land in the south is rolling hills, whereas the far north of Scotland comprises numerous low mountains, with the highest being Ben Nevis, whose sheer cliffs rise from near sea level to 4,406 feet, as the highest point. Although almost 26 percent of its land is arable, only 1 percent of the population actually farms, with three-quarters working in service industries. The United Kingdom has 7,723 miles (12,429 km) of coastline on the English Channel to the south, the North Sea along the northern coast, the Irish and Celtic seas along the western shores, and the North Atlantic Ocean in far northwest coasts of Scotland (CIA *World Factbook*).

A long-standing global financial and economic power, the United Kingdom has struggled in the post–World War II era to reestablish its position. Many believe that the military and financial power of the United Kingdom has been in dramatic decline, indicated by the rise of the U.S. hegemony. Although this decline is seen in absolute terms, it must be noted that the present situation should not be compared to the state at the height of its colo-nial power. In relative terms the United Kingdom has a large economic and military strength for a country with its size and population (Martin and Garnett 1997).

The government of the United Kingdom has been scaling back its ownership in private industries as part of the guidelines stipulated by the European Union. More recently the economy of the United Kingdom has passed through the global recession of 2000 with only a mild downturn in its overall economic position. The GDP of the United Kingdom is $1.782 trillion (GDP per capita is $29,600) and growing at an annual rate of 1.8 percent, ranking it as the seventh-largest global economy. The service sector comprises the largest share (79.5 percent) of the national economic strength, followed by the indusial sector (19.1 percent) and a small efficient agricultural sector (1.5 percent) (CIA *World Factbook*).

The United Kingdom's political system has evolved over the last 400 years. Although it has no formal constitution, one can point to a number of major documents as well as the body of common law as a proxy. The head of the state is the British monarchy, which appoints the head of government, the prime minister. In the modern era the party that wins the majority in parliamentary elections is awarded this post. The prime minister appoints the government of the state and the various cabinet-level positions within it. The Parliament is bicameral, having a lower House of Commons and an upper House of Lords. The House of Commons has 659 seats; members of Parliament (MOP) are elected for five-year terms in single-member districts, unless the prime minister calls for elections at an earlier time. The second house, the House of Lords, is one of the famous oddities of the British parliamentary system. The House of Lords is made up of approximately 689 "peers." There are 571 life peers (those chosen for their seat by merit—for example, Baroness Margaret Thatcher), 92 hereditary peers (those with family positions on the House of Lords), and 26 clergy (the high positions within the Church of England). Legislation can begin in either house of Parliament, while the House of Lords cannot issue legislation that deals with taxation. Presently the Lords have the power only to delay legislation that has been passed by the Commons, prior to royal assent. Importantly, the House of Lords is the final court of appeal for civil cases in the United Kingdom. The twelve Lords of Appeal, commonly known as the Law Lords, make such rulings (British Parliament Website).

The island of Britain was conquered by Julius Caesar in 50 B.C. After numerous attempts to control the local populations in the north of the country, the Romans completed Hadrian's Wall in the second century to deter these northern invaders. In the eighth century the Viking forces from the lands were attacking the coastal regions of Britain and in 865 launched a full-scale invasion of the country. By the tenth century the Danes controlled all of England. This ended in 1066 when England was conquered by the Normans, which were led by the duke of Normandy who became William I of England (Schama 2000).

William I established a strong feudal system and central bureaucracy that oversaw the king's policies. In 1171, Henry the II undertook the conquest of Ireland. The friction that existed between the king and the nobles led to one of the most famous documents, the Magna Carta, signed in 1215. Edward I began the conquest of the Kingdoms of Wales and Scotland. The Hundred Years' War began in 1337 over the question of the succession of the French throne that was challenged by Edward III.

The rise of the Tudor family in 1485 began one of the most tumultuous eras in

Table 1   United Kingdom: Key Statistics

Type of government	Constitutional monarchy
Population (millions)	60,441,457 (July 2005 est.)
Religions	Anglican (COE) and Roman Catholic 66%, Muslim 2.5%, Presbyterian 1.3%, Methodist 1.3%, Sikh 0.8%, Hindu 0.8%, Jewish 0.6%
Main industries	Electric power equipment, automation equipment, shipbuilding, aircraft, motor vehicles and parts, electronics and communications equipment, metals, chemicals, coal, petroleum, paper and paper products, food processing, textiles, clothing, and other consumer goods
Main security threats	Terrorist threats; Spanish claims over Gibraltar; resurgent threat within Northern Ireland; various claims to maritime rights between Argentina, Denmark, and Iceland
Defense spending (% GDP)	2.4 (2003)
Size of military (thousands)	212 (2004)
Number of civil wars since 1945	1
Number of interstate wars since 1945	0

Sources
Central Intelligence Agency Website. 2005. CIA *World Factbook*. http://www.cia.gov/cia/ publications/factbook/ (accessed May 15, 2005).
International Institute for Strategic Studies (IISS). 2004. *The Military Balance 2004–2005*. London: IISS and Oxford University Press.

England. Under Henry VII the United Kingdom made the religious split from the Roman Catholic Church to become the Church of England (COE). This was done after the papal refusal to grant a divorce to the king from Catherine of Aragon. Under Queen Mary I, Catholicism was revived as the state religion, but was short-lived. The coronation of Elizabeth I reestablished the COE as the official religion of the state that continues today. The Elizabethan age saw the rise of international trade and exploration. This expansion of the country's navy led to the eventual defeat of the Spanish Armada in 1588 for dominance of the high seas (Stater 2002).

The Stuart royal family began with the accession of James I in 1603, which united the Crowns of England and Scotland. It was under James's son Charles I that the policies of the monarchy led to a bloody English civil war in 1642. This civil war against the royalists was led by the famous lord general of the army Oliver Cromwell, whose forces won over the royalists and led the revolution. This resulted in the trial of King Charles I for treason and his beheading in 1649. The English monarchy was abolished and the Rump Parliament governed the country until Cromwell abolished it in 1653. Cromwell established a military regime called the Protectorate with himself as lord protector of the realm. With the death of Cromwell, Parliament asked the son of Charles I to become king in 1660, beginning "the Restoration." As an indication of lingering anti-Catholicism, in the Glorious Revolution, Parliament offered the protestant William III the throne over the son of the Catholic James II in 1689. Soon after, the Act of Union signed by the Scottish Parliament established the unified kingdoms of England and Scotland in 1707, and the seat of government became the Parliament in Westminster. Throughout the 1700s, the United Kingdom's attention was focused on its large colonial empire. Even though the British Empire was firmly entrenched in India, the loss of the North American colonies was a great setback to the economic and territorial desires of the king. In 1801, the Irish Parliament was suspended and was absorbed by the British Parliament (Stater 2002).

The United Kingdom in the late eighteenth and nineteenth centuries was the locus of one of the most important changes in human society—the Industrial Revolution. This gave the United Kingdom an advantage in the production of finished goods to strengthen its already dominant international trade regime. It was under the monarchy of Queen Victoria that the United Kingdom saw the apex of its industrial and military powers. Under the political leadership of Benjamin Disraeli and William Gladstone, Britain undertook a number of conflicts in Africa, Egypt, and Afghanistan (Black 2004; Judd 1996).

The end of the Victorian era saw the rise of Germany as a military and economic rival. The relative isolation from European affairs was shattered by the events that led to World War I. The German violation of Belgium's neutrality in its attempt to conquer France led to the declaration of war in 1914. As part of the victorious allied forces in World War I, Great Britain lost more than 700,000 soldiers. The nation also saw the decline of its economic strength, only to be made worse by the postwar global economic de-

pression. Prior to the outbreak of World War II, the United Kingdom undertook a policy of appeasement with the newly rising German power. This appeasement policy can be seen most clearly in the Munich Pact of 1938, signed by Prime Minister Neville Chamberlain. After its invasion of Poland in September 1939, Great Britain again declared war on Germany. After the failure of British forces to stem the rising German power, Chamberlain resigned and was replaced by Winston Churchill. Britain was part of the Allied forces of the USSR, the United States, and the remaining French Free Forces under Charles de Gaulle. In the end the triumphant Allies incurred more than 420,000 dead and massive economic losses when German forces surrendered in May 1945, followed soon by the Japanese in September 1945 (Prior and Wilson 1998; Williamson 1998).

The postwar rebuilding of the devastated country was done through large loans made by the United States under the Marshall Plan. Through the newly reelected Labour Party, the government established large nationalization programs in medical services and communications. Following World War II, many of the colonial states that brought Great Britain to power also provided problems for the country. The nationalization of the British oil fields in Iran, the South African apartheid, and the Suez Canal crisis brought Great Britain into numerous disagreements with these colonies. As the British Empire became too costly, many of the former "jewels" were yielded their sovereignty. This decolonization process was made even more complicated with Spanish demands for the return of the island of Gibraltar (Judd 1996). The Conservative government of Margaret Thatcher came to power in 1979, ending the socialist policies that had been prevalent since the end of the war. It was during this government that Great Britain fought the conflict over the Falkland Islands. More recently the British government of Tony Blair has been the most vocal supporter of the United States. This support has caused some domestic upheaval, as the British army has been deployed in both the Afghanistan and Iraq conflicts in 2003.

Regional Geopolitics

The United Kingdom benefits from its proximity to the peaceful and stable European democracies. Even its relations with Spain over the island of Gibraltar are cordial. Historically Great Britain has been able to shield itself from many of the international conflicts that have taken place on the continent, content to weigh in only when it suited national interests. This has been less the case in the domestic conflict over Northern Ireland. Although the current environment is peaceful, this has not always been the case. The visible conflict between the British forces stationed in Northern Ireland and the Irish Republican Army (IRA) has taken on an international standing alongside the Middle East conflicts. This long-standing civil conflict that began in 1968 has seen calm since the signing of the Good Friday Agreements in 1998 and the establishment of a power-sharing government.

The United Kingdom actively involves itself in many international peacekeeping missions within Europe, notably in Kosovo and Serbia. The forces that are contributed to such missions are significant, given the overall size and structure of the military. These troop deployments were established to end the ethnic violence in the region and as such are viewed positively by most Britons. The United Kingdom has seen an increase in attention paid to continental security policy, particularly with the expansion of NATO membership to eastern European countries. The expansion of the Atlantic alliance that has been dominated by the United States and United Kingdom might indicate that the United Kingdom will play a more active role as guarantor of security and stability on the continent.

Conflict Past and Present

Although best known for a number of films, the Anglo-Zulu War was one of the defining events in British foreign policy in Africa. Beginning in the 1840s the British began expanding the African Empire to take advantage of the economic riches in the southeast part of southern Africa. The British established a number of colonies along the boarders of the Zulu area known as Zululand. The high commissioner in South Africa, Sir Henry Bartle Frere, believed that a strong Zulu kingdom was a threat to British colonial interests. Frere began making severe demands of the Zulu king Cetshwayo kaMpande, effectively enticing him to war. Frere believed that the Zulu army would acquiesce or be quickly defeated by the British army (Morris 1986).

The Anglo-Zulu War began on January 11, 1879. The British troops, under the command of Lt. Gen. Lord Chelmsford, invaded Zululand through Rorke's Drift. Yet the technologically superior British could not match the numerically superior Zulu, and on January 22, 1879, the troops under the personal command of Lord Chelmsford were defeated at Isandlwana Mountain. In what was seen as one of the worst defeats in British colonial history,

1,300 British and their allies were routed by 24,000 Zulu troops. Soon after the defeat at Isandlwana, Zulu reserve forces pressed on to raid the British post at Rorke's Drift. One hundred forty-five British, many of whom were awarded the Victoria Cross for their bravery, held off the assault of more than 3,000 Zulu.

The battle at Isandlwana Mountain greatly diminished the strength of the Zulu army, leaving King Cetshwayo with little resources to mount an offensive on British positions. Through March of that year British troops were redeployed to South Africa from across the British Empire to strengthen Lord Chelmsford's forces. On March 28 the British commander attacked a Zulu stronghold at Hlobane Mountain, but found himself in battle with the main Zulu army. The next day the Zulu attacked the British forces, but were unable to make gains.

On April 2, Lord Chelmsford broke through the Zulu forces around the besieged mission station of Eshowe. These two defeats demoralized the Zulu and proved to be turning points in the war. Lord Chelmsford continued to advance toward the Zulu capital, Ulundi. On July 4, Chelmsford defeated the Zulu army in the last great battle of the war and razed Ulundi and captured King Cetshwayo. After defeating the remaining supporters of King Cetshwayo, the British established thirteen pro-British chiefdoms under British authority (Morris 1986).

A second major conflict that soon followed the Zulu War pitted the British against the Boers for influence in South Africa. The United Kingdom wished to control all of South Africa, but two Dutch Boer republics (Transvaal and the Orange Free State) did not wish to be part of a new British authority. The discovery of gold in Transvaal in 1886 led many

from around the world to become prospectors and minors in the region. The establishment saw the influx of people (Uitlanders, or newcomers) as a threat to the independence of the Transvaal republic. In 1890, the Transvaal government restricted the presidential and parliamentary (Volksraad) elections to those who had been in the country for fourteen years or more. The government established a second Parliament that was elected by naturalized citizens who had lived in the country for two years or more. The conflict became even more entrenched with the appointment of Joseph Chamberlain to the Colonial Office in 1895. The colonialist Chamberlain pushed very strongly for Transvaal to fall under the British flag, raising Boer suspicions of British intent. Chamberlain and High Commissioner Alfred Milner began urging the United Kingdom to intervene on behalf of the English-speaking South Africans and the Uitlanders and their opposition to the Boer government. This situation was complicated by Milner's walking out of the Bloemfontein Conference in June 1899 between the Boer government and the Transvall government led by President Paul Kruger (Nasson 1999).

With the deployment of British military forces to South Africa in September 1899, the leaders of Transvaal and the Orange Free State believed that the British intended to resolve the conflict with military force. The Transvaal government issued an ultimatum to the British, calling for them to remove all troops within forty-eight hours or face war. The British ignored this ultimatum, and war was declared on October 12, 1899. Initially the Boer forces were very successful in their assault on British forces, which led to the replacement of British General Buller with

General Frederick Sleigh as commander-in-chief. General Sleigh's successes let to the surrender of 4,000 Boer troops within the Orange Free State and the capture of its capital on March 13. This campaign continued, and by May 31 Johannesburg was captured, and five days later the capital of Transvaal, Pretoria, was captured. Many British forces believed that the war was to be over by January 1901, and General Sleigh himself returned to England. The Boer resistances initiated well-planned attacks against the remaining British forces but were put down only after the draconian tactics of the new British commander-in-chief. Peace negotiations began on March 23, 1902, and Boer leaders signed the Treaty of Vereeniging on May 31. The treaty stipulated self-government to Transvaal and the Orange Free State and pardoned Boer soldiers who pledged their loyalty to the British Crown (Nasson 1999).

The United Kingdom was protected from many of the continental conflicts that led to the Napoleonic Wars. The conquests of Napoleon in Germany led to the formation of the Third Coalition (formed by Great Britain, Austria, Russia, and Sweden) to provide a balance to rising French might. In 1805, the Royal Navy won the historic battle of Trafalgar, defeating the combined Spanish and French navies, which prevented Napoleon from attempting to invade England. Realizing that a military victory against the British was not possible, Napoleon attempted to isolate the United Kingdom economically from the Continental System. By 1808 the United Kingdom was the only European power that was not under French control (Gulick 1955).

The British military rose to challenge the French in what became the Peninsular War, which raged from 1808 to 1814.

Buoyed by the revolution of Portuguese forces against Napoleon, the British invaded Spain. In 1809, the duke of Wellington freed Portugal of the French and began an attack on French forces in Spain that lasted almost four years. By 1813, Wellington had driven the French from Spain and began a direct attack against France. It was only after Napoleon's 1814 abdication, following his disastrous invasion of Russia, that the Peninsular War was over.

On March 20, 1815, while deliberating the Congress of Vienna, Napoleon escaped Elba and returned to France to once again establish his control over Paris. Napoleon believed that the best course of action was to attack the more isolated armies of Britain and Prussia along the northwestern part of France. The British forces engaged the French in battle south of Waterloo at Quatre Bras Belgium. With the arrival of the Prussian reinforcements, the combined forces defeated Napoleon on June 22. Napoleon surrendered himself to a British warship and became a prisoner of war on the island of Saint Helena (Gulick 1955).

The War of 1812 marked a low point in the relations of the United States and the United Kingdom. The increasing hostilities between the United Kingdom and France led to a mutual maritime blockade. This blockade stipulated that third-party ships could not trade with France (nor conversely Britain) without first landing at British (or French) ports. This policy led to numerous U.S. seizures by the British, impressments (forced conscription) of citizens, and violations of U.S. neutrality. War was officially declared on June 18, 1812, and the British forces in Canada won a number of early battles against the Americans, particularly at Detroit. Although suffering a notable defeat by the USS *Constitution*, the Royal Navy reestablished its dominance of the sea by 1813. In August 1814 the British won a victory at Bladensburg, Maryland, and took Washington, burning the U.S. Capitol and the White House. Once the war reached an impasse in late 1814, with no decisive victories on either side, Great Britain offered to end the war. This led to the Treaty of Ghent, which was signed on December 24, 1814, in which the British ceased hostilities and relinquished control of the Great Lakes to the United States.

In the 1830s, the East India Company used shipments of opium into Canton as a means of balancing the financial costs of Chinese finished goods and tea. The social effect of opium use on the Chinese population was becoming a major liability to the Chinese. As a result, the imperial government made opium illegal in 1836 and began an aggressive campaign to stop its sale and importation. In 1839, the imperial commissioner of Canton, Lin Tse-hsü, began enforcing the ban on opium by destroying a large quantity of opium confiscated from British merchants. As a result of Tse-hsü's tactics of pursuing foreign nationals in violation of Chinese law coupled with the trade restrictions, the British responded by sending gunboats to attack several Chinese coastal cities in June 1840.

The superior military technology of the British army and navy led to continual Chinese defeats. As a result the Chinese were forced to sign the Treaty of Nanjing (1842) and the British Supplementary Treaty of the Bogue (1843). These treaties stipulated that British citizens were subject only to British law (even on Chinese soil), removed Chinese trade restrictions, opened major seaports, and ceded Hong Kong to the British. Two years later China

signed similar treaties with France and the United States. A second conflict broke out in 1856 after the Chinese illegally searched a British-registered ship, the *Arrow*, in Canton. As a result British and French troops attacked the Chinese, eventually taking Canton and Tianjin. This second conflict led to the Chinese acceptance of the Treaties of Tianjin (1858). This forced China to open eleven more ports and allow Christian missionary activity and the complete legalization of opium. China responded with an attempt to block the entry of European diplomats into Beijing, and the exuberant British enforcement of the new treaty led to a rekindling of the conflict in 1859. As a result, British and French forces occupied Beijing. The official end of the conflict came with the Beijing Conventions of 1860, which reaffirmed the Treaties of Tianjin (Melancon 2003).

The rise of European nationalism in the 1800s and the conflicts over national

---

Sidebar 2   Shortest International Conflict in History

The shortest international conflict to ever occur took place between the United Kingdom and Zanzibar (now part of Tanzania) on August 27, 1896. The conflict broke out when the sultan of Zanzibar ordered his navy (which consisted of one ship) to fire on a British man-of-war. Admiral Sir Harry Rawson returned fire, sinking the ship, and demanded that the sultan surrender. The war lasted from 9:00 to 9:45 A.M., a total of forty-five minutes.

Source
Anglo-Zanzibar War: http://www.guinnessworldrecords.com/ (accessed May 20, 2005).

interests laid the foundations for World War I. German colonialism led the state to expand its naval powers, which threatened Great Britain's hegemony of the seas. Eventually the Germans declared war against France on August 3, 1914. The German invasion through Belgium violated the neutrality of Belgium, and soon Great Britain declared war on Germany in retaliation. The war quickly escalated to include most of Europe with the battle lines drawn between the allies (Belgium, Great Britain, France, Russia, and Serbia) versus the Central Powers (Austria-Hungary, Germany, and the Ottoman Empire) (Prior and Wilson 1998; Williamson 1998).

The German Schlieffen Plan called for an attack on the flank of the French to quickly win the Western Front to ensure that the Germans did not fight a two-front war. This desire was not realized, and the first Battle of the Marne in 1914 set the tone of the conflict of bloody trench warfare along the rather static Western Front. One of the most significant defeats for the allied forces took place in the ill-fated Gallipoli campaign. This was undertaken in 1915 to force the Ottoman Empire to withdraw from the conflict and open the supply route to Russia through the Dardanelles. After the inability for the Royal Navy to open the straits, a joint army force of Australian, New Zealand, and British troops landed on the Gallipoli Peninsula. Turkish forces prevented the allied advances and greatly outnumbered the combined forces. After the loss of some 46,000 troops, the allies retreated on January 9, 1916.

The United States joined the allied forces by 1917, first landing in France, and might have helped turn the tide of the war. Although the war on the Western Front was a continual stalemate, the British forces succeeded in defeating the Ottoman Empire in the Middle East, allowing a redeployment of troops to France. The German forces began a massive counteroffensive in the second Battle of the Marne in July 1918, but were repelled. By late 1918 most of the Central Powers were defeated, and Germany finally capitulated and signed an armistice on November 11, 1918.

The rise of nationalist military regimes in Europe underscored World War II. In 1938, then chancellor of Germany, Adolf Hitler, began demanding the rights of Germans living in Czechoslovakia. In an attempt to defuse the conflict, British Prime Minister Neville Chamberlain met with Hitler in what became known as the Munich Pact. The United Kingdom and France allowed Germany the occupation of the Czech Sudetenland. Yet the peace that was to be ensured by the Munich Pact was never realized, because Germany continued with the occupation of all of Czechoslovakia by March 1939. At this time Great Britain began creating the antiaggression front, which included France, Turkey, and Poland, as a way to speed the rearmament of the nations for another war against Germany. With the signing of the Soviet-German nonaggression pact, Germany invaded Poland on September 1, 1939, and Great Britain declared war on September 3 of that year. Britain provided a naval blockade of Germany, and France militarized behind the Maginot Line (Winks and Adams 2003).

On May 13, the Germans outflanked the Maginot Line cutting off Flanders, forcing a massive evacuation of more than 300,000 Allied troops at Dunkirk to the United Kingdom. Once France fell in late June, the German military began a massive bombing campaign in August

1940 against the United Kingdom. The campaign was then known as the Battle of Britain. It wasn't until 1941, when Germany (and the Axis powers) invaded the Soviet Union, that Great Britain had any allies. To prevent the economic and military collapse of the United Kingdom, the United States passed the Lend-Lease Act in 1941. This gave the president of the United States the ability to transfer war materials to the United Kingdom. By the end of the war, the United Kingdom and Commonwealth was the recipient of $31 billion in U.S. aid. It wasn't until December 1941 that the United States entered the conflict by declaring war on both Japan and Germany.

The first major victory for the Allied forces took place in North Africa when the British general Montgomery defeated the Germans at Alamein in October 1942. This victory paved the way for the U.S.-led invasion of Algeria and the eventual victory in North Africa by the Allies by May 1943. These forces then invaded and liberated Italy, which surrendered on September 8. By 1944, the bombing of German industry had reduced its ability to continue to resupply German forces. On June 6, 1944, the Allies invaded France at Normandy, and on August 15 they invaded southern France. These victories led to the eventual defeat of Germany in France by October and underscored the unconditional surrender of Germany on May 7 (Winks and Adams 2003).

The Suez War began on July 26, 1956, when the Egyptian president Abdel Nasser nationalized the Suez Canal. This conflict has been seen as one of the clearest examples of the dissolution of the British Empire. Although Egypt had gained much of its independence from the United Kingdom in 1922, the end of

World War II increased Egyptian desire for independence and economic self-sufficiency. In many ways the crisis began by U.S. and British decisions not to finance the construction of the Aswan Dam. This decision was in response to the close ties that the nationalist Nasser had fostered with the Soviet Union. In reaction to the decision to withdraw funding from the dam, Nasser declared martial law in the Canal Zone and took control of the Suez Canal Company.

On October 29, 1956, Israeli troops invaded Egypt's Sinai Peninsula. The following day Britain and France offered to temporarily occupy the Canal Zone and demanded that Israeli and Egyptian troops withdraw from the canal. Nasser refused the terms of the British and French Plan, and on October 31 Egypt was attacked. The Soviet Union threatened to respond to this invasion on Egypt's behalf. Alarmed by the quick escalation of the crisis, the UN General Assembly adopted a resolution on November 7, 1956, that called for the United Kingdom, France, and Israel to withdraw their troops from Egypt immediately.

Given domestic opposition to the war and the threat of Soviet intervention, the United Nations evacuated British and French troops on December 22, and Israeli forces withdrew in March 1957. Prime Minister Eden was forced to resign his office because of the combined opposition of the Labour Party and his own party over the botched invasion of Egypt. In many ways the end of the Suez War marks the end of the British Empire and the transfer of influence to the United States (Schonfield 1969).

On April 2, 1982, Argentina invaded a number of small islands known as the Malvinas (or the Falklands) that lay off its eastern shores in the South Atlantic. The

1,800 inhabitants of the islands were of British origin, and most spoke English, but the Argentinean government believed that British possession was a national affront. Much to the surprise of Argentina the United Kingdom ordered the Royal Navy to retake these islands. Although much stronger, the British military was almost 8,000 miles away, and the nearest British airfields were 3,000 miles away on Ascension Island.

On May 3, the Royal Navy sank the Argentinean cruiser the *General Belgrano,* killing 368 people. The following day an Argentinean missile sank the HMS *Sheffield* destroyer, killing 22 British sailors. British Special Forces and Royal Marines landed at San Carlos on May 21, taking the Argentines by surprise, but efforts to resupply these troops cost the Royal Navy four vessels. One of the largest setbacks for the British took place on June 8 as their forces began their assault on the main port of Stanley. The supply ship the HMS *Sir Galahad* was destroyed with almost 200 soldiers on board. Even so the 10,000-strong Argentine forces in Stanley surrendered on June 14, ending the conflict. At home the Falkland War was seen as a triumph for the United Kingdom, although internationally it was seen as having been unnecessary. The Argentinean government was humiliated, and the invasion of the island was seen as an attempt to divert domestic attention away from its poor economic policies. Overall the conflict saw the death of 655 Argentines, 255 British, and 3 Falkland Islanders (BBC Website).

More recently, and perhaps most visible of the current British operations, is Operation Telic in Iraq. As part of the U.S.-led Coalition forces, the United Kingdom deployed 46,000 troops to de-

militarize Iraq. This was the culmination of the low-level tensions that the United Kingdom faced in enforcing the no-fly zones. This operation has been contentious both domestically and internationally—particularly in the UN Security Council, with the threat of a French veto over UN support. On the one-year anniversary of the Iraqi invasion, some 26,000 individuals protested this operation on the streets of London. The Royal Navy currently has deployed the HMS *Norfolk*, HMS *Kent*, and the RFA *Bayleaf* to the Gulf. The army contingent consists of the 3rd Division and the 20th Armored Brigade, along with the support staffs of military hospitals and engineers (UK Ministry of Defense: Operation Telic Website).

The United Kingdom has played an active role in a number of military missions established by the United Nations and NATO. Currently as part of the UN/NATO force, the United Kingdom has approximately 5,000 troops stationed in the Balkans. The United Kingdom has 1,400 troops as part of the 3,400-large SFOR II Multinational Brigade Northwest deployment alongside five other nations. The United Kingdom has been part of KFOR since October 2002 and presently has 1,400 troops stationed in Kosovo. The United Kingdom is also part of the UN mission in Cyprus (UNFICYP, with 431 troops) that exists to prevent fighting between the NATO countries of Greece and Turkey on the island and to oversee a de facto cease-fire. The United Kingdom is also a part of the mission in Georgia (UNOMIG, with seven observers), particularly overseeing the security stability in Abkhazia, Georgia. In Africa, the United Kingdom provides peacekeeping forces in the Congo (MONUNC, with six observers) to ensure the delivery of humanitarian relief and disarmament. Similarly in Sierra Leone (UNOMIL, with twenty-one observers), forces have been deployed to assist in providing security for government offices and to ensure humanitarian relief supplies. There are 300 British soldiers as part of the UN-ISAF in Afghanistan, complemented by the Royal Air Force. The United Kingdom is also a contributing member to the UN's Standby Forces Arrangement as a way to speed in the deployment of UN-backed forces (UN Website).

Alliance Structure

Throughout the Cold War British defense policy was nearly indistinguishable from NATO policy. It relied on the U.S. nuclear guarantee of extended deterrence to levy against the Soviet Union, a foe beyond British capabilities. Yet with the collapse of the Soviet Union and the reduction of its military threat, NATO remains central to the United Kingdom's defense strategies, and nearly all of the British military can be assigned to NATO. Moreover, the United Kingdom contributes almost £110 million yearly to NATO's budget. This has been coupled by the strong relationship with the United States in pursuing these goals. Furthermore, the United Kingdom believes in strengthening the "European pillar" of the European Union, but believes this role should be within NATO rather than through a separate European force. Redefining the role of the European Union and the Common Foreign and Security Policy (CFSP), especially in light of NATO expansion, has been one of the most contentious issues in British defense and is likely to remain so in the future. Currently there are approximately

2,600 troops as part of the NATO forces in Bosnia, Kosovo, and the former Yugoslav Republic of Macedonia (fYROM) (Foreign and Commonwealth Office Website).

The United Kingdom was one of the original architects of the United Nations and holds a permanent seat on the Security Council. In 2001 the United Kingdom contributed almost £275 million to the United Nations, with £158 million allocated for peacekeeping, making it the fifth-largest contributor. The United Kingdom has been part of a number of the UN-backed peacekeeping missions in 2004. Currently the United Kingdom contributes either military or financial support for UN missions in Bosnia (1,400 in SFOR II), Kosovo (KFOR, 1,400), Cyprus (UNFICYP, 431), the Congo (MONUNC, 6), Georgia (UNOMIG, 7), and Sierra Leone (UNOMIL, 21). There are 300 British soldiers as part of the UN-ISAF in Afghanistan, complemented by the RAF. The United Kingdom is also a contributing member to the UN's Standby Forces Arrangement as a way to speed in the deployment of UN-backed forces (United Kingdom Permanent Mission to the United Nations Website; *Military Balance* 2004).

Great Britain's foreign policy toward European integration is marked by caution and pragmatism. This could be in part from its geographic separation from the continent and the lack of a common military and economic history with the dominant states of France and Germany. This pragmatism could also be a remnant of the French veto (under de Gaulle) of UK membership. Although it is a part of the political structure of the European Parliament and its common market, the United Kingdom decided not to join the currency regime of the Euro. These policies were established under the Treaty of

European Union (or the Maastricht Treaty) ratified in 1993. Maastricht also codified the Western European Union (WEU, organized in 1948 in part as a defensive organization now subsumed by OSCE) as the military arm of the European Union. The defensive nature of Europe has always been a concern for the NATO-minded British. In 1995, members of WEU, NATO, and the European Union established the Eurocorps. These forces were deployed in 2003 to replace NATO troops in Macedonia (European Union Website).

The United Kingdom is also a member of the Organization for Security and Co-Operation in Europe (OSCE), joining as a founding party in 1973. During the Cold War OSCE was established to promote East-West cooperation. More recently in Kosovo, Bosnia and Herzegovina, and Macedonia, OSCE has played a visible role in crisis management and postconflict rebuilding (Organization for Security and Cooperation in Europe Website). The nations of OSCE came together at the Paris summit to sign the Charter of Paris, which ensured the territorial integrity of Europe and limited the number of conventional troops on the continent.

As a founding partner of the Council of Europe, the United Kingdom helps promote democracy and human rights within Europe. Beginning in 1949, the council has expanded its membership to currently include forty-five states. The council has established a number of institutions that help further its mission, including the European Court of Human Rights, councils for social cohesion, and public health initiatives. The United Kingdom contributes $27,663,878 (approximately 12 percent) toward the total budget of the council (Council of Europe Website).

Size and Structure of the Military

The Ministry of Defense (MoD) was reorganized in 1964 to streamline and coordinate the smaller postwar Ministry of Defense, the Admiralty, the War Office, the Air Ministry, and the Ministry of Aviation. A more dramatic restructuring, called the Strategic Defense Review, took place in 1998 as a way to reevaluate UK force deployment and composition in the changing security environment. The secretary of state for defense is a cabinet-level position directly responsible for the defense bureaucracy and the formation of defense policy. This position, and the three support ministries beneath it, are directly accountable to Parliament. There are three staff members that support this office: (1) the minister of state for the armed forces, who is responsible for operational issues of the armed forces; (2) the undersecretary of state for defense and minister for defense procurement, who is responsible for defense equipment imports and exports; and (3) the undersecretary of state and minister for veterans, who is responsible for public service, veterans affairs, and environmental issues involving the defense industry (United Kingdom Ministry of Defense Website).

Beneath these defense ministers are two principal positions that have similar organizational status: the first is the chief of defense staff (CDS), who is the head of the armed forces and is the principal military adviser; the second is the civilian permanent secretary, who is in charge of policy, finance, and administration within the MoD. Reporting to the permanent secretary are (1) the Defense Procurement Agency, which is led by the chief of procurement, who is responsible for all equipment procurement for the armed forces; (2) the Defense Logistics Organization, led by the chief of defense logistics, who provides logistical support for the armed forces; and (3) the chief scientific adviser. Reporting jointly to the CDS and the permanent secretary is the second permanent secretary and the vice chief of the defense staff who are joint heads of the civilian central staff. One of the largest bureaucratic staffs within the UK government is the civilian central staff. In 2000 there were almost 105,000 civilians employed—90,600 within the United Kingdom and 14,100 overseas.

Reporting to the CDS are the heads of the single-service staffs of the navy, army, and air force and their support positions. The defense policy of the United Kingdom is made under the authority vested in the Defense Council, chaired by the secretary of state for defense. Those who sit on the Defense Council include the four ministers as well as ten senior military and civilian staff. These three branches of service comprise the Service Board, which reports to the Defense Council (United Kingdom Ministry of Defense Website).

The total armed forces of the United Kingdom are 212,660 active duty forces (trained and untrained Regular Forces, Full Time Reserve Service, and Gurkhas) and 272,550 reservist forces (*Military Balance* 2004). The United Kingdom currently holds 185 strategic warheads on four Vanguard class nuclear-powered ballistic missile submarines (SSBNs). These warheads are deliverable by the Trident II D-5 missile system, which is MIRVed (multiple independent reentry vehicles) and has a range of 12,000 kilometers. Each SSBN carries up to sixteen SLBMs, each containing eight reentry vehicles. The Strategic Defense Review stipulated that all Tridents were to contain three MIRVs, or forty-eight nontargeted warheads per boat. Importantly, the review noted that only one SSBN is placed on active patrol at any given time. The United Kingdom also possesses a ballistic missile early warning system stationed at Fylingdales (*Military Balance* 2004).

There are 116,670 active soldiers in the British army (including 3,750 Gurkhas and 1,140 Full Time Reservists). The MoD, and more specifically the Army Board, broadly controls the British army. Many of the important overseas operations (Cyprus, the Balkans, Iraq, Afghanistan) are controlled directly by the MoD. The British army was reorganized in April 1995 into the Land Command and is located at Erskine Barracks, Wilton, near Salisbury. With a budget of more than £3.7

Table 2　UK Nuclear Armament Levels, 1953–2004

War- heads	1 (0.06%)	10 (0.31%)	30 (0.14%)	310 (0.81%)	280 (0.73%)	350 (0.75%)	350 (0.64%)	300 (0.47%)	300 (0.54%)	300 (1.11%)	185 (0.85%)	185 (0.85%)
World Total	1,557	3,267	22,069	38,118	38,153	46,830	54,706	63,417	55,863	27,131	21,871	20,150
Year	1953	1955	1960	1965	1970	1975	1980	1985	1990	1995	2000	2004

Sources

Carnegie Endowment for International Peace. "Proliferation News and Resources." http://www.ceip.org/files/nonprolif/default.asp.

International Institute for Strategic Studies (IISS). 2003. *The Military Balance 2003–2004*. London: IISS and Oxford University Press.

Norris, Robert S., and Hans M. Kristensen. 2002. "Nuclear Notebook." *The Bulletin of Atomic Scientists* 58, no. 4:103–104.

billion, the Land Command controls 70,000 troops, as well as all of the army's fighting equipment in eight organizational formations. The Ready Divisions, the 1st Armored Division in Germany, and the 3rd Division in the United Kingdom are part of NATO's Allied Rapid Reaction Corps. There are three Regenerative Divisions, the 2nd Division in Edinburgh, the 4th Division at Aldershot, and the 5th Division at Shrewsbury. Such divisions are responsible for nondeployable units that would provide the core to any newly formed divisions if needed. The overseas detachments include those forces stationed in Belize, Brunei, Canada, Nepal, and Kenya. This structure includes the Embedded Units that make up the Land Command operations. These include the 16th Air Assault Brigade, based in Colchester, the Allied Command Europe Mobile Force (Land), with its headquarters and logistic elements at Bulford, and an infantry battalion at Dover.

Such units employ both the *Challenger 2* and *Challenger 1* main battle tanks, which have been used in both Iraq and Bosnia. Moreover, the rapid deployment of forces has seen the increase in use of the Scimitar/Sabre/Spartan platform armored vehicles for infantry and armored infantry deployments. The army air brigades use the Lynx AH-1/-7/-9 helicopters as their main antitank helicopters. The assault capabilities of this force are complemented by the Apache and Apache Longbow helicopters and Gazelle reconnaissance helicopters (British Army Website).

There are 42,370 active sailors in the British Royal Navy (including 1,000 Full Time Reservists). As part of the 1999 reorganization implemented by the Fleet Future Integrated and Rationalized Study Team (Fleet First), the Royal Navy was restructured to streamline the deployment of naval forces. The commander-in-chief (CINC) and deputy CINC are responsible for the training, capability, resources, and general organization of the fleet staff. The fleet staff is organized into six primary units. There are three flotillas (Denvonport, Portsmouth, and Faslane), the Fleet Air Arm (naval air force), the Royal Marines, and the Fleet Auxiliary (support ships). There are four nuclear-powered ballistic missile submarines, three listed as operational, and six operational attack submarines. The Royal Navy also has two operational aircraft carriers and one helicopter carrier. These vessels are the main operational stations of the Fleet Air Arm. This force consists of twenty-eight Sea Harrier aircraft and a helicopter force of thirty-eight Sea King and Merlin, forty-eight Lynx, twenty-nine Sea King Commando, and nine Gazelle helicopters. Other major vessels include six operational destroyers out of eleven total, with six more slated for service by 2007 (Royal Navy Website).

There are 53,620 active members of the Royal Air Force (including 350 Full Time Reservists). First reorganized in 2000, and again in 2003, the Royal Air Force (RAF) was reorganized into two commands—Strike Command and Personnel and Training Command. These forces employ the attack aircraft of the Harrier, Jaguar, and Tornado aircraft. These aircraft will be augmented by the Typhoon craft, also known as the Eurofighter. In 2002, Strike Command employed about 5,600 civilians and 29,600 soldiers. The chief of the air staff, who operates within the MoD, leads this new command structure. Under this position is the air chief marshal at High Wycombe, who is responsible for the Strike Command and controls the RAF aircraft worldwide. There are three domestic groups, one operation unit for overseas deployments, a Cyprus unit, a Gibraltar unit, and a force stationed on Ascension Island (Royal Air Force Website).

Budget

The military expenditures of the United Kingdom totaled $36 billion in 2002, a $6.5 billion decrease from 1992. The total number of individuals employed in British arms productions was 240,000 as of 2001. The most recent data available estimate that the United Kingdom spends $3.89 billion on military research and development (10 percent of total military expenditures), and such expenditures are increasing. The United Kingdom is one of the major arms-producing countries in the world. The United Kingdom ranked fifth as a global supplier of military arms from 1998 to 2002, with sales totaling $4.8 billion for the same period. The United Kingdom also ranked ninth as a recipient of armaments, spending $3.1 billion for the 1998–2002 period. Three of the largest arms producers in the world are located in the United Kingdom. The largest of these is BAE Systems, which is the third largest in the world, with almost $14 billion in sales in 2000 alone. Rolls Royce and GKN are also major arms producers, but their total production numbers place them respectively fourteenth and fifteenth globally (*SIPRI Yearbook* 2003).

Civil-Military Relations/The Role of the Military in Domestic Politics

There are rather positive relations between the military and the political government of the United Kingdom, with a respect for the ideal of military subordination to the civil authority. In the past there has not been much of a link between a domestic military service and homeland defense. Given the UK's island status, such protection was ensured by the Royal Navy. Coupled with the apolitical nature of many within the British military and the nonvisibility policy mandated to ensure public safety, there might be a gap between military and civilians within the United Kingdom. In some ways this decoupling has led to disparate social policies, including issues of homosexuality in the military and military family financial support. The largest segment of the population that joined the military (those not going to university) is shrinking, making military recruitment and retention difficult. Yet the military of the United Kingdom is highly professionalized and remains outside much of the political decision making within the MoD. Any political debate that does take place on military issues by active soldiers is often done behind the closed doors of Whitehall (Strachan 2003).

Terrorism

The United Kingdom has been one of the most visible states in the fight against terrorism. The goals of this fight are the removal of terrorism as an international threat and the protection of the territory and people of the United Kingdom. Soon after the terrorist attacks of September 11, 2001, the United Kingdom (alongside the United States) deployed to fight Taliban forces in Afghanistan. By March 2002, there were more than 1,700 troops stationed in Afghanistan as part of the Task Force JACANA. This force has now evolved into the International Security Assistance Force (ISAF), which was created by the United Nations. Of the 5,000 troops from the eighteen countries supporting the ISAF, 2,000 were British.

Domestically the United Kingdom has established two new Ministerial Committees as part of a three-tiered government scheme to coordinate antiterror policies. The topmost level is the War Cabinet (DOP(IT)), chaired by the prime minister, which oversees the operations of all other government agencies. The newly established DOP(IT)(T) committee, chaired by the home secretary, coordinates domestic security. Last, there is the Civil Contingencies Committee (CCC), also chaired by the home secretary, which coordinates national emergency services similar to the Federal Emergency Management Agency (FEMA) in the United States. One of the more controversial aspects of the United Kingdom's "War on Terrorism" was the passage of the Anti-Terrorism Crime and Security Act in 2001. It enlarged the ability for the security agencies (both the MI5 and MI6) to fight terrorists within the United Kingdom. One aspect of this "War on Terrorism" is the very active enforcement of laws banning terrorist financing. The United Kingdom has frozen more than $100 million from more than 100 organizations (Foreign and Commonwealth Office Website).

The United Kingdom is particularly familiar with terrorism, given the past conflict with the Irish Republican Army (IRA) in Northern Ireland. The "provisionals" of the IRA took part in the systematic terrorist campaign against the British government. The most dramatic attack took place in 1974, when a pub in Birmingham was bombed, killing nineteen people. This caused the British Parliament to pass the Prevention of Terrorism Act and led to a crackdown on terrorism. Some of the tactics used by the British-supported Royal Ulster Constabulary (RUC) police force led to protests in Belfast and the hunger strikes and deaths of ten Irish inmates (most famously Bobby Sands). The Protestant-led RUC was ac-cused by the IRA of employing shoot-to-kill orders and providing paramilitary forces with information on IRA members. By the early 1990s both sides of the conflict were beginning to tire, and the parties began a series of peace negotiations. The IRA questioned these negotiations after the expulsion of the IRA's political party Sinn Féin following terrorist bombings on London's Canary Wharf in 1996. The negotiations were restarted in 1997 after the decisive victory of Tony Blair, who made Northern Irish peace a priority in his campaign. This led to the signing of the Good Friday Accords in 1998, which has demilitarized the conflict.

Relationship with the United States

The common cultural and linguistic heritage facilitates relations between the two countries. The strategic interests and close military relationship that was established by President Franklin D. Roosevelt and Prime Minister Winston Churchill during World War II fostered such relations (Kimball 1997). Throughout the Cold War the United Kingdom was seen as the "perpetual ally" of the United States. This role developed as a result of the ability of the United Kingdom to influence the United States, given the particular role that the United Kingdom plays in European security. In Europe this influence might be tempered by a number of factors. Even though Germany might have a larger economy, its military history, combined with French "aloofness," has left the United Kingdom to play a dominant role in European security with the United States.

Relations between the United Nations and the United Kingdom are at their strongest since the end of World War II. The United Kingdom is the most visible supporter of U.S. foreign policy in Iraq, and alongside Spain, it is the only European military contributor. Even at the expense of his domestic support, British Prime Minister Tony Blair has consistently reiterated his support of the conflicts. The decision to participate in the Iraq War was a watershed moment for the Blair government, because it was seen as a choice made in support of the United States rather than of France and Germany. This does not mean that the United Kingdom blindly follows U.S. security policy, but it does remain a pragmatic link between the United States and Europe. Moreover, the United Kingdom also sees itself as the "second in command" of NATO, behind U.S. leadership, as a liaison between the United States and Europe (Martin and Garnett 1997).

The Future

The United Kingdom has a strong history of commitment and desire to remain committed to the multilateral nature of peacekeeping. The UK military establishment has recognized that this process might be slower than unilateral action and is attempting to streamline the decision-making process. Even so the United Kingdom still relies on NATO to define its security policy within Europe and the United States to provide the context for other major international missions. The shift away from large-scale troop deployments actually favors the structure of the UK military. The ability for the UK forces to rapidly deploy in a number of areas was one of the defining characteristics of the Strategic Defense Review.

Deployments are more likely to use small military forces complemented by helicopter and fast armored vehicles for support. Even with this shift in defense strategy, the United Kingdom recognizes the changing role of their enemy. The use of terrorism as a military strategy has altered the ability for the Ministry of Defense to provide security in the United Kingdom and abroad. This must be done despite increasing pressure from within the country to reduce overall military expenditures. Much of this pressure came from the fact that there was no strategic threat to the United Kingdom or its overseas territories. The Ministry of Defense believes that these economic pressures force it to scale back on its overall personnel force posture while increasing its spending on military technology to offset this reduction (United Kingdom Ministry of Defense Website).

References, Recommended Readings, and Websites

Books

Black, Jeremy. 2004. *Parliament and Foreign Policy in the Eighteenth Century*. Cambridge: Cambridge University Press.

Chuter, David. 1997. "The United Kingdom." In *The European Union and National Defense Policy*, John Howorth and Anand Menon, eds. London: Routledge, p. 105.

Gulick, Edward Vose. 1955. *Europe's Classical Balance of Power*. Ithaca, NY: Cornell University Press.

Judd, Denis. 1996. *Empire: The British Imperial Experience from 1765 to the Present*. London: HarperCollins.

Kimball, Warren F. 1997. *Forged in War*. Chicago: Ivan R. Dee.

Martin, Laurence, and John Garnett. 1997. *British Foreign Policy: Challenges and Choices for the 21st Century*. London: Pinter.

Melancon, Glenn. 2003. *Britain's China Policy and the Opium Crisis: Balancing Drugs, Violence, and National Honour, 1833–1840*. Aldershot, UK: Ashgate.

The Military Balance, 2003–2004. London: International Institute for Strategic Studies.

Morris, Donald R. 1986. *The Washing of the Spears: A History of the Rise of the Zulu Nation under Shaka and Its Fall in the Zulu War of 1879*. New York: Simon and Schuster.

Nasson, Bill. 1999. *The South African War, 1899–1902*. New York: Oxford University Press.

Prior, Robin, and Trevor Wilson. 1998. "Eastern Front and Western Front, 1916–1917." In *World War I: A History*, Hew Strachan, ed. Oxford: Oxford University Press, pp. 187–190.

Schama, Simon. 2000. *A History of Britain: At the Edge of the World? 3000 BC–1603*. New York: Hyperion.

Schonfield, Hugh. 1969. *The Suez Canal in Peace and War, 1869–1969*. Miami: University of Miami Press.

SIPRI Yearbook 2003. New York: Humanities Press.

Stater, Victor. 2002. *The Political History of Tudor and Stuart England: A Sourcebook*. London: Routledge.

Williamson, Samuel R. 1998. "The Origins of the War." In *World War I: A History*, Hew Strachan, ed. Oxford, UK: Oxford University Press, pp. 9–25.

Winks, Robin W., and R. J. Q. Adams. 2003. *Europe, 1890–1945: Crisis and Conflict*. New York: Oxford University Press.

Articles/Newspapers

Gordon, Philip H. 2002. "France, the United States and the 'War on Terrorism.'" Brookings Institution. http://www.brookings.edu/fp/cusf/analysis/terrorism.htm (accessed May 20, 2005).

Norris, Robert S., and Hans M. Kristensen. 2002. "Nuclear Notebook." *The Bulletin of Atomic Scientists* 58, no. 6:103–104.

Strachan, Hew. 2003. "The Civil–Military 'Gap' in Britain." *Journal of Strategic Studies* 26, no. 2:43–63.

Websites

Britain's Small Wars: http://www.britains-smallwars.com/main/index1.html.

British Army: http://www.army.mod.uk/.

British Broadcast Corporation (BBC): http://www.bbc.co.uk.

British Embassy in the United States: http://www.britainusa.com/.

British Parliament: http://www.parliament.uk/.

Carnegie Endowment for International Peace. "Proliferation News and Resources." http://www.ceip.org/files/nonprolif/default.asp.

Central Intelligence Agency. The *World Factbook*. http://www.cia.gov.

Council of Europe: http://www.coe.int.

European Union: http://europa.eu.int/.

Foreign and Commonwealth Office: http://www.fco.gov.uk/.

North Atlantic Treaty Organization: http://www.nato.int.

Nuclear Threat Initiative: http://www.nti.org.

Organization for Security and Cooperation in Europe: http://www.osce.org/.

Royal Air Force http://www.raf.mod.uk/

Royal Navy: http://www.royal-navy.mod.uk/.

United Kingdom Ministry of Defense: http://www.mod.uk.

United Kingdom Ministry of Defense: Operation Telic: http://www.operations.mod.uk/telic/index.htm.

United Kingdom Permanent Mission to the United Nations: http://www.ukun.org/.

United Nations (UN): http://www.un.org.

United States of America

Steven B. Redd

Geography and History

The United States is bordered by Canada to the north and Mexico to the south and the Pacific and Atlantic oceans to the west and east, respectively. The total area is approximately 9,629,091 square kilometers, making it the third-largest country in the world. Its terrain is varied: low mountains and hills in the east, an extensive central plain, and mountains in the west. The climate is primarily temperate. Alaska consists primarily of broad river valleys and rugged mountains, and Hawaii has a volcanic topography. The estimated population as of July 2003 was 290,342,554, also making it the third largest in the world. The dominant religion is Protestant (52 percent), although there is no state-sponsored religion, and freedom of religion is expressly granted in the country's Bill of Rights.

The United States of America was formed when colonists broke away from Great Britain in the latter half of the eighteenth century. Representatives from the original thirteen colonies officially declared their independence from Great Britain on July 4, 1776. The United States was recognized as a new nation following the Treaty of Paris in 1783. Over the ensuing two centuries, colonization expanded westward and thirty-seven additional states, and the District of Columbia, were formed, including the noncontiguous states of Hawaii and Alaska.

The government is a constitution-based federal republic with a strong democratic tradition. It is divided into three branches: the executive, legislative, and judicial. The president serves for a term of four years and is nationally elected. The legislative branch consists of a bicameral Congress. The Senate is composed of 100 members, two from each of the fifty states. One-third of the senators are up for reelection every two years with the term of service being six years. The House of Representatives consists of 435 members, and all are up for reelection every two years. In both the Senate and the House the members are popularly elected. The two primary parties in the United States are Democrats and Republicans. The judicial branch of government consists of the Supreme Court (nine members who are appointed for life by the president with confirmation by the Senate), the U.S. Courts of Appeals, U.S. District Courts, and state and county courts.

The United States has the largest and most technologically powerful economy in the world. It has a per capita GDP of $37,600 and a market-oriented economy, run by private individuals and businesses. State and federal governments purchase most of their goods and services from the private marketplace (CIA 2004). The 2002 estimated GDP was $10.45 trillion with GDP per capita the same year estimated at \$36,300. The 2002 real GDP growth rate was 2.4 percent. The composition of GDP by sector is as follows (2002): agriculture—2 percent, industry—18 percent, and service—80 percent. In 2002, the inflation rate was relatively low at 1.6 percent, and unemployment was 5.8 percent. The United States is the leading industrial power in the world and one of the most technologically advanced with major industries including telecommunications, steel, petroleum, consumer goods, motor vehicles, aerospace, chemicals, lumber, electronics, food processing, and mining (CIA 2004). Chief export partners include Canada, Mexico, Japan, and the United Kingdom, and chief import partners are Canada, Mexico, China, Japan, and Germany (see Table 1 for a summary of key statistics pertinent to the United States).

Regional Geopolitics

The guiding principle for U.S. security concerns in the region has historically been the Monroe Doctrine of 1824 and the Roosevelt Corollary of 1904. The Monroe Doctrine stipulated that the United States would not allow European interference in the Western Hemisphere (Hastedt 2003), and the Roosevelt Corollary stated that the United States would use force if necessary to protect its interests in the Western Hemisphere.

A current concern of the United States in the Western Hemisphere entails ensuring that democracies throughout Latin America remain functioning and stable. Only one country in the region is not officially considered a democracy: Cuba. Latin America has had a history of military rule and usurpation of power. At the time of this writing (2004), Haiti is experiencing a threat to its democracy, and there is fear that the government will fall. In fact, CNN has reported that the rebel groups challenging President Jean Bertrand Aristide consist of forces dissolved by Aristide more than ten years ago (CNN 2004). There have also been recent problems with the government in Venezuela.

Table 1   United States of America: Key Statistics

Type of government	Constitution-based federal republic
Population (millions)	290.3 (2003)
Religion	Protestant 52%, Roman Catholic 24% (2002)
Main industries	Petroleum, steel, motor vehicles, aerospace, telecommunications, chemicals, electronics, food processing, consumer goods, lumber, mining
Main security threats	Terrorism, economic/security threats in key regions
Defense spending (% GDP)	3.3% (2002)
Size of military (thousands)	1,427 (2003)
Number of civil wars since 1945	0
Number of interstate wars since 1945	4

Sources

Central Intelligence Agency Website. 2004. CIA *World Factbook.* http://www.cia.gov/cia/publications/factbook/ (accessed May 15, 2005).

Correlates of War (COW). http://cow2.la.psu.edu (accessed March 1, 2004).

International Institute for Strategic Studies (IISS). 2003. *The Military Balance 2003–2004.* London: IISS and Oxford University Press.

Sarkees, Meredith Reid. 2000. "The Correlates of War Data on War: An Update to 1997." *Conflict Management and Peace Science* 18:123–144.

The other primary security concern for the United States is its borders and their susceptibility to drug traffickers and terrorists. The Mexican border is especially problematic. The government has undertaken several measures to slow the volume of drugs coming over the borders as well as to prevent terrorists from crossing into the United States. Besides increased surveillance of the borders, the United States has also implemented measures to reduce the threat of terrorism, either from individuals or devices, by increasing security at the nation's international airports.

Conflict Past and Present
Conflict History
The founding of the United States of America can be traced back to its conflict with Great Britain over independence. The First Continental Congress met in 1774 to object to British interference in American affairs (Dye 2001). The Revolutionary War began shortly thereafter on April 19, 1775, and lasted until October 1781. The U.S. victory in 1781 did not end U.S. problems with Great Britain. The United States declared war on Great Britain on June 12, 1812. The primary cause of the War of 1812 centered on the impressment of American sailors by the British. Additional ongoing disputes between the two included British attacks on the USS *Chesapeake*, disagreements over the Northwest Territories and the Canadian border, and Great Britain's attempts to impose a blockade on France during the Napoleonic Wars (History Central 2004).

By and large the United States endeavored to stay out of European conflicts for the first century and a half of its existence. Instead, the United States became involved in conflicts directly related to its expansion westward. The first interstate war for the United States following the War of 1812 was partly the result of Manifest Destiny, the "belief in the inevitability that the United States would spread democracy throughout the North American continent" (Fiorina and Peterson 1999, 666). The Mexican-American War lasted from 1846 to 1848 and was also partly a result of the Texas War of Independence. After Texas declared its independence in 1836, hostilities continued along the Texas-Mexico border. When the U.S. Congress admitted Texas into the union on December 29, 1845, the dispute intensified, and the fighting began on April 25, 1846. The U.S. victory in the war was significant, because the land acquired from Mexico later became the states of Arizona, California, Nevada, New Mexico, and Utah. The outcome of the war did not ease the tensions between the United States and Mexico, and the rivalry continued until 1893 (Diehl and Goertz 2000).

Another consequence of U.S. westward expansion was the ongoing conflict between settlers and the native Indians. The largest of these conflicts was the intrastate war between the United States and the Sioux Indians in 1876. This approximately nine-month-long battle for the Black Hills of South Dakota also included Cheyenne and Arapahoe Indian tribes under Sitting Bull and Crazy Horse. This war was also made famous by the overwhelming defeat of General George Armstrong Custer at the Battle of Little Bighorn.

One of the bloodiest conflicts in U.S. history was the Civil War, which lasted from 1861 to 1865. To summarize, this war between Northern and Southern states centered around states' rights and slavery issues, with the Southern states favoring the practice of slavery and construing states rights more broadly than did the states in the North. South Carolina was the first state to secede from the Union on December 20, 1860, and the ensuing war resulted in more than 364,000 battle deaths and thousands more from disease and privation (Dye 2001; Sarkees 2000). In 1865, the North succeeded in defeating the South on the battlefield, and the Union was preserved.

The U.S. arrival as a major power in the world arena was manifest through its actions with respect to Spain in 1898. On February 15, 1898, Spain sank the battleship USS *Maine* in Cuba's Havana harbor. The United States responded by declaring war on Spain on April 25, 1898. The war was fought in both the Philippines and in Cuba and lasted approximately four months. "The war ended with the signing of the Treaty of Paris on December 10, 1898. As a result Spain lost its control over the remains of its overseas empire—Cuba, Puerto Rico, the Philippine islands, Guam, and other islands" (Library of Congress 2004).

The United States did not stay out of conflict for too long. With its acquisition of the Philippines from Spain in 1898, the United States now had influence in East Asia. During this time, many European nations such as France, Germany, Great Britain, and Italy, as well as other major powers such as Russia and Japan, had been carving out "spheres of influence" in China. In general the idea was to open up China and its vast resources to trade with the outside world. U.S. Secretary of State John Hay suggested an "Open Door" policy in China for all interested powers. At the same time in China, Empress Dowager Tsu Hsi was rallying her country to resist the encroachment from the foreign powers.

One particular group formed, calling itself the Fists of Righteous Harmony. Foreigners called the group Boxers because of the group's fixation with the martial arts. These Boxers first attacked Western missionaries and Christians and then turned on the Western diplomats (Bianco 1971). The United States, allied with Russia, Japan, Great Britain, and France, sent troops to rescue the diplomats in 1900, and China was defeated in a campaign that lasted approximately two months and led to the opening up of China until World War II.

World War I started in 1914 with the assassination of Austria's Archduke Ferdinand in Serbia. After the Serbian government refused to turn over those responsible for the assassination, Austria-Hungary declared war on Serbia. Soon nation after nation came to the defense of the two principals, and a world war engulfed Europe. Although the United States remained neutral, it did continue to export goods to Allied countries, particularly to Great Britain and France. Germany countered by promising to use submarines to sink any and all ships transporting goods to the Allied forces. On May 7, 1915, a German U-boat sank the *Lusitania*, a British passenger vessel that also happened to be carrying U.S. citizens on board. This attack began to change U.S. public opinion toward the war in Europe, although Woodrow Wilson still argued for neutrality and was reelected in 1916 emphasizing this in his campaign. However, Germany announced a new submarine offensive in January 1917 and hinted that it would be willing to support Mexico in a bid to recapture territories in Texas and Arizona (Spartacus Educational: WWI 2004). Wilson subsequently asked Congress in April for permission to go to war, which Congress approved several days later. The United States declared war on Austria-Hungary later that year in December. The Allied forces eventually won the war, and the armistice was signed in November 1918—but not before the United States had lost more than 116,000 soldiers in combat. Ziegler (1997) notes that the U.S. entry into the war was one of the primary reasons for the success of the Allies.

Events started to heat up again in Europe after Adolf Hitler rose to power in Germany. Germany first invaded Czechoslovakia on March 15, 1939, and then Poland on September 1, 1939. Great Britain and France immediately declared war on Germany, but the United States declared that it would remain neutral. However, President Franklin D. Roosevelt, in a radio address to the U.S. public on December 17, 1940, argued, "we should do everything to help the British Empire to defend itself" (Spartacus Educational: FDR 2004). This was the beginning of the "Lend-Lease" program, which was officially passed by Congress as the Lend-Lease Act on March 11, 1941, wherein the United States pledged to help any country defend itself against the Axis powers by transferring, exchanging, selling, and/or lending equipment and material (Spartacus Educational: WWII 2004). Japan, an ally of Germany, attacked the U. S. naval fleet at Pearl Harbor on December 7, 1941. Approximately 2,400 servicemen were killed and 18 warships and 188 aircraft were destroyed in the surprise attack. The United States declared war on Japan the next day, December 8, 1941, and subsequently declared war on Germany on December 11, 1941.

Eventually, Allied forces defeated Germany in the spring of 1945. However, the United States was still meeting with significant resistance from the Japanese in the Pacific theater. President Harry S Truman, who had replaced Roosevelt after his death, made the decision to use a new secret weapon that the United States had been working on for some time: the atomic bomb. On August 6, 1945, the United States dropped the first atomic bomb on Hiroshima and then three days later, on August 9, it dropped another on Nagasaki. Exact figures concerning the number killed by these two nuclear bombs are unavailable, but most estimates range from a low of 120,000 to a high of 275,000 (Barash 1987). Japan surrendered the next day on August 10, 1945. In all, more than 405,000 Americans were killed, but the United States and its Allies were victorious in defeating Nazi Germany.

The joy over the Allied victory in World War II was short-lived as the United States and its Western Allies realized that a new threat had emerged: the Soviet Union. The United States viewed the Soviet Union as an expansionist power with a governing ideology, communism, which was antithetical to U.S. interests in freedom, liberty, and democracy. For the next forty years, until 1989, the United States and the Soviet Union would be locked in an ideological battle that came to be known as the Cold War because of the lack of direct confrontation between the two superpowers. Instead, the two enduring rivals (Diehl and Goertz 2000) engaged in several proxy wars and clashed with each other via a nuclear arms race (Barash 1987). The two nations indirectly clashed primarily in the Middle East and East Asia. However, they would eventually confront one another in places such as Latin America and Africa, as the Soviet Union endeavored to support communist movements and the United States did whatever it could to prevent these same movements from taking hold. Perhaps the most volatile confrontation between the two nations was the Cuban missile crisis. The Soviet Union placed ballistic missiles in Cuba, and when the United States found out, it ordered a blockade around Cuba. The nuclear forces of each country were put on alert, and eventually the Soviet Union backed down and agreed to remove its missiles from Cuba. In return, the United States promised not to invade Cuba and to remove its Jupiter missiles from Turkey (Allison and Zelikow 1999).

The primary policy guiding the United States was the Truman Doctrine of containment, which was based on George Kennan's 1947 treatise on "The Sources of Soviet Conduct," published in *Foreign Affairs.* Truman—and Kennan—argued, "that the United States must help other nations to maintain their political institutions and national integrity when threatened by aggressive attempts to overthrow them and to institute totalitarian regimes" (Jordan, Taylor, and Mazarr 1999, 68).

The Korean War was part of this Cold War and the policy of containment. On June 25, 1950, North Korea, backed by the Soviet Union, invaded South Korea. The United States quickly came to the defense of South Korea, as did other nations through the auspices of the newly created United Nations. Among the allies to the United States and South Korea were Turkey, Australia, France, Belgium, Great Britain, and Canada. Interestingly, though, Congress never formally declared war against North Korea.

On June 30, 1950, President Truman authorized General Douglas MacArthur to employ ground troops to stop the advancing North Korean forces (Stoessinger 2001). However, he was also instructed to steer clear of the Manchurian and Soviet borders (Korean War 2004). Initially, U.S.

and UN forces fought only against Soviet-backed and -supported North Korean troops. That would soon change with the September surprising and successful amphibious U.S.-led attack at Inchon, which in effect surrounded the North Korean forces. The U.S. and UN forces were faced with a dilemma: end the attack against North Korea at the original line of demarcation between North and South Korea, the 38th parallel, or continue to pursue the North Koreans across the 38th parallel. Complicating matters was the threat by China to insert itself into the conflict should U.S. and UN forces cross into North Korea.

The UN General Assembly, by majority rule, approved the U.S. decision to not only destroy the North Korean forces but to also, under the auspices of the UN, unify the entire country (Stoessinger 2001). Truman, however, was concerned about China's threats to intervene, but MacArthur and the State Department concluded that this was not likely. Moreover, General MacArthur and others concluded that even if China were to invade, it could not do so effectively and U.S. forces would be able to handle this new development. On October 26, 1950, Chinese forces attacked U.S. and South Korean forces with surprising success. The attacks continued for about a week, but the Chinese then withdrew. MacArthur mistakenly believed that the Chinese forces were smaller in number and in need of rest and regrouping. MacArthur decided to make a "final offensive" push toward the Yalu River, but was met with an overwhelming and decisive defeat at the hands of the Chinese (Stoessinger 2001). The Korean War lasted another two and a half years and ended in a stalemate with the demarcation between North and South Korea back at almost the same place as it was before the war. More than 54,000 U.S. soldiers died in the Korean War, and the United States still to this day maintains a force of approximately 40,000 troops along the Demilitarized Zone (DMZ) between North and South Korea.

Stoessinger (2001) notes that the Vietnam War was the most divisive conflict domestically since the Civil War and the longest war in U.S. history. The breadth and length of the Vietnam War prevent a detailed analysis in this venue, but this entry will provide a brief historical and policy account of the war and how it influenced future U.S. national security policy. In the initial aftermath of World War II, Truman did not see Vietnam, or its ruler Ho Chi Minh, as a threat to the West. However, Truman came to believe that the Cold War was not only being waged in Europe, but that it had also moved to Asia. By 1950, the U.S. State Department "asserted that the recognition of Ho Chi Minh by the USSR, China, North Korea, and the East European nations ended any speculation as to the fate of Vietnam under Ho, who was now described as a lifelong servant of world Communism" (Stoessinger 2001, 84). Truman ended up focusing on the Korean War, but he did send material aid to French forces.

Dwight D. Eisenhower increased aid to the French to the point that by 1954, the United States had paid more than 50 percent of the cost of the war in Indochina, approximately $1 billion (Stoessinger 2001). The French made a last stand at Dien Bien Phu and requested U.S. intervention, arguing that without it Indochina would be lost. Eisenhower decided against intervening, partly because he feared Chinese involvement and also because he believed Congress would not support U.S.

involvement in another war in East Asia (Stoessinger 2001; see also DeRouen 2003). However, while France was in the process of exiting Indochina, Eisenhower was still committed to maintaining a presence in Vietnam. The Geneva Accords of 1954 called for a cessation of hostilities in Indochina, provided for a provisional military demarcation line at the 17th parallel, and created the independent sovereign states of Laos, Cambodia, and Vietnam (Stoessinger 2001). The United States never signed the Geneva Accords but did promise not to threaten or use force to disturb the settlement. To prevent any further communist encroachment in Asia the United States created the Southeast Asia Treaty Organization (SEATO), whose members were the United States, Australia, France, New Zealand, Pakistan, the Philippines, Thailand, and Great Britain (Jordan, Taylor, and Mazarr 1999), and the United States decided to consider South Vietnam a separate state. By the end of Eisenhower's administration, the United States had more than 1,000 military advisers in South Vietnam.

During the brief presidency of John F. Kennedy, the United States deepened its commitment to Vietnam such that by the end of 1963, it had increased the number of military advisers in Vietnam to approximately 17,000 (Stoessinger 2001). A key point here was the influence of Kennedy's vice president, Lyndon B. Johnson, in committing the United States to further involvement in Vietnam. After visiting South Vietnam to lend encouragement and support to President Ngo Dinh Diem, Johnson stated in his report to President Kennedy that "The battle against Communism must be joined in Southeast Asia with strength and determination to achieve success there. Vietnam can be saved if we move quickly and wisely"

(Stoessinger 2001, 91). After Kennedy's assassination, the Joint Chiefs of Staff, Secretary of Defense Robert McNamara, and others advised Johnson to increase the level of commitment to the war on communism in Indochina. In August 1964, the United States began a massive bombing campaign brought on by incidents in the Gulf of Tonkin—considered in some circles as manufactured—and the subsequent Gulf of Tonkin Resolution passed by Congress (Stoessinger 2001; see also Austin 1971). Eventually, Johnson realized that even with the massive escalation of the war, the United States was losing, and he therefore decided to halt the bombing in March 1968. Johnson, himself, was the other casualty in this period of the Vietnam War, and he decided not to run for reelection in 1968.

Richard M. Nixon was elected president in 1968 and began the process of "Vietnamization," whereby the United States would gradually turn over the conduct of the war to the Vietnamese, and U.S. forces would be withdrawn (Stoessinger 2001). The United States began withdrawing its force of more than 500,000 ground troops in June 1969. However, Nixon realized that as a result of the United States doing so the South Vietnamese government would be vulnerable to North Vietnamese forces. Therefore, while the United States was reducing its ground forces in Vietnam, it stepped up its ground attacks in neighboring Laos and Cambodia—purported Vietcong strongholds—and increased aerial bombing of Vietnam, Laos, and Cambodia (Stoessinger 2001). Eventually, both domestic and international opposition to the destruction and devastation wrought upon Vietnam, Laos, and Cambodia, combined with the cost of the war and mounting U.S. casualties led

Nixon to sign a cease-fire on January 23, 1973. By 1975, South Vietnam was conquered by the North. The United States suffered more than 58,000 casualties and countless others injured as a result of the protracted war in Vietnam (Sarkees 2000).

The Vietnam War also had a profound influence on future U.S. foreign policy processes and outcomes and the interaction between Congress and the White House (Jordan, Taylor, and Mazarr 1999; Meernik 1993). The War Powers Resolution passed in 1973 was at least partly a result of President Nixon's bombing campaign and Congress's subsequent efforts to constrain the president's war powers. The Vietnam War has often served as a historical analogy for both those opposed to and those in favor of uses of force, with the former arguing that new conflicts will end up as tragically as Vietnam and the latter arguing the opposite. "Vietnam" became a code word for U.S. forces getting bogged down in an unwinnable war. In fact, Yuen Foong Khong (1992, 259–260) stated, "In the aftermath of expelling the Iraqis from Kuwait by use of overwhelming force, President George H. W. Bush claimed that the United States had also kicked the Vietnam syndrome."

On August 2, 1990, Iraqi forces, led by Saddam Hussein, invaded Kuwait. The U.S. and UN reaction was swift—by the end of that same day the UN Security Council passed a resolution by a vote of 14 to 0, demanding Iraq immediately and unconditionally withdraw from Kuwait (Stoessinger 2001). Hussein refused to comply with the UN resolution. The United States began to deploy a massive number of troops—eventually totaling more than 500,000—to Saudi Arabia, while President Bush crafted a coalition supporting the eventual ouster of Iraq from Kuwait. The allied forces included Saudi Arabia, Egypt, Italy, France, Great Britain, Canada, and others. The UN Security Council announced on November 29, 1990, that Saddam had to withdraw from Kuwait by January 15, 1991 (Stoessinger 2001, 201–202). Bush then turned his attention to Congress and narrowly obtained a resolution authorizing force: Senate 52 to 47, and House 250 to 183. Saddam did not withdraw, and the Persian Gulf War began on January 16, 1991. The United States and its allies achieved a decisive victory in expelling Iraq from Kuwait in only eighty-six days and with a loss of 268 U.S. lives. However, the allies did not pursue Saddam Hussein into Iraq, and he remained in power. This eventually led to a second war with Iraq, which is discussed in the next section.

To be sure, the United States was involved in many more conflicts than those discussed here (DeRouen 2001b). On many occasions the United States engaged in uses of force short of war such as the *Mayaguez* rescue mission in 1975 (Head, Short, and McFarland 1978; Lamb 1989), the Tehran hostage rescue mission in 1980 (Hollis and Smith 1986; Smith 1984/5), Grenada in 1983 (Beck 1993), Panama in 1989 (Gilboa 1995/96), Somalia in 1992 (Burk 1999), and Kosovo in 1999 (Daalder and O'Hanlon 2000; Hendrickson 2002; Paris 2002), just to name a few. The general characteristics of these conflicts were that the goals were usually more political in nature (Blechman and Kaplan 1978; DeRouen 2001b; Meernik 1991) and the duration of conflict shorter. In only 2003, the United States used force short of war to topple the Taliban regime in Afghanistan because of that regime's support of the terrorist organization al-Qaeda.

Current and Potential Military Confrontation

The current and potential future military confrontations for the United States primarily revolve around problems in the Middle East and East Asia. Diehl and Goertz (2000) identify U.S. enduring rivalries with North Korea and, of course, Iraq. The United States has also had stressful relations for the last two decades with Iran, and there is also the possibility of conflict with China should its relations with Taiwan sour to the point of armed conflict. Some might even point to rising tensions with Syria because of its support of terrorist organizations. Interestingly, with respect to Iraq, Iran, and North Korea, the chief problems concern these nations' possession of, or attempts to produce or acquire, weapons of mass destruction (WMD). One of the chief security concerns of the United States is terrorism, and this issue is discussed in the section on terrorism.

U.S. action against Iraq began to accelerate after the September 11, 2001, terrorist attacks against the World Trade Center towers and the Pentagon. Saddam Hussein had throughout the 1990s failed to abide by various UN resolutions requiring him to disclose the extent of his nuclear, chemical, and biological weapons programs (Butler 2000; McCarthy and Tucker 2000). Former chief UN weapons inspector for the United Nations Special Commission (UNSCOM) Richard Butler detailed his attempts to ascertain the extent of Iraq's WMD programs and how his investigations were ultimately terminated in December 1998 (Butler 2000).

In September 2002, the Bush administration released a document entitled *National Security Strategy for the United States of America*. In this document, the administration outlined, among other things, the need to defeat terrorism and to prevent threats from WMD, using pre-emptive strikes if necessary (U.S. White House, NSC 2004; see also Tanter 2004a). In December 2002, the administration released another document entitled *National Strategy to Combat Weapons of Mass Destruction*. This document contained information on U.S. plans to aggressively counter the proliferation of WMD and target threats to the United States (U.S. White House: WMD 2002; see also Tanter 2004b). Within this context, the Bush administration began to make a case demanding that Iraq disclose its WMD programs since it had failed to do so under previous UN resolutions in the 1990s.

President George W. Bush asked for, and received in October 2002, resolutions from both the House and Senate to use force in Iraq. On November 8, 2002, the UN Security Council unanimously passed Resolution 1441, which required Iraq to provide "immediate, unimpeded, unconditional, and unrestricted access." Iraq was warned that if it failed to do so, "it [would] face serious consequences as a result of its continued violations of its obligations" (United Nations 2004). Iraq failed to comply with UN Resolution 1441, so the United States, Great Britain, and other countries resolved to use force to compel Saddam Hussein to comply with the resolution. However, several other countries such as France, Germany, and Russia, and various domestic opponents, opposed U.S. calls to use force, instead arguing for more time to conduct inspections of Iraq.

The United States, Great Britain, and other allies proceeded despite the objections of other UN Security Council members, and on March 19, 2003, the Iraq War began. Militarily, Iraq was quickly defeated, and the president announced on May 1 that major combat operations had ended. Saddam Hussein went into hiding but was eventually found and captured on December 14, 2003. The primary objective of the United States since its military victory in Iraq has been to rebuild Iraq and to help it establish a stable and democratic governing system. Coalition efforts in this endeavor have been complicated by repeated terrorist attacks on coalition troops and on Iraqi citizens in general by those loyal to Saddam Hussein or those who simply oppose the coalition presence in Iraq. The plans for Iraq's future have included a Transitional National Assembly, which was elected on January 30, 2005, voting for a new constitution/government to occur in October 2005, and election of a permanent government in December 2005 (U.S. White House: Iraq).

U.S. efforts with respect to North Korea and Iran center around nonproliferation goals. In the 1990s the United States attempted to negotiate with North Korea to end its nuclear weapons programs. In October 1994 the two countries signed the Agreed Framework, which was supposed to result in North Korea suspending or at least severely cutting back on its plutonium production (Bermudez 2000, 189). On April 24, 2003, North Korea admitted that it had nuclear weapons and threatened to export nuclear materials unless the United States agreed to bilateral negotiations with North Korea (Federation of American Scientists: DPRK 2004); however, some scientists are not convinced that North Korea has actually constructed a nuclear device (New Scientist 2004). North Korea also withdrew from the Nuclear Non-Proliferation Treaty. Since that time the United States has attempted to convince North Korea to allow International Atomic Energy Agency (IAEA) inspectors back in and to cease nuclear weapons production and proliferation. Negotiations between the two countries are ongoing.

The U.S. rivalry with Iran began with the Iranian revolution in November 1979, when students stormed the U.S. Embassy and took U.S. diplomats hostage. These hostages were held for 444 days and finally released on January 20, 1981. The Ayatollah Khomeini assumed the leadership of Iran and established an Islamic republic that was hostile to the United States and most other Western states. Even after the death of the ayatollah in 1989, the U.S.-Iran relationship has remained strained. Iran has been accused of sponsoring the terrorist group Hezbollah (as has Syria) (British Broadcasting Corporation 2002). Currently, the main concern the United States has with Iran is its efforts to produce WMD, particularly nuclear weapons. The Federation of American Scientists (Federation of American Scientists: Iran 2004) reports that the IAEA has been investigating Iran and has found that it has violated the terms of the Nuclear Non-Proliferation Treaty. In February 2004, the IAEA discovered that Iran had not disclosed to nuclear inspectors that it had blueprints for an advanced centrifuge design with the purpose of enriching uranium (Federation of American Scientists: Iran 2004). The United States is also concerned with Iran's efforts to produce and acquire chemical weapons (Giles 2000).

The United States has also had an enduring rivalry with Cuba. However, since the fall of the Soviet Union, the threat from Cuba has dissipated. The United States has still refused to lift the embargo on Cuba, and the current policy toward Cuba is focused on promoting a peaceful transition to a democratically elected government and respect for human rights (U.S. Department of State 2001).

Alliance Structure

Perhaps the first point to mention with respect to U.S. alliances is that the U.S. did not have any for the first 132 years of its existence (Gibler and Sarkees 2004). The U.S. hesitancy to formally ally with other countries represents its isolationist foreign policy, especially in the realm of conflict and war. The first "official" alliance for the United States was an entente with Japan from 1908 to 1910. It also formed an entente with Great Britain, France, and Japan in the interwar period from 1921 to 1931. Then from 1936 to 1945 it had an entente with most of the nations in Latin America. The first defense pact alliance for the United States was signed in 1947, and is still in force today, with these same Latin American nations adding in most of the Caribbean countries. Cuba withdrew from the alliance on January 22, 1962.

The most important alliance for the United States historically and even today is its defense pact with many western European countries vis-à-vis the North Atlantic Treaty Organization (NATO), formed in 1949. The original signatories were Belgium, Canada, Denmark, France, Great Britain, Iceland, Italy, Luxembourg, The Netherlands, Norway, Portugal, and the United States. Greece and Turkey joined in 1951, West Germany in 1955, and Spain in 1981 (the United States also signed separate bilateral defense pacts with Canada in 1958 and Spain in 1970, although the separate bilateral alliance with Spain was terminated in 1981). By signing the treaty "the Parties agree that an armed attack against one or more of them in Europe or North America shall be considered an attack against them all" (NATO 2004). The primary purpose of NATO was to protect its member nations from the Soviet Union and its expansionist activities.

NATO encountered a dilemma then with the fall of the Soviet Union in the late 1980s. Many wondered whether NATO could survive, given that its raison d'être was now gone. Instead of folding, NATO revised and extended its membership. In 1990, it added a unified Germany, and in 1997 the Czech Republic, Hungary, and Poland were added as part of the defense pact. The addition of the latter three East European countries was part of NATO's 1994 Partnership for Peace, a program designed to provide for a closer relationship with the former Soviet republics (Sarkesian, Williams, and Cimbala 2002). NATO's expanded membership was an expression of its interest and willingness to take the lead in preventing or lessening the impact of humanitarian disasters, conflict management and resolution, and ultimately preventing conflict wherever and whenever possible (Sarkesian, Williams, and Cimbala 2002). In 1997, NATO even made provisions for Russian involvement through the NATO-Russia Founding Act. Russia was not given a veto over NATO decisions, but it was given the opportunity to consult with NATO members on security issues (Sarkesian, Williams, and Cimbala 2002). Numerous other countries in central and eastern Europe are on a waiting list to join NATO. NATO has moved from an organization whose primary purpose was collective security against a threatening Soviet bloc to a more proactive democracy and peace-fostering organization.

The next several years of alliance activity signaled the U.S. decision to end its self-imposed isolation from the rest of the world's security concerns. In 1951, the United States signed defense pacts with the Philippines, Australia, and New Zealand. In 1952, the United States signed a defense pact with Japan that is still in force today. The United States signed a mutual defense treaty with South Korea at the conclusion of the Korean War.

The United States entered into a defense pact with the Republic of China (Taiwan) in 1954. However, with the normalization of relations between China and the United States first begun in 1972 under President Richard Nixon and then finalized under President Jimmy Carter and the signing of the Taiwan Relations Act, the official relationship with Taiwan was terminated in 1979. Again, and somewhat similar to South Korea, although the U.S. relationship with Taiwan is "unofficial," it is generally understood that the United States is a close ally of Taiwan. In fact, President George W. Bush, in an interview with ABC news, stated that the United States would do "whatever it takes" to defend Taiwan from a Chinese attack. In a subsequent interview with CNN he further stated that "our nation will help Taiwan defend itself. . . . At the same time, we support the one-China policy, and we expect the dispute to be resolved peacefully" (CNN 2001). Most U.S. presidents have been vague on the subject of the China-Taiwan dispute, but it is generally understood that the United States would probably not allow China to forcibly unite the two countries. Along these lines, from 1998 to 2002, the United States supplied more arms to Taiwan than to any other country (Stockholm International Peace Research Institute [SIPRI] 2003).

Four other alliances are worth discussion: Egypt, Saudi Arabia, Pakistan, and

Israel. It is probably not correct to think of the current interactions between the United States and Egypt as an "alliance," but the two countries have established a working relationship over the last two decades. During much of the Cold War, the United States and Egypt were on opposite sides, primarily because the United States supported Israel, and Egypt and Israel were enemies. In fact, Egypt and Syria launched a surprise attack on Israel during the Jewish Yom Kippur feast in 1973 and were supported and supplied by the Soviet Union. The United States supported and supplied Israel, and eventually Israel was victorious. However, President Carter and his national security adviser, Henry Kissinger, succeeded in getting Egypt's president Anwar Sadat, and Israel's prime minister Menachem Begin, to meet at Camp David, Maryland, in 1978 to discuss the possibility of peace between the two countries. Eventually, the two sides signed a peace agreement, which is commonly referred to as the Camp David Accords (Stiles 2002). The United States is Egypt's primary supplier of arms (SIPRI 2003), and Egypt ranks second in amount of arms received from the United States in the period 1998–2002. The United States has also enlisted the help of Egypt in fighting the "War on Terrorism" and in the Middle East peace process.

The United States has approached Saudi Arabia and Pakistan in a similar fashion, that is, soliciting their help in fighting terrorism. Historically, the relationship between the United States and Saudi Arabia has been friendly and revolves around oil. The United States pledged to protect Saudi Arabia as early as 1945 (Jordan, Taylor, and Mazarr 1999). Recently, though, the United States has been pressuring Saudi Arabia

to assist in the "War on Terrorism" by first ending its funding of suspected terrorist organizations (Egypt also has problems with terrorists residing in the country). Moreover, fifteen of the nineteen September 11, 2001, hijackers were from Saudi Arabia (*Economist* 2003). Saudi Arabia has also been involved in assisting in the monetary aspects of the "War on Terrorism" (the same dynamics of ending domestic sources of terrorism and helping in the "War on Terrorism" are also occurring between the United States and Pakistan). Historically, the U.S. relationship with Pakistan has been more complex because of Pakistan's relationship with both India and China. Recently, however, the two nations have been closely allied in carrying out the "War on Terrorism." On March 4, 2003, Pakistan's ambassador to the United States, Ashraf Jahangir Qazi, made the following statement, "There has recently been a series of articles calling into question the value of Pakistan's partnership with the United States and the war against terrorism, . . . [but] since 9/11, since the launch of Operation Enduring Freedom, Pakistan has become a critical and crucial ally of the United States" (*Stanford Daily* 2003). He further noted that Pakistan had captured approximately 500 suspected al-Qaeda terrorists and handed them over to U.S. authorities. The most interesting point for U.S. national security is that these three countries are not democracies. In fact, the United States has faced criticism because of its alliances with these countries and their questionable records regarding human rights. However, because of the roles they play in the U.S. "War on Terrorism," each plays a very important part in the overall national security strategy of the United States.

Jordan, Taylor, and Mazarr (1999, 401) state, "Since 1948, one of the most enduring features of U.S. policy in the Middle East has been a commitment to the security of Israel." The reasons for the U.S.-Israel alliance are varied. Jordan, Taylor, and Mazarr (1999, 401) further note that many view Israel as a reliable ally and a democratic nation in a region of the world wherein just about every other country is either anti-American or undemocratic. From Israel's founding in 1948 until around 1966, the United States primarily supported Israel by providing economic and financial aid, but very little military aid. However, in 1966, the United States changed its policies and began to supply Israel with military arms and is currently Israel's largest supplier of weaponry. This is not to suggest that the relationship between the United States and Israel is without problems. The United States has continually directly pressured Israel to work with its Arab neighbors to establish peace in the region. Various presidents have also attempted to serve as intermediaries between Israel and Arab states in constructing peace treaties, such as the 1978 Camp David Accords, the 1993 Oslo Accords, and the Wye River Accords in 1998. The latter two accords sought to facilitate peace agreements between Israel and the Palestinians. Although the alliance between Israel and the United States is not officially a defense pact or any other type of alliance, there is no question that the United States is committed to the preservation of a free and democratic Israel.

Size and Structure of the Military

The U.S. military is primarily a volunteer force. The drafting of military-age young men has occurred at various times previous to major conflicts such as the Vietnam War. As of 2003, the U.S. military consisted of 1,427,000 active troops (excluding the Coast Guard), with another 1,237,700 in the Reserves, which includes the National Guard. Military forces are generally divided among four groups with the numbers in each group listed in parentheses: army (485,000), navy (400,000), air force (367,600), and marines (174,400). By law, the Coast Guard (37,582 military; 6,750 civilian) is also a branch of the armed forces, but in peacetime is under, and funded by, the Department of Homeland Security.

The Department of Homeland Security was created in the aftermath of the terrorist attacks on the United States on September 11, 2001, and is headed by the homeland security adviser. This new department was created to "develop a comprehensive strategy to secure the USA from terrorist attacks or threats, while coordinating all relevant activities in the executive" (SIPRI 2003, 54).

The United States is involved in numerous deployments of forces throughout the world. Some are considered peacetime support forces, some are involved in UN and other peacekeeping operations, and still others are actively engaged in various conflicts. As part of the European Command, the United States has forces in Germany, Belgium, Greece, Italy, Luxembourg, the Mediterranean, The Netherlands, Norway, Portugal, Spain, Turkey, and the United Kingdom. As part of the Pacific Command, the United States has forces in Singapore, Japan, South Korea, Guam, Australia, Diego Garcia, and Thailand. As part of the Central Command, the United States has forces in Bahrain, Iraq, Kuwait, Oman, Qatar, and the United Arab Emirates (UAE). As part of its Southern Command the United States has troops in Honduras. As part of its Northern Command (newly created in 2002), the United States has troops in Bermuda, Cuba, Iceland, Portugal (Azores), and the United Kingdom. U.S. forces abroad as part of UN and peacekeeping operations include Bosnia, Egypt, Ethiopia, Eritrea, Georgia, Hungary, Kyrgyzstan, Middle East, Tajikistan, Uzbekistan, and Serbia and Montenegro. Operational deployments for the United States currently ongoing include troops in Afghanistan, Iraq, and Liberia.

Another key aspect of the U.S. military concerns its possession of nuclear weapons, with nuclear forces considered to be a vital part of U.S. deterrence and war-fighting capabilities. U.S. nuclear forces are structured in a strategic triad: land, sea, and air (see Table 2). The land leg of the triad consists of approximately 500 Minuteman missiles, with some having the capability of carrying 3 warheads per missile, for a subtotal of 1,200 warheads, and approximately 40 MX missiles, with each carrying 10 warheads, for a subtotal of 400 warheads, for a total of 1,600 land-based ICBM warheads (MX missiles are currently being destroyed with dismantling scheduled for completion by the end of 2005; thus, only Minuteman missiles will remain, reducing the overall ICBM total to 1200). The air leg of the strategic triad primarily consists of B-52H and B-2 bombers, with the B-52H carrying approximately 860 warheads on 56 combat-ready aircraft, and the B-2 deploying approximately 800 warheads—which can also be deployed on the B-52H—on 16 combat-ready aircraft. It should be noted that the warheads in the B-52H are primarily delivered by means of an Air-Launched Cruise Missile (ALCM), whereas the warheads in the B-2 are actually bombs. The sea leg of the triad is composed of 10 Trident D-5 and 8 Trident C-4 submarines. Each Trident D-5 submarine carries 24 Submarine-Launched Ballistic Missiles (SLBM) with 8 warheads each for a subtotal of 1,920 warheads (IISS 2003, 18). SIPRI (2003) lists the total number of Trident D-5 warheads at 2,112. Each Trident C-4 submarine carries 24 SLBMs with 6 warheads each for a subtotal of 1,152 warheads. SIPRI (2003) lists Trident C-4 warhead totals at only 576. The total number of sea leg warheads according to IISS is listed as 3,072, whereas SIPRI lists the total at 2,688. The number of strategic nuclear warheads totals 5,948 (SIPRI 2003). The United States also has other

Table 2   U.S. Strategic Nuclear Forces (January 2004)

Leg	Type	Designation	Warheads
Land	LGM-30G	Minuteman III	1,200
Land	LGM-118-A	MX/Peacekeeper	290
Sea	UGM-96A	Trident I (C-4)	432
Sea	UGM-133A	Trident II (D-5)	2,304
Air	B-52H	Stratofortress	860
Air	B-2	Spirit	800
Total			5,886

Source
Stockholm International Peace Research Institute (SIPRI). 2004. *SIPRI Yearbook 2004: Armaments, Disarmament and International Security.* London: Oxford University Press.

nonstrategic nuclear forces in the form of bombs and *Tomahawk* cruise missiles, making a grand total of 7,068 active nuclear warheads (another 380 warheads are spares and an additional 3,000 are kept in the reserve stockpile) (SIPRI 2003).

Another important issue related to nuclear weapons is the numerous bilateral and multilateral treaties signed by the United States. The United States has signed and ratified the 1925 Geneva Protocol, prohibiting chemical and biological warfare; the 1963 Partial Test Ban Treaty (PTBT), prohibiting the testing of nuclear weapons in the atmosphere or under water; and the 1968 Nuclear Non-Proliferation Treaty (NPT), prohibiting the transfer of nuclear weapons to nonnuclear states (SIPRI 2003). The United States also signed and ratified the 1972 Strategic Arms Limitation Talks Treaty (SALT I), which placed ceilings on the production of various strategic nuclear missiles, and the 1987 Intermediate-Range Nuclear Forces Treaty (INF), which obligated the United States and Soviet Union to destroy intermediate-range ballistic missiles deployed in Europe (Barash 1987; SIPRI 2003). The United States also signed and ratified the Strategic Arms Reduction Talks Treaties (START I and START II, although the START II Treaty is not in force because Russia withdrew after the United States abrogated the ABM Treaty and because in some respects the SORT accomplishes some of the same goals), which required both sides to reduce the numbers of their offensive strategic nuclear missiles in successive years (SIPRI 2003).

The United States also signed and ratified the 1972 Anti-Ballistic Missile Treaty (ABM), which prohibited each side from building a national missile defense system. However, the United States officially withdrew from the treaty on June 13, 2001, citing the need to develop a national missile defense system in order to protect itself from "rogue" nations possibly intending to launch nuclear missiles at the United States. In 1996, President Bill Clinton signed the Comprehensive Nuclear Test Ban Treaty (CTBT), which prohibits all nuclear weapons testing, but the United States failed to ratify the treaty, and it was not in force as of 2004. On May 24, 2002, President George W. Bush and President Vladimir Putin of Russia, in a surprise development, announced their signing of the Strategic Offensive Reductions Treaty (SORT). The treaty requires both sides to reduce their nuclear warheads to 1,700–2,200 by December 31, 2012 (Federation of American Scientists: SORT 2004). The U.S. Senate ratified the treaty on March 6, 2003, and the Russian Duma did so on May 14, 2003 (SIPRI 2003).

Budget

The national defense budget for 2002 was $362.1 billion. The estimated 2003 defense budget was $382.6 and did not include supplemental appropriation totals for the war in Iraq. Future defense budgets are proposed to increase in successive years to approximately $480.9 billion in FY2008. The defense budget breakdown for 2002 is as follows: (1) Military Personnel—$86.9 billion, (2) Operations and Maintenance—$116 billion, (3) Procurement—$61.6 billion, (4) Research and Development—$48.7, (5) Other (includes Defense Health Program, Inspector General and Drug Interdiction, and Chemical Agents and Munitions Destruction)—$18.8 billion, and (6) Military Construction, Family Housing, Revolving and Management Funds, and Department of Energy Defense-Related Funds—$30.4 billion.

The defense budget has been undergoing what is often referred to as a Revolution in Military Affairs (RMA), a revolution designed to transform the U.S. military "into a lighter, more agile and technically advanced fighting force" (IISS 2003, 233). The U.S. military is generally considered the most technologically advanced fighting force in the world, as evidenced by the war in Iraq wherein the military heavily relied upon precision-guided munitions and superior ground and air forces. However, critics point out that, although the RMA has proposed many significant operational and technological changes, actual results have been slow in coming and that many existing programs, for example, legacy platforms, have continued to be perpetuated.

Perhaps the most significant change to the defense budget centers on efforts to combat terrorism. SIPRI (2003) notes that the Department of Homeland Security was allocated $36.2 billion in the 2004 budget. Other budget efforts to combat terrorism include $2.3 billion (FY2004) to various partner countries such as Jordan, Pakistan, Turkey, and Afghanistan (SIPRI 2003). Many additional programs have been created to deal with the threat of terrorism: the Terrorist Threat Integration Center (TTIC), Talon, Guardian, the Joint Program Executive Office for Chemical and Biological Defense (JPEO-CBE), Project Bioshield, Customs and Border Protection (CBP), and the Container Security Initiative (CSI).

The U.S. military has also endeavored to improve its maritime, aerospace, and ground forces. The U.S. Navy (USN) has a new strategic concept entitled Sea Power 21, which is focused on a "global conception of operations" (IISS 2003, 16). Along these lines the USN has requested adding an additional "seven vessels: one

SSN *Virginia*-class nuclear submarine; three DDG-51 *Aegis*-class destroyers; one LPD-17 *San Antonio*-class amphibious transport ship; and two auxiliary cargo and ammunition ships" (IISS 2003, 234). The USN also plans to purchase 100 new aircraft, including "42 F/A-18E *Super Hornets,* 15 T-45 trainers, 13 MH-60S helicopters and six MH-60R helicopters" (IISS 2003, 235). The USN will also procure 267 tactical Tomahawk land-attack cruise missiles. The U.S. Air Force (USAF) has several technological advancements under way. It is currently adding to its Predator Unmanned Aerial Vehicle (UAV) family, and it has begun work on a new project entitled FALCON, from Force Application and Launch from CONUS, which is a drone that when launched from the United States could hit any target in the world within two hours (IISS 2003). The U.S. Army has developed the Stryker AFV, a brigade that is designed to be deployed within ninety-six hours and able to operate without support for seventy-two hours. Other programs include the Future Combat Systems (FCS) and Objective Force with the necessary armored vehicles.

The United States has also been developing several facets of a missile defense system for the newly created Missile Defense Agency. The total budget for missile defense in both 2003 and 2004 was approximately $7.7 billion with a requested budget of $9.2 billion for FY2005 (SIPRI 2004). The projects to be funded include land-based interceptors, Aegis-equipped ships, the start of a space-based kinetic energy interceptor program, and the Patriot Advanced Capability (PAC)-3 program.

The U.S. Agency for International Development also expends funds under its international affairs budget. The total 2002 estimated budget was $24.4 billion to support various endeavors such as Voluntary Peacekeeping Operations, contributions to UN and other Peacekeeping Operations, the Economic Support Fund, Non-Proliferation, Antiterrorism and Related Programs, and International Disaster Assistance (IISS 2003).

The United States produces, imports, and exports a wide range of arms. Types of arms produced in the United States include fixed-wing aircraft, rotorcraft (helicopters), tactical and strategic missiles, satellites, surface ships, submarines, and torpedoes. Expenditures on military equipment and military R&D in the United States in 2002 were $83.6 billion and $50.6 billion, respectively (SIPRI 2003). The top five U.S. arms-producing companies as of 2002 were in rank order Lockheed Martin, Boeing, Raytheon, Northrop Grumman, and General Dynamics (SIPRI 2003). Perhaps the biggest development in the arms industry in the United States is a trend toward concentration and consolidation of arms producers, which SIPRI (2003) notes is guided by changes and adjustments to U.S. doctrines of war fighting and military technology, instead of by lack of demand. This trend toward concentration is illustrated by the 2002 acquisition of the aerospace and information technology company TRW by Northrop Grumman as well as other recent acquisitions (see SIPRI 2003 for more detail).

The United States is the leading supplier of arms and arms transfer agreements in the world, both in terms of total value as well as in terms of its percentage of the world's countries. The total value of arms transfers in 2002 was $10.2 billion, and the total value of arms transfer agreements in 2002 was $13.3 billion. In 2002, the U.S. share of global arms deliveries was 40.3 percent, and the U.S. share of global arms transfer agreements was 45.5 percent (IISS 2003). For the period 1998–2002, the major recipients of arms from the United States in rank order were Taiwan, Egypt, Saudi Arabia, Turkey, Japan, the United Kingdom, Israel, and South Korea (SIPRI 2003). The United States also imported approximately $761 million worth of arms for the period 1998–2002 primarily from the United Kingdom, Italy, Germany, and other countries.

Civil-Military Relations/The Role of the Military in Domestic Politics

The military is civilian controlled, with the president of the United States serving as commander-in-chief. Next in authority in the military is the secretary of defense, who is also a civilian. He is advised by, among others, the Joint Chiefs of Staff, which comprises one representative from each branch of the armed forces. The chairman of the Joint Chiefs of Staff heads the Joint Chiefs of Staff. Sarkesian, Williams, and Cimbala (2002, 145) note, "Throughout the history of democracies, the role of the military has rested on absolute civilian control over the military. This is engrained in the U.S. system, as well as in the U.S. military institution and mind-set."

Generally and historically speaking, the relationship between the military and U.S. civilians has been benign, even during times of war. Allan Millett (1979, 11; quoted in Sarkesian and Williams 1994, 211) stated,

World War II marked a watershed in the history of American civil-military relations. . . . Even under the extraordinary stresses of global war, the

American system of civil control had not been appreciably altered.

This is not to imply, however, that the relationship between civilians and the military has always been smooth. The Vietnam War caused many in the public to be distrustful of the military and to doubt its ability to wage war effectively. Likewise, many in the military began to be increasingly frustrated with U.S. leadership and effectiveness (Sarkesian and Williams 1994). The 1991 Persian Gulf War helped to repair the civilian-military rift. As Sarkesian and Williams (1994, 218) state, "For many, it not only relegated Vietnam to the dustbin of history but highlighted the renewed effectiveness of the U.S. military."

The Persian Gulf War notwithstanding, many still point to the potential for a greater disconnect between the military and civilians. Ole Holsti (1998) conducted extensive surveys and found among other things that military officers were more likely to identify themselves as conservative and Republican. Moreover, as Sarkesian, Williams, and Cimbala (2002, 148) state, "Many in the military already feel estranged from civilians, whom they see as undisciplined, irresolute, and morally adrift." To potentially complicate matters further, national security leaders such as the president, his advisers, Defense Department appointees, and members of Congress and their staffs are much less likely than previous generations to have any military experience (Sarkesian, Williams, and Cimbala 2002). These authors conclude that there is no real danger of the military defying civilian authorities. Instead, the primary concern most likely centers around the possibly widening gap between the cultures of the military and the U.S. public.

Terrorism

On September 11, 2001, al-Qaeda terrorists, using commercial airliners, flew planes into both World Trade Centers in New York City and the Pentagon, killing approximately 3,000 people (see Sidebar 1). Both World Trade Centers collapsed, and the Pentagon was significantly damaged. A fourth plane was hijacked but failed to reach its intended target, instead crashing into a field outside of Pittsburgh, Pennsylvania. The events of this day profoundly altered the psyche of the

---

Sidebar 1   Al-Qaeda Attack on September 11, 2001

In the worst terrorist attack on U.S. soil, approximately 3,000 people were killed. One hundred fifteen nations had citizens who were killed in the attacks. In addition to the human toll, the economic ramifications were also devastating. More than 146,000 individuals in New York City lost their jobs, with an economic loss to the city totaling approximately U.S.$105 billion. The estimated cost of the cleanup alone was U.S.$600 million.

Sources

NewYorkMetro.com. 2004. "9/11 by the Numbers." http://www.newyorkmetro.com/news/articles/wtc/1year/numbers.htm (accessed May 14, 2005).

VikingPhoenix.com. "Remembering the Victims and Heroes of September 11, 2001." http://vikingphoenix.com/news/stn/2003/911casualties.htm (accessed May 14, 2005).

U.S. public and led the Bush administration to declare a "War on Terrorism." U.S. national security policy in the ensuing years has focused primarily on fighting terrorism in various forms.

The United States not only wanted to target those terrorists directly responsible for the attacks of September 11, 2001, al-Qaeda, but it also wanted to identify and eliminate the Taliban regime in Afghanistan that supported al-Qaeda. The United States quickly destroyed the Taliban regime and continued to capture al-Qaeda members, with the primary target being al-Qaeda's leader, Osama bin Laden. As of this writing the United States has still not captured bin Laden. The United States also turned its attention toward other state sponsors of terrorism. In his 2002 State of the Union Address, President Bush identified Iraq, Iran, and North Korea as an "axis of evil" (Bush 2002). The United States has also identified Syria and Libya as state sponsors of terrorism. The central objective for the United States vis-à-vis these countries is to identify their capabilities with respect to WMD, keep them from proliferating weapons or technology to other countries or terrorist groups and ultimately convince them to give up desires to acquire WMD or give up the weapons themselves if they already have them.

Another primary goal of the United States with respect to terrorism is to prevent another direct attack on the homeland and also to prevent attacks against interests and allies. As discussed previously, the United States has undertaken several measures to accomplish these goals, including the creation of the Department of Homeland Security and several additional counterterrorism programs. The United States has also enlisted the support of its allies in combating terrorism around the world.

The Future

The United States is the world's lone remaining superpower. Its military is the most superior and technologically sophisticated of any in the world. It emerged from its half century of conflict with the Soviet Union victorious and without rival. Yet, the events of September 11, 2001, and recent disagreements with allies and domestic discontent regarding the 2003 Iraq War, illustrate that the United States is not the world's hegemon and that the international arena is not unipolar. Instead, perhaps Samuel Huntington (1999, 36) is correct in asserting that we have a "uni-multipolar system with one superpower and several major powers" (italics in original). Whether or not he is correct, it will be crucial for the United States to ensure the cooperation of current and future allies in the fight against terrorism and the proliferation of WMD (Jordan, Taylor, and Mazarr 1999).

Perhaps the biggest security threat for the United States in the foreseeable future is from terrorism and/or the proliferation of WMD. Very few, if any, countries can directly challenge U.S. military supremacy, but WMD in the hands of those willing to use them or more conventional terrorist attacks on the United States could severely threaten the U.S. economy and by extension its national security. Terrorist attacks, either conventional or using WMD, are also a threat to key allies, and such attacks could destabilize vital geostrategic regions such as the Middle East, East Asia, and western Europe. The United States is also concerned about regional instabilities in the Middle East between Israel and its Arab neighbors, Iraq and its transition to a stable democracy, and in East Asia with North Korea, China, and Taiwan. The United States will continue to work through NATO regarding its security concerns in Europe. In other areas, the United States will continue to promote democratic institutions and economic free trade as a means to ensure amicable relations.

In order to combat these threats, the United States will continue to increase the size of its military budget. It will also continue to develop and fund a national missile defense to address the proliferation of WMD. Moreover, the United States is likely to continue the revolution in military affairs (RMA), which holds that "further advances in precision munitions, real-time data dissemination, and other modern technologies, together with associated changes in war-fighting organizations and doctrines, can help transform the nature of future war and with it the size and structure of the U.S. military" (O'Hanlon 2001, 87). Domestically, the United States will continue to focus on antiterrorism efforts via the Department of Homeland Security. Although many aspects of U.S. national security look favorable, the threat of terrorism and proliferation of WMD still cast a shadow toward the future.

Sidebar 2   U.S. Defense Budget in Comparative Perspective

The 2002 U.S. defense budget of U.S.$362.1 billion was greater than the combined budgets of all NATO, non-NATO Europe, Russian, Middle Eastern, central Asian, and East Asian (including Australia) defense budgets combined (U.S.$361.1 billion). In fact, the U.S. defense budget for 2002 was only slightly less than the combined budgets of all other countries for which data was available (U.S.$389.6 billion). To be sure, the United States contributes to the defense budgets of many of these countries through its alliance relationships, but the comparison still is noteworthy.

Source
International Institute for Strategic Studies (IISS). 2003. *The Military Balance 2003–2004.* London: IISS and Oxford University Press.

References, Recommended Readings, and Websites

Books
Allison, Graham, and Philip Zelikow. 1999. *Essence of Decision: Explaining the Cuban Missile Crisis.* 2d ed. New York: Longman.
Art, Robert J., and Kenneth N. Waltz. 2003. *The Use of Force: Military Power and International Politics.* 6th ed. Lanham, MD: Rowman & Littlefield.
Austin, Anthony. 1971. *The President's War.* Philadelphia: Lippincott.
Barash, David P. 1987. *The Arms Race and Nuclear War.* Belmont, CA: Wadsworth.
Barash, David P., and Charles P. Webel. 2002. *Peace and Conflict Studies.* Thousand Oaks, CA: Sage.
Beck, Robert J. 1993. *The Grenada Invasion: Politics, Law, and Foreign Policy Decision Making.* Boulder, CO: Westview.
Bermudez, Joseph S., Jr. 2000. "The Democratic People's Republic of Korea and Unconventional Weapons." In *Planning the Unthinkable: How New Powers Will Use Nuclear, Biological, and Chemical Weapons,* Peter R. Lavoy, Scott D. Sagan, and James J. Wirtz, eds. Ithaca, NY: Cornell University Press, pp. 182–201.
Bianco, Lucien. 1971. *Origins of the Chinese Revolution, 1915–1949.* Stanford, CA: Stanford University Press.
Blechman, Barry, and Stephen Kaplan. 1978. *Force without War.* Washington, DC: Brookings Institution.

Burke, John P., and Fred I. Greenstein. 1989. *How Presidents Test Reality: Decisions on Vietnam, 1954 and 1965.* New York: Russell Sage Foundation.

Butler, Richard. 2000. *The Greatest Threat: Iraq, Weapons of Mass Destruction, and the Crisis of Global Security.* New York: Public Affairs.

Daalder, Ivo H., and Michael E. O'Hanlon. 2000. *Winning Ugly: NATO's War to Save Kosovo.* Washington, DC: Brookings Institution.

DeRouen, Karl R., Jr. 2001a. *Historical Encyclopedia of U.S. Presidential Use of Force, 1789–2000.* Westport, CT: Greenwood Press.

———. 2001b. *Politics, Economics, and Presidential Use of Force Decision Making.* Lewiston, NY: Edward Mellen.

———. 2003. "The Decision Not to Use Force at Dien Bien Phu: A Poliheuristic Perspective." In *Integrating Cognitive and Rational Theories of Foreign Policy Decision Making,* Alex Mintz, ed. New York: Palgrave Macmillan, pp. 11–28.

Diehl, Paul F., and Gary Goertz. 2000. *War and Peace in International Rivalry.* Ann Arbor: University of Michigan Press.

Dye, Thomas R. 2001. *Politics in America.* 4th ed. Upper Saddle River, NJ: Prentice-Hall.

Feaver, Peter. 2003. *Armed Servants: Agency, Oversight, and Civil-Military Relations.* Cambridge, MA: Harvard University Press.

Feaver, Peter, and Christopher Gelpi. 2004. *Choosing Your Battles: American Civil-Military Relations and the Use of Force.* Princeton, NJ: Princeton University Press.

Fiorina, Morris P., and Paul E. Peterson. 1999. *The New American Democracy.* Needham Heights, MD: Allyn & Bacon.

Fry, Earl H., Stan A. Taylor, and Robert S. Wood. 1994. *America the Vincible: U.S. Foreign Policy for the Twenty-First Century.* Englewood Cliffs, NJ: Prentice-Hall.

Gaddis, John Lewis. 1992. *The United States and the End of the Cold War: Implications, Reconsiderations, Provocations.* New York: Oxford University Press.

———. 1997. *We Now Know: Rethinking Cold War History.* New York: Oxford University Press.

Giles, Gregory F. 2000. "The Islamic Republic of Iran and Nuclear, Biological, and Chemical Weapons." In *Planning the Unthinkable: How New Powers Will Use Nuclear, Biological, and Chemical Weapons,* Peter R. Lavoy, Scott D. Sagan, and James J. Wirtz, eds. Ithaca, NY: Cornell University Press, pp. 79–103.

Haass, Richard N. 1999. *Intervention: The Use of American Military Force in the Post–Cold War World.* Washington, DC: Brookings Institution.

Hastedt, Glenn P. 2003. *American Foreign Policy: Past, Present, Future.* 5th ed. Upper Saddle River, NJ: Prentice-Hall.

Head, Richard G., Frisco W. Short, and Robert C. McFarland. 1978. *Crisis Resolution: Presidential Decision Making in the Mayaguez and Korean Confrontations.* Boulder, CO: Westview Press.

Hendrickson, Ryan C. 2002. *The Clinton Wars: The Constitution, Congress, and War Powers.* Nashville, TN: Vanderbilt University Press.

International Institute for Strategic Studies. 2003. *The Military Balance.* Oxford: Oxford University Press.

Jordan, Amos A., William J. Taylor, Jr., and Michael J. Mazarr. 1999. *American National Security.* 5th ed. Baltimore, MD: Johns Hopkins University Press.

Khong, Yuen Foong. 1992. *Analogies at War: Korea, Munich, Dien Bien Phu, and the Vietnam Decisions of 1965.* Princeton, NJ: Princeton University Press.

Lamb, Christopher. 1989. *Belief Systems and Decision Making in the Mayaguez Crisis.* Gainesville: University of Florida Press.

Lavoy, Peter R., Scott D. Sagan, and James J. Wirtz, eds. 2000. *Planning the Unthinkable: How New Powers Will Use Nuclear, Biological, and Chemical Weapons.* Ithaca, NY: Cornell University Press.

Levering, Ralph B., Vladimir O. Pechatnov, Verena Botzenhart-Viehe, and C. Earl Edmondson. 2002. *Debating the Origins of the Cold War: American and Russian Perspectives.* Lanham, MD: Rowman & Littlefield.

McCarthy, Timothy V., and Jonathan B. Tucker. 2000. "Saddam's Toxic Arsenal: Chemical and Biological Weapons in the Gulf Wars." In *Planning the Unthinkable: How New Powers Will*

Use Nuclear, Biological, and Chemical Weapons, Peter R. Lavoy, Scott D. Sagan, and James J. Wirtz, eds. Ithaca, NY: Cornell University Press, pp. 47–78.

Meernik, James. 1991. "Presidential Decision-Making and the Political Use of Military Force." Ph.D. dissertation, Michigan State University.

Melanson, Richard A. 2000. *American Foreign Policy since the Vietnam War: The Search for Consensus from Nixon to Clinton.* 3d ed. Armonk, NY: M. E. Sharpe.

O'Hanlon, Michael E. 2001. *Defense Policy Choices for the Bush Administration.* 2d ed. Washington, DC: Brookings Institution.

Pillar, Paul R. 2001. *Terrorism and U.S. Foreign Policy.* Washington, DC: Brookings Institution.

Renshon, Stanley A., ed. 1993. *The Political Psychology of the Gulf War: Leaders, Publics, and the Process of Conflict.* Pittsburgh, PA: University of Pittsburgh Press.

Sarkesian, Sam C., and John Mead Flanagin. 1994. *U.S. Domestic and National Security Agendas: Into the Twenty-First Century.* Westport, CT: Greenwood Press.

Sarkesian, Sam C., and John Allen Williams. 1994. "Civil-Military Relations in the New Era." In *U.S. Domestic and National Security Agendas: Into the Twenty-First Century,* Sam C. Sarkesian and John Mead Flanagin, eds. Westport, CT: Greenwood Press, pp. 207–222.

Sarkesian, Sam C., John Allen Williams, and Stephen J. Cimbala. 2002. *U.S. National Security: Policymakers, Processes, and Politics.* 3d ed. Boulder, CO: Lynne Rienner Publishers.

Sobel, Richard. 2001. *The Impact of Public Opinion on U.S. Foreign Policy since Vietnam: Constraining the Colossus.* New York: Oxford University Press.

Stiles, Kendall W. 2002. *Case Histories in International Politics.* 2d ed. New York: Longman.

Stockholm International Peace Research Institute (SIPRI). 2003. *SIPRI Yearbook 2003: Armaments, Disarmament and International Security.* London: Oxford University Press.

_____. 2004. *SIPRI Yearbook 2004: Armaments, Disarmament and*

International Security. London: Oxford University Press.

Stoessinger, John G. 2001. *Why Nations Go to War.* 8th ed. Boston: Bedford/St. Martin's Press.

Thompson, William R., ed. 1999. *Great Power Rivalries.* Columbia: University of South Carolina Press.

Wiarda, Howard J., ed. 1996. *U.S. Foreign and Strategic Policy in the Post–Cold War Era: A Geopolitical Perspective.* Westport, CT: Greenwood Press.

Ziegler, David W. 1997. *War, Peace, and International Politics.* 7th ed. New York: Longman.

Journal Articles/Newspapers

Burk, James. 1999. "Public Support for Peacekeeping in Lebanon and Somalia: Assessing the Casualties Hypothesis." *Political Science Quarterly* 114:53–78.

Gibler, Douglas M., and Meredith Reid Sarkees. 2004. "Measuring Alliances: The Correlates of War Formal Interstate Alliance Data Set, 1816–2000." *Journal of Peace Research* 41:211–222.

Gilboa, Eytan. 1995/96. "The Panama Invasion Revisited: Lessons for the Use of Force in the Post Cold War Era." *Political Science Quarterly* 110:539–562.

Glaser, Charles L., and Steve Fetter. 2001. "National Missile Defense and the Future of U.S. Nuclear Weapons Policy." *International Security* 26:40–92.

Hollis, Martin, and Steve Smith. 1986. "Roles and Reasons in Foreign Policy Decision Making." *British Journal of Political Science* 16:269–286.

Holsti, Ole R. 1998. "A Widening Gap between the U.S. Military and Civilian Society: Some Evidence, 1976–1996." *International Security* 23:5–42.

Huntington, Samuel P. 1999. "The Lonely Superpower." *Foreign Affairs* 78:35–49.

Kennan, George. 1947. "The Sources of Soviet Conduct." *Foreign Affairs* 25:566–576.

Meernik, James. 1993. "Presidential Support in Congress: Conflict and Consensus on Foreign and Defense Policy." *Journal of Politics* 55:569–587.

Millett, Allan R. 1979. "The American Political System and Civil Control of the Military: A Historical Perspective." Mershon Center Position Papers in the Policy Sciences, Ohio State University.

Paris, Roland. 2002. "Kosovo and the Metaphor War." *Political Science Quarterly* 117:423–450.

Posen, Barry R. 2001. "The Struggle against Terrorism: Grand Strategy, Strategy, and Tactics." *International Security* 26:39–55.

Sarkees, Meredith Reid. 2000. "The Correlates of War Data on War: An Update to 1997." *Conflict Management and Peace Science* 18:123–144.

Sloan, Stanley R. 1995. "U.S. Perspectives on NATO's Future." *International Affairs* 71:217–231.

Smith, Steve. 1984/5. "Policy Preferences and Bureaucratic Position: The Case of the American Hostage Rescue Mission." *International Affairs* 61:9–25.

Werner, Suzanne, and Douglas Lemke. 1997. "Opposites Do Not Attract: The Impact of Domestic Institutions, Power, and Prior Commitments on Alignment Choices." *International Studies Quarterly* 41:529–546.

Websites

British Broadcasting Corporation. 2002. http://news.bbc.co.uk/2/hi/middleeast/1908671.stm (accessed March 1, 2004).

Bush. http://www.whitehouse.gov/news/releases/2002/01/ 20020129–11.html (accessed March 1, 2004).

Center for Defense Information. http://www.cdi.org (accessed March 1, 2004).

Central Intelligence Agency. http://www.cia.gov/cia/publications/factbook/geos/us.html (accessed March 1, 2004).

CNN. 2001. http://edition.cnn.com/2001/ALLPOLITICS/04/25/bush.taiwan.04/ (accessed March 1, 2004).

———. 2004. http://www.cnn.com/2004/WORLD/americas/02/26/haiti.revolt/index.html (accessed March 1, 2004).

Correlates of War. http://cow2.la.psu.edu (accessed March 1, 2004)

Department of Defense. http://www.defenselink.mil/ (accessed March 1, 2004).

Economist. 2003. http://www.economist.com/displayStory.cfm?story_id=1973895 (accessed March 1, 2004).

Federation of American Scientists: DPRK. http://www.fas.org/nuke/guide/dprk/nuke/index.html (accessed March 1, 2004).

Federation of American Scientists: Iran. http://www.fas.org/nuke/guide/iran/nuke/ (accessed March 1, 2004).

Federation of American Scientists: SORT. http://www.fas.org/nuke/control/sort/fs-sort.html (accessed March 1, 2004).

History Central. http://www.multied.com/1812/declares.html (accessed March 1, 2004).

Jane's. http://www.janes.com/ (accessed March 1, 2004).

Korean War. http://www.korean-war.com/TimeLine/1950/06–25to08–03–50.html (accessed March 1, 2004).

Library of Congress. http://www.loc.gov/rr/hispanic/1898/intro.html (accessed March 1, 2004).

NATO. http://www.nato.int/ docu/basictxt/treaty.htm (accessed March 1, 2004).

New Scientist. http://www.newscientist.com/news/news.jsp?id=ns99994594 (accessed March 1, 2004).

Spartacus Educational: FDR. http://www.spartacus.schoolnet.co.uk/USArooseveltF.htm (accessed March 1, 2004).

Spartacus Educational: WWI. http://www.spartacus.schoolnet.co.uk/FWWusaG.htm (accessed March 1, 2004).

Spartacus Educational: WWII. http://www.spartacus.schoolnet.co.uk/2WWlendlease.htm (accessed March 1, 2004).

Stanford Daily. 2003. http://daily.stanford.edu/tempo?page=content&id=10527&repository=0001article (accessed March 1, 2004).

Tanter. 2004a. http://www.lib.umich.edu/govdocs/iraqwar.html#regime (accessed March 1, 2004).

Tanter. 2004b. http://www.lib.umich.edu/govdocs/iraqwar.html#warus (accessed March 1, 2004).

United Nations. Security Council. http://ods-dds-ny.un.org/doc/UNDOC/GEN/N02/682/26/PDF/N0268226.pdf?OpenElement (accessed March 1, 2004).

U.S. Department of State. http://www.state.gov/p/wha/rls/fs/2001/2558.htm (accessed March 1, 2004).

U.S. White House: Iraq. http://www.whitehouse.gov/infocus/elections/ (accessed May 26, 2005).

U.S. White House: NSC. http://www.whitehouse.gov/nsc/nss.pdf (accessed March 1, 2004).

U.S. White House: WMD. http://www.whitehouse.gov/news/releases/2002/12/WMDStrategy.pdf (accessed March 1, 2004).

Venezuela

Joakim Kreutz

Geography and History

Tribes such as Carib, Arawak, and Chibcha originally inhabited the territory of present Venezuela with distinctly different Andean and Caribbean cultures. Christopher Columbus's third trip to the Americas, the first time his expeditions landed on continental land, arrived August 2, 1498, at the mouth of the Orinoco River. The expedition continued to sail along the Venezuelan coast before witnessing the gold carried by native tribes in northern Colombia that created the legend of El Dorado and further Spanish interest. In 1499, Alonso de Ojeda named the country Venezuela ("Little Venice"), after seeing the stilted houses the natives had built at Lake Maracaibo. Exploration was slower in Venezuela than in neighboring areas, but in 1567 Diego de Losada defeated local tribes and founded Caracas. Venezuelan territory became administered under the Spanish Viceroy in Santo Domingo until, in 1739, present-day Colombia, Venezuela, Ecuador, and Panama formed the Spanish New Granada ruled from Bogotá. The main export was cocoa, which attracted large Spanish immigration in the following centuries and also led to an influx of slaves from Africa.

Disgruntled plantation owners that opposed the Spanish control of the colonial economy led to the first independence movements in the late eighteenth century. When Jose Bonaparte removed the Spanish king Fernando VII in 1810, the Creole elite in Venezuela attacked and removed the local governor. On July 5, 1811, Venezuelan independence was declared by the national congress followed by a civil war between different factions of the independence movement. Spain retook the territory, but the independence movements in the region were unified under the leadership of Venezuelan Simón Bolívar, who defeated the Spanish in 1819–1823. The former Spanish colonies in northern South America became united as Gran Colombia. Following years of political turmoil and the death of Bolívar in 1830, Gran Colombia collapsed and established the states of Colombia (including the territory of present-day Panama), Venezuela, and Ecuador (History of Venezuela 2000).

Since February 3, 1999, the president of the Republica Bolivariana de Venezuela has been Hugo Chávez, and Jose Vicente Rangel has been vice president since April 28, 2002. Since the election in 1998, there has been a constitutional change, and Chávez was reelected in July 2000 under the new constitution for a period of six years.

The president is elected by a plurality vote for six years. The president then appoints members of and heads the cabinet. The president is the chief of state, the head of government, and the commander-in-chief of the armed forces (Szajkowski 2004, 526). In the new constitution there is a unicameral Asamblea Nacional, consisting of 165 seats, with election every five years. Three seats are reserved for the indigenous peoples of Venezuela.

The highest judicial branch is the Tribuna Suprema de Justicia, with magistrates elected by the National Assembly for a single twelve-year term. Since 1989, governors and mayors have been elected directly in the districts, whereas before the president appointed them.

The country is administered as one Distrito Federal (federal district), twenty-three Estados (states), and one Dependencia Federal (federal dependency), consisting of eleven island groups, or seventy-two islands.

Venezuela borders Colombia to the west, Brazil to the South, and Guyana to the east. Just across the small Golfo de Paria to the northeast of Venezuela is the island of Trinidad, and the Dutch Antilles lie a short distance north of the coastline.

The area of Venezuela is 912,050 square kilometers. The northwest is divided between the Andean Mountain range and Maracaibo lowlands. Most of the country is located on plains that rise into the Guiana highlands in the southeast.

The country is rich in mineral resources, such as petroleum, natural gas, iron ore, gold, bauxite, and other minerals, as well as hydropower and diamonds, but has become very dependent on its oil production, because oil early on became the most important source of national revenue.

The region of Latin America is generally considered to have the most unequal income distribution in the world, where the poorest 20 percent of the population receives 4.5 percent of the income, and the wealthiest 10 percent receives 40 percent (World Bank 2000). Even though the Venezuelan economy in general showed

Table 1   Venezuela: Key Statistics

Type of government	Federal republic
Population (millions)	25 (July 2003)
Religion	Roman Catholic 96%
Main industries	Petroleum, iron ore mining, construction materials, food processing, textiles, steel, aluminum, motor vehicle assembly
Main security threats	Regional instability from Colombian civil war, coup d'etat, or civil war, possible United States involvement
Defense spending (% GDP)	0.9 (1999, higher at present)
Size of military (thousands)	82.3 (2002)
Number of civil wars since 1945	2
Number of interstate wars since 1945	0

Sources
Central Intelligence Agency Website. 2005. CIA *World Factbook.* http://www.cia.gov/cia/ publications/factbook/ (accessed May 15, 2005).
DCP (Democracy Coalition Project). 2003. *Defending Democracy: A Global Survey of Foreign Policy Trends 1992–2002.*
Eriksson, Mikael, ed. 2004. *States in Armed Conflict 2002.* Uppsala, Sweden: Uppsala Publishing House.
International Institute for Strategic Studies (IISS). 2003. *The Military Balance 2003–2004.* London: IISS and Oxford University Press.

some growth in the 1990s, the percentage of population that suffered from poverty increased from 39/49 percent (urban/rural areas) in 1990 to 47/56 in 1999. In roughly the same time period (1990–2000), the unemployment rose from 10.2 to 14.5 percent (Valenzuela 2002, 1–2; CIA *World Fact Book* 2004

Regional Geopolitics

Relations between Venezuela and neighboring states have been most intense, both in a positive and a negative way, with Colombia, since they both separated from Gran Colombia in 1830. The two countries have had the most trade and cross-border economic cooperation, but also suffered some cases of fierce competition. In the late 1960s, relations turned very sour after Colombia tried to negotiate contracts with foreign oil companies to do exploratory drilling in the Golfo de Venezuela. The Venezuelan government protested and pointed out that the Golfo was an inland waterway that belonged to Venezuela. In 1971, the two states agreed to suspend further exploration until the border dispute was settled.

Following a short—and failed—Venezuelan initiative of negotiations in 1979, the situation became tense in the first half of the ensuing decade. Several incidents of shooting in the Golfo were reported, as both countries engaged in a minor arms race and increased their forces along the borders. Another round of talks failed in 1986, and Venezuela rejected a proposal to submit the dispute to the International Court of Justice. In August 1987, the Venezuelan government claimed that a Colombian warship had penetrated the border, and both sides mobilized, but because the Venezuelan forces at the time were far superior, nothing happened (U.S. Library of Congress 1988).

More recently, the current Colombian civil war has spilled over the borders into Venezuela. The Colombian antigovernment guerrilla FARC-EP has bases on Venezuelan territory, and the illegal Colombian paramilitary organization AUC claimed in 2002 that it had clashed with FARC-EP across the border and also that it was involved in training right-wing Venezuelan paramilitaries called AUV. The Colombian government has repeatedly accused Venezuela of supporting FARC-EP, a claim that is usually denied, but in 2002 a Venezuelan television program showed documentary footage of Venezuelan troops participating in FARC-EP operations. The pictures were allegedly from 2000. As a result of the intense conflict in Colombia, the neighboring countries have strengthened their border forces for several years.

Another effect of the Colombian conflict is an influx of refugees. It has been estimated that between 1950 and 1988, more than 1 million Colombians have entered Venezuela. Lately, the refugees have mostly consisted of people forcibly removed by FARC-EP or AUC in their competition over territory and control of drug trafficking. After Venezuelan troops clashed with Colombian paramilitaries in late 2003, the Venezuelan border forces were further strengthened (U.S. Library of Congress 1988; Valenzuela 2002, 6–7; Kreutz 2005; Sanchez 2003b, 12–30).

A connected issue is Venezuela's stance in relation to the large-scale, U.S.-sponsored antinarcotics and guerrilla initiative "Plan Colombia." The plan was launched in 2000 and immediately received serious criticism from President Chávez. He opposes the idea of the United States as a global hegemon and declares that Plan Colombia is a step toward "Viet-namization" of the conflict rather than re-specting the national sovereignty of the states in the region (DCP 2003, 217).

There is a long-standing dispute over the eastern border of the former British colony of Guyana, which was decided by the United States in 1899. Venezuela claims that Great Britain—at the time—received more than they were entitled to, and this issue has been discussed various times. The last time the issue of border claims was revived was in 2000 by Hugo Chávez.

In the 1960s and 1970s, Venezuela sup-plied economic assistance to neighboring Caribbean island states such as Trinidad and Tobago, Costa Rica, Honduras, and Puerto Rico, with the intention of in-creasing industrial developments in those countries.

Venezuela had the strongest reaction of any country to the *autogolpe* (self-coup) crisis in Peru in 1992. Not satisfied with the quiet diplomacy preferred by most members of the Organization of Ameri-can States (OAS), Venezuela advocated stronger measures. It recalled its ambas-sador from Lima, called for official con-demnation of Peruvian leader Alberto Fu-jimori, and was in favor of the exclusion of Peru from the Rio Group as well as the freezing of approved loans by the IDB (Inter-American Development Bank). The reason behind the intense reaction was probably then President Carlos An-drés Perez's experience of a coup attempt in Venezuela only two months earlier (DCP 2003, 218).

Venezuela participated in the interna-tional trade embargo that followed the 1991 coup in Haiti and also chose to uni-laterally suspend the oil supply to Haiti. The ousted leader, Jean Bertrand Aristide, spend some of his time in exile in Venezuela, and when he was reinstated in 1993, his former hosts were one of the first Latin American countries to support his return (Babulin et al. 1999; DCP 2003, 218).

Because of Venezuela's strong condem-nation of coup attempts in the region, it came as somewhat of a surprise that its response to the short-lived coup in

---

Sidebar 1   The "Curse" of Oil

It has been recorded that having ac-cess to natural resources such as oil can be a curse for the economic growth of a country. The income from oil exports is not distributed through-out society, and usually rests with a small part of the population. Since the 1920s, oil has contributed to more than 50 percent of Venezuelan export earnings and more than 50 percent of government income. Until the late 1970s, it seemed as if the country had managed to avoid the negative effects of this type of economy. The govern-ment created a democracy based on a high level of social welfare spending. Eventually, corruption and clien-telism created a situation where the government agencies started to bor-row from abroad to cover their ambi-tious projects and wages. Since 1980, the economies of only three countries in Latin America (Nicaragua, Haiti, and Guyana) have performed worse than that of Venezuela.

Sources
Barrios, Harald, Martin Beck, Andreas Boeckh, and Klaus Segbers, eds. 2003. *Resistance to Globalization: Political Struggle and Cultural Resilience in the Middle East, Russia, and Latin America*. Münster: Lit Verlag.
Gruben, William C., and Sarah Darley. 2004. "The 'Curse' of Venezuela." *Southwest Economy* 3:17–18.

Ecuador in 2000 was so weak. Allegations of close ties between the Ecuadorian coup leader, Col. Lucio Gutierrez, and Hugo Chávez have led some to speculate that the Venezuelan government covertly supported the attempt (DCP 2003, 219).

Conflicts Past and Present

Conflict History

The indigenous tribes of Carib, Arawak, and the Chibcha originally inhabited the territory of present-day Venezuela. The first European to record a visit to the area was Christopher Columbus, who arrived in 1498 on his third American journey. The exploration of Venezuela was slower than in the mineral-rich areas in the West, and the area was largely independent even though it nominally was under the control of Bogotá.

Toward the end of the eighteenth century, there was a growing opposition to the Spanish colonialists all over South America. Plantation owners that were disgruntled with the colonial monopoly of trade initiated the first independence movement under Fernando de Miranda in the late eighteenth century. It took until the Spanish kingdom was weakened by the Napoleonic Wars in Europe for a successful rebellion to take place in 1810. The following year, an independent republic in Venezuela was declared, but fighting within the independence movement led to reconquest by the Spaniards a few years later. The different movements in the northern part of South America united behind Venezuelan Simón Bolívar, who created an army of native fighters and British mercenaries and defeated the Spaniards in 1819–1823. Venezuela, Ecuador, and Colombia (including present-day Panama) united as Gran Colombia, but regional tensions and the death of revolutionaries Bolívar and Antonia José Sucre in 1830 led to the dissolution of the union into three separate states.

Following the establishment of Venezuela, a period of some thirty years under different dictatorships and overthrows culminated in the civil war of 1859–1863 between centralist and federalist factions. The latter grouping won, but a series of

---

Sidebar 2   The Revolution Will Not Be Televised—The Movie

At the time of the attempted coup in 2002, a television crew from Irish TV (Radio Telifís Éireann) was doing a program about Chávez. The crew managed to shoot pictures of opposition figures who claimed that they had engineered the coup, and had deliberately directed Chávez and anti-Chávez demonstrations until they came face-to-face and violence erupted.

In general, the award-winning report that was broadcast by RTÉ under the title *Chávez: Inside the Coup* contradicted explanations for the coup given by several observers as well as the U.S. State Department and U.S. President George W. Bush. Chávez supporters have since discredited the movie and, as of May 2005, no U.S. television channel had aired it. A longer version, however, has been shown in selected theaters.

Sources
   "The Revolution Will Not Be Televised." www.chavezthefilm.com (accessed May 14, 2005).
   Sweet, Frederick. 2003. "Media Concentration Undermines Democracy." *Intervention Magazine,* April 5. http://www.interventionmag.com.

coups, many nonviolent, led to a continuation of authoritarian rule for almost another century. Most influential of the rulers were Antonio Guzman Blanco (1870–1888), Cipriano Castro (1899–1908), and Juan Vincente Gómez (1908–1935).

During this time period, there was still some confusion about border territories, because after Gran Colombia disintegrated, the boundaries were not clearly set. Venezuela claimed some territory along the eastern border of what was then the British colony of Guiana. This dispute was actually left over from Spanish colonial times, because the borders Venezuela wanted would give them territory previously claimed by the Spanish. The British disagreed, arguing that they had acquired the territory from the Dutch in 1810. In 1841, the British established a provisional border, which was contested by Venezuela.

The dispute became heated when gold was discovered in the area, and in 1887 Venezuela broke off diplomatic connections with Great Britain and sought aid from the United States. After some failed U.S. attempts at mediation, the U.S. Secretary of State Richard Olney in 1895 made a broader interpretation of the Monroe Doctrine and demanded arbitration. The British were unwilling to comply, and U.S. President Grover Cleveland declared that it was the duty of the United States to determine the boundary, and Great Britain had to accept whatever their determination was. Neither side was prepared to go to war over the issue, and the British sent a conciliatory note recognizing this interpretation of the Monroe Doctrine. In 1899, a U.S.-appointed commission established the border, generally being favorable for Great Britain.

Three years later, Venezuela had to cancel the repayment of loans, because the finances of the Cipriano Castro administration were in chaos owing to mismanagement and civil disturbances. The creditors, consisting of Great Britain, Germany, and Italy, sent a joint naval expedition to blockade and shell the Venezuelan coast. Germany had already explained its actions to the United States, which—according to the Monroe Doctrine—was the hemispheric power. After U.S. mediation, the claims were adjusted in 1903, and, following a ruling in The Hague Tribunal, it was decided that Venezuela should repay the blockading countries before they paid any other creditors.

Oil was discovered in the territory early in the twentieth century, and from the 1920s onward, the petroleum industry grew and paid for the investments in infrastructure by the authoritarian rulers. This led to increasingly close relations with the United States, because many of the investments came from companies based in North America.

The civil-military relationship in Venezuela contrasts that of most other South American countries, where the armed forces in general have been largely disconnected from political movements but at times have intervened in order to protect the various countries from bad political decision makers. In Venezuela, the military during the leaderships of Juan Vincente Gómez (1908–1935) and Marcos Pérez Jiménez (1948–1958) became closely connected with the leaders, to the point that the armed forces almost had the status of the presidents' private army.

It took until 1945 before Venezuela experienced democracy for the first time. Following the dismantling of the long dictatorship, the ruling AD (Acción Democrática) Party assumed it had the backing for a program of radical reforms. This proved not to be the case, as important civilian sectors joined the military in the 1948 coup that led to the return to authoritarianism under Pérez Jiménez (Mares 1998, 69).

After large landowners and other important figures of the "civilian" elite openly rejected the Jiménez dictatorship in 1958, the military removed their support and participated in the transition to democracy. Since then, the majority of the military has voluntarily rejected involvement in domestic politics. Following the establishment of the joint civilian-military transitional government in 1958, there were a few attempts by dissident military factions to overthrow the government, but pro-government forces and immediate public reaction through mass demonstrations in support of democracy crushed the rebellions (Mares 1998, 63).

In 1960, the ruling Democratic Party split, and one opposition faction called MIR (Movimiento de la Izquierda Revolucionaria: Movement of the Revolutionary Left) emerged. In 1962, MIR merged with the communist FALN (Fuerzas Armadas de Liberación Nacional: The National Liberation Forces), which maintained an armed insurgency for a few years in the 1960s. The conflict was mostly based around urban warfare and terrorist acts, but because the expected revolutionary support did not follow, the activities grew sparser. The majority of the largely urbanized and middle-class Venezuelan society responded with revulsion, because the terrorist activity was perceived as an irritation to daily life (Saavedra 2003b, 197). In 1966, the guerrillas declared an end to the armed revolutionary tactics, and after a general amnesty in 1969, the conflict was over.

The few remains of the movement merged in 1973 into the OIR (Opción de Izquierda Revolucionaria). In general,

however, the Venezuelan society was the most stable in South America, with functioning democracy and civil-military relations as well as higher per capita income, best-organized labor organizations, and a larger middle class (Falcoff 2003).

The country suddenly became very wealthy in the 1970s because of the energy crisis, and a lot of the money was put into building a strong military. The country became dependent on oil revenues and was not prepared for the 1980s decline in oil prices, which led to a deep recession, accelerated by corruption and economic mismanagement. An example cited by Falcoff is that "in the late '80s (Venezuela) [was] spending roughly the same proportion of their GNP on health and education as France—with nothing resembling a French result" (2002, 5).

The increasing budget deficit and foreign debt led President Carlos Andrés Pérez to impose big budget cuts in 1989. The economic crisis of 1989 led to large-scale antigovernment demonstrations and the "Caracazo" riots, where the army was used against protesters and several hundred people were killed (Trinkunas 2001, 5).

In the mid-1980s, there had been several incidents of shooting between Colombian and Venezuelan forces in the Golfo de Venezuela over a contested and oil-rich border area. The countries were also engaged in a minor arms race and increased their forces along the borders. In August 1987, the Venezuelan government claimed that a Colombian warship had penetrated the border, and both sides mobilized, but because the Venezuelan forces at the time were far superior to the Colombian forces, nothing happened (U.S. Library of Congress 1988). The conflict was still not settled, and as the Venezuelan defense spending decreased in the early 1990s, there were renewed discussions over the future of the area. Venezuelan President Pérez stated that he was willing to accept some Colombian sovereignty in the area if the dispute could be settled. This statement was perceived as downplaying the importance of the Venezuelan armed forces, and disgruntled military leaders became discontent with the activities of the president (Pion-Berlin and Arceneaux 2000, 431).

The measures taken to halt the deteriorating economy were not successful—or not enough—and created increasing opposition to President Pérez, even within his own party. Between September 1991 and the end of January 1992, there were more than 900 organized protests against the president, and more than half were violent enough to require police intervention. A group of young officers decided that the time was ripe for a coup and attempted to seize power in February 1992. One of the leaders among the young officers was Colonel Hugo Chávez. There was no public protest of the coup, but all organized sectors of society rejected the attempt, and pro-government forces defeated the rebels. Interestingly enough, in a poll taken two weeks after the failed coup, 45 percent of the population thought the young officers would have done a better job than the sitting president.

As it was, in November the same year, a group of more senior military officers also attempted a coup but largely met with a similar result, even though the clashes this time led to more casualties. President Pérez had lost all domestic support, however, and in June 1993 he was impeached as a caretaker government administered new elections (Mares 1998, 60, 67–68).

After winning the elections in December 1993 as an independent candidate, and faced with another economic crisis,

President Rafael Caldera decided to suspend some constitutional rights and give the police the power to detain people and enter homes without warrants as well as seize property without compensation. In July 1994, the Congress voted to restore the civil rights, but Caldera resuspended them and challenged the congress to put the matter up for a national referendum.

Following his release from prison in 1995, Hugo Chávez went to Cuba, where he was greeted as a great revolutionary hero and established good personal contacts with Fidel Castro. He then returned to Venezuela to compete in the upcoming presidential elections under a revolutionary political umbrella. In a populist campaign that drew strong parallels between Chávez and the national hero Simón Bolívar, he proclaimed himself to be against the United States, globalization, and economic liberalism and instead offered a "Bolivarian Revolution" as a national solution to the country's problems. His arguments worked, as a wave of support from left-wing sympathizers and the poor population led to his victory in the 1998 election (DCP 2003, 217, 220).

Current and Potential Military Confrontation

Following the inauguration in February 1999, Chávez acted swiftly. He reorganized the public administration along military lines and appointed more than 176 active duty and retired military officers to senior ministerial, vice-ministerial, and senior policy positions in government agencies unrelated to defense (Trinkunas 2001, 2, 6).

Chávez's populist policies alienated the middle and upper classes as well as parts of the military, which began considering his rhetoric a liability. At the same time, the emergence of independent media sources such as the newspapers *El Nacional* and *El Universal* led to an increased public debate of Chávez's policies and a chance for opponents to criticize them. These have led to the increased political mobilization of the Venezuelan society and have contributed to the strong reactions that occur among the general public after every controversial decision. The political opposition to Chávez unified in 2000 under the name CD (Coordinación Democrática) and also received support from both trade unions and private sector organizations (Falcoff 2002, 7; Szajkowski 2004, 526).

In April 2002, disgruntled officers of the air force and army seized power and declared that businessman Pedro Carmona was head of a caretaker government, supported by a large section of the civilian elite and labor organizations. Chávez supporters took to the streets, and the governments of Argentina, Mexico, and Paraguay quickly declared that the new government was illegal. After two days in power, Carmona was forced out of office, as Chávez-faithful members of the armed forces counterattacked, eventually resulting in a purge of suspected disloyal officers from the military. The political situation continued to be tense, as the economic crisis and accusations of undemocratic behavior fueled a harsh debate between further radicalized pro- and anti-Chávez movements (McGirk 2002; Meltzer 2002, 1–2).

Later in the year, large-scale demonstrations demanding Chávez's resignation led to clashes on the streets. A group of military officers and civilian supporters declared themselves as legally in rebellion against the government, because the constitution permitted rebellion against an authoritarian regime. As the economy worsened, the Chávez administration tried to extract an increasing amount of capital from the state-run oil company PDVSA for different projects. This, in combination with Chávez's attempts to replace the technocratic management with political allies, led to the next major crisis. The employees of PDVSA—the main source of wealth for the Venezuelan economy—became disgruntled with the political involvement and in December 2002 started a strike that continued until mid-February 2003. In response to the strike, the Chávez administration sacked 5,300 company employees, including 700 executives (of a total prestrike employee count of 33,000), and the military was ordered to work to keep oil production up. This action has allegedly created further criticism of Chávez within the armed forces (Falcoff 2003, 2; Szajkowski 2004, 526; Campbell 2003, 2–7).

The strike was enhanced by large-scale anti-Chávez demonstrations that erupted into riots as the police force responded with tear gas and rubber bullets. There were some concerns about how the military would react in the situation, but the armed forces commander, General Garcia Montoya, declared his support of Chávez, and the armed forces focused on oil refinery operations and distribution of supplies. International concern led to the establishment of a "Group of Friends," consisting of the United States, Mexico, Brazil, Chile, Spain, and Portugal, to find a negotiated settlement to the crisis. Before any initiatives had been launched, however, the strike ended in early February 2003 (Castañeda 2003, 75; Meltzer 2002, 1).

There were concerns that the aftermath of the strike would create further political violence, because the Chávez administration has been criticized for its poor human rights record. Several of the labor organization leaders fled the country in the ensuing months, fearing government repression, and there were some suggestions that political murders were being committed. In May 2003, a conciliation agreement was signed between the opposition and the government, in which both sides agreed to refrain from violence. As part of the agreement, a disarmament of civil society was also stipulated, and the opposition started a campaign to collect signatures for a possible recall referendum (EIU 2004; Webb-Vidal 2003, 17).

Chávez also faced some internal opposition from within the government movement (Movimiento Quinta República) and among the parts of the armed forces that supported the attempted overthrow of government in 2002 (Valenzuela 2002, 4).

In the early months of 2004, the situation was chaotic with pro- and anti-Chávez rallies involving tens of thousands of people almost daily. Clashes between supporters occurred, and parts of Caracas were inaccessible, owing to roadblocks and burning barricades. During, for example, the last weekend of February, at least 5 people were killed and 100 injured in the political protests. The opposition once again gathered signatures for a recall referendum, and Chávez agreed to abide by the result if enough signatures were presented. He also publicly declared that he easily would win a referendum, and he initiated several projects in early 2004 to strengthen his popularity among the poorer sections of the population. These initiatives, among them unconstitutionally forcing the Venezuelan Central Bank to release U.S.$1 billion for agriculture reform, have only increased the criticism of Chávez for trying to impose a Cuban-style command economy. Another suggestion floated by the Chávez administration was the decriminalization of theft of food and medicine in cases of hunger or need (*Strategic Survey* 2004).

The previous attempt by the opposition to gather enough signatures for a referendum, in December 2003, was blocked when election officials declared that some of the signatures were fraudulently obtained. Chávez blamed the United States for being behind the campaign against him and declared that any U.S. attempt to remove him from power would mean the end of Venezuelan oil exports to the United States (Sanchez 2004b; Campbell 2004; Sanchez 2004a; Fletcher 2004; Sanchez 2003a).

When the Venezuelan Electoral Council evaluated the signatures in late February 2004, they demanded further information on the list submitted and declared that 800,000 signers should reaffirm their signatures and submit fingerprints. This led to criticism from the observers of the Organization of American States and the Carter Center, and the minority members of the council walked out. Symbolically significant was also the resignation of the Venezuelan ambassador to the UN, Milos Alcalay, in protest of the situation in the country (Johnson 2004).

Alliance Structure

Venezuela is not a member of any military alliances, but there have been suggestions that the Chávez administration has initiated working relationships with the Cuban military. As the controversy over domestic politics continues, Venezuela seems to have fewer political allies.

The country has been a member of the United Nations since November 15, 1945, and recognizes the UN charter with all its obligations. Venezuela is a member of OPEC, something that at times has strained relations with the United States (EIU 2004).

It has been instrumental as a member of the OAS (Organization of American States), even though there is currently some friction in the relationship. As the current president of OAS, the Colombian César Gaviria has tried to negotiate a settlement of the political dispute in Venezuela; Chávez has been less active internationally. Some U.S. sources have made calls for the Venezuelan membership to be suspended, but other members such as the Argentine and Brazilian presidents Nestor Kirchner and Luiz Inacio Lula Da Silva, respectively, have argued that it is better to maintain a dialogue with the Chávez administration in order to settle the situation (Johnson 2004).

Venezuela's wealth from oil revenue, its previously close relationship with the United States, and its strong civil society made it different from most other South American countries. It became involved in economic assistance during the 1960s and 1970s to increase industrial development in neighboring Caribbean island states such as Trinidad and Tobago, Costa Rica, Honduras, and Puerto Rico. This period also led to an increased economic and political involvement on a regional level.

In 1973, Venezuela became a member of the Andean group that previously included Colombia, Bolivia, Chile, Ecuador, and Peru. Chile left the organization in 1976, but the cooperation eventually led to the establishment of the LAFTA (Latin American Free Trade Association) and ALADI (Asociación Latinoamericana de Integración, Latin American Integration Association) in 1980.

In 1983, Colombia initiated the Contadora Group with Mexico, Venezuela, and Panama, which eventually merged with the Support Group to form the present Rio Group.

Size and Structure of the Military

In August 2002, the Venezuelan military consisted of 82,300 troops. Of this number, the army comprised 34,000, the navy 18,300 (including 500 naval aviation and 7,800 marines), and the air force comprised 7,000. In addition, the army had an estimated 8,000 reserves and 23,000 members of the National Guard (Fuerzas Armadas de Cooperación). Some 31,000 members of the military were made up of conscripts, as Venezuela requires up to thirty months of mandatory service, which varies between regions.

Most of the conscripts (27,000) were active in the army, which was divided into nineteen battalions and one aviation regiment. Sixteen of the battalions were designated as infantry, rangers, or counterguerrilla forces, leaving one battalion each for artillery, cavalry, and airborne forces. The aviation regiment of the army had at its disposal twelve aircraft and twenty-six helicopters, including seven attack helicopters.

The rest of the conscripts were enrolled in the navy, which consisted of five commands, with the main headquarters in Caracas. The other two main bases were in Puerto Cabillo for submarines, frigates, amphibious units, and service and Punto Fijo for the patrol units. All five commands were involved in patrol missions and served as part of the territorial defense.

The fleet was boosted in 2002, when it received the first two of its commissioned updated frigates and as the process of acquiring an additional supply ship (decided on in 2001) continued. After they acquire the new ship, the navy will be able to carry out limited regional deployments. The fleet included two submarines of the Sabalo (T-209/1300) kind, six frigates, six boats for patrol and coastal combat, four amphibious units, and six other vessels for support and miscellaneous assignments. All of these were housed at one of the main navy bases.

The command for fluvial (river) forces had a headquarters at the minor base of Ciudad Bolivar and a strong presence as well at the base in El Amparo, which served as headquarters for the Aruaca River.

The coast guard operated under the naval command and control but was organizationally separate, with bases in Maracaibo and La Guaira. The coast guard had at its disposal two offshore, sixteen inshore, and twenty-seven river patrol boats.

The navy also included 7,800 marines and a naval aviation command with bases in Puerto de Hierro, La Orchila, and Turiamo. The naval aviation comprised three aircraft, nine armed helicopters, and 500 troops. In addition to the naval strength of Venezuela, it should also be noted that the National Guard had at its disposal fifty-two inshore patrol vessels.

The air force comprised some 7,000 well-trained troops, including a few conscripts who were mainly involved in maintenance and supporting roles. Venezuela has put a lot of focus on developing a strong air force, and their 125 aircraft and 31 armed helicopters make them substantially stronger than, for example, neighboring Colombia (*The Military Balance 2002–2003*).

The Venezuelan armed forces have a tradition of noninvolvement in civic projects, but the implementation of "Plan Bolívar" in 2000 led to an increasing involvement of the military in areas of infrastructure maintenance. It should also be reiterated that the armed forces were ordered to participate in government attempts to keep oil production going during the strike in December 2002–February 2003 (Trinkunas 2001, 6).

Budget
The defense budget was increased from 949 billion bolivar in 2000 to around 1.400 billion bolivar in 2001 and was expected to continue on that level in 2002 (*The Military Balance* 2003). The fluctuation in the value of currency led to a yo-yo effect in the defense budget as viewed in U.S. dollars. It was U.S.$1.395 million in 2000. The increase represented U.S.$1.933 million in 2001, but then—although remaining basically the same—owing to fluctuations in value, it represented just U.S.$1.053 million in 2002.

The biggest difference between the 2001 and 2002 budgets was the increase, from 201 billion to 229 billion bolivar, for the Guardia Nacional (GN). This increase is in line with reports that the Chávez administration wanted the GN to take a more important role in Venezuelan security, but it has also been suggested that the increase was a reward for the branch's loyalty to the president (*The Military Balance* 2003; Perlo-Freeman 2003).

Many analysts believe that increased revenue coming from the recent rise in oil prices following the war in Iraq will be used to increase military spending accompanied by additional organizational and personnel changes. It has further been claimed that the military staff have been promised substantial salary increases, with as much as 30–45 percent in the coming years (EIU 2004).

Civil-Military Relations/The Role of the Military in Domestic Politics

Despite the abundance of coups during the first century of the Venezuelan state, there were few that led to actual clashes. In most cases, someone close to the previous ruler initiated the coup when the former was abroad, and the armed forces accepted the new government. During the dictatorships of Gómez (1908–1935) and Jiménez (1948–1958), the military became closely connected to and controlled by the leader. However, it maintained a certain independence, because the military leadership had close connections to the business community and local elites. When society seemed to have lost faith in Jiménez, the armed forces participated in safeguarding the transformation to democracy. The military has a constitutional possibility to intervene in the case of a national political crisis, but this "tutelary" role has rarely been used (Valenzuela 2002, 5).

In the 2000 revised constitution, some military matters were transferred back to the armed forces after previously being under civilian control, such as the powers over promotion.

Until 2000, there was a practice of appointing a member of the armed forces as minister of defense, which was part of the chain of command. In the revised constitution, both of these features have changed. Currently, there is a civilian appointed as minister of defense, and the position is no longer officially recognized as part of the chain of command. The new organization has been criticized, because the minister of defense now has limited ability to influence the armed forces. Although the minister of defense is a civilian, he has no civilian staff and his office is removed from the Defense Ministry, which has been moved to the former air force headquarters (Trinkunas 2001, 6; Fishel 2000, 9–10).

Aside from their independence concerning military matters, the armed forces in Venezuela have been proud of their lack of involvement in internal politics. At present, the Chávez administration wants current and former military leaders to have increasing political power. Most analysts suggest that there is a divide in the military, as indicated by the attempted coup of 2002, between those who are faithful to Chávez and a faction that wants to be removed from the political role increasingly being assigned to the military. The latter faction used to be strong in the navy, partly based on the navy's desire to continue joint U.S.-Venezuelan exercises (Castillo et al. 2001).

Terrorism

Since the short terrorist campaign in the 1960s, there has not been much terrorist activity in Venezuela. It can be argued that because terrorism is aimed at destabilizing a society, there is not much use for it in Venezuela, because its society is already unstable due to the political situation.

It seems that a more viable terrorist threat would come from groups involved in the Colombian conflict. The FARC-EP, the ELN, and the AUC are all included on the U.S. and Colombian lists of known terrorist groups. Even though Chávez uses the term "terrorists" to describe his domestic enemies, he has refused to expand the terminology to incorporate leftist Colombian groups, despite pressures from Colombian authorities to do so since 2001.

Following the breakdown of the Colombian peace talks in early 2002, FARC-EP withdrew to bases in the border area between Colombia and Venezuela. FARC-EP had strong support among civilians in the area, following a wave of cross-border attacks by the AUC in the late 1990s to establish and control drug routes. In June 2002, a videotape was released, indicating that a newly formed paramilitary organization called AUV (Autodefensas Unidas por Venezuela, United Self-Defense Units of Venezuela) was committed to stop left-wing intrusion into the country. The AUV were allegedly trained and supported by the AUC, but no action of the AUV has been recorded and Venezuelan security forces have no further evidence that the group exists (Szajkowski, 2004, 526).

In February 2003, two bombs detonated in Caracas, which was the first occurrence of "modern terrorism" in Venezuela. The bombs were placed at the Spanish Embassy and the Colombian consulate, and leaflets were left at the scene, claiming that the urban militia of the FBL (Fuerza Bolivariana de Liberación, Bolivarian Force for Liberation) was responsible for the bombings. The FBL was a small rural group from the area bordering Colombia, with strong links to the FARC-EP and alleged links to former officials of the Chávez government.

The leaflets demanded the expulsion of U.S. and Spanish ambassadors and the OAS secretary-general and former Colombian president Gaviria from Venezuela. Gaviria was present in Caracas at the time attempting to mediate between Chávez and the opposition.

The timing of the blasts is interesting, because only two days earlier, Chavéz had accused the U.S. and Spanish governments of taking the side of his opponents, and shortly before that, Colombian president Alvaro Uribe Velez had criticized the Venezuelan "ineffectiveness" in policing the border between the two countries (Webb-Vidal 2003, 14–15).

In a statement on January 2003, the commander of the U.S. Southern Command, James Hill, declared that Islamist group such as Hizballah and Hamas were operating out of Venezuela's Margarita Island, but no proof of that has been forthcoming. If there is a connection to these groups, it is most likely to be in the form of economic support, because investigations concerning fund-raising had been initiated in the area by the FBI-DISIP in late 2001 (Webb-Vidal 2003, 16).

Relationship with the United States

Since 1895, when Venezuela received U.S. backing for their interpretation of the legal international framework in the region, the United States and Venezuela had a good working relationship, and U.S. companies pursued business interests related to the emerging Venezuelan oil industry.

The 1954 Inter-American Conference in Caracas led to the declaration against communism in the American hemisphere. When Vice President Richard Nixon had a tour of the region in 1958, his visit was marred by riots in Peru and Venezuela. Following the success of the Cuban revolution, the United States implemented a new, more directly interventionist approach in its national security doctrine, focusing on internal threats from its allies instead of just external enemies (Huggins 1991, 145).

Following the establishment of democracy, President Rómulo Betancourt (1959–

1964) laid the foundations for a foreign policy intent on limiting Venezuela's dependence on the United States. Following the successful revolution in Cuba, Venezuela did not immediately cancel relations with the Castro government, but when Cuba became involved in supporting a communist insurgency in Venezuela in 1962, Venezuela acted to get Cuba excluded from the OAS.

During the 1970s, relations between the United States and Venezuela became strained, because Venezuela's membership in OPEC was against U.S. wishes. As a consequence, the 1974 U.S. Trade Act explicitly excluded Venezuela and Ecuador because of their membership in OPEC. The same year, Cuba and Venezuela reestablished diplomatic contacts, and Venezuela has been a firm advocate of lifting U.S. sanctions against Cuba ever since (DCP 2003, 219–220). The Venezuelan nationalization of the oil industry in the mid-1970s also led to worsening relations with the United States.

Throughout the 1980s and 1990s, relations between the two countries became increasingly better as a result of the growing regional economic cooperation and dialogue, but after Hugo Chávez was elected president in 1998 on an outspoken anti-U.S. platform, the political relations have suffered (Casteñeda 2003, 67). It should be noted, however, that the economic connections between the United States and Venezuela are still very good, because the United States is by far Venezuela's largest trading partner (CIA *World Factbook* 2004).

A thorny issue is the Venezuelan stance on the large-scale, U.S.-sponsored antinarcotics and antiguerrilla initiative "Plan Colombia." When the plan was launched in the late 1990s, it immediately received serious criticism from President Chávez. He opposes the idea of the United States as a global hegemon and claims that Plan Colombia is a step toward "Vietnamization" of the conflict by meddling in what Chávez considers to be domestic politics.

The theme of national sovereignty was used again when Venezuela energetically rejected U.S. proposals for sanctions and condemnation of what international observers declared to be fraudulent Peruvian and Haitian elections in 2000. Venezuela claimed that elections were a sovereignty issue and that the Peruvian and Haitian governments were the ones who should decide the fairness of the process (DCP 2003, 219).

Because part of Chávez's popularity is built on his image of challenging the United States, there have been several incidents when he has embraced authoritarian leaders. In addition to his relationship with Fidel Castro, he has also had public meetings with Saddam Hussein and Moammar Qaddafi (DCP 2003, 220). Following the events in the United States on September 11, 2001, and the ensuing "War on Terrorism," which included U.S. engagements in Afghanistan and Iraq, Chávez's anti-U.S. stance has gotten stronger. He acknowledges that the United States at present is pursuing an interventionist foreign policy (Saavedra 2003, 216) and has on several occasions voiced his concern that his administration is targeted.

However, since Venezuela at present is the fourth-largest oil exporter to the United States, there are also strong motives to maintain good relations between the countries. Venezuela is dependent on its oil exports, and U.S. attempts to avoid being dependent on Middle Eastern oil means that it would have a hard time replacing the 10–15 percent of its total oil imports that is provided by Venezuela (see Table 2). Chávez is aware of this relationship, and it can be argued that he uses his anti-American rhetoric mainly as a means to increase domestic support against an increasingly vocal opposition.

It did not do much in the way of changing Chávez's concern about U.S. intentions when the United States had little to no reaction to the coup attempt in 2002. It can be claimed that the U.S. Department of State was concerned with other areas at the time, but the virtual nonresponse was perceived by Chávez as a sign of unofficial support for the coup plotters. The United States did commit, after fierce lobbying by other Latin American states, to participate in the "Group of Friends" initiative that was established in January 2003 to resolve the political crisis during the PDVSA strike. Because the strike ended before the group made any attempts to settle the conflict, no major improvement in U.S.-Venezuelan relations was recorded (Castañeda 2003, 75).

In 2003–2004, President Chávez made repeated statements that the United States had been behind the coup attempt against him in 2002 and that the antigovernment opposition in Venezuela was supported and instigated by the United States. He also made threats that should the United States make any attempts to kill him or remove him from power, Venezuela would cut off the oil supply to the United States (Fletcher 2004; Reuters March 1, 2004).

The Future
It is very difficult to predict the future for Venezuela. Regardless of what happens, the conflict between Chávez supporters and the opposition will continue to make the situation tense. It is possible that the conflict in Colombia will spill over fur-

Table 2   U.S. Oil Imports from Venezuela (Selected Years)

Year	Size*	Share (%)**
1960	911	50%
1965	994	40%
1970	989	29%
1975	702	12%
1980	481	7%
1985	605	12%
1990	1,025	14%
1995	1,480	17%
1996	1,676	18%
1997	1,773	17%
1998	1,719	16%
1999	1,493	14%
2000	1,546	13%
2001	1,553	13%
2002	1,383	12%

 * Thousand barrels per day
 ** % of total U.S. oil imports

Source
U.S. Energy Information Administration: http://www.eia.doe.gov.

ther into Venezuelan territory, creating additional political and social problems. Following the extended engagement by the United States in Iraq, it is not likely that Chávez's claims of a U.S.-orchestrated invasion will materialize, and the political situation in Venezuela does seem to have calmed down in mid-2004. It could be assumed that the strong commitment and tradition of noninvolvement by the armed forces in political matters makes a coup less likely, but Chávez has politicized the military elite through his connections within the armed forces and his attempts to remove critical voices from the military. Most of the opposition, including the critical voices from the military, has focused on trying to find a way to democratically replace the president. The increase in criminality following the economic crisis also contributes to the tenseness of the situation, but the political situation in Venezuela is at present too complex to adequately predict what will happen in the future.

References, Recommended Readings, and Websites

Books

Atkins, G. Pope. 1999. *Latin America in the International Political System*, 3d. ed. Boulder, CO: Perseus Books.

Barrios, Harald, Martin Beck, Andreas Boeckh, and Klaus Segbers, eds. 2003. *Resistance to Globalization: Political Struggle and Cultural Resilience in the Middle East, Russia, and Latin America*. Münster: Lit Verlag.

DCP (Democracy Coalition Project). 2003. *Defending Democracy: A Global Survey of Foreign Policy Trends 1992–2002.*

Eriksson, Mikael, ed. 2004. *States in Armed Conflict 2002*. Uppsala, Sweden: Uppsala Publishing House.

Huggins, M. K., ed. 1991. *Vigilantism and the State in Modern Latin America*. New York: Praeger Publishers.

Mares, David R., ed. 1998. *Civil-Military Relations: Building Democracy and Regional Security in Latin America, Southern Asia, and Central Europe.* Boulder, CO: Westview Press.

The Military Balance 2002–2003. 2002. London: International Institute for Strategic Studies, Oxford University Press.

Silva, Patricio, ed. 2001. *The Soldier and the State in South America.* New York: Latin American Studies Series.

Strategic Survey 2003–04. 2004. London: International Institute for Strategic Studies, Oxford University Press.

Szajkowski, Bogdan, ed. 2004. *Revolutionary and Dissident Movements of the World*, 4th ed. London: John Harper.

Valenzuela, Pedro, 2002. *Conflict Analysis: Colombia, Bolivia, and the Andean Region.* Stockholm: SIDA (Swedish International Development Cooperation Agency).

World Bank. 2000. *2000–2001 World Development Report: Attacking Poverty.* Washington D.C.: World Bank. *Also:* http://www.wds.worldbank.org/servlet/WDS_Ibank_Servlet?pcont=details&eid=000094946_01083004025527.

Articles/Papers

Babukin, Sergei A., Andrew C. Danopoulos, Rita Giacalone, and Erika Moreno. 1999. "The 1992 Coup Attempts in Venezuela: Causes and Failure." *Journal of Political and Military Sociology*, 1:141–154.

Campbell, Duncan. 2003. "Chávez Tries to Steady the Ship as Strike Peters Out." *The Guardian*, February 7.

———. 2004. "Chávez Calls Bush 'Asshole' as Foes Fight Troops." *Reuters News*, February 29.

Casteñeda, Jorge G. 2003. "The Forgotten Relationship: Rethinking U.S.-Latin American Ties." *Foreign Affairs* 3:67–81.

Castillo, Hernán, Laura Rojas de Perez, and Vilma Petrásh. 2001. Conference on Political and Economic Insecurity: Civil-Military Relations in Venezuela. Center for International Private Enterprise. http://www.cipe.org/whats_new/events/conferences/lac/venezuela/index.htm.

EIU (Economist Intelligence Unit). 2004. "Whose Side Is the Army On?" *Riskwire*, March 5.

Falcoff, Mark, 2002. "The Future of Democratic Institutions in Latin America." Paper presented at the Conference of the Bretton Woods Committee, Washington, DC. December 12.

———. 2003. "Is There Hope for Peace in Venezuela?" *Latin American Outlook.* Washington DC: AEI Online, http://www.aei.org, February 1.

Fishel, John T. 2000. "The Organizational Component of Civil-Military Relations in Latin America: The Role of the Ministry of Defense." Paper presented at the Latin American Studies Association Meeting, Miami, FL. September 16–18.

Fletcher, Pascal. 2004. "Venezuela's Chávez Says U.S. Seeking His Overthrow." *Reuters News*, January 12.

Gruben, William C., and Sarah Darley. 2004. "The 'Curse' of Venezuela." *Southwest Economy* 3:17–18.

Johnson, Stephen, 2004. "Venezuela Erupting." *National Review Online.* http://www.nationalreview.com/comment/johnson200403051032.asp.

Kreutz, Joakim. 2005. "Dictionary of Non-State Conflict in the World." http://www.ucdp.uu.se.

McGirk, Jan. 2002. "Venezuelan Countercoup Returns Chávez to Power." *The Independent*, April 15.

Meltzer, Judy. 2002. "Between Coup and Chaos: Political Standoff in Venezuela." *Focal Point* 5:1–2.

Perlo-Freeman, Sam. 2003. "Survey of Military Expenditure in South America: Background Paper for the *SIPRI Yearbook 2003*." http://projects.sipri.se/milex/mex_s_america_bg_03.pdf.

Pion-Berlin, David, and Craig Arceneaux. 2000. "Decision-Makers or Decision-Takers? Military Missions and Civilian Control in Democratic South America." *Armed Forces and Society* 3:413–436.

Saavedra, Boris. 2003. "Confronting Terrorism in Latin America: Latin America and United States Policy Implications." *Security and Defense Studies Review* 2:192–220.

Sanchez, Fabiola. 2003a. "Thousands Rally in Support of Chávez." *VOA News*, December 6.

———. 2003b. "Venezuela Steps up Border Defense." *BBC News*, December 30.

———. 2004a. "Venezuela in Tumult over Recall Vote." Associated Press, February 13.

———. 2004b. "Tensions Soar ahead of Venezuela Recall Ruling." Channel_news_asia, March 3.

Sweet, Frederick. 2003. "Media Concentration Undermines Democracy." *Intervention Magazine.* April 5. http://www.interventionmag.com.

Trinkunas, Harald A. 2001. "A Crisis in Civil-Military Relations in the Andes?" Paper presented at the Latin American Studies Association Meeting, Washington, DC, September 5–8.

U.S. Library of Congress. 1988. "Colombia: Country Study." http://lcweb2.loc.gov/frd/cs/cotoc.html.

Webb-Vidal, Andrew. 2003. "Embassy Bombs Mark New Phase in Venezuelan Crisis." *Jane's Intelligence Review* 4:14–17.

Websites

Armada de Venezuela (The Navy): http://www.armada.mil.ve.

Central Intelligence Agency (CIA). The *World Factbook.* http://www.cia.gov (accessed March 21, 2004).

Ejercito Venezolano (The Army): http://www.ejercito.mil.ve.

Fuerza Aérea Venezuela (The Air Force): http://www.fav.mil.ve.

Guardia Nacional de Venezuela (The National Guard): http://www.guardia.mil.ve#.

History of Venezuela, 2000. http://www.venezuelatuya.com/historia/eng.htm.

Ministerio de la Defensa: http://www.mindefensa.mil.ve.

The Revolution Will Not Be Televised. http://www.chavezthefilm.com.

U.S. Energy Information Administration: http://www.eia.doe.gov.

The Former Yugoslavia: Croatia, Bosnia-Herzegovina, and Serbia-Montenegro

Shale Horowitz

Geography and History

Croatia, Bosnia-Herzegovina, and Serbia-Montenegro are three of the five successor states of the former Yugoslavia—Slovenia and Macedonia being the other two. Croatia is shaped like an open book with the binding on the west side. Most of Croatia's northern, inland part is flat plain, and the southern, coastal part is mountainous and studded with islands. Bosnia—most of which is wedged into the middle of the "Croatian book"—is covered with mountains, except for a small area of plain along the northern border with Croatia. Serbia-Montenegro lies to the east of Bosnia and of the northern and southern parts of Croatia. Serbia-Montenegro is a flat plain in the north and mountainous in the south.

Yugoslavia was formed after World War I from the independent states of Serbia and Montenegro and former Austro-Hungarian Empire territories, including Slovenia, Croatia, and Bosnia-Herzegovina (henceforth, "Bosnia"). After being occupied by Nazi Germany in 1941, Yugoslavia was carved up. The next four bloody years combined a war of resistance against foreign occupiers with interethnic and ideological civil war. In 1945, Yugoslavia was reassembled under an independent communist regime. Following decades of decentralization, the death of regime founder Josip Broz Tito in 1980, and finally the decline and collapse of the Soviet Union's eastern European empire in the late 1980s, Yugoslavia broke up under interethnic stresses in 1991–1992.

The main source of the recent conflicts is familiar. The successor states and their dominant ethnic groups insist that the interrepublic boundaries inherited from the former Yugoslav state are inviolable. On the other hand, regionally concentrated ethnic minorities in Croatia, Bosnia, and Serbia have insisted on political and territorial self-determination—on what amounts, formally or informally, to secession. Moreover, these minorities have been able to count on varying levels of assistance from neighboring states dominated by their ethnic kin (Lake and Rothschild 1998; Van Evera 1994).

Among the Yugoslav successor states, only Slovenia is both internally homogeneous and without regionally concentrated ethnic kin in neighboring states. In Croatia, Croats—Roman Catholic, Serbo-Croatian speakers—are almost 90 percent of the population. But Croatia possessed a large concentration of Serbs—Orthodox Christian, Serbo-Croatian speakers—along its westernmost borders with Bosnia. Croats also make up about 15 percent of the population of neighboring Bosnia, concentrated in the southwestern Herzegovina region and in smaller clusters in northern and central Bosnia.

Bosnia's other main ethnic groups are Muslims, at around 40 percent, and Serbs, at around 30 percent. The Muslim population—also Serbo-Croatian speaking—was concentrated in central and eastern Bosnia, with an additional enclave around Bihać in western Bosnia. The Serb population was concentrated in western and eastern Bosnia, on both sides of the central strand of cities with large Muslim populations. In general, the Muslim and Serb populations were more interpenetrated with one another than either was with the Croat population, making it easier for both groups to ally tactically with the Croats than with one another. Serbia-Montenegro is a loose federation, and in recent years tiny Montenegro has moved toward independence. Montenegrins, like Serbs, are Orthodox Christian, Serbo-Croatian speakers. But a distinct geography, history, and culture lend them a dual identity as both Serbs and Montenegrins. Within Serbia-Montenegro, Serbs make up a bit more than 60 percent of the population, Montenegrins about 5 percent, Albanians 14 percent, and Hungarians 4 percent. The Al-

banians are concentrated in the southern Kosovo region, where, in the early 1990s, they constituted about 90 percent of the population. (The Hungarians are concentrated in the northern region of Vojvodina, where Serbs form the predominant population.) In Macedonia, which borders Serbia to the south, the population is about 65 percent Macedonian and 25 percent Albanian. Macedonia's Albanians are concentrated along the borders with Serbia's Kosovo region and with Albania proper (Central Intelligence Agency 2003; Karatnycky et al. 2001). (See Tables 1-3.)

Croatia demanded the right to secede from Yugoslavia and insisted both that its own boundaries were sacrosanct and that Croat regions of Bosnia had a right to affiliate with Croatia. The Bosnian Muslims demanded the right to secede from Yugoslavia and insisted that Bosnia's boundaries were sacrosanct, that is, that the Bosnian Serb and Bosnian Croat regions had no right to affiliate with their mother countries. Serbia insisted that the other republics had no right to secede from Yugoslavia and that Serbia's boundaries were sacrosanct, that is, that the Kosovo Alba-

Table 1   Croatia: Key Statistics

Type of government	Presidential/parliamentary democracy
Population (millions)	4.4 (July 2003)
Religion	Roman Catholic 87.8% (2001)
Main industries	Transport equipment, textiles, chemicals, tourism, agriculture (2001)
Main security threats	Civil and territorial conflict in Bosnia-Herzegovina, which would also likely involve Serbia
Defense spending (% GDP)	2.4% (2002)
Size of military (thousands)	20.8 (2002)
Number of civil wars since 1945	2 (1941–1945, 1991–1995)
Number of interstate wars since 1945	1 (1991–1995), same as second civil war

Sources

Central Intelligence Agency Website. 2003. CIA *World Factbook.* http://www.cia.gov/cia/publications/factbook/ (accessed May 15, 2005).

International Institute for Strategic Studies (IISS). 2003. *The Military Balance 2003–2004.* London: IISS and Oxford University Press, p. 69.

Table 2 Bosnia and Herzegovina: Key Statistics

Type of government	Federal democracy
Population (millions)	4.0 (July 2003)
Religions	Muslim 40%, Orthodox 30%, Roman Catholic 15% (2000)
Main industries	Metals, mining, transport equipment, textiles, agriculture (2001)
Main security threats	Internal civil and territorial conflict, which would also likely involve Croatia and Serbia
Defense spending (% GDP)	4.5% (2002); more reliable unofficial figures are 10.5% (2000) Muslim and Croat combined and 6.5% (2000) Serb
Size of military (thousands)	19.8 (2002), of which 9.2 Muslim, 4.0 Croat, 6.6 Serb
Number of civil wars since 1945	2 (1941–1945, 1991–1995)
Number of interstate wars since 1945	1 (1991–1995)—same as second civil war

Sources

Central Intelligence Agency Website. 2003. CIA *World Factbook.* http://www.cia.gov/cia/publications/factbook/ (accessed May 15, 2005).

International Institute for Strategic Studies (IISS). 2003. *The Military Balance 2003–2004.* London: IISS and Oxford University Press, p. 67.

Stockholm International Peace Research Institute (SIPRI). 2003. *SIPRI Yearbook 2003: Armaments, Disarmament and International Security.* London: Oxford University Press, p. 359.

Table 3 Serbia and Montenegro (Formerly the Federal Republic of Yugoslavia): Key Statistics

Type of government	Presidential/parliamentary democracy
Population (millions)	10.7 (July 2003)
Religion	Christian Orthodox 65% (1991)
Main industries	Machinery and transport equipment, chemicals, textiles, agriculture (2001)
Main security threats	Renewed civil conflict in Kosovo; civil and territorial conflict in Bosnia-Herzegovina, which would also likely involve Croatia, and in Macedonia
Defense spending (% GDP)	4.9% (2001)
Size of military (thousands)	74.2 (2002)
Number of civil wars since 1945	3 (1941–1945, 1991–1995, 1998–1999)
Number of interstate wars since 1945	1 (1991–1995)—same as second civil war

Sources

Central Intelligence Agency Website. 2003. CIA *World Factbook.* http://www.cia.gov/cia/publications/factbook/ (accessed May 15, 2005).

International Institute for Strategic Studies (IISS). 2003. *The Military Balance 2003–2004.* London: IISS and Oxford University Press, p. 83.

Stockholm International Peace Research Institute (SIPRI). 2003. *SIPRI Yearbook 2003: Armaments, Disarmament and International Security.* London: Oxford University Press, 356.

nians had no right to secede. If the other republics insisted on seceding from Yugoslavia, then the Croatian Serbs and Bosnian Serbs had a right to secede and affiliate with Serbia. The Kosovo Albanians wanted to form a republic separate from Serbia within Yugoslavia and wanted independence in the event of Yugoslavia's breakup. Macedonia's Albanians were also restless, although not so outspokenly secessionist as their brethren in Kosovo.

In Yugoslavia's last years, all the republics held elections. With the breakup of Yugoslavia, the successor states evolved into democracies. During the war and in the early postwar years, Croatia, Bosnia, and particularly Serbia had authoritarian-leaning leaders. All attained higher levels of democracy as these leaders passed from the political scene. There are great economic disparities among the successor states. Roughly, wealth declines as one moves southeast from Slovenia. Slovenia is not far below the level of Portugal, the poorest western European country. Late Yugoslav statistics place Croatia at about two-thirds the level of Slovenia, Serbia excluding Kosovo at about half, Montenegro, Bosnia, and Macedonia at around one-third, and Kosovo at 10–15 percent. Although Slovenia and to a lesser extent Croatia have important capital-intensive manufacturing sectors, most industry in the region is labor intensive. Outside of Slovenia, agriculture still occupies 15–20 percent of the workforce and, of course, more than that in the poorest regions (Plestina 1992; World Bank 1996, 188–189, 194–195).

Regional Geopolitics

The retreat and collapse of the Soviet Union produced a power vacuum in eastern Europe, which the European powers and the United States were not anxious to fill. The region's long-standing ethnic and territorial tensions, which had been controlled by overwhelming Soviet power, were left to be resolved locally. The most serious of the resulting conflicts have occurred among the major ethnic groups of the former Yugoslavia. These include territorial conflicts among Croats, Bosnian Muslims, and Serbs; between Serbs and Albanians; and between Macedonians and Albanians. There are other ethnic conflicts in eastern Europe and the Balkans. Some have been violent, but are now stalemated—such as those in Moldova and Cyprus. Others could become violent, but have so far remained under control—such as those in Romania, Ukraine, Estonia, and Latvia.

Regional stability depends largely on whether internal politics in Russia leads to active intervention to expand Russia's sphere of influence or territory, particularly in states with large Russian diasporas (Moldova, Ukraine, Estonia, and Latvia). It also depends on judicious U.S. and European use of carrots and sticks—particularly the carrots of entry into the North Atlantic Treaty Organization (NATO) and the European Union (EU), the sticks of economic embargos, and, under certain conditions, military intervention. Any further conflict spillovers are likely to be based on ethnic or religious ties that are carriers of political identity. For example, Albania might support ethnic Albanians in Serbia's Kosovo region or in northwest Macedonia, whereas Bulgaria might support Macedonians against Albanians. The biggest nightmare is that Greece and Turkey might support (respectively) Christian Orthodox and Muslim brethren in Serbia, Macedonia, or elsewhere and that this might escalate into direct conflict.

Conflict Past and Present

Conflict History

Yugoslavia emerged from World War I, incorporating lands coveted by Italy and Hungary. The Croats and Slovenes agreed to a union largely to protect themselves from Italy and Hungary. Serbia was primarily interested in the fate of the borderland Serbs of Croatia and Bosnia—so called because these Serbs live on the borderlands between the old Habsburg and Ottoman empires, well to the west of Serbia proper. The preexisting Serbian state and army was duly expanded to encompass all of Yugoslavia. Not surprisingly, postwar democracy showcased tensions between Serbs and Croats, with borderland Serbs, Slovenes, and Bosnian Muslims carving out mediating political niches. From 1929, a Serbian royal dictatorship exacerbated the grievances of non-Serbs, especially of Croats (Rothschild 1974, 201–280).

After German forces overran Yugoslavia in April 1941, the victor divided the spoils. For example, Slovenia was divided between Germany and Italy. Hungary took a bite out of northern Serbia, and Italy tore off large chunks of coastal Croatia. Germany added Bosnia to what was left of Croatia and installed a puppet regime run by the extremist Croat Ustaša movement. Kosovo and western Macedonia were added to Italian-dominated Albania. Bulgaria acquired the rest of Macedonia. The Ustaša regime, sometimes using Bosnian Muslims as auxiliaries, mounted a campaign of murder, expulsion, and forced assimilation against the borderland Serbs of Croatia and Bosnia. These policies pitted Croats and Muslims against Serbs. Tito's communist Partisans, although built around a borderland Serb core, benefited from a panethnic appeal and emerged as the most effective resistance force. The Red Army's victorious drive through eastern Europe guaranteed Tito's postwar accession to power. By the time the war ended, more than 10 percent of Yugoslavia's population had perished.

Although initially an orthodox communist, Tito resisted Joseph Stalin's effort to assert control over Yugoslavia. In 1948, Stalin openly broke relations. From the outbreak of the Korean War in 1950, Yugoslavia became a de facto ally of NATO against the common Soviet threat. Tito tried to burnish his ideological legitimacy by developing a more moderate type of socialism, involving greater personal freedom, as well as political and economic decentralization. At first, Tito adopted a Soviet-style strategy for dealing with ethnic identity. The dominant ethnic groups received their own republics, while power remained centralized in the party and army controlled by Tito. But Tito's decentralization began an institutional process of devolving power to the ethnically based republics.

From the mid-1960s, this process transferred important economic and cultural policymaking powers to the republic level. The process culminated in the new constitution of 1974, which upgraded Serbia's two autonomous regions (Kosovo and Vojvodina) into de facto republics, established a collective presidency to succeed Tito, and decentralized more state powers. By these half measures, Tito achieved the feat of alienating the dominant ethnic group, the Serbs, without satisfying the Croats and Slovenes. Even the smaller, poorer minorities—the Bosnian Muslims, Albanians, and Macedonians—remained loyal mainly out of a desire for protection against the Serbs, and in the case of the Bosnian Muslims, also the Croats. From the 1960s, ethnic tensions were exacerbated by economic difficulties. These were worsened in the 1970s by the oil shocks, rising debt burdens, and high inflation. As long as Tito was in power, he could serve as the final arbiter of the ethnic and economic cleavages. After his death, Yugoslavia limped along for as long as the external Soviet threat persisted (Cohen 1995, 21–38; Meier 1999, 1–34; Ramet 1992; Rothschild 1993).

In the late 1980s, Mikhail Gorbachev's liberalization policies lifted the threat of Soviet intervention and repression. This led to mobilization for political change across eastern Europe, including Yugoslavia. Loyalty to a common Yugoslavia was limited to a thin crust of better-educated urban "Yugoslavs," particularly the children of ethnically mixed marriages. The overwhelming majority still identified predominantly with their ethnic group. The ethnic groups with the strongest grievances were the Serbs, the Croats, the Slovenes, and the Albanians. Initially, the conflicts were most strongly articulated through the Serbian and Slovenian Leagues of Communists (LCs). Here the republic-level Leagues of Communists felt most secure and most successfully caught the nationalist wave. Slovene and most other ethnic leaders seem to have been genuinely committed to the collective ideals and interests of their people. On the other hand, Serbian leader Slobodan Milošević seems to have viewed pursuit of collective ideals primarily as a means to take and keep power. Milošević used the Serbian media and a series of heavily publicized mass rallies to champion Serb grievances—to demand that Serbian control be reasserted in Kosovo and Vojvodina and that Serb minority rights in Croatia and Bosnia be protected. Meanwhile, Slovenian communists and noncommunists competed in criticizing the centralization of power in Yugoslavia, in demanding de facto independence for Slovenia through a radical "confederalization" of Yugoslavia, and in criticizing the methods and goals of Milošević's Serbian nationalist movement.

Milošević used his rhetoric and rallies to consolidate control over the Kosovo and Vojvodina LCs. Combined with support from the sympathetic Montenegro LC, this gave Milošević control of four of the eight votes on the collective presidency—putting him within one vote of controlling the Yugoslav state and army. These events pushed the initially hesitant Croatian LC into line with that of Slovenia and frightened the more careful Bosnian and Macedonian parties. Deadlock ensued. Milošević's Serbia pushed to recentralize power within the Yugoslav state, Slovenia and Croatia insisted on de facto independence, and the Bosnian and Macedonian LCs clung nervously to the status quo.

As time passed, nationalist parties won elections in all the republics. LCs remained in power only where, as in Serbia and Montenegro, they reinvented themselves early on as nationalist parties. First, in April–May 1990, center-right nationalist parties came to power in Slovenia and Croatia. Elections in the other republics followed in November–December 1990. In Bosnia, a combination of Muslim, Serb, and Croat anticommunist parties, with irreconcilable national self-determination goals, unseated the LC. Only in Macedonia did a center-left LC manage to remain in power by forming a coalition with an Albanian nationalist party. The federal-level LC largely ceased to function.

Slovenia and Croatia set a deadline of June 1991, at which time they promised to declare independence if their self-determination demands were not met. Milošević warned that if Slovenia and Croatia had a right to secede from Yugoslavia, then so too did the Croatian and Bosnian Serb borderlands have a right to secede from their republics and affiliate with Serbia. Bosnian Muslim leader Alija Izetbegović insisted that Bosnia would not remain within a Serb-dominated rump Yugoslavia. Repeated efforts at a negotiated compromise foundered on irreconcilable demands for ethnic self-determination on overlapping territories. Slovenia and Croatia started to procure arms secretly and to reform their police and territorial reserve units into more conventional military formations. Encouraged and supported by Milošević, the borderland Serbs of Croatia began to seize control of their local administrations. Clashes with Croatian police and paramilitary units multiplied (Cohen 1995, 45–222; Meier 1999, 35–180; Silber and Little 1996, 31–153).

On June 25, 1991, Slovenia and Croatia declared independence. The Yugoslav People's Army (JNA) initiated some desultory military actions in Slovenia. But Slovenia contained no significant Serb minority, and a collective presidency without Slovenia was controlled by Milošević's Serbia. Hence command of the JNA fell into Milošević's hands, and an agreement was quickly reached on Slovenia's withdrawal from the Yugoslav Federation. Croatia was a different matter. Croatia's borderland Serbs, supported by JNA forces and Serbia-based paramilitaries, quickly seized their regions of predominant settlement clustered along the Bosnian border. Less successfully, JNA forces and Serbia-based paramilitaries also attacked along Serbia's border with Croatia in an effort to consolidate transport corridors to Croatia's regions of Serb settlement. Ethnic Croats were driven (or

"cleansed") from Serb-controlled regions. A January 1992 cease-fire left about one-third of Croatia's territory in Serb hands (Goldstein 1999, 212–238; Silber and Little 1996, 154–204).

In 1991, a similar process gathered momentum in Bosnia. The three nationalist parties that formed a coalition government—the Muslim Party of Democratic Action (SDA) led by Izetbegović, the Serb Serbian Democratic Party (SDS) led by Radovan Karadžić, and the Croat Croatian Democratic Union (HDZ), a branch of the governing nationalist party in Croatia—were unable to cooperate. The SDA's dominant wing favored a leading, state-constituting status for Muslims, along with a greater political role for Islam—although Izetbegović acknowledged that these were long-term goals and that a secular, multiethnic transition period would be necessary. The SDA's secular nationalist faction, led by Haris Silajdžić, emphasized a multiethnic Bosnian identity and culture. Both factions favored a centralized Bosnian state. The SDS favored a centralized Yugoslavia, in which the position of Serbs would be elevated. If Bosnia became independent, it sought de jure or de facto secession of heavily Serb regions and their affiliation with Serbia. Again, the HDZ was a controlled offshoot of the ruling party in Croatia. It supported Bosnian independence from Yugoslavia, followed by secession of heavily Croat regions and their affiliation with Croatia. The HDZ's less influential central Bosnian wing, which represented Croats surrounded by Muslims and Serbs, was more favorable to maintaining the territorial and political integrity of Bosnia. In short, each ethnic party wanted to achieve far-reaching self-determination and territorial gains for its own group at the expense of the other two groups.

The parties could agree only on purging LC loyalists. They proceeded to divide up the government, colonize their respective ministries, and establish local control in their predominant regions of settlement. The SDA established a commanding position in the central government in Sarajevo, the capital city. By late 1991, with fighting under way in Croatia, first Bosnian Serbs and then Bosnian Croats set up autonomous regions, while all three groups built up paramilitary forces. Milošević partitioned the large JNA contingent in Bosnia, leaving heavily armed, Bosnian Serb JNA elements to fuse with Bosnian Serb paramilitaries. In September 1991, the United Nations Security Council, anxious to "do something" about Yugoslavia's descent into war, imposed an arms embargo on all parties to the fighting. This had the easily foreseeable, but unintended effect of locking in much of the initial military advantage of the Serbs, who "inherited" the support of the JNA. In October, Muslims and Croats outvoted Serbs in Parliament to opt for Bosnian independence from Serbian-dominated Yugoslavia—although the Muslims and Croats did not agree on what should happen following independence. International mediation efforts failed to bridge disagreements on allocating territory and governmental powers among the ethnic groups. After an independence referendum passed with Muslim and Croat support, Bosnia declared independence on March 3, 1992.

The referendum and declaration triggered a fevered struggle for local control across Bosnia. In April, Izetbegović ordered a military mobilization in Sarajevo, and the Serb siege and shelling of the city began. JNA forces and Serbian paramilitaries invaded eastern Bosnia from Serbia, while forces from Croatia proper reinforced Bosnian Croats in northern Bosnia and in the southern Herzegovina region. As in Croatia, Serb forces used exemplary atrocities to drive out non-Serb civilians. Media reports of this "ethnic cleansing," of the siege of Sarajevo and other predominantly Muslim cities, and, finally, of a Sarajevo breadline shelling led the Security Council to impose the first of a series of economic sanctions against Serbia and Montenegro. "Ethnic cleansing" tactics were reciprocated by Croat and Muslim forces, with the three ethnic populations gravitating to their regions of military control.

Serb forces made rapid advances in eastern and western Bosnia, seizing about two-thirds of Bosnia's territory. But Croat and Muslim forces held a north-south corridor in central Bosnia running through Sarajevo, and Croat forces also held most of the southern region of Herzegovina. From late 1992, Croat-Muslim military cooperation broke down under the stress of territorial disputes, allowing the Serbs to make further advances. From April 1993, heavy fighting broke out between Croats and Muslims, with Muslims overrunning some of the more vulnerable central Bosnian Croat communities. In February 1994, a Sarajevo marketplace shelling was the final catalyst for a U.S.-brokered alliance (the "Washington Agreements") among Croatia, the Bosnian Croats, and the Bosnian Muslims. The United States informally supported the arming and training of the Croatian army and the Muslims. In exchange, Croat-Muslim fighting was ended and a unified Federation of the Bosnian Croats and Muslims was formed.

A shift in the military balance was already evident in the limited Croat-Muslim offensives of November 1994. In the spring and summer of 1995, Muslim offensives led the Serbs to overrun the internationally sanctioned civilian "safe areas" of Srebrenica and Žepa. Thousands of Muslim men and boys were massacred outside of Srebrenica. In May 1995, a Croatian offensive seized important territories in western Slavonia and in Herzegovina. In August, Croatia reconquered its own Serb borderlands. As Croats were once driven from Serb-held territory, Serbs were now driven from the same borderlands. Following yet another Sarajevo marketplace shelling, large-scale NATO air strikes pounded Serb targets in Bosnia. Meanwhile, a Croat-Muslim offensive drove Serb forces from the Bihać area and much of western Bosnia, threatening the main Bosnian Serb city of Banja Luka.

On August 29, Milošević imposed binding joint negotiating authority on the Bosnian Serbs, who had hitherto resisted diplomatic settlement proposals. Over the next two months, tentative agreements were reached on most outstanding issues in Croatia and Bosnia. NATO bombing ended in exchange for Serb withdrawal of heavy weapons from around Sarajevo. A cease-fire was agreed to and implemented. In November–December 1995, the Dayton Peace Agreements were negotiated and signed, ending all fighting in Croatia and Bosnia (Burg and Shoup 1999, 46–188; Silber and Little 1996, 205–344).

Dayton committed Serbia to withdraw from eastern Slavonia, the only Croatian territory still under Serb control. In Bosnia, the Bosnian Serbs gained a formerly Croat-held northern area linking western Bosnia with eastern Bosnia, and the Muslims gained Serb-held neighborhoods and environs of Sarajevo and a corridor to the long-besieged eastern city of Goražde. About half of Bosnian territory was allocated to a Serb republic and the other half to the Croat-Muslim Federation. The federation was itself divided de facto into Croat- and Muslim-controlled zones. Although Bosnia's nominal territorial integrity was preserved, a weak central state was created, with strong group veto powers in the upper and lower legislative houses. The international Office of the High Representative has override powers to implement the agreements, supported by overwhelming NATO enforcement power. (See Table 4.) The High Representatives have felt forced to use their decree powers liberally.

Nominally, there is full economic integration and a right of refugees to return to their homes. In practice, significant informal barriers exist. Refugee returns have been particularly slow, and the overwhelming majority of refugees will never return to their homes—usually because it is undesirable or unsafe. The international administration has been more successful in imposing competitive elections, which have slowly injected competition and political turnover into the monolithic ethnic one-party systems left over from the war. The continued NATO presence and the prospect of future integration into the European Union are vital stabilizing forces. However, war and "ethnic cleansing" have done their work, and Bosnia will remain three separate nations for generations to come (Burg and Shoup 1999, 360–381; Chandler 2001).

Against the background of the events in Croatia and Bosnia, the story of Serbia's Kosovo region in the 1990s is familiar. Kosovo was restored to direct Serbian rule in the late 1980s, as part of Miloševićs prewar drive to power. Serbs replaced Albanians in the state administration, and Albanians became marginalized

Table 4   International Administrative Entities in Bosnia and Kosovo

	Office of the High Representative in Bosnia	*United Nations Mission in Kosovo (UNMIK)*
Founded	December 1995, as part of the Dayton Agreement.	June 1999, by UN Security Council Resolution 1244.
Mission and Powers	Has decree powers to implement the civilian provisions of the Dayton Agreement in Bosnia. Does not command supporting military Stabilization Force (SFOR), which is NATO dominated.	To provide an interim civilian administration for Kosovo and to facilitate reconstruction and local autonomy pending a final political settlement. Some functions are delegated to the European Union and Organization for Security and Cooperation in Europe. Does not command Kosovo Force (KFOR), which is NATO dominated.
Leadership	High Representative (HR) is nominated by Steering Board of Peace Implementation Council (PIC). The PIC consists mostly of European countries, along with Canada, Japan, the United States, and a number of non-European Muslim countries and international organizations. The Steering Board consists mostly of the larger countries.	Head of Mission is appointed by the UN secretary-general. The UN Security Council approves the nomination of the HR.
Achievements	Since the Dayton Agreement, has helped to maintain peace, hold elections and marginalize extremists, rebuild infrastructure, and institute legal and economic reforms.	Provided emergency aid and helped to rebuild infrastructure and public services. Elections have allowed for some local self-rule.
Failures or Limitations	Has facilitated only limited return of refugees and has not managed to alter the postwar informal status quo of three ethnically distinct nation-states.	Has failed to prevent continued interethnic violence, mostly directed against Serbs. Economic recovery has been slow. Bernard Kouchner, former head of UNMIK, criticized the lack of clear political objectives.
Outlook	Continued gradual progress in areas of achievement, continued stagnation in areas of failure or limitation.	Continued political stalemate, complicated by interethnic violence and a weak economy.

Sources
http://www.unmikonline.org.
http://www.euinkosovo.org.
http://www.nato.int/kfor/welcome.html.

and impoverished. Moderates, led by communist-era academic luminary Ibrahim Rugova, long managed a nonviolent response to Serbian rule—knowing that Milošević and Serbian public opinion supported a potentially devastating "military solution" to armed resistance. However, in 1997, arms made available by a breakdown in order in neighboring Albania, combined with rising frustration, led to a surge in guerrilla and terrorist attacks by the Kosovo Liberation

Army (UCK). Serbian reprisals often targeted bystanders as well as fighters and their supporters. In June 1998, intensified Serbian attacks on UCK base areas drove 10,000–20,000 Albanians across the border into Albania. An international uproar led Milošević to accept foreign observers in October, but atrocities against Albanians continued.

In January 1999, the United States threatened to counter with air strikes unless Kosovo's autonomy was restored. Talks in February and March at Rambouillet led to belated UCK, but not Serbian, acceptance of an autonomy plan. In March, international monitors were ordered out, and ethnic cleansing of Albanians intensified. NATO air strikes commenced. In June, after an intense bombing campaign that extended to targets throughout Serbia, Milošević accepted the autonomy plan, and Serbian forces withdrew from Kosovo. As Albanian refugees returned, most Kosovo Serbs were duly driven out in their turn and the rest confined to ethnic ghettos. A UN-led international administration was set up, which governs Kosovo to this day. (See Table 4.) There is no definite plan to turn over full authority to the Kosovo Albanians. This is because the Albanians would use it to pursue political independence. The international community is—for the time being at least—committed to keeping Kosovo as an autonomous region within Serbia, pending a negotiated settlement between Serbia and the Kosovo Albanians. In practical terms, however, Kosovo is unlikely to be directly governed by Serbia for the foreseeable future. The loss of Kosovo devastated Milošević's popularity. Following a disputed presidential election in 2000, mass demonstrations and security force defections toppled Milošević. He was soon extradited to The Hague to stand trial for

---

Sidebar 1   Slobodan Milošević on Trial

On May 24, 1999, Slobodan Milošević was indicted by the International Criminal Tribunal for the former Yugoslavia (ICTY). Including a number of additional and amended indictments, Milošević is accused of war crimes, crimes against humanity, genocide, and violating the 1949 Geneva Conventions during the Croatia, Bosnia, and Kosovo wars.

Milošević also is accused of participating in a "joint criminal enterprise" that sought "the forcible removal of the majority of the Croat and other non-Serb population from the approximately one-third of the territory of the Republic of Croatia that he planned to become part of a new Serb-dominated state"; "the forcible and permanent removal of the majority of non-Serbs, principally Bosnian Muslims and Bosnian Croats, from large areas of the Republic of Bosnia and Herzegovina"; and "the expulsion of a substantial portion of the Kosovo Albanian population from the territory of the province of Kosovo in an effort to ensure continued Serbian control over the province." After falling from power, Milošević was turned over to the ICTY for trial. He has pled "not guilty" on all counts, and his trial is under way.

Sources
International Criminal Tribunal for the Former Yugoslavia (ICTY) Website. http://www.un.org/icty/cases/indictindex-e.htm (accessed May 14, 2005).

BBC News Website. http://news.bbc.co.uk/1/hi/in_depth/europe/2001/yugoslavia_after_milosevic/default.stm (accessed May 14, 2005).

war crimes (Malcolm 1998; O'Neill 2002). (See Sidebar 1 on the trial of Milošević.)

The Kosovo conflict soon spread to the Albanian regions of neighboring Macedonia, but prompt international intervention and a flexible Macedonian political system have so far stopped a slide into full-scale war. Albanians constitute about 25 percent of Macedonia's population. Since Macedonia's first free elections were held and independence was achieved in 1990–1991, Albanian parties have regularly participated in governing coalitions while clamoring for greater minority rights and improved social services. As violence intensified in neighboring Kosovo in 1997, interethnic political disputes and clashes multiplied in heavily Albanian regions of Macedonia. Although the Albanian parties showed restraint, the activities of the Kosovo Liberation Army captivated the imagination of Macedonian Albanians. This influence grew when more than 300,000 Kosovo Albanians temporarily took refuge in Macedonia in 1999—before returning to their homes after NATO pressure pushed Serbian forces from Kosovo. The established Macedonian Albanian parties continued to broker compromises with the ruling ethnic Macedonian parties (Krause 2000).

However, in 2001, a National Liberation Army—with the same Albanian language acronym (UCK) as the Kosovo Liberation Army—launched an insurrection in Albanian areas. As Macedonian army forces ineffectually responded, the insurrection spread rapidly across the Albanian-populated areas. Largely under international pressure, ethnic Macedonian parties formed a government of national unity and signed the Ohrid Agreement. The agreement's main provisions improved the constitutional status of Albanians, made Albanian a second official language, created an ethnic minority veto for constitutional changes and issues important to the minority community, and provided for increased representation of Albanians in the state administration. In exchange, the UCK agreed to lay down its arms, and NATO- and EU-sponsored forces were sent in to police the agreement. Despite delays, the Ohrid Agreement has been implemented. In the 2002 elections, a UCK-backed Albanian party eclipsed the older Albanian parties and entered the new coalition government (Krause 2002, 2003).

Current and Potential Military Confrontation

In the near future, is violent conflict likely to recur in Croatia, Bosnia, Kosovo, or Macedonia? Here there are two main factors to discuss: the preferences of political leaders and their constituents, and balance of power and other material constraints that affect cost-benefit calculations about alternative political and military strategies. After looking at how present conditions compare with ideal self-determination and territorial objectives, we can ask how likely it seems that any party would choose war in an effort to achieve more of its goals.

Consider first the contested Serb borderland areas of Croatia. After these areas were reconquered by Croatia in late 1995, the overwhelming majority of the local Serbs fled for their lives. Croatia has formally agreed to allow these Serbs to return to their homes. However, a combination of informal official resistance and local hostility is likely to keep most Serbs from returning. Croatia is the winner and has no significant unsatisfied goals within its own territorial boundaries. Serbia and the Serbs are the losers in the

Croatia war, but they have bigger problems to worry about and are in no position to contest the outcome. Securing the Serb republic of Bosnia, and of course retaining sovereignty and some kind of Serb presence in Kosovo, are more important to most Serbians than going to war again for the self-determination of Croatia's borderland Serbs. Moreover, the Croatian army emerged as the most formidable in the region in 1994–1995, so there is little chance that Serbia could win in a conventional war. Given Croatia's informal alliance relationship with the United States since 1994, this conventional balance of power will not change anytime soon. With the flight and expulsion of the borderland Serbs, there is no realistic low-intensity guerrilla strategy available either.

If Croatia goes to war again, then it will probably be in Bosnia rather than in Croatia proper. However, Croatia and the Bosnian Croats have done quite well in Bosnia. The Bosnian Croats hold most of Herzegovina, although many central Bosnian Croat communities have been devastated. Although the Bosnian Croats have not been able to detach Herzegovina from Bosnia and formally affiliate or merge with Croatia, they are self-ruling and unchallenged in their de facto statelet, which is an informal protectorate of Croatia. Thus the Bosnian Croats, supported by Croatia, are most interested in keeping what they have politically and territorially. Although the Bosnian Serbs suffered a significant defeat in late 1995, they retain about half of Bosnia's territory, in which they too are self-ruling and unchallenged. They would like more territory, but the balance of power has become highly adverse to them—particularly because most in Serbia proper would prefer to keep the status quo in Bosnia and to

focus on protecting Serbia's claims and interests in Kosovo.

Thus, the Bosnian Muslims are the most aggrieved group in Bosnia and are most likely to challenge the status quo by seeking more territory and more centralization of state power. Many have argued that U.S. military support has significantly increased Muslim military power and thus increased the likelihood of renewed fighting in the event of a NATO withdrawal. But, first, a NATO withdrawal is extremely unlikely without a follow-up, EU-based deployment. Moreover, the Bosnian Muslims cannot fight the Bosnian Serbs and Serbia without support from the Bosnian Croats and Croatia. But the Bosnian Croats and Croatia have most of what they want and hence have no interest in strengthening a Bosnian Muslim entity that would later be likely to threaten them. Hence, renewed conflict seems unlikely in Bosnia, particularly if a significant NATO or EU military presence remains in place.

In Kosovo, it is the Albanians that have most of what they want. True, there is not yet an independent Albanian state, and Albanian self-government is constrained by an international superstructure. Yet, informally, the Albanians have gained a self-ruling statelet. If the Albanians defy the United States and the European powers by moving unilaterally toward independence, they risk driving out the international presence, leaving them to face Serbia alone. (See Sidebar 2 on ongoing ethnic violence in postwar Kosovo.) This risks losing remaining Serb-populated areas of Kosovo, and maybe more. Serbia is not yet reconciled to losing Kosovo and would probably act to defend the remaining Kosovo Serbs and to secure historically important religious sites. Large-scale fighting could lead to large Albanian refugee flows and territorial losses. For as long as the NATO or EU military presence lasts, however, Serbia will not intervene militarily in Kosovo.

In Macedonia, the Albanians have gained close to the maximum that ethnic Macedonians are willing to grant and the Western powers are willing to support. If the Macedonian Albanians insist on moving toward separation from Macedonia, they will have to fight Macedonia alone—and Macedonia would probably be aided

---

Sidebar 2   Continuing Ethnic Violence in Kosovo

As Serbian armed forces withdrew in 1999, Albanian paramilitaries and mobs drove about 200,000 Serbs from Kosovo. This "reverse ethnic cleansing" also confined the remaining Serb population of about 100,000 to the North Mitrovica area and to smaller enclaves or ghettos elsewhere in Kosovo. The United Nations Mission in Kosovo (UNMIK) and Kosovo Force (KFOR) presence have since managed to control ethnic violence—although small-scale attacks, usually by Albanians against Serbs, have occurred regularly.

On March 17, 2004, rumors circulated that two Albanian boys had drowned after being chased into a river by Serbs. Subsequent anti-Serb rioting and Serb retaliations killed about thirty people. Approximately 3,000 Serbs from smaller enclaves south of the Ibar River fled or were evacuated, and rioters burned down their houses to prevent them from returning.

Sources
Associated Press, March 18, 2004.
Irish Times, March 22, 2004.
Ottawa Citizen, March 20, 2004.

---

by Serbia and Bulgaria. However, because of the Albanian predominance in the western parts of Macedonia adjoining Kosovo and Albania, such a conflict is probably one that the Macedonian Albanians can win. This is because, unless the Macedonian army is willing and able to use a strategy of ethnic cleansing, it cannot control and govern the ethnic Albanian areas without popular consent. In such a situation, in the face of ongoing bloodletting, ultimate partition of Macedonia would become likely. The question is whether this outcome would be worth the human and economic devastation that would be necessary to achieve it. The Ohrid Agreement concessions, which grant Albanians a high degree of local self-rule along with a constitutionally protected minority status, make it less likely that most Macedonian Albanians would be willing to pay the high price of achieving independence.

It must be kept in mind, though, that these apparently reassuring arguments assume two things. They assume some degree of moderation in the self-determination and territorial demands of the main ethnic groups, that is, a willingness to sacrifice some important goals to conserve goals already achieved and to build a better economic future. They also assume that political decision makers are accountable to such a moderate population, or, failing that, they assume at least a moderate political leadership. Ideological moderation is more likely among the peoples that have achieved most of their goals, or that at least would otherwise have to defy a highly adverse balance of power—that is, it is most likely among the Croats and least likely among the Macedonian Albanians.

Accountability of political decision makers might be more difficult to achieve—particularly among the peoples with weaker, less democratic political institutions. The danger is that ideological fanatics or political careerists—the two types can be difficult to distinguish—will unilaterally pursue violent strategies as a means of pursuing their own goals. Recall that such strategies have been a staple of politics in the region. Serbia's Slobodan Milošević and his clients among the Croatian and Bosnian Serbs, the leaders of the Kosovo Liberation Army, and to a somewhat lesser extent the leaders of the National Liberation Army in Macedonia all show that political figures can unilaterally initiate conflict intended to polarize public opinion in a manner that strengthens them vis-à-vis more moderate politicians. The less legitimate or well institutionalized are the existing representatives, the greater the scope for extremist political entrepreneurs to initiate conflict and to gain politically from it. Much depends on whether important international actors discourage and punish such polarizing political strategies.

Alliance Structure

None of the alliances or collaborative relationships to be discussed is formally enshrined in a treaty—at least not yet. But informal alliances or relationships have been important. Like formal alliances, they reflect more or less durable confluences of national interest.

Consider first international attitudes toward the initial breakup of Yugoslavia. Following long-standing tradition, the European Community (EC) and the United States initially emphasized that Yugoslavia's international and internal (interrepublic) boundaries were inviolable—unless all the concerned parties voluntarily agreed on adjustments. How-

ever, after Serb forces initiated wars in Croatia and Bosnia, the EC and the United States recognized the successor republics and their boundaries and imposed economic sanctions on Serbia and Montenegro. Within the EC, Germany was much more keen to recognize the successor republics—particularly Slovenia and Croatia—than were Britain and France. The United States initially deferred to the EC, viewing Yugoslavia as being of greater interest to the western European powers. Given the great power democracies' aversion to casualties and memories of Nazi Germany's "quagmire" in Yugoslavia during World War II, there was at first no thought of military intervention. In response to international economic sanctions, Milošević dropped overt claims to an enlarged Serbia and supported the Croatian and Bosnian Serbs based on the principle of self-determination.

As fighting and ethnic cleansing spread from Croatia to Bosnia, limited humanitarian intervention followed. United Nations peacekeeping missions were sent in to separate hostile forces and to provide aid and assistance to civilians. Serb sieges of Bosnian Muslim cities, most notably Sarajevo, led the Security Council to designate some as demilitarized "safe areas." These rules of engagement were not observed by any of the ethnic groups, but the Serbs were guilty of the most egregious violations. Differences of opinion soon emerged between Britain and France on the one hand and the United States on the other. As Serb-on-Muslim atrocities continued to appear in the news, the United States increasingly favored a "lift and strike" strategy—in which the arms embargo would be lifted to strengthen the Bosnian Muslims and air strikes against the Serbs would be used to enforce compliance with international norms. Britain and France, which supplied large numbers of peacekeepers, viewed these U.S. plans as half baked and dangerous. The United States seemed intent on getting involved in the fighting, but without any plan for an overall settlement. This would create an open-ended commitment, which the Bosnian Muslims would have an incentive to exploit for their own ends. In the process, the British and French peacekeepers would serve the Serbs as attractive targets for retaliation and hostage taking. These were indeed important issues. "Lift and strike" advocacy proved the entrée to taking more direct responsibility to broker and back the Croatian-Muslim alliance, support it with air strikes, and impose the diplomatic settlement at Dayton. Once the United States proved willing to act to impose a coherent settlement, the western European powers provided diplomatic and military support under the NATO umbrella. NATO forces remain in Bosnia to this day as guarantors of the more enforceable parts of the Dayton Agreements (Burg and Shoup 1999, 189–316).

The Bosnia precedent made Western intervention much easier once Milošević embarked on a new military adventure in Kosovo in 1998. By early 1999, the United States and NATO were not only threatening Milošević with air strikes, but also demanding that Kosovo's Yugoslav-era autonomy be restored. Following months of air strikes and with NATO forces massing on Kosovo's Albanian and Macedonian borders, Milošević backed down. NATO-dominated forces remain in Kosovo. Similarly, when an Albanian rebellion broke out in Macedonia in 2001, the United States and the western European powers pressured the Macedonian government to make the Ohrid Agreement concessions, while NATO and the EU provided troops to help disarm the rebels and reduce tensions.

The U.S.-led NATO interventions created informal alliances with Croatia and the Bosnian Croats, the Bosnian Muslims, the Kosovo Albanians, and in a way with both Macedonia and her Albanian minority. However, the alliances extend only as far as the common stakes in the currently existing diplomatic settlements. As discussed, allies that are unhappy with their settlements risk losing U.S. support by challenging the status quo. It should also be mentioned that, because of likely objections from Russia and China, the UN Security Council did not authorize the U.S.-led interventions in Bosnia and Kosovo. All countries and entities involved in these conflicts aspire to NATO and EU membership as a means of guaranteeing their military security and improving their economic prospects. However, this will not occur until the conflicts seem enduringly stabilized. This is because the member countries of NATO and the EU, and particularly their great power leaders, do not want to internalize unresolved grievances and cleavages.

Size and Structure of the Militaries

The armed forces of Croatia, Serbia-Montenegro, and of Bosnia's Croat-Muslim Federation and Serb republic are limited under the Dayton Agreements. All of the armed forces have contracted significantly since the wars ended. Croatia's armed forces, while retaining substantial reserves, are transitioning to the smaller, more professional contingents necessary for the anticipated entry into NATO. Out of 20,800 active troops in 2002, 14,050 were in the army and the remainder about evenly split between the navy and air force. There were also about 10,000 paramilitary police suited for local defense. These smaller forces are well trained and relatively mobile and still primarily concerned with territorial defense and with potential operations in Bosnia. Croatia has contributed small contingents to a number of international peacekeeping and state-building efforts.

Bosnia has two formally distinct armed forces—one for the Croat-Muslim Federation and another for the Serb republic. In practice, the federation armed forces are for the most part divided into Muslim and Croat contingents. Joint institutions include a federation-level Ministry of Defense and general staff, and some military formations. By 2002, the Dayton troop reductions had brought the Muslim forces down to 9,200 regulars, the Croat forces to 4,000, and the Serb forces to 6,600—although reserves for each group are approximately ten times larger. Heavy equipment is mostly held in storage under NATO control. Approximately 12,000 NATO troops, along with smaller contingents from other countries, remain on the ground to enforce the Dayton Agreements. As the new order has taken hold, the international forces have been scaled down. Largely owing to training and aid from the United States, the Muslim and Croat forces are better trained and armed, and more mobile, than the Serb forces.

Serbia-Montenegro's armed forces are those of Serbia, with Montenegro controlling only small, light Interior Ministry and police forces. In 2002, Serbia's active forces remained at a high level of 74,200, including 3,800 in the navy and 8,000 in the air force. There were then an additional 35,000 Ministry of Interior troops. These large forces are a legacy of the far-flung military commitments and repressive domestic politics of the Milošević era. The post-Milošević reformist governments have started to reduce troop numbers to free up resources for improved training and more modern equipment (Bellamy 2002b; Gow 2002b; International Institute for Strategic Studies 2003, 66–67, 69, 83–84; Stockholm International Peace Research Institute 2003, 320–322).

Budget
Military spending has come down dramatically from wartime levels. By 2002, it had fallen to 2.4 percent of GDP in Croatia, to 4.9 percent in Serbia-Montenegro, to around 10.5 percent in Bosnia's Croat-Muslim Federation, and to around 6.5 percent in Bosnia's Serb republic. Although Croatia no longer provides direct financial support to the Bosnian Croat forces, the United States and a number of Muslim countries provide substantial aid to the Croat-Muslim Federation. Serbia-Montenegro allocates significant funds for the Serb Republic forces (Institute for Strategic Studies 2003, 251–255; Stockholm International Peace Research Institute 2003, 320–322, 355–356, 359).

Civil-Military Relations/The Role of the Military in Domestic Politics
The officers' corps of the JNA was heavily Serb. This reflected the Serbs' demographic preponderance, but was also a legacy of the Serbs' strong military tradition—including the central role of borderland Serbs in the World War II–era partisan movement. Unquestioned control over the JNA was the bedrock of Tito's personal power and authority. In multi-ethnic Yugoslavia, particularly after Tito's decentralizations weakened the

federal-level League of Communists, the JNA was also the main guarantor of Yugoslavia's territorial integrity. As in other communist countries, the ruling party used a variety of institutional and ideological levers to inculcate political loyalty and deference in the JNA—to make sure that the "Bonapartist" temptation would never threaten Communist Party power.

This effort was so successful that the JNA failed to act as Milošević's struggle with Slovenia and Croatia was tearing Yugoslavia apart. By default, this allowed Milošević to "Serbianize" the JNA and make it serve his own ends. Milošević did not allow the JNA to pursue plans to keep Slovenia within the federation. This gave his federal presidency faction effective control, allowing Milošević to commit the JNA to the Croatia war and, less than a year later, the Bosnia war. Non-Serb conscripts defected en masse. Milošević was also able to purge the officers corps repeatedly, removing both those loyal to their ethnic groups and to Titoite Yugoslavia, and leaving a more careerist Serb rump—although independent officers were purged as late as November 1998. Once the wars in Croatia and Bosnia were under way, Milošević decided to support the Croatian and Bosnian Serbs at arm's length—hiving off local chunks of the JNA and using money, arms, and a common officers' pool to influence them from Serbia. Within Serbia, Milošević also built large Interior Ministry and police forces as more reliable counterweights to the Yugoslav army. Up to the end, Milošević planned to use force if necessary to protect his power. He fell from power only when, after losing the 2000 federal Yugoslav presidential election and then trying to annul the outcome, the Interior Ministry and police forces as well as the army refused to fire on opposition demonstrators in the capital.

The post-Milošević government took steps to depoliticize the security forces and dismantle Milošević's far-flung patronage network. In March 2003, old regime and organized crime elements threatened by these reforms assassinated Prime Minister Zoran Djindjić. In the ensuing state of emergency, further efforts were made to make the security forces more neutral and professional. Given Serbia's economic difficulties, the prospect of Western integration will be vital to keeping reformists in power and to depoliticize the armed forces (Gow 2002a; Gow and Zveržanovski 2003; Vasić 1996).

In Croatia, the armed forces were created from scratch amid the war against Serb insurgency and invasion. In the process, the military was heavily politicized by Franjo Tudjman's Croatian Democratic Union (HDZ) government. Using the military emergency as a justification, Tudjman marginalized the Parliament in the process of making military strategy, appointing military leaders, and allocating the military budget. Over time, there were increasing signs that the security forces were being used to harass the internal political opposition and its budget used to build patronage networks for the ruling party. This arrangement did not become deeply unpopular for as long as the war lasted and the government appeared to conduct it responsibly. Thus, government legitimacy remained strong until well after the war was won in late 1995—with the exception of a brief period in 1993–1994, when fighting with the Bosnian Muslims threatened to undermine Croatia's international support and to prevent it from recovering its own Serb-held borderlands.

From late 1996 onward, the HDZ's rough treatment of the political opposition and independent media, along with continued economic difficulties, gradually eroded its legitimacy. After the HDZ lost power to a Social Democrat–led coalition in January 2000, efforts were made to restore parliamentary oversight; to increase transparency in national security planning, military appointments, and budgetary procedures; and to professionalize military recruitment, promotion, and training. This process was given greater legitimacy because it was perceived as necessary to gain Croatia's ultimate entry into NATO and the EU (Bellamy 2002a, 2002b, 2003).

As war loomed in Bosnia in 1991 and early 1992, the three ethnic groups built separate paramilitary forces. After war broke out, the Serb forces were wrapped into the local JNA forces. Since the war ended in late 1995, elements of these forces have sheltered the wartime leaders, Radovan Karadžić and Ratko Mladić, from the International Criminal Tribunal for the Former Yugoslavia (ICTY). Other elements have supported more moderate Serb leaders, who seek to build a future by cooperating with the NATO protectorate. The Bosnian Croats' Croatian Defense Council (HVO) was from the outset controlled from Croatia proper, and Croatian army units fought alongside HVO units throughout the war.

The Bosnian Muslims' Army of the Republic of Bosnia and Herzegovina (ABH) was formed mostly from local territorial defense and police units. Heavily criminal paramilitaries played an important role in the initial defense of Sarajevo. Some had ties to SDA factions and were not broken up until late 1993. In the isolated western Muslim enclave around Bihać, the local notable Fikret Abdić built up a paramilitary following that was able to compete for local authority until late 1994. After the federation was formed with the Bosnian Croats in early 1994, arms became more readily available, and training and political reliability improved. Since the end of the war, U.S. aid and training has made the ABH into a formidable force, and a more competitive political environment has made the ABH less a creature of the SDA. Just as there remain three de facto statelets within Bosnia, there remain three armies under the command of the leaders of the three ethnic groups. International efforts to integrate Muslim and Croat forces within the Muslim-Croat Federation have so far been limited—because the Bosnian Croats (supported by Croatia proper) view this as establishing de facto Muslim dominance (Kadić 2004; Vasić 1996).

Terrorism

Suppose that terrorism is defined as intentionally attacking civilian populations on a large scale to achieve political goals. In that case, all sides engaged in terrorism in the Croatia, Bosnia, and Kosovo wars. Milošević and his minions have the distinction of initiating its use and of perpetrating by far the worst atrocities. He and many others have been or will be tried for war crimes by the ICTY.

However, there is deep ambivalence, and sometimes hostility, toward these trials in Croatia, Bosnia, and Serbia. In Croatia and Bosnia, most Croats and Muslims feel that their "own" alleged war criminals are being punished for responding in kind—and even then acting with greater restraint—in a total war initiated by Milošević. If leaders of an ethnic group initiate the use of ethnic cleansing, the target group is arguably forced into a zero-sum struggle. If members of the initiating ethnic group are left unmolested on territory currently controlled by the target group, the initiating group members are likely to try to seize the land as future opportunities permit. Many would say that it is expecting unrealistic self-sacrifice to assume that, in such cases, a strategy of ethnic cleansing should never be reciprocated. Most Serbs, on the other hand, view the international community as a hostile dupe—as unfairly singling out "their" war criminals, largely because it respects the rights of self-determination of all the Yugoslav peoples except the Serbs.

During the desperate early days of the Bosnia war, when the Bosnian Muslims were trying to build up an army while avoiding total defeat, there was an international arms embargo in place. Under these circumstances, arms, money, and volunteers were welcome from across the Islamic world—including from some of the quasi-official Saudi charities with extensive links to al-Qaeda and other terrorist groups. Even after the United States and its allies became the main sources of arms and training, these charities retained local organizations that sought to promote Wahhabi Islam among the Bosnian Muslims. Soon after the September 11, 2001, attacks, the Bosnian Muslim-dominated authorities in Sarajevo raided the office of the Saudi High Commissioner for Aid to Bosnia and Herzegovina. Bosnian and U.S. officials said that the raid turned up before-and-after pictures of al-Qaeda attacks on U.S. targets, information on the use of crop dusters and on forging U.S. State Department identification cards, and maps of Washington, D.C., with marks over government buildings. At around the same time, six Algerian suspects, including an employee of the Saudi High Commissioner, were arrested and sent to the U.S. base at Guantánamo Bay (*Associated Press*, February 21, 2002).

The Bosnian Muslim leadership and population are relatively secular and moderate. Moreover, good relations with the United States are the key to Bosnian Muslim security and political survival in the region. As a result, it seems highly unlikely that the Muslim regions of Bosnia will develop into a significant haven for international terrorists. There have been reports of links between elements of the UCK and international terrorists. Again, however, the Kosovo Albanians and their leaders do not have an incentive to provide bases for use against their U.S. protectors. This is not to say that extremists have not done so or will not do so, but such extremists have greater difficulty operating against what are widely perceived to be the best interests of their own ethnic group. The situation in Macedonia is similar, but seems more unstable.

Relationship with the United States

As already discussed, the United States initially "delegated" management of Yugoslavia's death throes to the EC and the European great powers. When the European powers proved unwilling to respond to the ongoing bloodletting with more than diplomatic pressure, economic sanctions, and peacekeeping efforts, U.S. policymakers warmed up to the idea of military intervention—particularly with the election of President Bill Clinton in November 1992. However, fear of a "quagmire"—an indeterminate and bloody conventional commitment—led U.S. policymakers to focus on the options of lifting the arms embargo and using air strikes. As European diplomats long argued, these policies alone could not work without the will to change the balance of power on the ground toward achieving a stable diplomatic settlement. The sensational atrocities that the Bosnian Serbs steadily provided for the international media were pivotal in selling the idea of a U.S.-backed Croat-Muslim alliance leading to a Dayton-type settlement—selling it strategically to policymakers and politically to the public.

Milošević might have calculated that the United States would not intervene in Kosovo because the Albanians did not provide reliable ground auxiliaries. The Albanian guerrillas could not realistically defeat the Yugoslav army, and even if they did, they would seize independence rather than settle for autonomy. The United States would not want to send the message that aggrieved minorities can elicit international intervention and achieve independence by provoking atrocities against their civilian populations. However, the U.S. public is more averse to guerrilla warfare than to conventional warfare. After Serb conventional forces were defeated, the Albanian population could be counted on to be friendly. Hence, once NATO forces started massing on Kosovo's borders, Milošević understood that he had to withdraw to avert a military disaster, which could have led directly to his overthrow.

Since Dayton, the United States has retained informal alliances with Croatia and the Bosnian Muslims. Both continue to receive arms and training from the United States, and for the reasons discussed previously, both are unlikely to challenge the U.S.-brokered status quo. The Kosovo Albanians, too, are protected by the United States and NATO and are unlikely to challenge the status quo. Relations with Serbia are complex. Although most Serbs remain deeply resentful toward the United States, the one-time Serbian opposition that now governs needs U.S. and EU trade, investment, and aid. These actual and potential economic benefits offer an important means of fending off a political comeback by Milošević or a challenge by nationalist extremists such as Vojislav Šešelj. Most Serbs are aware that military adventures have brought them disaster and that European integration offers the most secure future. They are also aware that the only way for Serbia to regain all or part of Kosovo is to sit tight and restore relations with the United States and the EU. Then, it is possible that Albanian moderates will agree to partition Kosovo in exchange for formal independence or that Albanian extremists will gain influence and alienate their foreign protectors.

The Future

If the political status quo is compared to widely held objectives of the main ethnic groups and leaders, some conjectures can be made about the near future. Renewed conflict seems least likely in Croatia and most likely in Macedonia. It also seems unlikely in Bosnia, but somewhat more likely in Kosovo. Croatia won a complete victory within its own territory. Serbia is unlikely to attack its most militarily formidable foe to restore Croatia's borderland Serbs when the destiny of Kosovo and Bosnia's Serb republic are higher priorities. In Bosnia, the Croats have again achieved most of their objectives—large territorial holdings with de facto self-rule, although not secession and affiliation with Croatia. The Bosnian Serbs ended up with territorial holdings and a level of self-rule that is impressive given the balance of power at the time of Dayton. They would be wise to embrace a tacit alliance with the Croats to maintain the status quo against the strengthened and relatively disaffected Bosnian Muslims. Such common Croat-Serb interests in the status quo make it almost suicidal for the Bosnian Muslims to return to war to gain territory and greater centralization of state power. The problem in Kosovo is that the stronger Serbs are more aggrieved by the status quo. That is why a long-term, NATO-led international military presence is more crucial to maintaining peace in Kosovo than in Bosnia. In Macedonia, it is only the threats of limited casualties and greater economic hardship that deter the Albanian minority from fighting for a Kosovo-like, quasi-independent status.

International military forces are much more able and willing to keep conventional forces apart—as in Bosnia and Kosovo after ethnic cleansing and separation—than to police semilegitimate diplomatic settlements of low-intensity conflicts—as in Macedonia. This point is also relevant to the question of whether in-group "spoilers" (Stedman 1997)—leaders that provoke and sustain conflict to pursue political power or seek extremist ideological objectives—are likely to be able to trigger renewed conflict. Tactically speaking, this is more difficult where ethnic groups are already separated and conflict takes the form of attacks across well-demarcated cease-fire lines. Only in Macedonia is this conflict-driven separation process more incomplete. Another important factor is progress of legitimate political institutions. It is more difficult for extremists to seize the agenda and undermine moderates with some record of accountable, effective governance. In these terms, the Bosnian Muslim political system seems

more stable and more likely to deliver some goods than that of the Kosovo Albanians. In Macedonia, the Albanian parties have enjoyed impressive access to governing coalitions. Moreover, the Ohrid Agreement made important policy concessions to the Albanians. However, the situation could easily deteriorate again if economic conditions do not improve more quickly.

This point again raises the issue of international intervention—this time in the form of carrots. Across eastern Europe, the prospect of entry into the EU, and in appropriate cases also NATO, has been important in helping to push through often-controversial political and economic reforms. In some cases, it has helped in adopting policies to address interethnic grievances and conflicts. If the EU wants to prevent chronic instability and even a return to full-scale conflict in Kosovo and Macedonia, it should be more aggressive about pushing feasible settlements. In Macedonia, this was not done until it was almost too late, and it is not clear that the Ohrid Agreement alone will suffice to deliver longer-term stability. In Kosovo, there is a widespread sense of dashed expectations and drift under the UN-led administration. Of course, it requires unusual foresight and political will to push conflicting ethnic groups into difficult compromises—even after the bodies start piling up.

References, Recommended Readings, and Websites

Books
Bellamy, Alex J. 2002a. "'Like Drunken Geese in the Fog': Developing Democratic Control of Armed Forces in Croatia." In *Democratic Control of the Military in Postcommunist Europe*, Andrew Cottey, Timothy Edmunds, and Anthony Forster, eds. Basingstoke, UK: Palgrave, pp. 174–193.

————. 2002b. "A Revolution in Civil-Military Affairs: The Professionalization of Croatia's Armed Forces." In *The Challenge of Military Reform in Postcommunist Europe: Building Professional Armed Forces*, Anthony Forster, Timothy Edmunds, and Andrew Cottey, eds. Basingstoke, UK: Palgrave, pp. 165–182.

————. 2003. "A Crisis of Legitimacy: The Military and Society in Croatia." In *Soldiers and Societies in Postcommunist Europe*, Anthony Forster, Timothy Edmunds, and Andrew Cottey, eds. Basingstoke, UK: Palgrave, pp. 185–202.

Burg, Steven L., and Paul S. Shoup. 1999. *The War in Bosnia-Herzegovina: Ethnic Conflict and International Intervention.* Armonk, NY: M. E. Sharpe.

Central Intelligence Agency. 2003. *World Factbook.* Washington, DC: CIA. http://www.cia.gov/cia/publications/factbook/

Cohen, Lenard. 1995. *Broken Bonds: Yugoslavia's Disintegration and Balkan Politics in Transition.* 2d ed. Boulder, CO: Westview.

Goldstein, Ivo. 1999. *Croatia: A New History.* London: Hurst.

Gow, James. 2002a. "The European Exception: Civil-Military Relations in the Federal Republic of Yugoslavia (Serbia and Montenegro)." In *Democratic Control of the Military in Postcommunist Europe*, Andrew Cottey, Timothy Edmunds, and Anthony Forster, eds. Basingstoke, UK: Palgrave, pp. 194–211.

————. 2002b. "Professionalization and the Yugoslav Army." In *The Challenge of Military Reform in Postcommunist Europe*, Anthony Forster, Timothy Edmunds, and Andrew Cottey, eds. Basingstoke, UK: Palgrave, pp. 183–193.

Gow, James, and Ivan Zveržanovski. 2003. "Legitimacy and the Military Revisited: Civil-Military Relations and the Future of Yugoslavia." In *Soldiers and Societies in Postcommunist Europe*, Anthony Forster, Timothy Edmunds, and Andrew Cottey, eds. Basingstoke, UK: Palgrave, pp. 203–216.

Institute for Strategic Studies. 2003. *The Military Balance 2003/2004.* London: Institute for Strategic Studies.

Kadić, Amel. 2004. *Civil-Military Relations in Bosnia and Herzegovina: Democratic Control of the Armed Forces.* Geneva: Geneva Centre for the Democratic Control of the Armed Forces.

Karatnycky, Adrian, Alexander Motyl, and Aili Piano. 2001. *Nations in Transit 1999–2000: Civil Society, Democracy and Markets in East Central Europe and the Newly Independent States.* New Brunswick, NJ: Transaction.

Lake, David A., and Donald Rothchild, eds. 1998. *The International Spread of Ethnic Conflict: Fear, Diffusion, and Escalation.* Princeton, NJ: Princeton University Press.

Malcolm, Noel. 1998. *Kosovo: A Short History.* New York: New York University Press.

Meier, Viktor. 1999. *Yugoslavia: A History of Its Demise.* London: Routledge.

O'Neill, William G. 2002. *Kosovo: An Unfinished Peace.* Boulder, CO: Lynne Rienner Publishers.

Plestina, Dijana. 1992. *Regional Development in Communist Yugoslavia: Success, Failure, and Consequences.* Boulder, CO: Westview.

Ramet, Sabrina P. 1992. *Nationalism and Federalism in Yugoslavia, 1963–1991.* 2d ed. Bloomington: Indiana University Press.

Rothschild, Joseph. 1974. *East Central Europe between the Two World Wars.* Seattle: University of Washington Press.

————. 1993. *Return to Diversity: A Political History of East Central Europe since World War II.* 2d. ed. Oxford, UK: Oxford University Press.

Silber, Laura, and Allan Little. 1996. *The Death of Yugoslavia.* Rev. ed. London: Penguin.

Stockholm International Peace Research Institute (SIPRI). 2003. *SIPRI Yearbook 2003: Armaments, Disarmament and International Security.* London: Oxford University Press.

Vasić, Miloš. 1996. "The Yugoslav Army and the Post-Yugoslav Armies." In *Yugoslavia and After: A Study in Fragmentation, Despair and Rebirth,* David A. Dyker and Ivan Vejvoda, eds. London: Longman, pp. 116–137.

World Bank. 1996. *From Plan to Market: World Development Report 1996.* Washington, DC: Oxford University Press.

Journal Articles/Newspapers

Chandler, David. 2001. "Bosnia: The Democracy Paradox." *Current History* 100 (March):114–119.

Krause, Stefan. 2000. "Macedonia 1999: Surviving a Year of Crises." Prague: Transitions Online. http://knowledgenet. tol.cz/look/knowledgeNet/article.tpl?Id Language=1&IdPublication=12&NrIssue =13&NrSection=17&NrArticle=4835 (accessed May 1, 2004).

———. 2002. "Macedonia 2001: Into the Quagmire." Prague: Transitions Online. http://knowledgenet.tol.cz/look/ knowledgeNet/article.tpl?IdLanguage= 1&IdPublication=12&NrIssue=15& NrSection=17&NrArticle=4525 (accessed May 1, 2004).

———. 2003. "Macedonia 2002: Inching toward Normalization." Prague: Transitions Online. http://knowledgenet. tol.cz/look/knowledgeNet/article.tpl?Id Language=1&IdPublication=12&NrIssue =16&NrSection=17&NrArticle=9185 (accessed May 1, 2004).

Stedman, Stephen John. 1997. "Spoiler Problems in Peace Processes."

International Security 22 (Fall): 5–53.

Van Evera, Stephen. 1994. "Hypotheses on Nationalism and War." *International Security* 18 (Spring):5–39.

Websites

Government of the Federation of Bosnia and Herzegovina: http://www. fbihvlada.gov.ba/.

Government of the Serb Republic (Bosnia): http://www.vladars.net/.

Government of Serbia and Montenegro: http://www.gov.yu/.

International Criminal Tribunal for the Former Yugoslavia: http://www.un. org/icty/.

Office of the High Representative in Bosnia: http://www.ohr.int/.

Republic of Croatia Homepage: http:// www.hr/.

Stabilization Force (NATO-Led Mission in Bosnia): http://www.nato.int/sfor/.

Transitions Online: http://www.tol.cz/.

United Nations Interim Administrative Mission in Kosovo: http://www. unmikonline.org/.

APPENDIX

Research Institutes, Think Tanks, and Other Organizations with Interests in Defense/Security Issues

The following list of Websites represents a cross section of international research centers. The ISN site is an excellent gateway site. It offers a useful starting point for research on defense and security issues. It is also a great link to other institutes and is relatively easy to navigate. Many of the sites offer useful information on the topics discussed in the essays in this book. It was intended to provide a variety of information from both developed and developing countries. Some of these sites might appear a bit one-sided or even biased. For example, opinions on the Middle East or India-Pakistan disputes can vary wildly. Readers are urged to enlist several viewpoints and perspectives so that his or her research and understanding can be more fully informed. This list was compiled using several search engines.

Asia-Pacific Center for Security Studies, USA
www.apcss.org/

Begin-Sadat Center for Strategic Studies, Israel
www.biu.ac.il/soc/besa

Canadian Institute of Strategic Studies, Canada
www.ciss.ca/

Center for Strategic and International Studies, USA
www.csis.org/

Centre for Defence Studies, England
www.kcl.ac.uk/depsta/wsg/cds/

Centre for Defence Studies, Zimbabwe
www.uz.ac.zw/units/cds/

Centre for Military and Strategic Studies, Canada
www.stratnet.ucalgary.ca/

Institute for Defense Studies and Analysis, India
www.idsa-india.org/

Institute of Strategic Studies, Pakistan
www.issi.org.pk/

International Institute for Strategic Studies, England
www.iiss.org/

International Relations and Security Network, Switzerland
www.isn.ethz.ch

National Institute for Defense Studies,
Japan
www.nids.go.jp/english/

Olin Institute for Strategic Studies, USA
www.wcfia.harvard.edu/olin/

RAND Corporation, USA
www.rand.org/

Strategic and Defence Studies Centre,
Australia
www.rspas.anu.edu.au/sdsc/

U.S. Army War College, USA
www.carlisle.army.mil/ssi/

U.S. Institute of Peace, USA
www.usip.org/

INDEX

AURI. *See* Indonesian Air
Force
Austerlitz, 229, 651
Australia: alliance structure
for, 43–45; casualties for,
46 (table); civil-military
relations in, 48; combat
deployments by, 46
(table); conflicts for,
42–43; future of, 50–51;
geography/history of,
37–40; independence of,
37–38, 42, 43, 48; key
statistics on, 38 (table);
Melanesia and, 548;
military size/structure for,
45–48; Oceania and, 545;
population of, 37; regional
geopolitics of, 40–42; U.S.
relations with, 49–50, 890;
Vanuatu and, 555
Australia and New Zealand
in the Malayan Area
(ANZAM), 497
Australian Armed Forces,
branches of, 45
Australian Army, 45, 47
Australia-New Zealand
Agreement. *See* Canberra
Pact
Australia New Zealand
Army Corps (ANZAC),
44, 49, 496, 499–500
Australia-New Zealand-
United States Treaty
(ANZUS) (1951), 44, 49-
50, 497, 501, 502–503, 551
Australian Police, 548
Australian Women's Army
Service (AWAS), 45
Austria: alliance structure
for, 62–64; civil-military
relations in, 67; conflicts
for, 58–62; future of,
68–69; geography/history
of, 55–56; independence
of, 56, 57, 62, 68; key
statistics on, 56 (table);
military size/structure for,
64–66; neutrality of, 62,
63–64, 66, 68; regional

geopolitics of, 56–58; U.S.
relations with, 68
Austrian Army, 69;
constitution and, 67;
structure for, 65–66
Austrian Empire,
Netherlands/Spain and,
746
Austrian Federal
Constitution, 62, 63
Austrian State Treaty (1955),
57, 62
Austro-Hungarian Army,
670
Austro-Hungarian Empire,
55, 57, 59, 883; collapse
of, 632; Germany and,
246; Serbia and, 882;
Yugoslavia and, 921
Austro-Prussian War, 230
Autodefensas Campesinas
de Córdoba y Urabá
(ACCU), 173, 175
Autodefensas Unidas de
Colombia (AUC), 176,
178, 184, 905, 915, 916;
drug trafficking and, 175;
as terrorist organization,
182; Colombian armed
forces and, 175;
demobilization of, 177;
FARC-EP and, 169, 175;
kidnappings by, 173
Autodefensas Unidas por
Venezuela (AUV), 905,
916
Avanti!, Mussolini and, 365
Aviano, 368
Avibrás Aerospace Industry,
78
Awami League, 270, 575
AWAS. *See* Australian
Women's Army Service
Axis of evil: Iran and, 311,
320, 405, 530, 898; Iraq
and, 530, 898; North
Korea and, 530, 898
Axis Powers, 207; Argentina
and, 21, 32; Germany and,
247
Ay, Manueal Antonio, 471

Ayub Khan, Muhammad,
583
Ayuthaya Kingdom, 820
Azad Kashmir, 568
Azerbaijan, 671, 674;
Armenia and, 839; Iran
and, 313; Russian treaty
with, 675; Spain and, 753;
Turkey and, 839, 843, 854
Azeris, 307
Aznar, Jose Maria, 659
Azores, 655, 656, 659, 660
"Aztec Eagles" Squadron
201, 481
Aztecs, 463
Az-Zawahri, Ayman, 218

Baader, Andreas, 258
Baader-Meinhoff Gang, 258
Baathist regimes, 654,
692–693; in Syria, 407,
781, 784, 786, 788, 793
Babangida, Ibrahim, 520
Babenberg family, 59
Badawi, Abdullah bin
Ahmad, 454, 459, 460
BAE Systems, 874
Baghdad Pact (1955):
Pakistan and, 578; Syria
and, 790; Turkey and, 844
Baha'is, 307
Bahasa Indonesia, 288
Bahasa Melayu, 445
Bahrain: banking/commerce
in, 695; Iranian claim to,
693; overthrow plot
against, 311; Saudi Arabia
and, 694, 695
Baïdoa, 233
Bainimarama, Voreqe
(Frank), 553, 559, 560
Baja California Norte, 463
Bakassi Peninsula, 516, 517
Baku, 672, 839
Balearic Islands, 743, 750,
754
Balfour Declaration (1917),
342, 343
Bali, 286; bombing in, 48,
304, 453, 456, 459, 491,
501–502, 504, 548, 609,
824, 830

About the Editors

Karl DeRouen Jr. is associate professor of Political Science at the University of Alabama. His research interests are conflict processes and international political economy. His recent work has appeared in *British Journal of Political Science, Journal of Conflict Resolution, Journal of Peace Research, International Studies Quarterly, American Politics Research, Civil Wars,* and others.

Uk Heo is associate professor of Political Science at the University of Wisconsin–Milwaukee. He is author, coauthor, or coeditor of five books. His works on international security and political economy have appeared in *Journal of Politics, British Journal of Political Science, Political Research Quarterly, Journal of Conflict Resolution, International Studies Quarterly, Journal of Peace Research, International Interactions, Comparative Politics, Comparative Political Studies,* and others.